Poverty, Wealth
Dictatorship, Democracy

Resource Scarcity and the Origins of Dictatorship

Jack Barkstrom

Pericles Press
Englewood, Colorado

Pericles Press

8200 South Quebec Street
Suite A-3 159
Englewood, CO 80112

Library of Congress Catalog Card Number: 98-96403

ISBN 0-9610224-0-X

Contents

PART I   **A THEORY ABOUT RESOURCES**

1.	Introduction	1
2.	Resources and a Theory	15
3.	The Resource Mechanism: How Resource Availability Determines the Type of Government	25

PART II   **THE ANCIENT WORLD**

4.	Athens: Silver, Ships, and Grain	61
5.	Sparta: Dictatorial Democracy and a Society Under Siege	79
6.	Rome: Out of Work, Out of Bread, Out of Control	90

PART III   **WORLD IN TRANSITION**

7.	France and the French Revolution The Political History	116
8.	France and the French Revolution The Economic History	135

PART IV   **THE TOTALITARIAN STATE**

The Soviet Union:

9.	Russia and the October Revolution	158
10.	1917 - Background to Revolt	171
11.	The Russian Civil War (1918-1921)	189
12.	The Communists in Power (1921-1938)	208
13.	The Economics of the Russian Agricultural Sector	230
14.	The Collectivization of Agriculture (1929-1933)	260
15.	Russian Industry and the Revolution	294
16.	The New Economic Policy and the Five-Year Plans	312
17.	The Role of Scarcity In Political and Economic Controls	333

Nazi Germany:

18.	Background to Fascism and an Overview of Nazi Germany	352
19.	The Nazi Dictatorship (1933-1939)	374
20.	German Economic Resources and the German Economy	386

PART V   MODERN DEMOCRACY

21.	The United States and the Great Depression: Too Much Credit, Too Little Cash	414
22.	American Democracy and Patterns in Economic Development	430

PART VI   THE GLOBAL MARKETPLACE

23.	The Global Market: More Profits, Less Employment, Never-Ending Competition	457
24.	The New World Economic Order	475
	Notes	490
	Index	520

The story of government really begins with the invention of writing. Yet the origins of government can be traced to an earlier time - prehistory - the period of time before the recording of history. Political concepts such as democracy and dictatorship, similarly, belong to the written age, yet find their origins in a distant past. Belonging to the written age, they would seem a part of the advance of civilization. Only democracy, the model for man's noblest aspirations, seems in keeping with that spirit. Dictatorship, with its appeal to the basest of human emotions and a capacity for evil, seems more of a throwback to an earlier, primitive, period in human development.

Governments, whether they are democratic or dictatorial, may belong to the written age. In reality they are products of an earlier era. Democracies and dictatorships are determined at the time geologic forces allocate resources to future nations.

PART I

A THEORY ABOUT RESOURCES

CHAPTER 1

INTRODUCTION

The theory of this book can be summarized in three sentences. The amount of resources which a country has determines whether it will become a democracy or a dictatorship. Countries which possess large amounts of resources will become democracies. Countries where resources are scarce will become dictatorships. If the basic premise can be summarized so quickly, the question is how the theory operates. What is the resource "mechanism?" In other words, how does scarcity or abundance operate to create a repressive or free society? The mechanism can be explained best in the context of a dictatorship. Violence, economic unrest, and unemployment are key ingredients in the dictatorial equation. While dictatorships have been universally condemned for their treatment of individuals, few societies are willing to tolerate widespread violence or an environment of turmoil. Governmental repression historically has been a response to long-term violence and unrest. The economic link between resource scarcity and repression is that large-scale violence often has its origins in scarcity. Scarcity, under certain circumstances, can lead to improvements in business services. However, if scarcity becomes severe, competition has a tendency to lead to violence.

This book is both a political and an economic study of dictatorships and democracies spanning some 2,500 years of history. Seven countries and their governments have been included as case studies. Three are from the ancient world - Athens, Sparta, and Rome. Four are more recent - Revolutionary France, Nazi Germany, the Soviet Union, and the United States. The study begins with Athens and Sparta, two contrasting governments - Athens, the model for democracy, which established itself around 490 B.C., and Sparta, a dictatorship, known more for the bravery and fighting ability of its soldiers. The fight-to-the-death defense of the pass at Thermopylae in 480 B.C. against the Persian invaders is legendary. Leonidas and his 300 Spartans stood alone against the Persian army's band of 10,000 "Immortals." For public consumption, Sparta promoted the sacrificial exploits of its armies. It erected a column with the names of Leonidas and his soldiers on it to commemorate their sacrifice.[1] Yet Sparta had a dark side. The Spartan state governed with the help of the Krypteia, Sparta's secret police. In contrast to the honor earned by the deaths of Leonidas and his 300 Spartans at Thermopylae, the Spartan government sanctioned dishonorable conduct at times. In 424 B.C., on the pretext of honoring members of a subjugated neighboring tribe who had fought for Sparta, the Spartan government secretly put 2,000 of its former soldiers to death.[2] In some ways it seems incomprehensible that a Greek city-state, some 2,500 years ago, could reach a level of sophistication sufficient to incorporate a secret police into its governing structure. Athens and Sparta differed in their economic practices as well. Athens was a powerful trading society while Sparta relied on a system of forced agricultural labor.

Rome serves as the third example of the economics and politics of the Ancient

World. It experienced periods of strong economic growth with democratic tendencies, yet encountered both economic hard times and political repression. From Ancient Rome, the study moves forward some 1,800 years, to Revolutionary France. The French Revolution is remembered more for the extreme violence which occurred. While political events attract most of the attention, the economic problems of France during the time period were severe. Germany, prior to the Nazi takeover, similarly experienced economic hardship. If the Soviet Union represented a different form of dictatorship than Germany, it too experienced both political and economic turmoil. The last study in the book is the United States, the foremost modern democracy. While it has had periods of political unrest, it has enjoyed both political freedom and economic prosperity for much of its history.

In the area of historical analysis, it can be dangerous to make generalizations about societies or governments. One generalization which appears to be true however, is that democracies require a lot of resources. Ancient Athens and the United States, perhaps the most notable examples of democracy, were blessed with vast resource reserves. The amount of resources these two democracies possessed, were not just a little above average in amount. Those reserves were on the order of "colossal" or "vast," held in amounts which positively dwarfed resource reserves of other countries. Another generalization is that dictatorships are associated with resource scarcity. This book would argue that resource scarcity causes dictatorship. Others would dispute that assertion. They would argue that dictatorship, because of its restrictions on personal and economic freedom, contributes to economic problems. Whether scarcity contributes to, or is caused by, dictatorship, there is an association between a lack of resources and dictatorial government.

The Berlin Wall, which came down in November 1989, has come to symbolize the ultimate triumph of freedom over the bankrupt ideas of the communist system. The Soviet Union would manage to last until 1991, but the communist economic experiment in was over. The defeat of communism and the adoption of Western free market ideas were expected to make the former Russian republics prosperous democracies with flourishing economies. Despite the introduction of Western business solutions and modern management techniques, the former states of the Soviet Union have continued having problems. The problems have been explained away: 70 years of Soviet mismanagement could not be corrected overnight; it would take some time for a free market system to right all the wrongs; or the Russian people did not have any experience with democracy. The U.S., it was pointed out, has had nearly 200 years of democratic traditions to work with. Yet, these answers - 70 years of central planning and a lack of democratic traditions - do not seem to account for the current economic and political problems experienced in the former Soviet republics. It might be pointed out that the Russian people have had a long experience as traders - the "capitalist spirit" was alive in Russia for hundreds of years before the October Revolution of 1917, it survived 70 years of Soviet rule, and it is very much alive today.

The Twentieth Century has been witness to a worldwide struggle between two conflicting ideologies: communism and democracy. As prominent as Russia has been in the ideological debate, this book is not just about communist dictatorships or the Soviet Union. (Nazi Germany was also a dictatorship, even though Hitler did not pattern his regime after Lenin's.) Nevertheless, Russia commands a special place in any discussion. There are four preliminary questions about Russia and the communist system which may help to explain this book's theory. First, was communism the cause of the economic problems in the Soviet Union or was it the result? Second, was communism really a failure in Russia? Third, was the suppression of the free market equivalent to the control or elimination of market forces? Fourth, if critics said that communists had destroyed the market, did what they say accurately reflect what was taking place?

Did communism cause Russia's problems? Conventional wisdom in the West holds that difficulties began when the free market was destroyed by the Bolsheviks. This book's thesis suggests instead that economic problems and the totalitarian nature of her government were caused by an underlying scarcity of resources. Central planning was not the cause of scarcity in the Soviet Union; it was a response to it. Conversely, it is not clear that capitalism has been responsible for the development of democracy in the U.S. This book's argument is that both democracy and capitalism in the U.S. developed because the U.S. possessed large amounts of resources.

Was the communist experiment a failure? Communism in Russia has been condemned for both its political and economic faults. Politically, the government took away many personal freedoms, and economically, industrial output fell far short of that in the West. Yet, in absolute terms, were these failures of such a magnitude that they signified complete societal collapse or, was it more a case of life being difficult? Failure may be a term better applied to societies in which destruction is complete. In addition, it is not clear that success or failure are terms which can be applied to political and economic forces, even if they seem to battle each other at times. Political and economic systems do not technically win or lose. They seek to exist in a state of equilibrium. In Russia, as in all societies, the economic and political systems approached a state of equilibrium - the system as whole had not failed. Central planning, the basis of the Soviet economic system, represented the point where the underlying economic forces roughly balanced the political forces.

In restricting the free market did Soviet authorities exercise control over the market? The assumption has long been that the controlled economy of Russia represents the economic opposite of Western capitalism and that the choice, where market systems are concerned, is between the operation of the market and a government-controlled system. Because capitalism has emphasized market operations, it is believed that market forces are somehow the monopoly of the free market or that they only operate in free market systems. But do market forces just disappear in a controlled economy? - or do they continue to exist? - and if they exist, how does the government reach an accommodation with them?

What was taking place under communist rule? Communists claimed that they had created an alternative to capitalism, implying that the market itself no longer operated in

Russia. Their capitalist critics seemed to confirm that assertion, charging that the Bolsheviks were out to destroy the free market. However, was the market eliminated in Russia simply because both sides said that it was? If the debate between communism and capitalism suggested that result, the argument relied heavily on what the communists said they intended to do. Because they said that they intended to destroy capitalism, that must have been what happened; because they intended to create a communist system, they must have created a communist system. The focus on intent became so intense that everything attempted in Russia became tainted by what Soviet leaders said. Even the factory assembly line could not escape such scrutiny. However similar it might be to that of Western factories, it somehow operated differently because it was installed in a communist-run Russian factory.

Did Soviet leaders succeed in imposing an alternative, non-market, system on Russia, as the rhetoric of both sides suggested, or was the reality something else? The evidence suggests that they were not entirely successful in breaking away from a capitalist model, however much they claimed to despise it. Why were they unable to make a complete break, and, just as importantly, why did their system not measure up to its Western counterparts? Perhaps it was a case of trying to operate a capitalist system in an economic climate, a hostile environment, for which it was not suited. That hostile environment was created by Bolshevik leaders through their writings and speeches - or so the West believed. Yet, if the climate in Russia was a hostile one, it may have had little to do with rhetoric and everything to do with a scarcity of resources.

For Russia, the question has always been - what led to communism? Therefore the focus has been on the conditions and events surrounding the October Revolution of 1917. Perhaps the reason is that the transition to dictatorship occurred rather quickly in Russia. Lenin forcibly dissolved the Constituent Assembly, the newly-elected legislative body, in January 1918, less than four months after seizing power. By July he would not even tolerate press criticism from his own Bolshevik newspapers, adding their names to the list of outlawed publications. Yet, a more critical question might be, not what led to communism, but what led from communism to dictatorship?

These four points should provide a framework from which to begin. They are not intended to ignore the serious problems which Russia has experienced. Communism and central planning in Russia have been labeled a total failure with good reason, at least from a manufacturing perspective. Food lines, with day-long waits for food in Moscow and other Soviet cities are well-known, as are empty store shelves. Foreigners complain about the quality of accommodations and food in Russian hotels and Russians have often been heard to complain about the quality of Russian apartments and Russian goods - "shoddy merchandise" is a commonly-used term. In contrast, manufacturers in the U.S. and other Western countries have largely set the standard for success. In fact, if manufacturing quality and quantity is the standard by which economic systems are judged, then the Soviet system is, by almost any standard, an abject failure.

At the same time, it seems somewhat surprising that, for a failure, the Soviet system has been the most talked about, the most studied, the most analyzed, and the most reviled. In fact, as "failures" go, it has been subject to some of the most intense scrutiny of any "failure" in history. Perhaps that is because, for all the examples used to prove the "failure" of the Soviet system, the one proof lacking is actual "failure," i.e., the total societal collapse of Russia. For years Western writers pointed to signs which indicated the imminent collapse of the Soviet Union. The Soviet Union always seemed to be on the verge of collapse. Unfortunately, when the "imminent" collapse did not occur as predicted, Western writers had to be content with "proof" of the next best thing - "failure." Empty store shelves, shoddy merchandise, lack of consumer choice, and lack of personal freedom - all were offered as proof of the failure of Soviet rule.

Judging success or failure by the quality or quantity of manufactured goods is one possible standard - although it is subjective and somewhat elusive. (It might be well to note that success or failure will always depend on the standard applied, and a manufacturing standard is only one standard.) At the country level, as mentioned above, there is a more absolute standard which might be appropriate - survival. Success is measured simply by the survival of the society - period. When economic and political systems are judged, in absolute terms, there are only two alternatives - survival and/or total collapse.

Often forgotten are examples of civilizations which simply disappeared because their economic and political systems actually did fail. In the 1920s archaeologists investigated ruins found in the Indus Valley of northern India. The cities of Mohenjo-daro and Harappa provided evidence of a fairly advanced civilization, which came to be known as the Harappa Culture. The cities established themselves around 2400 B.C. The site at Mohenjo-daro revealed a city with regularly laid-out streets, a granary, a large public bath, a water supply system, and surprisingly, earthenware pipe connections at individual houses to a sewage system which emptied into a central drainage system. This drainage system was even equipped with manhole covers over access holes at regularly spaced intervals which provided access for cleaning. It appears that earthquake activity may have caused what is known as tectonic uplift, a lifting of the earth's surface, which, in turn caused the Indus River to change course. This may have dried up the region near Mohenjo-daro. Another possibility is that the tectonic uplift blocked the path of the Indus river and its waters backed up, forming a stagnant lake around Mohenjo-daro - a process called "ponding." It would have been impossible to grow crops in the inundated fields, and as some evidence suggests, the ponding may have been so extensive that the streets of the city were themselves submerged. At any rate, sometime around 1800 B.C. Mohenjo-daro and other nearby Harappan settlements appear to have been abandoned.[3]

The Maya, in Central America, provide another example. Archaeologists define the period from around 250 to 900 A.D. as the Classic period in Maya culture. It was during this period that the stone monuments, paved roads, and buildings were created. The 9th Century A.D. is generally used to mark the collapse of Maya civilization. Current theory suggests that a combination of deforestation, erosion, and overcultivation resulted in a shortage of cultivable land. This, in turn, undermined the agricultural productivity of the region and the land was unable to sustain the population. The great stone buildings and monuments in the Mayan cities were abandoned to the encroaching jungle.[4]

East of Egypt, in the Jordanian desert, lies a limestone plateau. In a sandstone fault in the plateau, some 2,800 feet above sea-level, can be found the ruins of the city of Petra. Sometime in the fourth century B.C., a nomadic tribe from northern Arabia, known as the Nabataeans, established Petra as their capital. Petra was strategically situated along the north-south caravan route between Arabia and Damascus, as well as an east-west route between Egypt and Mesopotamia. Nabataean engineers constructed an 88,275 cubic foot reservoir, known as Al Birka, 'the pool,' to hold water from springs and the occasional rainstorm. An aqueduct carried water down to Petra itself. Petra, taking advantage of its location, flourished. At one point it supported a population of 20,000. It survived into the second century A.D. when the Romans took control and made it part of the new province of Arabia. Unfortunately, the trade routes which formerly passed through Petra became untenable and caravans moved farther north. Petra, with its reservoir, was abandoned to the desert in the third century and forgotten. It was not heard of again until its redis-covery in 1812. Perhaps an indication of the relative swiftness with which desert climate could triumph was the fact that kilns found in Petra had been left full of pots and clay vessels - still waiting to be fired.[5]

What standard can be used to judge the success or failure of any given society or economic and political system? The Harappans, the Maya, and the Nabataeans, - three cultures, three time periods, three different locations, and three "models" of societal collapse - serve as examples of the absolute standard which can be applied to economic and political systems, when the term "failure" is used. While the Soviet Union was not a failure in an absolute sense, Soviet society certainly experienced problems. If communism was not the cause of Russia's economic problems, what factors were at work? There are several concepts which may help to explain the interaction between political and econo-mic forces, both in Russia, and in a wider context.

First, there is a distinction between political and economic power. This needs to be explored in conjunction with the interaction of these two forces. Stating that power can have either an economic or a political origin may be overstating the obvious. However, a discussion of the origin and operation of these separate power bases may prove useful. Second, there are, in economic terms, regional economies, almost "mini-economies" which operate within the total economy of a country. Their boundaries might be said to be the normal or "natural" limits of the economic forces within a given region. Third, there is the political conception of a country, such as Russia, i.e., what is it that people believe their country is, in a geographical sense? At times, the results of this political concept can bring political forces into conflict with the economic forces generated by the regional economies. Fourth, there is the economic concept of monopoly. Conditions conducive to monopolis-tic power bring certain economic forces into play. In Russia, it was forces created by monopolistic conditions which played a significant role in the implementation of a Soviet or communistic system.

The distinction between political and economic power is the first concept. Anyone who has followed elections in the United States or other Western democracies is well aware that economic forces clearly can influence political decisions. Rising unemployment figures tend to make incumbent politicians nervous. To restate an obvious point, it might be said that economic and political forces are somewhat independent of each other. It might be said, in one sense, that the power of economic forces remains something of a constant: rich agricultural land or mountains with veins of pure gold or silver will always be sought after. However, geological and climactic conditions have not always conveniently concentrated agricultural or mineral wealth in one place or country. As a result, economic power is not uniformly distributed, nor, based on resource potential, is economic power of the same magnitude. Even within a single country or region, economic strength can vary. Because of these factors, economic power might be better measured in relative terms, particularly in relation to political power. Economic forces can be strong or weak - both in relation to political forces and in relation to other economic forces.

An example may serve to illustrate the differences between economic and political "power" and how these two forces interact. We will imagine two kingdoms in the Ancient World. The one "resource" possessed by the first kingdom is a rich gold mine, situated on a mountain overlooking a river, which also serves as the border between the two kingdoms. The sole resource of the second kingdom is fertile agricultural land., lying directly across the river from the gold mine. The king of the first land has located his capital city a great distance from the gold mine. Impassable desert, fierce tribes, and a mountain range lie between the gold mine and the king's capital city. Both the gold mine and the agricultural land represent sources of economic power, since both have value to someone.

Economic forces would be strongest between the gold mine and the agricultural land. Gold would be used to purchase agricultural products or land. Agricultural products would be used to buy gold. The mine owners or gold producers see agricultural products, such as wheat, to be commodities they would like to have. Economic ties, i.e., economic forces, would be weakest between the capital city and the gold mine and/or agricultural region. Economically, there are two reasons for this circumstance: 1) agricultural produce is a commodity of value to the mine owners and gold is a commodity of value to the agricultural producers; and 2) the mountains, hostile tribes, and desert represent economic barriers to trade, i.e., they are physical obstacles which increase costs. The physical barriers represent economic counterforces, which inhibit movement. Political power is represented by the king. The king wants the gold moved to his capital He will use political power, i.e., his army, engineers, and administrative system, to move the gold over the mountains and across the desert to his capital, i.e., in a direction contrary to that of the natural economic forces. The army will guard the gold shipments or control the hostile tribes and the engineers and administrators will develop some sort of desert transport system. Using political power to counteract economic forces however, means the expenditure of the kingdom's resources. (In one sense this means that even political power has an economic foundation.)

The scenario can be changed to illustrate an alternative situation. What if the capital of the first kingdom is not located across a desert and mountain range, but instead is located in the second kingdom, across the river, in the middle of the agricultural land. In this case, economic and political forces are not in conflict. The normal operation of econo-

7

mic forces will bring the gold to the capital city, in accordance with the king's political wishes.

This example illustrates the distinction between economic and political forces and the problems likely to arise when they do not work in conjunction. A second factor at work, particularly in Russia, was the existence of many independent regional markets operating within the overall framework of the entire economy. While these regions are part of the total economy, they both support and compete with the economies of other regions. Just as economic forces impact the overall economy, so too do economic forces work within and between any of the economic regions themselves. Physical factors or obstacles operate to aid, obstruct, or block the operation of economic forces. Geographical distance is one such factor, for example. It operates to limit the size of a market - the greater the distance which grain must be shipped, the greater the cost. The presence of a market, such as a city, or any area of concentrated population, is another "physical" factor acting on market forces. In some cases it serves to expand an economic region since it attracts resources.

The existence of regional markets within a country, in some ways acts as a natural limit on size. People living within an economic region grow to think of themselves as part of that region, since they tend to limit business dealings to that economic region. The size-limiting aspect of regional markets stands in contrast to the third factor, the political conception of Russia as a single geographic region. Russia's problem was that the conception of Russia, in the minds of its leaders, was geographically larger than Russia's economic regions suggested. Politically, Russia was far greater in physical size than Russia's economies could comfortably maintain - the Russian "state" was overextended. In the context of the example of the two kingdoms, the king, viz., Russia's political leadership, wanted to transport the gold across the desert, while the mine owners, viz., the economic regions, wanted only to trade it across the river - the beginnings of a potential conflict.

The existence of opposing concepts, regional economies acting to constrict Russia and political ideas seeking to expand it, provided only two ingredients. The other ingredient was related to the term monopoly. Monopoly, in the context of the Soviet Union, has often been used to describe the control exercised by the Soviet planners over economic resources. Central planning, it has been said, involves a state-run monopoly. Monopoly, in this context, has some very unflattering connotations. On the other hand, its reputation in Western economies is not much better - it has some unflattering connotations there as well. In political sense, it can take on connotations of conspiracy - monopolistic conspiracies are seen in dealings by "Big Oil," i.e., the major oil companies, by steel producers, or by any number of other large-scale industries. Monopolies, despite their sinister reputation, hold a fascination as well. Conspiracies fascinate us - at least in the U.S. Monopolies, by their nature, have a conspiratorial aspect - they are carried out by a small group or even one company and they operate unseen, through hidden market forces. For that reason, the term monopoly has taken on a sinister aspect; monopoly is personified as an evil company gouging the public through its monopolistic control of the market. Communist theorists have long alleged a conspiratorial, monopolistic control of the world's resources by capitalists or big industrialists.

Yet, the term monopoly, apart from its highly-charged political sense, has a less sinister economic meaning. In an economic context monopoly can be used to describe a market situation or set of conditions. It might be added, as well, that in any monopolistic situation, there are forces present contributing to exploitation as well as forces present which counteract monopolistic tendencies. Above all, it should be kept in mind, that the power of monopolies, in one sense, is imaginary. The power of monopoly operates, not through physical control of the purchaser, but based on the strength of the desire for a product.

To explain monopoly, it might be helpful to provide a working definition. What is known as a pure monopoly exists when there is one firm which supplies a product in a given market area. According to economists there are, in fact, very few examples of pure monopoly situations in the real world, despite the accusations made against "Big Oil," or companies associated with similar industries. A major reason for the scarcity of true monopolies is the presence or possibility of substitute products. True monopolies can usually exist only where there are no substitute products.

Contrary to popular notions, monopolistic power is not an irresistible force holding absolute power over a market. There are market forces, in a free market, which operate to counteract monopolistic tendencies on the part of most companies. One market "force" which limits higher prices, or price-gouging, is the presence of potential competitors. Companies which increase profits by charging more for a product find that the higher prices attract competitors, who, on entering a market, will seek to undercut their competitors. Another market force limiting the actual power of the monopolist is the buyer's incentive to find or develop substitutes.

One might use the trucking industry in the U.S. to illustrate how market forces work to limit monopolistic power. For suppliers in the U.S., be they manufacturers of consumer goods or farm products, transport is crucial to operations. Monopolistic theory holds that, while trucking companies might wish to raise prices because they have control of road transport, market forces will limit such tendencies. The possibility of substitution acts to hold prices down. First, if transport prices become exorbitant, producers may be tempted to form their own trucking lines or buy existing trucking firms. New competitors may find the market tempting as well. Second, producers may opt for substitute transport, such as river barges or railroads.

Turning now to the Soviet Union, how do monopoly principles operate within that economy? As indicated above, monopoly, in relation to the Soviet Union, is not restricted to state-controlled institutions. Two points about economic conditions in a monopolistic situation should be emphasized: 1) the monopolist's power is based on both the strength of the buyer's need for a product as well as the buyer's inability to find substitutes; and 2) the strength of the monopolist's power over a given market (or conversely, the buyer's dependence on the monopolist's product) may be a symptom of an inherent weakness in that market. In relation to the second point, it could be said that economic strength is derived from the possession or creation of a commodity of value to someone else. The gold mine in the example of the two kingdoms represents a source of economic power to its owners. Economic dependence on a would-be monopolist's product implies a two-fold weakness, first, that the buyer cannot obtain a substitute product and second, that the buyer does not have any other product or commodity of value to someone else. The dependent buyer, in other words, has no independent source of economic power.

Siberia can serve as a starting point to illustrate the operation of the rules of "monopoly" in the economic context. Perhaps, more to the point, the Siberian fur-trader, can serve as an example. More infamous for Stalin's use of its salt mines as political punishment, Siberia is both beautiful and inhospitable. Anyone who chooses to live there must be very tough and very resourceful. In the economic context, however, Siberia serves as the perfect example of how "substitution" can counteract the forces of "monopoly." The Siberian fur trader would have liked to have any number of manufactured goods. However, only three would be "essential;" a rifle and ammunition, a steel knife, and spring traps. Given the resourcefulness of these individuals, even these items were never essentials. They were valued because they made trapping and working easier, but there were substitutes available. In the area of transport, it's doubtful if any firm could have created a monopoly attempting to deliver such items. An increase in delivery cost would simply prompt the fur trapper to make a trip to the nearest trading settlement or town to obtain the items himself.

The one commodity crucial to all economies and societies is food. Even here, the Siberian fur trapper was at an advantage. Flour from Russia's grain producing regions was, no doubt, an extremely valuable product. Yet, while sought after, there were other food products which could be used instead. The fur trapper could obtain those products himself by hunting. The sinister power of monopoly is, in a sense, imaginary and ephemeral, since it depends on the buyer's perceived need for a product. Monopoly, in the economic sense, does not draw its strength from physical control or restraint over the buyer; its power is derived from the strength of the market, i.e., the buyer's need or desire for a product. The fur trapper was largely immune to such market forces. At the extreme, should prices become too high, he could resort to the ultimate in substitution, and simply move. Economically, Moscow's hold over the fur trapper was tenuous.

In contrast to the fur-trapper, Russian city-dwellers had fewer options. For them, however, their limited options had both a psychological and an economic aspect. Psychologically, city-dwellers were reluctant to leave the city. Leaving the city was probably always an option - even when government restrictions on personal freedom were greatest. What held the city-dweller however, was often more a psychological attachment to urban life. Once established in the city, people tended to lose the resourcefulness which was second nature to the Siberian fur-trapper. In addition, they became attached to their occupation or profession. As workers in the U.S. have recently discovered, changing jobs, or professions, requires a great deal of effort - there is an inertia which is involved. Life in the countryside was harsh, and once people became accustomed to the city, their perception of how hard country life could be grew.

Economically, city-dwellers, were at a disadvantage in two ways: 1) they did not have access to substitute products or the wherewithal to produce them; and 2) they lacked, in many ways, the resources or power to create products which could be marketed to the outside world, a source of economic power of their own. In the context of "substitution," they had traded off many of the resources which made substitution possible. The Siberian fur-trapper, when confronted by the need for food or by high prices, could often gather or hunt for food within a short distance of camp. In addition, he had some market forces on his side - the fur pelts he got from trapping had an economic value, i.e., they commanded a price in the outside world. This provided him with an economic power he could create on his own. The city-dweller, in contrast, was almost totally dependent on others for that most important of commodities - food. To be sure, even in the area of food commodities, substitution was possible - cheaper items could be substituted for more expensive items, such as meat. However, for Muscovites and residents of other cities, this option was limited.

For the monopolist, intent on increasing profits by raising prices, a captive market and the lack of alternative substitutes would seem ideal. In Russia, however, a monopolistic situation without countervailing controls was only part of the problem. There was another factor at work - the presence of alternative markets for the monopolist. What happens if the monopolist chooses not to exploit the captive market? A market which is ripe for exploitation by a monopolist may, in reality, not be the "golden opportunity" it appears. The buyer's very dependence on a single product may be evidence that the underlying market is quite weak. It implies a lack of resource diversity and a lack of real economic strength. While the monopolist can fully exploit the market, he may realize that even full exploitation will bring limited benefits. Efforts spent in other markets with other products are likely to be more profitable.

The monopolist is often pictured as the conservative industrialist, similar in character to Ebenezer Scrooge. To understand the Russian economic situation, particularly after the October Revolution, it may be helpful to view monopolistic forces and markets from a somewhat different perspective. Shortages of food have often been the focal point for criticism of the Soviet system, and food is the major product on which Moscow and other Russian cities were dependent. For the producer, the economic problem is not simply one of charging the highest price for grain. There is also the problem of keeping costs low. The grain producer, offered the same price by a buyer located in a distant city and a buyer close at hand, is likely to opt for the geographically closer market. Shipping costs to distant markets will eliminate any profit. It was a "monopoly" situation involving food production which was Moscow's dilemma. In Russia, monopoly power was not held by a small group of industrial firms, instead, it was held by agricultural producers in the aggregate. A "monopoly" controlled by agricultural producers represented the economic side of the equation.

On the other side of the equation was the political power, represented, in part by the Soviet government, in part by the cities. Stalin's industrialization plans needed to be financed and the cities needed to be fed. The government competed against the cities for grain and the cities competed against each other. There were any number of cities between Russia's grain-producing regions and Moscow. It will be recalled, in the example of the two kingdoms cited earlier, that the king in his faraway capital had one option available to counteract economic forces. He could use his political resources to physically move gold from the mine to his capital. In very simple terms the market was weak. The government as well as the cities, like the king's capital, lacked the economic power to move grain from producing regions to the cities. On the other hand, Russia's political leaders controlled the army which could carry out political orders. Political and military power was a crude way to make up for deficiencies in economic strength.

The problem which confronted Stalin in 1929, pushing him to collectivization and to centralization, was not so much that the agricultural monopoly used its power to extort economic concessions from Moscow in the form of higher grain prices, although producers often did withhold grain in expectation of higher prices. The real problem was that the agricultural producers largely ignored Moscow. That, at least, is part of the scenario in the context of Russia.

A discussion of monopolistic economic forces and imbalances between economic and political forces, while far-ranging, seems somehow mundane in comparison to the political events which transpired in Russia. While estimates of the total number of deaths which occurred during the Stalin era differ, they are in the millions. Yet, we will leave Russia for the time being and turn to examples of other governments. In Ancient Rome and Nazi Germany other economic forces came to the fore.

The concept of work, and the need for a job, is as old as history. In ancient cultures, not as efficient as modern societies, the need and demand for labor was so high, that unemployment was virtually unheard of. However, once economies reached a point beyond subsistence-level production, unemployment surfaced. Ancient Rome was successful in conquering distant lands and administering a far-flung empire, yet even Rome had a problem with unemployment. Rome also presents politically somewhat of a paradox. Notwithstanding Rome's military success in subjugating far-off lands, there seems to have been a reluctance to resort to military force as a political option in the city itself. Roman politicians, at least, discovered that the easier path was to buy off the masses than to use physical force to control them. Expediency involves offering something of advantage rather than doing something right or just; taking the easy way out, in other words. Roman politicians probably didn't discover the concept, but their financial support of the Roman Circus to win the favor of the masses, gave expediency a greater prominence.

Kings, despite the temptation to rule by fear and the use of physical force, discovered that persuasion was a less costly means of administration. In more primitive agricultural societies, kings, in one sense, worried more about the power held by competing noblemen than about the diluted power of the individual citizen, particularly if the populace was dispersed over the countryside. In medieval Europe, for example, the peasants were less of a problem than the manor lords who held power locally. City-states, such as Rome, in contrast, presented a more complex problem. People who were unhappy, were not only conveniently located in a place where they could complain to others about their problems, they were just as conveniently in a position to act on their grievances. The physical threat represented by a mob can only be countered by physical force, unless there are means to appease the mob or its leaders.

There are any number of reasons people will complain to (or about) political leaders. In Russia, in simple terms, the complaint was about a lack of food. In Rome, the complaint was more about jobs, although there were problems as well with the food supply. Jobs, in and of themselves, are not quite as important as the fact that they represent a means of obtaining food and necessities. In nearly all cases, economic problems boil down to a need to obtain necessities, especially food. However, in Rome (and Nazi Germany as well), the economic focus was more on jobs, i.e., while the underlying problem in the economies of Russia, Ancient Rome, and Germany was food, the specific economic problem involved in Rome and Germany was related to jobs and unemployment.

While there are differences between Ancient Rome and Nazi Germany, they have two things in common, an unemployment rate approaching or exceeding 30 percent and a disturbingly high level of violence and civil unrest. Rome, from around 133 B.C. until the ascension of Julius Caesar in 48 B.C., was plagued by street violence. Gangs of unemployed workers fought political leaders and attacked each other. Rome's achievements in engineering and governmental administration in the context of Empire are somewhat offset by its reputation for barbarity. Roman citizens enjoyed the life and death struggles of gladiatorial contests in which the loser was put to death. But Romans were not content to serve merely as spectators. The deadly gladiatorial contests, for which Rome is famous, were mirrored in the street fighting. At some elections, citizens showed up to vote armed with bows and arrows, intent, not just on defeating the politicians of the opposing party, but on killing their supporters. Many times they were successful. Germany, prior to Hitler's rise to power, experienced similar problems. Clashes between Nazi supporters and communists in 1932 and 1933 culminated in bloody riots, fatal to many of the participants.

There is something else which Ancient Rome and Nazi Germany shared - both turned to public works to help solve problems of unemployment and both used some form of political repression. Caesar Augustus, who came to power in 31 B.C., engaged in public works projects which included new buildings as well as the renovation of existing structures. He also established a 3,000 man security force as part of the army, but with responsibility only for the city of Rome. In Germany, Hitler turned to public works as well. The unemployed were hired for community projects and in a major program to construct a national system of roads. The Gestapo and SS were Hitler's instruments of political repression. It was the SS which would administer the Death Camps while the Gestapo would seek to identify "enemies of the state."

Nazi Germany is separated from Ancient Rome by almost 2,000 years of history. It seems somewhat surprising that, despite the technological differences, both the problems and solutions appear to be much the same. That "sameness" or constancy over time is perhaps what this book is really about, for in a sense, the political and economic forces which showed themselves at the beginnings of human history have remain unchanged. While modern economies have become more complex and sophisticated, they have, at heart, remained the same as their ancient counterparts. Food and employment remain perhaps the two elements unchanged in all history; food still an essential commodity; employment still an essential element of participation in an economy.

Russia, Ancient Rome, and Nazi Germany provide examples of different economic and political forces at work. In reality, the forces at work were the same; the difference was in the magnitude and origin of the conflicting forces. Russia's response was different than that of Rome and Germany, but it was confronted by different economic circumstances. In Russia actual scarcity caused unrest, while in Rome and Germany, unemployment was the immediate problem. The remainder of this book explores in greater detail how the economic circumstances faced by different governments have provoked different responses.

CHAPTER 2

RESOURCES AND A THEORY

This chapter discusses four topics: first, how resources are defined; second, how resources are measured; third, how democracies or dictatorships are defined and classified; and fourth, how resource availability is associated with governmental development. More specifically, the fourth area is about relative resource availability, i.e., abundance and scarcity, and its relationship to the evolution of dictatorships and democracies.

Resources can be defined in several ways. A classic definition, in relation to countries, normally involves natural resources: something that a country or state has and can use to advantage; actual or potential forms of wealth. Resources can be defined in a broader sense as well: a resource is something that lies ready for use or that can be drawn upon to take care of a need. In the context of this book, the second, broader definition is the one which applies. Boiled down to its simplest terms, a resource is something which someone needs or can use, or, in monetary terms, something someone will pay for. Human needs are so varied that resources have been divided into different categories. One of the more common designations is applied to those resources supplied by nature - natural resources. Natural resources include energy resources, such as coal, oil, and water power, mineral resources such as iron and copper, and farming resources, such as arable land.

Natural resources is the broadest category of resources. Yet there are other classifications. Some represent sub-classifications or special categories of natural resources, such as water resources or agricultural resources. Others are simply desig-nations based on special markets or specialized fields of activity, such as technological resources or human resources. What the various classifications have in common is a relationship to some human need. For every human need imaginable there has probably been a corresponding resource available with a special resource term applied. People who want to borrow rely on banking or financial resources. Travelers depend on transportation or travel resources.

In one sense we tend to think of resources in terms of things which do not change over time. Perhaps this is because when we think of resources, it is the hard metals, such as iron or copper, which come to mind. Yet the concept of a resource also contains an element of change; there is something fluid in the nature of resources. No matter what material, mineral, or energy source is involved, it does not become a resource until it is needed in some way. In economic terms, something does not become a resource until it can be incorporated into an economy. There is, in other words, a time element involved in the notion of what a resource is. Uranium is perhaps one of the best examples of this resource property. It had no value as an energy resource prior to the Twentieth Century. In fact, probably its only value as a resource prior to World War II was as a ceramic additive. Uranium oxide was valued from 1896 on by the ceramic industry because, when added to clay, it produced an intense red color in kiln-fired ceramic ware.

Demand for energy has been a human constant since the Ice Age. Uranium, with its high energy output, was thus always a potential resource. Yet, there were a number of obstacles in the way of its reaching the status of an actual resource. First, unlike wood or coal, uranium requires sophisticated processing before its energy can be released. Such technology was not even available until the 1940s. Second, the energy produced in nuclear reactors is difficult to exploit in the absence of electricity and an electrical transmission system. Nuclear power produces energy by converting heat to electricity and electricity was little understood until the second half of the Nineteenth Century. Even after a basic understanding was achieved, the creation of a power system to deliver it took some time - electrical power is itself dependent on a fairly intricate infrastructure of power lines and electrical relays for distribution.

Iron provides a good example of how things we designate as resources can change over time. While the underlying element or substance can remain essentially unchanged over time, its inclusion in the group of things we call resources depends on whether it is being used by someone at a particular time. Because modern industrial economies incorporate iron in so many areas, iron has almost become synonymous with the term resource. Iron is important in automobiles and building construction. Yet even iron, for all its importance today, would not be defined as a resource for all times or in all civilizations. Iron is the second most abundant metal in the earth, after aluminum.[1] Iron objects began appearing as early as 5000 B.C.,[2] although its first major use may have been in Egyptian weapons, around 2000 B.C..[3] From about 1100 B.C. until around 900 B.C., iron became more common, but it is not until 900 or 800 B.C. that the Age of Iron is said to begin.[4] (Because the use of iron was a gradual process around the Mediterranean, the beginning of the Age of Iron can be dated anywhere from 1200 B.C. to 800 B.C., depending on the source.)[5] Steel, the tough alloy of iron, began to be used about the time of Christ.[6]

With the advantage of 3,000 years of technology and the knowledge of the modern blast furnace, it may be a little difficult to understand the beginnings of iron use. The first iron used was called sponge iron, which is basically the run-off from heated iron ore. The reason sponge iron was used was because ancient metallurgists had invented no container to hold molten metal.[7] The Hittites, who lived in what is now Turkey, are said to have been the first people to understand the technology of iron-smelting, the process which separates impurities from pure metal.[8] Whether the Hittites carried their process as far as steel development is not clear. Steel is an alloy of iron containing at least one other element, usually carbon.[9] The ultimate achievement in iron technology involves an understanding that the absorption of carbon by iron, known as carburization, and rapid cooling, known as quenching, in combination will produce a stronger product.[10]

Iron and steel held many advantages, even in the Ancient World, over other metals. They made superior agricultural implements and weapons. However, it was not until the arrival of modern industrialization that iron and steel became "true" resources. Machinery and construction requirements provided an economic need for iron and steel.

Other minerals and substances have become resources at different times. Bronze, generally an alloy made of copper and tin, favored by the Ancient World, was made as early as 3700 B.C..[11] Tin, as a resource, was so valuable that Phoenicians shipped it from Cornwall in England, from 1500 to 1200 B.C. Britain supplied 100 tons annually in 500 B.C..[12]

Human or country needs, in the resource sense, could be divided into actual and hypothetical or abstract needs. Hypothetical needs will always be there, although they are unlikely to be fulfilled. These are the "...nice to have, but probably not likely." A cure for disease fits in this category. More practically, there are improvements in machinery or implements, which would be helpful, but may not have been thought of. Ancient farmers who had to use wooden plows to break up the soil no doubt longed for some improvement, and clearly "needed" the advantages of the modern steel plow. That need however did not have any relation to a resource. The technology did not exist at the time to fulfill the need. Resources can only come from something concrete - an existing use or an existing technology. On the other hand, substitution, the economic counterforce to monopoly, discussed in the introduction, has its counterpart in the resource realm as well. There are certain needs which can be met by substitutes. Steel arrowheads were no doubt an improvement over their predecessors, but stone would serve as well. An iron cup might last longer than a ceramic one, but a ceramic cup would hold liquid just as well.

There are thus two points which could be made about resources. First, to be a resource, a resource must, not just fulfill a need, but fulfill that need in a way or at a price which makes the resource practical. Second, the value of a resource depends on its uniqueness; if substitutes can be found which can be economically acquired, the resource loses some of its value. A resource, in one sense becomes less of a resource as it is less needed. Substitute products diminish other resources because they reduce the need for the primary product. The value of gold and silver stemmed from the fact that, while rare, they were still attainable. The other source of their value as resources was that their appearance, e.g., gold's lustre, could not be duplicated. There were no substitute products, in other words.

If price were any indication, gold would probably be considered one of the more crucial resources. In fact, because it is used as a standard for trade, its value is un-challenged. Yet, it is some of the "cheaper," more plentiful, food items which, in the aggregate, are more important resources. Resource needs might be thought of in terms of a series of concentric circles. The center of these circles represents the strongest resource needs of people or countries. Necessities, such as food clothing, water, and fuel, are what comprise the core of these circles. While food items individually may cost very little, in the aggregate these items represent the strongest resource needs of any society. Deprived of these items, humans cannot survive. Therefore water and agricultural resources represent the heart of resource requirements; the possession of such resources absolutely essential. This may explain why Petra, the desert city, flourished and then so suddenly died. The scarcity of water in the vicinity of Petra, increased Petra's value as a source of a rare resource, but also made Petra's hold on life extremely precarious. The closer a resource or resource need comes to being necessary for sustaining life, the more crucial that resource becomes for a society, and in turn, for an economy. Technology crucial for war, such as iron and steel technology for weapons, may seem to be at the outer edge of needs. However, if one thinks in terms of ancient governments, the inability to defend land or a country against an invading army meant that that army could completely deprive a country of food and thus could totally threaten its survival.

While it is true that minerals or substances must be incorporated in an economy to become resources, it could also be said that necessary substances, such as food or water, have represented unchanging "needs" over time. Since they have always been necessary for survival, they have always been part of every economy. Food and water resources, thus represent "constants," over the course of human history, in terms of resources. Minerals, such as iron, have been valued as resources (or not) based on the economic and technological level of a civilization at any given time or geographical location. Food and water resources have always been and will always be valued.

The problem for most countries, nations, or governments is that resources have not been evenly distributed throughout the world. Good fortune, in the area of resource distribution, has often been the result of chance. Geological and climactic conditions have often played a major role in determining whether a country is rich or poor in resources. Mineral deposits, such as gold, can often be found only in areas far away from agricultural land, e.g., in the middle of deserts or high in the mountains. The income received for gold or other precious metals often is offset by the costs of extraction and transport. As the Phoenicians discovered, an important element in bronze, tin, needed to be brought from Britain. The United States, once a major producer of oil, now finds itself more and more dependent on the Middle East for oil.

Having provided a rough definition of resources, the question becomes how to measure the amount of resources which a country has. It may sound simple. If you want to find out how much iron ore a country has, go out and measure the size of the reserves. The equation becomes more complex however, if you try to factor in technological resources. For example, what if a country has large reserves of iron ore, but no technological capabilities for processing that ore? What if it has some technology, but the technology is obsolete?

Technological resources are, by one definition, the means by which a society provides for its members. They are, in other words, the means by which "knowledge" translates physical resources into the end or "delivered" product, e.g., how iron ore is transformed into iron metal or steel and delivered to the consumer in final product form. In that sense, they are a separate resource. In another sense however, they become part of overall resource availability. and the resource need, in turn, is measured by the monetary value placed on a given resource. The amount of resources a country has may be determined by the monetary value of the resources. This monetary value, however, may be more than just the value of unprocessed resources in the ground. A country might also be said to have or possess the "value" of "inputs" it adds to a product, i.e., a country's resources include those technological resources which add value to the unprocessed resource. The amount of resources possessed by a country may thus be related to the question - How much are those resources valued by someone? or, more simply, how much do they cost?

Since the theme of this book is that the amount of resources possessed by a country determines the type of government, measuring the amount of resources of a given country can be important. Through geological testing it is possible to determine the amount of mineral or energy reserves present in a given area, i.e., the physical quantity which exists. However, measuring the physical quantity or amount of a given substance is not the same thing as determining the amount of a resource. That is because the concept of a resource includes not just the physical substance, but also the economic need. A resource combines an abstract with a physical component. The physical component is the resource itself; the abstract component is the human need or market demand for the resource.

Oil reserves may serve to illustrate this distinction. Assuming reserves are 1 billion barrels, how are oil "resources" measured? Does a country possess a physical resource of 1 billion barrels? or does it possess the value of the 1 billion barrels at a given point in time? The price of oil in the last few years has ranged anywhere from $10 per barrel to $30 per barrel. In monetary terms does the country possess a resource worth $10 billion or worth $30 billion? A more abstract question perhaps is whether the country "has," "possesses," or "owns" the reserves it holds without selling or does it really only possess those resources which it sells on the market. A resource, by definition, exists only in relation to a market or to market demand. Put another way, iron, as a metal and physical substance, exists in the earth, independently of whether there is a market for iron; iron as a resource exists only to the extent there is a market for iron.

When the market value of a given material or product falls to zero, that material ceases to be a resource. As dependent as modern industrialized economies are on iron, the thought that iron might stop being a resource seems somewhat incomprehensible. Yet if one journeys back several thousand years to a time before iron smelting had been developed, it is possible to understand that resource is a term which would not apply to iron in that time period. In one sense we tend to think of things as either being resources or not, based on the physical quantity. If there is even minimal demand, the physical quantity seems to determine the concept of how much of the resource exists. In that context, the 1 billion barrels of oil is the same amount of resource, whether its value is $30 per barrel or $1 per barrel. That is the physical side of the concept of a resource. Yet, conceptually, it could be said that the actual "amount" of a resource can decrease based on the loss of demand for that resource - the abstract side of the resource definition plays as big a role. If that is the case, when the price of oil drops to $1 per barrel, a country has lost resources, even though it still may physically possess the 1 billion barrels in oil reserves.

Another aspect of resources and need is that there is a geographical side of resource demand. It is not the absolute, physical quantity of a metal or resource which a country has, but the amount a country has in relation to the total supply. The question may not be simply whether there is a general need or demand for a resource, but whether there is a demand from a particular country. For example, the Organization of Petroleum Exporting Countries (OPEC), in the recent past, has had problems policing production by its member countries. In order to maintain the world price for oil at a certain level, individual countries were assigned a production quota. So long as the price stayed high, the temptation for individual countries was to exceed the quota, since greater production at the higher price meant more hard currency could be brought in. When overproduction occurred resulting in a glut, the price fell. In resource terms, there was a general level of demand for oil. When the world need could be fulfilled by a number of different producing countries, the need or demand for oil from any one country was diminished. Individual countries "lost" resources as a result.

There is another complicating factor in determining "how much" a country possesses. That factor is related to the overall market demand both internally and in relation to other countries. This is related to what might be called the "constant" aspect of resource needs and the "relative" aspect. The constant aspect relates to the ability of a country to fulfill the basic needs of its population. A country must be able to satisfy the needs of its people for food, clothing, water, and shelter or it will always be considered resource poor. It does not matter whether it satisfies such markets by producing internally what it needs or by trading some resource for necessities. The external market or the relationship of a country's internal resources to world resources is another aspect. Economics, by one definition, is the allocation of scarce resources. By way of illustration, this means that the desert traveler who only has so much money may be forced to decide whether to spend the money on water or on some product. Between countries, the economic value of one country's products is relative to that of products of other countries. Need is both a function of population and of a population's decisions on how to spend its income. The value of one country's resources is measured by the price on the world market. As illustrated by changes in the world price for oil, the relative value of individual resources changes over time.

The amount of resources possessed by one country is affected or determined by yet another factor, the costs or outflows required to market a product, i.e., the costs involved. In accounting terms, for most revenues generated by a company, there are corresponding expenses which operate to reduce or offset the value of the revenues. Inflows, or incoming assets, are reduced by outflows, or outgoing assets. A country might view its precious metal reserves as resources, i.e., potential sources of revenues or hard currency. On the other hand, it must not only take the costs of producing and delivering resources into account, but also the costs of buying resources from other countries. This may be better understood if resources are thought in terms of, not the physical quantity or substance, but rather the monetary value. Everything must be translated into monetary terms. Thus, from the value of oil in the ground must be subtracted the costs, of refining the oil, of building any pipelines to carry it, and any other costs of transport or delivery.

Viewing resources as the hard currency or market price at the time a resource reaches the market, simplifies matters in some ways, complicates it in others. It simplifies things because the amount of resources can be calculated simply by multiplying a given quantity of the resource by the market price at a given point in time. It complicates things because viewing resources as nothing more than the sum total of costs and/or revenues brings in some "intangibles" which affect the price. For example, the ability to transport grain by ship requires good harbor facilities, i.e., places where the landing place is deep enough to load a ship without running the ship aground. A country which can produce grain because of rich agricultural land, but which has a rocky coastline, must expend resources on land transport in order to get the grain to market. Harbor "resources," i.e., places where boats can get in close enough to land to allow them to take on cargo, reduce the costs of transport.

There is probably less of a tendency to think of harbors as being resources. There is something of an intangible aspect to harbor "resources." At least harbors as resources do not immediately spring to mind if we are asked to list resources. Perhaps this is because the needs they satisfy are difficult to measure. Iron or gold ore, as resources, can be quantified and valued fairly easily. In contrast, how is it possible to determine the monetary value of a harbor which is one or two meters deeper than another harbor? Is the cost measured by multiplying the number of times the shallower harbor must be dredged to keep it from silting up, or is it measured by the costs of freeing ships which run aground in the shallower harbor? What about the value of the shipping routes planned by shipowners because ships incur damage at one port or harbor, but not another? Resource availability changes, if one begins to think of resources, not as physical quantities, but as a series of revenues and costs. Harbor resources take on a more tangible or concrete form when viewed from a strictly cost perspective. A good harbor adds to value while a bad harbor subtracts from the value of physical resources which finally reach the market.

Similarly, the amount of gold or oil available as a resource depends on whether the gold or oil is located only one mile or 1,000 miles from a point where it can enter a market. A 1,000 mile pipeline, with its construction and maintenance requirements, by adding to the cost, decreases the amount of oil resources available. Russia, for example, is said to be rich in resources. In terms of reserves in the ground, without including transport costs, this is probably true. However, Russia's vast size increases costs and reduces the resources available.

Resources, in the end, can be reduced to a series of arithmetic pluses and minuses. Even the greatest resource reserves of iron, gold, or oil amount to nothing more than a set of numbers on a balance sheet. At the same time, calculating resource availability can be somewhat complex, and determining "how much" or "how many" resources a country has in relation to other countries can include many variables. As the commercial geographer George Chisholm observed, different parts of the world yield different products or provide the same products under conditions unequally favorable.[13] The variety of products found in different places is either the result of original distribution, e.g., the natural or geologic deposit of minerals, oil, or forests, or artificial production, i.e., cultivation or manufacture. Artificial production of agricultural products, in turn, depends not just on the presence of fertile soil, but also on favorable climactic conditions. Availability is further compounded by problems of distance, ease of transport, labor costs, and transport availability. Vegetation growth of any kind requires both heat and moisture. The complete lack of water resources, as in desert regions, makes crop growth nearly impossible. Yet too much water after harvest can cause problems in storage with mold and fungus; keeping grain dry after harvest is a cost which impacts resource availability.

Consumers rarely think about the production processes or travel routes taken by the products they buy. They are only aware of the final cost of the product. If "hidden" costs make it difficult to quantify resource availability, they may not be that critical in any overall assessment if the analysis involves the impact of resources on governments. Resource availability, insofar as it impacts governments, is measured on a grand scale. The discussion to this point has dealt with the difficulties in both defining and measuring resources. Such problems are probably inevitable when dealing with a concept which combines the material with the abstract. In one sense, many overlooked costs are important because they affect resource availability, in another sense, exact measurement is not crucial. Where resource differences between rich and poor nations have existed they have been quite large, not simply a matter of a few hidden costs. Measuring how rich or poor a nation is, in terms of its resources, is only the economic side of the equation. Governments represent the political.

The remaining discussion in this chapter is not intended to establish the link between wealth and democracy or between poverty and dictatorship. Its purpose, instead, is to provide a background to an analysis of governments and an introduction to a discussion of the relationship between resources and governments. This book's thesis does suggest that if the measurement of resources is accurate enough to label a country as wealthy or poor, it will also indicate whether that country will be a democracy or a dictatorship.

Classifying governments may not be as difficult as defining or measuring resources, but it does present some unique problems. The first question to decide is whether a country is a democracy or a dictatorship. Governments sometimes provide outward signs of political leanings, but such clues often prove deceptive. Communist governments tried to give themselves a democratic appearance by calling themselves "democratic republics" or "people's republics." Both democracies and dictatorships can have parliaments or legislative bodies and elections have been held under all kinds of regimes. For countries which have been labeled dictatorships, the next question is - what kind of dictatorship is it? Dictatorships are not all the same. While they are all repressive, some are more repressive than others and the methods of administration are often different.

Modern dictatorships have been given several different labels, usually based on the philosophy of the political leadership - communist, socialist, or fascist. There is also the all-encompassing designation - totalitarian. One problem in finding a precise definition of any one of these terms is that each term is really a combination of political and economic concepts. Communism as a term, for example, describes both a repressive political system and a centrally planned economic system.

For this book's purposes, governments fall into one of three categories: 1) democracies; 2) fascist regimes; and 3) communist regimes. Perhaps the most practical way to define these terms is to use the characteristics of the governments which have come to be most closely associated with each. The United States thus defines democracy, the Soviet Union or Russia defines communism, and Nazi Germany defines fascism. Without getting into the political philosophy of totalitarian regimes, one common characteristic of all dictatorships is a secret police. Democracies, such as the United States, generally do not maintain a secret police. The Soviet Union had the KGB and Nazi Germany had the Gestapo. A second distinguishing characteristic of dictatorships is that political opposition is suppressed and usually defined as criminal conduct. In democracies, political opposition is treated differently than actual "criminal" conduct; criminal conduct being defined by anti-social acts such as murder, theft, or violence against individuals. Dictatorships place restrictions on individual freedoms, whereas democracies do not. These represent the major distinctions between democracies and dictatorships. On a second level, how does communism differ from fascism?

On the political level, fascism, as exemplified by Nazi Germany, appears to be a more "democratic" type of dictatorship, at least superficially. In fascism, power appears to be somewhat more dispersed, with somewhat more emphasis on consensus among the leadership. In the Soviet Union, particularly under Stalin, there was less subtlety and less concern about building support for policies. At the same time this somewhat oversimplifies what happened under Stalin's rule, since he also had to work at building support among Party representatives. The other major distinction between Nazi Germany and the Soviet Union is at the economic level; the Soviet Union chose central planning whereas Germany maintained or chose a more capitalistic or relatively freer market-oriented system.

The discussion here is only intended to loosely define the three types of political systems and to identify some of their major characteristics. The question becomes what the relationship is between resource availability and the type of government which develops? The next chapter takes a more detailed look at the resource mechanism. In concluding this chapter's discussion, it may be helpful to simply restate the general thesis of this book, in particular its application to fascist and communist regimes.

Democracies will develop in countries which have a large amount of resources, i.e., rich countries will become democracies. Dictatorships are the result of resource scarcity, i.e., poor countries will become totalitarian. As between communist and fascist dictatorships, communist dictatorships result from conditions of severe resource scarcity.

Fascist dictatorships are midway between democracies and communist governments, in terms of resource availability. The thesis may be summarized as follows:

RESOURCE AVAILABILITY/PRODUCTION

TYPE OF GOVERNMENT	PER CAPITA
DEMOCRACY	High resource availability Resource rich
FASCISM	Medium resource availability
COMMUNISM	Scarce resource availability Resource poor

CHAPTER 3

THE RESOURCE MECHANISM: HOW RESOURCE AVAILABILITY DETERMINES THE TYPE OF GOVERNMENT

A secret police force has been the common identifying characteristic of dictatorship. If dictatorships share that distinction, they have one other thing in common - they are born out of violence and turmoil. Violence at the street level is mirrored by a reactionary violence on the part of governments. For some reason, it is the governmental response which is remembered; the societal violence which precedes it is either overlooked or forgotten. Part of the reason totalitarian regimes are vividly remembered is the staggering number of victims. Hitler's Nazis may have killed some 11 million people. Estimates of the number of dead blamed on Stalin's rule in the Soviet Union, have gone as high as 65 million.[1] In just nine months of the Terror during the French Revolution some 16,000 people were guillotined.[2] The Spartan killing of the 2,000 helots by the Krypteia in 424 B.C. represented only a partial count of Sparta's victims.

This chapter looks at the role of violence in dictatorial development. Understanding how violence impacts society and government is key to an understanding of the resource mechanism. (The resource "mechanism," as introduced in the first chapter, is essentially the way in which resources "operate" on an economy to bring about either democratic or dictatorial government.) Violence, as generally defined, is limited to actual physical force; it conjures up images of real acts, such as riots or killings. Violence however, can have an impact, whether it actually occurs or not. The mere threat of violence is often enough to motivate people. One of the more vivid images of war has been the sight of lines of refugees fleeing advancing armies. Where individuals are concerned, threats can be as effective as actual acts at provoking a response. What the response is will often depend on the situation. Sometimes people will flee violence, sometimes they will resort to violence themselves. In ancient Rome gangs of people routinely roamed the streets looking for rival gangs to fight. Romans would later be branded as barbaric for merely watching bloody gladiatorial contests in the Coliseum. The gangs may have lacked the formal discipline of regular army units, but they fought with intensity. Some only had stones to fight with while others fought with swords or even bows and arrows. If some of the weapons were crude, every confrontation left dead or seriously wounded participants.

Governments, like individuals, are often confronted by violence. Like individuals, their response to violence can vary. When faced with an invading army or serious rebellion, some governments or government officials will choose to flee. At other times governments may choose to confront violent situations with military force. Not every governmental effort is successful. Nevertheless governments have acquired a formidable reputation when it comes to the ruthless use of force. Despite such notoriety, the resources at their disposal are often not extraordinarily greater than those possessed by individuals. When Caesar Augustus finally acted against the Roman mobs, his soldiers had the same weapons available to the rioters - swords and spears. What made the soldiers more effective was organization and training.

In some ways there is little difference between the way governments react to situations and the way individuals respond. The military units may have been more effective than the rioters when they were ordered to attack, but their method of putting down unrest involved arming individual soldiers and ordering them to engage members of the mob in combat. Similarly, governmental actions are not really differentiated by a lack of emotional involvement. If governments cannot feel fear or anger, the people who lead them can. Governments, after all, are made up of individuals. If the government response differs from that of the individual, it is in the organizational nature of the response. Governments react to situations through the agencies or special bureaucracies they have set up. Caesar Augustus, for example, did not respond to mob violence by personally leading his soldiers against the rioters. He gave orders to his military staff.

Bureaucratic organizations, whether they are governmental or not, are by nature slow and methodical. They require meticulous planning when they are created and are designed primarily to minimize mistakes, rather than to take decisive action. This does not mean that organizations cannot be modified to make speedy decisions. Roman army units could quickly form to meet any military or physical threat. What it means instead is that, if a given situation is likely to demand an immediate response, an organization or bureaucratic agency must be in place before the expected problem arises. If the government wishes to respond to acts or threats of violence, it must have a police force or army organization set up in advance.

Bureaucracies are often criticized as being "unthinking" or "uncaring." If they suffer from a lack of creativity, that deficiency normally involves situations which are outside their limited experience. They are, in a way, designed for thinking, even anticipating future situations and responses. Unfortunately, whatever creativity they possess is narrowly focused. Governments, by design, must operate through their bureaucratic structures. While bureaucratic patterns of thinking are a disadvantage in many situations, they nevertheless represent a step above the highly emotional thinking of the mob. Though limited by a lack of imagination, bureaucracies can anticipate future problems. It is the bureaucratic capability to think about the future which allows violence to play such a key role in the resource mechanism.

Governments, in contrast to the mob, do not simply react to the immediate situation, they anticipate possible future problems. Though government bureaucracies have a limited imagination, the fact that they can anticipate future events at all gives them an almost human quality. Unlike the mob, which instinctively reacts only to the moment, the immediate provocation, bureaucracies can "think" about the future - and that future can frighten them. That fear can prod governments into action, even if the threat is an imaginary or exaggerated one. If government agencies are gifted by a primitive imagination, they also can count on the support of other bureaucratic organizations which think along similar lines.

Bureaucracies are best suited to situations where goals are clearly defined and boundaries set. Directing a police organization to control actual outbreaks of violence may provide the necessary guidance for efficient bureaucratic operation. Asking a bureaucracy to widen its authority to include preventing future or potential violence is asking for trouble. The difficulties of estimating what potential violence might be are extreme and the organization has little idea of the boundaries which may exist. Once set in motion, bureaucratic operations take on a life of their own - they do not necessarily stop once the original problem has been solved. A police force may quash a riot but continue making arrests long after the riot is over. If the goal is unclear, the organization can never be certain if it has been achieved.

Potentially all governments, whether democracies or dictatorships, face both a real and an imagined threat of violence. Most societies have had to adjust to a certain level of violence and most governments face some opposition. Similarly, all governments, whether democracies or dictatorships, have created similar administrative structures to deal with real or potential problems. What, then, distinguishes the two types of government? The CIA is the American counterpart to the Russian KGB, yet the existence of the CIA does not mean that the United States is in danger of becoming a dictatorship. Are dictatorships merely more paranoid or sensitive to imagined threats than democracies? The simple answer is that societies from which totalitarian regimes emerge appear to be under much greater strain.

If dictatorial regimes are more sensitive to threats of violence, the danger is not simply that violence will occur, but that it will be of a more severe nature when it does occur. There is an inherent instability in the society which surrounds them and it takes only a small spark to make them explode. For this reason, totalitarian societies might be labeled as violent or referred to as "pressure cooker" societies. What might be said about dictatorships is that they exist in an environment of violence. They are not simply brutal and violent themselves. The societies from which they emerge are, by nature, violent.

Crime is a type of violence which can be measured. If nothing else, statistics on criminal activity can be compared to earlier levels of crime. Statistics are available on the number of murders, rapes, or robberies or, in the case of widespread unrest, the number of riots or occurrences of arson. The problem with a term such as violence, if it is to be used to label a society, is that it is not always exact. What is a "violent" society? A major problem, in the context of this book's "violence mechanism," is that violence includes both real acts and potential or threatened acts of violence. Where violence can assume an abstract form, such as a conspiracy or a threat of future violent action, quantification becomes harder. There are fewer statistics available and those that are available may not be reliable.

Where unrest is concerned, totalitarian regimes present a curious paradox. Many dictatorships are relatively free of violence. The effectiveness of secret police tactics clearly accounts for its absence. Nevertheless, without the existence of violence, it is difficult to offer proof of a relationship between violence and dictatorship. It would be naive to assume that the long periods of outward calm exhibited by totalitarian societies is an indication that they have solved their domestic problems or that the theory of a "resource mechanism" suggested by this chapter can be dismissed. Sparta provides an example of a society where years of calm only served to mask the potentially explosive level of violence present.

Around 650 B.C. Sparta put down a revolt of a neighboring tribe and enslaved the defeated Messenians. The Spartans were intensely hated, not merely for their conquest, but for their methods of rule. Spartan military training required their recruits to infiltrate Messenian villages and randomly kill anyone they suspected might revolt. Despite such activities, to outward appearances Messenia gave every indication of being content with Spartan rule. Any signs of discontent did not reach a level which was noticeable or publicly noted, at any rate.

In 465 B.C., a violent earthquake destroyed much of the city of Sparta, possibly killing as many as 20,000 of her inhabitants.[3] Far from sympathizing, the Messenians saw the destruction as an opportunity to revolt. Whether from Spartan overconfidence or Messenian hatred, in one encounter the Messenians killed every man in a company of 300 Spartan hoplites sent against them. In Sparta's case, the potential for violence, even the seriousness of the threat, can be inferred from the intensity of the fighting, once it broke out. From a causal standpoint, one problem is that the Messenian response can itself be seen as a response to years of provocation by the Spartan government. The problem, from the standpoint of logic is - if Spartan repression was a response to violence, why was the repression taking place before the Messenians had revolted. The answer is that the violence the Spartans were responding to was the violence of the Messenian war in 650 B.C.. The Spartan perception was that the Messenians represented a continuing threat.

Characterizing a society as violent or not is only one obstacle. It is a difficult hurdle to overcome. Assuming that actual violent acts can be accurately measured, it becomes necessary to calculate the more abstract "potential" violence and add that to the total. What counts as a potential act of violence? - a criminal conspiracy which was discovered by the policy and only prevented from being carried out by the arrest of the conspirators? - or an undiscovered conspiracy which was abandoned before it was put into action? Assuming that obstacle can be overcome, this book's thesis requires still another logical step - establishing a link between the overall level of violence and government repression. Assuming a society can be proved to be violent, how does that violence produce dictatorship?

Why and how nations turn from democracy to repression is an age-old question. It is a perplexing problem, given the revered status of democratic government. If democracy has long represented the ideal, dictatorship has long been the norm. Over the course of human history dictatorships appear to far outnumber democracies. Why have so many governments chosen the path of totalitarianism? This book's premise, that violence is the primary force behind totalitarian governments, is only one theory. Other theories are based on notions of morality. Dictatorships can be explained in terms of good and evil, according to some - dictators are simply evil people. Still other theories, if not based directly on notions of evil, at least attribute dictatorships to some deliberate choices made by leaders. There is also the related belief that governmental "bureaucracy" should share some of the blame.

Some of these theories suggest one simple answer. On closer examination, even simple answers may not seem so simple. Does the concept of "evil" take into account the complex governmental structures involved in governing? As dictatorial governments go, none have been considered as evil as Nazi Germany or Stalinist Russia. Yet to dismiss or try to explain both these governmental systems with the word evil leaves many questions unanswered. Neither Hitler nor Stalin acted alone. They each headed huge governmental bureaucracies. If evil is the explanation for dictatorship, was it limited to the man at the top, Hitler or Stalin, or did it permeate the entire governmental system? Were Hitler and Stalin evil to begin with or did they only become that way after they came to power? Was the evil only confined to those in power or did it extend to the populace as well? (The accusation has long been made that most Germans must have known what the Nazis were doing at their death camps.) Is evil based on the intent to do something bad, or is it related more to the number of evil deeds involved? For example, were Nazi Germany and the Soviet Union evil because Stalin and Hitler deliberately had innocent people killed, or more because the victims numbered in the millions?

What about theories which are based on some deliberate choice? The repressive nature of the Soviet Union, for example, has been attributed, in the popular mind, to the fanatical beliefs of Bolshevik leaders. If not always necessarily evil, the theory suggests that dictatorships contain elements of calculation and deliberation. There is a dogmatic, unbending determination to accomplish a goal. Dictatorial regimes, according to this argument, are repressive because people get in the way of some greater goal. It suggests that individual personalities, like those of Stalin and Hitler, or the decisions of leadership, are a key ingredient in totalitarianism. Dictatorial actions, in other words, are not simply an irrational response to societal turmoil.

These alternative explanations of the origin of dictatorship have some basis in fact and logic. From the perspective of evil, neither Hitler nor Stalin felt bound by the normal rules of human conduct - where political opponents were concerned, murder was simply one option among many. Stalin rarely judged political killings in a moral light; if he did, they were not something which weighed terribly on his conscience.

In both Nazi Germany and the Soviet Union the majority of deaths and political killings came long after most serious opposition to the government had been suppressed. Between 1929 and 1933, Germany had had to contend with unemployment and increasingly violent confrontations in her streets. Once Hitler was appointed chancellor in January 1933, the Nazis began arresting and killing many of their political opponents. By summer, they had eliminated the opposition and were in complete control of the government. The arrests and murder did not stop. In fact, the vast majority of deaths caused by the Nazis would come after they had crushed their opposition. In Russia, similarly, the period of greatest societal violence, the civil war, had been long over by the time Stalin began moving against the peasants in 1929. Because of the sheer number of deaths associated with forced collectivization, there is a temptation to attribute every evil aspect of communist rule to Stalin. In actuality, the time lag between the period of greatest violence, the civil war, and the governmental response was much shorter. It began almost as soon as the civil war was over. Bolshevik suppression of political opposition, more accurately, never stopped. In 1920, during the civil war, the Bolsheviks had established 84 concentration camps. The end of the civil war did not see a reduction of that number, but rather an increase. There were 315 camps in October 1923.[4] The problem, from a logical argument standpoint, is that the tempo of repression increased as the level of violence receded.

What makes governmental action more perplexing, in the case of Germany and Russia, is that the government response seems out of all proportion to the provocation. The phrase "disproportionate response" has come into greater prominence recently in diplomatic circles. It refers to an overwhelming use of force in a situation where the provocation is relatively small. It contrasts to a "measured response" when talking about the use of military force, meaning that an action by one party is answered with a similar action in retaliation. There is a certain element of disproportionate response when considering the actions in Germany and Russia. Whether the wholesale killing or imprisonment of political opponents was justified in either country, it is at least understandable. Hitler and Stalin however, did not stop with political opposition, where the state terror apparatus was concerned. Hitler, after eliminating the active opposition, targeted Jews. Stalin, not content with suppressing his political enemies, went after the peasants.

Governments can also choose to directly avoid the issue of violence or even to delay any confrontation. During the French Revolution, political leaders seemed more willing to exploit mob anger in battling their opponents than to control the fury of the rioters. Politicians openly courted mob support, since it proved useful in dealing with their rivals. For a time the goal was to guillotine political opponents, not maintain civilized debate, and mob support proved an invaluable tool to that end. In the end however, such government inaction only put off the inevitable decision to end the violence.

Based on the contradictions of Germany, Russia, and Revolutionary France alone there might be a temptation to dismiss any connection between violence and governmental repression as simply too tenuous. The government response to violence seems late in coming at times, an overreaction at others. Yet it may be possible to account for some of these discrepancies. The slowness of the governmental response, by itself, is probably insufficient grounds for dismissing an argument - governments are notoriously slow to respond to most situations. If there is a time lag between the period when violence occurs and the point at which a government will respond, that lag can be attributed, in part, to the large societal resources required to put down violence. The violence itself tends to hinder normal operations. Violence disappears, it might be argued, not because the threat of violence is overrated, but because the repressive measures employed by government are so effective.

Why would the government response to violence, under a dictatorship, be such an extreme one? The problem is not so much that a governmental response is totally un-expected in the face of a violent threat. Most societies troubled by crime have expected their governments to establish a police force. The problem instead is that the nature of repression is in a category of its own. Repression, in contrast to a general reaction to violence, cannot be considered an ordinary or normal response - it is a very specific and very extreme reaction. An argument for the connection between a limited governmental response and violence seems plausible because it is more obvious. An argument which attempts to link violence to extreme measures, such as torture and murder, seems weaker, because it is not immediately apparent.

Drawing conclusions about a direct link between repression and violence then is difficult for several reasons. First, a long period of time may elapse between the first appearance of violence and any governmental response. An immediate reaction to any stimulus provides greater certainty when investigating causation. Second, there is an inability to correlate the level of violence with the intensity of the governmental response. Any response which closely mirrors the original input suggests a closer connection. Third, much of the societal violence seems to disappear once dictatorial regimes are in power. From an evidentiary standpoint the loss of evidence muddies the waters. What these three possibilities suggest is, not so much that the theory is wrong, but rather that it is difficult to prove.

Despite the ease with which totalitarian governments are grouped together, they often have little in common except a secret police. Even the personalities of the leadership of Germany and Russia were different. If Hitler and Stalin shared a single trait, it was that they were master politicians. Their styles of leadership were radically different however. Hitler's strength was his oratory, the charismatic ability to sway crowds; that and his single-minded devotion to his ideas. Stalin's political strengths were found in his behind-the-scenes ability to make alliances, his patience, attendance to detail, and his sense of timing. More the pragmatist and down-to-earth party member, he rarely challenged the intellectual leadership of the communist party in the early years, at least not on an intellectual level. Despite such differences both Hitler and Stalin each took their countries down the path of dictatorship.

The remainder of this chapter covers three topics. The first is a more detailed look at the resource mechanism, the way in which resources impact the political process. The second is a brief explanation of the function of governments in general and the impact of violence on political decisions. The third is an analysis of the relationship between resources, unemployment, and violence.

THE RESOURCE MECHANISM IN OPERATION

The discussion in this chapter has suggested that violence is the engine which drives governments into dictatorship. Violence is clearly a component of the resource mechanism, which provides the centerpiece of this book's theory. The resource mechanism might be understood in terms of a general process. It could be described as the way in which the economic power of resources is translated into political power. Resources, at some point, enter a nation's economy, with a corresponding impact on the economic system. The economic system, in turn, impacts the political system, forcing the political leadership to make decisions to counteract the economic pressures. The term "mechanism" suggests an image of motion - the smooth, continuous operation of a one small part of larger piece of machinery. The general perspective of the mechanism is one view. The resource mechanism can also be approached by breaking it down into two parts. It contains essentially two components, a political component and an economic component.

While the field of economics has traditionally been considered a realm separate and apart from that of politics, throughout history economics has had a closer association to politics than might appear. The political leadership, even in ancient times, universally took an interest in commerce and exploitation of natural resources. The irrigation system developed in Sumer before 2000 B.C. was administered by the government. Bribery and corruption of government officials by contractors, an obvious example of the impact of economics on political decisions, is not a modern phenomenon. It was a problem for ancient Egypt and Rome.

When the political issue is dictatorship, the connection between economics and politics is not a matter of a few small bribes. In dictatorship, what serves as a bridge between the political and the economic is violence. At first glance violence is likely to be classified as some form of political expression. The violence of the American Revolution clearly falls into the category of political expression. Yet, on closer analysis, violence is not itself always political. Labor unrest, in which violence is directed at an employer or employees, while having political associations, is not so easily categorized as political. It is likely to provoke a political response on the part of government if severe enough and of long enough duration. Violence, according to the resource mechanism, bridges the gap between the economic and the political by posing two questions. Violence - its existence, its severity, and its suppression - is a political question which governments must confront in the real world. Violence - its origins or causes - on the other hand, is primarily an economic question created by the resource hand dealt each country. The key question, where violence is concerned, is how violence impacts government. The key question, on the resource side, is how resources play a role in violence.

The resource mechanism, at a basic level, is tied to the instinct for survival. Notions of survival - the fight-to-the death battle with the sabre tooth tiger - seem almost quaint today, given the productive capabilities of modern industrial societies. Yet, to those forced to confront the powerful forces of nature and a hostile world, survival was not some abstract idea discussed around the campfire at night. Survival, to ancient peoples, was an obsession.

Survival is no less important to modern man than it was to the ancients, despite the fact that modern people give it little thought. What has changed, particularly for in-dustrial societies, is the way in which the struggle for survival is carried on. In ancient times, the tribe survived by hunting game or by scavenging for food. Now the individual survives by participating in the market. The market serves as the source of the food once provided by the land. If it allows the individual to avoid the dangers of the hunt or the time involved in scavenging, the market does not totally free the individual from making some kind of effort to survive. What the market did, was not to free the individual from work demands, but rather to exchange one type or work for another. Instead of participating in the hunt, the individual had to find work. The price of participation was a contribution of something of value, either a product or an individual's labor.

Survival has oftentimes been more a matter of luck than of planning. Danger can take many forms, from the ever-present problems posed by insufficient food production, to the more dramatic problems posed by weather, such as tornadoes or flooding. Danger often arrives unexpectedly. The Black Death devastated the population of Europe in the 14th Century at a time when other threats seemed under control. Threats, in dramatic forms such as the plague, have represented the exception rather than the rule, over the course of history. Hunger and its relative, starvation, has been a constant threat. Modern agricultural technology has seemed to overcome the problem of hunger, but maintaining an adequate food supply will always require extra effort. The demand for food has been the one constant in the economic equation, whether the economic unit was the tribe or an entire nation. Threats to the food supply could be classified as economic threats, in that they raise economic problems and can be countered by economic measures. In contrast to the Black Death, threats to food supplies can be dealt with through economic solutions, such as increased production or trade or storage.

Threats which are of an economic nature generally fall into one of two categories. The first involves a failure at the group level to produce. The second involves a failure at the individual level. The group involved, in the prehistoric period, could range from a family or clan to a tribe, and, in more sophisticated societies, a city-state or civilization. Group failure often spelled disaster for the clan or tribe. A long period of drought could mean crop failure. The disappearance of game from a productive hunting region could also mean starvation. Civilizations, like the smaller clans or tribes, could also fall victim to group failure. The disappearance of civilizations, such as the Maya, suggests the consequences of group failure at the larger societal level.

Individual failure was probably a rare phenomenon in prehistoric cultures. The physical difficulties of basic food production were so great that individuals came at a premium. That is not to say that individual failure did not occur. Most clans or tribes could sanction non-productive or troublesome individuals by ostracizing them from the tribe, an all-but-certain death sentence in the primitive world. Individual failure could occur through age or injury as well. The tribal solution was often to leave such individuals to die.

The dynamics of failure, at the individual level, changed with the coming of the market. If the tribe was more willing to intercede on behalf of the individual because his services were needed, market economies were not. The market, in contrast to the tribe, did not need a formal vote to ostracize a non-productive individual. It simply ignored him. Primitive though ancient economies may have been, by modern standards, they represented a significant advance in productive capacity over the tribal system - particularly in agriculture. The ability to create an agricultural surplus had given an impetus to market development. If the market did not dominate every aspect of an individual's life, it nevertheless controlled the one aspect necessary to survival - the economic realm. The individual was free to leave a city, to grow or hunt his own food - if he or his family wanted to face bandits or hostile tribes or if he was willing to risk the weather. As a practical matter however, if the individual wanted to survive he was forced to participate in the market. He had to recognize market rules and to respect concepts of property.

One question which may arise is why the emphasis has been on "failure," as in group production "failure" or individual production "failure." Using the term seems to frame the discussion in negative terms. Why not focus on the "success" of the market or the "success" of the individual? The reason is because economic "failure," rather than success, is what triggers violent political upheaval. Any threat to human survival comes, not from the economic success of the tribe or civilization, but from its failure or collapse.

It may be helpful to give different labels to the economic difficulties of the group and of the individual. The group failure - the inability of the group to provide for its members - might be more understandable if it is called a "failure of delivery." It represents a failure of the economic system to physically deliver goods to the consumer. In essence, it is a condition of scarcity, whether the scarcity involves food or manufactured goods. The individual may want to bargain, but there is nothing to bargain for. The failure of the individual economically might be called a "failure of participation" - the individual is unable to participate in an economy even if the economy is relatively productive. It is one way of saying that the consumer is unemployed or has no savings. In this situation there might be an inability to buy goods because they are too expensive, i.e., the goods are available, but the individual cannot afford them.

Failure of delivery and failure of participation involve two sides of the economic coin, since they represent two entirely different economic problems. If they differ economically, they nevertheless represent a single political problem - both conditions pose a threat to the individual's survival. It might be said that, even if the economic conditions of scarcity or unemployment are different, the economic impact is identical. If an individual cannot obtain a needed item, it doesn't matter whether the reason is because the economic system cannot deliver the item or because the individual cannot afford it. Failure of delivery implies, at its worst, total economic collapse. Failure of participation implies, at its worst, complete exclusion from the market. The worker, in other words, has nothing which the market considers of value, not even his labor. There is a complete lack of economic bargaining power or a lack of economic resources. In resource terms, labor has lost its value as a resource, i.e., something needed by someone. (It may be helpful to recall the example of the Siberian fur-trader. The fur-trader would rarely be a victim of a failure of participation. He had physical resources available, in the form of furs from trapping, as well as the technical skills to either supply his own personal needs, or to enter the economy. In other words, with resources available he could create economic bargaining power.)

Scarcity of goods, or scarcity, is a more readily understood concept than "failure of delivery." Similarly, it may be more useful to use the term "unemployment" as shorthand for failure of participation. Failure of participation really encompasses more than just unemployment. Employment or work, despite the emphasis on the work ethic or the "need" to work, is not necessary to fulfill a basic human drive. Economically, the market has never retaliated against individuals who do not work. The market may deny access to its benefits to those who do not work, but it does not actively seek to punish them. What the market is concerned with is economic resources or, more specifically, monetary resources or savings. Individuals with large savings accounts do not need to work. Failing that however, individuals, in order to participate in an economy, must have employment to create economic resources.

By themselves, scarcity and unemployment simply represent economic conditions. They differ from other economic circumstances because, not only do they have a direct impact on people, but also because the effect they have represents the most direct threat to survival. There are other economic circumstances which create problems, but which have a less drastic impact. Price increases in raw materials, for example, will impact businesses in some way, possibly forcing them to adjust their purchases. Such increases however cause fewer problems for people, and the problems appear in less direct and less threatening ways. It is because people serve as intermediaries between economic conditions and the political system that scarcity and unemployment are political problems. People have a number of options available to express their feelings, and violence is one of those options. If elections do not work or if the political leadership is otherwise unresponsive, the most commonly used means of expressing political dissatisfaction will be violence. Violence will nearly always have a political impact, whether it originates in economic problems or not.

Violence, in its various forms, has always been a threat to human survival. It is a perplexing phenomenon. Rather than diminishing with the advancement of human civilization, in contrast to hunger, it seems to keep pace with population increases. Agricultural production was improved, in terms of yield and productivity, by the development of civilization. The threat to survival from crop failure became less, in other words, as societies became more complex. Paradoxically, the threat of violence seemed to grow, not diminish, as populations increased and civilizations became more complex. Inter-tribal warfare and banditry gave way to organized war and large-scale battles between the armies of neighboring city-states. As populations and cities grew, so did crime.

Scarcity and unemployment, as threats, seem a far cry from the threat posed by the Black Death. Yet, in the context of human existence, and particularly the conditions created by market forces, scarcity and unemployment are not the economic equivalent of the placid mountain lake or babbling country brook either. The instinctive "fight or flight" response to danger is a description of the response to situations humans perceive as dangerous. Individuals who feel threatened will react to the threat in some way. The problem, in confronting any economic system, is that there is no clearly defined enemy to either confront or to run away from. The hunter may either fight a lion or choose to retreat, but the hunter has few doubts about who the enemy is. Perhaps the instinctive human response, when faced with no clear enemy, is to strike out at the most convenient enemy available, i.e., the thing that one believes to be an enemy or whatever most resembles an enemy.

In April 1789 crowds of laborers in Paris worked themselves into a frenzy over fears of a possible cut in wages. The object of their anger was a wallpaper manufacturer named Réveillon. Réveillon made the mistake of suggesting that lower bread prices would allow for lower wages. He had made the suggestion at an electoral meeting. He had not actually demanded wage cuts and he was not even present when the crowds gathered. Nevertheless the crowd interpreted his statements as a threat. The workers had suffered through a terribly long winter in which food was scarce and work unavailable. Troops ordered out to maintain order somehow allowed the crowd to gain access to Réveillon's factory, which they proceeded to destroy. In restoring order, the troops fired on the crowd, injuring or killing several hundred people.

If the resource mechanism could be illustrated by a single historical happening, it would be the Réveillon riots, as they came to be known. Compressed into a period of just two days, all the elements of the mechanism were there - scarcity, unemployment, violence, and finally government repression. What is more, the violence which did occur could be directly tied to dissatisfaction over economic conditions, and economic conditions which were related to both scarcity and unemployment. Unfortunately, the riots, if they represent a near-perfect example, are something of an exception. Violence, when it occurs, may not have any obvious connection to economic conditions.

THE FUNCTION OF GOVERNMENTS

Scarcity, unemployment, and violence clearly shape societies and impact governments. To understand their influence and how they interact, it may be helpful to look at governments and what their function is. We might define governments to be organizations created by societies to provide services to or to carry out the wishes of the citizens of the society. There are problems confronted by societies which individuals cannot solve or which people cannot provide on their own. Recent criticism of government focuses on its inefficient nature. The private sector, it is said, is a much more efficient provider of services. The criticism, in many cases, is a valid one. Perhaps that is why, even in the ancient world, the duties assigned governments were somewhat narrow. Governments normally took on the overwhelming jobs, such as maintaining armies and fighting invaders, or the jobs which no one else wanted, such as the administration of court systems.

Any threat to survival which was big enough to threaten an entire culture or civilization was, without much thought, assumed to be the government's responsibility. Anything which caused disruptions in an otherwise dependable food supply was seen as a threat. As a result, some of the first duties of ancient governments were to control floods and provide irrigation, as in Egypt and Sumer, or to administer grain storage, as in Mohenjo-daro. War has always been a threat. The resources required to fight an invading army are clearly beyond the capabilities of the individual and war, as a result, became the province of governments. If disasters could not be prevented, then governments were asked to help after they occurred. The task of dealing with natural disaster situations such as flood, storms, or fire were also assumed by governments. Even modern governments have stepped in to provide flood or tornado relief or to aid victims of famine and earthquake.

Criminal conduct, while rarely reaching the level of violence associated with war, nevertheless can pose a serious threat to the individual. Because the resources required are beyond the capabilities of most individuals, controlling crime became another function of government. Governments carried out this responsibility by creating police forces. However, even if controlling crime is a legitimate concern of government, there is a big difference between maintaining a police force and creating a secret police. What governmental function does a secret police serve? From an administrative standpoint alone, a secret police is a cumbersome organization. The duties of a regular police force in combatting everyday crime can absorb large amounts of resources. Adding another agency or organization which must keep track of untold numbers of individuals adds an even greater burden.

In contrast to citizen requests for governmental aid following an earthquake or flood, where the demand for governmental involvement is clear, there is unlikely to be a great popular clamor for a secret police force. People are not going to ask for a service which allows their government to imprison or kill them arbitrarily. That would suggest that, having eliminated all other threats, people would accept a threat from the government itself. The perception is that a secret police is often a direct response to political dissent. In the case of the Soviet Union, the belief is that the secret police were created to deal specifically with political opposition to communism.

What function does a secret police serve? The answer clearly is not an easy one. However, there may be two possible alternatives which partially explain their existence. The first is that people will demand protection from what they perceive as the more dangerous threat. If a secret police represents a threat, it is seen as less of a threat than the alternative. The second is that the decision to create a secret police is not made by the populace, but by governmental leaders. What gave this particular governmental decision such devastating effect was the fact that the tribal governing structure was gone. Advanced societies, to deal with their more complex problems, created bureaucratic structures which were no longer accountable to the society as a whole. Bureaucracies operate independently of the societies in which they exist.

There is one other factor which must be considered in trying to understand any decision to create a secret police. The assumption is that decisions about repression are made in an atmosphere of calm. Against such an assumed atmosphere, it is easy to conclude that the choice was a simple moral question of right or wrong. Yet, we tend to condemn dictatorship from a distance and the debate is conducted under conditions of relative quiet. However, what if the events leading up to the decision involve violence and chaos? Dictatorships often find themselves squarely in the middle of upheaval and turbulence. If the decision to resort to a secret police can be condemned, whatever the cause, the decision may at least be more easily understood, when it is made under conditions of stress.

The legitimate governmental function of secret police forces and the reasons for their creation are somewhat of an academic exercise. The answer to the puzzle may be found in some universal element, or in the conditions unique to each country. What may be said is that secret police have been one of the constants throughout history. We lose sight of them in one country, then find them reappearing in another. Regimes in different countries, even in different times, have maintained secret police forces. Russia had the KGB, Nazi Germany had the Gestapo, Sparta had the Krypteia, and Rome had its cohortes urbanae. What these governments had in common was a secret police force; what their societies shared was a period of large-scale violence and civil unrest.

It may be helpful to look at the problems faced by the government and society of ancient Rome. The Soviet Union, while offering a modern example of dictatorship, instantly provokes controversy because of the ideological nature of communist dictatorship. Rome, free of the baggage associated with Russia and separated from us by some 2,000 years of history, offers a unique perspective on economic problems and social unrest. Rome certainly had its share of political troubles. Perhaps the most famous assassination of all time took place in Rome, with the murder of Julius Caesar. (Fame was a long time coming, since it took William Shakespeare's play to establish Caesar's legendary status.) Despite Shakespeare's writing, the reasons for the assassination are less than clear. In fact, Shakespeare's focus on the ambition and personal rivalries of Caesar's killers sheds very little light on either Caesar or Rome. To modern eyes Julius Caesar comes off as neither total tyrant nor total hero. The play gives the impression that Rome was normally a peaceful place - political assassinations were rare. In some ways that impression is correct, in other ways, it is misleading. Julius Caesar's killing was not the only killing which took place, just the most prominent. Rome, in fact, went through a long period of political violence.

Violence in Rome was not directed at the government as such. Instead, violence was directed at opposition parties. In fact, the violence was not even directed at leaders of the opposition parties, but at opposition supporters. Armed mobs supporting one political leader showed up to vote and then attacked and counterattacked armed mobs supporting other political leaders. While there is some justification for allowing the free expression of political views, few societies can afford the violent type of political expression which prevailed in Rome.

One final point should be made in relation to violence in general. Democratic governments, in contrast to dictatorships, have been relatively free of both violence and political repression. The four dictatorships examined here - Sparta, Rome, Nazi Germany, and Stalinist Russia - suffered through periods of civil unrest and violence and the response of each was nearly identical - political repression. Whether it is felt the violence was justified or not, was politically inspired or not, the root cause and ultimate effect were the same. Ancient Athens and the U.S. are examples of relatively peaceful and also relatively free societies. Athens shows little evidence of political repression. It had no secret police, in contrast to Sparta, and appears to have been relatively free of widespread violence or major political dissent. The United States, in turn, largely escaped political repression. The American Civil War, the use of troops to put down labor unrest, and the excesses of the McCarthy period are examples of government involvement in ideological disputes, but they seem to represent the exception. For the most part, the FBI and CIA, counterparts to the KGB, have remained free of involvement in domestic political disputes.

RESOURCES, UNEMPLOYMENT AND VIOLENCE

The discussion, to this point, has focused primarily on the political operation of the resource mechanism - the purpose of governments in general and their response to violence in particular. The remaining discussion of this chapter is intended to examine the economic side of the mechanism. The economic component can be divided into two parts. Both relate to unemployment. The first is the relationship between unemployment and violence, in the case of dictatorship, (or employment and societal calm, in the case of democracy). The second is the relationship between unemployment and resource scarcity. The discussion here is an attempt to suggest how the resource mechanism might work. It is not necessarily intended to prove that the resource mechanism is true. Rather it is intended to explain how it works, if it is true. If the mechanism is an accurate theory of what takes place, in other words, this is the way it is likely to operate.

Scarcity and unemployment have been mentioned as significant components of the resource mechanism. (Unemployment, as used here, can be actual or merely threatened - it represents a condition of job insecurity. Unemployment, as mentioned, refers to both actual unemployment as well as a lack of savings or monetary resources on the part of workers.) Both can produce violence, either by operating together, if the Réveillon riots are any indicator, or by operating independently. The threat of job loss or a reduction in wages, "milder" forms of unemployment, have often been a source of violence. The American labor movement has a history of violent confrontation. The Haymarket riot of 1886, the Homestead strike of 1892, and the Ludlow massacre of 1914, are all examples of confrontations which resulted in death to some of the participants. Perhaps the worst confrontations occurred during the railroad strike of 1877. Striking workers, protesting wage cuts, confronted federal troops, state militia, or local police in Pittsburgh, Baltimore, Chicago, and St. Louis as well as in other cities across the U.S.. Some 100 people were killed by the time the strike was over.

The connection between unemployment and violence can be traced back even further. At the time when ancient Rome was experiencing periods of mob violence, it was also experiencing grain shortages and high unemployment. Unemployment in Rome, at times was as high as 30 percent. Unemployed workers joined street gangs and from 100

B.C. on there were frequent riots with death the result for participants. Nazi Germany suffered through its greatest period of street violence and riots from 1930 to 1933 when it was also experiencing its highest level of unemployment. In 1932 when unemployment was around 5.5 million, out of a possible work force of 18 million, 82 people were killed in June and July in political riots. In 1933 unemployment reached 6 million. By August, 160 people had died in connection with violent political activity.[5] Support for a connecting link between economic difficulties and violence is also provided by ancient Athens, although from a somewhat different perspective. During her building campaign of 435 B.C. Athens attained nearly full employment - she also suffered little violence or political unrest during this time. In the United States unemployment has remained at a relatively low five to seven percent and production has been fairly high; violence and political unrest have also been relatively infrequent occurrences.

If scarcity was not an obvious partner in many of the strikes and confrontations, it always lurked in the background. Workers, focused on the immediate battle with employers over wage cuts, or the larger war with the economy over jobs, would occasionally provide evidence that wages, even jobs, were not their only concern. The rallying cry of New York's unemployed in the flour riots of 1837 was "Bread, Meat, Rent, Fuel." Like the French mob which targeted Réveillon's factory, the American rioters focused their anger on a single enterprise, that of a flour merchant. It took a combined force of police and state militia to stop the rioting, but not before the crowd had managed to break into the building and loot the flour.

The scarcity which triggered both the Réveillon riots of 1789 and the flour riots of 1837 has been seen throughout history. The types of hardships involved, shortages of food or fuel, in fact, seem to define our concept of scarcity. It can be caused by war, by physical problems with agricultural production, or by economic collapse. There is either an inability to produce enough for a populace, or an inability to deliver what is produced. The connection between such scarcity and violence is readily apparent. Although such scarcity seems to have an association with conditions of violence, there is no connection between scarcity and unemployment - or at least there is no connection which is readily apparent. The resource mechanism suggests that there should be a connection.

In one sense, there is little distinction between one form of scarcity and another. A scarcity of food, in a resource sense, is no different than a scarcity of iron or coal. Scarcity will cause an increase in prices, whether the commodity is food or minerals. However, for purposes of the resource mechanism, it may be helpful to divide the concept of scarcity into two different forms. The first form is the "absolute" scarcity associated with a lack of consumer goods, particularly food. The second form is an "inflationary" or relative scarcity, the scarcity associated more generally with shortages of industrial resources. (Describing a relative shortage as "inflationary" is somewhat misleading. All shortages, even "absolute" shortages lead to inflation. As goods become more scarce, their price will increase.) This type of resource scarcity, such as a shortage of oil or copper, will reveal itself through inflationary increases in the prices of such minerals as they become scarce.

Economists tend to view employment as a function of economic growth. (Growth, as measured by the gross national product (GNP), now gross domestic product (GDP), is the market value of all goods and services produced in a country in a year.) If economic growth slows, unemployment will increase; as growth increases, unemployment will fall. This might be described as a "growth" theory of unemployment. While the specific cause of unemployment is elusive, it is believed to be related to the upturns and downturns of the business cycle. The business cycle, in turn, is driven by changes in aggregate demand, i.e., an economy's total demand for products.[6]

The resource mechanism would explain unemployment in terms of a "resource" theory or, more accurately, a "cost" theory. Unemployment is not a function of growth, but is a function instead of resource costs. The theory, which can be divided into two parts, explains unemployment in terms of the impact of resource costs on market demand. Unemployment, in the first instance, is a function of demand. Jobs are dependent, not so much on economic growth, but on demand for particular products. As long as consumers sustain the market by buying products, there will be jobs for workers. Market demand, in the second instance, is essentially a function of cost. When costs increase, product prices go up, which will, in turn, weaken market demand. In order to maintain market share producers will look for ways to cut costs. Often labor is the cost they will cut, either by reducing wages or by laying off workers. What part does resource availability play in demand or in unemployment? Resource costs, like other costs, will impact prices. Increased raw material costs, which will result when there is scarcity, potentially threaten workers with job loss because they threaten market share.

The resource theory is similar to the growth theory in its focus on aggregate demand and the business cycle. Where it differs is in its approach to market demand. The growth theory assumes that market demand is related in a general way to growth. As an economy grows, there is an increase in demand which will translate into employment growth. Growth fluctuates in accordance with the business cycle. The resource theory ties demand to specific products and the costs associated with individual markets. The resource theory does not totally discount growth as a factor in demand. Demand depends as much on consumer income, as on producer cost reductions. If consumers have more money to spend - the normal result of a growing economy - demand will increase.

The resource theory differs from the growth theory in one other significant way. The growth theory suggests that employment is a "function" of the business cycle, i.e., is caused by it. It is not clear however, that growth actually causes an increase in the employment rate. It may be that employment increases are more an accompanying circumstance which is observed to occur during a period of growth. Growth and employment, in other words, are really just indicators, used to measure a business cycle. The resource theory argues that market demand is actually a function of cost, not simply an observed phenomenon which correlates with the business cycle.

It is ironic that the market, which exerts such a strong influence on production and employment, encounters a product for the first time only at the end of the journey, once the physical production process has been completed. A product begins the journey as nothing more than the raw materials which enter a factory to be processed. Economists use the term inputs to describe everything that goes into manufacturing a product or providing a service. Inputs include such things as raw materials (iron or gold) and labor. Outputs are what comes out of the manufacturing process. Outputs are, in other words, the final product. Manufactured goods are obviously outputs, but outputs can be anything, including services. Economists label the total process as production, which is the process by which inputs are transformed into outputs. This transformation takes place through a recipe and technological process. The recipe is the percentage of various ingredients added, such as iron and carbon in steelmaking, while the technological process involves the temperature and length of time the ingredients are processed.

The market operates according to a number of rules, including the "laws" of supply and demand. The law of demand, in general, is that the lower the price of an item the more of that item buyers will purchase. The law of supply is that the higher the price of an item the more of that item a supplier will produce. The market price and quantity is generally the point at which buyers and sellers agree on the price purchasers will pay and the quantity producers will produce. If price goes above the market price, buyers stop buying the product, a surplus results and the price drops. At prices below the market price, producers stop making the product, shortages occur, and prices move back up.

When a producer finds that he cannot sell products at a given price, his usual reaction will be to lower the price until buyers start to buy again. Since every component of a product adds to its cost, the elimination or reduction in cost of any input will help to reduce the product's cost on the market. Reductions in labor costs, like other inputs, will reduce the cost of the product. They normally are accomplished either by reducing wages or by laying off workers. The global economy of the 1990s, with its emphasis on competition, has pressured firms to cut costs. If technological advances are offered as the hope of real cost reductions, the temptation is still strong to seek cost savings in the area of labor. While workers are easily the first victims of cost-cutting measures, they nevertheless depend on those cost-cutting measures for employment because their jobs are totally dependent on their firm's share of the market.

The market views a product, not so much as a physical object, but as a cost. What the market sees is really a total of the individual costs which go into making the product. The manufacturing process, however complicated, is largely hidden from view. Costs, of course, are the financial side of the physical processes or functions involved in manufacturing. The manufacturing process initially might be broken down into four categories: 1) raw materials; 2) production, the combination of recipe, ingredient, technology and labor which is involved in producing a product; 3) transport; and 4) labor. This combination of substances, processes, and activities comes close to describing how a producer gets a product from the factory to the market and into the hands of the consumer. There are as many costs involved as there are things which need to be done to deliver a product or things which can happen to a product before delivery. Handling and storage usually are other activities which add to cost. Additional costs in international trade stem from language differences and translation requirements. There are costs associated as well with changes in exchange rates. Production costs can include costs associated with preventing destruction of the product. Producers sometimes have to absorb costs resulting from natural destructive forces such as wind, drought, hail, or flood or plant or animal pests, such as locusts and rats or fungi which can attack wheat or other grains.

For simplicity, just six factors will be considered as essential to production:

1. Raw materials
2. Production/manufacture
    Recipe, ingredient, technology and labor
3. Transport
4. Handling
5. Storage
6. Labor

Delivery of any product to the market will involve some aspect of these six steps before it reaches the buyer or consumer. Labor, though listed as a separate item, is involved at nearly every stage of the production process. How extensive each step is depends on the type of product. Steel may demand more of technology, with specific recipe and ingredient requirements, but require less, in terms of storage or handling. Agricultural products may be less demanding, in terms of harvesting efforts, while requiring more commitment to plant cultivation and irrigation or fertilization. Automated manufacturing may demand huge investments in technology, while minimizing the use of human labor.

The final cost to the consumer will equal the sum of each of the six factors plus whatever profit charge is associated with delivery. There may be times when a producer will sell below cost to maintain a market. In the long run however, no producer can sell below actual cost and still remain in business. While it is possible to introduce efficiencies into any one of the six steps which will reduce product cost, it is not possible to eliminate the cost of any single step entirely. The result is a constant internal pressure on all producers to cover costs by increasing prices. The problem is that the market exerts a constant external pressure on producers to cut costs.

The market, through supply and demand, creates a dilemma for all producers. Join the market by agreeing to its demands to reduce prices - and go broke. Stay out of the market by getting out of production altogether (or by keeping prices high) - and go broke. The market does not care what the decision is, but it will exact a price for participation. The price is that the producer who does choose to compete must submit to market rules. However, there really is just one rule - in order to survive, the producer must remain competitive. Market economists would be quick to point out that is the whole point - competition is what the market is all about. That assertion restates the obvious, but overlooks a more subtle point. The producer's problem is not so much that, by entering the market, he submits to market rules relating to competition. The real problem is that the producer, in trying to compete, has conceded a total dependence on the market for survival. (A distinction needs to be made between a broad concept of the market, as represented by the "free market" and the much narrower market for individual products.

The market the producer relies on is the market for his specific product.) That dependence is not just a problem for the producer alone. Any employee of a business, by agreeing to work for the employer becomes dependent as much on the market, as on the employer, for work.

A dependence on the market is unavoidable, given the complexities of the modern economy. It should be emphasized however that "dependence on the market" takes place at two levels. All individuals within a market society are dependent on the market in a general sense. Individuals don't need to grow or gather their own food when they rely on the market. The market serves as both "grocery store" and "delivery boy." If this general market frees producers from many concerns, they must be completely on guard at another level. It is the specific market for their product which needs to be watched, not just the overall performance of the economy. Businesses may have to function within the context of an overall economic system, but market dependence is tied to individual products.

There is another point related to dependence on individual markets. If companies are totally dependent on markets, it may mean that expectations about success, based on the apparent rules of the competitive game are simply irrelevant. "Being competitive," in other words, does not, by itself, guarantee control of any market. Competition, in the context of the wider market, means that companies are in a continual struggle with other companies for survival. That companies may be dependent on individual markets within the wider economy only suggests that competition in particular industries will mirror the competition taking place in the economy as a whole.

Competition has taken on a special meaning since the advent of the global marketplace. In fact, competition today has almost come to be synonymous with the market, while seemingly losing contact with its economic origins. No longer does it describe the economic relationship between companies and the market. Competition has come to mean a high-intensity form of "busy-work" - an atmosphere of hard work and struggle for its own sake, evidenced by high-tech communications and advanced manufacturing technology. If the desire to get ahead is an admirable quality, the new emphasis on competition suggests that it is sufficient by itself. An emphasis on high-intensity competition suggests that, even if businesses are dependent on a market, they can "do" something about a market which is unresponsive. Firms can "do" any number of things - lower prices, advertise - in order to increase market share. Everything they can "do" however is really a passive activity in terms of the market. It is really only the customer who takes an active role - there is nothing a company can do which will guarantee consumer purchases. Consumers make active choices when they buy products, and the market might be described as "active" for that reason, however companies play no active role in market choices. They can advertise, in hopes of influencing consumer choices, but advertising campaigns can fail.

Total quality management (TQM) is a recent trend in management. The goal of TQM is to improve product quality. There is a strongly held belief that many firms, particularly in the U.S., have lost their competitive edge because they are no longer interested in serving the customer. If TQM has improved many products, there is the suspicion that it is almost more of an advertising gimmick than a true conversion to customer service. What seems to drive TQM and other customer-oriented trends, is the belief that demand can be controlled, even manipulated. Market demand, given that assumption, is a function more of advertising than of substantive differences between products. Advertising is based largely on the assumption that it is possible to differentiate one product from another. Luxury car manufacturers, for example, try to differentiate their cars from those of their competitors by emphasizing quality and prestige. The alternative to a "niche" or differentiation strategy, is a strategy which involves price competition, where a producer competes with other producers by lowering prices.

The amount of money devoted to advertising luxury or specialty products in the U.S. would suggest that most competition is for special niche markets and that markets are sustained by advertising alone. Despite that impression, most marketing strategies, even in ancient markets, have involved some form of pricing competition. The market demand which sustains individual markets in most cases is thus a function of the price the consumer must pay. (Price for the consumer will translate into cost when applied to the producer.) Cost, (or price) when all is said and done, will determine market share.

Competition can, in the end, be reduced to nothing more than a battle between competitors over the lowest price they can offer. Low price, market economists would argue, is one of the great benefits of competition - for the consumer. What is less obvious is the downside. Any market demand which can be sustained only by price reductions is inherently unstable, and for any business, a dangerous ally in the struggle for survival. The danger however, is not limited to just the business itself. Workers who depend on the business for their jobs, are at the mercy of product markets as well. Employment, like business, is a function of market demand.

The classic view of the labor struggle pits management against labor. Business leaders have long suggested that organized labor is the enemy of business, while the market is their friend. Even while the market pressures them to reduce costs, they defend the market as the ideal - competition is good, they assert, because competition makes business stronger. How the market views businesses is another question. The market seems unconcerned about the existence of individual businesses or even whether a producer participates in the market. Employers often believe that their business benefits from some privileged economic status, qualitatively different from that of labor. Yet the market makes little distinction between business owners and employees. This is nowhere more evident than in the competitive pressures surrounding costs. The market is single-minded in its focus on reducing prices. Business owners are only too aware that the market's sole concern is competition - and a desire for ever lower prices. The market is not concerned about how a producer reduces costs. To the market, there is no difference between cost reductions achieved by wage cuts and those achieved from production efficiencies. It does not reward employers who achieve cost reductions through greater efficiencies in production processes. It does not punish employers who force workers to accept lower pay.

Market demand is everything, when it comes to survival. Businesses depend on demand for the revenues which keep them afloat while workers depend on demand for employment. The market, in other words, plays a dual role, supporting both businesses and employment. Low product cost is important to maintaining markets, which are crucial to employment, whatever labor demands for higher wages may suggest to the contrary.

Current economic theory suggests a complex relationship between market demand and employment, particularly when employment is explained in terms of the business cycle. Unemployment will rise or fall depending on whether an economy is in expansion or contraction, according to that explanation. The relationship, in fact, may be much simpler, if it is explained in terms of the specific relationship between demand and employment. What creates a demand for a product involves many of the same elements which sustain a demand for labor. In summary form, it may be helpful to compare product demand components with the requirements for employment.

BASIC COMPONENTS OF PRODUCT DEMAND
(PRODUCT MARKET)

1.　　Market Demand (Intangible) (Why the customer buys.)
　　　　a.　　Consumer Need
　　　　b.　　Cost

2.　　Physical Production and Distribution (Tangible)
　　　　(What the customer gets and how it is delivered.)

BASIC COMPONENTS OF EMPLOYMENT DEMAND
(LABOR MARKET)

1.　　Market Demand (Intangible) (Why the worker works.)
　　　　a.　　Consumer Need
　　　　b.　　Cost

2.　　Physical Production and Distribution (Tangible)
　　　　(What the worker does and how it's delivered.)

At this level, the product market and the labor market appear to have similar, even identical, elements. A more detailed breakdown of these elements may suggest why there is such a close relationship between product demand and the demand for labor.

COMPONENTS (DETAIL) OF PRODUCT DEMAND
(PRODUCT MARKET)

1.   Market Demand (Intangible) (Why the customer buys.)
      a.   Consumer Need
      b.   Cost
            1)   Raw materials
            2)   Production/manufacture
                     Recipe, ingredient, technology (and labor)
            3)   Transport
            4)   Handling
            5)   Storage
            6)   Labor

2.   Physical Production and Distribution (Tangible)
      (How a product comes into existence.)
            1)   Raw materials
            2)   Production/manufacture
                     Recipe, ingredient, technology (and labor)
            3)   Transport
            4)   Handling
            5)   Storage
            6)   Labor

COMPONENTS (DETAIL) OF EMPLOYMENT DEMAND
(LABOR MARKET)

1.   Market Demand (Intangible) (Why the worker works.)
      a.   Consumer Need
      b.   Cost
             1)   Raw materials
            2)   Production/manufacture
                     Recipe, ingredient, technology (and labor)
            3)   Transport
            4)   Handling
            5)   Storage
            6)   Labor

2. Physical Production and Distribution (Tangible) (Continued)
   (What the worker does and how it's delivered.)
   a. Production/manufacture
      Recipe, ingredient, technology and labor
   b. Transport
   c. Handling
   d. Storage

What supports the product market as well as the labor market is one common element, a basic demand for a product. Basic demand will be influenced by the price at which the product is sold. Since any of the six listed factors of production will add to a product's final cost, they each can influence demand as well. In practical terms, an increase in the cost of any one of the six functions will mean an increase in the final market cost of the product, with a resultant loss in market share and a corresponding loss in employment. The raw materials, such as iron ore, which go into a product, are the most likely culprits when resource scarcity is mentioned. Resource availability however can impact product cost at other stages of manufacture, even when the resource is not an ingredient of the product. Transport costs, for example, will be affected by the availability of motor fuel, while manufacturing costs will be impacted by fuel demands related to heating factories.

If the area of transport seems an uncomplicated one with few cost variables, that impression is deceptive. Goods are moved in a wide variety of ways. *Chisholm's Handbook of Commercial Geography* groups transport methods into eight categories: 1) human porterage; 2) animals; 3) roads and motor vehicles; 4) railroads; 5) ropeways and cableways; 6) inland water transport; 7) ocean transport; and 8) air transport.[7] One factor is the size of the carrier, such as a truck or ship, which will determine how much, in volume, of a product can be carried. Water transport, despite a relatively slow speed, has the capacity to carry large volumes of material. Another factor is distance, i.e., how far must something be transported? This affects the speed of delivery. In addition, when transport uses fuel, such as coal or oil, increased distance means increased fuel costs. Another factor is the difficulty of transport. Road and motor vehicle transport costs increase when infrastructure, such as roads or bridges, is not in good repair.

LABOR RESOURCES - THE PARADOX OF ABUNDANCE

Because business strategies relating to the market are often cost-driven, cost is an obsession for management. If cost, in such instances, acts as a motivational force for efficiency, in other cases, it also serves as a measurement of resource availability. Cost increases are often the first sign that a resource is becoming scarce. Cost decreases are normally a sign that a resource is becoming more abundant. The fact that cost provides a rough measure of resource availability presents something of a puzzle, where labor resources and the resource mechanism are concerned. Labor resources, if cost is an accurate indicator, have evidenced signs of progressively greater availability over the course of human history. In nearly every society, from ancient Greece and Rome, to Revolutionary France and Nazi Germany, economic pressures have forced wages continually lower.

According to this book's thesis, an abundance of resources tends to favor democracy, because resource availability reduces the level of tension in a society. However, the evidence relating to the impact of labor resources on society seems to contradict or defy the logic of the resource mechanism. Instead of having a calming effect, the greater availability of labor has resulted in greater turmoil. The immediate cause of the railroad strike of July 1877 was the implementation of a 10 percent wage cut by the Baltimore and Ohio Railroad. The problem was not that it was unexpected, but that it came on top of other cuts which had been implemented by the railroads in the preceding years. In July 1892 strikers at the Carnegie Homestead works fought Pinkerton detectives in a day-long battle which left 16 dead. The immediate cause of the fighting was Andrew Carnegie's attempt to get rid of the union. The real substance of the battle was Carnegie's desire to cut labor costs. If the strike provided the most dramatic episode of the conflict, the Homestead strikers were fighting a less-visible battle with technology and with an increasingly abundant supply of labor. Carnegie's plants, by 1910, would need fewer workers as a result of technological improvements and those workers still there were making only 80 percent of the wages paid in 1890.

A similar labor situation occurred in Athens in the Seventh Century B.C., where men who worked the land, known as *hektemoroi*, or sixth-parters, were so desperate for work that they were willing to give up a sixth of their produce in order to hold onto their land. If the bidding between these tenant farmers was an indication that labor resources were abundant, it also contributed to political unrest sufficiently serious to force the government to intervene and promote reform. In Rome a labor shortage caused rural dwellers to flock to the city. When the shortage later turned into a glut Rome had to contend with violent mobs of unemployed. In France landowners found so many potential tenants seeking land that land went to the highest bidder. Workers in Paris found themselves engaged in a similar competition for the few jobs available. If the French Revolution could be partially blamed on a glutted labor market, it clearly was no ordinary labor dispute.

Does the simultaneous existence of abundant labor resources and societal violence throw the resource mechanism into question? Or, despite the seeming contradiction, do these circumstances provide additional support for the thesis? Is labor such a unique resource that the results can be explained as an anomaly? It might be easier to use a gimmicky approach and define resources differently. Resources could be defined so as not to include labor. Labor, after all, doesn't have the "feel" of a real resource, like a mineral, such as copper, does. Unfortunately that would eliminate many intangible types of resources, such as technological or harbor resources. The fact that there has been a need for workers in nearly every economy suggests that labor must be considered a resource, under any conceivable definition.

To reconcile labor abundance with the resource mechanism, it may be helpful to review the resource mechanism and its relationship to this book's overall theme. The mechanism predicts that, when scarcity reaches such a level that it poses a serious threat to survival, it will create pressure on the political system through an expected increase in violence. Scarcity, in this context, revolves around the resources essential to human survival, such as food or fuel. The overall theory of this book predicts that resource abundance will allow democracy to develop because abundance contributes to a reduced level of violence.

That violence can occur, even under conditions of abundance, (if abundance is measured in terms of labor alone), is illustrated by the events during the period between 1877 and 1894 in America. The nationwide railroad strike of 1877 was one of the first large-scale labor uprisings. In addition to property damage in the millions of dollars, some 100 people died. Another 16 were killed during the Homestead strike of 1892 in Pennsylvania, and 34 were killed in the unrest surrounding the Pullman strike in 1894. The Long Strike in the anthracite-mining region of Pennsylvania was ended in 1877 with the hanging of twenty Irish miners, members of an organization known as the Molly Maguires. That labor struggle had produced 63 unsolved murders between 1860 and 1867.[8] Such violence took place against a background of labor abundance.

In its battle with labor, industry had a number of weapons in its arsenal. However, it was the large supply of labor and the desperate need for work which proved the most effective. Over 20 million people immigrated to America between 1870 and 1910.[9] If companies were willing to risk a confrontation with unions, it was because of the vast pool of potential workers. When they wanted to break a strike, employers hired new immigrants or brought in workers from outside a region.

The surprising thing is not that violence occurred, but that it did not happen more often. The events of 1877, 1892 and 1894, however dramatic, represented a rare failure on the part of industry. The failure was not so much that industry had allowed its relations with labor to deteriorate. The failure was more that industry had allowed the conflict to reach the stage where two large armies faced off against each other. Federal troops or state militia were the weapon of last resort. It was not that employers were averse to using violence, it was more that it was most effective against individuals or small unarmed groups, even if the confrontations were violent. To be sure, many other weapons involved some form of coercion. Companies routinely fired individual workers involved in union activity, then blacklisted them to prevent them from finding new jobs. Companies enlisted the aid of the courts and the legal system in attacking labor. When the Homestead strike was over, union members faced indictment on 167 counts of murder, rioting, and conspiracy. When most were acquitted or the charges dropped, 35 union leaders were charged with treason against the state of Pennsylvania.[10]

The existence of violence during a period of resource abundance, (even if the availability is limited to labor resources), is clearly a contradiction, if this book's thesis is to be believed. Labor itself is something of a contradiction, in an economic sense. It has properties which clearly mark it as a commodity in the market. It can be measured, like other commodities, and, like other commodities, is subject to the laws of supply and demand; its value goes up and down with fluctuations in the market. Yet, labor possesses two qualities in particular which flow from its human dimensions and distinguish it from every other traded item. First, labor is the only resource which combines the power of thinking with the ability to act. People, as a result, can draw conclusions about their condition and additionally, can act on the basis of those conclusions. The danger for the political system is that their reactions can involve violence. Second, labor is subject to human limitations in physical and biological terms. People have to eat. Food intake, for example, must provide a minimal level of calories on a daily basis. If oil and coal can neither think nor act, they do not need to be fed either.

Perhaps the heart of any reconciliation of labor abundance, in a resource sense, with labor unrest, in a political context, involves an understanding of the difference between the economic concept of "employment" and the worker's notion of what a "job" is. Put another way, what does the market expect of the worker, in offering employment, and what does the worker need from the job that's offered? The term "job" can be used in three different contexts: 1) economic; 2) psychological; or 3) biological. The first, the economic or market concept, views labor as a commodity and a job as nothing more than the trade-off between labor and the market. A laborer works a day in return for a wage. The second, the psychological, involves the personal satisfaction obtained from work. A career, for example, combines the market concept of a job with the personal choice of doing something rewarding. The third, the biological, involves the minimal biological requirements needed for survival. Whatever the market may suggest about employment, people are subject to human limitations. The worker must be paid enough to buy food.

The concept of a "job," whether economic, psychological, or biological, is very broad. A job is simply a general economic classification applied to a particular worker for what he or she does. Whether a worker works two or 80 or 90 hours a week, it is all just one job. Work could be broken down into smaller individual units, such as hours or minutes, but the concept of a job is really related to the individual. A worker may have two or three jobs and work so many hours a week, but we normally do not subdivide a 40-hour a week job into 40 separate jobs of one hour each.

If Andrew Carnegie and the railroad owners felt any moral obligation toward their workers, it was satisfied by giving them an economic "job." At the wages paid, it was little more than a job title. Carnegie's concept of what a job was, in economic terms, did not go very far toward meeting the physical needs of workers. What industrialists, as well as workers, were up against were human limitations, both inside and outside the factory. It was not just the long hours or hazardous conditions found in the factory itself which were a problem. It was also the economic circumstances which the worker had to endure at home. Wages were barely enough to feed, clothe, and house workers and their families. An increasing supply of labor allowed Carnegie and the railroad owners to cut labor costs while still providing what would be called "jobs." However, each round of wage cuts brought workers closer to the brink. Carnegie was vaguely aware of how hard some of the work was and seemingly oblivious to the conditions under which his workers

51

lived outside the factory. As he saw it however, his only responsibility was to give workers a chance. If they wanted to better themselves, it was up to them to work hard.

The dilemma for workers was that the market only gave them two choices. They could choose not to work at all, avoiding the strikes and battles with business, but not have any money, and risk being excluded from the market. The other choice was to accept work in the steel mills or on the railroads, but at wages which were minimal. If that choice gave them access to the market, it was not full access.

The economic pressure on survival, through wage cuts and loss of jobs, was what created such an explosive political situation. The paradox between abundant resources and societal violence can be reconciled, if viewed from the personal level of the worker. Even as labor became a more abundant resource, in relation to the overall economy, critical resources, such as food, became less available at the individual level. Food may have been available to the economy as a whole but it was a scarce commodity, in relation to the individual worker. The low wages which followed on the heels of labor abundance made food too expensive to afford.

There may be another explanation for the paradox. The assumption is that wages were falling because of the abundant supply of labor. An abundant supply would cause wages to fall. However, wages may have been declining for another reason - labor was losing its value. The market did not need that many workers because it did not need all the products they produced. Our assumption is that there are no limits on the ability of the market to expand. It may be a holdover from prehistoric days when the fear was that insufficient production would lead to starvation. Instinctively we produce for the sake of production - more and more goods are produced at a faster and faster pace. The feeling is that because we need to produce, the market must accept everything we make. Since we can never produce enough, anything and everything we produce will find a market. It appears however that the world's markets are finite, not infinite.

If markets do not have the capacity to absorb all of our products, they do not need all of our workers. The paradox is that the more workers are capable of producing, the less they are needed. From a resource standpoint, as labor increases in abundance, it does not become cheaper, it simply ceases to be a resource. Andrew Carnegie and the railroad owners demonstrated that an abundance of labor allowed them, initially, to squeeze the workers with ever lower wages, then to exclude them from an economy altogether.

The natural consequence of an abundance of labor is a competition for jobs. Competition, whether it is in the labor market or elsewhere, is viewed favorably by most economists. Their argument is that it brings efficiency to the market - companies and workers will be motivated to increase productivity. In reality, this type of competition often has been symptomatic, not of economic health, but of serious underlying problems. Such problems have not been confined to the American economy of the late 1800s. The competition among the sixth-parters of ancient Athens or the peasants of France, for land, did not increase productivity or produce economic well-being.

At least two major economic problems are evidenced by competition in the labor market, if Athens and France are any indication. First, it is symptomatic of an economy which is undiversified, with markets concentrated in limited areas. The result is a dangerous overreliance by workers on a single market for employment. They are forced to compete because there are no alternative labor markets to move into. Second, it suggests that the markets which are available are extremely weak. Businesses, which battled tooth and nail with labor, in the end were overwhelmed by the market themselves, because demand was insufficient to support production.

Athens and France provide examples of economies where market opportunities were limited. If there had been greater economic diversity, landowners would probably have put their efforts into other commercial ventures. Instead they chose to make their money from their tenants. The farmers themselves saw no better opportunities outside agriculture and chose to compete for the limited land available. Normally people will move rather than endure poor working conditions or low wages. This situation contrasts with that of Rome in the Second Century B.C.. Latin towns complained that, because of a favorable job market in Rome, people were leaving the towns to work there.

It was not the fact of competition alone, which made the late 1800s in America so violent, it was more the fact that the competition was carried on at an unusually intense level. At the philosophical level, businessmen such as John D. Rockefeller and Andrew Carnegie, created an atmosphere of ferocity. The willingness to use physical threats against competitors, in the case of Standard Oil, or even to sanction the killing of striking workers, as Carnegie did, went far beyond the economic rules of supply and demand. While this survival-of-the-fittest mentality suggested economic strength, the background against which the competition took place suggests substantial economic weakness. At the economic level, businesses were struggling to keep their heads above water. While a Darwinist outlook may have encouraged a competitive mentality, weak market demand is what motivated businesses to cut costs. The physical confrontations with labor, the resort to imported labor, and the general willingness to exploit workers were indicative of how competitive the economic environment had become - they went far beyond normal cost-cutting measures. The panic of 1893 provides a rough way of gauging market conditions. The railroads, which had been at the forefront of the battle against labor, themselves fell victim to the economic war in the panic of 1893 - 156 went bankrupt. They were not the only victims. Over 16,000 businesses failed that year.

The lack of alternative markets for labor and the competitive environment for producers are only symptoms of market weaknesses. There was another problem lurking in the wings. Market demand is not just a function of cost. Costs represent only the seller's side of the market. Market demand also depends on buyers, i.e., people who have money to spend. If the railroad and steel industry seemed obsessed with labor costs, that was not their only focus. Andrew Carnegie took a serious interest in technology. If Carnegie represented business at its most arrogant, in terms of the treatment accorded to his workers, he also represented the free market at its best, in terms of innovations. Carnegie was motivated by competition to improve productivity. If he did try to keep labor costs down, he also was quick to develop or adapt technology which would make his entire operation more productive. The problem was not so much that Carnegie or the railroads focused on labor costs alone. It was more that their entire focus was on costs, when costs represented only half the problem of the market.

The market, as buyer, plays two almost diametrically opposing roles. It both fights producers by pressuring for reductions in costs, while at the same time sustaining them by buying their products. Consumers want to buy at the lowest price. The market, as adversary, continually pressures producers to reduce costs and cut wages. In its other role it sustains business by providing a market for what the producer makes. The market is made up of consumers with money. If businesses viewed their workers strictly as costs which needed to be reduced, they overlooked the fact that, workers as consumers helped to sustain demand.

This section has tried to explain why an abundance of labor resources is indicative, not of wealth, but of resource scarcity or poverty and is associated with economic problems. As indicated, part of the explanation may lie in the uniquely human nature of labor resources and part of the explanation may be found in the economic circumstances which create such an "abundance." It is not difficult to understand why such circumstances would contribute to violence.

Were the results of competition limited to efficiency and innovation, it would be categorically labeled as beneficial. Competition is relentless however. The pressure to cut costs does not stop with innovative equipment or more efficient production. Competition, taken to extremes, will eventually impact workers, resulting either in lay-offs or in subsistence-level wages. Individuals can neither provide for current needs nor put aside savings for the future in such circumstances. While layoffs and wage-cuts clearly are economically significant, their real impact may come in the political sphere. The more far-reaching economic consequence of unemployment may be the fact that it undermines demand. Each worker who is laid off may mean one less cost to worry about but it also means one less consumer who can buy products.

RESOURCE SCARCITY AND UNEMPLOYMENT

The problem of labor abundance in the context of overall resource availability is helpful to an understanding of the resource mechanism. All that is left, in terms of the mechanism, is the connection between resource scarcity and unemployment. Of the links in the mechanism, the weakest is perhaps that between scarcity and unemployment. The evidence of an association between violence and scarcity is fairly strong, as is the evidence of a connection between violence and unemployment. Scarcity and unemployment however, have no apparent connection. For example, if iron or copper become scarce, does that scarcity automatically translate into unemployment? Higher prices can be expected if aluminum production declines, but are they enough to predict layoffs? The basic answer is yes. Scarcity will first make itself felt in cost increases, but the impact will not stop there. Cost increases, once incorporated into product prices, will weaken demand and cause a loss of market share. Producers will either need to cut costs or accept a loss of market share. Either option is likely to bring layoffs or wage cuts.

If resource scarcity is only moderately severe, then the impact over a whole economy is likely to be only mild unemployment. Producers can compensate for mild fluctuations in resource prices. However, where resource scarcity is severe, then unemployment is likely to be fairly high. It is this severe type of scarcity which is relevant to situations where dictatorships will develop.

HUNTER-GATHERER SOCIETIES - LIFE BEFORE THE MARKET

Was it the market that propelled mankind from prehistoric cave-dweller to builder of civilizations? Market advocates, in their enthusiasm, at times seem to make that claim. The desire to accumulate personal fortunes motivated early people to produce surplus food and goods. That personal effort and energy powered early civilizations and allowed them to do great things - or so the argument goes. Apart from the historical support which early civilizations lend to market arguments, do places such as Sumer, Egypt or Athens, have anything to tell us? If they do, is their message limited to that of supporting cast member to the market's central role?

What would early civilizations teach about the market? What would a primitive tribe, a clan of hunter-gatherers, have to say about an industrial economy? Prehistoric peoples barely produced enough food to keep themselves alive. Modern agriculture can feed whole nations. On the other hand, perhaps today's economy places too great an emphasis on production - at the expense of other areas of economics. The economies of the ancient city-states and especially the economies of prehistoric tribes are treated with disdain, precisely because they lacked the ability to produce on the grand scale of today. By modern market standards they were failures. Yet, if production and productivity were the solution to all problems, why does unemployment still exist, and why do companies in the business of producing goods go bankrupt? If the overriding economic problem throughout history has been an inability to produce enough goods, why does increased production not bring a permanent solution to any and all economic problems?

Whatever their inadequacies, tribal economies nevertheless are important - for two reasons. First, the economic environment in which tribal economies operate is much simpler to understand, yet involves many of the same economic principles which govern the modern market. Second, the tribe represented a social organization which combined economic duties with political responsibilities. If market analysis tends to view economic problems in isolation, this book's thesis demands that economic problems and political decisions be looked at in combination.

The significant date, for most hunter-gatherer economies, is not when they began, but when they ended. Histories have largely been written about the cultures which emerged from early peoples, rather than the peoples themselves. The Indus civilization may have developed as early as 6000 B.C., while the fertile crescent of the Tigris and Euphrates began to show signs of civilization perhaps as early as 5500 B.C., as did Egypt. What distinguishes a hunter-gatherer culture from a civilized culture is primarily a lack of permanent connection to the land. Hunter-gatherers did not systematically raise livestock or cultivate crops, but instead wandered in search of game or plants and berries which grew wild.

There may be a temptation to dismiss hunter-gatherer societies as immune to market forces and therefore irrelevant to the market. Yet, the tribe, and its members, because they had needs, collectively represented a crude form of market "demand." The tribe's productive capabilities were too limited to create a surplus sufficient to sustain a full "market" system, as we know it. At the same time the tribe's needs, in a more narrow sense, did create markets or demand for particular products, such as meat. The economic laws of supply and demand both theoretically applied. However, because it was nearly impossible to find or produce enough food, demand tended to be the dominant economic law. Since demand was infinitely beyond the capabilities of production to satisfy, there were few limits on the amount which could be produced. The rule was to produce as much as possible.

The hunter in the hunter-gatherer group or tribal society was really a combination producer and buyer. As a consumer of meat, the hunter was a buyer. As the person who did the hunting, he was a producer. As a user of tools, the hunter was a buyer, and therefore represented the demand side of the market; as a maker of tools, he was a producer, and represented the supply side of the market. More broadly, the tribe's need for food created a market for meat and hunting services, which, in turn, gave the hunter his "job."

In prehistoric societies the laws of supply and demand served a single goal - survival. Demand was largely limited to food, clothing, heat, and shelter. The need for such products might be described as a "core" or primary market around which all human activities are centered. Since the need has been a constant, the market has remained a central one, even to the present day. Modern agriculture and production has facilitated the supply of core products, in fact, has seemingly diminished their importance. In reality this market is important because it is key to survival.

Keeping in mind the importance of this core market, it may be helpful to divide it in two and to illustrate this division using the prehistoric hunter as an example. The division is between a direct or primary market and an indirect or secondary market. The hunter was involved in both. The primary market involved the supply or production of game or meat. The goal of the hunter was to obtain the food necessary for survival. It would be called a direct or primary market because food or products necessary for survival were the primary goal of all human activities. The indirect or secondary market involved activities of importance to the primary market, but not directly connected to its activities. The indirect market involved the production of the tools the hunter needed to kill game, such as bows, arrows, and spears. Economists would sometimes label such production as a roundabout method of production.

The secondary market was important, even to survival, but it was only indirectly associated with hunting, the primary activity. Both the primary and secondary markets had an associated primary and secondary method of production; the primary method of production involved killing game, while the secondary method of production involved chipping arrow- or spear-heads from stone and making arrows, for example. This division of markets and production techniques or technology into a direct and an indirect category really describes the beginnings of specialization, a system in which the final product is produced using a series of separate steps.

Market price in early societies was measured, for either market, not in terms of money, but in terms of time. A single arrow might take several hours to make. While the hunter might like to have 10 to 20 arrows for a hunt, he could get by with four or five. As a "buyer," the hunter knew he needed more than one arrow for any given hunt, because he might miss or a single arrow would not bring the animal down. Therefore, he knew he needed to put in enough time to make several arrows. As "supplier," on the other hand, the hunter knew that time spent making arrows was time which could be spent actually hunting game. Spending time making arrows when the hunter already had a supply and would be wasting time was equivalent to saying the price was too low.

Hunter-gatherer economies operated in a world where demand so overshadowed supply that demand became an obsession. The hunter could never produce enough to saturate the market. The economic consequence was a system which highly valued labor. The social result was a tightly-knit social community which both helped the individual and yet controlled him as well.

THE LURE OF THE MARKET - TRANSFORMATION TO MARKET ECONOMIES

The market economy has had a long association with cities. Whether the market was the driving force behind the rise of cities or whether the conditions which favored one were ideal for the other, is not clear. An agricultural surplus was a prerequisite to both. What probably served as the greatest incentive for the growth of civilization was not so much the desire for personal gain, but the interest in a stable food supply. If early tribes found freedom in a wandering life, they also were burdened with insecurity. Since a reliable food supply was one of the best defenses against hunger, one of the earliest collective tasks undertaken by governments was the development of irrigation systems and grain storage systems.

The possibility of producing enough food to withstand periods of drought or locust infestations was an appealing one to early man. Tribal efforts often fell short in the battle against nature. Since food production and survival remained the key to survival, early civilizations tended to develop where natural forces could be tamed or were suitable to agricultural exploitation. Societies focused their energies on collective agricultural problems.

Once the tribal society moved beyond subsistence level production economic relationships changed. It was not that the economic forces at work were necessarily different, it was more that an increase in the size and complexity of production brought some underlying defects of a tribal market to the surface. A change from subsistence level production contributed especially to a change in the nature of employment. It did this in three ways. First, food and agricultural products would change in nature from necessities to commodities. Once they had been special because necessary for survival; now they simply became one more thing to be exchanged in the market. More efficient production of a greater variety of crops meant there were now surpluses. In a market economy where money and price had come into play this would mean that different crops could begin to serve as substitute products to keep price low.

Second, a change from subsistence level economies meant that the supply or production side of the market functioned more and more independently of the demand side. Productive ability and capacity, in a sense, became divorced from the market. As technology made production more efficient, it was possible to physically produce items at a faster rate than an economy could absorb them. Increased efficiency on the production side, particularly in agriculture, provided ancient societies with protection from food shortages and famine. At the same time, the increased productive capacity created areas of inefficiency in the market. Increased market size meant less market information. The market in a tribal economy was small enough to provide information to the producer about how much needed to be produced. The person who made arrows, for example, knew whether he had enough for a hunt and only needed to produce what he needed at any particular time. In contrast, producers in larger market economies found it more difficult to tailor production to changing market conditions

Third, a change from a subsistence level production meant an increase in specialization. Workers began to move from the direct production of necessary items to employment in indirect types of manufacture or service. Workers, in other words, no longer gathered or hunted their own food directly. Instead, they specialized in areas where the final product was itself only an intermediate product in the chain of production of necessities. Specialization, for example, meant that agricultural laborers were involved in only a specialized portion of production; rather than gathering foods for personal consumption, they only partially participated in production by trimming trees or crushing olives for oil in exchange for a wage.

If specialization brought increased productivity, it served to transform labor into a commodity, in the same way it transformed agricultural products into "commodities." The part workers played in production became smaller and smaller. Each specialized task reduced the importance of that job to the overall process. This was true even in such "non-productive" areas as grain harvesting. The search for fruits or grains had consumed large amounts of time for prehistoric peoples. Following the rise of the city-state, agricultural efforts were expanded to include irrigation, structured cultivation, and storage. The actual harvesting or gathering of grain, while crucial, became a relatively smaller part of the overall production process. In addition, the work no longer resembled the tribal methods of production. Greater numbers of workers became involved in secondary or indirect employment, i.e., workers no longer provided for themselves. They no longer went out from camp every day to gather berries or hunt animals. Instead, they carried wood or stone from one part of a city to another in exchange for a wage.

Accompanying these changes was a shift in power. Power, in nearly every culture, has often been associated with control of the resources or activities deemed most valuable.

Hunters, in tribal economies, were a valuable resource because they actually provided the game. The switch to domesticated cattle, sheep, or goats put the hunter out of business. Animals no longer were hunted, they were herded. To the newly emerging city-states, physical labor, such as hunting or gathering, became less central to agricultural production. Power shifted to landowners because land was viewed as more critical to agriculture than labor. While harvesting a crop was an essential step in the delivery of the product, a crop such as olives meant year-round care. There would be no crop unless the fields were irrigated and weeds pulled. While in any one year, any group of people could harvest olives, over time the trees, without care, would disappear. The cultivation of crops required stability and therefore Greek and Roman law protected the landowner. The landowner was seen to play the most important role in production.

Placing an exact value on labor is not a problem of ancient economies alone. Workers in the 1990s are finding that, while a job is still necessary for survival, establishing the value of specific skills is largely subjective. The value of labor decreases where jobs require few skills, where there is an oversupply of "interchangeable" workers, and where any particular job plays only a small role in the final product. The specialized nature of present-day jobs has become dissociated from the final product and from the product market itself. In such a situation it becomes almost impossible to prove to a potential employer that individual skills are of any particular value.

If the market did displace the tribe and labeled all economic endeavors as "commodities," it also encouraged innovation, particularly in the area of trade. Some believe that accounting was the original reason writing was developed, not so much to communicate, but to keep track of business transactions. The invention of money was a response to the difficulties presented by reliance on a barter system. King Croessus of Lydia (560-546 B.C.), in what is now western Turkey, is believed to have been the first ruler to issue a coin backed by any government. Such advances suggest that the advantages of the market were immediately obvious to everyone and that most were eager to join. In fact, there was a good deal of coercion involved in the market and in the societal changes taking place. It was not so much that tribes or peoples had a clear choice - either join a market or opt out. It was more that most faced pressures to change on several fronts - and the pressures did not all originate in the market. It may not have been the allure of the market which contributed to the rise of city-states so much as the desire to escape raids by neighboring tribes. If one looks at the various civilizations which arose around the Mediterranean one can see the practical reasons for many of the changes. Population increases made old tribal ways impractical. As more fields came under cultivation, game simply disappeared. The ability to freely wander in search of food, was drastically curtailed as tribes began to stake claims to particular lands.

If the pressures on the tribe were not all of an economic nature, the impact of the changes was not limited to the economic sphere. Many tribes watched their political power erode. The source of the tribe's power had come from its ability to provide safety for its members - it provided food and protected them from hostile neighbors. That capability was undermined by the market's seemingly unlimited potential. The market seemed to offer "guarantees" of a stable food supply and protection from armed attack. The producer in the market economy began to look more and more to the market for survival. If the tribe offered family and personal bonds, it could not compete with the market's ability to provide a secure environment.

Whether tribal societies willingly embraced the market or were simply forced to accept it as inevitable, the reliance on the market for survival was probably the most far-reaching effect of the new civilizations. In return for acceptance, the market promised to deliver large quantities of goods and security from want. What the market got in return was ultimate control over the production process and the workers who were part of it. Employment came to depend, not on the skills of the worker or the physical ability to produce, but rather on market demand. The social consequence was a loss in importance for the individual, the erosion of tribal support, and the decline of tribal controls. In prehistoric times, tribes had been victimized by resource scarcity. In giving themselves so completely to the market, the descendants of tribal members were victimized once again by resources. Cheap resources were crucial to maintaining the market demand which provided employment. When resources became scarce the employment promised by the market as a replacement for the prehistoric struggles of the tribe simply disappeared.

PART II

THE ANCIENT WORLD

CHAPTER 4

ATHENS - SILVER, SHIPS, AND GRAIN

Athens, in 500 B.C., was just one of many Greek city-states vying for trade and power around the Mediterranean and Aegean Seas. That changed in 483 B.C., when a very rich vein of ore was discovered at the Laurium silver mines, not far from Athens. Athenians were divided over the question of what to do about the discovery. Some wanted to distribute the wealth among Athens' citizens. Others saw the need to prepare for war. Just seven years before Persia had sent a small expeditionary force against Greece. It had been defeated by the Athenians at the Battle of Marathon in 490 B.C. Themistocles, one of Athens' leaders, persuaded the Athenian Assembly to invest the money in a fleet of ships.[1] The decision proved fortuitous.

What Themistocles proposed was an ambitious project. Nevertheless, when the inevitable Persian invasion came in 480 B.C., the Athenians had built a powerful fleet of 200 triremes. The naval confrontation between the Greek and Persian fleets would take place at Salamis, an island across the straits from Athens. The Greeks had managed to assemble a force of 379 triremes, but they were still outnumbered. Only by tricking the Persians into sailing into the straits were the Greeks able to win the battle. The Persians are said to have lost 200 ships.

The struggles with Persia have been portrayed in epic terms. Small, heroic Greek city-states banded together against a much more powerful adversary, who was determined to enslave them. Athens and Sparta, as the leading states, came to symbolize the determination of all peoples to be free from tyranny. Leonidas and the 300 Spartans who sacrificed themselves at the pass of Thermopylae, more than anything, embodied that spirit.

In the eyes of history, the leadership role in the Persian War reinforced, even enhanced, Athens' image as a model of democracy. The democratic ideals which governed the conduct of politics in Athens could be extended to the outside world. So strong were her beliefs in democratic government that she would sacrifice everything to preserve freedom, not just for herself, but for all of Greece.

The war with Persia, however much it symbolizes the eternal struggle against tyranny, may represent something else - the not-so-clear political and economic situation which existed in the Mediterranean world at the time. If Athens was engaged in a crusade for freedom and democracy on behalf of all the Greeks, she was rather selective about the battles she fought. In addition, for some of the Greek states the war came too late. The Greek settlements on the eastern coast of the Mediterranean had fallen to Persia some 50 years before and, despite pleas to Sparta, had received no help from Greece. If the war has been portrayed as a clash between two cultures, it ignores the fact that there were Greeks who fought on the Persian side. The Persian navy which confronted the Greeks at Salamis was not entirely Persian. It had its share of Greek sailors, contributed by the city-states to the east. To make matters even more confusing, less than a hundred years after the Persian armies had been driven from Greece, both Athens and Sparta would ask for her help when they were fighting each other. Persia would finance Sparta's navy in the final years of the Peloponnesian War (411 B.C.- 404 B.C.). In 398 B.C. Persia put its fleet under the command of an Athenian general named Conon, who methodically attacked Sparta's navy until 393 B.C.. One of the great ironies was that the Long Walls, the link between Athens and her port and a symbol of Athenian power, were rebuilt with Persian help in 393 B.C..

Perhaps the confusing struggles with Persia in the larger world are symbolic of something else - a less than clear understanding of Athenian democracy. Athens has come to symbolize Greek culture, democratic ideals, and everything that is heroic in mankind. As the first model for democracy, Athens' position is unlikely to ever face serious challenge. At the same time, part of Athens' reputation is based on things which have little to do with either democracy or government. We know Athens, as much for her architecture and great philosophers, as for her democratic form of government. The buildings of the Acropolis mark Athens as one of the truly great civilizations. The Parthenon alone, viewed against a backdrop of mountains, paints an heroic picture, as if to say 'great things happened here.' That 'aura of greatness' is enhanced by the reputation of philosophers such as Socrates, Plato, and Aristotle. Yet, as much as we stand in awe of Athens for her achievements, we only have a vague idea of how her government actually functioned.

The irony of any association with philosophy is that the democratic experiment was largely over by the time the philosophers arrived on the scene. Aristotle was born in 384 B.C. when Athens was already in decline. Plato, born in 428 B.C., did see some of Athens' most productive years, yet would enter the world of philosophy late. Athens, where its image was concerned, led a charmed life. Even Socrates' death at the hands of the state did not seem to tarnish that image. The focus was on Socrates' life, not on the actions of the state which put him to death. His death, if anything, added to Athens' heroic stature - Greek philosophers were willing to die for their beliefs.

If the notion of Athenian democracy seems ill-defined, it may be helpful to at least provide a time frame for its existence. Athenian democracy, at its point of highest development, seemed to coincide with the rise and dominance of the Athenian Empire. The Empire lasted only 50 years. It began in 454 B.C. and ended in 404 B.C.. (The Parthenon, by comparison, took 15 years to build (447 B.C. to 432 B.C.).) The beginning, 454 B.C., is somewhat arbitrary and the end, 404 B.C., ignores a brief non-democratic period in 411 B.C.. If mere form were one of the criteria for democracy, it could be said that democracy survived until 422 B.C., when the Macedonians forced a constitutional change. By that time Athens was a democracy in name only. Dating Athens' democratic period is inexact because many of the governmental structures we associate with democracy, such as the popular assemblies, evolved over a long period of time - they did not suddenly spring to life in 454 B.C..

The seeds of empire were sown in 483 B.C. with the silver discovery at the Laurium mines. The fact that Athens had added 200 triremes to her fleet by 480 B.C. testifies to her economic potential. There is less confusion about the date the Empire came to an end. The Athenians, who had begun so confidently with the victory at Salamis in 480 B.C., saw their fleet destroyed in 405 B.C., and found themselves blockaded in their city by a Spartan-led navy. There were no battlefield heroics at the end. Athens was starved into surrendering in 404 B.C..

This chapter begins with a brief look at the Confederacy of Delos and the events leading up to 454 B.C., then focuses on Athenian history in the Sixth and Fifth Centuries, B.C., roughly from 594 B.C., the date of the Archonship (or leadership) of Solon to the death of Socrates in 399 B.C.. During this time period Athens went from poverty to prosperity and back again. She also experienced periods of unrest, calm, and political chaos. The relationship between economic problems and political unrest is looked at next. Finally, the chapter looks at the relationship of all these factors to the resources available to Athens, the part resources played in the unrest during different time periods, and the government response.

THE CONFEDERACY (LEAGUE) OF DELOS

The silver strike at the Laurium mines in 483 B.C. serves as an introduction to the economic side of Athenian democracy. It was something of a prelude to empire as well. The story of the Athenian Empire really begins in 479 B.C., when the Greek armies, under the leadership of Sparta, decisively defeated the Persians at the battle of Plataea, a city allied to Athens located near Thebes. The prestige of the victory and Sparta's military capabilities should have provided her with an opportunity to lead a united Greece. The problem was that, once the Persian armies had retreated, the war would no longer be fought on land. With no fleet of her own, Sparta had to rely on the naval resources and experience of her allies, a fact which undermined her credibility. In addition, her generals were not immune to bribes, even bribes offered by Persia. Athens, with a powerful navy, should have been an obvious alternative to Sparta, but she was mistrusted by many of the Greek states. The states in Asia Minor nevertheless realized that naval power was their only hope against Persia. Overcoming any misgivings, the Greek states formed a naval alliance with Athens in the winter of 478-7 B.C.. This alliance came to be called the Confederacy of Delos, because it was headquartered on the sacred island of Delos.

Although the original intent of the Confederacy was to serve as a defensive alliance against Persia, Athens found it a convenient excuse for action against other Greek cities. First, city-states which had not joined were forced to become members. Next, states which wanted to leave were subjugated. The island city of Thasos revolted in 465 B.C., but was defeated in 463 B.C. and forced to pay tribute to Athens. Finally, Athens moved the treasury from Delos to Athens in 454 B.C.. It is this date which has been chosen to mark the formal beginning of the Athenian Empire.

The formation of the Confederacy marked a significant change in Athenian foreign policy. Up to that time Athens had mostly limited military involvement to Greece itself.

Now she chose to pursue an aggressive policy, involving military confrontation with a major power outside of Greece. The Confederacy had resource implications as well, and for Athens, these may have been of greater significance. The Confederacy represented a financial windfall, far beyond anything Athens could have dreamed of. She was not just rich. The Laurium silver had made her rich. She became wealthy on a scale which could barely be measured, let alone comprehended. In 478-7 B.C. alone, the Confederacy had revenues of 460 talents. Just five years before Athens had begun her fleet of triremes with 100 talents of silver.

ATHENS FROM SOLON (594 B.C.) TO SOCRATES (399 B.C.)

For those unfamiliar with the history of Athens, the first question may be - just who was Solon and what was the archonship? As to the second question, the archonship was the leadership position of Athens. The archon was a regent or ruler. The archonship had its origins in the Eleventh Century B.C., according to tradition, in 1088 B.C. Prior to that time Athens had been ruled by a king. The Medontids, a powerful Athenian family, overthrew the royal family, but rather than assuming the office of king, they established the archonship. At first, archons were appointed for life and were members of the Medontid family. Around 753-2 B.C., the lifetime term was reduced to 10 years and, in 683-2 B.C. the term was reduced to one year. The Medontids at some time during this period lost their claim to the archonship and any member of the nobility could be elected. In one sense the archonship was an aristocratic office, since the nobility by-and-large controlled political office. In another sense it was largely an acknowledgment that power in Athens had shifted from the individual or family of the king to leaders of the commercial class; the source of political power was no longer the personal or military prestige of the king, but the money-making ability of the business leaders of Athens.

Solon, appointed Archon in 594 B.C., is said to have been a descendant of one of the early kings of Attica, the region in which Athens was located. In addition, his father was a nobleman connected with the Medontid family. The reasons for Solon's appointment perhaps tell more about Solon and the part he played in Athenian history than his family background. Those reasons also say a great deal about the economic conditions of Athens in 594 B.C. It was said that the common people were weighed down with debt. Those who worked the land paid the rich one sixth of their produce. Others pledged themselves as collateral for loans. Creditors thus could seize debtors when they failed to repay as promised; some were sold as slaves to foreigners while others were enslaved at home. Children were even sold by their parents. Such oppressive conditions prompted discussions of possible solutions. There was talk of setting free those who had been enslaved and of redistributing the land.[2] It was at this time that many began to view Solon as someone who could solve Athens' problems since he was widely regarded as a neutral party in the dispute between the rich and the poor. One commentator, Phanias of Lesbos, suggested that, far from being a neutral party, Solon expediently promised each party what they wanted, telling the poor that the land would be redistributed and the rich that they would still be able to enforce the laws relating to personal security and slavery.[3]

Solon's reforms, after assuming the archonship, were carried out on two levels, one substantive, the other procedural. At the substantive level, Solon instituted what was called the *Seisactheia*, under which all debts were cancelled or discharged and individuals could no longer give themselves as security for a debt. He also freed those who had been sold into slavery as a result of their personal security.[4] At the procedural level Solon reformed the governmental system. In another concession to the increasing economic basis of political power, Solon changed the requirements for political office. Wealth, rather than noble birth, became the criterion for office. He created four classes of citizens, based on how wealthy the individual was. The four classes were: 1) 500-bushel men, those with an annual income of 500 bushels or measures or more; 2) knights, with incomes between 300 and 500 measures (or able to afford a horse and pay the horse tax); 3) teamsters, with incomes between 200 and 300 measures; and 4) thetes, with incomes less than 200 measures.[5] Another major change was the enlargement of the legislative bodies. The Assembly was the major law-making body. The thetes were now allowed to sit as members of the Assembly.[6] Solon established the Council of Areopagus, which he divided into two bodies. The upper body consisted of those who had held the position of archon. The second body was composed of 400 men, 100 from each of the four classes. The Council of Areopagus was intended to deliberate matters before they were debated in the Assembly.[7]

From a Twentieth Century perspective, even the existence of a representative Assembly and its expansion to include the thetes, the poorest of the four classes of citizens, suggests that Athens had finally become a democracy. In reality, the steps Solon took toward putting a democratic mechanism in place masked underlying problems which Solon's reforms did not cure. Only eleven years later, in 583 B.C., an archon named Damasias tried to transform his archonship into a permanent tyranny and managed to hold office until 581 B.C. The end of Damasias' brief dictatorship did not end Athens' political problems. Political fighting caused Athens to split into two parties, called the Shore or Coast, and the Plain. The members of the Plain party wished a return to the old aristocracy, while the Shore party, largely supported Solon's reforms.[8]

Whether Athens, in fact, remained calm in the period immediately following Damasias' attempted coup, historical records do not show. When the political story resumes, Athens is actually moving away from democracy. Some time before 561 B.C. Athens had been involved in a dispute with the city of Megara over possession of the port city of Nisaea, which lay to the west of Athens. Megara had captured Nisaea, but in 570 B.C. Athens managed to recapture it. The leader of this successful expedition was called Pisistratus. Playing on his success, Pisistratus formed the Hill party, so-called because its members were from the hills or highlands above Athens. But Pisistratus also recruited many of the thetes in Athens itself, who, as Plutarch points out, still had grievances against the rich.[9] In 561 B.C. Pisistratus concocted a scheme to seize power. He appeared in public one day with a self-inflicted wound and alleged that the wound was the result of an assassination attempt. One of his supporters then introduced a resolution in the

Assembly granting Pisistratus a bodyguard of 50 men. Whether the number was 50 or greater, Pisistratus used the bodyguard later to seize the Acropolis and assume control of Athens.[10]

Pisistratus held power for five years, when the Plain and Shore parties united and drove him out. However, around 550-49 B.C., Megacles, the leader of the Shore party, allied himself with Pisistratus, on condition that Pisistratus marry Megacles' daughter. However, this alliance did not last and Pisistratus was exiled again, probably in the same year as his restoration to power. Pisistratus went north to Macedonia and spent 10 years building a power base and an army. Around 540-39 B.C. he landed his army at Marathon, site of the future battle with the Persians, marched to Athens, and seized power. He held power there until his death, sometime in 528-7 B.C..[11]

While Athens probably remained relatively calm under Pisistratus, it was clearly not democratically governed. Pisistratus maintained a small army of mercenaries in Athens and also held the children of some of the noble families as hostages. At the same time, he did not simply do away with the governmental structure. The changes which Solon had made remained and the structures of government, such as the Assembly, were left largely intact.

When Pisistratus died in 528-7 B.C., he was replaced by his eldest son Hippias. Hippias, while maintaining a dictatorship, appears to have relaxed its hold somewhat, because he allowed some of the enemies of his father's tyranny to hold political office. Cleisthenes, for example, whose family had gone into exile when Pisistratus came to power, was archon in 525-24 B.C. However, the somewhat benevolent nature of Hippias' rule changed after 514 B.C., when his brother Hipparchus was assassinated. Following this killing, one of Athens' leading families, the Alcmaeonids, left Athens, either exiled or compelled to leave. Hippias however, was not left free to rule unhindered. The Alcmaeonids first organized a group of exiles who seized a fortress at Leipsydrion, north of Athens. This effort was soon abandoned. The Alcmaeonids then persuaded the Spartans to intervene and in 510 B.C. Hippias surrendered to a Spartan force under the Spartan king Cleomenes and left Athens. It was said that the Spartans may have feared some of Hippias' dealings with Persia.[12]

The departure of Hippias did not mean a return to democracy. Party politics came to the fore again. In some ways the new struggle was played out along rich and poor lines. The rich and many of the backers of Hippias now threw their support behind Isagoras, who was elected archon in 508-7 B.C. The opposition turned to Cleisthenes, an Alcmaeonid. Cleisthenes, despite Isagoras' archonship, succeeded in getting new democratic measures passed in the Assembly, whereupon Isagoras asked Sparta for help. The same Spartan king, Cleomenes, who had ousted Hippias, returned to Athens. Not only did Cleisthenes leave, but Isagoras had Cleomenes expel 700 Athenian families, believed to oppose him. Unfortunately for Cleomenes, he had only brought a small group of soldiers with him and angry Athenian citizens blockaded him in the Acropolis for three days before he surrendered.[13]

When Cleisthenes returned, he instituted political reforms of a different nature.

Solon's reforms had been aimed at changing the nature of political power from one based on heredity or noble birth to one based on wealth. Eligibility for public office was expanded, under Solon, to include wealthy individuals; no longer was power restricted to members of the nobility. The reforms were simply an acknowledgment that the nature of political power had changed. In one sense his reforms were somewhat limited, since they dealt primarily with the grievances which the newly rich had against the old nobility. Yet the grievances which were the source of Athens' problems in the eighty or so years since the reforms were those of the poor against the rich. To be sure, Solon had tried to address the most serious of the inequities. Yet the continuing disparity between the rich and poor resulted in a kind of class warfare which often erupted into violent confrontations. Politicians could expediently appeal to the grievances of the poor, as Pisistratus did. What Cleisthenes did was to try to contain the forces which the division between rich and poor created.

Cleisthenes created a governmental structure in which political power was divided geographically. One of the practical problems encountered after Solon was that power could coalesce around a geographical region. Pisistratus, for example, had established a political base using the tribesmen who lived in the hills, when he formed the Hill party. Each region, when left alone, served as a source of independent power. Eliminating the power of every region was impractical. Yet allowing it to operate at the governmental level made it impossible to control. The solution, instead, was to break up or confine this power. Cleisthenes' specific solution was to create 10 geographical "tribes." All of Attica, the region around and including the city of Athens, was divided into 30 *trittyes*, or districts. Attica was also geographically divided into three regions: the city, the coast, and the inland. Each tribe included three trittyes, one from the city, one from the coast, and one from the inland. Instead of allowing the different regions to use their power against each other, power was confined to individual tribes. In effect, before the grievances of the hillsmen reached the Assembly or full governmental level, they would have to be dealt with at the tribal level. At the governmental level, Cleisthenes changed the Council of Four Hundred to a Council of Five Hundred, 50 members of which came from each of the 10 new tribes. The Council of Five Hundred had formal responsibility for the introduction of legislation in the Assembly.[14]

Following the institution of these reforms Athens had external matters to worry about. In 506 B.C. Attica was invaded by a combined army of Spartans, Boeotians, and Chalcidians, but the invasion was repelled. In 499 B.C. Greek colonies in Ionia, along the Eastern shore of the Aegean, revolted against Persia. Athens sent some ships and a force of soldiers which captured the city of Sardis in 498 B.C. In 494 B.C. Persia managed to capture the city of Miletus and bring the rebellion to an end. Darius, Persia's ruler decided to punish Athens for her role in the revolt, but the Persian force which landed at Marathon in 490 B.C. was defeated. The repulse of the Persian force served only as a prelude to the full-scale Persian invasion in 480 B.C..

Following the defeat of the Persian force at Marathon, the Athenians added a new procedure to their governmental system - ostracism. Whoever was ostracized had to leave

Athens for a period of ten years. Ostracism was carried out by a vote of the citizens in the Assembly. Whoever received the most votes had ten days to leave Athens. While the sanction involved a ten-year exile, the ostracized individual did not lose his citizenship nor his property rights. The first ostracism took place in 487 B.C..

Other than the use of ostracism as a new political sanction, Athens appears not to have introduced any other new political innovations in this time period. The preoccupation with the Persian threat may have reduced any interest in tinkering with political institutions. However, the Persian fleet was decisively defeated at Salamis and its army was defeated at Plataea. In addition, shortly after Plataea, an Athenian naval force defeated the Persians at Mycale in the eastern Aegean and managed to reignite the revolt against Persia which the Ionian Greeks had begun in 499 B.C. The Battle of Mycale and the renewed revolt of the Ionian Greeks perhaps marks the beginning of the alliance known as the Confederacy of Delos, discussed briefly at the beginning of this chapter. It was officially organized in the winter of 478-7 B.C. The Confederacy supported itself by a levy on its member states, either an in-kind contribution of ships or by the payment of money. It is said that the first levy in 478-7 B.C., resulted in a total contribution of 460 talents.[15] (As noted, the silver strike at the Laurium mines may have brought in around 100 talents in 483 B.C. It was these funds which Athens used to construct her fleet.[16])

Initially, the Confederacy's purpose was that of a defensive and offensive alliance against Persia. However, the Athenian general Cimon, possibly in 468 B.C., destroyed a Phoenician fleet and defeated a Persian army at the river Eurymedon in Pamphylia in Asia Minor, effectively eliminating Persia as a threat. Perhaps Athens concluded that Persian power was on the wane, even before this victory. While perhaps using the threat of a Persian resurgence as the moral justification for its actions, Athens resorted more to pure force and military coercion in Confederacy operations. The Confederacy turned its operations against its own members - or against those city-states in proximity to Athens which were not members. First, around 472-1 B.C., Athens forced the city of Carystus to join the league. Then, in 469 B.C., when Naxos tried to secede from the Confederacy, the allies attacked her and forced her surrender. Next, it was Thasos' turn to revolt in 465 B.C., resulting in surrender two years later. Athens largely dropped the pretense of a voluntary alliance when it moved the treasury from Delos to Athens in 454 B.C. - and charged an administrative fee of one-sixtieth of the tribute for safeguarding the funds there.[17]

Athenians made additional changes to their governmental rules during this time period. Sometime between 463 B.C. and 461 B.C., Ephialtes, one of Athens' political leaders succeeded in taking away many of the powers of the Council of Areopagus. They could no longer punish public officials for legal violations and many of their powers were transferred to the Assembly or the Council of Five Hundred. Pay for judges was initiated and the archonship was also made a paid office. In 458-7 B.C., the teamsters or zeugitae, the third class of citizens, were made eligible for the archonship.[18]

In 459 B.C. Athens found itself in a war, first with Corinth, then with Sparta and Aegina, Athens' island competitor. In 451 B.C. however, a Five-years' Truce was concluded which put an end to the fighting temporarily. At the end of this period, another peace treaty, for thirty years, was concluded. In 449 B.C. a peace had also been negotiated with Persia. The peace, in effect, removed the justification for the continuation of the Confederacy. Pericles, then-leader of Athens, however, proposed that Athens should maintain a fleet and for this purpose, had a right to continued use of the League treasury funds. Pericles proposed, in addition, that Athens would use the funds to rebuild her temples, since they had been destroyed as a result of Athens' defense of Greece. Instead of disbanding the Confederacy and discontinuing the contributions the Confederacy was to continue as before. Athens embarked on a huge building program. Construction of the Parthenon was begun in 447 B.C., and was completed in 432 B.C.

It was in 432 B.C. that a series of events plunged Athens and Sparta into war. The first phase of what became known as the Peloponnesian War lasted until 421 B.C. when a negotiated peace ended the fighting. Fighting resumed in 418 B.C. In 416 B.C. the city of Segista in Sicily, requested Athens' help against the city of Selinus. Athens agreed to the request and an expedition was sent in 415 B.C. This expedition undertook a siege of the city of Syracuse in 414 B.C. Although Athens sent a second expedition in 413 B.C. to help, the Athenians failed and their army was destroyed. The defeat of the Athenian army at Syracuse showed Athens to be weakened, perhaps mortally wounded, and the members of the Confederacy took it as signal to revolt in 412 B.C. Encouraged by Sparta, first Chios, then Miletus, Teos, Lebedus, Methymna, Mytilene, Cyme, and Pocaea declared their independence. Athens was not finished however. She attacked Chios and took Mytilene back. The navies of Athens and Sparta battled back and forth for several years. Athens won naval victories at Cyzicus in 410 B.C. and at Arginusae in 406 B.C. But in 405 B.C. the Spartan admiral Lysander surprised the Athenians at Aegospotami when the Athenians had left their ships and gone ashore for the day. Out of a fleet of 180 ships only 20 escaped. The Spartans executed 3,000 prisoners, all those captured in the battle.[19] Lysander then blockaded Athens which, with its people starving, finally surrendered in 404 B.C.

The government of Athens, during this period, had undergone some changes. In 411 B.C., those who favored rule by some form of oligarchy, i.e., rule by a small number of individuals, devised a plan to transfer power from the Assembly to a body which became known as the Council of Four Hundred. The transfer was effected at a meeting of the Assembly held just outside the walls of Athens. The Assembly was persuaded to abolish the existing magistracies, while five officials were then chosen. These five in turn, were to appoint 100 individuals who, in turn, were to chose 300 additional individuals. This Council of Four Hundred was vested with absolute power. The Four Hundred only held power for four months, from June to September, and then were deposed. Power was formally transferred to a body known as the Five Thousand. Yet the political divisions had become so great that, for a time, two groups vied for power over Athens, one group in Athens, the other at Samos. Finally in 410 B.C. the divided rule ended and power was exercised solely from Athens.

Athenian government changed once more following her surrender to Lysander and the Spartans. Under Spartan oversight, the Athenian Assembly, in 404 B.C., transferred power to a body called the Thirty, which would draft new legislation. The Thirty then appointed a Council of Five Hundred. A police force, the Eleven, was also chosen. The Thirty next proceeded to execute many of Athens' prominent citizens. As part of their activities, the Thirty enrolled a group of 3,000 citizens, allowing them to bear arms, and also providing that anyone not among the 3,000 could be tried by the Thirty without trial. The unpopularity of the Thirty caused them to ask Sparta for troops to maintain order. However, armed resistance by Athenian exiles eventually brought the rule of the Thirty to an end in 403 B.C. The political divisions in Athens were not completely healed. Some of the Thirty had moved to Eleusis, further up the coast from Athens. In 401 B.C. Athens attacked Eleusis and executed the leaders it captured. If the Thirty had been eliminated, Socrates' death in 399 B.C. suggests that democracy had been restored in name only. Officially Socrates was charged with impiety, a religious crime, although the reason he was charged at all may be more related to political fears. Whether the newly-restored government is totally to blame is subject to debate. Socrates could have fled Athens, but chose to remain and accept his death sentence. The events of 399 B.C. provide a convenient stopping point for a discussion of Athens' political history. The next section deals with the economic aspects of Athenian history.

OVERVIEW OF ATHENS' ECONOMIC HISTORY

Athens' economic history, like her political story, is a series of ups and downs. One economic thread which runs throughout Athens' political history is the political problem caused by dissatisfaction among the poor and the resentment felt toward the rich. Solon attempted to deal with these problems in 594 B.C., yet he was unable to provide Athens with any permanent solution. The increasingly bitter rivalry between the haves and have-nots was a symptom of one particular problem - what to do about those who had no real place in the economy, yet whose very presence was a source of political power. Athenian political leaders never did come to grips with this particular problem. If the economy would not accept them, politicians were tempted to play on their resentments, in their bids for power. The temptation to use the extraordinary wealth provided by the treasury of the Confederacy proved too much for Pericles. It amounted to nothing more than buying off the unemployed. it provided no permanent solution to economic problems. When the revenues ran out, politicians once again had to confront the underlying problems.

Perhaps the two most common solutions to Athens' employment problems were the settlement of Athenian citizens on lands taken from defeated enemies and public works projects. Resettlement might seem like the ideal solution, and from Athens' perspective, it was. Unfortunately, it tended to bring Athens into conflict with other peoples. In rallying the Greek states against Persia, Athenian leaders had appealed to notions of democracy and freedom. When there was a falling out with other Greek cities, democratic ideals were cast aside. Time and again Athenian armies and navies wiped out rebellious cities, sometimes exterminating their populations, often replacing the defeated inhabitants with Athenian citizens.

In 506 B.C., after defeating the Chalcidians in battle, 4,000 Athenian citizens took over lands located in the Chalcidian plain. At Scyros in 474-3 B.C., an Athenian force sold the population into slavery, once the victory had been achieved. In 450 B.C., after capturing the city of Histiaea, in Euboea, Pericles drove its inhabitants out and replaced them with settlers from Athens. A similar fate happened to Potidaea in 430 B.C. - defeat, expulsion, and settlement by Athenians. In 427 B.C., when the city of Mytilene surrendered following a revolt, the Athenian Assembly voted to put the male population to death and to sell the women and children as slaves. The Assembly later changed its mind, but the vote to overturn the sentence only just carried. When the island of Melos surrendered in 425 B.C., men of military age were killed, the inhabitants enslaved, and a settlement of Athens established. Of course the Athenians sometimes were on the receiving end. One Athenian settlement force in Thrace was surrounded and wiped out in 463 B.C.

Public works projects were the other solution to unemployment or discontent among the Athenian masses. The biggest public works project was that undertaken by Pericles beginning in 447 B.C., with the start of construction on the Parthenon. It lasted until 432 B.C. Public works were also used in 410 B.C. by Cleophon. There was something of a public works or make-work aspect to many of the public services Athenian citizens were asked to perform. Ordinary citizens, without training, were allowed to serve as judges. Citizenship was the only criteria for becoming a judge after 462-1 B.C.. Judges were chosen by lot from a list of 6,000. Individuals got on the list simply by signing up. This may have served to promote fairer treatment of the poorer classes. On the other hand, in complex cases involving disputes between members of the same class, judgments by untrained individuals would tend to hinder just verdicts.

Although such innovations have been lauded as major advances in participatory government, they often failed to provide safeguards from potential abuses. Ostracism, the proceeding by which citizens could be exiled from Athens, was originally intended to limit political power. The story is told that at one ostracism, Aristides, one of Athens' political leaders was asked by an illiterate citizen to write Aristides' name on the potsherd in order to vote for his ostracism, although he did not know who Aristides was. Aristides had been given the name "The Just." When Aristides asked why the individual wished to ostracize him, the individual is said to have replied that he was tired of hearing him called "The Just."[20] If the story suggests that voter cynicism and dissatisfaction are not a new phenomenon, it also points to the potential abuses inherent in the use of ostracism as a mechanism of government. Somewhat overshadowed by the story itself is the fact that the individual was illiterate. While participatory government is a worthy goal, allowing individuals who could not even read to make decisions of this magnitude is not a credit to the name of Athenian democracy.

Resettlement and public works are suggested as the two solutions Athenian politicians had resort to in connection with Athens' employment problems. To provide some perspective on Athens' economic problems, it may be helpful to contrast two periods of time: the first, the time of Solon, the second, the time of Pericles. Looking at 594 B.C., when Solon instituted his reforms, it is clear that Athens was suffering serious economic problems. As discussed, those who worked the land endured severe economic privations. Moving forward some 150 years to 447 B.C. and Pericles' public works projects, it can be seen that the economic situation had completely turned around. Pericles' programs brought full employment to Athens and a period of prosperity.[21] What had happened in the interval between these two leaders?

ECONOMIC CHANGES FROM 594 B.C. TO 399 B.C.

To understand the economic changes which took place at Athens, there are three political developments and their time periods which should be kept in mind. The first occurred in 594 B.C. with the reforms of Solon. This involved the creation of the four classes of citizens based on wealth. The second involved the reforms of Cleisthenes and the creation of the ten tribes. This occurred around 508-7 B.C. The third was the transformation of Athens from just another city-state into a city-state with mastery of the Athenian Empire, which began after 478-7 B.C. when the Confederacy of Delos was formed. The economic complaint voiced in Solon's time was the inability of those working the land to make ends meet - suggesting that Athens relied on local agriculture for both products and employment. Perhaps the major economic question is what caused the transformation from an economy based on farming to one based on sea-trade? Athens' geographic location had remained unchanged - even when Athenian workers were mostly farmers, Athens had a port from which it could ship and receive goods. Did forests suddenly start to grow in Attica, creating a supply of ship's lumber which hadn't existed before? Or was the change to a sea-based trading economy the result of new cities and markets caused by a population increase around the Mediterranean? Or, another possibility, had production techniques of different localities around the Mediterranean world created changes in the production and availability of products? Egypt, for example, no longer a major military power, now served as a major grain producer for the Mediterranean. Or, still another possibility, did the Phoenician fleet of Persia or the navies of Athens' rival Greek cities combine to limit Athens' trade? For whatever reason, Athens seems to have relied more on land and agricultural production than on the sea, for economic growth. Despite its location, it appears to have been slow to exploit its geographical position.

When Themistocles proposed that the revenues from the silver mines at Laurium be used to construct a fleet of ships in 483 B.C., it seems clear that Athens was not a sea power. It is also clear that, following the defeat of the Persians and the formation of the Confederacy of Delos in 478-7 B.C., Athens was not only a sea power, but was on the way to becoming the dominant power in the Aegean and Eastern Mediterranean. For some 70 years, from 478-7 B.C. until her defeat in 404 B.C., her navy ruled. For a little over 30 of those 70 years, roughly from 447 B.C. to around 415 B.C., her economy prospered.

72

Whether the war with Persia or the Peloponnesian War were the only factors in these changes, it is clear that economic changes were occurring. To understand more fully the changes, it may be helpful to return to economic conditions in Solon's time.

Some indications of the economic changes taking place can be discerned from the writings related to the period following Solon's archonship. Historical data is admittedly scarce for much of this period. Plutarch, a source for some of the stories, wrote his histories some 400 to 500 years after they took place. He wasn't born until 45 A.D. Nevertheless, it is possible to get an inkling of the economic changes through the few references he makes to the plight of the thetes and to comments about other aspects of the economy.

There are indications that several factors were at work in the Athenian economy in Solon's time. It appears that the soil in Attica was wearing out and that agricultural productivity was declining. Indirect evidence of soil and agricultural decline is provided by the problems of the sixth-parters. Plutarch provides more direct evidence when he states that Solon recognized that Attica was poor and unproductive and that the soil yielded only a bare subsistence to those who worked it. Plutarch also states that large numbers of people were moving to Athens from the country, another indication that people were giving up on the economic prospects in the countryside.[22] The other side of the coin, in regard to the movement to Athens, is that it indicates an expanding economy with the growth of economic and job prospects there. Solon and the Athenian political leadership also took steps to actively encourage trade and manufacturing, as opposed to agriculture. One law passed at this time excused sons from parental support if the sons had not been taught a trade by their parents. It is said that Solon also ordered the Council of Areopagus to inquire about the employment or professions of individuals and to punish people found to have no occupation, a law somewhat at odds with Athens' more democratic reputation.[23]

Bury and Meiggs argue that Athens, while a major exporter of olives and oil, had by this time become dependent on the import of other agricultural products, particularly grain.[24] Solon is said to have banned exports of all agricultural products, except oil.[25] They argue that this measure was not intended to encourage the olive industry, but instead was intended to discourage the sale and export of what few grain crops Attica did produce herself.[26] The export of olive oil and a reliance on imported grain may be the first major examples of specialization and comparative advantage.

When Pisistratus formed his Hill party, sometime before 561 B.C., the evidence suggests that, while the Athenian economy had shifted from agricultural employment to an urban trade and manufacturing base, Athens was in recession or more seriously, a depression. The thetes, it was said, had serious grievances against the rich. A revolution was even expected.[27]

The evidence is somewhat scarce for economic conditions at the time of Cleisthenes's reforms after 508 B.C. The fact that Cleisthenes defeated his opponent Isagoras through an appeal to the people suggests a large urban population. The Spartan king Cleomenes is said to have expelled 700 families at Isagoras' urging, a surprisingly large number, suggesting the existence of a large middle class and an economy robust enough to support it.

Greek playwrights, from time to time, would include a deity in a play. The god would be brought onto the stage by means of a mechanical device and the entrance came to be known as deus ex machina, literally, the god from the machine. Often the only reason the gods were included in a play was to artificially extract the hero or heroine from a situation they could not otherwise escape from. Although the term had its origins in the Greek stage convention, it came to mean any plot or story which was rescued by some artificial or improbable event or character. Perhaps there was something of the deus ex machina in Athens' good fortune. She had been rescued from an impossible economic situation by an out-of-the-ordinary event. In fact, it was not just one event, but two. The first was the Laurium silver strike, the second was the windfall provided by the Confederacy. The revenues from the Confederacy were of a magnitude unheard of in Greece. In 431 B.C., at the start of the Peloponnesian War, the League treasury contained around 6,000 talents. This was the amount which remained after 15 years of public works projects in Athens. In addition, annual revenues were around 1,000 talents.

Athens was struck twice with good fortune. At a superficial level, the only difference between the silver strike at Laurium and the appropriation of the League's funds is that the amount received from the Confederacy was much greater. From another perspective however, the two events can be differentiated for what they say about Athenian political leadership and its approach to economic problems. Themistocles, who persuaded the Assembly to invest the Laurium silver revenues in a fleet, was willing to experiment with novel ideas which promised long-term solutions. Pericles, on the other hand, can be criticized for taking the easy way out. Rather than looking for new approaches to problems such as unemployment, he used what was conveniently available, the League funds. His public works projects, as Plutarch notes, spread much of the wealth among Athenian citizens and provided work even for unskilled laborers.[28] At the same time, what Pericles did amounted to nothing more than political appeasement of the lower classes. It was a time-honored practice among Athenian politicians, but it was not on a level with Themistocles. (The only other Athenian idea which was new or which came close to matching Themistocles' level of sophistication was that of extorting monies from other members of the League. Whatever it says about Athenian morality or principles, it did promise long-term financial returns.)

Pericles can be criticized politically for resorting to public works projects to control potential unrest. If those projects are evidence of Athenian wealth, they also hint at an underlying economic problem - market demand under normal economic conditions was inadequate to accommodate the Athenian work force. Public works projects were an artificial stimulus for demand. They were extraordinary measures, in an economic sense, because they were not part of normal market operations.

Twentieth Century economists would immediately recognize the dangers posed by any policy involving massive government spending. The Athenian economy would begin to overheat. Increased demand would contribute to inflation. That, in fact, occurred.

Government policy however, represented only a temporary difficulty. What the public works program hints at is problems permanently buried in the market system - a labor force which was superfluous in a normal economy. It was as if, out of a hypothetical work force of 50,000 people, there was only employment for 30,000. The only way to incorporate the excess 20,000 workers, would be to use artificial methods, such as that provided by public works projects. The effect was similar to the use of credit to sustain demand in modern times.

One problem appears to have been that the Athenian market was close to the saturation point. Neither the domestic nor the foreign market could absorb any more goods or provide employment for any more workers. The other problem, closely related to market saturation, may have been something more fundamental. The "efficiency of the market," did not appear to have universal application. Some areas of the market were more efficient than others. The physical side of production seemed to gain in efficiency while the financial or economic side seemed to fall behind, particularly where labor was concerned. Advances in productive capability could not be translated into a corresponding benefit for labor.

The physical efficiency of the market was apparent in the increased output of goods, even in the falling level of wages. However there was an inefficiency about the way in which the market provided economic benefits and employment to the worker. If the market was efficient at providing goods, it was not the most efficient method of guaranteeing economic survival. It was as if the market could operate at nearly 100 percent efficiency in terms of supplying the market with goods and satisfying consumer demand, but was only 60 or 70 percent efficient when it came to generating jobs. The problem was not simply that inefficiency occurred from time to time. The problem was that it was a permanent fixture of the labor market in a market economy. Basing employment on a market system which, by its nature, was motivated to eliminate labor altogether created an irreconcilable conflict. An infinitely expanding market seemed to offer the only solution to this dilemma. As Athens discovered however, markets in the real world tend to have limits. If the League treasury allowed Pericles to artificially create new markets, it did not solve the underlying problem of a market-based employment system.

POLITICAL UNREST FROM 594 B.C. TO 403 B.C.

Athens, from Solon's time down to Socrates' death in 399 B.C. went through cycles of political unrest and calm. In addition, political unrest and violence varied in intensity during these different cycles. The two worst periods of political violence occurred toward the end of the Athenian Empire, first with the rule of the Four Hundred in 411 B.C., and second, with the rule of the Thirty in 404-403 B.C. In contrast to these two periods, there is the relative calm which settled over Athens during the time when Pericles led her, from around 447 B.C. to the outbreak of the Peloponnesian War in 431 B.C. There is evidence that, at other times during this period, Athens was deeply divided, the discontent simmering just beneath the surface. Ephialtes, one of the leaders of Athens' democratic parties was assassinated around 461 B.C., just before Athens entered her most prosperous and tranquil political period.

When Solon instituted his reforms in 594 B.C., Plutarch says that Athens was on the brink of revolution.[29] The first major act of political violence following the reforms was the seizure of the Acropolis by Pisistratus with his armed bodyguard in 561 B.C..[30] Whether Pisistratus' resort to the use of an invading army in 540 B.C. to seize power really would be considered the type of violence associated with an internal resource scarcity is somewhat questionable. There were many Athenian citizens who did rally to his cause when he landed at Marathon and fought other Athenians in a battle at a place called Pallene. To the extent that Athenians fought on both sides, the actions would probably be classified as internal violence. Pisistratus rule, in some ways was relatively benevolent. He remained in power until his death in 528-7 B.C.. Athens appears to have remained relatively calm during his tyranny. It should be kept in mind however, that part of the reason for calm was the standing army Pisistratus kept in Athens - that, and the fact that he kept the children of some noble families as hostages.

Following the death of Pisistratus in 528-7 B.C., Athens was ruled by his son Hippias. It appears the transition was relatively smooth, since Athens remained calm until 514 B.C., when Hippias' brother, Hipparchus, was assassinated. Following this assassination, Hippias' rule became more despotic. A rival Athenian family, the Alcmaeonids, now began to actively foment rebellion, first gathering an armed force of exiled Athenians, and then, when that attempt failed, persuading the Spartans to intervene, resulting in the ouster of Hippias in 510 B.C. However, with Hippias' departure, political fighting at Athens brought a request for Spartan intervention again in 508-7 B.C. The result this time was the expulsion of the 700 families. The armed resistance of the Athenian citizens, who attacked the small Spartan force, succeeded in defeating them. It was following this intervention that Cleisthenes instituted the reforms involving the ten-tribe structure containing the 30 trittyes. Perhaps the external threat following Cleisthenes' reforms, first by the Spartans and their allies in 506 B.C., and then by the Persians, served to limit internal conflict. Not until 461 B.C. with the assassination of the democratic leader Ephialtes, is the relative calm broken. Following this murder Athens appears calm through the leadership of Pericles, from 447 B.C. on, through the first phase of the Peloponnesian War, from 431 to 421 B.C., and the renewal of the war in 418 B.C.

The disaster of the Athenian expedition at Syracuse in 413 B.C. did not bring an immediate end to Athens' political calm, but political fighting began after this catastrophe. What was different about political disputes after 413 B.C. was that they were not settled within the framework of rules relating to discussion or debate. Instead the political game rules now expanded to include assassination as a means of settling scores. In 411 B.C. the oligarchic political leader, Antiphon of Rhamnus, plotted with other supporters of an oligarchy to take over the Athenian government. Androcles, a democratic leader, was murdered, as were several other democratic leaders. Hyperbolus, an exile, was also murdered. Following the choosing of the Four Hundred, supporters of the oligarchy, with an armed body of around 100, entered the building where the Assembly was meeting and forcibly dismissed the council. The rule of the Four Hundred lasted only from June to September. The seizure of the government brought a reaction from the democratic forces serving in the Athenian navy at Samos. One of the oligarchic conspirators, Phrynichus, was himself assassinated. An Assembly voted to oust the Four Hundred and Antiphon, the leader of the conspiracy, was executed together with another conspirator. the restoration of the democratic party following the ouster of the Four Hundred managed to restore political calm to Athens for a number of years. However, the calm was broken again following the capitulation of Athens to Lysander in 404 B.C.

It was in 404 B.C. that Lysander helped bring the Thirty to power in Athens. One of its first acts was to place the leading democrats on trial and to have them executed for conspiracy. The Thirty began systematically executing people, often without the benefit of trial. First, it was individuals considered to be of bad character. Next, prominent democratic leaders were condemned. Finally, members of the oligarchic party who did not approve of the actions of the Thirty were condemned. They even turned on one of the members of the Thirty, a man named Theramenes, and condemned him to death when he opposed them. The Thirty also requested that Sparta send troops, which Sparta agreed to. However, the democratic leaders who had escaped Athens soon created an armed force capable of opposing the Thirty and their Spartan garrison. The two armed forces attacked each other at a place called Munychia, just outside Athens. Critias, the leader of the Thirty, was killed in this battle, along with 69 of his followers as were many among those opposing the Thirty. In May of 403 B.C., only nine months after coming to power, the Spartans arbitrated a settlement between the opposing forces and the Thirty were removed from power.

ATHENIAN RESOURCES, VIOLENCE, AND POLITICAL REPRESSION

In 413 B.C. the Spartans established a military force at Decalea, which lies northeast of Athens. From this post they were able to raid most of Attica, stopping agricultural production there, but more importantly, forcing the closure of the silver mines at Laurium. The Athenians were so short of funds that they took to melting the gold offerings to the gods in order to mint coins. It had taken just 18 years to dissipate the financial resources of an empire, 6,000 talents worth, in 431 B.C., in a war they would eventually lose. Accompanying this loss was a change in the political environment in Athens. It was in 411 B.C. that the political murders of Androcles and other leaders of the democratic party took place. This was followed by the replacement of the council with the Four Hundred. The Four Hundred only ruled for four months, from June to September, but democracy was only restored after violent fighting.

The rule of the Four Hundred in 411 B.C. and later, of the Thirty, both provide examples of government repression. That their rule coincides with a substantial drop in financial resources and an increased tempo of violence provides support for this book's thesis. Athens had remained relatively calm while the Empire, and its monies, existed.

At the same time, the evidence is rather thin for other periods of time, where unemployment and violence are concerned. There had been obvious periods of repression in earlier times, during the rule of Pisistratus, from 540-39 B.C. to 528-7 B.C. and the rule of his son Hippias, from 528-7 B.C. to 510 B.C.. Historians, such as Plutarch, provide glimpses of a society divided by wealth and full of tension.

The scarcity of hard data for both population and economic output for much of Athens' history makes resource availability, particularly on a per capita basis, difficult to calculate, except in very broad terms. The Athenian economy underwent dramatic changes over time, although scarcity seemed to follow each change. For example, in Solon's time, the economy was based largely on agriculture. At the same time agricultural resources were in decline as the land became less and less productive. Workers who pinned their hopes on the rising urban economy of Athens found that it was no guarantee of wealth. Perhaps the strongest evidence of resource scarcity are the references to the extreme divisions between rich and poor.

CONCLUSION

This chapter has dealt with the problem of resource availability and political repression from the perspective of a single society. From this perspective, the focus is on how Athens' political system changed over time. The key question, in Athens' case, was how the same government and society responded to changes in resource availability. The next chapter focuses on Sparta. In one aspect, Sparta should be looked at in the same way as Athens, i.e., by comparing one period in Spartan history with another. In another sense, however, Sparta's importance as an economic and political model lies in the fact that it existed at the same time as Athens. The two states also shared a common cultural heritage. Differences in time and culture are variables which might impact the development of economic and political systems. Using countries with similar backgrounds existing in the same historical time period however, may serve to negate or eliminate these factors as explanations for the democratic or totalitarian nature of governments. More specifically, since Athens and Sparta had a common heritage, the explanation for their differing political systems will not be found in their cultural background.

CHAPTER 5

SPARTA: DICTATORIAL DEMOCRACY AND A SOCIETY UNDER SIEGE

The Spartan king Cleombrotus led his army south, past Mount Helicon, to Creusis, on the Corinthian Gulf. He had been ordered to march against Thebes, which, in the shifting alliances of the Greek world, was now Sparta's enemy. From Creusis the army turned northeast - toward Thebes. They would submit, he would make sure of that. At a place called Leuctra, the Spartans found the Theban army.

The Spartans should have had the advantage. Not only were her hoplites the best in all of Greece, they also outnumbered the Thebans. If the odds seemed to favor the Spartans, the Thebans seemed unconcerned. Despite appearances, the advantages were not all on the Spartan side. For one thing, the Thebans could be expected to fight well when they were defending their homeland. In addition, their cavalry was far superior to that of the Spartans. Above all, they had a brilliant tactician, Epaminondas, leading them. It was not tactics alone which would decide the battle. Epaminondas had also molded the Theban army into a force about equal in fighting ability to the Spartans, with a high level of confidence, almost overconfidence. Among the Theban ranks was an elite group of shock troops, numbering 300, called the Sacred Band. Drawn from Thebes' noble families, these hoplites had undergone extensive training.

As if to openly flaunt their defiance, Epaminondas ordered the Theban hoplites into formation directly opposite the main force of Spartans. The Spartans may not have noticed anything unusual about the Theban lines, or, even if they did, may not have thought anything about it. The normal battle deployment of Greek hoplites was a phalanx formation of interlocking shields 12 rows deep. The Theban lines were not just the normal 12 rows deep, or even 24 - they were 50 lines deep.

If the battle formation of the Theban army suggested defiance, Epaminondas seemed almost cautious in actually committing his troops to battle. He did not order the Sacred Band to open the battle by charging the Spartan lines. Instead he waited for the Spartans to give him an opening. The Spartans, for their part, did not immediately charge the Theban lines either. Instead they tried to maneuver their forces around the Thebans before actually moving to the attack. In doing so they had broken formation and, without the protection offered by the phalanx formation, were temporarily vulnerable. It was at this point that the Theban cavalry charged. They drove the Spartan horsemen back onto the infantry lines. The horses and riders knocked down some soldiers and distracted others and the confusion left them momentarily unprepared to fight. The Sacred Band now charged and the Theban forces concentrated their attack on the weakened point in the Spartan lines.[1] The Spartan king, who was directing his forces from near the breach, was mortally wounded in the fighting and almost his entire bodyguard, some 300 men, wiped out. The Spartans fell back, followed closely by the Theban hoplites. Conceding defeat the Spartans asked for a truce to bury their dead. In all, some 400 Spartan citizens fell at Leuctra, out of a total of 1,000 killed in their entire army.[2] Expecting a continuous string of victories, the unexpected disaster at Leuctra, in 371 B.C., marked the end of Spartan dominance of the Greek world.

Despite the defeat at Leuctra, the legendary fighting ability of Sparta's soldiers endures. Like Athens, Sparta is remembered more for the impressions of its culture than for the specifics of its history. If Athens' reputation revolves around its democratic philosophy, Sparta is known for the "Spartan" lifestyle of its citizens. Sparta took pains to cultivate this image among its Greek neighbors. While Spartan soldiers were not victorious in every encounter, Sparta emphasized the courage and single-minded devotion of its soldiers, even in defeat. Sparta might lose in battle, but defeat would be extremely costly for enemy armies. The Spartan reputation was held in such awe that, when a force of only 120 Spartan hoplites actually surrendered to a force of several thousand Athenians on the island of Sphacteria in 425 B.C., the whole Greek world was said to have been amazed - it was thought that Spartan soldiers would always prefer death to surrender.[3]

This chapter follows Sparta's political and economic history from its beginnings, around 800 B.C. until 371 B.C., the date of the battle of Leuctra. The chapter begins with a general overview of Spartan foreign policy and history and the role played in the wider Greek world. Sparta rarely took an interest in political affairs outside her region. Her dominance of Greece and participation in the outside world would be relatively short, some 32 years, from 404 B.C. until 371 B.C.. The chapter then looks at Sparta's social and political development as well as her economic history. Finally, it examines the relationship between periodic eruptions of violence and Sparta's resources and the governmental response. That response might be summed up in a single word - Krypteia - the Spartan secret police, mentioned earlier.

SPARTA AND GREECE

Sparta, in contrast to Athens, was an inland city. She had started out as four settlements, Pitane, Limnai, Kynosoura, and Messoa.[4] Situated in the south of the large peninsula known as the Peloponnese, which lent its name to the long drawn-out war with Athens, Sparta was part of a region or district called Laconia. Sometimes called laconians, for their district, the Spartans were known for saying very little. The spirit of the region survives today in the term 'laconic,' meaning brevity of speech. The Spartans called themselves by another name as well, the Lacedaemonians, when they were referring to the Spartan political state. Sparta lay south of the ancient city of Mycenae, fortress city of the warrior kings who ruled the Greek world from 1600 to 1100 B.C.. Where Athenians seemed to fight among themselves, the Spartans seem to have fought more with their neighbors. West of Sparta, separated from Laconia by the Taygetos mountain range, lay the district of Messenia. After conquering other neighboring cities in Laconia itself, Sparta went to war with Messenia. It is believed the First Spartano-Messenian War began around 740 B.C. and ended around 720 B.C. Sparta acquired an area called the Stenyclarus Plain and the inhabitants of Messenia became helots or captives.[5] While succeeding militarily against the Messenians, Sparta failed in such endeavors against Argos, the city controlling the district known as Argolis to the immediate north of Laconia. Around 669-8 B.C., Sparta had gone to war with Argos, but her army was decisively defeated at Hysiai.[6] The defeat was the signal for a revolt in Messenia and the Second Spartano-Messenian War began. Sparta emerged the victor again, probably around 650 B.C., only this time she annexed the whole district of Messenia.

Sparta attempted to repeat her success against Messenia by going to war with Tegea, her neighbor to the north. The first and second Spartano-Tegeatan wars lasted from around 575 B.C. to 545 B.C. Sparta failed to conquer Tegea however and she turned her attention once again to Argos, her rival to the north. Sparta managed to defeat the Argives at Thyrea, possibly in 547 or 544 B.C. and annexed Thyrea and the southern part of Argolis.[7] Argos itself was not conquered however. Later, in 494 B.C., the Spartans would inflict a decisive defeat on the Argives at Tiryns, although Sparta did not annex Argos as a result.[8]

From around 479 B.C. until 465 B.C., Sparta was at war with Tegea again.[9] There is reason to believe that in 465 B.C. or just before, the Spartans killed some helots who had sought religious sanctuary. Shortly after the killings a major earthquake struck Sparta, brought on by the murders of the helot suppliants, or so some Spartans believed. The earthquake precipitated a revolt among the helots. A Spartan force of 300 soldiers was annihilated at a place called Stenyclaros.[10] The Messenian helots, following Stenyclaros, chose to make a stand against Sparta at the fortress city of Ithome, near Messene. They managed to withstand a siege, lasting at least four and possibly as many as nine or 10 years. Sparta even asked the Athenians for help. The helots who managed to hold out were, in the end, allowed to leave the Peloponnese.[11]

Sparta, following the end of the rebellion, apparently reestablished its control at home sufficiently to send armies into Attica nearly every year of the Peloponnesian War. Despite outward appearances however, Sparta may not have felt that secure. In 424 B.C., when the Athenians had landed forces at Pylos, a small promontory in the western Peloponnese, the Spartan government made a proclamation to the helots. The helots were to choose from their number those who had done the greatest service to Sparta on the battlefield. The impression was given that those chosen would be granted their freedom as a reward for their service. The 2,000 chosen were paraded around the temples in Sparta in a celebration of their freedom. The Spartans secretly put all of them to death.[12]

In 421 B.C. Sparta and Athens agreed to a peace for a period of 50 years. Unfortunately the situation in Greece was not stable enough to support what was called the Peace of Nicias. Both Athens and Sparta entered into various alliances with other Greek states. Athens allied itself with Argos, Sparta's long-standing adversary. Sparta invaded Argos in 418 B.C. and the invasion resulted in a negotiated 4-month peace. However, Athens sent an army under Alcibiades, who persuaded Argos to disregard the truce. An

Athenian-Argive army then invaded Arcadia, a district north of Sparta. This force first captured the city of Orchomenus and then moved to take Mantinea, north of Tegea, another of Sparta's long-standing enemies. However a Spartan army defeated the force at Mantinea. This resulted in the overthrow of the government at Argos. The new government then entered into an alliance with Sparta. The fighting for the first few years took place mostly at sea, but in 415 B.C. Athens sent its ill-fated expedition against Syracuse. Sparta, perhaps sensing that Athens would be preoccupied with its naval expedition in the west, sent an army into northern Attica and built a fort at a place called Decelea, in 413 B.C. From Decelea, the Spartan garrison began sending raiding parties into Athens' agricultural districts, disrupting food production. Finally, when Athens surrendered in 404 B.C., Sparta maintained a garrison for a time there. Sparta apparently was secure at home during this time.

Sparta now attempted to rule what had been the Athenian Empire in Athens' place. While Sparta produced some gifted administrators, such as Lysander, the general who defeated Athens in 404 B.C., they were hampered by an unwieldy administrative system. Athens had been largely content to collect tribute from its allies, while leaving their internal governmental and administrative systems alone. Sparta, in contrast, attempted to directly administer each city, often maintaining a garrison to enforce Spartan rule. The internal politics at Sparta also caused her to view the actions of her own administrators with suspicion. Lysander, for example, was recalled to Sparta largely because he had adapted too well to the foreign culture surrounding the royal house at Samos when he governed there.

Sparta has been compared unfavorably with Athens because of her methods of foreign administration. She tended to replace every democratic government with an oligarchy and to maintain her control with a garrison. Athens' democratic image, in fact, is enhanced because her administrative methods were more liberal and she installed democratic governments. Sparta clearly did not favor democracy. Yet, it may be unfair to view Spartan administration as a departure from the standard set by Athens, because it is not clear just what standard Athens was setting. Athens may not have installed garrisons in the cities where she introduced democracy, but she didn't need to. She could control wayward states with her navy. With the military resources at her command, she had the luxury of deploying troops quickly wherever they might be needed.

While Sparta's methods can be criticized for being heavy-handed, a more basic administrative problem was that they required a heavy commitment of resources. In addition to finding enough soldiers to man the garrisons, she had to find administrators for each city. Compounding this problem was the fact that many of her old adversaries were reasserting themselves. To the east, Persia had recovered much of her strength following the invasion of Greece and the revolt of the Eastern Greeks. Where she had helped Sparta toward the end of the Peloponnesian War, she now offered Athens her help. In Greece itself, many of Sparta's old adversaries were recovering as well. Argos, Corinth, Thebes, and Athens would enter into alliances designed to end Spartan rule.

Sparta became entangled in a war with Persia only a few years after Athens had surrendered her empire. Persia, around the end of the Peloponnesian War, had been governed by Darius. On his death, his eldest son, Artaxerxes, ascended the throne. Cyrus, another of Darius' sons, served as satrap, or governor, over the region of Asia Minor. Cyrus decided to take the Persian throne from his brother, Artaxerxes, and recruited an army of Greek mercenaries to help him. In the spring of 401 B.C. this army set out for Susa, the capital of Persia. The army reached Cunaxa, not far from Babylon, in the summer, and defeated the Persian army there. Unfortunately, when the battle had been won, Cyrus saw his brother and, in an attempt to personally kill him, charged into the midst of the Persian army and was himself slain. While Artaxerxes kept his throne, Cyrus had changed the political situation in Asia Minor prior to the expedition. He had fomented a rebellion of the Ionian Greek cities in a neighboring satrapy, governed by Tissaphernes. Fearing the reassertion of Persian power following the failure of Cyrus' expedition, the rebellious cities appealed to Sparta. Having committed an act of war against the Persian king by supplying Cyrus with troops, Sparta committed troops to help the Greek cities.

Sparta, under her king Agesilaus, carried on successful campaigns in Asia Minor for several years. However, the Persians put together a large Phoenician fleet command-ed by Conon, an Athenian admiral, which destroyed the Spartan fleet at Cnidus in 394 B.C. The Spartan defeat at Cnidus brought the rebellion to an end. The Greek cities in Asia accepted Persian rule and threw out the Spartan garrisons. Sparta was also having problems closer to home. In 396 B.C., Pharnabazus, one of the Persian satraps, sent an emissary to some of the Greek states to try to create an anti-Spartan alliance. Whether it was because of this emissary, or for other reasons, Thebes provoked Sparta, and in 395 B.C. Sparta sent two armies against Thebes. However, one of the armies, under Lysan-der, got trapped between a city it was attacking and a Theban army. Lysander was killed in the fighting and a force, sent from Athens to help Thebes, caused the second Spartan army to withdraw. In July of 394 B.C. a Spartan army defeated a combined army from Thebes, Athens, and Argos at Corinth, but could not destroy the army. A second battle in 394 B.C., at Coronea also brought victory to Sparta, but again left the defeated armies intact. The allied forces, rather than confront Sparta armies directly, tried to contain Sparta by building fortified walls across the Isthmus at Corinth. Athens rebuilt her fortifications in 393 B.C., torn down as a result of the peace settlement following her surrender in 404 B.C.. In 387-6 B.C., the Persian king Artaxerxes mediated a peace settlement.

Sparta used the breathing space provided by the settlement to consolidate her position in the Peloponnese, attacking Mantinea, to her north, in 386-5 B.C. In 382 B.C., an oligarchic party, friendly to Sparta, overthrew the ruling party at Thebes. Spartan strength was such that she extended her influence far to the north, into Chalcidice and Thrace, causing a defensive alliance of the cities, known as the Chalcidian League, to be disbanded in 379 B.C.. Yet this achievement may have represented the apex of Spartan influence; circumstances were beginning to operate against her. In 379-8 B.C. the Thebans overthrew the Spartan-supported government and threw out the garrison which helped to maintain it. In 378 B.C. Athens entered into an alliance with Thebes. Athens then resurrected its old naval confederacy and its fleet defeated the Spartans at Naxos in 376 B.C.. During this time, the Theban army began to have some successes against the Spartans.

News of the defeat at Leuctra caused a democratic revolt of states all over Greece. The cities of Arcadia, the region north of Sparta, formed an alliance against Sparta and a capital was established at a place called Megalopolis. When this federation ousted a pro-Spartan government at Tegea, Sparta responded by invading Arcadia. The federation appealed to Thebes for help and she agreed to the request. By the time the Theban forces arrived the Spartans had withdrawn. It was decided to invade Laconia itself. Although the army did not capture Sparta, it did manage to reach the outskirts of the city, in itself a severe blow to Spartan prestige. On leaving Laconia, the army went west, into the district of Messenia. Here, it did more than damage Spartan prestige. The Thebans reestablished the independence of Messenia and founded the city of Messene on Mount Ithome. Sparta, in 370-69 B.C., with the founding of Messene, had now lost nearly one-third of its geographical size.

SPARTA'S SOCIAL AND POLITICAL SYSTEM

The city of Sparta might be viewed as nothing more than the capital of the Lacedaemonian state, much as Athens was the seat of government of Attica. There were some similarities to Athens. Athens had based its four citizenship classifications, 500-bushel men, knights, teamsters, and thetes, on wealth. Sparta, similarly, used wealth as the yardstick for citizenship, although wealth was a relative term. For Spartans, wealth meant a minimal contribution to the military mess, whereas Athenians were only considered wealthy if they had incomes above the 500-bushel level. If Sparta used wealth as a criterion for citizenship, it was less refined in its classification system. It only made a distinction between citizens and former citizens, those who could no longer contribute to the mess. It did not divide citizenship into different categories. Sparta, like Athens, allowed slavery, although the Spartan system of slavery may have involved a greater element of physical coercion.

Sparta, as a capital city, did differ from Athens in one respect. Where all the inhabitants of Attica were governed directly by Athens, not everyone living in Laconia fell strictly under Spartan rule. There were autonomous city-states which had submitted to Spartan sovereignty. Residents of these states, the perioeci, while being granted certain privileges, were not considered full citizens of Sparta. Unlike the Spartans who could not meet their mess obligations however, the perioeci were ineligible for citizenship.

The highest class in Spartan society was that of Spartan citizens, the Spartiatai. The Spartiatai, however, came to be divided into two classes, 1) the 'homoioi' or Peers and 2) the 'hypomeiones,' or Inferiors.[13] The Inferiors were those who could not

84

contribute to the monthly mess or syssitia. The homoios, or Peer, to retain full citizenship, had only two obligations: 1) contributing to the syssitia and 2) performing military service. After the Spartiatai, the next class was the perioeci. The perioeci were, for the most part, citizens of independent city-states in Laconia. They sought a close allegiance with Sparta for protection. The primary obligation Sparta imposed on them was military service, since Sparta apparently did not ask for any type of tribute from them. In other respects they were freemen who supported themselves primarily through farming and sometimes manufacturing.[14] Sparta's lowest class, after the perioeci, was that of the helots. The helots were essentially slaves, a status imposed on them as a result of Sparta's wars of conquest. Some were conquered people in the immediate vicinity of the city of Sparta. Others, like the Messenian helots, lived some distance from Sparta. The helots had few rights. They could be killed by Spartan authorities without trial. They were primarily agricultural laborers who worked plots of land for their Spartan masters. The only restriction which worked in their favor was a limitation on the amount of agricultural produce which they could be required to turn over to their masters; they paid a fixed amount.[15]

The Spartan government presents a contrast to Sparta's societal structure. The paradox of Sparta is that, while the societal treatment of the helot population was repressive, the government operated as a democracy. The constitutional basis for governing was one of equality. At the same time, the constitutional rights of participation in governmental decisions were accorded only to the Peers.

Sparta's governmental structure was somewhat unusual. She had two kings. While many of their original powers gradually were curtailed, one function they kept was that of leading the army in time of war. Only one king however, was chosen to lead at any given time. This was the reason the Spartan king Cleombrotus was personally involved in the fighting at Leuctra. Below the kings was a body of 30, called the Gerusia or Council of Elders. It was made up of 28 members chosen by acclamation in the Spartan Assembly, plus the two kings. The 28 members chosen by the Assembly had to be members of the nobility and over 60 years of age, although they were chosen for life. The primary duties of the Gerusia were to prepare matters for the Assembly and to act as a court of justice in criminal matters. There was an executive body, similar in some respects to the Gerusia, called the Ephorate. It was made up of five ephors, or representatives of the Assembly, who served for terms of one year. The Ephorate appears to have been a counterweight to the power of the king, an executive body representative of the Assembly. The ephors did have the authority to indict the king and force him to answer charges before them. Two of the five also accompanied the king on military expeditions. The ephors also had final jurisdiction in civil cases.

The Assembly of Citizens was Sparta's popular legislative body. Spartan citizens over 30 years of age were members. In general the drafting of laws was left to the ephors and kings, with the Assembly either approving or disapproving decisions. The Assembly did elect members of the Gerusia as well as the ephors. Formal approval by the Assembly was required for proposals to become law. The one check on the

Assembly's law-making power was the requirement that laws had to be formally "proclaimed" or officially read, before the Assembly was dissolved. If the Gerusia or magistrates disapproved of a proposal they could dissolve the Assembly without making an official proclamation, preventing the proposal from being enacted.

It is not known how the unique form of government at Sparta, with its division of power between two kings and five ephors, came into being. One theory held that a man named Lycurgus, who lived around 885 B.C., created the Spartan constitution. Another theory held that there was no such person; the stories surrounding Lycurgus were all a myth intended to explain the development of the Spartan constitutional system. There is some evidence that the ephorate, as an office, came into being in 755-4 B.C. and that the office may have originally been created, not to limit, but to help the king, whose administrative duties increased following the annexation of Messenia.[16]

The creation of the ephorate is only part of what came to be known as the 'Lycurgan reforms.' Perhaps the most significant accomplishment of these reforms was not the establishment of a particular governmental institution, such as the ephorate. Instead, it was the complete transformation of all of Spartan society from a simple agricultural society into a perpetual armed camp. In essence, these reforms provided that Spartan citizens were no longer to engage in agricultural production or manufacturing. They were instead to continually train for war. Farming was to be done by the helots. There is some speculation that this change occurred after the Second Spartano-Messenian War. Sparta came to the conclusion, during that war, that the only effective method of fighting was using hoplites, heavy armed infantry, in phalanx formation. The phalanx was a compact, massed unit, with deep ranks, overlapping shields, and forward-extending spears. The phalanx, to be effective, depended on extensive training. It was felt that the only way to provide sufficient time for training was to free the Spartan citizen from all other duties. The land taken from the Messenians was divided up among the Spartan citizens in the form of kleroi, or allotments, the citizens were given helots to work the land, and the Spartans were to devote their life to military training.[17]

The significance of this change lay, not so much in the transformation of Sparta into a total military society, rather it was found in the division of land among all of Sparta's citizens, rather than a few wealthy individuals. Sparta, in some respects, seems to have been suffering from problems similar to those of Athens, i.e., a division in Spartan society between the rich and poor. Instead of giving the conquered land to the nobility, while leaving Sparta militarily weak, the new land division distributed the conquered land more equitably, and provided a means of gaining military superiority. The Lycurgan reforms represent both the first and final major change in the form of Sparta's constitutional changes. There appears to have been a continuing struggle between the ephors and the kings. However, where Athens' story involved a more or less continual expansion of democratic power, Sparta's basic political form stopped evolving after the Lycurgan reforms.

If the Assembly created some semblance of democracy, the Krypteia, Sparta's secret police, clearly set Sparta apart from Athens. Whatever role the Krypteia played, it was not publicly discussed in Sparta. What is known about it comes primarily from an incident which took place in 397 B.C.. One of the Inferiors, named Cinadon, plotted to overthrow the Spartan government. He enlisted a number of other Inferiors in the scheme, but the Krypteia learned of the plot and arrested him secretly. Based on what he had said, he did not intend to limit his accomplices to other Inferiors, but to all the people subject to Spartan rule. The secret police tortured and then executed him.

SPARTA'S ECONOMIC HISTORY AND CONDITIONS

Spartan economic history in some ways parallels that of Athens. Sparta experienced the same disparity in economic circumstances between rich and poor. Economic scarcity in Sparta, however, played itself out on two levels. On one level, there was the economic battle between the Spartan citizen and the helots, those who had been conquered in war, such as the Messenians. At another level, an economic battle was also taking place between Spartan citizens themselves, i.e., between the Peers and Inferiors. The evidence suggests that, either the productivity of the land was declining or that an increase in population was putting pressure on what resources there were. It is generally recognized that the Spartan citizen population was in decline, however, the overall population in the Peloponnese may have been increasing. In any event, the conspiracy of Cinadon and the growing number of Inferiors, suggests that resources, in relation to the Spartan population, were becoming scarce. The perpetual war footing which Spartan society placed itself on may have masked some of these problems, but it could not eliminate them.

Just after the end of the First Spartano-Messenian War, around 720 B.C., the Spartan king Polydoros is said to have distributed, or at least tried to distribute, some 3,000 to 4,500 kleroi, or allotments of land, to Spartan citizens. The allotments were made out of the Messenian land captured in the war. It appears that Spartan society was being divided by the disparity between rich and poor. While Polydoros was king, a dissatisfied group, called the epeunaktai, is said to have plotted a rebellion, however, the plot was discovered and foiled, and the plotters were forced to leave Sparta. In addition, an aristocrat named Polemarkhos assassinated the king.[18] It appears, as well, that the division between rich and poor continued to be a problem for the Spartans even some 50 years later. In 676-673 B.C. they invited Terpander, a poet, to visit Sparta, in hopes that he could find a solution.[19]

Following the end of the Second Spartano-Messenian War, probably around 650 B.C., Sparta is believed to have divided the conquered land into 9,000 lots, with a lot, or kleros, being given to each Spartan citizen. Ownership of the kleros remained with the state, although the Spartan citizen had effective control of the property. Several helots were assigned to each kleros. The Spartan did not work the land himself, but relied on the labor of the helot for the monthly contribution to the syssitia. Until the helot revolt in Messenia in 465 B.C., following the earthquake, the system worked. Unfortunately, the physical interference in the economic order, limits the ability to draw conclusions about the economic changes which may have been occurring.

Cinadon's conspiracy provides some information about economic conditions. Cinadon is said to have remarked, when he was enlisting people, that there were so few Spartan Peers, in comparison to the number of the Inferiors, perioeci, and helots. His statement suggests that production from the kleros was declining. There is another indication of a decline in agricultural productivity. Although the date is uncertain, it is believed that sometime after 404 B.C., the ephor Epitadeus, got a law enacted allowing for the transfer of property by Spartan citizens. This law specifically allowed the transfer of the Spartan's kleros. It is not clear whether this brought an immediate transfer of property or whether there was a long-term process involving a transfer of landholdings from poor citizens to the rich. By around 240 B.C., the number of Spartan citizens who held kleroi had dropped to 700.[20]

SCARCITY, VIOLENCE AND REPRESSION

The growing number of Inferiors is perhaps the strongest evidence of resource scarcity in Sparta. The major economic resource was land and productive land was becoming scarce. Resource availability, especially the availability of agricultural resources, fluctuated very little over time; scarcity was constant, competition was almost a given. If there was scarcity, it is difficult to draw any conclusions about its relationship to violence. Open violence was a rare occurrence in Sparta. The eruptions of violence which occurred, such as the Second Spartano-Messenian War and the revolts of the helots in 465 B.C. and again, in 369 B.C., following Leuctra, were related more to the military opportunities Spartan misfortunes presented for revolt, rather than to fluctuations in economic circumstances. Economic conditions were universally bleak and it was only the continual readiness and training of the Spartan hoplites which prevented a continual state of open warfare.

References to the Krypteia are perhaps the strongest indication that the Spartan government had an established mechanism for dealing with dissent. Plutarch reported that the magistrates would send young men out into the countryside, armed only with daggers, empowered to kill any helots they encountered on the roads at night. Sometimes they would kill helots working their fields during the day as well.[21] Plutarch had trouble believing that the Spartans would have resorted to such extreme measures unless circumstances forced them to it. He felt such orders only came about following the earthquake and revolt in 465 B.C..[22]

Xenophon sheds more light on secret police operations when he discusses the circumstances surrounding Cinadon's conspiracy. The ephors learned of Cinadon's plot, significantly, through an informer. Because they were unsure of the number of people who might be involved, they wanted Cinadon arrested outside the city limits of Sparta. They laid their plans in secret. Cinadon had apparently worked for the Krypteia himself, since the ephors used the ruse of a mission to arrest certain persons in the city of

Aulon to get him out of the city.[23] He was given a list of the names of those to be arrested, with no mention of charges, except for one woman said to be corrupting the Spartans who visited Aulon.[24] When Cinadon was arrested he was tortured and the persons he named were in turn arrested. The conspirators were flogged through the streets and executed.[25] The killing of the 2,000 helots in 424 B.C. is one other piece of evidence suggesting that the Spartan government might resort to repressive measures to control its subjects.

CONCLUSION

This chapter has followed the history of Sparta through a series of wars. Following the Second Spartano-Messenian War, around 650 B.C., Sparta instituted its Lycurgan reforms. These reforms distributed the conquered land in Messenia among Sparta's citizens, but forced them to adopt a way of life involving continual training in order to keep the lands they had won. Sparta represents a situation where the economic forces were totally at variance with the political forces. The Messenian helots, from an economic standpoint, clearly had no desire to farm the land for their Spartan masters. The only way to get the helots to produce in such a situation was through the use of military force and physical threats. Once Sparta's ability to physically enforce its system was gone, the system could no longer be maintained.

The next chapter looks at Rome. Rome is instructive for several reasons. In some ways it faced the same problems encountered by both Athens and Sparta. Rome is instructive because its economic and political situation contains similarities to both Athens and Sparta, yet also involved differences as well. Rome, like Athens, was an urban center, attracting laborers who found work in a diversified market. Rome, like Athens, became an industrial economy, (at least industrial by ancient standards) dependent on imports, and the labor of others, for its food supply. Unlike Athens however, Rome eventually incorporated military force into its governmental mechanism. In this aspect, Rome was similar to Sparta. Sparta however, was largely an agricultural economy, in contrast to Rome. Rome differed from Sparta in one final respect. Rome somehow found a way to balance the economic and political forces which threatened it. The Roman government managed to stay in power longer. In contrast to Rome, Sparta, as an economic and political system simply proved too fragile to last. When Thebes intervened in the Peloponnese in 369 B.C., the Spartan system, for all the toughness of its hoplites, simply disintegrated.

CHAPTER 6

ROME: OUT OF WORK, OUT OF BREAD, OUT OF CONTROL

Tiberius Gracchus might have done well to heed the omens. First, the man who kept the crows Rome used for the auspices, the omen-readings taken from the flights of birds, came to Tiberius' house and the crows refused to eat food placed before them. They wouldn't even come out of their cages. Finally, after their keeper shook the cages, one actually did venture out. Even then, it only stretched and walked around a bit, still ignoring the food that was offered. Then, when Tiberius was leaving for the Capitol, he stumbled in his doorway and hurt his foot, a bad omen in itself. Finally, as he walked to the Capitol, some crows fighting on the roof of a building dislodged a stone, which fell on Tiberius' foot. This was an even more ominous sign. It meant, not just that his stumbling was a bad omen, but that the omen related specifically to him.[1] Yet one of his followers suggested that it would be a disgrace for a grandson of Scipio Africanus, the man who had defeated Hannibal, to let a raven frighten him. Tiberius continued to the Capitol.

Unfortunately, Tiberius, in recent actions had offended the Roman Senate and on this particular day, they finally acted. Tiberius signified to his followers that his life was in danger by raising his hand to his head, but his opponents reported to the Senate that the gesture meant that he was asking for a crown. On being informed of this, some of the senators strode out of the Senate, followed by their supporters, armed with clubs and staves. The senators and the men with them were sufficiently large in number to intimidate the crowd surrounding Tiberius. Forcing their way through the crowd, they came directly after Tiberius, and when he stumbled in trying to escape, they fell on him and clubbed him to death. In all, over 300 people were beaten to death by the senatorial mob. The bodies of the dead, including that of Tiberius, were thrown into the Tiber river.[2] The death of Tiberius occurred in 133 B.C. It had been 400 years since Rome had experienced such bloodshed. While wholesale death in battle had become commonplace for Rome, civil unrest had been almost nonexistent during this time.

This chapter looks at Rome from around 500 to 27 B.C.. In 500 B.C. Rome's republican form of government was just beginning to take shape. In 27 B.C. Caesar Augustus would bring the democratic experiment to an end. A major focus is the latter part of that time period, from 133 on. The structure and operation of the Roman government is then looked at. Next the chapter analyzes the economic history and then the civil unrest, followed by the part economic forces played in civil unrest and violence. Finally, it looks at the effect the violence and civil unrest had on the form of government Caesar Augustus implemented.

Roman history during this time might be divided into two periods. The first period, the time of the Gracchi (133 B.C. to (121 B.C.), was marked by unemployment and civil disturbances. Tiberius Gracchus was succeeded by his brother, Gaius Gracchus, who met a similar fate in 121. Like the democratic parties in Athens, the Gracchi attempted to distribute land to the poor. The difference is that, where the democratic parties in Athens were largely successful in implementing their reforms, the Gracchi only succeeded in getting themselves killed. In the second period, beginning around 91 B.C., Roman history became a series of interventions by large armies. Unable to solve problems of civil unrest peacefully, Rome found itself at the mercy of any soldier charismatic enough to rally troops to his standard. For a period of time, these commanders fought the Roman mobs as well as each other. Julius Caesar managed to gain control briefly, but he was assassinated in 44 B.C.. Finally Octavian was able to eliminate his political opponents and establish complete control in 27 B.C., when he became Emperor.

There is a tendency to view Rome's government, especially that part embodied by the Senate, as an extremely aristocratic and conservative structure, which either totally oppressed the masses or avoided contact with the lowly plebs other than at gladiatorial contests, or similar "bread and circus" events. Yet the Roman Senate is probably unfairly portrayed as a group of reactionary aristocrats protecting the interests of the rich, thinking and acting in the same way. Even given its generally conservative nature, there were senators who seriously worked at reform. Unfortunately not all problems have a legislative solution and often the solutions tried prove inadequate. If the government could redistribute land or vote to provide grain to the people of Rome, it could not raise agricultural productivity of depleted soil or redesign an economy to incorporate the unemployed.

EARLY POLITICAL HISTORY

Rome supposedly had been founded in 753 B.C., although it had some form of settlement prior to that time.[3] It apparently started out simply as a convenient marketplace for the region along the Tiber river. The famous Roman Forum originally had been a low-lying swampy area which had been drained by the Cloaca Maxima (the Great Drain). Although Rome was apparently an early Etruscan settlement, the Romans came to view their Etruscan ancestors as having more of a distant influence than any direct connection; their original rulers, the Etruscan kings, they came to view as foreign despots. It is believed that just after 510, the last Etruscan king, Tarquinius Superbus (Tarquin the Proud), was deposed and driven from Rome.[4]

Having gotten rid of its kings, Rome began to quarrel with neighboring cities in central Italy. After 500, due to fighting with hill tribes, Rome formed alliances with other cities, known as the Latin League, and began to set up settlements in nearby areas.[5] Some 100 years later, in 396, Rome captured and destroyed the neighboring city of Veii. In 387-6, Rome was itself captured by an invading army of Gauls. The Gauls were bought off and left. Rome was left free to concentrate on local problems. It went to war with its Samnite neighbors in 343, but by 338, had largely subjugated the neighboring towns. Then, from 327 to 304, Rome fought another war with the Samnites, known as the Second or Great Samnite War.

POLITICAL HISTORY FROM 298 B.C. TO CAESAR AUGUSTUS

The Third Samnite War began in 298 and lasted until 290. While Rome was ultimately successful, the war caused a great deal of hardship among the plebs. Rome took the unusual step of appointing a dictator, Quintus Hortensius, in 287, to deal with the resulting disturbances.[6] In 291, before the Samnite war ended, Rome established a colony at Venusia, which was in the southern part of the Samnite territory. By expanding into this area, Rome increased the geographical size of its territory. This action also brought Rome into contact with the Tarantines, now not so distant neighbors in the south of Italy. Their capital was at Taras. Thurii, a former Greek colony, and a rival city of Taras, asked for Rome's help in 282. When Rome agreed, it got into a war with the Tarantines, who, in turn asked the ruler of Epirus, King Pyrrhus, for help. King Pyrrhus agreed to help and invaded Italy with a large mercenary army. However, while he managed to defeat the Romans in battle, he was not able to gain a decisive victory and the Tarantines concluded a peace with Rome in 272. This effectively gave Rome control of all of Italy.[7]

The conclusion of peace with the Tarantines only served as a preliminary step to another war. In 264 a dispute over control of Syracuse, the Sicilian city which had brought disaster to the Athenian expedition, now brought Rome into conflict with Carthage. When the First Punic War ended in 241, Rome not only acquired a navy, but also was successful in taking Sicily away from Carthage.

In 225 Rome defeated an invading army from Gaul. Then, in 219, the Carthaginian general Hannibal, captured the city of Saguntum in Spain, resulting in a declaration of war by Rome. Despite success on the battlefield in Italy itself, Hannibal could not bring Carthage victory in the war. In 204, Scipio landed a force in Africa and defeated the Carthaginians decisively at Zama in 202, effectively ending the Second Punic War. Shortly after the end of the war, in 200, Rome decided to go to war with Macedonia. In 197 the Romans defeated the Macedonian king, Philip V, in Thessaly. Then, from 192 until 189, Rome was at war with Antiochus III, monarch of the Seleucid Empire in Syria. When this war ended Rome was effectively in control of Asia Minor. Following this war, Rome was involved in what became known as the Third Macedonian War with Perseus, son of Philip V., from 171 to 168. Following the conclusion of this war, Rome enjoyed some 20 years of peace. Then, in 149, fearful of a revived Carthage, Cato the Elder persuaded Rome to declare war against its old rival. The Third Punic War ended in 146 when Scipio Aemilianus captured the city of Carthage, tore down its walls, and sold its people into slavery.

Having eliminated most external threats around the Mediterranean, Rome had to deal with internal conflicts. Slaves in Sicily rebelled in 139 and the First Slave Revolt was not quelled until 132. Before this war was even over, the city of Rome experienced problems itself. It was in 133 that Tiberius Gracchus tried to initiate reform and was killed, along with his 300 followers. His brother, following in his footsteps, was killed in 121, along with 3,000 of his followers. Rome was not finished in Africa however. From 112 to 105, its armies had to fight the Numidian leader Jugartha. In 104 the Second Slave

Revolt in Sicily began, and lasted until 100. In 95 Rome experienced rioting from dissatisfied workers. Then in 91, Marcus Livius Drusus (the Younger), as tribune, tried to give the Italian allies the rights of Roman citizenship. (The Italian allies were residents of the cities in Italy which had been conquered or made treaties with Rome. They often provided many of the soldiers for Rome's successful armies.) He was assassinated. While his death did not necessarily cause the revolt, the Italian allies went to war with Rome in 90. Known as the Social or Marsian War, it lasted until 87.

In 88, one of the Roman generals, Lucius Cornelius Sulla, set the precedent for Roman armies. Sulla was ousted from command of an expedition against King Mithridates VI of Pontus in Asia Minor by the tribune Sulpicius Rufus. Rather than retiring gracefully, Sulla instead marched his army on Rome and took over the government. Despite the uncertainty of such a situation, Sulla nevertheless led an expedition against Mithridates. When he left, another general, Cinna, seized control with his army. Cinna would remain in control until Sulla returned in 82. Sulla ordered his army to march on Rome and the government was once again in his hands. Sulla had a "bodyguard" of 10,000 men, called the Cornelii, which he now loosed on Rome. It is said that they massacred almost 10,000 people, including 40 senators and 1,600 knights.[8] Sulla now proclaimed himself dictator, although he chose to leave the governmental institutions largely intact. Rather then abolishing the Senate, he increased its size, from 300 to 600, and admitted many of the knights to membership. Sulla abdicated the dictatorship in 80 and died in 78.

The precedent of an armed march on Rome, as begun by Sulla, continued. Marcus Lepidus, one of Sulla's lieutenants, tried to take Rome in 77, but was defeated. His defeated soldiers however, found a new leader in Sertorius in Spain. To defeat Sertorius, Rome turned to Gnaeus Pompeius Magnus, Pompey the Great. One of Sertorius' lieutenants murdered him in 72, ensuring Pompey's success. Rome again experienced difficulties with its slave population. Spartacus led another slave revolt in 73, but was defeated in 71. In 67 Pompey was given the task of subduing the pirates who were preying on Mediterranean shipping. He succeeded in this task within three months. Yet Rome was not free of internal problems. In 63 Catiline tried to organize a government takeover, but the plot was discovered. Cicero executed some of the accused conspirators, effectively ending the 'Catiline conspiracy.' If the political leadership needed to deal with Rome's social and economic problems, it chose instead to offend, almost simultaneously, three leaders with the military capability to exact revenge - Pompey, Crassus, and Julius Caesar. In what became known as the First Triumvirate, these three entered into an agreement in 60 whereby they would give their support to each other so as to effectively control Rome.

Though only an informal arrangement, one of the first successes of the Triumvirate was to give Caesar the consulship in 59. Caesar paid one of his political debts by then sponsoring a land bill for Pompey's veterans. He paid another debt by giving Crassus' supporters some tax concessions. Caesar, in turn, received the governorship of the province known as Cisalpine Gaul and Illyricum, now Dalmatia. What he wanted however, was not just a territory to govern, but an enemy to conquer. He found this in the

Gauls and from 58 to 51 he subdued the Gallic tribes and managed to carry out a successful invasion of Britain. In 56 the three triumvirs renewed their arrangement, resulting in the election of Pompey and Crassus to the consulship in 55. However, Caesar's daughter, who was married to Pompey, died in 54, weakening the relationship. This was followed by the death of Crassus in 53. He was killed leading an expedition against the Parthians, in what is now Turkey. Caesar and Pompey initially maneuvered on the political front, avoiding direct armed confrontation. However, the political maneuvering ended in January 49, when Caesar led a single legion across the Rubicon river, the border between Cisalpine Gaul and Italy. The war which followed lasted four years, with Caesar emerging the victor in 45. This culminated in his being appointed dictator for life in February 44. His dictatorship lasted barely a month, ending with his assassination on March 15 in 44. Ironically, this was only three days before he was scheduled to leave Rome to lead an expedition in the East.

In 43 Antony, Octavian, and Lepidus formed the Second Triumvirate, which was granted a formal five-year appointment. One of the immediate results of this coalition was the death of 300 senators and 2,000 knights, together with the defeat of several armies led by their political rivals. The Second Triumvirate was renewed for a five-year period, in 37. However, Lepidus attempted to lead his armies against Octavian, failed, and was forced to step down. In 31 Agrippa, Octavian's general, defeated the combined forces of Antony and Cleopatra at a place called Actium, on the Greek coast. Agrippa's legions put a final end to their challenge in Egypt. Both committed suicide in 30, following the defeat of their armies. Octavian was now left to establish his own form of government.

What Octavian created came to be known as the principate, in which Octavian, known after 27 as Caesar Augustus, was the principal leader of the state, or princeps. Like Sulla and even the members of the First Triumvirate, Octavian largely left the governmental structure intact, at least superficially. He chose instead to rule behind the scenes, manipulating the choice of leaders and the results of elections. For example, he was elected consul eight years in a row, in the first years of his rule. The changes which Caesar Augustus instituted in Roman government could involve an extensive discussion. However, for purposes of an economic analysis, the principate provides a convenient place to end a discussion of Rome's political history. The political history of Rome is a story of change, from periods of calm at home to violent upheaval, culminating in the civil wars between Julius Caesar and Pompey and between Octavian and Antony.

ROMAN GOVERNMENT - THE SENATE AND MAGISTRACY

If the turbulence of Roman society suggests almost continuous change, the turmoil was not reflected in the governmental structure of Roman government itself. Its origins can be dated from around 510, the time of Tarquin the Proud, the last Etruscan king. Like certain modern governments, such as the United States, the Roman governmental system involved two more or less "representative" bodies, a Senate and a popular assembly. The Roman Senate often seems a focal point for an analysis of Roman government. It was an important governmental body in Rome, although its prestige perhaps has been enhanced by the abilities of its members. It did produce some distinguished orators, such as Cicero. Yet the Senate did not have the power to make laws. It did prepare the legislation which the assemblies would approve. Without the power to enact laws, how did the Senate attain such prominence? First, it did have the authority to issue decrees. A decree, while not formally a law, could empower magistrates to use extraordinary means to restore order. Second, it administered the finances of Rome and controlled foreign policy. Third, though without formal legislative powers, its members, because they were largely wealthy individuals, were able to influence the assemblies and magistrates.[9]

The Senate originally began as a relatively small body, containing only 100 members, but fairly early in Rome's history, was expanded to 300 members. In 80, the dictator Sulla doubled the size of the senate to 600 members. Julius Caesar increased its size again to 900. In its early years, membership in the Senate was largely restricted to patricians, i.e., members of the original citizen families. Later, membership in the Senate became automatic once an individual had been elected to the magistracy.[10] By nature the Senate was a conservative body, perhaps because its members came from the privileged classes. Wealth was clearly a prerequisite to Senate service, because Senators were not paid for serving. When Rome's political climate had become totally polarized following the Gracchi, the especially conservative members of the Senate called themselves optimates, or better class, while the reformers, mostly outside the Senate, became known as populares.

The magistracy, the "executive" branch, in contrast to the conservative and aristocratic nature of the Senate, was a no-nonsense office. Perhaps because Rome's early history involved a series of military confrontations with its neighbors, the magistrates were given a fair amount of leeway in the execution of their duties and in the interpretation of the law. The magistracy, although it included the highest executive position, that of consul, actually involved a number of different government offices with varying degrees of responsibility. The office of consul could be said to be the highest ranking magistracy in Rome. In some ways the powers of this office corresponded roughly to those of a modern executive, such as the President of the United States, although there were two consuls in power at the same time, rather than one individual. Roman tradition held that two consuls had immediately assumed power in Rome when Tarquin was expelled in 510.[11]

Rome conferred two forms of power on magistrates. There was a general power, known as potestas, which was the power to enforce the legal duties of a particular office. This power was conferred on all magistrates. The other form of power was imperium, or supreme authority. Supreme authority included, not just the general power associated with potestas, but additional powers, such as command of the army and the power to pass death sentences.[12] Consuls, holding the highest office of the magistracy, were granted imperium, and as such, held the most power in the government. At the same time the consulship contained somewhat contradictory elements, in terms of its power. At the upper limits of power, consuls held authority which was theoretically supreme. They could both command the army or order individuals to be put to death. Cicero, who was consul in 63, used his power of imperium to order the execution of five followers of Catiline, accused of plotting a revolt.[13] Consuls were not responsible, in carrying out their duties, to either the Senate or the Assembly.[14] If they felt they needed additional support, they could have the Senate vote them a special decree, the senatus consultum ultimum, the final decree of the Senate, which authorized them to use whatever means necessary to restore order.[15] The senatus consultum ultimum was the power requested by Cicero, in dealing with the Catiline conspiracy, before exercising his power of imperium. Interestingly, Julius Caesar, in the Senate debate, opposed the executions.

In contrast to the "absolute" power conferred on the consuls, at the upper extreme, there were two formal restrictions which limited the exercise of this power. First, each of the two consuls had absolute veto power over the actions of the other. Second, the consuls were only elected for terms of one year.[16] (A dictator, in terms of power, was given a special advantage. He had the power of two consuls and therefore did not have to deal with the problem of the consular veto. While the term dictator has come to mean anyone with absolute authority, Rome specifically provided for appointment of dictators in military emergencies. They were appointed by a consul for a term of six months, after proposal by the Senate.[17]) There were some informal restrictions as well. While the consuls were elected by the popular Assembly, they originally were required to be members of the Senate. In addition, the fact that they served for only one year, meant that, once their term was ended, they lost the immunity conferred by the office - they might be subject to the wrath of their colleagues in the Senate or to the whims of future consuls.[18] Cicero, for all the decisiveness of his actions involving the Catiline conspirators, was criticized throughout the remainder of his political life for acting illegally in executing the men without trial.

Political power in Rome, like that in Greece, changed over time as economic power shifted away from the original families controlling the city. The relationship between the magistracy and the Senate reflected those changes as well. Senate membership originally was limited to those aristocratic families who founded Rome. Senate membership was a prerequisite to election to the chief magistracy position, the consulship. In later Roman history however, the situation became reversed. An individual, first elected to a magistracy by one of the popular assemblies, was automatically admitted as a member of the Senate for life.[19] The change from an hereditary-based political structure to an economic-based system was formally recognized in 180. By that time, the system was so widely accepted by Romans that a standard progression of office was established, known as the cursus honorum, or course of honors. An individual gained experience in government and administration, starting with the lowest office, quaestor and moving up to consul and censor.[20] In the later republic plebeians were admitted to the Senate. The restriction which limited membership to the patrician class, i.e., the large landowners, was dropped.[21]

THE POPULAR ASSEMBLIES

Rome had, not just one, but three popular assemblies. The assemblies, as a whole, were known as comitia, derived from the word comitium, meaning an assembly place.[22] In one sense, there was an ascending scale of relative power for each type of assembly, related to the wealth of its voting members. At the bottom was the concilium plebis, whose membership was limited to Rome's poorest citizens, the plebeians, i.e., plebs, or common people. Though clearly a less powerful body than the Senate, the concilium plebis nevertheless gained in power as the plebs increased in numbers. It had grown sufficiently in power to be represented by 10 tribunes or tribuni plebis in 449. In the Second Century B.C. the stature of the tribuneship had grown to the point where tribunes were qualified to become senators.[23] The tribunate, as an office, was intended to be one of the checks on the abuse of power, since it had been established to provide some protection to the plebeians from the actions of the patricians. In rare circumstances, during the later Republic, the tribunes had a veto power even over the actions of the Senate. The tribunes, like the consuls, were elected for a term of one year.[24]

At a level above the plebeian assembly, was the comitia tributa, or assembly of the tribes. Representing the 35 tribes of Rome, it had somewhat more responsibility. It served as an appeals court in non-capital cases and elected some of the lesser magistrates. It also enacted some legislation. Another assembly, the comitia centuriata, was at a higher level still. It could not be summoned unless the magistrate held imperium power. A measure of its importance is the fact that it decided whether to declare war. It served as the court of appeals in capital cases and also elected the higher magistrates. It appears that this assembly had assumed the functions of an earlier fourth assembly, known as the comitia curiata.[25] One limitation on all the assemblies was the fact that they only voted yes or no on measures which had been placed before them, after discussion by the Senate. The impact of voting was therefore somewhat undercut by a lack of debate. Since there was no formal discussion of legislation there would be no opportunity to amend what had been proposed and therefore little input in the drafting.[26]

ROMAN SOCIAL CLASSES

Rome could be described as having only two social classes, with one thing in common. The two classes were the rich and the poor. What they shared was a perpetual state of war with each other. The rich were represented by the patricians, the large landowners who led Rome when she overthrew the Etruscan kings. While the patricians held a great deal of power, that power began to decline over the course of the republic. Conversely, the power of the poorer classes, the plebeians, began to grow - at the expense of the patricians. In part this was due to fundamental changes in the Roman economy; in part it was due to the growing number of plebs. Some of the plebeians became quite wealthy as a result of the changes. However, the majority of plebs benefitted very little, contributing to the bitter hatred the plebs had for the patrician class.

Those who were able to succeed in the new environment were eventually given recognition as a distinct class - the equites or knights. While the knights were entitled to admission to the Senate, many chose not to exercise that privilege, since senators were forbidden to engage in commercial enterprises. The knights represented the rich entrepreneurial class, in wealth, a class midway between the plebs and the patricians.[27]

ROME'S ECONOMIC HISTORY

In some ways, Rome's economic history parallels that of Athens. Perhaps this was related to similarities in agricultural methods - an unmechanized, yet specialized, form of production, adapted to depleted soils. The agricultural economy relied on fewer workers, and often those who worked the fields were slaves. Industrial production, similarly, was specialized, yet far below the standards set by modern economies. Rome, like Athens, found itself inundated by agricultural workers seeking employment in the city, and like Athens, would turn to public works projects to solve an economic problem which otherwise seemed insoluble. In its reliance on public works projects, Rome all but conceded that its economy was incapable of accommodating the growing number of people who relied on it. Perhaps Rome did stumble on a novel solution. Whereas Athens used its military forces to keep its allies in line, Rome used its armies to provide its residents with work.

Early Roman history suggests that economic conflict was present almost as soon as Rome threw out the Etruscan kings. The early Roman agricultural laborers, like their Athenian counterparts, the sixth-parters, found agricultural production to be inadequate. There were often grain shortages and many of the plebeians fell into debt. Like the Athenians, the laborers in Rome pledged themselves as security for loans. On default they fell into a condition known as nexus, i.e., "men in chains." While not technically slaves, such men lived in virtual servitude to their creditors, and could be included as part of an inheritance.[28] The plebeians had very few weapons with which to fight back against economic conditions. However, there was one which they did find was effective to a certain degree, even against the laws favoring their creditors. Called a secessio, or secession, it was the ancient equivalent of a strike, a form of collective bargaining. The plebeians would physically leave Rome until their demands were met. It is believed they resorted to this tactic five times during the Republic, the first time being in 494.[29] This secessio proved effective, since the authorities agreed to the creation of the tribuni plebis or tribunes of the people. The tribunes had the power to protect plebeians from being seized by their creditors.[30]

The secession of 494 did not provide a permanent solution to the problem of insufficient agricultural production. Around 471 there was a dispute between the landowner patricians and the plebeians about public lands. The plebeians wanted these lands distributed while the patricians wanted the land kept public, since they had the use of it in such circumstances. The plebs were strong enough to wring another concession from the government, the creation of the plebeian assembly, the concilium plebis. Twenty years later, in 451, plebeian unrest over economic circumstances caused further disruption and changes in Roman law. The violence was sufficiently great to result in the suspension of consular elections and the appointment of a commission of ten patricians to write down all the laws. The Twelve Tables, as this collection of laws became known, represented a diminishing of the power of the patricians. Prior to the Twelve Tables, the college of priests, the pontifices, all patricians, had been responsible for the interpretation of the law.[31]

Rome's early economic history suggests that, in part, the military conflicts Rome had with its neighbors involved competition for land and agricultural resources. Around 444 Rome's lands were proving insufficient to support her population and she was enduring periods of famine. She needed more land to feed the population and the city of Veii stood in the way.[32]

The annexation of Veii did not solve the economic problems of the plebeians. The number of debtors continued to grow. Licinius and Sextus, who served as tribunes from 376 to 367 passed legislation providing that interest already paid on a debt should be subtracted from the remaining principal. Debt-limiting measures would be introduced four more times in the next fifty years. They also attempted to limit the amount of land any single individual could own. Another measure suggests, as well, the growing power of the plebs. In 367-366 they got a measure passed providing that one of the consuls should always be a plebeian.[33]

The consul Poetelius, around 326, also sought a solution for the problem of debt. While he may not have stopped the practice of the sale of a debtor into hereditary servitude, he apparently provided some due process by requiring a court decision before the step could be taken. In 312 the censor Appius Claudius began two of Rome's first public works projects, the Aqua Appia, a major waterway, and the Appian Way. Sons of former slaves were also admitted to the Senate.[34] Economic difficulties continued to plague the plebeians. Many plebeians who served in the army during the Samnite war, returned to find their farms in decay. Attempting to regain production, these plebeians fell into debt. They apparently resorted to such violent measures to redress their wrongs that the Senate authorized the appointment of a dictator, Quintus Hortensius, to restore order in 287. Quintus, in a major concession to the plebs, provided that the resolutions passed by the concilium plebis would have the force of law, something they had not had prior to this time.[35]

In 283 Rome annexed the Ager Gallicus, a region south of the Po river, which it had taken from the Gauls. It used some of this land to found some colonies, but most was left vacant. At the end of the First Punic War, in 241, Gaius Flaminius proposed that this land be distributed among the returning soldiers. It appears that their farms had gone to ruin while they were away fighting. The fact that the soldiers would want to exchange their old holdings for land in the Ager Gallicus suggests that agricultural methods had depleted the soil in the regions closer to Rome, making it unproductive. There was opposition from many in the Senate who owned the rights to leaseholds in the region. Rather than attempt to force the measure through the Senate, Flaminius took the measure to the plebeian council in 232 and passed it there. An invasion by the Gauls in 225 put an end to the effective implementation of the plan, making its passage a somewhat futile exercise. The proposal however, was important for the "psychological" impact it had on Roman legal concepts - and for the precedent it set for the future. It was also an indication of the weakening power of the patricians and the Senate. Politically, it planted the idea of passing legislation without having to go through the Senate.[36]

The Second Punic War ended in 201. Hannibal's almost superhuman exploits during the war seemed to dwarf all other adversaries of Rome. Yet the wars fought in the east against Philip V and Antiochus took a toll on the Roman soldier. While, compared to the war with Carthage these wars may seem small, they required some 47,000 soldiers each year. In the period between 200 and 168, the Roman army fielded as many as 130,000 soldiers each year, if the Italian allies and Italian Greeks are included in the number.[37] Since many of these soldiers were small landholders, their absence had an impact on Roman agriculture. The agricultural sector was changing, although war-time service of the small landholder was not the only factor at work. In fact, it was not just the agricultural sector which was changing; the entire Roman economy was undergoing change.

In a narrow sense the agricultural sector of the Roman economy had to absorb a host of operational changes. In a broader sense however, such changes were just part of an adjustment on the human or labor side of the economy. Changes in agriculture contributed to the new trends, but they were only one aspect of the change. At the technical or operational level, Italian agriculture became more specialized. In fact, the entire Mediterranean economy became more specialized - and more competitive. Sicily, Sardinia, and Egypt, the grain supplier for Athens, proved to be better grain-growing regions than most of Italy, although Campania, the region southeast of Rome, still provided Rome with wheat. The specialized production and competition proved to be a two-edged sword however. For the populace of Rome, specialization meant more efficient grain production and cheaper bread; for the small landholder, competition meant revenues below those needed to sustain production. Small farmers simply could not operate their farms economically. Farms in the Italian peninsula switched to raising cattle or producing grapes and olives.

Three factors contributed to this change. First, soil in some parts of Italy had been depleted, making it less suitable for crops such as wheat. Second, specialized production of grain in areas outside of Italy meant lower prices for Italian farmers and less incentive to produce wheat. Third, growth of a market for other agricultural products, with correspondingly higher prices, provided an incentive to growers to switch to products such as meat, wool, leather, and especially wine and oil. The destruction of Carthage contributed to this trend. Carthage had been an economic rival and supplied grapes and olive oil to the Mediterranean. Almost by default, Italy inherited the market.[38] The combined effect of these three factors was to encourage large-scale farming. The specialized nature of production was better suited to the large landhold, rather than the small holder.

If more efficient production methods represented major advances on the technical side, they had an impact at the human level. Labor markets changed. At a time when specialization reduced the overall need for skilled workers, the availability of slave labor reduced demand even further. Foreign wars provided Rome with a large pool of slave laborers. The First Punic War, for example, brought 75,000 prisoners of war. Returning Roman soldiers found themselves competing for work at home against the very enemies they had faced in battle. Slave holders were able to drastically reduce labor costs - as well as the corresponding bargaining power of free labor. The wars also changed the dynamics of land ownership. Soldiers who either did not return or who, on returning, found their property too far ruined to rescue, provided the Roman government with large amounts of public land. In fact, governmental holdings amounted to one-fifth of the land in the Italian peninsula. The Roman government would lease this land to individuals, subject to the payment of a rental. While small holders could obtain such leaseholds, economic circumstances were slowly eliminating their holdings. It was probably a push/pull situation in which large holders wanted the smaller holders out and the small landholder perhaps saw economic opportunities elsewhere in Italy. Small holders, in any event, began to sell to large landowners, or lost their properties when they could not pay off mortgages to the large holders. Sometimes physical violence was used against the small holders.[39]

Despite such problems Rome itself seemed to prosper. If small farmers were struggling, the greater productivity which accompanied the agricultural changes seemed to provide Rome with a surplus of food and goods. For a time Rome's prosperity offered the small holder a promising alternative. After 200 she became a very busy place, with a lot of construction, requiring a large number of workers. Some idea of Rome's attractiveness can be surmised from actions she took in 187 and 177. Roman authorities expelled large numbers of non-Roman Latins at the request of Latin authorities. It seems that so many people had left to find work in Rome that the Latin towns were having problems meeting the military levies Rome required under the treaties with each town.[40] At mid-century Rome also stopped sending out colonies, a measure she used from 200 to 160, to deal with excess people residing in Rome. Yet Rome's period of economic prosperity was coming to an end.

After 146 Roman authorities, to provide employment, embarked on large-scale public works projects. Quintus Metellus built temples to Jupiter Stator and Juno Regina. The Aqua Marcia, or Marcian Aqueduct, was built in 144 at a cost of 180,000,000 sesterces.[41] The Aqua Appia and Aqua Anio Vetus were repaired, beginning in 144. Such large expenditures represented a serious drain on government funds and around 140 Rome began to cut back on public works. Political leaders began to look for alternative solutions. Gaius Laelius, consul in 140, proposed that the public lands, now effectively in the hands of the large landowners, be returned to state control and redistributed among the landless. While the proposal did not pass, the idea was not dead either.[42]

In some ways Rome's poorest class, the plebs, comprised in large part of laborers, had benefitted from the regional specialization which both the Italian and Mediterranean economies had undergone. The changes in agricultural production brought a greater variety of goods to Rome. In addition, the efficiencies resulting from specialization reduced prices in Rome, providing her people with more discretionary income, and contributing to the growth of markets which would provide employment for her workers. Specialization however, was not without its problems. The Roman laborer, like his Athenian counterpart, discovered that he had given up his economic independence. Having tied himself to the market by leaving his farm and moving to Rome, he became subject to the ups and downs of market forces. It was not really a voluntary decision, since legal and economic forces in the country worked against him. Those same forces also prevented a return to the country, once the decision had been made; few former farm owners could raise the capital necessary to buy back their holdings and small holdings, even if reacquired, were not economically viable.

Another problem, at the macro-economic level, was that specialization had been carried too far. More specifically, Rome was too reliant on one or two regions to supply her market needs. This became apparent in 135 when slaves in Sicily revolted. For three years the slaves managed to hold off the legions of Rome. Sicilian grain exports accounted for one-third of Rome's grain supply and the war seriously reduced those exports. Increased pirate activity around the Mediterranean limited shipments from Egypt and elsewhere, and the combination of circumstances made the grain shortages worse.[43] Even before the slave revolt, grain prices had been on the increase. Between 140 and 124 prices rose 1200 percent throughout the Mediterranean.[44]

The Roman Republic formally came to an end in 31, with the defeat of the forces of Antony and Cleopatra at Actium. Yet, what historians call the "Fall of the Republic," refers not to the year 31, but to the period of time from 133 to 31.[45] This time period, from the tribuneship of Tiberius Gracchus to the victory of Caesar Augustus, was marked by growing violent civil unrest and by increased military intervention in governmental affairs. Tiberius Gracchus, in 133, attempted to harness the growing political strength of the plebeians residing in Rome. Economically, the plebs appear to have been hit from two sides. From one direction they were hit by shortages; they perhaps suffered the most from the increase in grain prices and they also bore the brunt of the grain shortages which hit Rome. The other attack came on the employment front. Unemployment was on the rise. Whether the increase in grain prices was the major cause of unemployment or not, it undoubtedly was a contributing factor. An increase in prices would have destroyed disposable income, reducing the markets on which employment was dependent.

Tiberius Gracchus became tribune in 133. The economy was giving mixed signals at the time. It is clear that the plebs were experiencing economic problems; many were unemployed and the number of unemployed seems to have been on the increase. At the same time the large landowners were maintaining and trying to increase the size of their holdings, an indication that there were still markets for their products. The measure which Tiberius proposed, in itself, provides some insight into the economic difficulties Rome was experiencing. What Tiberius proposed was to enforce the Lex Licinia of 366, a law which limited individual land holdings to 500 jugera of land (roughly 310 acres), and to distribute the excess land to the poor and homeless in Rome. It is somewhat difficult to determine Tiberius' motives. Politically, it was a popular measure with Rome's poor, so Tiberius may be viewed strictly as an opportunist. At the same time, there were other factors which may have been involved. One of those factors was the difficulty in finding enough men for military service. There was a property requirement for military service, and without land, the plebs in Rome were not qualified to serve.[46] Many in the Senate, in fact, probably agreed that Rome's survival required a dependable pool of army recruits. In addition to the evidence of economic problems suggested by Tiberius' proposals themselves, there were other indications of existing economic conditions. Tiberius observed, for example, that the countryside was largely deserted of its native inhabitants, supplanted by slave laborers.[47]

Ten years after Tiberius' death, in 123, his brother Gaius Gracchus was elected tribune. Rome had not solved her economic problems. In fact, they were getting worse. In addition to the continuing problem of unemployment, Rome had to deal with grain shortages and inflationary food costs. Gaius' program included a law to distribute public land among the poor.[48] To deal with unemployment, Gaius looked to more public works projects, such as road construction, and to colonization.[49] Gaius' program was a public acknowledgment of growing food shortages. He established public granaries and provided for public subsidies of grain prices.[50] Gaius made powerful enemies, however, and in 121, he suffered the same fate as his brother.

Gaius' death clearly did not solve Rome's economic problems. It did however, eliminate a leader around which political forces could coalesce. The Jugerthine War, which began in 112, may have provided a partial solution to the problem of unemployment. Gaius Marius, elected consul in 107, found many of his recruits from among the unemployed. In fact he ignored the requirement that soldiers own property. Following the conclusion of the war in 105, Rome had to deal with the Second Slave Revolt in Sicily, starting in 104. Before the revolt had been put down, in 100, Rome had to contend with threats from the Germanic Cimbri and Teutonic tribes in the north, ending in 101. This fighting however, provided a relatively short period of relief. Unemployment continued to plague Rome - as did grain shortages. Saturninus, elected tribune in both 103 and 100, instituted monthly grain distributions.[51] In 91, Marcus Livius Drusus the Younger, son of one of the rivals of Gaius Gracchus, was elected tribune. He renewed the ideas of colonization and land distribution to deal with the plight of Rome's poor. While he championed the cause of the Italian allies, he lost some of their support, by linking their demand for full citizenship with a requirement that large landholders among the allies give up their excess public landholdings.[52] He was assassinated in the same year he was elected tribune.

Drussus' assassination contributed to the tensions between Rome and the Italian allies, leading to the Social War, which lasted from 90 to 87. At the end of the Social War, Lucius Cornelius Cinna, was elected consul in 87. Driven out of Rome by Octavius, he gathered an army together and retook it. His rule was significant, economically, for one measure in 86, a law which eliminated three-quarters of all debt in Rome, a hint of continued economic problems.[53] When Sulla became dictator in 81, one of his solutions for Rome's unemployment problems was the forced settlement of 100,000 of his legionnaires in colonies scattered throughout Italy.[54] He also embarked on a building program which included the construction of a new records office, the Tabularium, and the renovation of the Senate house.[55] In 63, Catiline, of the patrician class, ran for consul. His program called for, not only land distribution, but also debt cancellation. Unlike Cinna's debt cancellation in 86, which included three-fourths of all debt however, Catiline proposed a general cancellation.[56] His proposals, while popular with veterans and the people generally, naturally created a coalition of lenders and landowners in opposition. Catiline was defeated and, concluding that his only chance for political power lay in outright revolt, openly joined an army of his supporters and was killed when Roman armies suppressed the revolt.

Cato the Younger, tribune in 62, increased the free grain distributions to Rome's poor.[57] This was increased further in 57 by the tribune Clodius, who provided for an unlimited distribution, free of charge.[58] Julius Caesar found, in 45, that Rome still had not solved her economic problems. The magnitude of the unemployment problem can be discerned from the number of Rome's unemployed civilians Caesar included in the colonies he settled - the figure was 80,000. This was in addition to the soldiers he found land for.[59] The problem of debt had reappeared. While Caesar had been in Egypt in 46, one of the tribunes had called for the cancellation of all debts. Caesar's solution was, not to cancel all debt, but instead, to cancel any unpaid interest accruing since the Civil War had begun. About one-fourth of the accumulated debt was eliminated as a result.[60] Caesar also used public works projects to deal with unemployment. He built the Basilica Julia as well as the Forum of Julius Caesar, a temple of Mars, and a theater on the Capitoline Hill.[61] Caesar also relied on the dole. Suetonius says that there were 150,000 households receiving free grain.[62] The problem would continue under Caesar Augustus. Despite his ability to eliminate political rivals, he still had to provide for people on the dole, even using his own funds in 23.

The number receiving grain at the time of the Gracchi was estimated at around 50,000. In 63, it had grown to 200,000, and had increased further, to 260,000 in 58.[63] In 53, the number probably would have been around 285,000. Suetonius says that Julius Caesar found the number of households on the dole to be 320,000, but later reduced the number to 150,000.[64] It is clear from the figures that the economic forces at work in Rome were too weak to supply her with food. At times this weakness resulted in food shortages; at other times, it simply forced the government to take extraordinary measures to make up for the deficiencies. Figures for colonization are another indication of the extent of the unemployment problem. From the Gracchan period to 118, between 50,000 and 75,000 citizens were involved in colonization. From 118 to the time of Sulla, another 225,000 colonists were sent out.[65] Julius Caesar's 80,000 figure was that for only a single year.[66]

POLITICAL UNREST - THE INCREASING TEMPO OF VIOLENCE

Political unrest and violence did not begin with the death of Tiberius Gracchus in 133. It had been present before that time. With the Gracchi, however, there was an increase in intensity; there was also an increase in the number of deaths with each new incident. The number of deaths from political violence seem small in the beginning. The attack on Tiberius and his followers resulted in 300 deaths from the attack itself, with additional numbers in the executions which followed.[67] When Gaius Gracchus was killed in 121, the number of deaths increased to 3,000.[68] Sulla, in 82, put 40 senators and 1,600 knights to death.[69] He is also said to have massacred 6,000 people in the circus immediately after he took Rome, together with another 12,000 at Praeneste.[70] The Second Triumvirate, on assuming power in 43, had 300 senators and 2,000 knights put to death.[71] These deaths, for the most part, are related to events in Rome itself. They do not include deaths which occurred in the battles between the rival armies during the various insurrections.

The deaths which occurred in 133, 121, 82, or 43, in sheer numbers, represent only the most sensationalized and dramatic aspect of the killings which went on in Rome. In fact, death in some form of mob action became more and more common as the Republic approached its final days; it was almost an everyday occurrence. Less apparent, from the figures, is the strength of the street gangs and mobs which began to terrorize Rome. They attacked Roman citizens, Roman politicians, even other gangs. At the same time, while politicians were frequently the target of these gangs, they were also perpetrators of the violence. It was politicians who often provided the money which fueled the gang violence, but the employment of gangs was not confined to one particular party. Both the aristocratic landholders and the popular democrats found a following among the unemployed poor who inhabited Rome.

The attack on Tiberius and his followers in 133, represents a watershed, in terms of the change it brought to the domestic political scene; an explosive reaction to which Rome was unaccustomed. There is perhaps a tendency to view the struggle in black and white terms, a conservative and reactionary Senate against a progressive and democratic movement of the people. Tiberius takes on the robes of a martyr, a popular hero killed in the service of the people. In reality, Tiberius had some supporters in the Senate who were aware of the need for economic reform. In addition, not all opposition was based solely on the reactionary instincts of Rome's landed aristocracy. Scipio Aemilianus, an opponent of Tiberius' measure, was against it because he championed the cause of the Italian allies and the land measure would have forced many of that group to relinquish their excess lands.[72] The plebs, for their part, looked back nostalgically to life on the land. They may have taken an overly overly optimistic view of their chances for economic success on redistributed land. Many had been forced to leave the land because production was insufficient to sustain the small holder.

It is not entirely clear whether the death of Tiberius and so many of his followers was the result of a deliberate plan or more a spontaneous outburst. There is some evidence that there was a conspiracy to assassinate Tiberius himself; it was alleged that some of the property-owning faction had hired some ruffians to kill him.[73] At the same time, Tiberius offended many by his own actions. When he could not persuade a fellow tribune, Octavius, to vote for his proposals, Tiberius had the Assembly vote Octavius out of office.[74] It appears that, when the attack on Tiberius came, it was the work of the followers and slaves of the large landholders, possibly the clientes, those who attached themselves to wealthy patrons.[75] At a latter point in time, the mobs would be the homeless, unemployed ruffians, who would attach themselves to anyone willing to pay. Tensions, at any rate, were high in Rome. The attack was sparked by Tiberius' act in raising his hand to his head, interpreted by some as a request for a crown. The ex-consul Nasica then led some senators and other armed men down to the Capitol, where they clubbed Tiberius and his supporters to death. Other of Tiberius' supporters were arrested and executed later.[76]

The Senate adhered to procedural requirements in the killing of Gaius Gracchus in 121. Opimius, an opponent of Gaius, had been elected consul. There was clearly tension between Gaius and Opimius. After Opimius had conducted a sacrifice, one of his attendants made the mistake of insulting a crowd consisting of supporters of Fulvius Flaccus, an ally of Gaius. The crowd immediately turned on him and stabbed him to death. This gave the Senate an excuse to invoke the senatus consultum optimum, granting Opimius dictatorial powers.[77] While both sides were armed, Opimius' forces proved to be stronger and better organized. There was even a contingent of Cretan archers among them. Fulvius occupied and fortified the temple of Diana. While some wanted to negotiate, Opimius sent his soldiers against the position. They routed the forces, hunted down Gaius and Fulvius and killed them. In all, some 3,000 were killed in the fighting or its aftermath. One ghoulish aspect of the engagement was that Opimius offered to pay its weight in gold for the head of Gaius.[78]

If order had been restored to Rome, the underlying problems had not been addressed. Signs of trouble reappeared when a speaker named Saturninus was elected to the tribuneship in 103. After service in the Senate, he would be reelected tribune in 100. He revived some of the Gracchan program, providing for monthly grain distributions and renewed colonization. However, there were other, more disturbing aspects of his political program. In the election of 101, for the tribuneship, Saturninus hired thugs to murder his opponent, Nonius. In 100, a colleague of Saturninus named Gaius Servilius Glaucia ran for the consulship, and his opponent, Memmius, was murdered with the complicity of Saturninus.[79] The murders were only the most blatant of his actions. He was more systematic in his exploitation of the discontent of the unemployed in Rome. Unlike Tiberius or Gaius Gracchus, who merely appealed to the poor, Saturninus hired the street toughs to intimidate his political opposition.

Saturninus went so far as to use his influence to interfere with the daily proceedings of the Senate. In 102, for example, he found an impostor named Equitius and attempted to foist him off as a son of Tiberius Gracchus. The two consuls objected that Equitius was not a Roman citizen. One of the consuls then sought to eject Saturninus from the Senate, at which point the mob of Saturninus' followers attacked the consul. At another time, a capital charge was brought against Saturninus for publicly abusing an embassy from Mithridates. When the trial was held, a mob of such size was present that the jury acquitted Saturninus.

Saturninus, too late, discovered that popularity with the masses can be rather fickle and the mob somewhat difficult to control. In passing a bill providing for Marius' veterans, he included provisions which seemed to many Romans to favor the Italian allies over the Romans. He also wanted to grant citizenship to the allies. The senatorial faction now had an issue they could use against him and they played on the hatred of the lower classes, creating their own mob faction.[80] The murder of Memmius, the opponent of Glaucia, proved to be the catalyst for final action. A mob besieged Saturninus and Glaucia on the Capitoline hill and the Senate ordered Marius to restore order with an army. Saturninus' party surrendered after their water supply was cut off.[81] Marius locked the men in the Senate house to prevent them from being lynched, but this was not enough to satisfy the rabble. A crowd climbed to the roof and threw tiles down on the prisoners until they were all dead.

In 91 Marcus Livius Drussus was elected tribune. He resurrected Saturninus' program with proposals for land distribution, colonization, and cheap grain. He also adopted Saturninus' method of political operation, employing street gangs to help carry out his program. Unfortunately, he made the same mistake as Saturninus, in proposing full citizenship for the Italian allies. While he managed to force his measures through, with the help of the street gangs, he was assassinated, and his legislation was declared illegal by the Senate. As if to emphasize the contempt Rome felt for the allies, the tribune Quintus Varius, forced through a measure making any attempt to gain them citizenship illegal. The Italian cities chose to revolt and it was not until 88 that Rome would be able to defeat them.

The end of the Social War did not bring calm to Rome. In 88 a man named Sulpicius Rufus became tribune. He is said to have maintained a private army of 3,000 swordsmen and surrounded himself with a bodyguard of 600 men. He referred to these men as his anti-Senate.[82] Sulpicius championed the cause of the Italians. One of the measures he supported was to enroll the new Italian citizens in all 35 of Rome's tribes, instead of just 10. This would have strengthened the voting power of the Italians. Just after the start of the Social War, Rome had sought to win over the Italians by granting them full voting rights in Rome. However, the Roman legislators sought to dilute this grant by assigning the Italians to only 10 of the 35 tribes, ensuring that they could be outvoted.

Rome was ready to embark on its campaign against Mithridates in the east at this time and was gathering an army together for this purpose. Sulla had been given command. Sulpicius, however, took this command away and conferred it on Marius. Sulla and Pompeius were consuls at the time and tried to prevent a vote on these measures by decreeing a suspension of all public business. Sulpicius then led a mob against the assembly, resulting in the deaths of several people, including the son of Pompeius, although Pompeius himself escaped. At sword point, Sulla was forced to go to the house of Marius. Although not killed, when he returned he had the decree cancelled.[83] Sulla managed to escape Rome and reach the army. When Marius sent his officers to take command, they were stoned to death. In return, Marius put to death the friends of Sulla. Instead of embarking for the east, Sulla marched his six legions, around 36,000 men, against Rome and succeeded in capturing the city. Sulpicius was betrayed by a servant and killed, but Marius managed to escape.[84] Sulla chose not to remain in Rome. Having set up a government, he set off with the army against Mithridates.

Almost as soon as Sulla had left, Rome fell back into the now-familiar pattern of violence. In 87 Gnaeus Octavius and Cinna became consuls. The two immediately began fighting each other. In a pitched battle in the Forum, it is said that 10,000 were killed and Cinna was forced to flee Rome.[85] He found support with the garrison at Capua. He was joined by Marius, who set about raising an army in the countryside. Their supporters in Rome attacked and killed Octavius in the Forum. Their army now entered Rome and they engaged in a series of reprisals. Several political leaders were executed. Marius, in addition, maintained a bodyguard of 4,000 slaves, called Bardyiae. The Bardyiae engaged in a series of arbitrary killings, on the orders of Marius. Their excesses finally became intolerable to Cinna and his ally Sertorius. Sertorius, with his army, had them surrounded in their camp one night and killed them all with volleys of javelins.[86] Marius died in 86, leaving Cinna to rule alone. Although Rome experienced less bloodshed during the remainder of Cinna's rule, the political killings were not all over. In 84 Cinna was killed by his troops in a mutiny and Marius Gratidianus, a nephew of Marius, who had tried to stabilize Rome's currency, was killed by his brother-in-law, Catiline.

Sulla and his army in the East, had defeated Mithridates' armies, captured Athens, and concluded a peace. Although Sulla was forbidden from bringing his army into Italy, in 83 he defied this order and invaded Italy. In 82, following a battle outside Rome, Sulla captured the city. A bloodbath followed. It is said that the number of killings exceeded those which had taken place while Marius was in power. Like Marius, Sulla maintained a personal bodyguard of ex-slaves, called the Cornelii. Their number is said to have been 10,000, not just the 4,000 of Marius' bodyguard. Whether the number of reported deaths can be relied on, they were clearly very high: some 40 senators, 1,600 knights, 6,000 prisoners following the capture of Rome, and 12,000 at Praeneste. Apart from the ruthless manner in which he dealt with his enemies, Sulla did manage to secure colonies for some 120,000 men who had been part of his 23-legion army. Sulla abolished the distribution of grain.

Sulla's abdication came in 80. Two years later, Marcus Lepidus, a follower of Sulla, became consul, and attempted to undo the constitutional structure established by Sulla. At the end of his consulship, he was given Gaul as his province. He apparently felt his political opportunities were greatest in plotting revolt. He managed to raise a force of Etruscans and other disaffected individuals and marched on Rome. The Senate passed an emergency decree and the army defending Rome defeated his forces. Even after the defeat, the survivors numbered 20,000, most of whom fled to Sertorius in Spain. Rome sent an army under Pompey to deal with the problem in 77. Pompey brought hostilities to an end when Sertorius was murdered.[87] Rome's focus shifted from Spain to Italy in 73, when there was a slave revolt, led by Spartacus. Crassus was given command after several Roman defeats, and finally caught and killed Spartacus in 71. Joined by Pompey's army at the end, both Crassus and Pompey chose to disband their respective forces, rather than fight each other and agreed to jointly stand for the consulships of 70.

In 67 Pompey was given command of an army to deal with the pirate problem in the Mediterranean. He managed to complete the job in three months. Mithridates was again causing problems in the East, and Pompey was given command, when the Roman armies refused to obey their general, Lucullus. Fortuitously, shortly after Pompey's arrival, Mithridates' forces fell apart, and he committed suicide. Pompey did not return to Rome until 65. Rome remained relatively quiet in his absence, however the underlying pressures were beginning to build again.

In 63 Rome had to contend, not with an army, but with a disorganized plot among its leading citizens. The conspiracy would be named for its supposed leader, Catiline. Catiline had come from a patrician family, had served under Sulla, and, prior to the conspiracy, had killed his brother-in-law Marius Gratidianus in 84. He served as praetor in 68 and was given a province in Africa to govern. The result of his two-year rule was a charge of embezzlement. This charge disqualified him for the consulship in 65 and in 64. To gain popular support, he proposed a new Gracchan program, including land distribution and debt cancellation. A moderate faction, fearful of the effects of his program, persuaded Cicero to run against him for the consulship in 63, and Cicero defeated him. Catiline did not immediately come out openly for revolt. In November, however, some of his supporters were careless and discussed a planned march on Rome with some foreign envoys. While the evidence was not strong enough to prove Catiline himself was involved, it was sufficient for Cicero to act. He arrested five of the leaders, persuaded the Senate to agree to their execution, and immediately carried out the decree. There were some, including Julius Caesar, who argued that the conspirators should be given a trial.

If Cicero's actions tarnished his career, they effectively ended the conspiracy. Catiline decided that his army in Etruria could not surprise Rome and sought to escape north. Two armies were sent against him, he was trapped near Pistoria in January 62, and he and his supporters were annihilated. While the destruction of Catiline's army meant the end of the rebellion, it did not end the fear of revolution in Rome. Cato was so afraid of revolution that he persuaded the Senate to provide for a monthly ration of grain, at an annual expenditure of 7.5 million drachmas.[88]

In 60 Pompey, Crassus, and Julius Caesar, formed the First Triumvirate. On one level, it was an agreement to share power in Rome. On another level, power could not be shared if it could not be acquired. The Triumvirate was, in reality, powerless to deal with the forces of violence operating on the streets of Rome. Perhaps some indication of their frustration was the fact that Julius Caesar and Pompey, instead of opposing the violence, incorporated street tactics in dealing with their political opponents. When Caesar was opposed in his proposals for Pompey's veterans, he unleashed a mob on the Senate.

Pompey also brought his soldiers into the city. In one incident, the consul Bibulus, while opposing Caesar's measures, was attacked by a crowd. Someone grabbed the fasces of his lictors (the minor officials who preceded the magistrates) and broke them, while someone else dumped a bucket of dung over Bibulus' head. Several tribunes escorting him were wounded. When the Forum had been cleared of opposition, the laws providing for the distribution of land were passed. The violence during the remainder of Caesar's consulship became so bad that Bibulus shut himself up in his house for the last eight months of his term and most of the senators stayed away from meetings presided over by Caesar.[89]

At the end of his consulship, Caesar left Rome to assume the governorship of Cisalpine Gaul and Illyricum. (One of the reasons he was eager to leave Rome was to avoid prosecution for the actions taken during his consulship.) For the next six years, Rome would be subjected to the excesses of a man called Clodius. Surrounding himself with a group of ex-slaves, he attracted a following among the street toughs and unemployed. He would subject Rome to continuous mob rule and killings until he himself was killed in January of 52. It is difficult to get a clear picture of Clodius. He would be described as a rogue, born with the ability to both charm and persuade - had he opted for a conventional political career, he would have been quite successful. In some ways his political life was a joke and some of his antics show an amusing side - from a distance of some 2,000 years. In 62 he was indicted on a sacrilege charge. He had dressed in women's clothes and tried to participate in one of the religious rites restricted to women - at Caesar's house. He escaped punishment by bribing the jury at his trial. In other ways his actions were tragic - many of his followers or rivals were killed as a result of what he did.

Clodius, on entering the tribunate in 58 immediately proposed the free distribution of grain. Another step, which may have proved as important in maintaining the level of violence, was his proposal to reinstate the collegia. The collegia were groups of tradesmen, usually living at a subsistence level because of competition from slaves. They had been abolished in 64 because it was believed that it was too easy for politicians to buy their services.

Clodius soon acquired a bodyguard of armed slaves and focused on his first target - Cicero. Cicero apparently was unable to view the political situation in Rome realistically. Only the triumvirs held sufficient power to control Clodius, yet Cicero refused to come to any accommodation with them - he even rebuffed Caesar's attempts at a reconciliation. Clodius, as tribune, introduced legislation specifically aimed at Cicero and his conduct in suppressing Catiline's conspiracy. Clodius' legislation provided that anyone who had executed a Roman citizen without trial would be banished. Initially the battle between Clodius and Cicero took on elements of a public relations contest. Cicero dressed as if in mourning to try to sway public opinion. Clodius' gangs when they met him on the street threw stones and mud at him. When the Senate attempted to show Cicero its support by declaring a period of mourning, Clodius had the Senate house surrounded by armed men.[90]

None of the triumvirs would help, so Cicero left Rome for Macedonia. After he had gone, Clodius' gangs burned down his house and country villa. The triumvirs soon discovered that, with Cicero out of the way, Clodius was free to attack them. It appears Clodius was working on Caesar's behalf. His first target after Cicero was Pompey. He attacked the arrangements Pompey had made for the conquered countries and even prosecuted some of Pompey's friends. Almost comically, during the trials, Clodius would goad the crowd when Pompey appeared in court - Clodius would stand at one side asking questions and signalling the crowd to answer with Pompey's name. There was a sinister aspect of the proceedings however when a servant of Clodius was discovered with a sword trying to reach Pompey.[91]

Pompey, having been the target of Clodius, now sought to have Cicero recalled. Clodius passed a law forbidding the Senate from even discussing the matter. As if to emphasize his determination, Clodius turned a band of gladiators loose on the assembly to prevent a discussion of the recall in 57. The tribunes Quintus Fabricius and Marcus Cispius were attacked and many of their followers slain in the Forum. The Senate eventually decreed that no public business should be carried on until Cicero's recall.[92]

Pompey decided to fight Clodius on his own terms and found his own champion in a man named Titus Annius Milo. Elected tribune in 57, Milo hired his own gang of gladiators or street fighters and ordered them to attack Clodius' gangs. In addition, Milo took Clodius to court - he tried to prosecute Clodius twice in 57 for acts of violence. By that summer Pompey felt strong enough to more openly confront Clodius. In September, having assembled a large force of armed men, Pompey escorted Cicero's brother to the Forum, where he presented a petition for Cicero's recall. In the fighting which ensued, several people were killed or wounded, but Clodius was driven out and the recall measure was introduced.[93] Rome, at the time, was also beset with yet another grain shortage. Although Clodius charged that the scarcity had been artificially created for the benefit of Pompey, Cicero, on his return, moved the Senate to place Pompey in charge of grain procurements.[94]

Once restored, Cicero, like Pompey, attached Milo to his cause and Rome became spectator to a series of actions and counter-actions at the street level. The first to strike was Cicero. When Clodius happened to be out of town, Cicero went up to the Capitol with a crowd of supporters and tore down the tablets on which the measures passed by the tribunes were recorded.[95] Clodius' forces retaliated by attacking the workmen rebuilding Cicero's house. Cicero himself was even attacked on the Sacred Way. Clodius ran for the aedilship of 56. (Coincidently or not, election to this position provided Clodius with immunity from prosecution for the charges Milo had lodged against him.) Clodius seized on the shortcomings of the Triumvirate and made them his target; the high price of grain and a shortage of money was causing a great deal of dissatisfaction with the Triumvirate at the time. His gangs turned their attention to Pompey, who began to employ men from the country to fight back.

The triumvirs held their meeting at Luca in April of 56, aware of the growing dissatisfaction in Rome. It was agreed that Crassus and Pompey were to stand for the consulship of 55. Caesar agreed to help Crassus and Pompey in the elections. In return, he was to be given command of his provinces for another five years.[96] The elections were bloody. Cato, for the Senate, persuaded his brother-in-law, Lucius Domitius, to fight the election. On one occasion, when Domitius' party was going down to the Forum, the supporters of Crassus and Pompey ambushed them. The torch-bearer was killed and several others were wounded. Pompey and Crassus had themselves proclaimed consuls. When it came time to confirm Caesar's command and to vote themselves provinces and armies, they surrounded the assembly with armed men. Cato was thrown out of the assembly and those who resisted were killed.[97]

In 53 Crassus would be killed fighting the Parthians in the East, formally bringing the First Triumvirate to an end. It had begun to exhibit signs of strain prior to this time. Pompey had been married to Caesar's daughter, who died in 54. Her death reduced the chances of further cooperation between the two men. Pompey now decided to use the services of Clodius, in spite of the treatment Pompey had received from Clodius at an earlier time. When Clodius ran for the praetorship in 53, Pompey supported him. Clodius, for his part, focused his anger on his personal antagonist, Milo. Milo was running for the consulship and Clodius supported another candidate against him named Hypsaeus. Clodius bragged that Milo wouldn't stay alive, yet Milo seemed unperturbed, spending lavishly on gangs and crowds. The elections were constantly postponed as a result of almost continuous fighting. According to Plutarch, things got so bad that candidates would bribe people in public. While the politicians may have intended to buy votes, the people receiving the money went to the Forum to fight for their candidates - armed with bows and arrows and swords and slings. The places where elections were held were often stained with blood and fouled with dead bodies.[98] Perhaps it came as a relief to Rome when Clodius was finally killed in January 52. Even in death he seemed to cause trouble. His followers burned his body in the Senate house, which caught fire and burned down as a consequence.

Milo, for his part, did not escape completely. He was prosecuted for the murder of Clodius - by Pompey. To provide security at the trial, Pompey posted soldiers around the Forum. While this measure may have kept the crowds at bay, its real purpose may have been to frighten Cicero, who was defending Milo. It was successful in that regard, for Cicero was too shaken to say anything in Milo's defence. Milo was condemned, although, in view of his actions, his sentence was somewhat mild - he was forced into exile.[99] Milo apparently felt his true calling was that of a leader of the street people. In 48 he came out of exile at the request of then-praetor Rufus Caelius, with the goal of recreating his urban armies. His dream was short-lived - he was captured at Cosa and executed.[100]

The deaths of Clodius and Milo did not eliminate discontent in Rome. Neither did those deaths totally stop the violence. The fighting simply moved from the streets of Rome to the battlefields of Italy. However, their deaths removed two leaders around which the discontented could rally and at least somewhat dampened the most extreme actions of the Roman mob. It provides a convenient stopping point for a discussion of violence. The next section looks at the ways in which Rome responded to the violence.

THE GOVERNMENTAL RESPONSE

From around 133, the time of the Gracchi, until Octavian took the title of Caesar Augustus in 27 B.C., the political situation in Rome can only be described as chaotic. While Augustus managed to bring stability to Rome, the methods employed were anything but democratic. He created a security force called the cohortes urbanae, totaling about 3,000 men, regarded as part of the army, but assigned to the city of Rome alone. Armed police were stationed in areas of the city prone to violence. Augustus also outlawed the collegia, the workmen's guilds where Clodius had found the recruits for his street gangs.[101] For much of the period from the Gracchi down to Caesar Augustus, it would be accurate to describe the governmental response to violence as repression. When Crassus and Pompey defeated Spartacus in the slave uprising in 71, they crucified 6,000 slaves. As if to reinforce the idea that Rome would not tolerate revolt, the crucifixions did not occur at a single location. Instead the 6,000 crosses were placed beside the road all the way from Rome to Capua. The only problem, in speaking of a governmental response, is that it is hard to tell whether any legitimate government existed for much of the time. Whatever faction managed to seize the reins of power by killing more of their opponents constituted the government. It was often the case of a bigger mob intimidating a smaller or weaker mob. Whether it was mob rule or a "legitimate" governmental decision, the result was the same - some form of repression.

An inexact measure of the increasingly repressive atmosphere in Rome was the resort to the Senate's ultimate emergency decree, the senatus consultum ultimum, which allowed the magistrates to use any means necessary to restore order to Rome. Its use coincides with the increasing level of street violence which accompanied the increasing economic problems Rome was suffering. It was first used against Gaius Gracchus in 121, then against Saturninus and Glaucia in 100. It was voted against Sulla in 83, although his more experienced army proved that success in implementation depended on the military resources the Senate could command. It was voted next against Lepidus in 77, against Catiline in 63, in 62 when Rome experienced civil disturbances, and in 52 against Clodius. It was also voted against Julius Caesar in 49, against Caelius in 48, in the disturbances of Dolabella in 47, against Octavian in 43, and finally, against Salvidienus Rufus in 40.[102]

The action of the Senate in voting the senatus consultum ultimum represents the most extreme of measures. It differs somewhat from what would be expected of a dictatorship in the sense that it was employed only in exceptional circumstances. A dictatorship, almost by definition, incorporates physical repression on a continuous basis. Perhaps one explanation for the difference is that, by the time the measure was voted, civil unrest was at a point which left little room for maneuvering or compromise. The commanding generals, with a directive to restore order, were confronted by what amounted to a fully armed military opponent. There was little possibility of employing half measures. Its relatively rare use perhaps is a concession to its effectiveness. The forces charged with enforcing the decree engaged in such indiscriminate killing that they not only eliminated those responsible for the existing problems, but also those who might be expected to cause trouble in the future. Augustus, in contrast, had the "luxury" of employing preventive, though repressive measures. The populace was disarmed, the collegia were disbanded, and the cohortes urbanae, no doubt, operated swiftly to quell any violent outbursts or mob actions before they had a chance to work into full-scale riots. While the Senate's decrees may not themselves be proof of dictatorship, it is clear that the atmosphere for much of the period during and following the Gracchi, was dictatorial.

CONCLUSION

The principate, the form of government which Augustus settled on to rule Rome, was clearly a dictatorship. In some ways it seems relatively benign, especially when compared to the examples of dictatorship seen in the Twentieth Century. The principate is somewhat difficult to classify, at least in terms of the type of dictatorship it would be defined as. Whatever the ultimate form of its government however, Roman society clearly contained the three ingredients most closely associated with dictatorship - scarcity, unemployment, and violence.

Rome's leaders found themselves in a quandary. Roman agriculture had proved itself efficient enough to support a fairly large urban population - at least at a subsistence level. Yet it was not efficient enough to permanently sustain that population. The economy, which had been productive enough to attract workers from the country, had dried up. The combination of legal ownership of the land, the change in agricultural production methods, and slave labor, operated to prevent those who had left from returning. One solution tried by the political leadership was to send out colonies in an attempt to reintegrate ex-soldiers or the unemployed back into the agricultural economy. Unfortunately, the land often proved to be unproductive and the new settlers viewed Rome as both a cause of their problems and a potential solution. The only advantage for Rome was that the ex-soldiers lost the training and military edge which would have made them a more potent threat. The armies the Senate sent out were better organized, recently trained, and more experienced. Trying to force workers back into an agricul- tural economy might have been one solution, but it would have been extremely costly and probably unworkable.

Augustus' solution was to allow the unemployed to remain in Rome, but disarmed and subject to the threat of physical force in the event of unrest. Augustus also maintained people on the dole and provided them with what the market could not. It meant that his government had to use its political capital to make up for what the economic forces could not provide on their own. While there was a political cost involv- ed in maintaining an armed force to control unrest, that cost to Roman society was still less than the cost incurred as a result of the continuous violence.

The next chapter shifts to a more recent economy, that of Revolutionary France. France, like Rome, economically and politically, contained elements of scarcity, unemployment, and violence. While France was beginning to industrialize, its economy contained a large agricultural component. Agricultural production had reached the stage where farmers were struggling. France also had to endure a period of mob rule. The only difference was that mob violence was more formally incorporated into the mechanism of government.

PART III

WORLD IN TRANSITION

CHAPTER 7

FRANCE AND THE FRENCH REVOLUTION
THE POLITICAL HISTORY

In the city of Lucerne, Switzerland there is a sculpture of a mortally wounded lion, a spear embedded in its side. In its final death-throes, tears stream down its face. Mark Twain is said to have remarked that it was one of the saddest sculptures ever done. The sculpture was not created to depict a successful hunt or nature scene. It was instead a memorial to the members of the Swiss royal guard of Louis XVI of France. On August 10, 1792 a force of around 20,000 French National Guardsmen mounted an assault on the Tuileries Palace, defended by only 1,200 men. Whether Louis was hoping to appease the opponents of the monarchy or merely trying to prevent further bloodshed, he finally ordered the Swiss to surrender. Whether the National Guard were willing to accept the surrender, many among the bystanders were not. Without firearms the mob attacked the Swiss with knives, pikes, and hatchets, even fists and clubs, killing nearly every one - in all some 600 soldiers.

The theme of the French Revolution - liberty, equality, and fraternity - originated, in part, from the idealism of the American fight for independence. Yet, perhaps no political event inspires as much horror or terror as the French Revolution. In fact, it is probably not so much the events of the Reign of Terror which bring an involuntary shudder - it is the method in which they were carried out. Specifically, what lends such a macabre atmosphere to the Revolution is the image of the guillotine. Whenever the French Revolution and the Reign of Terror are mentioned, it is the guillotine which instinctively comes to mind. Ironically the guillotine, the machine which conveyed such a horrific image of death, had evolved from another method of execution which tended to give executions an heroic atmosphere. French nobility had been granted the "privilege" of choosing beheading for capital crimes. Perhaps beheading invoked images of a battlefield death. The other irony was that the guillotine was intended to ease the suffering when the condemned were executed.

The guillotine was not named for its designer, but rather for the person who conceived of the general idea of a swift execution method in December 1789, a deputy to the French National Assembly named Dr. Joseph-Ignace Guillotin. Oddly, Dr. Guillotin was not intending to frighten people with a macabre invention, but was interested in eliminating some of the cruder practices surrounding the execution process. In addition, while Dr. Guillotin's name was immortalized by the contraption, his proposal was largely ignored in 1789. The first prototype was built by a German piano maker in April 1792, tested on corpses, and used in its first execution on April 25, 1792.[1] In June and July 1794, at the height of the Reign of Terror, its use had increased to the point where there were some 26 executions a day, for a total of 796 for the month of Messidor. (The new French month of Messidor included the months of June and July.)[2] It eliminated members of the royal family - the King was executed on January 21, 1793 - as well as the leaders of the Revolution. Danton and his followers were killed on April 5, 1794, while Robespierre, who ordered the deaths of so many others, fell victim to the guillotine himself, on July 28, 1794.

The French Revolution and its immediate aftermath, in context, represents the very briefest periods of time, perhaps 15 years. It seems much too short a period for a serious discussion of either the history of France or an analysis of the French economy. Economic changes are measured seemingly, not in years, but in decades or even centuries. Perhaps the French Revolution has been chosen more for its concentrated levels of violence, than for its economic lessons. At the same time the events provide any number of clues to economic conditions and the changes taking place in France. Discussion of the French Revolution has been divided into two sections. This chapter, for the most part, concentrates on the political history and major events of the Revolution. The political history begins on July 14, 1789, the day the Bastille fell and ends with the coronation of Napoleon as Emperor in 1804. The next chapter focuses on the economic side of the Revolution, beginning around 1775, with what was called the "Flour War" and continuing through the Revolution and its aftermath. A formal discussion of violence follows the economic history. Because violence figures so prominently in the political history of the Revolution, there is almost no need for a separate discussion, except to show the relationship between economic conditions and the violence. Chapter Eight ends with a discussion of the measures taken by the government to bring the violence under control and an analysis of the type of government instituted by Napoleon.

THE REVOLUTION BEGINS

The fall of the Bastille, which occurred on July 14, 1789, is generally regarded, more or less, as the formal beginning of the French Revolution. The "Fall of the Bastille" has always sounded a dramatic note, conjuring up images of a bold strike for liberty. A patriotic crowd, intent on bringing down the Ancien Regime, finally takes action. The revolution, which would eventually bring down much of the "evil" French aristocracy, had a somewhat inauspicious beginning. The armed mob which stormed the Bastille July 14 numbered only around 800 or 900. (The day before it was estimated that the rebellious crowd which gathered in Paris had numbered some 80,000.) The defenders numbered only 124, 82 invalides pensioners, i.e., disabled pensioners, and 32 Swiss guards. At the same time, the "victory" had come at a very high price - of those besieging the fortress, 98 were killed and 73 were wounded.[3] One of the defenders was killed. The effort expended seems somehow out of proportion to what was achieved - in fact only seven prisoners were liberated - and none were political prisoners. Included among the seven freed that day were four forgers and two lunatics - perhaps not the political catch expected.

Freeing political prisoners was always a worthy goal, but what the crowd wanted on July 14 was more practical. Its real goal was to obtain the gunpowder which had been moved to the Bastille for storage.[4] The Bastille, by 1789, had fallen into disuse - largely ignored as a means of political repression. Its reputation as a place of horrors had been created some 150 years before when Cardinal Richelieu imprisoned opponents of the king.[5] Whatever sinister reputation remained for the Bastille was enhanced in the weeks prior to its fall by the presence of the Marquis de Sade. Improvising a megaphone, from his cell, he made hourly announcements to the citizens of Paris of an impending massacre of the prisoners planned by the governor of the Bastille, Bernard de Launay. This proved too much for the governor, who had de Sade moved to another prison on July 5.[6]

Paris was in an excited state that summer. De Sade, with his irritating rantings, hardly posed a political threat to the French Crown, but de Launay feared his effect on the crowds. It was the crowds, growing larger and more restive through the early months of 1789, which de Launay was really afraid of. The crowds however represented mostly the working classes and Louis had bigger things to worry about. While aware of the need to keep the populace in line, he focused his attention on those who represented a more immediate threat to his power. The nobility, like the Paris crowds, were beginning to openly question the Crown and they were finding a voice through representative bodies such as the Estates General and the Assembly of Notables. The Estates General was a national popular assembly, the body charged with representing the "people" of France. The Assembly of Notables was a representative body, but primarily responsible for the interests of the nobility and clergy. Louis found that both groups did not like his policies. Somewhat ironically, the dispute involved, not so much an ideological battle over the authority of the king or the representative assemblies, rather it involved money. The Assembly of Notables particularly disliked Louis' proposals for taxes they would be asked to pay. In February 1787 Louis had convened the Assembly of Notables only to see it dissolved in May of that year when it would not agree to his budgetary proposals. Surprisingly, its members argued that they did not have the legal authority to approve new taxes. That was the prerogative of the Estates General.[7] Although the Estates General had not been convened since 1614, political pressure began to build to have it meet. So, in August 1788, it was announced that it would be convened in May 1789.

While opposition from the Assembly of Notables and the convening of the Estates General represented political defeats for the king, they did not represent an overt threat to civil order in France. That threat came from the crowds which were gathering in the streets of Paris. Even if the Estates General did not physically threaten the king, its existence and the actions of its members served as a source of inspiration for the masses of Paris. The leaders of the Estates General were able to put their grievances against the Crown into words, although the poor citizens perhaps understood only a portion of the fine legal points discussed. They took to heart the arguments which laid the blame for social problems at the feet of a privileged Crown and an arrogant nobility. Perhaps they better understood, or at least admired, the actions of the newly established National Assembly. On June 17, 1789, members of the Third Estate, one of the three groups making up the Estates General, had voted to call themselves the National Assembly.[8] When Barentin, the king's representative, on June 23, ordered the Estates General to disperse, Mirabeau, on behalf of the National Assembly, defied the demand - only bayonets could force the Assembly to disband, he said.[9] While the Parisian crowds may not have understood the underlying political debate between the Crown and Assembly, Mirabeau's defiance conveyed a direct meaning, as did the king's decision to allow the Assembly to stay.

It was the king's misfortune to be indecisive in times of crisis. Tactically the king, more than once, made the mistake of an irresolute and wavering defense. He often vacillated, one minute bluffing with a show of military force, the next completely caving in. That indecisiveness apparently began to infect his troops. On the evening of June 22-23, when the king had decided to dismiss Necker, his popular Minister of Finance, a crowd invaded the palace grounds, but the soldiers stationed there refused a command to fire on the people.

The king's indecision was only one factor in the events leading up to the Bastille's fall. That alone would not have triggered events. It was, in fact, the growing size and restiveness of the crowds assembling in the streets of Paris which led to the attack of July 14. That circumstance, in turn, can be traced to economic conditions in Paris. Even in January 1789 Paris was suffering severe unemployment.[10] Unemployment however, was not just a problem of the city. Peasants and laborers in the country were suffering as well. Many thought that employment prospects in Paris would be better. They weren't. But those traveling to Paris in search of work added to the number of unemployed and homeless who resided there. The large numbers, by themselves, might not have been the deciding factor for revolution. The dissatisfaction however, was feeding off the political defiance and discontent of those making up the National Assembly. The political leaders of the National Assembly and the crowds in the street found a common ground in their dislike of the French aristocracy. Each act of defiance tended to reinforce the beliefs and actions of the other group.

The first serious mob action occurred in April 1789. One of the poorer districts of Paris was the Saint-Marcel. A rumor had been making the rounds in the district that some manufacturers intended to cut wages. The object of these rumors was a wallpaper manufacturer named Réveillon, whose factory was located in the next district, Saint-Antoine. On April 27 a crowd gathered and began to march towards Réveillon's factory. At first numbering only 500, it grew to around 3,000. Led by cries of death to the rich and the aristocrats, the crowd intended to march to Réveillon's factory. Some government officials were successful in dissuading the crowd from continuing to the factory aided, no doubt, by a company of soldiers which blocked the way to the factory. What was left of the crowd however, chose another target, the house of Henriot, a saltpeter manufacturer. Entering the house, they went from one floor to another, smashing furniture and throwing household possessions into the street, where they set them on fire.[11]

The next day the crowd returned, only this time it numbered between 5,000 and 10,000. Again it was blocked by a contingent of French guards at the gates of Réveillon's factory - until the wife of the Duc d'Orleans persuaded the guards to let her take her carriage through their lines. The momentary parting of the soldier's ranks gave the crowd an opportunity to break through. Following just behind the carriage, the crowd was able

119

to reach the factory (where Réveillon's home also was located). They repeated their actions of the day before, destroying his house and factory and setting fire to everything they could. When reinforcements arrived, the crowd pelted the soldiers with stones and tiles. Warning shots were fired into the air at first, but then the soldiers fired on the crowd itself. The dead were officially numbered at 25, although it was rumored the actual number was even higher. Another 300 were injured.[12]

The Réveillon riots, as they came to be known, were the beginning. Next there was the incident of the crowd's invasion of the palace courtyard on the night of June 22. Some of the guardsmen who refused to fire on the crowd that night were imprisoned in the Abbaye prison. A crowd entered the prison on June 30 and forced their release.[13] On July 9 the crowds targeted the *barrièrs*, or governmental customs posts, scattered throughout Paris. In four days of rioting they destroyed 40 out of 54 customs posts. Nearly all receipts and registers were burned. The customs posts served as a target probably because they were the most obvious symbol of an oppressive governmental system; the taxes collected also added to the cost of food. (The ferocity of the attacks suggests a spontaneous outburst. There are indications, however, that there was not only a plan of attack, but that money was behind it. Two of the posts which survived were operated by the Duke of Orleans. The Duke of Orleans, although a member of the nobility, had decided early on that greater political opportunities lay on the side of revolution. He even went so far as to set up headquarters in the Palais Royal. From there, he and his staff of journalists and writers had begun to distribute pamphlets and broadsides - all aimed at the government. It appears money was also being given out as well. Whether money was the attraction or not, each evening thousands would gather at the Palais Royal for the latest news.)[14]

The specific chain of events leading to the attack on the Bastille, began on Saturday July 11. On that day the king finally removed Necker as Minister of Finance, sent him into exile, and replaced him with the Baron de Breteuil. The news reached Paris the next day. From the Palais Royal, speakers harangued the crowds, attacking the decision. Carried away by their own rhetoric, the speakers emphasized the dangers posed by their "enemies." Camille Desmoulins, one of the speakers, was in the middle of a speech when he claimed he saw police arriving - a massacre was about to take place.[15] One after another, the speakers issued a call to arms - the people needed to defend themselves against their enemies. These speeches prompted some action. One crowd went to the Paris wax museum and borrowed the wax busts of their two heroes-of-the-hour - the exiled Necker and the Duke of Orleans. The Opéra was invaded by another crowd, numbering some 3,000, and forced to close, out of mourning for Necker. Other theater owners decided it might be advisable to show themselves sympathetic to the marchers and closed as well. Increasing in determination, the crowd began to call for and actually to search for arms. In the Tuileries, there was some action when a troop of cavalry tried to clear the gardens of people who had congregated there. Ominously for the regime, the gardes françaises, or French Guard, the governmental troops charged with responsibility for order in Paris, formed up against the cavalry, ready to attack. The cavalry retreated.[16]

The cavalry, in fact, abandoned the city.

The crowds now expanded their search for arms and, in addition, added grain to their list of things to look for. The monastery of Saint-Lazare, north of Paris, was invaded and ransacked on Sunday, July 12. Businesses of gunsmiths and armorers were visited and arms taken. Throughout the day on Monday, July 13 the crowds continued their search. On the morning of July 14, a crowd, numbering perhaps as many as 80,000, went to the Hotel des Invalides and distributed some 30,000 muskets.[17] The Bastille was the place where the powder was stored and this became the next target. During most of the day, there was a standoff, with the defenders firing into the crowd. Finally around 5:00 p.m., while negotiations were underway, a drawbridge was lowered and the garrison surrendered. The killing of July 14 did not end with the surrender. Having suffered 83 deaths that day, not including the 15 who died later, compared to a single death among the defenders, the crowd was not in a forgiving mood. Unfortunately, the Bastille commandant, de Launay, provided the crowd with the excuse they wanted. While being marched to the Hôtel de Ville he was attacked several times and finally kicked one of his captors, at which point he was knocked down and shot. His head was then severed, stuck on a pike, and paraded through the streets of Paris, along with that of another captive. Two other Bastille defenders were hung.[18]

THE WIDENING CONFLICT

Civil order in Paris was deteriorating. On July 22, the intendant of Paris, Bertier de Sauvigny and his father-in-law Foulon, a minister in the government formed after Necker's dismissal, were lynched. Like de Launay, their heads were paraded through the streets of Paris. The crowd stuffed grass in Foulon's mouth, symbolic of their belief that he had tried to starve Paris. Unrest in Paris was spreading to the countryside as well. France, as a whole, was suffering from bread shortages and rioting and looting occurred in many cities. Mobs attacked the town hall in Strasbourg. Granaries were looted in Rouen. Even where there was not a total breakdown, there was change. The governmental bodies of Louis' regime were replaced by revolutionary committees. Citizens' militias were formed throughout France. Bands of unemployed roamed the countryside, causing what was known as the 'Great Fear.' Farmers, believing the roaming groups were hired by the aristocracy, armed themselves. In addition, many, seeing the loss of governmental authority, decided to go after the tax collectors, as well as many of the landed nobility. Tax records were destroyed and manors looted and burned.[19]

The next logical step after the systematic destruction of tax records was the decision to stop paying future taxes as well. Many farmers took this step, in combination with a refusal to pay rents to landlords as well. The members of the National Assembly, in spite of their own disagreements with the king over taxes, realized that whatever government would emerge would still require revenues. At first, they urged the French citizenry to continue paying their legal obligations. However, many in the Assembly concluded that such an appeal was now unrealistic. Bowing to the inevitable, on the evening of August 4,

121

the leaders of the Assembly decided to abolish feudalism in France. Starting out at a somewhat slow pace, the evening degenerated into a bidding war, primarily aimed at pleasing the French citizenry. The basic proposals were themselves a dramatic change in French law. Serfdom and labor services were abolished. The speakers, one after another moved to take away as many aristocratic privileges as possible. At the same time, many remained loyal, and protective of their own specific privileges. While few privileges remained when the night was over, the reasons for the removal of certain privileges were political; August 4 proved to be an evening of attack followed by retaliation. When a bishop proposed that the hunting rights of the country nobility be eliminated, a duke countered with a proposal that tithes be ended. Whether hunting rights were that valuable, the result for the Church was a near total loss of income for parishes, by the time all the various revenue sources were eliminated. When the city courtiers denounced the rights of country lords, the country lords proposed that courtier pensions should be abolished as well. In perhaps one of the first experiments in privatization of governmental services, representatives of towns and provinces renounced many of their legal rights. Magistrates gave up their salaries.[20]

On August 11, the National Assembly formally enacted many of the changes into law. While the peasants may have been grateful for the concessions, they were not incentive enough to get them to start paying taxes again. On August 26, the deputies tried to formalize their changes with the adoption of the Declaration of the Rights of Man and the Citizen, a preamble to the passage of a new constitution. It was felt by some that the king's approval was required if the declaration were to be legally binding. The king however, objected to some portions and would not officially approve the legislation. The king's refusal was a blow to the new political leadership. Other actions he took made them suspicious. He called in the Flanders Regiment and stationed it in Paris. This action caused some apprehension among the people, suggesting that he intended to move against them. On October 5 the alarm bells were rung and a crowd of women, possibly as many as 7,000, marched on the palace at Versailles. They sent a delegation in to meet with the king. In the evening Louis agreed to the Declaration of the Rights of Man. Despite this concession, not all the crowd left. Around 5:30 in the morning on October 6, a crowd found its way into the palace, killed two of the king's bodyguard, and raced through the palace, searching for the queen. (The heads of the bodyguards, like those of the earlier victims, were also paraded around on pikes, for the benefit of the crowds). The king was now persuaded to accept the offer of the Marquis de Lafayette to return to Paris, which he did, accompanied by a crowd of 60,000.

For most of the next two years, politically, Paris remained relatively quiet. The Constituent Assembly, the body charged with drafting a new constitution, produced a document which was accepted by the king on September 14, 1791. The king had tried to escape Paris on June 20, 1791, but had been captured and forced to return, where he was confined under house arrest. Significantly, while the new government had to deal with the political opposition of the king, the National Assembly, early on, passed a measure aimed at the excesses of the mob. Called the Martial Law against Tumults, and passed on

October 21, 1789, it allowed authorities to declare martial law. This included the power to call out the National Guard. They, in turn, could be authorized to fire on crowds. The end of this period of quiet was perhaps marked by the dissolution of the Constituent Assembly on September 30, 1791.

THE LEGISLATIVE ASSEMBLY

The Constituent Assembly was replaced by the Legislative Assembly, the legislative arm of the newly created government. Its first meeting was held on October 1, 1791. The Legislative Assembly immediately faced two problems. First, many priests and church leaders were refusing to accept the authority of the government, embodied in the new Civil Constitution of the Clergy. Second, the émigrés, the nobility who had left France, were causing trouble outside her borders. Many were attempting to raise armies to restore the monarchy.

The problem with the Civil Constitution of the Clergy was a difficult one. First passed in July 1790, the measure was intended to reorganize the Catholic Church structure in France. Some measures were somewhat innocuous, providing a pay structure for priests. Other aspects were a direct challenge to the Pope's authority, providing for the election of priests by local parishioners. On November 27, 1790, the Constituent Assembly had passed a measure requiring the clergy to take an oath to the new government, refusal being grounds for dismissal. In April 1791, the Pope had openly condemned the measure. When the Legislative Assembly met in October 1791 it had to decide what to do about the large number of clerics who were refusing to take the oath. By itself, the oath represented a mere ideological dispute. Yet, in a situation where popular support could hinge on a few crucial issues, a measure which was offensive to the largely Catholic population, represented an unnecessary burden on the new government. In addition, it represented a general threat to civil order. Even where it did not place Catholic believers in direct conflict with the government, it reignited the conflict between the Catholic and Protestant populations. In Nîmes in June 1790, for example, Protestant National Guardsmen fired on companies of Catholic National Guardsmen, igniting a four-day battle in which some 300 Catholics and 20 Protestants died.[21] Similar riots occurred in Avignon. About half of all priests would ultimately agree to take the oath, but the existence of such a large number of refractories, as those who refused to take the oath were known, represented a large group around which opposition to the government could coalesce.

The émigrés represented another problem for the Legislative Assembly when it convened in October 1791. It was in the German provinces of Trier and Mainz where the émigrés, supported by the German princes, were the most active, even trying to raise armies to invade France. Members of the Assembly felt compelled to take some action, if it was only to threaten the German princes. Louis was persuaded to issue an ultimatum on December 14 - if the German princes did not stop their activities, France would declare war, he said. (The king's vigorous defense of the government which had removed him from power, can be explained by his hope that his ultimatum might actually provoke an invasion by armies strong enough to defeat the shaky army of the constitutional government.) When the new government began raising an army of 150,000, the electors of Trier and Mainz decided the ultimatum should be taken seriously. The *émigrés* were told to leave. Their decision reduced the likelihood of war, until the Emperor Leopold countered with a threat of his own - if France actually moved against the two electors Austria would go to war. The French Assembly countered with the demand that Leopold would withdraw his threat or France would declare war. The death of Leopold on March 1, 1792 offered an opportunity to avert any conflict, but political leadership in the French government was pushing for war. Louis made the formal announcement on April 20 - France was at war. Probably overshadowed by the news of war was another event which occurred on April 25 - the guillotine was used to execute a highwayman.

The enthusiasm greeting the declaration of war received a setback when French troops broke and ran in their first encounter with the Austrians on April 28. While the Austrians had won the first battle, they would not actually invade France until the end of July. The Prussians, allies of Austria, would not enter the conflict until August, with an invasion of their own. War provided the people of France with an outside focus. However, political events in Paris moved almost independently. On June 13, 1792, the king dismissed several ministers of the governmental cabinet. Paris was suffering economic shortages and with tempers short, popular leaders had little difficulty organizing a mass protest, the purpose of which was ostensibly to intimidate the king into a reversal of his decision dismissing the ministers. An armed crowd of between 10,000 and 20,000, on June 20, marched to the Tuileries. They intended an impressive show, even dragging cannon up the staircase to the king's apartment. The king, by himself, had to endure two hours worth of angry threats, as the demonstrators marched by him. In the end he diffused the situation by swearing allegiance to the constitution and drinking to the health of the nation. He would not however reappoint the ministers he had dismissed earlier.[22] The king's firm response was perhaps his last great act of defiance.

When the Austrians invaded France in late July, their commander, the Duke of Brunswick, issued a Manifesto. The Austrians intended to restore order in France. They also intended to restore the king to power. In addition, they would hold Paris responsible for the king's safety - if anything happened to him the Austrian army would take revenge on the citizens of Paris. While the king may have welcomed the help of the Austrian army, the public statements by its leaders would only serve to antagonize and arouse the people of Paris, further undermining the king's already diminished authority. The Duke, just inside the borders of France was, as yet, in no position to provide any real help to Louis. When the news of the his pronouncements reached Paris on July 28, the reaction of the Assembly was to distribute arms to everyone. There were also increasing calls that the king be deposed.[23]

THE INSURRECTIONARY COMMUNE

The Legislative Assembly, the body which supposedly represented the French people, found, like the king, that it was exercising less and less control. It found, in 1792, that it had another competing "legislature" in the heart of Paris. Around Paris, each section, or political district, had its own representative assembly. These assemblies, in July began coordinating their activities through a central committee. The leaders of this committee were the most radical of the politicians, being at the forefront of those calling for the deposition of the king. The central committee had at its command an army of discontented, ever ready to confront the king - in fact the leaders had to exercise some constraint on the mob. By August 10 however, they felt the time had come to act. They rang the tocsins summoning their army of citizens early in the morning, informed the crowd that the central committee was now an insurrectionary commune, and ordered their army to march on the Tuileries. The king was not at the Tuileries, but the Swiss Guard was. Numbering around 900, together with some National Guard troops, the Swiss faced an attacking force of around 20,000. The Swiss held out for about an hour and then received Louis' note, written in the comparative safety of the Assembly building, ordering them to surrender. Out of 900, the crowd killed 600, some of whom had even surrendered. The attackers lost under 300. The crowds then moved through the streets of Paris, intent on eliminating every reminder of royalty. Even street signs were the object of attack - anything with the name 'king' on it was destroyed. The king was transferred to a fortress in the northeast of Paris, called the Temple.[24]

The physical seizure of Paris, represented a political victory for the new commune and the effective dissolution of the Legislative Assembly. While the Assembly formally enacted some legislation, in reality it became nothing more than a rubber stamp. The commune wasted little time in dealing with the perceived political enemies of the revolution. On August 21 the first political prisoner was guillotined. Following the Prussian invasion of France and the surrender of the garrison at the fortress of Longwy to the Prussians on August 26, Danton, one of the political leaders of the commune, initiated a search of dwellings in Paris for arms and suspects. There were 3,000 arrests which took place as a result of these searches, held on August 30 and 31.[25]

The Prussian army, following the fall of Longwy, at first decided to lay siege to Verdun, then decided to bypass it. On September 2 news of the movement of the Prussian army toward Paris caused a panic. The Parisian crowds, fearing the potential actions of the royalist 'traitors' still in Paris, decided even those in prison represented a threat. A group of priests being taken to the Abbaye prison were attacked when they arrived and 19 were killed. This was the start of what became known as the September massacres. Another hundred and fifty priests held the Carmelite convent were similarly attacked. Of this group 115 were killed. By September 6, when the attacks ended, some 1,400 prisoners had been murdered, about half the prison population of Paris.[26] Panic in Paris subsided somewhat after the French army managed to check the Prussians at Valmy on September 20.

While the crowd was involved in such actions, formal political power was being transferred once again. By the time the insurrectionary commune ordered the attack on the Tuileries on August 10, there was a feeling that the Legislative Assembly was too moderate. A new body was needed to draft any legislative changes. So a national Convention was called for. After primary elections in August, the Convention finally met on the day the battle of Valmy was fought. Its first act was to declare France a republic.[27] Having accomplished one goal, it set about accomplishing its second goal - deposing the king - a preliminary step toward the third goal - punishing him.

To put a king on trial was a momentous step, even for the most radical of the political opposition. At the same time, to condemn him without some formal trial made the delegates uneasy, since most of them were lawyers. So, on December 11, 1792 he had to appear before the members of the Convention to hear his indictment and present a preliminary defense of the charges. The formal, but brief trial, consisted, for the most part, of a speech by his lawyer defending his actions. The Convention had little trouble in a finding of guilt; it had a great deal of difficulty deciding whether to execute him or not. The roll call regarding the imposition of the death penalty occurred on January 15, 1793; 361 were in favor of death with 288 against. A second vote, specifically on granting Louis a reprieve occurred on January 18; 380 voted for death while 310 were against it. Three days later, on January 21, 1793, Louis XVI was escorted to the square named the place de la Révolution. He tried to speak to the crowd, but Santerre, the commander of the Guard, ordered a drum roll to drown him out. He was quickly strapped to a plank, thrust under the guillotine's blade, and beheaded. The crowd was ecstatic.

While the king's death may have brought immediate gratification to the crowd, the sense of accomplishment or even elation did not last long. On February 25, 1793, Paris was subjected to food riots which lasted for three days. While this may have been symptomatic of underlying problems, it was perhaps a minor inconvenience compared to the results of an earlier action by French political leaders. On February 1, 1793 the French government overconfidently declared war on both Britain and the Dutch Republic. The French army, in late 1792, had found success on the battlefield, first against the Prussians at Valmy, and then against the Austrians at Jemappes on November 3, 1792. The army was so successful that it had gained control of the Austrian Netherlands by the end of November. Yet, even before the February 1 declaration of war, French forces were being forced back. French forces were defeated at Neerwinden on March 18 by the Austrians.

THE REIGN OF TERROR

Foreign armies were not the only problem facing the government. Southwest of Paris, near the Atlantic coast, lay the department of the Vendée. A rural district, its occupants were primarily farmers - who came to hate the bourgeois leaders imposed on them by the authorities in Paris. On February 24, the Convention in Paris had decreed a levy for all of France, intended to raise 300,000 troops. Resentment soon gave way to physical resistance. Armed peasants by the thousands swarmed into towns, openly confronting the representatives of the Convention. In the town of Machecoul, an officer named Maupassant, was killed as he tried to talk to the mob confronting him. The mob then went through the streets of the town, killing over 40 people believed to be associated with the revolutionary government. Others were rounded up and imprisoned. Like the September massacres of Paris, the peasants set about slaughtering those imprisoned. Some were even forced to dig their own graves, being shot when the task was completed. In all over 500 were killed at Machecoul.[28] Machecoul was not the end of the revolt, only the beginning. It was not until December 1793 that the revolt was put down - in an even bloodier fashion than it began. Following a defeat at Le Mans on December 12, 10,000 retreating Vendéeans were said to have been killed by governmental forces, many of the dead including women and children. Another 3,000 were killed in the town of Savenay when they confronted the governmental forces.[29]

The political atmosphere in Paris, even before the Vendée uprising, was beginning to exhibit a certain paranoia. Calls were heard for trials of traitors and pressure began to build for the purging of political opponents of the regime. The first Revolutionary Tribunal was established on March 10, 1793. On April 1 the Convention decided to eliminate the deputies' immunity from arrest and on April 6 the Committee of Public Safety was created. It consisted of nine members elected from the Convention delegates. This was followed by the creation of a Commission of Twelve on May 20 which had a number of people arrested for insurrection. It soon lost political support and fell apart. Fears of insurrection finally materialized on May 31 when the 'insurrectionary committee' declared the ouster of the commune and tried to arrest a number of deputies. The leaders of this revolt had not properly organized popular support and it largely fell apart. However, they were better organized on June 2. Surrounding the Convention with more than 75,000 National Guard forces, supported by a large street crowd, they forced the Convention to vote the arrest of 29 delegates, including members of the Commission of Twelve.[30] Considering the alternatives available, their punishment was fairly mild - they were simply purged from the Convention.

While the purge resulted in a more unified political voice in Paris, the rest of France was moving in the opposite direction. In addition to the Vendée, some form of opposition to Paris sprang up in cities such as Lyons and Bourdeaux. The representatives of the Hérault department even tried to raise a force to march on Paris. Marseilles did manage to raise such a force and sent it off to recapture Paris. Its major achievement was the occupation of Avignon. In reality, the revolts, except in the Vendée, represented no real threat to the revolution.

On August 27, 1793, the port of Toulon surrendered to a British fleet. This bad news arrived at a time when economic conditions were deteriorating in Paris. Food was scarce, wages were low, and prices were on the increase. Many were convinced that traitors and opponents of the new government were behind most of the problems and that the government could do more to stop those who were hoarding food. On September 5 a crowd marched on the Convention and forced it to adopt tougher measures. For the most part, the primary action taken by the Convention on September 5 to implement the new 'terror' was the authorization of an armed force to operate in Paris. It was to include 6,000 infantrymen and 1,200 cavalry.[31] This authorization was followed by a more specific legal measure, the Law of Suspects, passed on September 17. While the measure represented something specific, its language was anything but. Conduct, personal contacts, or writings which showed someone to be an enemy of liberty, were grounds for arrest. This was followed on September 29 by the General Maximum Law, primarily a price control measure. The penalty for selling above the price allowed was having one's name placed on the suspect list. These first acts of the 'terror' turned out to be only preliminary measures.

On October 10, at the urging of Saint-Just, the Convention agreed to transfer its executive power to the Committee of Public Safety. The Convention was left with a general oversight. The emergency powers granted the Committee of Public Safety were to remain in effect until there was a peace. This formal transfer of power represented the beginning of the real Terror. Beginning with the execution of Marie-Antoinette on October 17, the Terror would claim some 16,000 victims. Following Marie-Antoinette, the victims were less the symbols of the old regime and more the immediate political opponents of the new leadership. After a trial, 21 members of the Girondin party were executed on October 21. By December 31 of 1793, 177 had been executed in Paris.[32]

Outside of Paris the Terror did not start out as slowly. Lyons fell on October 9 and Paris sent down a special mission to deal with the opponents of the regime. When the guillotine proved inadequate for a task which involved killing large numbers of people in a short time, a new method of execution was devised. From December 4 to 8, prisoners were tied together, lined up in a field, and shot at with cannon. Any survivors were bayoneted or shot. On a single day, one of those in charge boasted, 113 had been dispatched in this manner. When the government finished its executions in Lyons in April 1794, some 1,900 people had been killed.[33] At Nantes another method of execution was devised. Prisoners were tied up and placed in boats. Holes were made in the sides and bottoms which were covered over with planks. After the boats were towed into the center of the Loire river, the planks were removed, letting the water in. Between 2,000 and 4,800 may have died in this manner.[34]

In Paris itself the Terror seemingly subsided for a few months, providing a brief respite from the most extreme actions. The leaders of the revolutionary government than began to target each other. While France had real enemies to deal with, the focus became more and more the opponents within the Convention. In one sense the fighting involved nothing more than the infighting found in any political body; in another sense the game was played beyond the normal bounds of political struggle. Under more ordinary circumstances, the penalty for political defeat was a temporary loss of prestige, dismissal from a political post, or rejection by the voters, but these were not normal times. Those who were quick to grasp the nature of the game, too soon understood the possibility of the permanent elimination of potential rivals. There were pitfalls however for those clever enough to gain admittance. Those who eagerly condemned opponents to death only gained a true understanding of the stakes involved when they themselves became victims and stood face to face with the guillotine.

In December 1793 and January 1794, members of the 'Hébertist' faction, named after their leader Jacque-René Hébert, were arrested. Most were released in February. Far from being sobered by the experience, the Hébertists launched attacks on their enemies, stirred up the crowds, and even attacked those who had helped to get them released. On March 13 they, in turn, were attacked, and, on the following day, arrested. The charges were somewhat vague, but their trial begin on March 21. It ended on March 24, and all 20 were expeditiously sent to the guillotine the same day. No sooner were the Hébertists eliminated, than another target was found. The victims this time were a group which had been given the label of 'Indulgents.' So-called because it often favored an indulgent or more lenient policy toward political enemies. For example, the Indulgents opposed the trial of Marie-Antoinette and favored the early relaxation of the Terror.[35] Its most prominent spokesmen were Danton and Desmoulins. On March 30 Robespierre had an arrest warrant issued for Danton and the other Indulgents.

The original pretext for the charges involved corruption and "insider trading' in Indies Company stock, in which many had been involved. The charges against Danton did not include specific allegations relating to the Indies Company. He was charged only generally with anti-revolutionary and corrupt behavior. One of the charges was that he laughed whenever he heard the word 'virtue.'[36] It was believed, when Danton's trial began on April 2, that it would quickly be over. However, Danton immediately turned it into a public forum. Fearing the public might prove too sympathetic, the Revolutionary Tribunal concocted the story that those charged were involved in a plot. Prevented from appearing in their own defense, the accused were found guilty and executed on April 5.

In one sense, it is not surprising that Robespierre would see Danton as an enemy to be eliminated. In another sense, it is surprising that Robespierre would so quickly and completely give in to the urge to impose the death penalty on his political opponents. Robespierre had earlier, in fact, attempted to prevent the execution of Marie-Antoinette. Now he seemingly abandoned his earlier principles totally. In contrast to the actual morality of his proposed new governmental system, Robespierre, following the elimination of Danton, now tried to initiate a Republic of Virtue. A new body, the Bureau of General Police, within the Committee of Public Safety, was created on April 16 and Robespierre was appointed to serve on it. Though himself a lawyer, Robespierre oversaw passage of what can only be described as a highly illegal measure, the Law of 22 Prairial on June 10. It created an expanded list of criminal behavior. Even expressions of opinion were sufficient to warrant the death penalty. Statements 'slandering patriotism,' or involving the spreading of false reports, as well as those impairing the purity of the revolutionary government, were made criminal. In addition, those accused could not call any defense witnesses nor were they allowed a lawyer to defend them.[37] Its first victims were 54 individuals who had been involved in a plot against the government. One of those executed had even made an attempt on Robespierre's life on May 25, 1794.

The Law of 22 Prairial was more than sufficient to deal with actual plots against the members of the government. Many of the deputies, beginning to sense the possible danger of Robespierre and his laws, provided themselves with one out. On June 11, they passed a measure guaranteeing themselves immunity from the Law of 22 Prairial. Robespierre sensed that he needed to act against the growing opposition. On July 26 he delivered a speech before the Convention denouncing his 'enemies,' making threats against nearly everyone, and alleging the existence of a conspiracy. The battle having been joined, the contest came down to a series of parliamentary maneuverings - his opponents appealing directly to the Convention. Robespierre, having lost his support, was executed on July 28, followed by some 80 of his supporters.

THE COUNTER-TERROR AND THE DIRECTORY

With the death of Robespierre, the Convention began to rethink the nature of the revolutionary government. It was proposed that one quarter of the members of the Committee of Public Safety should retire every month. The proposal passed. The Law of 22 Prairial was repealed on August 1. The pace of executions fell sharply. In fact, in all of August 1794 there were only six people executed in Paris. The decision to slow the number of executions continued through the end of the year. From September through December, in Paris, only 40 people were executed. The Convention took back most of the extraordinary powers it had granted the Committee of Public Safety.[38] For the most part the Terror was over. Between March 21 and July 28, 1794, the Paris guillotine had dispatched some 2,156 prisoners. Of this figure 509 had been executed in the new revolutionary month of Prairial (May-June), followed by 796 in Messidor (June-July).[39]

In August the Convention took steps to reverse some of the results of the Terror. Those imprisoned as suspects were released - some 3,500 by the end of August in Paris. There was a perception that public opinion had swung decidedly against the actions of the revolutionary government. Those who had participated wholeheartedly in the excesses of the Terror became stigmatized as terrorists. Ex-prisoners now formed gangs seeking revenge on those who had imprisoned them. The Convention, stigmatized itself by the former actions of its members, was slow to punish them. At the same time, it began to feel the weight of the growing public disgust. Supporters of the Jacobin party, which had furnished some of the most extreme leaders, now found themselves on the defensive. Its members were attacked. In November 10, a speech threatening the anti-Jacobin forces provoked a crowd into stoning the building where the speech was made. On November 12, the crowd returned and beat up those they found inside. As if to show that it had undergone a conversion, the Convention ordered Carrier, the representative in Nantes who had overseen the executions by drowning, to the guillotine on December 16, 1794.[40]

France, in 1795, became subject to the counter-terror, or 'White Terror,' named for its believed association with the royalist cause. Armed companies were formed in various regions to take vengeance on the officials in charge of the terror of the year before - groups such as the 'Companies of the Sun' in Nîmes, or the 'Companies of Jesus' in Lyons. Mobs attacked and lynched former officials of the Terror. Mobs and local officials were aided by the Law of April 10, passed by the Convention in 1795. The law allowed officials to disarm those who had been actively involved in the Terror. In Paris, it affected 1,600 people. In the countryside, officials disarmed and jailed perhaps 80,000 to 90,000 people. The majority were released at the end of summer. However, in some localities, members of the counter-terror were not so lenient and retaliated in kind for the killings. On May 4, crowds in Lyons butchered over 100 prisoners. Similar massacres occurred at Aix, Tarascon, and Marseilles.[41]

While Paris remained relatively calm in the first half of 1795, it was suffering through food shortages. In April, short rations were reduced. Finally on May 20 workers in the poorer districts determined on a march on the Convention to demand action. A deputy who tried to stop the crowd from entering the hall was shot, then beheaded. The head was placed on a pike, carried at the head of those invading the hall. While some in the Convention were intimated, others summoned troops. Promised bread by the Convention, the crowd of around 20,000 dispersed the next day.[42]

Once order had been restored, the Convention moved decisively. Eleven Montagnard, or Mountain party, deputies who had offered support to the invading crowd were arrested. Five committed suicide and two were guillotined. The Convention also dealt directly with the marchers. The section (district) where the march had originated was surrounded by troops and ordered to surrender those who had killed the deputy on May 20. Its members were also ordered to surrender their arms. Following the surrender, those involved in the murder were executed, as were some of the troops who had joined the crowd. There were 3,000 arrests on the orders of the Convention, while the various sections disarmed almost as many on their own initiative.[43] The Convention's decisive actions put a stop to most internal opposition. In July, a major external threat was similarly dealt with when a British-supported invasion force of émigrés at Quiberon in Brittany was defeated.

On August 22, 1795 the Convention approved a new constitution. The right to vote was granted to all male taxpayers over 21, regardless of whether they owned property. However, there was a property requirement related to election to the national assembly. There were to be two chambers, the lower chamber, a 'Council of Five Hundred,' which would initiate legislation, and an upper chamber, a 'Council of Elders.' The upper chamber would not debate legislation, merely approve or reject it. Rather than a single head of state, or president, there were to be five Directors. The Convention added a measure, the Two Thirds Law, which required that two thirds of the members of the new councils had to be chosen from the Convention. Although the Two Thirds Law passed, it was not that popular.

The actions of the Convention were particularly disliked in Paris. On October 4, 1795, seven sections decided to act and declared themselves in insurrection. This time, the insurrection involved those with royalist leanings. While the National Guard units in these sections were mobilized, they promised to disband when faced by regular troops. However, rather than disband, they tried to march on the Convention on October 5. The insurgents numbered around 25,000 as against some 6,000 troops protecting the Convention. For most of the day there was a standoff, but finally the government troops were ordered to open fire with their cannon. Perhaps the main advantage for the Convention forces, despite their smaller numbers, was that the measures, including the Law of April 10, disarming the terrorists left the insurgents short of powder and shot. They nevertheless put up a ferocious fight. Hundreds died in the fighting, which lasted until October 6. The forces of the Convention had won.

The Convention took measures designed to reduce future threats. It was felt that opposition had been able to coalesce around the leaders of the local assemblies. Therefore, on October 10, the Convention abolished the assemblies of the sections. The National Guard units under the control of the sectional assemblies were also abolished. In place of the National Guard, the Convention created a Parisian Guard, which took orders directly from the Convention.[44]

The Directory, as the government was now known, still had to deal with rebellion. However, opposition was no longer an ongoing matter. Paris, and France, seemed to be experiencing extended periods of quiet. Discontent still existed, but it lacked effective leadership and the elimination of arms had lessened the likelihood of success in any uprising. Nevertheless, in early 1796, Francois Babeuf and others who favored a return to the days of the revolutionary government formed a secret committee, with the goal of bringing about a revolt. They set May 19 as the date of their intended coup. A little too inflexible, they failed to support a mutiny by units of the Police Legion on April 28. They themselves were arrested in May, although not executed until over a year later. In September 1796 a group of Jacobins, hoped to enlist troops stationed near Grenelle for an insurrection. The troops, rather than joining them, killed 20 immediately, and arrested another 30, put to death after trial.

It was in 1797 that the most serious governmental upheaval occurred, although it did not take place until September. In July, three members of the Directory, Barras, Reubell, and La Revellière, voted together to establish a working majority. Labelled the triumvirs by a critical press, they received help from Napoleon, then commanding the troops in Italy. He sent one of his officers, Augereau to assume control of the troops in Paris. The triumvirs were at odds with the Councils over leadership of the government. Royalist supporters even put together street gangs which occasionally challenged the regular troops. The triumvirs, on September 3, finally ordered troops to take positions around the legislative chambers. The minority members of the Directory were arrested, along with members of the Council. They annulled the results of elections which had been held that spring and replaced the two arrested Directors. What became known as the 'Second Directory' had begun.[45]

The Second Directory did not totally return to the days of the Terror, but during its rule, France became more totalitarian. Former nobles could be executed for simply residing in France. In fact, some 160 were actually put to death under the Directory. The Second Directory also passed measures requiring priests to take another oath of loyalty to the government, deporting many who refused. In May 1798, when the members of the Second Directory found the results of new elections not to their liking, they simply reversed them, purging those elected before they took their seats.

NAPOLEON BONAPARTE AND THE END OF THE REVOLUTION

The Second Directory lasted until June 1799. The French army had suffered a series of defeats and it was charged that corruption and mismanagement by the Directors were the cause. The Five Hundred, apparently feeling strong enough to question the actions of the Directory, was aided by the replacement of the most hard-line of several of the Directory members as well as the general loss of political support. The Directory remained in charge, although in a diminished political role. Finally, on October 10, 1799, Napoleon Bonaparte landed in France, having sailed from Egypt. With the connivance of his brother, the Councils were persuaded to move their meeting place outside Paris. The Councils, once there however, were not receptive to handing the government over to him. When Napoleon appeared before them on November 10 there was even a scuffle in the meeting hall, during which Napoleon received a cut. His brother persuaded the troops that Napoleon's injuries were the result of an assassination attempt and they obeyed orders to clear the hall. Sympathetic, or compliant members were later called back in to adjourn the Councils. For six weeks, the government was to be run by three Consuls, one of which was Napoleon.

Napoleon had a new constitution prepared by December 15, and put in place by December 25. The new constitution vested executive power permanently in the three Consuls, with Napoleon, as first Consul, having final authority in all decisions. It created a new legislative structure as well. The structure was innovative. The Senate's 60 members were appointed by the Consuls. The Legislative Body, consisting of 300 members, was not elected by popular vote. Its members, instead, were appointed by the Senate. The Senate also appointed the 100 members of the Tribunate, a body whose primary function was to discuss legislation - without being able to vote on it. The Senate, like its counterpart in ancient Rome, did have the power to issue an ultimate decree against those involved in civil disorder.[46] Napoleon created another body, the Council of State, which consisted of 40 members, appointed by him. Its main function was as an advisory board, or cabinet, which would provide him with expert advice in governmental matters.

In order to stay in power, Napoleon had two major problems to solve. First, he had to eliminate, or at least control, the royalists who wanted to bring back the monarchy. In this area he had to assure those who had benefitted from the overthrow of the monarchy. Second, he had to ensure stability by controlling the extremists at the other end of the spectrum, the sympathizers of the revolution.

The first goal was perhaps easier for Napoleon to achieve. He now commanded a strong army which royalist sympathizers could not match. They were persuaded to come to terms. In addition, he eliminated the laws which were directed against the émigrés, and invited them to return, having an amnesty declared in October 1800. He was given the perfect excuse to strike at the most militant of the revolutionary groups, the Jacobins, in December 1800. A bomb was exploded in Paris, intended for Napoleon. While it failed to kill him, it caused a number of deaths. While Napoleon became aware that the Jacobins were not involved, he nevertheless ordered the arrest of 130 Jacobins. Nine were executed and most of the rest were deported. Napoleon took another step toward stability in general in February 1801 by setting up special criminal courts, intended to deal mainly with the large number of crimes being committed throughout France by gangs. This measure was supplemented by an increased police presence. This was followed, in 1804, by the adoption of a new Civil Code of law.

In 1802 Napoleon had himself proclaimed Consul for Life. Rather than using the legislative body to pass favorable laws, he got the Senate to issue the senatus consulta. In 1804 he had himself proclaimed Emperor, reducing further the need for many of the now superfluous governmental bodies. Unquestionably, what Napoleon had created was a dictatorship. The Police Ministry, run by Joseph Fouché, was nothing more than a secret police with a network of paid informers. Mail was intercepted by his agents. Napoleon did not necessarily fear him, but attempted some curbs on his power by setting up independent police agencies which could compete with Fouché's agents. Napoleon, while professing loyalty to the principles of the Revolution, in 1803, brought back one of the practices of the Ancien Regime, the tracking of workers using the worker's passbook, or *livret*. The passbook would be given to an employer when starting work and given back when the employee left employment. In addition, local authorities had the power to require visas, based on the passbook, for travel through their districts in search of employment.[47]

How much of the relative calm which settled on France after 1800 can be attributed to Napoleon's reliance on the army, decisive action, and the presence of a secret police is difficult to determine. Napoleon was helped by some of the reforms he initiated and laws he passed. While not necessarily generating prosperity, his measures did at least create an atmosphere of stability. In February 1800 he established the Bank of France, a state-run bank. In August 1801 the French government initiated a policy of paying state creditors in cash and on time. Napoleon also took a less belligerent attitude toward the Catholic Church, formalizing an agreement in July 1801 which established Catholicism as the state religion, but with guarantees of freedom of religion.

The overthrow of the Directory in November 1799, effectively ended the governmental changes begun some ten years before. Napoleon's seizure of power is a convenient place to end the discussion of French political history during this period. The next chapter deals with the economic history of the revolutionary period. While it somewhat parallels the political history, it begins a few years before the start of the Revolution.

CHAPTER 8

FRANCE AND THE FRENCH REVOLUTION
THE ECONOMIC HISTORY

The death toll from the Reign of Terror is estimated at around 16,000. From this book's perspective, the question is whether economic factors played any role in the killings - or were the executions carried out for purely political motives? While the discussion in Chapter Seven suggests an underlying economic discontent among the populace of Paris, there is no obvious economic link between that discontent and the killings. The government, after all, carried out the executions, not the crowd. The official justification for the killings was purely political - those executed represented a threat to the new government. Official pronouncements aside, there are indications that the political power of the mob exerted a great deal of influence over governmental decisions. Some saw an opportunity to exploit that power while others had reason to fear it. While governmental leaders were willing to voice fears about the dangers posed by political opposition to the Revolutionary government, they were largely silent about the threat which emanated from the crowd. If the actions of the government can be seen in a purely political context at times, it was economic hardship which motivated the mob. The large numbers of hungry and unemployed provided a ready pool of "recruits" for the large urban armies which roamed the streets of Paris terrorizing the government and the people.

If a link between economic hardship and the violence of the Reign of Terror is not readily apparent, the Terror raises a unique question. Was the violence of the Terror a governmental response to political opposition and societal unrest, i.e., a repressive measure, or was it merely an extension of the violence engaged in by the mob? Both the Second Directory and the government of Napoleon would employ repressive measures, including the death penalty. At the same time, such measures were more focused and on a lesser scale than that of the Terror. Only 160 former nobles were executed by the Directory. Napoleon executed just nine Jacobins for the bomb plot of 1800.

The Terror, for all its prominence, represented only part of the violence which Paris was subjected to. Other instances of violence, if not equal in ferocity to the Terror, were more obviously linked to economic conditions. The crowd which invaded the Convention hall in May 1795, killing the deputy Feraud in the process, rallied to the cry of "Bread and the Constitution of 1793." A pamphlet circulating a few days before had been entitled "People's Insurrection to Obtain Bread and Recover Our Rights."[1] In February 1793, only a month after the death of Louis XVI, Parisians had rioted for three days over food shortages.

This chapter focuses primarily on the economic side of the French Revolution, although it concludes with a discussion of violence. As the discussion here and in Chapter Seven suggests, it is sometimes difficult to separate the political from the economic - economic conditions did impact the political process. For many of the poor in Paris, violence seemed the only way to express frustration about their plight or to get the attention of the political leadership. If nothing else, the examples cited illustrate the extremes to which economic conditions had driven people. If food shortages played a role in the political scene however, they were only one part of the larger economic picture.

FRANCE BEFORE THE REVOLUTION

The political violence which plagued the Revolution may have erupted in 1789, but the political inequities and grievances which prompted it had been present long before that date. France's economic problems, similarly, did not suddenly appear in 1789. Their origins can be traced back a number of years. The discussion of economic conditions in France begins with the year 1775, although that date is somewhat arbitrary. It was a year however, in which open opposition to government economic policy was strong enough to provoke a political response. It was in 1775 that France experienced what was called the 'Flour War.' It involved some two weeks of rioting, beginning on April 27. The rioting had not started in Paris but at Beaumont-sur-Oise, a town to the north. The cause of the riots was an increase in the price of bread, but they were something more than a local dispute with street vendors - rioters were bold enough to threaten the palace at Versailles. In the end the riots were quelled only after army troops were called in. Hundreds were arrested and two public executions were held.[2]

France would experience numerous riots during the next 20 years. Some involved complaints about prices; some involved complaints about wages. What they had in common was some form of economic grievance. The riots involved in the Flour War, stemmed from anger over price increases in basic foodstuffs. The Réveillon riots in April 1789 started out as a protest against a perceived threat to cut wages. The riots which occurred in Paris in February 1793 were over food prices and the attack on the Convention in May 1795 was caused by food shortages in Paris. To be sure, the rioting often took on political tones. The actions of the Paris mob were often motivated by the belief that scarcity and high prices were the result of a conspiracy between the aristocracy and political leadership to starve the people.

There might be said to be one overriding economic affliction which affected all of France in the period before the Revolution - scarcity. At the same time, scarcity took different forms, depending on the sector of the economy. In the rural areas, the most serious form of scarcity involved land. Where land was scarce, however, labor was plentiful. An increase in population led to a labor surplus. The result was a bidding war, a competition between peasants and laborers to acquire what land there was. Land-owners charged more to rent out land, while employers reduced the wages they paid. The number of peasants who lost their land was on the increase. While wages experienced a slow increase, it still was only a third of what prices increased.[3] In Paris, scarcity took two forms, both of which were problems for the poor. First, there were the actual shortages of food and consumer goods, which were a chronic problem. Second, there was a shortage of employment. Even where work could be found, the competition for jobs kept wages low. The actual shortages of foodstuffs and goods led to inflation, compounding the employment problem.

What would the expected impact of such an economic situation? Inflation and a lack of job opportunities would have reduced discretionary or spendable income, the lifeblood which helps to sustain markets. Depending on the severity of inflation, such a situation could prove devastating for the worker. Caught in a downward spiraling cycle, the worker would be dependent on potential employers, who, facing a reduction in overall demand and shrinking markets, would need fewer workers. That, in fact, appears to be what was happening in Paris. Not just workers were affected however. Even small business proprietors and artisans, more fortunate perhaps than the unemployed, were finding it difficult to make ends meet. Despite such difficulties, Paris nevertheless attracted people from rural areas. Peasants, who could no longer survive economically in the country, were drawn to Paris in hopes of finding work.

There is no question that changing economic conditions worked a hardship on workers. Viewed from a purely economic perspective however, it might be said that what was happening represented nothing more than the normal operation of the market. Inefficiencies were being eliminated, both in the countryside and in the cities. Even the shortages which plagued Paris could be explained in market terms - food producers simply did not find Paris to be a profitable market. They either sold elsewhere or held out for higher prices. The French economy, from a market standpoint, was in the process of eliminating its inefficiencies. Unfortunately, this was not the kind of solution French politicians were eager to explain to the citizens of Paris.

The 'Flour War' was prompted by a political decision which had been made in 1774. Ironically, it was not some despotic action by the monarchy which caused political unrest; it was instead a decision to let market forces operate freely. If the monarchy is to be judged by the policies of its ministers, the French monarchy was, in some ways, fairly progressive. In August 1774, Anne-Robert Turgot was appointed Comptroller-General. A believer in the free market, he decided that market forces should be allowed to operate in the grain market. Accordingly, on September 13, 1774, he lifted government restrictions on grain and flour prices. Unfortunately, he chose this action in a year in which there had been a bad harvest. When the resulting shortages caused prices to rise, angry consumers raided the Paris flour and bread markets and forced bakers to sell at the original price.[4] The 'Flour War' was not a good portent for the start of the reign of Louis XVI, whose coronation was held on June 11, 1775.

Lifting the governmental restrictions was a political mistake which would eventually contribute to Turgot's dismissal in May 1776. His September 1774 decision and the price increases which led to the 'Flour War' riots certainly did not make Turgot a hero to the French masses. At the same time, his financial policies were not based on currying favor with the aristocracy. He was, for the most part, simply a fiscal conservative. He had advised the king to bring spending under control when he first took office. He also advised against involvement in the American War of Independence - in her financial situation, France simply could not afford the expenditures such a war would entail.[5]

THE AMERICAN REVOLUTION, TAXES, AND A BALANCED BUDGET

Jacques Necker, the man who succeeded Turgot as Director of the Treasury in October 1776, brought to his post a reputation as something of a financial wizard. He was extremely popular despite the fact that he was neither French nor a Catholic, but Swiss and a Protestant. He may not have been more financially astute than Turgot, but he had better political instincts. Necker advocated government controls of the grain trade. This alone would not have antagonized Turgot; what made Turgot mad was the fact that Necker published his views in a book which came out around the time of the Flour War. Whether the timing was by design, the book made Necker into a popular hero. Necker was both intelligent and competent, yet he was, at the same time, a self-promoter and somewhat unscrupulous. Like Turgot, he was interested in establishing a sound financial administration for the French government. He tried to reorganize governmental accounting procedures and to overhaul the tax system. He was interested in eliminating the system where individuals could buy public office.[6] On the negative side, he was not above resorting to financial sleight of hand to promote himself. In 1781, he took the unprecedented step of publishing a balance sheet for the French government which showed a governmental surplus, even with expenditures for the American war effort. What he did not include in the balance sheet were the extraordinary accounts where expenditures for the war were actually being recorded. The French public was nevertheless convinced that the reported balanced budget was real - as were Necker's extraordinary abilities.[7]

Despite Necker's reputation, his political perception fell short. In May 1781, only three months after the balance sheet was published, Necker resigned. Believing the popularity which followed from the publication of the balance sheet gave him enhanced political power, Necker pressured the king to admit him to the king's inner council. Membership in the Catholic Church was a requirement for that position and the king refused the request.

Necker achieved a measure of revenge in 1785, when he published a book entitled *Administration des Finances* which was a defense of his term in office. It also served as a criticism of those in office in 1785. The criticism coincided with growing opposition to the economic and financial policies of the French government. Ironically, it was the continuation of one of Necker's policies, support for the American revolution, which contributed to the economic problems of the French government in 1785. Necker's successor, Joly de Fleury, in order to pay for the war, had made a decision to raise taxes.

Necker did not use tax revenues to pay directly for the war. Instead, Necker's mechanism involved large borrowings by the French government. Rather than appropriate tax revenues to pay directly for the war, the government borrowed money and used tax revenues to repay the loans and interest. Prior to Necker's resignation in 1781, this procedure did not put an undue strain on governmental finances. By 1785, however, the parlements, aware that taxes would need to be raised to pay for continued borrowing, began to object to the loans. Investors, as well, were apparently becoming skeptical about the liberal terms offered by the government. Subscriptions to the loans began to fall. At this point the king and his then-Comptroller-General, Calonne, determined that investor trust and belief in the financial soundness of the country depended on a broader show of support. The king, while wanting to impress investors still wanted to exercise control over the support he intended to enlist. The convening of the Estates-General, the traditional representative body of France, was discussed, but it was felt this body was subject to too many uncontrollable factors. As a result, the king, instead, authorized the convening of the ill-fated Assembly of Notables, a representative body whose members were chosen by the king, in December 1786.

The king, as well as Calonne, soon discovered that the Assembly of Notables, though believed to be more easily controllable than any Estates-General, was somewhat independent. Necker's presence was felt, even though he was not in office. Calonne, personally presiding over the Assembly, found his actions and statements contrasted with those of Necker. When Calonne announced the existence of a deficit, the delegates couldn't help but compare Calonne's deficit with the balanced budget achieved by Necker. While Calonne had advocated measures designed to stimulate the French economy - he resurrected the idea of allowing the market to operate in grain - he also had made a great many enemies, even among the delegates in the Assembly. The king, convinced of the soundness of Calonne's ideas, decided that someone else would be more successful in getting them adopted. Calonne was dismissed on April 8, 1787. Deciding that the Assembly of Notables was unlikely to adopt his suggested proposals, the king dissolved it just a month later, on May 25.

Prior to the dissolution of the Assembly, the king had found a successor to Calonne. On May 1 Brienne was appointed Chief of the Royal Council of Finances. It was Brienne who dismissed the Assembly of Notables. For the king, the Assembly's dissolution presented him with two immediate problems. First, it had not voted for new taxes. As a result, he lacked the formal approval of a representative body for new taxes. Second, the Assembly had drawn attention to the financial difficulties of the government. Confused by the explanations offered for the financial state of the treasury, the Assembly had demanded a permanent audit commission, prior to its dissolution. The king objected.

The king might have had fewer problems if he had himself seriously reviewed the revenues and expenditures of his government. Had the treasury been in a more sound financial state he could have avoided much of the legal confrontation with the parlements, the courts of law (not legislatures) which administered the thirteen jurisdictions into which France had been divided. His financial problems forced him to seek help from the judges of the parlements and the seriousness of the problem gave them a great deal of leverage. At the same time, what the parlements asked was not unreasonable. Like the budget committee of any organization, they wanted the king to provide information about the accounts.

While Brienne's reputation helped the government to obtain loans in May 1787 the parlements began to express reservations about the measures they were asked to approve, particularly those measures involving increased taxation. Brienne did advocate free trade in grain and the parlements agreed to this. However, when the Paris parlement was asked, on July 2, to extend the stamp duty, its reply was to refuse to approve the duty until it had seen the accounts and the increase had been justified. The king ordered the parlement to approve the measure anyway. The parlement maneuvered around the king's demand by arguing that only the Estates-General had the authority to approve a perpetual tax. The parlement made the same argument on July 30, when it refused to approve a territorial subsidy. Louis now resorted to an extraordinary measure, the *lit de justice*, literally the bed of justice. The bed of justice was a procedure in which the king presided over sessions of parlement from a canopied bed. The king probably undermined the intended gravity of his actions by falling asleep and snoring through part of the session when it was held on August 6. The result was a formal order by the king to register, or formally enact, the new taxes. The reply of the Paris parlement the next day, was to declare the king's actions illegal and without effect. This was followed on August 13 by a formal condemnation of the king's action. The king's reply, on August 15, was to exile the parlement of Paris.

While the king's attention was focused on the fight with the parlements, another battle was raging for public support. Not only did the sessions of the Paris parlement draw large crowds, but various political clubs and discussion groups formed. Pamphlets appeared in support of the actions of the parlement. In spite of the defiance by the parlement, it was possible to have the king's laws put into effect by having lower-level magistrates record them. While the king resorted to this mechanism, he may have been surprised by the opposition displayed even at this level. When the king's brother, with a guard as an escort, personally appeared at some of the courts, he was jeered. The king however, showed an unusual measure of resolve. Clubs were ordered closed and the streets were cleared and patrolled by the army.

Brienne, shortly after, proposed a compromise to the exiled parlement. He offered to introduce a five-year economic plan which would restore French finances by 1792 and would withdraw the stamp and territorial tax. In return the parlement would agree to approve a new loan and to a continuation of existing taxes. Despite the fact that some among the public accused the parlement of selling out in agreeing to the compromise, Brienne felt he had gained sufficient support among the members of the parlement to get his measures passed. The meeting, a Royal Session, was to be held on November 19. Since Brienne had the votes, the session was not to be as formal, nor as adversarial, as the *lit de justice*. Brienne's efforts at compromise were completely undone by the king. At the end of the session the king ordered the loans recorded as if the meeting had been a *lit de justice*. This action brought a protest from the Duke of Orleans, who told the king it was not legal. The king's reply was that it was legal because the king wished it. Defiantly, the parlement did not disband, even after the king had left. Instead, it formally protested by disassociating itself from the king's actions.[8]

The Paris parlement, by its actions on November 19, was not through with its protest. In April 1788, it issued several formal denunciations of the king's actions. On April 29, it even went so far as to forbid tax-collectors from bringing in collections from the new tax. On May 8 the king held another *lit de justice*. The seemingly simple act of registering laws, formally entrusted to the parlements, had proved to be a surprisingly large obstacle to the implementation of the king's edicts. Therefore he intended to transfer this duty to a Plenary Court. The parlements were to be transformed into courts of appeal. Along with this change, the king intended to institute other reforms of the judicial system. Some would have an economic impact on employees of the court system, such as the elimination of certain courts in the criminal justice system.

An attack on the political or economic power of two influential groups at the same time was probably unwise. Parlements throughout France protested the action. The courts in Paris only registered the new laws after they were forced to. Many of the parlements called for a meeting of the Estates-General. In Toulon, on June 7, when the parlement was exiled, riots resulted in the deaths of four people and 40 injuries, in what was called the 'Day of Tiles.' (Rioters had thrown tiles down on the troops from the rooftops.) On June 29, at Pau, rioters reinstalled the magistrates by smashing in the doors of the locked parlement building. Rioting law clerks and students took to the streets in Rennes in July. In response to the physical expressions of opposition to government policy, Brienne finally announced, on August 8, 1788, that the Estates-General would meet on May 1, 1789.

The decision by Brienne to convene the Estates-General would normally be considered primarily a political decision. Yet the decision, and particularly its timing, were heavily determined by economic factors. It was the financial situation of the French government, particularly as it stood on August 8, 1788, which played an important part in the timing of the announcement. A more long-standing financial problem, which contributed to the crisis in August, was related to the military. More specifically, the problem related to military pay and to budgetary cuts which had impacted the officer class. At a time when force was required to put a stop to mob action, many began to regard the soldiers as unreliable. Officers were reluctant to give orders to fire on rioters because they were unsure those orders would be carried out. Many of the soldiers were poor and served as a sympathetic audience for anti-royalist propaganda. The poor financial situation of the common soldier, contributing to an inability to maintain order, was only one part of the king's problem. The other was a more immediate financial dilemma.

The budget presented by Brienne was dependent on the government's ability to obtain short-term loans from private borrowers. Known as anticipations, these short-term loans used anticipated tax revenues as security. On July 13, 1788 a severe hailstorm destroyed crops around Paris. Investors believed that tax collections from farmers would be down the next year and, as a result, were reluctant to subscribe. Losing this source of cash, Brienne's announcement of the convening of the Estates-General was an attempt to restore investor confidence. It failed. On August 16, the government stopped further payments on outstanding loans and forced creditors to accept government notes. Brienne felt compelled to bring Necker back into the government. Necker agreed to return on August 24 and Brienne then resigned.

The question is how a single hailstorm could mean the difference between financial success and total disaster for the French government. That the French treasury was in such a precarious state is somewhat difficult to believe. Yet the economic story of the royal finances is perhaps a mirror of the Parisian and French economies as a whole. The French economy was itself balanced precariously between success and collapse. The story of financial policies up to 1788 has been included here, in part, because it provides some insight into the general economic forces at work in the French economy and how they impacted French politics and fiscal policy. It has also been included because it provides both direct and indirect evidence of scarcity which was plaguing the economy as a whole.

WEATHER PROBLEMS AND THE PRICE OF GRAIN

When Necker returned to power he reimposed government controls on grain - the one policy which made him popular with the French laborers. He was not, however able to come up with a workable solution to the chronic problem of shortages in Paris. His immediate successors discovered that their solutions were little better than those of the king. The economic story now shifts to the streets of Paris, which had to endure a series of Flour Wars. Inflation and shortages caused discontent which frequently erupted into violent confrontation.

Necker, looking forward from August 1788, could not know that grain prices, despite his efforts to control them, would continue to rise through July 1789, peaking the day the Bastille fell, July 14, 1789.[9] It might be said that many of the events of 1789 were determined by what happened in 1788. It perhaps would be too much to argue that the weather of 1788 was the cause of the downfall of Louis XVI. Yet, coupled with other economic circumstances, it played a major role. The hailstorm which struck on July 13, 1788, was particularly severe; severe enough to kill men and animals, in addition to the crop damage. The hailstorm was followed by drought which contributed to a poor harvest in 1788 as well.

Hail and drought were followed, in the winter of 1788-89, by severe cold. Rivers froze. Laborers in Paris, whose livelihood was related to river commerce, were directly impacted. Dockers, bargemen, and those who floated logs were thrown out of work.[10] With rivers frozen, water mills could not turn grain into flour and food transport became impossible. Yet the severe winter was not the sole cause of unemployment and economic hardship; other economic factors were at work as well. Overall income for the common laborer was relatively low. Even without the shortages of 1788-89, a laborer could spend up to half his wages on bread. In the spring of 1789 this increased to between two thirds and nine tenths.[11] With food absorbing such a high percentage of income, the demand for industrial goods dropped off. This, in turn, meant a fall in the market for workers, with a corresponding increase in unemployment. In Lyons, it was estimated that unemployment among silk workers was between 20,000 and 30,000.[12] France had concluded a commercial treaty with Great Britain in 1786. The import of cheaper goods was also having an effect on employment. Although unrelated to the weather, its impact was being felt at nearly the same time. Amiens, where goods would first arrive from England on their way to Paris, unemployment reached 46,000.[13] As high as that figure is, the hardship in Paris was perhaps greater. It was estimated that over 100,000 were receiving some form of charitable assistance there in the winter of 1788-89.[14] This figure was out of a total population in Paris estimated at between 524,000 and 660,000.[15]

Necker's decision to reimpose grain controls in August 1788 was exactly what the workers of Paris wanted. However, while it may have sounded like a simple action, there were, in fact, a number of actions which needed to be taken to implement it. Implementation involved more than the publication of a price list. Grain controls involved government purchases of grain and a ban on exports. The task was made more difficult by the fact that other countries were suffering through similar problems and were also in the market for surplus grain. The severe freeze, which had affected French transport, also created problems of delivery.[16]

Necker's decision, though primarily an economic one, had far-reaching political consequences as well. He focused primarily on the problems of the Paris grain market. In order to supply this market, he not only brought in supplies from outside France, but also from other regions within France. Regions such as Flanders, Artois, Picardy, and Normandy, as a result, experienced shortages in the spring of 1789. The bread riots, which occurred in these regions in May, contributed to the decision by the clergy, at the meeting of the Estates-General, to join the Third Estate in defying the king.[17]

Some of the underlying economic problems and problems of government intervention are hinted at in the actions taken against those violating price limits. The ceiling for bread was fourteen and a half sous, and 27 bakers were fined for exceeding that limit in February 1789. Their guild defended them. The defense was that, with shortages and the prices of wheat and ingredients so high, the bakers would need to either cheat on wheat or use substitute ingredients to bring their costs down sufficiently to be able to sell within the government ceiling.[18]

The severe winter, despite the economic hardship it brought, may have provided some benefit to Paris - it kept people off the streets. For it was at the end of April, when spring weather would allow people to move about more freely, that the Réveillon riots broke out. As discussed in Chapter Seven, what sparked the riots were remarks which Réveillon made at an electoral meeting. The misinterpretation of his remarks about lower wages were not helped by his advocating the deregulation of the grain trade. His argument was that deregulation would result in lower prices, which, in turn, would allow for lower wages. It was this part of his speech which created problems. After it was reported, the poorer workers focused, not on its free trade aspects, but on the reduction of wages. The reports and rumors began circulating among the workers, now congregating in the streets at the end of winter. It was interpreted as an actual threat to cut wages. The poor residents of the faubourg Saint-Marcel may have had other reasons to target Réveillon and his factory. He, in fact, paid his own workers well and even kept them on his payroll during slow periods. At the same time, he made an ostentatious display of his wealth, with furniture and a large library in the apartment above his factory. He also maintained a 2,000 bottle wine cellar, no doubt a source of resentment to the poor - as well as a temptation. Réveillon, served only as the immediate focus of the angry workers. The crowd resented the rich in general. As they marched they shouted "Death to the rich, death to the aristocrats."[19]

Whether Louis XVI had expected Necker to be able to resurrect the French economy, and with it, Louis' political fortunes, he dismissed Necker on July 11. It was only two days before that rioters had begun to attack the customs posts throughout Paris. These actions, which would result in the destruction of 40 of the customs posts in Paris over four days of rioting, were a combination of political and economic protest - a general attack on one of the more hated political arms of the regime and a chance to strike at an activity which added to the cost of goods. They were also not the only action against the customs posts. Rioters had also destroyed the toll-gates at Lyons.

The new National Assembly could not avoid the economic problems, even debating the necessity of price controls on grain from July 4 to July 7. The weather came into play on the economic scene again in July and August 1789. Mills were unable to grind grain into flour and, even if available, transport was difficult. The problem this time was not that the rivers had frozen over, but that they had dried up. The power supply for mills was gone. Bread prices, which had peaked on July 14, and then fallen, began to rise again. This time grain riots occurred in the outlying districts of Paris. Groups of women stopped grain convoys in Paris in September 1789. They also petitioned for price controls. The authorities ordered armed guards at baker's shops.[20] When the crowd marched on Versailles on October 4, one of their demands was for bread. Louis XVI, on his escorted return to the capital on October 6, thought it wise to provide the crowd with the flour stored at Versailles.

TEMPORARY STABILITY AND DECLINE AFTER 1792

Paris, following the events of October 1789, experienced fewer problems with its food supply for several years - save for the closure of a Monarchical Club in 1791 for selling bread at reduced prices. Unfortunately, the economic changes in Paris were not the result of an improving French economy. Instead they involved an economic sleight-of-hand by government officials. Paris authorities built up reserves for winter by shipping grain from the producing regions of northern France throughout the fall. Problems associated with a shortage of agricultural products were not solved however, they were simply transferred to different locations. While Paris was relatively well off, in terms of staples, such as grain, flour, and bread, that comfort was obtained at the expense of other regions of France. Such an artificial solution was difficult to maintain permanently. In the winter of 1791-1792 the resentment boiled over. The smaller towns of the north now had to confront angry consumers and food riots. Some confrontations went beyond simple price fixing; a mob lynched the mayor of Étampes in February 1792 after he refused to order price reductions. The government was forced to send in troops to regain control. Mobs destroyed warehouses at Dunkirk when an attempt was made to export grain from there.[21]

Paris did not avoid unrest altogether. A slave uprising which began in Saint-Domingue in 1791 nearly eliminated sugar exports to France and shortages began to be felt in January 1792. Crowds, in January and February, managed to get into warehouses and grocers' shops and forced sales at the old prices. Inflation, a more general symptom of shortage, made its appearance as well in 1792. Both the livre, the French pound, and the assignat, the state-issued bond secured by national land, fell in value. By March 1792, the livre was trading on foreign exchanges at only 80 per cent of its June 1791 price. The assignat's value had fallen by 37 per cent.[22]

SCARCITY, MOB ACTIVITY, AND THE TERROR

Mob activity in Paris for 1792 seemed to lessen until the storming of the Tuileries on August 10 and the massacres of September. If the crowd was not totally inactive, the protesters complained less about shortages. The Prussian and Austrian threats may have preoccupied many. The purely political focus of the crowd however, seemed to peak with the execution of Louis XVI on January 21, 1793. It would, once again, express concern about economic problems. Sugar prices in February were two to three times what they had been in 1790, due to the slave revolt. In addition a blockade resulting from the wars had severely restricted the flow of other imported goods. Coffee prices began to rise. The Convention and the Jacobin club received petitions calling for the imposition of a maximum, i.e., a maximum price for goods. Beginning on February 25, 1793, and lasting for the next two days, crowds once again invaded warehouses and shops. Store owners were forced to accept payment at the old prices. The government ordered troops in to restore order.[23]

The crowds began to focus on the delegates to the Convention. Despite their own lawless actions, the members of the crowd believed in the moral authority of the law. The will of the people, once enacted into law, carried greater weight. The trial of Marat, which resulted in his acquittal on April 24, served to stir the crowds. He had urged direct action against hoarders and speculators in a paper which was distributed after the February outbursts. Among the charges against him was one that this writing was an incitement to take action outside the law. Nevertheless, many began to call for government price controls again.

Montagnard delegates openly proposed controls in April. For economic reasons, the Girondins nevertheless found the courage to oppose their reimposition. That did not satisfy the crowd. On May 1, 8,000 demonstrators appeared at the Convention and demanded that price controls on bread be introduced. On May 2, the delegates passed a measure providing for price controls on grain and bread. They also added search and requisition authority for those who would be enforcing the law.[24] Lyons was also having problems with shortages. The cost of bread was nearly a third more there than its cost in Paris. A warehouse holding food intended for the army was invaded on May 24 and the supplies found there were paid for at "fair" prices, as determined by the crowd.

Having now intervened by imposing controls in May, the government took even stronger steps in July. Hoarding was made punishable with the death penalty on July 26. That food supplies had become a major concern of the government is illustrated by a note Robespierre wrote on his joining the Committee of Public Safety. He mentioned two priorities - food supplies and the law.[25] Toward the end of summer Paris was again experiencing shortages of flour. As in 1789, a drought severe enough to dry up many rivers, prevented the mills from grinding grain. The seriousness of the shortage perhaps can be understood from the perspective of the Paris Commune's Food Commission. In August its two agents told its commissioner Descombes that he could forcibly requisition grain - Paris was receiving only 100 sacks of flour a day and its normal requirement was 2,000.[26] Descombes would be sent to the guillotine on March 24, 1794, in part because his efforts to overcome the shortage failed.

Inflation remained high during the summer of 1793. Workers demonstrated on September 4 for bread and higher wages. This was followed, on September 5, by another large demonstration. Chaumette, one of the delegates, addressed the crowd, denouncing the shortages and the failure to apply the law. The Convention felt compelled to enact the measures which officially marked the beginning of the Terror. Shortly after, on September 9, news that the queen was plotting to escape, reinforced the idea that economic controls and political repression should be part of the same program. The General Maximum Law, passed on September 29, 1793, not only provided for the extension of price controls to non-food items, such as tobacco, but also made the selling of goods at prices above the maximum, a political crime. The solution of the Terror, which viewed nearly all economic problems in terms of consumer prices, was to focus exclusively on that economic area. The Girondins, executed in October, were not killed for any price violations, however. They were executed for their opposition, both political and economic, to the proposals of those in power.

In contrast to the arbitrary political actions taken against political opponents, the implementation of controls was taken with more systematic planning. On October 27, 1793 a Subsistence Commission, intended to deal with problems of national supply, was created under the Committee of Public Safety. It had rather extensive economic powers, such as authority over governmental purchases and grants, together with the regulation of exports and imports. It attempted to institute price controls, not only for Paris, but also for the rest of France. Taking costs into consideration, allowances were made for transport charges and for, what was considered, a reasonable profit. By February 21, 1794, it was able to issue a nationwide schedule of maximum prices.

While the French economy still struggled, there were indications that the decline it had suffered was beginning to reverse, or at least to slow. The assignat, for example,

146

whose value had dropped to 22 per cent of face value in August 1793, partially recovered, reaching 48 per cent by December.[27] The reduced value of the assignat had been one of the reasons Descombes, the food commissioner executed for failing in his job, had found securing food supplies for Paris to be so difficult.[28] Despite that hopeful sign, the Paris food supply continued to be a major headache. Those in charge of supply had to worry about nearly every aspect of production. Even the wagons bringing grain or flour into the city were subject to attack by mobs of hungry women in early 1794.[29] There were long lines for food outside bakeries and butcher shops in Paris. Individual towns, trying to feed their own citizens, seized whatever food supplies managed to come within their jurisdiction.[30] In February, a police spy named Charmont reported that he had heard of women complaining about standing in line until three in the morning to buy a chicken.[31]

Despite the harsh penalties for violations of the maximum provisions, market laws of supply and demand still proved too great a temptation for producers. Agents for the army were some of the worst offenders, ignoring the maximum when they needed to acquire beef or supplies. The army probably enjoyed a special type of immunity. Defending France against enemies aligned with the hated aristocracy, the army was the last organization any sane politician would dare accuse of being disloyal. The army purchases, not only provided producers with justification for selling above the maximum, they also reduced the supplies available for civilian use.

Politically, the shortages came to play a part in the destruction of the Hébertistes, condemned and executed in March 1794. Accusations of involvement in a plot against food supplies could be tantamount to a political or actual death sentence. Hébert's opponents used charges of involvement in a "starvation plot" to bring him down. Though largely based on allegations which were untrue, the accusers managed to eliminate political support for Hébert and his followers by accusing them of trying to starve Paris by sabotaging food supplies.

Scarcity and high food prices represented one side of the economic coin, low wages represented the other. Freezing wages, in the eyes of workers, was as bad as plot-ting to starve Paris. A tool for implementing wage controls was available. The Law of General Maximum, passed on September 29, 1793, had included a provision regulating wages, in addition to its price control mechanism. The more politically astute members of the commune chose not to enforce it. They realized that the laborers, in large numbers, were a political force which should not be antagonized. Robespierre, perhaps out of arro-gance, failed to see the political pitfalls of using that section of the Maximum. He impos-ed a freeze on wages a few days before his political opponents eliminated him. If the government seemed fully in control of the Terror, political power often was dependent on the number of troops one side could muster. When the Paris insurrectionary com-mune called for units of the National Guard to assemble in support of Robespierre on July 27, out of 48 sections, only 13 bothered to show up.[32] Those that showed up left in the middle of the night. Robespierre's opponents, in addition, were able to mobilize an armed force of their own to enforce the action against him. His forces had vanished by the time the final confrontation occurred and he had no armed force to defend himself on July 28.

147

EXPERIMENTING WITH MARKET FORCES

That Robespierre, who had seemed invincible when he brought Danton down in April, could himself fall in July, seemed inconceivable. It was only one of several "unforeseeable" events of 1794. Few could know, in July, that the coming winter would bring conditions as severe as those of 1788-89, with similar economic hardship in the spring of 1795. Few could guess, as well, that support for price controls would fall off among the poor. Price controls, the economic "plan" which had made Necker a national hero, which had been the overriding political "program" of the crowd, and which had been the most often heard demand of the mob, were now blamed for much of the scarcity which Paris was forced to endure. If the political winds were beginning to change, the Convention members were reluctant to commit to an immediate change of policy. Price (as well as wage) controls were continued in force for one year when the Maximum Law came up in September. By December however, the representatives had received sufficient indication of the change in mood to commission a report. Finally, on December 24, 1794, the Convention, on the basis of the report, voted to abolish price controls.[33]

The Convention did not wait until December to defuse another explosive issue - wage controls. The low wage rates imposed by Robespierre were raised on August 9. Yet that concession was not enough. Workers were struggling against the consequences of a scarcity which was driving prices up and they wanted wage rate maximums set even higher.

The hardships of the winter of 1794-95 did not cause the government to reimpose price controls. Political leaders avoided intervention in that area. However, the government did intervene in other ways in the economy. While the winter was severe, the government was perhaps more experienced and better prepared to deal with the problems. Frozen rivers once again stopped transport by barge and prevented mills from grinding grain. In February and March, though rationed, the bread supply still was sufficient to provide a pound of bread per day for those citizens of Paris in need. The elimination of price controls did make the replenishment of food stores more difficult. The government had provided no exemption for itself in the area of price controls and had to pay the market rate when it purchased food. Whether it was due to army requisitions or to low production, the price of meat in April had increased by 300 percent over its December 1794 price. Another economic indicator, the value of the assignat, also evidenced serious problems. In May 1795, it was worth only 8 percent of its face value.[34]

March 1795, despite the hope of spring, proved to be a difficult month. Lines grew longer outside shops, even where bread was available. In some districts the supply gave out completely. The Convention received petitions requesting better bread supplies. A forced requisition of farming areas was decreed and, in a novel attempt to at least reduce complaints about long lines at shops, the Convention decided that bread rations would be delivered directly to the people. The measures came too late or were insufficient to prevent bread riots at the end of the month. On April 1 a crowd of 10,000 marched on the

Convention and some of the marchers, demanding bread - and the constitution of 1793 - were able to enter the assembly hall. They eventually dispersed.[35]

The Convention was losing patience with such demonstrations and began to adopt a harder line. What may have provided the delegates with such newfound courage was the growth of a small "army" of Muscadins, the young counter-revolutionary force made up mostly of victims of the Terror or those with royalist sympathies. At the end of March it had voted a decree providing for punishment for attacks on the Convention. General Pichegru, a regular army general who had conducted operations in the Netherlands, was given command of police and army units in Paris charged with maintaining order. Following the events of April 1 it passed the Law of April 10, authorizing the disarmament of those who had been active during the Terror.[36]

The Convention did vote to supply Parisians with rice and biscuits, in addition to bread. Despite these measures, the Convention would have to endure one last outburst from the poorer sections. On May 20 a crowd gathered and marched on the Convention. The deputy Feraud was shot, then beheaded, as the crowd moved into the hall. As on April 1, there were demands for bread and the constitution of 1793. They also wanted legislation allowing compulsory food searches. The Convention's forces meanwhile assembled outside the hall. A standoff lasted until May 21. The situation was defused when the marchers agreed to disperse if they would be allowed to present a petition on behalf of the marchers. The petition included a demand for more bread.

The Convention, this time, reacted with more than threats or new legislation. Six of the Montagnard delegates who had supported the crowd were condemned to death. Gunners who had defected to the crowd were condemned to death as well. The Paris sections in which the march had been organized were surrounded by troops, those involved in the death of the deputy Feraud were identified and sentenced to death. All the Paris sections were now disarmed. By decree, the Convention had 3,000 arrested, and the sections, ordered to furnish the names of additional suspects, provided another 3,000 suspects.[37] The action taken to disarm the Paris sections was one of the last major official acts of the Convention. On August 22, 1795 it approved France's new constitution.

Between the approval of the Constitution and the official institution of the Directory on November 2, the Convention had one more serious uprising to deal with. Seven sections declared themselves in revolt in early October and succeeded in raising a force of 25,000 which marched on the Convention on October 5. While some of the insurgents had guns, in spite of the disarmament, they had no cannon, and little powder. While there was a standoff for a time, the Convention forces opened fire with their cannon. Though numbering only 6,000, the defenders were more disciplined and, after a six-and-a-half hour battle, were successful, although hundreds were reported killed. In one final action, aimed at curbing the unreliable National Guard, it was abolished and replaced by the Parisian Guard.

Paris, economically, had not recovered from the effects of early 1795. The severe winter, like 1789, had been followed by another dry summer. Prices remained high and went higher. The government imposed rationing. Despite shortages, which would continue into the spring, there were no more popular street demonstrations. The French economy probably reached its lowest level with the bankruptcy of the French government on September 30, 1797. Two thirds of the national debt was redeemed with a paper payment to creditors. The bankruptcy of the French government serves as a convenient stopping point for a discussion of economic conditions during the Revolutionary period. The French economy appears to have followed a slow period of economic recovery. The recovery was not a robust one; the French people did not suddenly begin living a life of luxury. On the other hand, Paris remained relatively free of the excesses of the crowd. The most serious of the violent outbursts had largely been brought under control.

THE VIOLENCE OF THE TERROR

The beginning of the Terror can be dated to September 5, 1793. The date is not significant for any government revelations about a new killing device, the guillotine. That had been in use since April of 1792. Nor is it significant for the number of deaths. Hundreds of aristocrats were not suddenly dragged from their homes and carted to the place of execution. No executions took place that day. In fact there would be only 177 executions by December 31.[38] Neither is September 5 of significance for the application of the death penalty in political cases. The ultimate political use of the death penalty had come on January 21, 1793, when Louis was beheaded. What September 5 is significant for is the creation of a bureaucratic mechanism. Despite what the name suggests the Terror was a bureaucratic operation, methodically carried out. If it would kill some 16,000 people over the next nine months, it took some time to organize.

One of the ironies of the Revolution is that, despite the seeming efficiency shown by the government in carrying out the Terror against secret plotters, it seemed totally inept when dealing with the very real and obvious threats posed by angry mobs. Only in May 1795 would the Convention finally resort to the obvious solution of disarming all the sections of Paris, but that had been accomplished only with the help of an organized military force. The practical problem for the government was that it lacked an effective mechanism for enforcing its will against the mob. Military forces, until 1795, had proved unreliable when confronting fellow citizens. Soldiers often showed sympathy for the demonstrators even as they held authorities in contempt. Louis XVI had had similar problems.

That the Terror was a bureaucratic operation is not surprising. What is puzzling about the Terror is that the bureaucracy would become much more efficient after September 5. The government, in fact, had the bureaucratic tools in place for a campaign of repression prior to that date. They were not considered that effective however. The Committee of Public Safety, the primary instrument of the Terror under Robespierre, was in danger of being replaced for its inability to deal with food shortages. What made September 5 a watershed date was the decision by the political leadership to make the new campaign a priority. It beefed up the bureaucratic apparatus with a force of 6,000 infantry and 1,200 cavalry. Perhaps more importantly, it chose to maintain the high priority after September. The initial force created was increased to around 40,000 by December. The question is why the political will could be sustained for such a long period of time. If the political forces represented by the crowd provided the initial impetus for the decision, why, after September, did politicians choose to continue the campaign, rather than ignoring it?

The crowd, on September 5, did march on the Convention, suggesting that physical intimidation played a part in the decision. Yet, far from being intimidated, there are hints that political leaders at the Convention manipulated the crowd to create a sense of popular support. Workshops were closed on the 5th, on the orders of government officials, ensuring that laborers would be out on the street.[39] In addition, not all the laws felt necessary for the Terror were pushed through on September 5. The death penalty for hoarding had been passed in July. The Law of Suspects, which provided extensive dictatorial powers, was not passed until September 17. The General Maximum Law, which dealt primarily with prices, but which included a provision allowing violators to be listed as suspects - political opponents - would not be passed until September 29. Significantly, the first major group of victims were politicians, 21 members of the Girondin party, executed on October 31, 1793.

If the threat posed by the crowd in September seemed manufactured, it contrasted to the real intimidation surrounding the arrest of the Girondins in June. Their political mistake was in vigorously opposing the imposition of price controls. The crowd had an issue, as well as a group, to focus on. Coupled with the demand for enforcement of price controls was a demand for the arrest of the Girondins. Many of the crowd, estimated as high as 80,000, were armed. As if that was not bad enough, the more formally organized military units turned cannon on the Convention. The Girondins were arrested. What is more, the political leadership did not release them, once the mob had dispersed.

The Convention did not need the actual presence of the crowd to fear its power. Simply knowing that it was willing to intervene was enough. But if the mob represented a potent force, it could be manipulated. At the same time, manipulation was not a simple matter. The crowd had its own ideas, and to be motivated into action, seemingly demanded a single idea or a clear theme. The most obvious theme related to economic conditions. Those who wanted to triumph politically merely needed to convince the people that their current opponents were responsible for economic conditions. One by one the various political factions or leaders fell victim - first, the Girondins, then the Hébertistes, and finally Danton. Robespierre had proved the most adept at manipulation. Yet the support of the crowd, even the crowd's political power, depended, not just on the ability to frame an idea, but also on economic realities. It may have been easy to create a clear picture of a villain - the Hébertistes were responsible for food shortages - it was more difficult to explain why conditions did not improve once the villains were removed. In the economic climate of 1794 it was difficult to gain an overwhelming advantage.

In some ways, the political power of the crowd was not simply in its physical size, but also in its intense enthusiasm. Robespierre fell, not so much because he had earned the mob's hatred, but because he had lost its fanatical support. If its power was eroding

151

at the time of his execution, the crowd was not yet finished. The Convention was still afraid to lift price controls. In dealing with that issue the Convention's tactic was not to oppose the mob. Instead it gave the sans-culottes exactly what they wanted - controls on prices. If they disliked higher prices however, they found the alternative, empty store shelves, even worse. Only when the Convention became convinced that the Parisian populace no longer wanted controls, did it eliminate them in December. What enabled the Convention to eliminate the remaining political power of the crowd was the creation of a reliable military force and the disarming of the sections in May 1795.

RESOURCES, VIOLENCE, AND REPRESSION

The Terror represented perhaps the longest sustained period of violence of the French Revolution. Making an exact correlation between the shortages which existed and violence is difficult however because the crowd remained relatively quiet while the government carried out the killings. Where there were spontaneous outbreaks, before and after the Terror, there nearly always was an economic connection involving shortages or scarcity. Shortage was apparent in the 50 percent increase in bread prices in 1775 in the aftermath of Turgot's decision to lift controls on grain prices. The result was the Flour War - two-weeks of rioting from Beaumont-sur-Oise to Paris, the use of troops to restore order, and two executions. The hailstorm of July 1788, in combination with the summer drought, had severely crippled the harvest of that year. The initial shortages of food stocks were compounded by transport and mill difficulties when cold weather froze rivers that winter. Scarcity again evidenced itself through increased bread prices. The scarcity was felt throughout France, not just Paris, and the result was an outbreak of rioting and vandalism in March and April. Not only did disturbances occur in market places but also in every conceivable place the hungry thought food might be hidden. Barns, warehouses, monasteries, and houses were invaded in the search for food. In Paris, the difficult winter added unemployment to problems of scarcity. The result was two days of rioting in April in which the houses of Henriot and Réveillon were destroyed, some 25 people were killed, and eight were executed.

In May Flanders, Artois, Picardy, and Normandy had to endure bread riots. The efforts to supply Paris with grain had made the general shortage worse in those regions. Yet Paris was still suffering shortages. In early July rioters protesting high prices in Lyons had attacked the city toll-gates. On July 12 rioters in Paris similarly destroyed 40 customs posts. The following day the monastery of Saint-Lazare was destroyed by a mob of the poor searching for the grain stored there. Bread prices, an indication of the continuing shortages, would reach their highest point on July 14. A crowd estimated at 80,000 broke into the Invalides that day and obtained the 30,000 muskets stored there, then moved on to the Bastille, in search of powder. In addition to the nearly 100 people who died in the storming of the Bastille, the mob killed de Launay, the commandant, and later that day Flesselles, the chief magistrate of Paris. On July 22, Sauvigny and Foulon would be lynched by a mob.

The march on Versailles on October 5, 1789 had been preceded by weeks of shortages. Food riots occurred in the market places around Paris and groups of women were even stopping grain convoys. Although the women who went to see Louis on October 5 numbered only 7,000, the number grew. The mob would kill two guardsmen at the Palace. Although Louis decision to return to Paris on October 6, mollified the mob, it did not end the shortages in Paris, which would endure another month of rioting at various market places.

Until July 1791, Paris saw few of the mass disturbances which marked 1789. A crowd of around 50,000 had assembled to sign a petition against the reinstatement of the king, discredited by his attempt to flee Paris. If the crowd was less restive than those of 1789, it did lynch two individuals it found hiding behind the altar at the Champ de Mars. The mayor of Paris declared martial law. When the troops called in were fired on, they responded by firing at the crowd. Around 50 were killed.

If the winter of 1791-92 was relatively free of food riots in Paris, it was because authorities had worked throughout the fall at building up food reserves. However such activities again created shortages in the regions where the grain was obtained and officials in those places had to contend with market riots. The mayor of Étampes was even lynched for refusing to lower prices. Mobs in Dunkirk destroyed warehouses holding grain for export. Paris did not escape all food-related troubles. Shortages of sugar, from the slave revolt in the West Indies, caused disturbances as crowds searched for sugar in warehouses and shops in January and February 1792.

The climb in prices which occurred during the spring of 1792 was evidence that scarcity was once again becoming a problem. The first major instance of unrest would occur on June 20 when a group of between 10,000 and 20,000 sans-culottes was bold enough to invade the Tuileries grounds, even dragging cannon up the steps. For two hours they would march past the king. While no one was killed, the marchers had been bold enough to make threats against the king. This action was a prelude to the violent confrontation of August 10, when National Guard forces stormed the Tuileries, killing the 600 Swiss, while losing around 300 themselves.

The King's death on January 21, 1793 only temporarily satisfied political demands. As in 1792 shortages of West Indies products, particularly sugar, were being seen in the shops of Paris, as a result of the British blockade. Other shortages were caused by the demands of the front. Army requisitioners had bought up commodities in the fall. On February 25 Paris was once hit by food riots lasting three days and requiring National Guard troops to restore order. Continuing shortages of bread led to an 8,000-strong demonstration at the Convention on May 1. The crowd wanted price controls. On May 24 a mob invaded a warehouse holding army provisions in Lyons. June 2 would see the largest demonstration. It was on that date that a crowd of onlookers and National Guard troops, estimated at between 75,000 and 100,000 would surround the Convention and force the arrest of the Girondins. Why the crowd was so adamant in its demands for the Girondins was related to their all-too-prominent opposition to price controls.

Shortages continued in June. Meat prices became the next target, but the availability of bread was still a concern. There were disturbances on June 25 related to soap supplies. The shortages of June would continue into July and August. Flour was a special problem because of the weather - water mills did not turn out flour because the summer drought dried up many rivers. Where Paris needed 2,000 sacks of flour a day, it only could obtain 100 in August.[40] But nearly every commodity was in short supply. On July 26 the Convention passed a law providing for the death penalty for hoarding. To the inflationary problems created by a lack of goods was a drop in the value of the assignat over the summer. On September 4, the day before the Convention decided to institute the Terror, workers had demonstrated for bread and higher wages.

The political program of the Terror was accompanied by an economic plan as well. A major demand of the sans-culottes had been enforcement of price controls. The General Maximum Law of September 29, 1793 indicated a willingness to put more government resources into that area. If public demonstrations subsided, it was not just the result of stricter enforcement of the Maximum Law, but also the steps taken to ensure better food supplies. Robert Lindet took over as head of the Subsistence Commission, with a staff of 500. It was recognized that one of the supply problems for Paris in the past had been the competing demands of the army for food. If Lindet could not ignore military needs, he could at least coordinate the job of provisioning both the army and Paris, giving Paris a higher priority than it had had.

It was apparent by March that government efforts were falling short. There were few large demonstrations - one section did organize a demonstration on March 6, but could not get any support from other sections - yet vendors had to contend with daily fighting at market stalls. While government efforts were not what they could have been, they were at least sufficient to meet basic needs. Workers at least did not see total economic collapse as a threat. They had to contend instead with a threat to their ability to participate in the economy. Robespierre, through the Committee of Public Safety, in April decided to focus on the portion of the Maximum Law dealing with wages and took steps to reduce what workers were paid. It was not popular with sans-culottes, already struggling to pay for basic necessities. If there were few mass demonstrations, it was partly because the Committee of Public Safety had taken steps to physically control the forces available to the communes - the Revolutionary Army used to enforce the Terror had been officially dissolved on March 27 - partly because it threatened to retaliate against protestors. In doing so however it undermined its own source of political power. The result was that, in the early morning hours of July 29, the section troops called out to defend the commune and Robespierre's government, decided to go home, in contrast to the Convention forces, which would arrive to arrest Robespierre.

Through the end of 1794, violence took the form of the counter-terror. It is not entirely clear why the sans-culottes forces, which had proved so formidable in street demonstrations a year before, were now on the defensive. It may have been that the populace had no specific economic grievance around which it could rally or was aware that the government had sufficient military forces, the angered Muscadins in combination with regular troops, at its disposal to at least neutralize any extreme popular actions.

Despite the counter-terror, in April 1795 the crowd would reappear. Some 10,000 people would march on the Convention on April 1. Economic conditions of scarcity had preceded the unrest. During the winter of 1794 the government had been able to at least provide bread, but not much else. However, by March, even bread was disappearing, resulting in longer lines at many shops. On March 22 a group of women went to the Convention to ask for more bread. This was followed a week later by bread riots in some of the sections. The crowd on April 1 would repeat the call for bread and the constitution of 1793. The response of the Convention was the Law of April 10 authorizing the disarmament of known terrorists. Conditions did not improve during April or May, but when the crowd again surrounded the Convention on May 21, it had enough military support to counter their threats. This time the government's response was not just a law, but repression. Its forces went on the offensive, surrounding the Saint-Antoine section on May 22, forcing the surrender of the mob's leaders, and executing nearly 40 people.

The actions of May 21 did not cause the government to reinstate the Terror. However, it probably reinforced the idea that the only response to mob violence was military force. On October 4, seven sections in Paris called on their National Guard units to march on the Convention and managed to attract some 25,000 people. The 6,000 Convention's troops under Napoleon would defeat the rebels, but only after a pitched battle on October 5. Again there was an economic element to the discontent. A dry summer which reduced wheat production combined with the British blockade and army demands to keep food stocks low. Parisians had been forced to accept rationing.

Parisians were also beginning to accept the fact that the government was making mass demonstrations difficult to stage. Even before the Directory was installed on November 1, the machinery which made the sections independent military and political "outposts" in Paris was overhauled. On October 10, shortly after the failed coup, not only were the sectional assemblies abolished, but the National Guard units as well. The only armed units operating in Paris were to be those of the Parisian Guard, which took its orders from the government. The restructuring of government was combined with a new decisiveness. When Police Legion units mutinied in April 1796, 17 of the ringleaders were executed. An attempted Jacobin coup in September brought another 30 executions.

Such measures could not solve economic problems or eliminate the grumbling and complaints which followed, as in early 1796 when shortages once again were seen. However, they were effective at preventing that discontent from growing beyond grumbling to open rebellion - or in limiting the ways in which revolt could be expressed. Napoleon escaped death on December 24, 1800, only because the bomb intended for him exploded after his carriage had passed. If the plan was ambitious for targeting Napoleon, a bomb plot executed in secrecy was hardly evidence of political strength. If anything it was testimony to the effectiveness of government measures as well as to the loss of power of political opponents.

REVOLUTIONARY FRANCE AND THE RUSSIAN REVOLUTION

In 1795, Francois-Noël Babeuf began publishing a journal called *Le Tribun du peuple*, (The Tribune of the People). A lawyer prior to the Revolution, Babeuf, in 1796, suggested in his journal that property be abolished and that there be an equal distribution of goods. Taking the side of the poor, in what he called a war between the rich and poor, Babeuf both criticized the government and called for the Constitution of 1793. He not only proved to be a major public relations headache for the government with his critical attacks on policy, he proved to be an embarrassment to the authorities by eluding capture for a number of months. He would finally be convicted and guillotined in May 1797.

Babeuf, with his philosophy of equal distribution of goods, represented perhaps the first modern proponent of a communist philosophy, or at least the first eloquent one. Karl Marx would not publish his works until the middle of the Nineteenth Century. The reference Marx would make to the "dictatorship of the proletariat," would not come until 1875.[41] Babeuf certainly struck a popular chord with his writings. In fact, the political popularity of the idea has a long history - it can be seen even in ancient Athens and Rome. Perhaps the appeal lies, not so much in the specific idea that goods should be distributed equally, rather it lies in the underlying theme. Those who do the actual work, i.e., the laborers or craftsmen, are the real contributors in society, not the owners or managers.

Babeuf's writings represented a preliminary outline of the communist philosophy implemented by Lenin in Russia. Babeuf's philosophy was not the only similarity between the two regimes. Both faced similar problems - and both resorted to similar solutions. The Subsistence Commission established in October 1793 was one of the first government agencies established in an attempt to coordinate and centralize administration of supplies. While perhaps not as extensive in scope as the efforts of Stalin's government nearly a century and a half later, it did represent a form of central planning. France also exhibited the political tension between the urban unemployed and the agricultural producers in the countryside which Russia would see; a disproportionate amount of political power existed in Paris while economic power was held by the countryside. If the Parisian crowds exerted political pressure to supply food at low prices, that power was at war with powerful economic forces, not only in the country, but also in the market stalls of the vendors consumers bought their produce from.

Natural disasters in the 1790s, such as hail and drought, resulted in shortages - and competition. Competition for grain supplies took place, not only between countries, but also between cities and governmental agencies. Governmental attempts to fulfill their requirements caused disruption which spilled over into political unrest. The same problems, the same attempted solutions, and the same results would be seen in Russia later.

Comparisons with Russia aside, France provides strong evidence for a connection between shortage, unemployment, and violence, on the one hand, and a dictatorial response on the other. The governmental response involved not only restrictions on personal freedom, but an increased governmental involvement in the economy. Economic improvement eventually allowed the French political leadership to relax some of the most restrictive political measures. Russia, with a struggling economy, kept its dictatorial apparatus in place, almost to the end of the Soviet regime. With France as an introduction, the focus now shifts to Russia.

PART IV

THE TOTALITARIAN STATE

CHAPTER 9

RUSSIA AND THE OCTOBER REVOLUTION

On December 1, 1934, Sergei Kirov, a secretary of the Communist Central Committee, was fatally wounded by an assassin - shot in the back with a revolver - outside his office in Leningrad. Leonid Nikolaev, a young member of the Communist Party was arrested at the scene. Two of Nikolaev's friends would later confess to involvement in the murder as well. Stalin, after being notified by phone of the assassination, took a train from Moscow and arrived in Leningrad the next day to take charge of the investigation. During the investigation Stalin personally interrogated Nikolaev about the crime. The indictment handed down on December 27, named not only the three main conspirators, but also a group of party members, which the indictment called the "Leningrad Center." Following a brief trial, all those named in the indictment were executed on December 30.

Perhaps the two undisputed facts of the case are that Kirov was shot on December 1, 1934 and that those indicted on December 27 were executed on December 30. It also appears certain that Nikolaev was the actual gunman. What is in dispute is the extent of Stalin's involvement in the crime. By one account, Stalin, through his subordinates, actively planned Kirov's assassination. According to this version, Nikolaev had been detained, prior to the assassination, carrying a briefcase which contained a loaded pistol and a map of Kirov's routes. Although he was questioned by the deputy director of the Leningrad secret police, Ivan Zaporozhets, he was released, on instructions from Moscow. He was detained and ordered released on one, or possibly two, other occasions. On the day of the assassination, Zaporozhets arranged for Kirov's guard to be away from the scene of the attack. Kirov's bodyguard, Borisov, on the following day, was beaten to death on his way to talk to Stalin, although the death was staged to look like a traffic accident.[1]

Other versions either contradict some of the facts or provide alternative interpretations. Nikolaev had been detained by the police, but only once, and he had not been acting suspiciously. The revolver used in the crime had been owned since 1918, and legally registered twice. Zaporozhets, the deputy director of the NKVD, (People's Commissariat of Internal Affairs) who supposedly questioned Nikolaev and aided him in the plot, had never met Nikolaev, and in fact, had been absent from Leningrad in the months prior to the assassination.[2]

Whether Stalin was directly involved in the plot or not, he did not seem particularly distressed by Kirov's death. The fact that he acted quickly and in such a sweeping manner suggests, either that he participated in, or knew about, the plot, or that he had been planning some form of political repression prior to December 1, 1934. Kirov's death did provide a good excuse to institute a crackdown, which came with surprising speed. On the evening of December 1, the same day the assassination occurred, Stalin had a decree issued which called for speeding up investigations of those accused of "terrorist acts." Much of the appeals process was eliminated - executions were not to be delayed by appeals - and capital sentences were to be carried out immediately following sentencing.[3] The immediate result was the acceleration of investigations and an increase in the number of executions, even before those charged in Kirov's death had been tried. On December 5, 37 were executed. Throughout December, in different cities, Stalin's newest orders were carried out - 29 shot in Moscow, 39 in Leningrad, 28 in Kiev, and nine in Minsk.[4]

Stalin also had 19 political opponents arrested and charged. Their trial took place in January 1935. In contrast to the death sentences handed out in December, the January defendants received prison sentences. About the same time, a separate set of "trials" was being held by a special board of the NKVD. The defendants in these inquiries, Communist Party members, were also sentenced to prison. This group was not even charged with involvement in Kirov's killing, simply with membership in the Leningrad and Moscow Center. In addition to these investigations and trials, former noblemen and officers, together with their families, were ordered deported from Leningrad.

The Kirov trials of late 1934 and the political trials of early 1935 were only a prelude to the Great Purges of 1936-1938 and the show trials which took place in those years. Arrests for the 1936 trials came in June of that year. Kamenev and Zinoviev, two opposition Party leaders, were arrested. They had been among those charged at the January 1935 trial and sentenced to prison following that trial. The brief 1936 trial lasted from August 19 until August 24. The defendants publicly confessed to their crimes, implicating themselves, not only in the Kirov assassination, but also in plots to kill Stalin and other Party leaders. They had no defense counsel and their confessions were the only evidence introduced in the trial. Kamenev, Zinoviev, and the other 14 defendants were shot following the trial.

A 1937 trial took place in January, resulting in a sentence of death for 13 defendants. The 1938 trial, in which 22 were charged, lasted from March 2 until March 13. Most, but not all, were sentenced to death - shot on March 15. Recorded on film, the damning confessions of the accused, provided evidence for a wide range of crimes - sufficient, under Stalin's standards, for a conviction. The filmed record, with the defendants coming across at times as automatons, also reinforced the image of communism and Stalin as an evil philosophy with an ominously inhuman capacity to control human thought. The trials and executions in Moscow, though they caught the attention of the rest of the world, were not the only trials and killings which went on during the Great Purges. Outside Moscow and out of the limelight, Stalin's government eliminated more Party members or potential opposition.

From one perspective, the assassination of Sergei Kirov can be viewed as a significant watershed event, a sudden reversal of an otherwise "liberal" policy; from another, as just one of a series of events on the road to total dictatorship. December 1, 1934 was significant in that it either triggered the events which followed or at least represented the date on which increased political repression began. It has less significance when viewed in the overall context of political repression in the Soviet Union. The forced collectivization of agriculture, a policy which resulted in untold deaths, had been urged by Stalin in December of 1929, and implemented in the spring of 1930, some five years before Sergei Kirov's death. While Stalin perhaps perfected the political trial, he had not been the first to use it. In 1928, in what came to be known as the Shakhty case, the Party had formally charged 53 engineers and technicians in the coal industry with "wrecking." Wrecking was essentially a charge of sabotage, which could mean anything from deliberately setting off explosions to wasting materials. While many of the accused were sentenced to prison, five were actually executed. One difference in the conduct of the political trials was that, once Stalin had gained control, the proportion of those receiving a death sentence increased. Where the number of the accused receiving the death sentence was relatively small in the Shakhty case, the relationship was reversed after Stalin's rise. The majority of those accused were shot, a minority were sentenced to prison.

ORGANIZATION OF THE DISCUSSION OF THE SOVIET UNION

This chapter focuses narrowly on the events surrounding the October Revolution, the Bolshevik seizure of power in Russia in 1917. It is intended to be only a brief history of the seizure of power. Many writings about the Russian Revolution have concentrated on the events of 1917 and the question of 'why' the communists came to power. In some ways there has been an assumption that dictatorship was a foregone conclusion, once communism managed to gain a foothold in government. This book's focus, as noted in the introduction, is, not so much on how the communists managed to come to power, but on why they turned to dictatorship, once they had gained control. The discussion of Russia actually extends over eight chapters, covering the period from the Russian Revolution through World War II. This time period was one of violent upheaval and brutal repression. Russia, as it existed prior to the Civil War, is discussed in Chapter Ten, while the Civil War itself is covered in Chapter Eleven. Chapter Twelve discusses communist rule between 1921 and 1938. The Russian agriculture sector of the economy is covered in Chapters Thirteen and Fourteen, with the latter chapter focusing on collectivization. Chapters Fifteen and Sixteen look at Soviet industry and the Five-Year Plans. Finally, Chapter Seventeen analyzes the role of resources and scarcity in the development of the Soviet economy.

In an attempt to establish the relationship between scarcity and repression, the discussion has followed a logical order. The premise of this book is that scarcity will lead to violence, and violence will, in turn, lead to repression. One way to establish that theory is to look first at resources and then to look at any resulting violence and repression. Previous chapters have begun by looking at the availability of resources, then moved to a discussion of the presence or absence of violence. If there was repression it was viewed in the context of the level of violence. This chapter, while generally following that sequence, takes a somewhat different approach. If scarcity will ultimately lead to repression, it should be possible to look at the end result, repression, and to work backwards to find scarcity present. In other words, if there is evidence of governmental repression, then it would logically follow that the society suffers from a scarcity of resources. With that in mind, the discussion begins by looking at the severity of repression in the Soviet Union under Stalin.

What is discussed in this chapter is the repression which can be quantified, e.g., the number of executions or the number of people imprisoned. It is not a complete discussion or analysis. Repression obviously can take many forms. In its less severe forms, it can involve anything from government censorship of the press to restrictions on artistic expression. At its most sinister, it can involve murder and imprisonment. While there is some dispute as to the exact number of deaths which occurred under Bolshevik rule, there is no question that the number was extremely high.

THE NUMBER OF VICTIMS

The Soviet Union and communist regimes in general, have come to define the term "totalitarianism." Stalin's rule has also been characterized, with some justification, as diabolically evil. In analyzing any totalitarian form of government however, there is a danger in using such loaded terms. The argument cannot realistically be framed in absolutes such as good or evil. Even in the Soviet Union the extent or severity of repression has not remained the same. There have been periods of extreme repression and periods in which restrictions have been relaxed. In judging the totalitarian nature of Stalin's regime, the question which needs to be asked is a cold-blooded one - How repressive was the Soviet Union under the communists or during Stalin's time, in terms of the number of victims?

While there is some discrepancy in the numbers, depending on the source, the figures given are consistently high. A *Pravda* article by V. Kumanov gave the figure 353,074 as the number shot in 1937.[5] (Medvedev's figure is 353,680.)[6] Another author, V. Popov, gave the figure 328,618 as the number shot in 1938.[7] There is an anomaly if the figures for these two years are compared with those for 1936 and 1939. The year 1937 represented a sharp increase from 1936 and the year 1939 showed a sudden reduction in the number executed compared to 1938. In 1936 only 1,118 were shot and 2,552 in 1939.[8] (Medvedev's figure for 1936 is 1,116.)[9] There are conflicting figures for the total number of executions which occurred during Stalin's time versus the number which occurred under Communist rule as a whole. One figure for the entire period from 1921 to 1953, 642,980,[10] is lower than the number occurring during Stalin's time, 786,098, in the period from 1931 to 1953.[11] Some perspective on the numbers is given by Roy Medvedev, when he notes that there were times in Moscow when the number of executions was as high as 1,000 a day, during 1937-1938.[12]

The number of people imprisoned, by one estimate, was around 11.8 million for the period from 1930 to 1953. In 1955 the secret police would admit to having had files on 9.5 million people, although it was claimed that many of the detainees were, in fact, involved in criminal activity.[13] The accuracy of any estimate is difficult to gauge because the Soviet government, in addition to imprisonment, could also exile political opponents. While not formally sentenced to prison, such individuals would be considered to be victims of political repression.

The intentional repression which occurred under the Soviet system, as represented by the number of people executed or imprisoned, is the primary focus of this book. Communist leaders have also been blamed for the mistakes and general shortcomings of the Communist system, not simply for deliberate acts. One aspect of this debate has involved the number of "excess" deaths, i.e., the number of deaths above what would be considered a normal mortality rate for the Soviet Union. There is disagreement in this area. At the low end are estimates suggesting that between 4 and 11 million died. Other calculations place the figure at around 20 million, or even as high as 40 million.[14]

On the basis of the numbers, there is little doubt that Stalin's regime would be judged an extremely repressive one. If this book's thesis is correct, repression, ultimately, is caused by resource scarcity. Having preliminarily "established" the dictatorial nature of Stalin's rule, the next step is to look for proof of resource scarcity and violence. The key question is - Does the evidence suggest an extreme scarcity of resources?

OCTOBER 1917 - THE STORY OF THE OVERTHROW

The October Revolution of 1917 began, not with a grand assault, but with the taking of small strategic positions throughout Petrograd. On the night of October 24, 1917, members of the Bolshevik party took over guard duties at key posts throughout Moscow, simply by telling the members of the regular army to go home. The story of the October Revolution has come down to us in epic terms, enhanced in status by John Reed's *Ten Days That Shook the World*, as well as by later events. Actual events were somewhat less heroic. Lenin, the Bolshevik leader, spent most of the crucial last days before the revolt in disguise - hiding until his party had seized control. Instead of a grand assault there were several smaller attacks organized. They immediately fell apart when the attackers were fired on. The violent takeover of the government, for which the Bolsheviks received the most criticism in the West, involved only five deaths, some press releases, and the seizure of some undefended buildings. It was not an auspicious beginning.

On October 10, 1917 there had been a secret meeting of twelve members of the Bolshevik Central Committee, at the apartment of Nikolai Sukhanov in Petrograd (St. Petersburg). Lenin pushed for an immediate armed coup against the Provisional Government. While Lenin's push for immediate action was rejected, he nevertheless got 10 votes in favor of his plan. Implementation began on October 21-22. It involved an effort to gain control of the military garrison in and around Petrograd, which numbered some 245,000. The Bolsheviks in early October had created a Military-Revolutionary Committee, known as the Milrevkom, charged with the defense of Petrograd. The fact that it was not a formal part of the government did not deter the Bolsheviks from asserting its authority over the Petrograd garrison.

On the night of October 21-22, the Milrevkom sent a delegation to the headquarters of the Military Staff, demanding that the Military Staff cede part of its authority to the Milrevkom. The demand was rebuffed. The Military Staff countered with a demand that the Milrevkom retract its orders. The Milrevkom then attempted negotiation. While it did not win, the negotiation provided Kerensky's cabinet with hopeful signs of a compromise and they persuaded Kerensky not to arrest the Milrevkom.

Whether that decision was "the" fatal blunder for Kerensky or simply one of a series of mistakes, is not clear. He put off immediate decisive action in the apparent belief that his forces could deal with the Bolsheviks at any time. He had also earlier alienated many members of the military by accusing General Kornilov, one of Russia's military leaders, and other officers, of treason (August 1917). He and his cabinet took preliminary action on the night of October 23-24, when four newspapers were ordered shut down - two Bolshevik papers and two right-wing papers. However, his attempt to organize a military defense was inadequate. He would not formally request troops from the front until the evening of October 24, although government troops on hand were ordered to various strategic positions around Petrograd.

In defending the government, Kerensky was handicapped in two ways. First, governmental operations were dispersed, the bureaucratic mechanism was weak, and the lack of leadership by Kerensky and those around him was a demoralizing influence on those within the government. From a military perspective, there were simply too many positions to defend around Petrograd and it was not clear to the defenders why any single position was worth defending. Second, Kerensky needed an enemy - a serious threat around which he could rally his forces. The Bolsheviks however were slow to provide him with any clear target.

The Bolsheviks were, in fact, both the enemy and a serious threat. Kerensky's problem was that he could not make the case that they were either. For one thing, he had compromised himself in August by appealing to the Bolsheviks for help in his attempt to fight the "conspiracy" against him by the generals. Having served as allies in August, it was difficult to argue with any credibility that they were enemies in October. For their part, the Bolsheviks made few overt threats against his government, even while they were putting their plan to overthrow it into operation. When faced with direct opposition, they sought compromise and "negotiated." In public statements they asserted they were not attacking the government, but defending the Revolution.

In spite of Kerensky's indecisiveness, his military forces actually made the first decisive move in the escalating battle with the Bolsheviks. Just after midnight on the night of October 23-24, governmental units took up positions at the Winter Palace and moved to occupy other strategic positions around the city. They closed down the two Bolshevik papers, and, in an attempt to disrupt communications for the Bolshevik command structure, disconnected telephone lines to Smolnyi. The Bolsheviks had convened the Second Congress of Soviets there and the military no doubt felt cutting off communications would help to contain the coup. To prevent the physical movement of Bolshevik troops, bridges over the Neva were ordered raised.

While the Bolshevik response was decisive, the Bolsheviks continued to avoid any all out or direct confrontation. Their first "victory" was the reopening, on October 24, of the two papers shut down the previous night. The Central Telegraph Office and the

Russian Telegraphic Agency were then occupied. The Smolnyi telephone lines were restored. The Bolsheviks would now attempt to disrupt governmental communications by disconnecting telephone lines to the Winter Palace.

These first Bolshevik victories may have been small, but they provided sufficient encouragement for further action. The next confrontation was another victory - the bridges over the Neva were lowered on the afternoon of October 24. As evening wore on, Bolshevik forces expanded control. While the Winter Palace remained under government control, seemingly unimportant positions were occupied throughout the city. The Bolsheviks took over post offices, railroad stations, and telephone centers. This part of the takeover proved bloodless. Loyal troops obeyed orders simply to go home - even though the orders were given by the Bolsheviks. Those who did refuse were disarmed. Surprisingly, the headquarters of the Military Staff itself, located in the Engineers' Palace, had not been guarded. The Bolsheviks took this simply by walking in and taking over from those on duty. The Winter Palace however, was still in government hands at midnight on October 24.

It still had not fallen at 9 a.m. on October 25 when Kerensky slipped out of the building in a U.S. embassy car, intent on reaching the front lines and bringing regular troops back. With Kerensky gone, government forces now found something Kerensky had not supplied - a real enemy and something to defend of more importance than a railroad station.

Despite the near total control of Petrograd by the Bolsheviks on the morning of October 25, Lenin hesitated at making any official proclamation regarding the takeover. He wanted the government ministers under arrest - then he would announce that the Provisional Government had been deposed. The ministers, perhaps surprised by the seemingly total victory of the Bolsheviks, waited inside the Winter Palace. At dawn the Bolshevik forces made their first attempt to take it. They moved toward the Palace - until the defenders started shooting at them. The attackers quickly retreated.

At 10 a.m. Lenin officially proclaimed the Provisional Government deposed, although the government forces still held the Palace and the ministers were not under arrest. The situation had not changed by 2 p.m. when the Bolsheviks received reinforcements, in the form of 5,000 sailors from the nearby naval base at Kronstadt. A second assault was attempted. It too fell apart as soon as it received gunfire from the Palace. At 6:30 p.m., the Bolsheviks tried to bluff the ministers into surrender by issuing an ultimatum - if the Winter Palace was not surrendered, then the cruiser *Aurora*, anchored in the harbor, would open fire, along with the fortresses Peter and Paul. The ministers ignored the ultimatum. At 9 p.m. the Bolsheviks made good on their threat - or at least tried to. While the *Aurora* did open fire, it had no live rounds. So it fired a single salvo of blanks. The Peter and Paul fortresses began firing around 11 p.m.. While their guns did have live rounds, only two rounds actually managed to hit the Winter Palace, out of the 30 to 35 fired. The two rounds which did hit did very little damage. Some of the Red Guard, a Bolshevik militia force, managed to get inside the Winter Palace through an unguarded entrance. However, when some of the defenders met them and ordered them to surrender, they obeyed.

The defenders inside the Winter Palace were not demoralized by the attacks of the Bolsheviks, as inept and ineffective as they were. However, when it appeared that Kerensky's promised help would not arrive in the immediate future, the defenders began to leave. The Cossacks and officers withdrew, leaving only the Women's Death Battalion and some cadets as the last defenders. Either because there was no command structure left, or because the defenders were concentrated on other things, the crowds besieging the Palace managed to approach in the darkness without being fired upon. Eventually some were able to enter the Palace. The weight of numbers was sufficient against the now small force still resisting. Once in Bolshevik hands the mob began to loot what treasures were left there. The ministers, who had remained in the Palace, were finally arrested at 2:10 a.m. on October 26.

The "violent" overthrow of the Russian government for which the Bolsheviks have been condemned, has perhaps been associated most closely with the events in Petrograd. Yet that violence involved only five deaths. It was in Moscow where the first serious violence would occur in the opening days of the Revolution. In the Moscow fighting, the Bolsheviks would still embarrass themselves, as at Petrograd, yet they would also display some of the determination which the Russian army would later show at Stalingrad and in other battles fought against the Nazi armies during the Second World War. The fighting in Moscow in the first days of the October Revolution would be house-to-house. In contrast to Bolshevik actions at Petrograd, where a few shots were enough to cause retreat, in Moscow they maintained a relentless assault.

The arrest of the ministers at the Winter Palace in Petrograd, had occurred just after 2 a.m. on the morning of October 26. Just four hours before that, in Moscow, at 10 p.m., the Moscow Revolutionary Committee (MRC) issued a statement that the Moscow garrison should only follow orders given by the Revolutionary Committee. The order had no legal effect, but the tactic of issuing such a statement had successfully confused those in charge at Petrograd. The next morning (October 26), the Revolutionary Committee moved to secure the Kremlin, the fortress in central Moscow. Two commissars appeared at the fortress, ordering the troops to hand over command. Since one of the commissars was the commanding officer of the troops stationed there, they obeyed. The plan was to distribute the weapons stored there to the Red Guard.

In contrast to Kerensky's actions at Petrograd, government leaders in Moscow were not caught completely off guard by the maneuverings of the Bolsheviks. The Socialist Revolutionary Party (SR), while a left-wing party, opposed the actions the Bolsheviks had taken at Petrograd. The SR leader in Moscow, V. V. Rudnev, began reporting to the Moscow Duma, one of the representative assemblies, what was happening in Petrograd, on October 25. One part of his report also referred to actions the Bolsheviks had taken in Moscow itself - the seizure of the post and telegraph offices. His report, and the more determined Moscow opposition to Bolshevik actions, provided support for the formation of the Committee of Public Security, intended to counter the Bolsheviks, at least in Moscow. A military force was assembled, which included cadets from the Moscow military academies.

Even as Rudnev put his defensive plans into operation, the Bolsheviks were moving. The October 26 attempt to gain the Kremlin was only one part of their plan. They had also moved in the outlying districts, where they were successful in gaining control. It was, in fact, to arm the workers that the attempt to take over the Kremlin was made. The Bolsheviks were thwarted in their plan to distribute the arms stored in the Kremlin by the arrival of the Committee of Public Security troops, who surrounded the Kremlin. The resulting stalemate caused both sides to enter into negotiations. Colonel K. I. Riabtsev, in charge of the SR forces, was expecting reinforcements and hoped to reduce the number of defenders inside the Kremlin. He did get the MRC to agree to withdraw one of the regiments inside the Kremlin, in return for which he agreed to withdraw his own forces. While reinforcements had been sent, few arrived to help Riabtsev - the Bolsheviks were able to persuade enough among them not to involve themselves.

The stalemate lasted through most of the day on October 27. Concluding that no further reinforcements could be expected, toward evening, Riabtsev ordered his forces to take up positions around the Kremlin. Fighting erupted after the forces were in position, resulting in heavy casualties. Riabtsev managed to secure the surrender of the Kremlin the next morning by telephoning those inside and convincing the defenders that the rest of Moscow was in the hands of the SR forces and that he would use artillery against the Kremlin if there was no surrender.

Despite this victory, the government hesitated. The MRC leadership was not arrested. Still hoping for regular reinforcements, the government tried further negotiation. The Bolsheviks, while negotiating, moved to recover their losses. The soldiers who had been forced from the Kremlin, began an effort to take the center of Moscow. They did not organize an all out assault. Instead they began fighting the government forces street by street, gradually pushing them back. Each side numbered around 15,000 soldiers. A 24-hour cease-fire was arranged, starting at midnight on October 29. Both sides expected reinforcements. Government reinforcements did not come. The Bolsheviks, in contrast, were able to call on surrounding towns for help. At midnight on October 30, they felt strong enough to resume fighting and broke off the cease-fire. For the next three days they would battle the loyalist soldiers in house-to-house fighting. The battle ended on November 2, when the Committee of Public Safety ordered its forces to surrender.

With only two cities under their control, the Bolsheviks did not have control of Russia. Gaining control of Petrograd and Moscow, as major political centers and sources of symbolic power, carried the Bolsheviks a long way toward that goal, however. At the same time, they had no government apparatus in place to take over other areas. The ability to physically assert control was limited, since he regular army was still fighting the German army. On the other hand, the use of force, in governing Russia was not really necessary in 1917. Much of the populace was indifferent. They were not that concerned about the fall of the Provisional Government, indifferent to the rise of the Bolsheviks.

Conventional wisdom in the West has it that the Russian people were "fooled" into supporting the Bolsheviks because they would not reveal their true intentions until after they had seized power - suggesting that the peasants would have marched on Moscow at the time, if they had known what was going on. It is true that the communists were not exactly forthcoming about their plans. While they had general goals, they provided no specific details or concrete plans. The term "socialism" was not a popular one and Bolsheviks purposely avoided using it in their first public statements. In fact they tried to give the impression that the overthrow of the Provisional Government was nothing more than a routine transfer of political power.

The control of Petrograd and Moscow, while it did not establish control of Russia as a whole, did provide a crucial foothold. In the period immediately following the October coup, the Bolsheviks acted to consolidate their power in the regions surrounding those two cities, as well as to begin to extend power to more distant regions. Consolidation in the Moscow and Petrograd area involved direct force, combined with coercive threats, while attempts at expanding long-term power in other areas involved a public relations battle and the use of political persuasion.

The disarray and seeming disorganization displayed by the Bolsheviks at Petrograd stood in sharp contrast to the discipline and effectiveness their forces would show in the regions nearby. All of Estonia came under Bolshevik control on October 27 when the Bolsheviks removed the Provisional Government representatives from power. Bolshevik infantry units from Latvia were ordered into the towns of Wenden, Wolmar, Walk, and Iuriev. The town of Walk was similarly taken over by military forces and the Second Congress of Soviets of Latvia in mid-November recognized the new Bolshevik regime as the legitimate power in Latvia.

CONSOLIDATION OF POWER - NOVEMBER 1917 - MAY 1918

The beginning of the Revolution can be dated to the events of October 24, when the Bolsheviks moved to take over Petrograd. The end of the Revolution is more difficult to determine. The Russian Civil War and the revolution would not be over until 1921 - it took that long for the Bolsheviks to achieve victory and to gain control of Russia. In another sense, the Bolsheviks achieved legitimacy on November 2, 1917, when the Provisional Government ordered its forces to lay down their arms and surrender the Kremlin. What occurred between 1917 and 1921 was the reaction of a government which had already achieved power.

In January 1918 the Bolsheviks seem to have been sufficiently in control to say that the first phase of the revolution was over. On January 5, a march was held in Petrograd, intended both to show support for the newly elected Constituent Assembly as well as opposition to Bolshevik policies. Troops, armed with rifles and machine guns, opened fire on the marchers, not once, out of panic, but several times. Between eight and 21 people were killed. In hindsight, it is not so much the fact that Bolshevik forces were bold enough to fire on unarmed demonstrators which is surprising, instead it is the lack of any real reaction. While condemned, the killings did not spark any activity on the part of the opposition.

The first indication of what Bolshevik government would be like came on October 27, 1917, when Lenin, without formal governmental approval, issued a Decree on the Press, which outlawed opposition newspapers. The measure was clearly aimed at the non-Bolshevik press, although by July of 1918, Lenin would also turn it against Bolshevik papers which criticized the government. A more far-reaching action was taken on November 4. In spite of Lenin's outlawing of opposition newspapers, there were a number of legislative and procedural safeguards in place which restricted his ability to enact laws. On October 26, Lenin had set up a Council of People's Commissars (Sovnarkom) which was the Bolshevik equivalent of the old Provisional Government. Sovnarkom was intended to be only a temporary body, which would govern until an elected Constituent Assembly was in place. Lenin was persuaded to act as president. An important legislative restriction on Sovnarkom was oversight by the Congress of Soviets, and by the Central Executive Committee, a body which included non-Bolsheviks. What Lenin wanted was the elimination of this oversight. In order to achieve this, he needed to persuade a majority of the members of the Central Executive Committee to give up this power. At a November 4 meeting, the preliminary vote was tied at 23-23. Lenin and Trotsky, who had no right to vote, announced that they were voting anyway and carried the motion with their two votes, 25-23. Sovnarkom was now free to issue decrees, without fear of having them reversed.

The first serious threat to the new government came, not so much from the defeated military forces of the opposition, but from civil servants in Moscow and Petrograd. They went on strike. While the Bolsheviks may have thought that the physical occupation of strategic positions alone would give them power, they soon found that the ability to keep those facilities in service was almost as important. The strike began in the governmental ministries. Instead of direct confrontation with the Bolshevik ministers, they used the opposite course of action - they went home. While the Bolsheviks issued orders there was no one to obey them. The strike spread from government agencies to other institutions. First, telephone and telegraph workers, then pharmacists, water transport workers, and schoolteachers joined the strike.

The most serious of the work stoppages involved the state financial institutions. The State Bank and State Treasury refused to honor requests for funds drawn by the Sovnarkom. The Bolsheviks first tried threats to obtain money. On October 30, private bank directors were threatened with arrest if they refused to honor Sovnarkom checks and drafts. The Bolshevik Commissar of Finance, V. R. Menzhinskii, on November 7 attempted to intimidate the State Bank by bringing a group of armed sailors and demanding a million rubles. For some reason he brought along a military band as well. Bank officials again refused to give him the money. Again on November 11 he tried the same tactic, using more troops. Once more the bank refused his request. On November 14, State Bank employees defiantly voted to continue the strike. At the State Treasury, a similar vote by the staff resulted in a decision to deny the Sovnarkom funds. The Bolsheviks lost patience on November 17 when Menzhinskii and his troops forced officials at the State Bank to open the vaults. Menzhinskii then appropriated 5 million rubles. While the resistance of the financial institutions was only one way in which anti-Bolshevik feelings were displayed, it was the reason Lenin would create the Cheka, the security police, on December 7, 1917.

Ironically, the Bolsheviks finally were able to break the strike by resorting to management methods more expected from their capitalist foes - they offered promotions to staff members who would agree to work for Sovnarkom. Combined with the physical occupation of buildings and the firing of uncooperative directors and managers the tactic brought some stability to governmental operations. The end of the strike would not come until January 1918. Its end however, meant the elimination of a small, but important, roadblock in the control of the Russian government. There were still legal obstacles to full control which remained. One of these was the Constituent Assembly.

The Provisional Government, in August, had called for elections for a new Constituent Assembly, to be held on November 12, 1917. While the Bolsheviks attempted to make it difficult for other parties to campaign, they nevertheless allowed the elections to take place, perhaps in the belief that they could win. They provided no specific details of their plans, relying instead on a more general appeal to the solidarity of the workers and on Lenin's belief that the SR members would defeat themselves. The appeal was unsuccessful, although the Bolsheviks, even with such a vague plan, did manage to come in second. Voter turn-out was high. In the countryside, voting percentages were as high as 80, even as high as 97 percent. In the capital cities, it reached 70 percent. Voting was by secret ballot.[15] When the voting was over on November 19, the SR's had captured 17,864,000, or 40 %, while the Bolsheviks received 10,649,000, for 23.9%. The Kadet Party received 2,099,000, or 4.7% and the Mensheviks received 1,158,000, or 2.3%.[16]

Despite the direction of popular opinion the results indicated, the Bolsheviks decided to challenge the results and to obstruct their implementation. Their first tactic was to postpone the originally scheduled November 28 meeting date for the Assembly. They charged that there had been abuses in the election procedures. When the Electoral Commission refused to hand over its files to Sovnarkom, the commissioners were arrested. When released from prison on November 28, they continued meeting, in defiance of M. S. Uritskii, the newly appointed Bolshevik head of the Electoral Commission. However Uritskii ordered the meeting place surrounded with larger and larger contingents of armed troops. The most decisive action was the outlawing of the Constitutional-Democratic Party. This was followed on November 28 by Lenin's order to arrest the leaders of the Kadet Party. While most were released later, two were murdered in the prison hospital by Bolshevik sailors.

Opposition to the Bolsheviks now grew more determined and serious, yet it also had a naive aspect. An extremist SR faction tried to assassinate Lenin on January 1, 1918, but the attempt was bungled and only succeeded in wounding slightly someone who was riding with Lenin. The assassination attempt was the more serious side of opposition. The naive side showed itself on January 5, 1918, the day the Constituent Assembly was scheduled to convene. Opposition leaders had called for a march and demonstration in Petrograd against Bolshevik policies and intended to show support for the Assembly. The naivety was not evidenced in the demonstrations themselves, but by the belief that mere shows of popular opposition would be enough to persuade the Bolsheviks to change policy. The Bolsheviks stationed troops armed with rifles and machine guns along the route of the march. There was more than one route the marchers intended to take. As the main march reached one intersection there were cheers for the Constituent Assembly - at which point the troops fired. While some demonstrators fell, the march nevertheless continued, and was fired on again as it proceeded. Other marches were similarly attacked. It is not known how many were killed - between eight and 21.[17] Fear of popular reaction may account, in part, for the fact that the soldiers were so easily provoked. Lenin apparently was unsure whether his forces could withstand a determined action by his opponents.

In spite of the promise which the election results held for democracy, the Constituent Assembly would last barely one day. Its one and only session opened at 4 p.m. on January 5, 1918 and was dissolved by the Bolsheviks sometime after midnight on the same day. The Bolsheviks, almost by sheer will and boldness, prevented the opposition from mounting any force effective enough to reverse the action. Neither the killings nor the decision to dissolve the Assembly provoked any determined national outburst. The Bolsheviks benefitted from several circumstances. First, there was no united opposition or single opposition party. What opposition leadership there was could not decide on a single plan or even to offer an alternative. Second, the opposition leadership seemed universally opposed to the use of force. Even when soldiers offered assistance to defend the Constituent Assembly, it was turned down.[18] Third, the majority of Russians were not committed to any great extent to the government represented by the Constituent Assembly.

By January 5, the best opportunities for toppling Lenin and his government had been lost. This chapter has provided a brief look at the events of the October Revolution. The next chapter looks at the political situation in Russia prior to the Revolution. The Bolshevik Revolution did not topple the Czar rather it brought down the Provisional Government. The Czar had handed over power in February 1917 to the Provisional Government. Two major questions are, why the Czar had felt compelled to relinquish power, and why the Provisional Government lasted for only a short time.

CHAPTER 10

1917 - BACKGROUND TO REVOLT

The Empress Alexandra would always be convinced that her husband, Czar Nicholas II, would not have abdicated if she had been with him when he was making the decision. Nicholas had had to contend with a mutiny of the soldiers in Petrograd, which began on February 26, 1917. Although control of Petrograd was almost completely lost, Nicholas became convinced that the rest of Russia was in revolt and irretrievably lost as well. He was not helped by the fact that the generals he listened to painted a gloomy picture of the situation. So, on March 2, he gave up the throne. On his abdication, power passed to what had been the Provisional Committee of the Duma. It would become the Provisional Government. It was the Provisional Government which the Bolsheviks would topple in October. Russia, in 1917, would thus experience two revolutions, one in February, the other in October.

The general view of the Bolshevik takeover is that, by some combination of fanaticism, trickery, and force, the Bolsheviks managed to subvert the popular will. Democratic forces, which would have provided a peaceful transition from Czarist rule to Western-style democracy and a free market economic system, were defeated by the totally ruthless actions of the Bolsheviks. In essence, the Russian people were tricked by noble-sounding ideas, which were totally at odds with the real plans of the Bolsheviks. In popular myth, the idealistic society promised by communist ideology proved so unworkable in practice that the 'dictatorship of the proletariat,' suggested by Marx could only be imposed by force. The free-market interpretation is that the Bolsheviks' major error was in suppressing the free market. The Bolsheviks chose to ignore human nature and the importance of the profit motive in the operation of political and economic systems. Individuals are motivated by profit, not idealism.

There is a good deal of truth in these popular interpretations. As to trickery, the Bolsheviks clearly lied when it suited them. In that they were not that different as politicians than others before or since. The charge that they used force to maintain control is also true. Lenin, the same "leader" who snuck around Petrograd in disguise while his followers were on the streets, was involved in giving the orders to the soldiers who fired on the unarmed demonstrators on January 5, 1918. Yet, even conceding these points, questions still remain regarding what happened in 1917.

The first question relates to the viability of the Bolsheviks as a political party. Assuming that there was dissatisfaction with the Provisional Government, how was it that the Bolsheviks, among all possible alternatives, were the party which was successful in achieving power? The second question involves really two separate, but related questions - what caused the growth of an opposition sufficiently strong and dissatisfied to force the Czar to consider abdicating? The related question is why, after only eight months in office, did the Provisional Government find itself without sufficient popular support to continue in office? Events suggest that, despite its good, i.e., democratic, intentions, the Provisional Government found the problems more difficult to solve than anticipated.

The first question - why the Bolsheviks? - has provided a number of possible scenarios. The Western perception is that they were ruthless fanatics who played by no rules. Democratic forces lost because they naively "played by the rules" while the communists used deception when the rules did not suit them and were not averse to using force when other methods failed. There is a good deal of truth in that charge. At the same time, the underlying assumption is that the Bolsheviks had almost no support at all. While the Bolsheviks were not the majority party, they did manage to gain 23 percent of the popular vote in the November elections for the Constituent Assembly. In addition, they managed to gain the support of a large number of troops, a crucial body of supporters.

A related assumption is that the Bolsheviks were fanatical believers in communist ideology. Communism was not simply a set of political ideas, it was a form of religion, a rival even to Christianity. While the Bolshevik leadership did hold strong beliefs in the rightness of its cause, this does not account for the substantial following among workers and soldiers. The likely cause of Bolshevik success is probably much simpler. In its basic form the core belief was that the rich were to blame for the problems of the Russian worker. The appeal of communism lay in an easily grasped concept - a 'conspiracy of capitalists' was to blame for all problems.

Apart from that anti-wealth message, a more basic explanation for Bolshevik success has nothing to do with philosophy, rather it has to do with practicality. Ultimately, some group would emerge on top, after all the political battles were over. The Bolsheviks just happened to be that party. It might be more accurate to say, not so much that the Bolsheviks won, but that the most ruthless group within their ranks won. Not every communist member supported the actions Lenin took. Victory required a measure of ruthlessness combined with political savvy, which they had. The various SR factions shared the anti-rich theme of the Bolsheviks, but they lacked the ruthlessness necessary to seize and maintain power.

There is one other element which has been often overlooked. Because the West has attributed an inhuman religious zeal to communists, it has been assumed that communist leadership was somehow immune to the attractions of power. Critics of communism seem to suggest that the Bolsheviks had some evil plan in place which guided them in the direction of Stalinism, even before the October Revolution had begun. A much less sinister interpretation is that, once in power, Bolsheviks succumbed to the temptations of power - and for reasons which had more to do with human nature than with communist philosophy. There is no reason to believe that the adage 'power corrupts, and absolute power corrupts absolutely,' did not apply to the Bolsheviks. What made the Bolsheviks different from the other SR parties was that, having tasted power, they did not want to relinquish it. It may explain why Lenin, who had been philosophically committed to helping the common laborer, would not only allow his troops to fire on unarmed workers on the afternoon of January 5, 1918, but would order them to do so.

The first part of this chapter focuses on events and conditions in Russia, from as far back as 1904 until the Czar's abdication in March 1917. The second section looks at events between March and October 1917 It is intended to provide a more in-depth explanation for the Bolshevik takeover. The third part looks at the political institutions which existed in Russia at the time. It has been asserted that Russia has no experience with democracy. It appears that there actually existed democratic institutions within the Russian system and more experience with the concept of democracy than such statements suggest.

THE END OF THE RUSSIAN MONARCHY

In order to understand what led to the abdication of Czar Nicholas on March 2, 1917, it is helpful to go back to events in 1904 and 1905. In December 1904, the dismissal of four workers at a factory in St. Petersburg led to a sympathy strike throughout St. Petersburg which would involve as many as 120,000 workers. At the time the Czar was viewed as somewhat of a benevolent monarch to whom the workers could appeal for help. The workers scheduled a procession to the Winter Palace which was to take place on Sunday, January 9, 1905. They hoped to present Czar Nicholas with a petition. The petition both listed worker grievances and asked for political changes. While the Czar was fully aware of the march, he felt that the police measures for controlling the crowd would be adequate and left the city the night before. When the march began, army soldiers had been posted at various points along the route to direct the crowd. While the crowd was primarily intent on marching to the Palace, many disregarded orders to turn back. When warning shots failed to disperse the crowds, the soldiers fired directly into the marchers. Some 200 people were killed and around 800 injured, although newspaper reports put the total number at around 4,600.[1] The incident became known as Bloody Sunday.

Bloody Sunday ignited the rest of Russia. There were protest meetings and additional factories went out on strike. A student walkout at the universities resulted, in March 1905, in a government-ordered closure of schools for the rest of the academic year. Demonstrations at other cities and confrontations with troops caused further deaths and injuries: 70 killed by troops at Riga in January; 93 killed in Warsaw; and around 2,000 killed, another 3,000 injured in Odessa in June.[2]

One result of the unrest was a decision, formally signed on February 18 by Nicholas, to create a representative assembly which would advise him on legislation. Like Louis XVI in France, prior to the outbreak of the Revolution, Nicholas found himself in a dilemma. Nicholas saw the assembly as more of a gesture to those demanding participatory democracy - a means of showing a public commitment to representative government without having to concede power. Nicholas' vision of the body was that of an advisory cabinet. However, like Louis, Nicholas found that, having agreed to the idea, he lost all control over its direction. Meetings throughout Russia pushed not for a mere advisory cabinet, but for a fully representative body which could draft legislation. The Czar was no doubt surprised when even the peasants got involved, sending him 60,000 petitions.[3]

On August 6, 1905, Nicholas released his proposal for the new body in a document which was called the Bulygin Constitution. It was the first formal statement about the State Duma, as the new representative body was called. Nicholas' interpretation was that it was to be merely an advisory body. Unfortunately, while it was perhaps the first Czarist concession that democratic representatives could play any role in decisions of the monarchy, it was a compromise which did not satisfy the opposition. The opposition, beginning with university students, developed the idea of pressuring the Czar for more concessions, and the strike was chosen as the instrument. Russia, in September and October, was once again hit with a wave of strikes. Most serious was a work stoppage of the railroad workers, which came in October, followed by stoppages by communication and service workers. By October 14, not only had the strike successfully halted rail traffic and telegraph communications, it had also virtually shut down the capital, St. Petersburg.

Nicholas wavered between bringing in the military to restore order and granting further concessions. The Czar opted for concessions and, on October 17, 1905, signed what became the October Manifesto which granted the new Duma the power to approve legislation. While it did not actually create a constitution, the concessions granted gave the impression that it had. The October Manifesto, on the surface, calmed some of the political waters, while creating other problems. Sergei Witte, Chairman of Nicholas' Council of Ministers, found it difficult to recruit cabinet members. Liberal opposition leaders were afraid that any participation in the government would compromise them with their followers. At the other extreme, Witte found that Nicholas and his supporters were reluctant to support him, out of distrust of the unwelcome democratic restrictions imposed on the Czar.

The difficulty in forming a working cabinet was the least of Nicholas' political problems. The mere fact that the Czar even issued the October Manifesto infuriated monarchists and right-wing parties, who felt that the Czar's authority should not be subject to any restrictions. On October 18, Jews throughout Russia were attacked in a series of pogroms - 500 Jews are said to have died in Odessa. Students and intellectuals were also attacked. In fact, anyone wearing eyeglasses ran the risk of being attacked, because glasses were associated with the hated intellectuals.[4]

Whether Nicholas actively encouraged his monarchist followers, he probably took some satisfaction in their actions. In any event, his failure to act decisively to curb his supporters, contributed to problems in the countryside. The peasants saw government complicity in attacks on Jews as tacit approval of attacks on landlords in general, who the peasants came to associate with the Jews. Surprisingly, much of the peasant violence was aimed at the land and property of the landlord, and few landlords were actually killed. The goal was primarily to drive the landlords off the land. To that end peasants largely confined their activities to the destruction of farm machinery and the non-payment of rent. While the number of deaths was small, the peasant outbreaks were not confined to a single outburst. Almost as soon as Nicholas issued his October Manifesto the peasant attacks began. Winter stopped the attacks, but they began again in the spring of 1906, resumed again in 1907, and even continued into 1908, when the government finally put an end to them.

While peasant unrest turned into a long-term expression of rural grievances, opposition to the government came into the open soon after the October Manifesto. The Moscow Soviet voted for an armed revolt against the Czar with the avowed goal of establishing a democratic republic. This time the Czar responded by calling in the army, which attacked on December 9, 1905. By the time the insurrection was over the death toll was above 1,000.

In spite of the disruptions, the implementation of the October Manifesto proceeded at a relatively fast pace. Whatever objections Nicholas had, he moved quickly. His advisers were given the task of coming up with a draft of what were called "Fundamental Laws," a more acceptable term for the constitution which Nicholas impliedly had promised in October. The final draft was completed and made public on April 26, 1906. It provided for a two-chamber parliament, consisting of a State Council, the upper chamber, and the State Duma, the lower chamber. The State Council was intended to be under the control of the Czar, with positions being filled by appointment of the Czar. The State Duma was an elected body, although Nicholas weighted the voting power so as to give wealthy landowners more power. The Czar could veto proposals of the Duma. While in theory the parliament had to approve the state budget, many expenditure items were not considered to be part of the budget. The Fundamental Laws represented a major concession to pressure for democratic reforms, however there was one provision which allowed for the passage of emergency measures. Article 87, as it was known, was in essence a ready tool for imposing martial law, if the Duma was not in session, or was not compliant enough.

The Duma's term was legally set at five years, although it was subject to dismissal by the Czar. Nicholas dissolved the First Duma on July 8, 1906, less than three months after its April 27 opening. The Second Duma would be convened on February 20, 1907 and sent home on June 2, 1907. Apparently Nicholas found the Third Duma, which convened on November 7, 1907, to be pliant enough, since it managed to survive until the end of its five-year term, in 1912. The Fourth Duma would officially convene on November 15, 1912. The Fourth Duma would last until March 1917, when, by agreement, whatever power it held was transferred to the newly formed Provisional Government.

THE IMPACT OF THE FIRST WORLD WAR

When the Fourth Duma opened in 1912, the political and economic situation in Russia was a good deal better than in 1905. Agricultural yields had been good and industrial production had been growing. While Russia's economy could be described as adequate for her normal economic stability, it was inadequate to support a war.

In April 1915 the Russian army was positioned in what is now Poland, facing a buildup of German forces. On April 15 the Germans began their offensive with an artillery barrage that devastated the Russian lines. By the time the German advance was

175

over in September, the Russians had abandoned the territory of Poland and Lithuania to the Germans. The retreat brought political problems for Nicholas. There was a feeling among the political leadership that part of the problem with the army's performance could be attributed to poor management. The members of the Duma wanted greater control over the conduct of the war. They pushed for another concession from the Czar - the power to appoint ministers - a power not granted under the 1906 laws. In return the Duma would support Nicholas.

The Duma had adjourned on January 9, 1915, before the German offensive had begun. The retreat of the Russian army in the face of the German assault however, convinced Nicholas to call the Duma back on July 19. Perhaps encouraged by the fact that Nicholas had felt compelled to recall the parliament, its members began to push for more concessions. Discussions were had until August 25, when the Progressive Bloc came out with a nine-point program which, in effect, gave the Duma control of the government. Actions by government officials would be subject to legal review and political prisoners were to be freed. While it did not seek specific power to appoint ministers, it did ask that Nicholas appoint ministers who the nation had confidence in.

The most serious obstacle to the proposals came from Nicholas. His ministers, in fact, were willing to step down. Nicholas however, was persuaded to adjourn the Duma on September 3, the date on which the special session would come to an end. He was apparently convinced that the concessions granted in 1905 had been a mistake. A confrontation was avoided when the German offensive ended in September and the push for governmental changes relaxed.

The end of the German offensive seemed to end Russia's problems at the front in 1915. However, a new set of problems arose at home which took the place of the problems at the front. In the fall of 1915 Russian cities began to experience food shortages. The shortages were coupled with the beginnings of inflation. Many of the problems could be traced to the war. The Russian economy was such however, that the impact of the war was felt differently depending on the section of the economy. It was the cities that took the brunt of the economic problems associated with shortage and inflation. The agricultural sector, paradoxically benefitted. While the cities, on the inflation side, paid more for food, the peasant producers were the recipients of the higher payments. Shortages which would normally be expected as a result of war were compounded by the way in which market forces operated in Russia. It had been more economical, prior to the war, for the region around St. Petersburg to obtain coal from England rather than from the southern regions of Russia. The German control of the sea lanes restricted this route, cutting off fuel supplies to the north.[5]

In spite of these problems, Russia managed to get through the winter of 1915-16 and through most of 1916. In the fall of 1916 however, the continuing shortages were more seriously impacting the cities, particularly Moscow and Petrograd. Both received only one-third of their food requirements. A fuel shortage in Petrograd meant that, even when there was flour, the bakeries lacked the fuel to bake it. In one sense the shortages did not directly cause Nicholas to abdicate; in another sense they were the crucial catalyst. In combination with other forces, the shortages proved too much for the Czar.

The Duma was scheduled to reconvene on November 1, 1916. Its members were ready to directly confront the Czar, not only over the government's handling of the war, but also over the power of the Duma. Nicholas' agreement to even set up the Duma had been a major political accomplishment in 1905 or 1906. In 1916, the members of the Duma were not content with the limited role assigned to them by the Czar. Whether they were justified in their belief or not, opposition members of the Duma became convinced, by September and October, that economic conditions in Petrograd had become so intolerable that there was likely to be some violent outburst, unless the Duma could somehow gain control. Their conviction was so strong that they were willing to accuse Boris Stürmer of treason, even though they knew the charges to be false. Stürmer, then-Chairman of the Council of Ministers, was not helped by his German surname. Nicholas, thinking he could appease the Duma, dismissed Stürmer on November 8. This victory did not satisfy the opposition, which became more strident in its criticism of the government. Nicholas however, would not dissolve the Duma, despite the criticism. The verbal attacks, in themselves, had no effect on the Czar's official powers. However, they seemed to contribute to a growing paralysis and isolation on the part of Nicholas. Nicholas had dismissed the First Duma in 1906 after only two months because it opposed him. In contrast, in October 1916 Nicholas response to attacks on the crown was to stop reading the daily newspapers.

The rebellion by members of the Duma represented the formal political opposition to the Czar. He also had to face the problems which the shortages created among ordinary citizens of Petrograd. An extremely cold winter wreaked havoc with transport and food supplies in Petrograd. The only benefit for the Czar was that it kept people inside. However, the shortages became so severe that, in February 1917, when it was rumored the government might impose rationing, people ventured out to buy what food they could find in stores. The shortages created a tense atmosphere, which showed itself in seemingly small ways - there was pushing and shoving in food lines and the large number of people quickly bought up what supplies were available. The size of the crowds was increased by the closure of factories as a result of fuel shortages.

Believing the discontent was not serious enough to threaten his regime, Nicholas left Petrograd for Mogilev on February 22. On February 23 Petrograd authorities had to deal with a socialist march organized around International Women's Day. Warm weather increased the number of people out on the streets. The ranks of the marchers were further swelled by striking workers protesting food shortages. The numbers were perhaps as high as 128,000. February 23 passed however, without violent confrontation.[6]

The next day continued warm weather brought more people out, perhaps as many as 200,000. Clashes began to occur between workers and police. Government authorities did not attempt any crackdown; the Cossack troops, the backbone of the Czar's guard, were present, but did nothing. Food stores were invaded by the crowd. Continued warm weather on February 25 brought more people out, perhaps as many as 300,000, and more confrontations with police. The violence began to escalate. Three marchers were killed near a shopping center and a police officer was beaten to death. The Czar cabled that evening that military forces should be used to put down the unrest. The authorities issued warnings which outlawed street gatherings, to go into effect the next day. During the night, police stations were attacked in some sections of Petrograd.

Whether the crowds took the announced measures seriously or not, they congregated on the streets on February 26, in spite of the presence of armed military units. At Znamenskii Square the first real confrontation occurred. Forty people were killed when troops opened fire.[7] It was not the only killing. Units elsewhere also fired on crowds. It was sufficient to convince many to go home. While the shootings may have convinced the crowds to leave, they also had a demoralizing effect on other soldiers.

Members of the Pavlovskii Regiment, when informed of the Znamenskii Square massacre, removed rifles from storage and took to the streets, intent on stopping the killing. When they received no support from other units, they returned to their barracks and their leaders were arrested. Nevertheless, their action persuaded other members of the regiment to refuse further orders to fire on civilians. By the morning of February 27, more soldiers, three regiments, in fact, took to the streets. One regiment killed one of its own officers. The mutinous troops then attacked police barracks and commandeered armored cars. Some released prisoners held in the Peter and Paul fortress, while others took over the Ministry of the Interior. Policemen were beaten to death and mobs looted shops and restaurants.

The situation in Petrograd had clearly gotten out of control. It may not have been the actual loss of control which worked against Nicholas. It may have been as much the perception of the loss of control and total hopelessness which political leaders conveyed to Nicholas. The members of the Duma and Nicholas' cabinet and many leading political figures, combined to persuade Nicholas that it was time for him to step down. On February 28, Nicholas began a train journey from Mogilev to Tsarskoe, where his wife was staying. He did not return to Petrograd. On March 1 Nicholas' train had only reached Pskov, army headquarters for the Northern Front. The commanding general, N. V. Ruzskii, had become convinced that the Czar should either grant greater power to the Duma or step down. On March 2 Nicholas was persuaded that the best course would be to step down. Before his abdication however, he took one last official action which confused the political situation. He ordered the Duma to adjourn.

The decision to adjourn the Duma split its membership. In September and October of 1916, many in the Duma had opposed the Czar and argued that the Duma should replace Nicholas. Now that the Duma had been adjourned however, some felt there was no legal basis for its assuming power - without some formal transfer of power or the official blessing of Nicholas, the Duma lacked legitimacy. The solution to this problem was the formation of a "Provisional Committee" consisting of 12 members of the Duma.

The Provisional Committee was faced with a dilemma the first two days of March. To openly defy the Czar, by forming a cabinet, risked retaliation should his military forces be successful in recapturing Petrograd. To side with the Czar and government authorities was to risk the wrath of the Petrograd mobs, very much in evidence around the city. The Provisional Committee opted for a middle course of action. While it did not officially disobey the Czar's decision, it sought support from the Petrograd Soviet's Provisional Executive Committee, known as Ispolkom. The Petrograd Soviet was perhaps the closest thing to a representative body for the workers and marchers of Petrograd. On March 1, the Provisional Committee began negotiations with Ispolkom about the formation of a new government. The Ispolkom, like the Provisional Committee, preferred not to accept any formal responsibility for governmental decision-making - on March 1, its members voted against joining the government. At the same time, it negotiated an eight-point program with the Provisional Committee on March 2, 1917. In return for adopting the program, the Ispolkom would support the new government. With the abdication of the Czar on March 2, the new government was free to go ahead with the formation of a new cabinet.

The events in Petrograd immediately preceding Nicholas' abdication, in themselves, tell a great deal about why the monarchy fell. The shortages and street demonstrations were clearly indicative of a society and government in turmoil. The actions of the Pavlovskii Regiment, in starting the mutiny, only hint at problems with the military. The breakdown of the military was an important factor in the fall of the monarchy. Logic would suggest that it was dissatisfaction and war weariness on the part of front-line troops which led to declining morale and a breakdown in discipline. The collapse of morale at the front however was not the immediate cause of the monarchy's fall, even if the war was the ultimate cause.

Russia relied on a combination military draft and reserve system to supply her military needs. Men who reached twenty-one were subject to the draft and three years of active service. Having completed active service, they became members of the reserve, which could be called to active duty in wartime. A large portion of the soldiers in Petrograd in February 1917 were a combination of new (and untrained) draftees and reservists. Many were peasants with little comprehension of the reasons for war and with generalized grievances against the monarchy. In addition their barracks were overcrowded. In the last few weeks before the mutiny, barracks designed for only 20,000 soldiers had to accommodate 160,000.[8] Government authorities contributed to the breakdown when they failed to institute a crackdown. Those guilty of leading the mutiny were only arrested; they were not executed. General S. S. Khabalov, military commander in Petrograd, overruled General M. A. Beliaev, Minister of War, who wanted the leaders executed. The rebellious soldiers got the impression that mutinous acts would go unpunished. The result was that, even when Nicholas would finally make the decision to use the army to restore order, his commanders could no longer count on their orders being obeyed.

The Provisional Government was, at least in name, the government of Russia from March until October 1917. The classic historical view is that it represented a short-lived experiment in democracy. That view sees the Mensheviks and their leader, Kerensky, as popular democrats who were undermined by the manipulative Bolsheviks. Yet, that reading suggests that the Provisional Government failed because of some action by the

179

Bolsheviks or that the Bolsheviks were the only problem facing the Provisional Government. The Provisional Government failed, not so much because it fell short of democratic principles, or because the Bolsheviks opposed democracy. It failed because it could not govern. If it formally took power from the Czar, it was unable to either control his government or to create an alternative structure to replace what had existed. The next section provides an overview of the rule of the Provisional Government.

THE FAILURE OF THE PROVISIONAL GOVERNMENT
MARCH - OCTOBER 1917

In some ways the Provisional Government made a good start. The collapse of order came so suddenly and seemed so complete that officials of the government feared for their lives in Petrograd. Between February 28 and March 1 many took refuge in the Taurida Palace, where the Duma was meeting. Alexander Kerensky, Minister of Justice in the new cabinet, refused to turn these officials over to the mobs then roaming Petrograd, even though he had been one of the most outspoken critics of the old regime.

The Duma unfortunately, had undermined the foundations of any new governmental authority even before assuming power, by asking the Ispolkom for help. Even though the Ispolkom had no formal legislative authority, it passed its own legislation. One of its first acts was Order No. 1, issued on March 1. In effect it sought to make the military a democratic institution. Military units were to elect soviet committees. The committees in turn were given control of all arms and officers were not to be allowed to carry arms. The Ispolkom, in addition, was empowered to countermand orders of the Provisional Government. The Ispolkom had no formal powers to enact any such order. To the troops at the front lines, any document which eased some of the burdens of military life was welcome. To have such a document proclaimed by an organization which at least seemed to be part of the government was enough to give Order No. 1 a semi-official status. Committees sprang up throughout the armed forces. In a way the Ispolkom's order enhanced its prestige, since it was popular, while undermining the authority of the Provisional Government. It provided some alternative governmental body to which the armed forces would give their allegiance.

Seeking an alliance with the Ispolkom was only the Provisional Government's first major mistake. It made a second mistake by formally dismantling the Czar's governmental administration. First, it eliminated the Department of Police by abolishing it on March 4, together with the Corps of Gendarmes, and the Okhrana, the political police. Then, it dismissed the Czarist governors and deputy governors on March 5, ordering the chairmen of the provincial zemstvo boards to take over such functions. The zemstvos were local self-governing assemblies which had their origins in the reforms Czar Nicholas I had instituted in 1864. The zemstvos, while eager to assume responsibility, were not really prepared for the detailed tasks day-to-day governmental administration required.

The Provisional Government made still another mistake. In its March 2 agreement with the Ispolkom, the Provisional Government had promised to begin immediate preparations for elections for a Constituent Assembly. While it did set up a commission on March 25 to deal with the problem, it produced no concrete plan even for the election procedures.

Not all of the problems which the new government had were of its own making. On April 20 a young socialist officer persuaded several units of troops stationed in Petrograd to participate in a protest march over the government's war policy. While the Bolsheviks would later deny involvement in a coup attempt, the next day they organized a larger protest in which armed marchers attempted to reach the center of Petrograd. Three people were killed when the marchers exchanged gunfire with supporters of the government. Opposition from the Ispolkom prevented the government from ordering troops out and the organizers were not punished. The protests and seeming government paralysis led Petrograd's commander, General Kornilov, to request reassignment. It also brought the resignation of the Minister of War, Alexandr Guchkov, on April 30 and an official confession from the Provisional Government, on April 26, that it could not administer the nation. The statement issued also sought to broaden its political support by bringing in new members. Following negotiations with the Ispolkom, a new cabinet was announced on May 5. Alexander Kerensky would move from his post as Minister of Justice to that of Minister of War. Ominously, on April 28, Lenin had established an armed militia of Bolsheviks, the Red Guard. The reason given for its creation was the protection of factories.

Kerensky, as Minister of War, sought to revitalize the army. He visited the front during May and June 1917, in anticipation of a June Russian offensive. The offensive which began on June 16 with a massive artillery barrage, came to an end on July 6, with a German counterattack. The repulse of the Russian army seemed to deflate Kerensky.

On July 3, the Bolshevik Central Committee formally called for the armed overthrow of the government. This was followed the next day, by a march by Bolshevik troops in Petrograd who were fired on during the march. Despite this display of determined opposition, the Bolsheviks were almost successful in bringing down the Provisional Government. The 8,000-man garrison of the Peter and Paul Fortress sided with the Bolsheviks and they managed to position troops at strategic locations throughout Petrograd. Workers and soldiers congregated angrily in front of the Taurida Palace, the seat of the Provisional Government, demanding it hand over power. Nevertheless the coup failed, apparently because Lenin hesitated at giving the orders which would complete the overthrow.

Lenin's indecisiveness was only one element in the coup's failure. Representatives of the Provisional Government were successful in turning some of the troops against the Bolsheviks when they released information concerning Lenin's dealings with the Germans. Even a hint of collaboration was sufficient to bring undecided units to the defense of the government. The crowds dispersed. Lenin went into hiding, then fled to the countryside on July 9. Following the collapse of the coup, the government arrested 800.[9]

Kerensky, following the coup, became Prime Minister. Yet despite Kerensky's seemingly increased political power, the actions of the Provisional Government provided mixed signals to its opponents. The units which had taken part in the July coup were disarmed and disbanded. Many of the soldiers stationed in Petrograd were ordered to the front. At the same time the Provisional Government was reluctant to place the coup leaders on trial. A commission appointed to prepare for legal proceedings was still working in October, but even then had not formally charged anyone.

Part of the reason for Kerensky's indecisiveness may have been that he viewed the forces loyal to the Czar as a greater threat to the new government than the Bolsheviks. Confident in his own political skills, Kerensky may have believed he could successfully manipulate the Bolsheviks to carry out his future political goals. In any event he may not have wanted to eliminate a force he might need in the future to counter a threat from the right. Kerensky's decision, on July 7, to exile the Royal family to Siberia, suggests that the threat of a counter-coup was a greater worry than the threat from the Bolsheviks.

The success of the German counteroffensive of July 6 alerted Kerensky to new problems in the military structure. The loss of discipline brought about by the Ispolkom decree needed to be reversed. Once again Kerensky had a chance to act decisively, but, in the end, failed. He felt that General Lavr Kornilov had the experience to take command and offered to make him Commander in Chief. Kornilov demanded, among other things, the restoration of the death penalty for insubordination and a reduction of the power of the political committees which Order No. 1 had encouraged. Kerensky agreed to the terms, although he may have known they would be unacceptable to the Ispolkom.

In August Kerensky and Kornilov would confront each other as a result of political ambitions and a misunderstanding. The confrontation would result in Kornilov's arrest on charges of treason made by Kerensky. Kerensky, for his part, would ask the Bolsheviks for help in defeating a "conspiracy of generals." Asking the Bolsheviks for help in August would make it difficult to find allies to fight them in October. August 1917 had perhaps one bright spot for the Provisional Government. It was announced on August 9 that elections for the Constituent Assembly would be held on November 12, to be followed by its first meeting on November 28.

In August a French intelligence report, probably incorrect, indicated that the Bolsheviks were planning another coup.[10] Kerensky is said to have requested a cavalry corps from Kornilov to defend Petrograd from the Bolsheviks, which Kornilov agreed to send. Kerensky would later allege that Kornilov had sent the troops in order to overthrow the Provisional Government.

August 26 appears to be the date that Kerensky became convinced that Kornilov was plotting against the government.. A number of misunderstood actions and conversations resulted in Kerensky's public accusation on August 27, that Kornilov was a traitor, which caused Kornilov to make an attempt at seizing control. Kerensky did not help his cause by leaving Kornilov in charge of the army, after having charged him with treason. Kornilov was subsequently arrested. Kerensky officially asked the Ispolkom for help against the generals. He also asked the Bolsheviks to use whatever influence they had with the soldiers to help him. In return, the Provisional Government released those

Bolsheviks who had been imprisoned. In spite of these gestures, Kerensky made no lasting friends among Bolshevik ranks.

Kerensky's obsession with a military conspiracy in August may have distracted him from the problems the government had at home. His treatment of Kornilov and other generals in August probably doomed any hope of support from the military when he would need it in October. Military matters would continue to distract Kerensky in the final two months of his regime. A German offensive would provide one of the final confrontations between Kerensky and the Ispolkom. It may have impacted the timing of the next Bolshevik coup attempt. The Bolsheviks had something else to worry about in early October. The elections and the November 28 convocation of a Constituent Assembly meant that a new government, with some claim to legitimacy, would take over. While the Bolsheviks were welcome to participate in elections they had little hope of winning a majority of the popular vote.

Between September 28 and October 8, 1917, German forces moved into the Gulf of Riga and occupied islands there. From these positions they could attack Petrograd. The Provisional Government felt more troops were needed at the front to meet this threat. Troops in Petrograd were reluctant to go and the Ispolkom was asked for approval. The Bolsheviks, not eager to provide the Provisional Government with help, instead voted to approve the creation of a "Revolutionary Committee of Defense," later renamed the Military-Revolutionary Committee, on October 9. In theory, it could operate both against the external threat from the Germans and the domestic threat posed by the Provisional Government. The next day the Bolshevik Central Committee would vote to approve its plan for the overthrow of the Provisional Government.

When the Bolsheviks actually began their final overthrow attempt in late October, it is estimated that the number of supporters among the garrison troops was quite small, possibly as low as four percent, or 10,000 men out of some 160,000 in the Petrograd area.[11] It seems inconceivable that this small a number could have been successful in pulling off a coup, or that they would be able to hold onto power, even if initially successful. At the same time, power in Russia, in light of her serious problems, depended, not so much on popular support, in terms of numbers of people who would vote, but on the number of people who were committed enough to fight.

With 20-20 hindsight, it is easy to see the mines hidden in the political landscape that was 1917 Russia. Kerensky's major mistake was in failing to see the Bolsheviks as the threat they were. Yet, from the perspective of his day, the political landscape is not so easy to read. The Czar had only abdicated in March. Loyalty to the Emperor among the followers of the Czar was still strong. Should the Czar return to power, the likelihood was that there would be retaliation for the overthrow. The Bolsheviks, for all the problems they caused, represented the one force which could counter the old regime's followers. Another of Kerensky's mistakes may have been to allow personal differences, particularly in his dispute with General Kornilov, to enter the larger arena of political ambition. He appears to have resented the popularity of Kornilov. His naivete lay, not in his commitment to democracy, but in his failure to understand the real forces at work during the period the Provisional Government was in power.

The next section provides a background and overview of the origins and histories of the various political parties. It also looks at the governmental and private political bodies which developed. The soviets, for example, were supposed to represent workers and peasants. While they were closely associated with the Bolshevik party, they were not identical to the Bolshevik party itself. The Menshevik party, while often linked, or even allied to, the Bolsheviks, had a somewhat different outlook.

RUSSIA'S POLITICAL LANDSCAPE

On February 19, 1861, Czar Alexander II signed a manifesto which freed some twenty-two and a half million Russian peasants. This was followed by other laws, passed between 1861 and 1865, which were intended to reform the Russian legal and governmental systems. Among the reforms was the creation of the zemstvo system, enacted into law in 1864. The zemstvos was a local assembly, consisting of three estates: landowners, peasant communities, and village or townspeople. The voting members of each estate elected delegates to local assemblies, which dealt with the administration of education, welfare, and health, together with the tax system. Following the assassination of Alexander II in 1881, his son Alexander III, incorporated the zemstvos into the civil service and curtailed their power.

When political leaders tried to use the zemstvos assemblies as a base for expansion of democratic political power Alexander III had them prosecuted. The "Zemstvo Liberals," sought to create a level of cooperation among the various zemstvo assemblies throughout the Russian empire. While Alexander was fairly successful at suppressing the Zemstvo Liberals, they did not disappear from the political scene altogether. They would reappear as the Konstitutional Democrats, the KD or Kadet Party, which was formed in October 1905. In the November 1917 elections for the Constituent Assembly the Kadets would come in third, with 4.7% of the vote, behind the SR and Bolshevik parties.[12] The Kadets could best be described as a liberal party, advocating some form of western parliamentary democracy.

The Socialist-Revolutionary Party (SR) had been established in 1902. Clearly more radical than the Kadet Party, its political philosophy centered on three ideas: anti-capitalism, terrorism, and the socialization of the land, by which they meant the elimination of private ownership of land. Instead ownership of land was to be held and managed by local governments. This common ownership was to ensure that peasants had an opportunity, if they wished, to receive a share of the land. The problem, as they saw it, was that poorer peasants were forced off the land by rich landlords or other peasants who were in a position to acquire most of the available land. The SR gained a strong following among the poorer peasants by calling for the "Black Repartition," which was a proposal to expropriate privately held land and redistribute it to the communes. This single proposal was one of the major reasons why the SRs were able to gain 40 percent of the vote in the November 1917 elections for the Constituent Assembly, frustrating Bolshevik

184

hopes for victory at the polls.

The SR, in the years immediately following its founding, was one of the most radical movements. In 1902, the year of its founding, it was responsible for the murder of the Minister of the Interior. The SR Combat Organization is said to have carried out hundreds of political killings between 1902 and 1908.[13] The dedication to violence and terrorism, central to its philosophy, earned the respect of other left-wing organizations, which considered the SRs to be the "true" revolutionaries. Given such a violent history, it is somewhat surprising that the Bolsheviks, rather than the SR, carried out the overthrow of the Provisional Government.

The SRs, by the time the Provisional Government was formed, had discarded much of their violent philosophy. While they made common cause with the Bolsheviks against the Czarist regime, they appeared to have mellowed when they became part of the Provisional Government. In some ways this cost them support. To many, over the course of 1917, they appeared indecisive and vacillating. The Bolsheviks, with their determined commitment to revolution, benefitted, in a way, from the same sense of admiration once reserved for the SRs. The loss of SR support between February and October 1917 was evidenced by the Moscow municipal elections in September 1917. Voter support for the socialist parties, including the SR, dropped by 375,000 voters. While the Bolsheviks received 188,100 votes, out of 380,000, the SR delegates only got 55,860.[14]

The two leading protagonists in the political arena that was 1917 were the Bolsheviks and Mensheviks. If the Bolshevik party gained a hard-line reputation, it was from the October coup. Its origins can be found, not in the terroristic SR, but in the more moderate Social-Democratic Workers' Party, founded in 1898. Its second meeting in 1903, known formally as the Second Congress, brought a name change and the creation of the Russian Social-Democratic Labor Party (RSDRP). The 1903 Congress, held in London, resulted in a split from which the Bolshevik and Menshevik parties came into being. The word bolshevik means majority, and the Bolsheviks, on one vote, happened to be in the majority. Their numbers, in fact, were smaller than those of the Mensheviks, which took their name from the Russian word for minority. By 1917 the roles had been reversed. It was now the Bolsheviks who advocated radical, even violent action, whereas the Mensheviks attempted accommodation and compromise. In summarizing the differences between the two parties, perhaps the key difference was that the Bolsheviks, under Lenin, favored revolution and the overthrow of the government, whereas the Mensheviks were in favor of gradual change from within the political system. The Mensheviks generally were more cooperative in their relations with other parties.

The word soviet, because of its incorporation into the governmental name, the Union of Soviet Socialist Republics, took on a more ominous connotation than its actual meaning warranted. Positive word association was limited as well by Bolshevik use of the soviet as a means of forcing through their political agenda. Bolshevik power, they said, was exercised on behalf of the soviets. The Bolsheviks found that the soviets could be easily manipulated if a particular vote was needed - it was possible to pack the meetings.

The soviets were primarily workers' organizations which had their origins in the labor strife which afflicted Russia in the early 1900s. They were nothing more than local councils, representative bodies, intended to provide some voice for the workers. In theory they were democratic bodies. In actuality they usually were led by intellectuals who wanted to identify or associate with the workers, but who tended to lead the soviets into more political areas. The first soviet had been formed in Ivanovo-Voznesensk in May 1905.[15] In some respects the soviets were nothing more than a formal version of the strike committee of a labor union, a worker's assembly intended to represent the workers in dealings with management. The St. Petersburg Soviet was perhaps the first major Soviet to be formed, beginning on October 13, 1905 as a strike committee. It contributed to the worker unrest which would shut down the capital and culminate in the Revolution of 1905. A Moscow Soviet was formed on November 21.

What gave the soviets power was not some official or governmental status but numbers. Even if they were more like fraternal or social organizations they attracted large numbers of people to their meetings. In this they contrasted with the Duma, which gained legitimacy from the Czar's decrees and a formal governmental adoption procedure. They also gained legitimacy - and power - by their ability to motivate people to act based on their pronouncements. At the same time the soviets were not an immediate success. On October 13, 1905 the St. Petersburg Soviet urged workers to continue the work stoppage then in effect. Since the work stoppage had already shut down St. Petersburg, the announcement had little visible impact. On October 15, 1905 the St. Petersburg Soviet issued an appeal to workers to close down shops which were not participating in the strike. (Part of the formal organization created on October 15 was the creation of the Executive Committee, the Ispolkom.) From the threat against non-participating shops, the Soviet came up with the idea of shutting down the Russian financial system. On December 2 the Soviet urged people to stop paying taxes, to take money out of their savings accounts, and to accept only gold or foreign currency as payment. This appeal brought results. While it did not bring about the collapse of the financial system, it got 260 Soviet deputies thrown into jail, on the orders of Peter Durnovo, Minister of the Interior. The St. Petersburg Soviet followed this with an appeal for a general strike set for December 8. Workers ignored this appeal.[16]

The fledgling Moscow Soviet, formed on November 21, 1905, took more drastic action, but also brought about more tragic consequences. It formally voted for an armed insurrection and was successful in bringing about a general strike on December 7. However, the unrest also caused a government crackdown which resulted in over 1,000 deaths. While there were some 50 soviets which were established in various cities in 1905, the suppression of the St. Petersburg and Moscow Soviets, virtually destroyed the soviets as political organizations, until 1917, when they would be revived.

On February 27, 1917, one day after the Volynskii Guard Regiment fired on the Znamenskii Square demonstrators, sparking the mutiny in Petrograd, there was a meeting to revive the Petrograd Soviet. Numerically, the new Soviet had grown considerably in size. Where, in 1905, there were some 500 deputies, in 1917, only several weeks into its existence, the deputies numbered around 3,000. Because the Soviet meetings often broke down into forums for speechmaking, the Executive Committee, the Ispolkom, became the real place where decisions were made. A curious aspect of the structure of the Soviet is that the members of the Ispolkom were not elected directly from the ordinary body of the Soviet delegates. Instead the Ispolkom were nominated by the various socialist parties. In one sense, this arrangement provided some form of representation to nearly every political party. In another sense, it increased the power of the smaller parties because each party was given three seats.[17]

The Petrograd Soviet, or more specifically, the Ispolkom, suffered from two defects in 1917. First, it had no official governmental status or legitimacy, like its predecessor, the St. Petersburg Soviet of 1905. Second, the Ispolkom was not democratically representative of the membership of the Soviet itself. Despite these deficiencies, the Ispolkom managed a coup in the first days March 1917 when it successfully negotiated the eight-point agreement with the members of the Provisional Government. The agreement gave it a form of legitimacy as well as power. This, in spite of the fact that, by a vote of 13 to 8, it refused to officially become a part of the Provisional Government.

The Ispolkom, with the passage of Order No. 1, also threw the Provisional Government into confusion. Order No. 1's call for the formation of "committees" in the armed forces was bad enough. When combined with Article 4's declaration that the Duma's military orders were to be obeyed only as they conformed to the wishes of the Soviet, it severely undermined the Provisional Government's authority. The Ispolkom had made gains - and had made them without having been formally empowered by any official body.

Just as the Ispolkom manufactured legitimacy simply by making public statements, it also created a governmental structure merely by assuming responsibility. On March 7, 1917, the Ispolkom established a Contact Commission, which reviewed the performance of the Provisional Government and reported on its compliance with the demands of the Ispolkom.

In establishing legitimacy, appearances began to take on almost as much importance as the substance. The left-wing parties furthered the prestige of the soviets by setting up formal gatherings which included representatives from throughout Russia. Two such gatherings were significant in 1917, the First and Second All-Russian Congress of Soviets. The First Congress took place on June 3, 1917. Whether, with their endless criticisms of the Provisional Government's bourgeois nature, they were anything more than rhetorical forums for radical debate, they at least furthered the impression that there was something of substance. The Second Congress, which finally opened on October 25, served as a backdrop to the October coup.

Throughout 1917 the Bolsheviks managed to manipulate the soviets in a manner which added to the prestige of the soviets, while reducing the authority of the Provisional Government. At the same time, the authority which was being established, was somehow beyond the normal political power associated with party politics. In some ways it came to resemble the aura of power accorded to the Czar and the more traditional institutions of the Czarist regime.

The soviet, as a newly created political body, proved to be an ideal tool for a party such as the Bolsheviks, intent on seizing power by any means. Superficially, it gave the workers and soldiers a sense of participation, while reserving real authority in the Executive Committee. The inclusion of workers and soldiers, even if not allowed a real say in decisions, provided a public relations advantage - the Bolsheviks could say any decisions were made on behalf of the workers represented in the soviet. In spite of these anti-democratic aspects, the structure of the soviets, even at the Executive Committee level, did include some checks on power. Each party started out with an equal number of representatives. Had the other parties been more aware, they had the means to at least check the excesses of any single political group. In the end, the Bolsheviks simply proved more tenacious than the other parties, and more adept at manipulating the political mechanism presented by the structure of the soviet.

The next chapter looks at the political events in the Russian Civil War itself in the years 1918 through 1921. Economic and political events exhibited a close relationship and many of the political decisions of the Bolsheviks can be seen to be a reaction to the economic circumstances existing at the time.

CHAPTER 11

THE RUSSIAN CIVIL WAR - 1918-1921

Around 4 in the morning on January 6, 1918, the acting commander of the guard came up to Victor Chernov, the Chairman of the Constituent Assembly, who was making a speech, and asked him to tell everyone to leave - the guard was tired, he said. Some minutes later Chernov adjourned the meeting. The one and only session of the Constituent Assembly thus came to an end after meeting for only 12 hours. Lenin and his Bolshevik followers made sure it never met again. On January 8 the Third Congress of Soviets opened. It declared the Sovnarkom to be Russia's legitimated government. The Sovnarkom, or Council of People's Commissars, had been a "government" body created by the Second Congress of Soviets at its October 1917 meeting. The Third Congress also gave the Russian government a new name, the "Russian Soviet Socialist Republic," changed in 1924 to the "Union of Soviet Socialist Republics."

The Bolsheviks would not be able to consolidate power for several years. However, they found surprisingly little resistance in the immediate aftermath of the dissolution of the Constituent Assembly. This chapter looks at the Bolshevik regime in the period of the Russian Civil War, i.e., from 1918 through 1921. The first half of the chapter follows the political events while the second half looks at the economic situation during that period. An attempt has been made to separate the history of political events from the economic situation in Russia. However, in some cases, the political events followed closely on, or were clearly a response to, economic problems.

POLITICAL HISTORY - 1918 - 1921

The new Soviet government in January 1918, as in November 1917, found itself short of operating cash. An immediate step taken to deal with this problem was a decree on January 21, defaulting on all government debt, both foreign and domestic. Naturally, this move was not received well by foreign governments. The new government's efforts to extricate itself from the war also worried the Allied governments. On March 3, the Russians signed the German version of the Brest-Litovsk Treaty. The terms required the surrender of large areas under Russian control - all of Poland and Finland and the Baltic states of Estonia, Latvia, and Lithuania were ceded. The treaty was ratified on March 14 by the Fourth Congress of Soviets. Following the collapse of Germany, the Soviet government would renounce the treaty (November 1918).

The ratification of the Brest-Litovsk Treaty, even with its disadvantageous territorial concessions, at least served to reduce a major political and economic drain on Russian resources. Having seemingly solved problems associated with the war, the Bolsheviks now had to face renewed economic turmoil at home. The populations of cities such as Petrograd had had to endure a harsh winter which disrupted food deliveries and fuel supplies. Unemployment was high - in Petrograd, in May 1918, it reached around 87 percent.[1] Residents of Petrograd were fortunate if they received four to six ounces of bread on any given day. Tensions finally erupted on May 8 at Kolpino, a town south of Petrograd. Unemployment there was even higher than in Petrograd - out of a work force of 10,000, only 300 had jobs. In the middle of a demonstration, troops were ordered to open fire. One person was killed.[2] In May and June elections for the Fifth Congress of Soviets, the Bolsheviks lost badly to SR and Menshevik candidates.

The Mensheviks, though aware of the discontent, chose not to exploit it. The Bolsheviks, by the inaction of the Mensheviks, received something of a reprieve. They showed little gratitude, however. Instead, they arrested those they thought were leaders of the opposition on June 13. They took the additional step of ordering new elections to the Fifth Congress of Soviets on June 16, while expelling Mensheviks and SRs from the soviets.

Despite these actions, the Bolsheviks lost badly, with the SR and Menshevik candidates garnering most of the actual votes. The Bolsheviks tampered with the results to obtain a majority. Bolshevik pressure tactics and the wavering of the Mensheviks and SRs allowed the rigged results to stand. While there were attempts to organize strikes and demonstrations, the workers were confused by the arguments of the Menshevik and SR leadership. They were convinced by the Bolsheviks that resistance was hopeless. When the call was made to strike on July 2, only a few of the plants joined.

On July 4, 1918, the Fifth Congress of Soviets approved the new Soviet Constitution. It was perhaps the only routine matter the Congress had to deal with. On the night of July 5-6, an anti-Bolshevik named Boris Savinkov, coordinated uprisings against the Bolsheviks in three cities, Iaroslavl, Murom, and Rybinsk. The Bolsheviks quickly put down the Murom and Rybinsk revolts, but Iaroslavl held out for over half a month, despite artillery and air attack. On the afternoon of July 6, two SR members assassinated the German ambassador, but staged the assassination to look like the Cheka's work. This was followed, in the evening, by a coup attempt by the Left SR. The Bolsheviks were unprepared, and virtually lost control of Moscow, save for the Kremlin. The Left SRs, instead of arresting the Bolsheviks, issued vague appeals to the Russian people, while relying on the possibility of German intervention. There was no coordinated uprising and a force, primarily Latvian infantry, overcame the rebels the next day. Surprisingly, the Bolsheviks dealt leniently with the coup leaders, executing some participants, but only imprisoning others.

The lenient treatment accorded to the Left SR in Moscow stands in contrast to events elsewhere. The murder of Czar Nicholas is believed to have taken place on the night of July 16-17 at Ekaterinburg, in the Urals. Using revolvers, a squad of 10 men shot Nicholas, his wife, and six other members of the royal family, together with their physician, cook and valet. Those who were not killed immediately were bayoneted. Some miles away, at Alapaevsk, on July 17, other relatives of the royal family were killed. Most suffocated after being thrown into a mine shaft which was then sealed shut. On July 21, at Iaroslavl, the starting point of the July 5-6 rebellion, the Bolshevik counterattack finally succeeded. Following the surrender, around 350 prisoners were taken outside the town and shot.[3] It was preliminary to the events of September, when what became known as the "Red Terror" would be instituted.

What triggered the Red Terror were two events which occurred on August 30, 1918. The first was the assassination of M. S. Uritskii, the chief of the Petrograd Cheka. The second was the attempted assassination of Lenin himself. The attempt on Lenin's life was carried out by a reincarnated faction of the SR, the SR Combat Organization. The Combat Organization had been responsible for giving the SR its reputation as a revolutionary group with the political assassinations it had carried out between 1900 and 1908. A woman named Fannie Kaplan had been chosen to carry out the killing. An earlier planned attack had failed when the would-be assassin changed his mind. Kaplan fired three shots from a Browning pistol, just as Lenin was about to get into his car following a speech he had made. Two of the bullets struck Lenin. Although one wound was nearly fatal, Lenin would recover, in spite of the fact that the bullets are said to have been poisoned with curare.

The Bolsheviks implied that the SR had been involved in the assassination plot, although when they made that charge they had not yet completed their own investigation. Kaplan had been captured close to where the attempt was made. While there probably would have been ample grounds to execute her following a trial, they chose instead to cover up her execution. On September 3 she was taken outside the Kremlin prison, to a small courtyard. Trucks parked nearby were started to muffle any sounds. She was told to walk toward a car parked in the courtyard and then shot in the back by the commandant of the Kremlin, on the orders of the Cheka.

On September 4 the Commissar of the Interior signed an "Order Concerning Hostages." The decree, calling for the arrest of Right SRs, authorized the taking of hostages, in anticipation of future attacks on Bolsheviks, and urged mass executions and mass terror. A second decree, adopted on September 5 called for placing enemies of the new government in concentration camps, as well as summary execution of those linked to conspiracies against the government. While these two decrees are generally considered the formal start of the Red Terror, the country began to get a glimpse of what was coming even before its official September start. As many as 882 executions may have taken place between January and June of 1918. It is believed the Cheka may have executed 1,115 in July alone.[4] At Nizhnii Novgorod on August 31 the Cheka arrested and executed 41 people. Another 512 hostages were executed in Petrograd that day, while in Moscow, former officials of the Czarist regime, already in prison, were shot.

By the time the Red Terror came to an end in 1920, thousands had been killed. Because the Cheka archives were destroyed, the actual figure is unlikely to be known. Estimates range from a low of 12,733 to 50,000, and even as high as 140,000.[5] The number of executions is only one aspect of the repressive nature of the Bolshevik regime. The number of concentration camps is another quantifiable measure. In spite of the fact that the use of concentration camps was advocated in the decree of September 5, implementation of that suggestion did not begin until after 1918. They were more formally provided for in a "Decision" by the Central Executive Committee of the Soviets (CEC) issued on April 11, 1919. Over the next year, this official commitment resulted in a series of camps being established. Some 50,000 prisoners are said to have been held at the end of 1920 in 84 camps. By October 1923, there were 70,000 inmates held in 315 camps.[6]

THE VOLUNTEER ARMY, THE WHITE GUARD, AND ORGANIZED OPPOSITION

On November 14, 1920, the army of the White forces evacuated the fortress of Sevastopol on the Crimean Peninsula. Over the next two days the White forces would evacuate their people from nearby positions, some 145,693 people in all, loaded on 126 ships headed toward Constantinople. It represented the final triumph of the Red forces over the White forces and the end of the Russian Civil War.

The odds of a Bolshevik victory looked particularly long in the early months of 1918, when their opponents joined armies vowing to defeat them. Yet, despite the fact that the Bolsheviks represented a minority, and an unpopular one at that, they somehow mustered the resources needed to win. What distinguishes the military aspect of the conflict from that aspect carried out in the voting booth? - How could a party which was unable to carry a popular election without resorting to fraud, manipulation, or physical intimidation possibly have won on the battlefield? Perhaps the simplest answer is that the Bolsheviks had a central core of committed supporters, surrounded by a sufficiently large body of people who were neutral or not sufficiently hostile to them politically to actively oppose them. They perhaps had one other advantage - there were no clear choices or good alternatives to Bolshevik rule. From a late Twentieth Century Western perspective, magnified by the events of the Cold War, the Bolsheviks are seen as the clearly evil choice, where the alternatives are seen in black and white terms.

In 1918 Russia people had many alternatives to choose from, yet none presented a clear improvement over Bolshevik rule. While the Provisional Government, from a Western perspective, is viewed as the good "democratic" choice, the experience Russia had had with that government was one of indecision and ineptitude. The other major alternative was the Czarist administration. It was not that popular either. One of the anomalies of the early days of Bolshevik rule is that many conservative "monarchists" actually supported the harsh measures of the Bolsheviks. It was felt a tough stand against opponents would end a chaos which the they saw as an even greater evil than Bolshevism itself. In the final analysis, the Bolsheviks won, not so much because they tricked people, but because they were able to control, and manage, the resources of force. Victory in any war requires both physical resources and a motivated army. While the Bolsheviks may have represented a minority in terms of popular opinion they were able to field an army of 3 million in 1919 as against White army numbers of only 250,000.[7]

It was the Bolsheviks who labeled their opponents as "Whites." The color white had been the color associated with the French monarchy and the Bolsheviks, no doubt, wanted to emphasize any connection the anti-Bolshevik forces might have with the deposed Czar. While the forces and armies which came to oppose the Bolsheviks were given the general label of Whites, they were not a single force. While all opposed the Bolsheviks, they were not all interested in restoring the monarchy. Many were fighting for the Provisional Government. The major White army was the Volunteer Army. The Cossacks were another part of the White armies although they sometimes fought with the Whites, sometimes did not. If central planning, the organizational solution of communism to economic problems, has been condemned for dragging down the Russian economy, decentralization and total independence, the option "chosen" by the White armies, did not operate to save them. Separated geographically by wide distances, they were often forced to fight independently of each other. It was difficult to learn what was happening, let alone to mount any kind of coordinated action.

The area of the Don, the land to the south of Moscow close to the Black Sea, was where opposition forces gathered, almost as soon as Petrograd had fallen in November 1917. What drew the generals and political leaders to the Don was perhaps the legends which came out of the Don. The Don was home to the Cossacks. They enjoyed a unique status - both the Whites and the Reds considered them as potential allies. Their horsemen had served the Czar as cavalry troops, yet they were also considered independent defenders of Russian liberty who would stand against oppression. Initially, the Whites had better reason to expect Cossack support. In the voting for the Constituent Assembly, Cossack voters had overwhelmingly opposed the Bolsheviks, giving around 98 % of their votes to non-Bolshevik candidates.[8] One reason for Cossack opposition to the Bolsheviks was the Land Decree, which had been issued on October 26, 1917.[9] The Land Decree provided for the expropriation of privately held lands and redistribution to peasant communes. While the land held by Cossack peasants was intended to be exempt from seizure, there were, in the land of the Don Cossacks, some 1.8 million non-Cossack peasants, of whom it was estimated that 500,000 were without land. If the Cossacks saw their lands as their own, they feared that the non-Cossack peasants viewed the land as available.

The presence of such a large group of non-Cossacks in the Don lands may have pushed Cossack leadership toward support of the White cause. At the same time, it presented a problem for the Cossacks, since it provided a reserve of potential recruits, only too ready to throw their support to the Bolsheviks. The conservative Cossack fear of unrest became a reality soon after the Bolsheviks had seized power in Petrograd. Toward the end of November 1917, at about the time the future recruits of the Whites were beginning to assemble in the Don area, a group of workers in Rostov took control of the city and proclaimed a Soviet Republic of the Don.

The Cossack leader Kaledin, who was confronted with a minor mutiny among his own followers, felt compelled to ask the newly- forming White army for help. Although the army numbered only 600, they were successful, on December 2, 1917, in taking back Rostov. This small victory provided some hope for the White cause when it formally became the Volunteer Army in mid-December 1917. It had, by that time, grown to just under 4,000 men.[10]

While the young Volunteer Army may have been small, the Bolsheviks felt the need to move swiftly to deal with it. Any armed force would be seen as a threat, however the Volunteer Army was particularly irksome because of the geographical area it had chosen as its base. The Don was next to the Ukraine, Russia's grain-growing region. The Germans wanted control of that area and the Bolsheviks felt compelled to control any military threat there. An army of some 6,000 to 7,000 men under the Bolshevik general Vladimir Antonov was sent south in December. The Red Army picked up support as it moved south, so that by the time it reached the land of the Don, its numbers had increased to 20,000. In contrast to the disorganization which the Bolshevik forces had displayed at the Winter Palace on October 25, the Red forces had heavy armament, with over 100 machine guns, field guns, airplanes, and an armored train.[11]

When the Red Army, which had been split, threatened to completely encircle the White forces, they began a retreat on February 22, 1918, south into the Kuban steppe lands which lay to the East of the Black Sea. The Volunteer Army had hopes of using the city of Ekaterinodar as a base. The workers of the city had other ideas. What happened at Ekaterinodar perhaps best illustrates the difficulties the Whites faced in trying to topple the Bolshevik government. Workers, on March 14, 1918, took control of the city. The Whites withdrew and returned again in April, at which time the Bolsheviks had a force of 18,000 ready to defend the city. On April 13, as the Whites were attacking the city, an artillery shell exploded inside the house used by the attackers. General Kornilov, the commander-in-chief, was killed. The Volunteer Army retreated. In June, what was left of the Volunteer Army would move once again into the Kuban steppes, while the Cossacks would move against the Bolsheviks in the fortress they had created at Tsaritsyn. The Volunteer Army, in spite of its retreat, was not through with Ekaterinodar. It returned to the city and captured it on August 16, 1918.

Perhaps the only thing that had saved the Volunteer Army from destruction was an advancing German army, which captured Rostov in May. The Germans had been quick to move east to take charge of the territories granted them under the terms of the Brest-Litovsk Treaty. In May the White forces also discovered the differences which lay between their goals and those of the Cossacks. The Whites thought of a war against the Bolshevik government as an idealistic struggle to create a Russian nation, whereas the Cossacks thought more in terms of a war of liberation of Cossack lands. These divergent views created a problem for both parties. The Whites, to a certain extent, viewed the Cossacks as some mythical force which could exist independently of the land. In reality, they were tied economically and socially to the land. While often willing to sacrifice their own lives in battle, it was another matter to subject their families to such risks. Unfortunately the fighting of the Russian Civil War was not limited to the battlefield. Both sides were often willing to torture and kill enemy soldiers and they were just as willing to subject noncombatants to the same rules. The leaders of the Volunteer Army, because they were less tied to the Don economically, to a certain extent, had the luxury of waging an ideological war. At the same time, they were economically dependent on the Don to sustain their war effort.

The Volunteer Army in the Don region was not the only White army to challenge the Bolsheviks. It was in Siberia where the Whites managed to achieve some early but decisive victories. A rival to the Bolsheviks, known as the Komuch government, was created in the spring of 1918. There may have been an inclination to oppose the government, but it did not show itself until the Czech Legion managed to score some victories against the Bolsheviks on its way home. The Czech Legion had confused and somewhat unusual origins. When the First World War began, the Austro-Hungarian army had within its ranks Czech and Slovak soldiers who disliked their allies, the Germans. These soldiers were among those captured by the Russians when they launched their first offensives of the war. A Czech, Thomas Masaryk, head of the Czechoslovak National Council, suggested that these prisoners might be persuaded to fight against the Germans and units were formed which fought with the Russians in 1917.

Following the signing of Brest-Litovsk, the Allies expressed an interest in the units. Initially, the Bolsheviks agreed to release the prisoners and to send them, as military units, to fight with the Allies. Because of fears of German U-boats, a decision was made to send the Czechs east across Siberia to Vladivostok. It was after German requests to stop the transfer that problems began. At Cheliabinsk, in Siberia, the local soviet arrested some Czechs involved in a fight with Hungarian POWs on May 14. The members of the Czech unit then seized the local arsenal and forced the release of the Czechs being held. Leon Trotsky, Commissar of War, arrested some Czech politicians in Moscow and ordered the Siberian soviets to disarm the Czechs. The Czechs, who had 20,500 men at various places along the Trans-Siberian railroad, retaliated by taking over the various towns located along the railway.[12]

On June 8, 1918 the Czech Legion, as it was known, took over the town of Samara. The Komuch government was formed shortly after. More formally known as the Committee of Members of the Constituent Assembly, it was formed by liberal and SR supporters. Samara had become something of an underground source of opposition to the Bolsheviks, since around 70 SR ex-deputies of the Constituent Assembly had moved to Samara following the dissolution of the Assembly. Like the Volunteer Army, the army organized by the Komuch government managed to score some early successes. In July, Ufa and Simbirsk were taken, followed by Kazan on August 7. The Czarist government had accumulated over 650 million rubles worth of gold reserves there, but the Bolsheviks left so quickly that the entire gold stock fell into the hands of the Komuch government.

With aid from Western nations, the White forces in Siberia began to constitute a serious military threat. In small battles they emerged victorious. In fact the Bolshevik army began to retreat. What saved the Bolsheviks was Trotsky, who arrived at the small town of Sviiazhsk with a special train, from which he could dispense food and weapons. By Bolshevik standards, the train was luxurious, containing not only a library, but also a garage with automobiles, and a radio station. Trotsky worked to restore order and morale on two fronts. In terms of the materials needed to fight, he made sure that the Red Army had whatever weapons and supplies were needed. He could even order ammunition directly from Moscow by direct wire from his train. At the same time, he worked to instill fear where inspiration would not work. He had the commissar and commander of one regiment executed when the regiment abandoned a position, along with randomly selected members of the regiment. Trotsky's logistics and morale-boosting efforts paid off. The Red Army, equipped with gunboats, bombers, and artillery retook Kazan on September 10, 1918. (For all the effort expended by Trotsky in Siberia, the actual forces involved were relatively small in the battles for Kazan. There were roughly 3,000 soldiers fighting for each side, both in the August battle as well as in the September recapture.)[13]

In the south, fighting shifted to the city of Tsaritsyn, somewhat north of, but roughly halfway between, the Black and Caspian Seas. The Bolsheviks, in June 1918, had retreated to Tsaritsyn before the German forces attacking Rostov. They spent most of the summer adding to the fortifications of the city. As early as June the Cossacks had started preparations for an attack. However, it was not until October that the first major attack would come. The Cossacks were unable to finish off the Red Army in Tsaritsyn, even though they besieged the city in late 1918. In January 1919, the Red Army would break out of the city to drive the Cossacks back.

The Red forces which faced the Volunteer Army following the rout of the Cossacks in January 1919 were numerically superior, three times those of the Volunteer Army.[14] The Volunteer Army turned to General Mai-Maevskii, just as the Bolsheviks had turned to Trotsky in the north. One advantage the Whites had in the spring of 1919 was the weather. Rainy weather made it difficult, not only for the Red Army to move, but also to communicate. The Volunteer Army, relying on the advantage of rail transport, moved more freely against their Red opponents. When dryer weather came in May, the Red armies found that White victories were not related to the weather. The Volunteer Army advanced along a broad front.

At the end of June the Volunteer Army stormed Tsaritsyn. While the success of the attack could be attributed in part to the aggressive leadership of General Petr Wrangel, the use of British tanks and armored cars no doubt were a major factor as well. The string of victories however, may have proved to be the undoing of the Volunteer Army. On July 3, General Denikin, the commanding general, announced that the Volunteer Army's next goal was Moscow. Although the Volunteer Army numbered over 100,000, it extended over an 800-mile front.

The Volunteer Army initially did well. Wrangel, in September, defeated a 50,000 man Red force sent against Tsarytsin. In mid-September, Denikin's main force besieged the city of Orël, only 220 miles south of Moscow, finally capturing it on October 14. While the main armies fought, a Cossack cavalry force rode through Bolshevik territory on a 500-mile rampage. From the north, another White army was moving against Petrograd. Despite this forward movement, the "unstoppable" White advance was beginning to run into trouble. It came, not from the Red Army attacking from Moscow, but from peasants in the Ukraine. Fearful that the Whites were about to reimpose Czarist rule, they revolted and Denikin was forced to send troops to put down the revolt.

Denikin had to weaken his front line at a time when the Red Army was being strengthened. Not only did Moscow put an additional 100,000 troops into the forces which lay between the advancing Volunteer Army and Moscow, they also supplied them with some 4,400 machine guns and 1,000 pieces of artillery.[15] A newly formed Red cavalry force also managed to defeat a Cossack cavalry force at Voronezh on October 24. The formation of a Red cavalry unit, an innovative military tactic for the Bolsheviks, proved to be one of the more important military decisions for the Bolsheviks. Providing the Red Army with greater mobility, the cavalry tipped the balance in the overall battle between the White and Red forces. Denikin, facing a much stronger Red Army, was forced to retreat almost as soon as Orël had been captured.

The Volunteer Army was not the only White force to experience problems with people in the lands it controlled. The White forces in Siberia also had difficulties with workers and peasants sympathetic to the Bolshevik cause. The loss of Kazan as a result of military action, in September 1918, was followed by the loss of the Czech Legion as a result of the end of the First World War - the Czechs decided it was time to leave. The various groups opposed to Bolshevik rule on November 4, 1918, had turned to Aleksandr Kolchak, a naval officer and Polar explorer. Through Kolchak's leadership, the White forces in Siberia were resurrected, capturing the city of Perm in December 1918, and advancing west and south, capturing Ufa in March 1919. Yet, even with these victories, Kolchak faced internal revolt. In December, a Bolshevik-led revolt of workers occurred in Omsk. The city prison was seized and prisoners freed.

White victories in the Siberian arena proved as ephemeral as those of the south. The Bolsheviks reorganized once more, this time under Mikhail Frunze, a former millworker. In April 1919 the Red Army launched an offensive which culminated in the recapture of Ufa in June. The Red Army continued to advance, inflicting serious losses on the retreating Whites who, by August had been reduced to a force of only 15,000. In retreat, they not only had to battle the regulars of the Red Army, but also local peasants and workers. Unable to obtain regular arms, many peasant groups used pitchforks or axes when attacking White supply trains or units. With White resistance collapsing, in January 1920 Kolchak would be handed over to the Bolsheviks, who would execute him in February.

The pattern of early White victories followed by relentless Bolshevik counter-attacks was repeated in the northwest. The Northwestern White Army, under General Nikolai Iudenich, moved against Petrograd on September 28, 1919. In a series of battles they continued to push the Red Army back and, by October 20, had nearly reached the city. However one of the White commanders failed to cut rail communications with the city when given the opportunity and the Bolsheviks again sent Trotsky to organize their defenses. On October 21 the Red Army mounted a counterattack which drove the White forces from their most advanced positions and continued to advance. The White army was driven back to the border of Estonia, conceding all the territory gained since September.

The capture of the city of Orël, which came on October 14, 1919 was the closest the Volunteer Army would come to Moscow. On October 24 their cavalry forces would be defeated at Voronezh. The Bolsheviks began to concentrate their forces as they moved south. They moved to split the Volunteer Army, one force moving south to Rostov, while their main army maintained pressure on the Whites at Orël. Realizing they simply could not hold the city, they had retreated. By February 1920, the Red Army had pushed them back to the Kuban river. The Volunteer Army was only able to halt the Red advance temporarily. As March came to an end the Reds had pushed the White forces into the port city of Novorossiisk. On March 26, 1920, the Volunteer Army had taken to ships, abandoning the city to the Bolsheviks, leaving behind some 20,000 soldiers unable to escape. Sailing to the Crimean Peninsula, their only real hope was to survive a little longer.

General Wrangel, in trying to hold the peninsula, began to fortify the Perekop Isthmus, the narrow strip of land separating the Crimea from the Ukrainian mainland. Despite the relative insignificance of the land area into which they had been forced to retreat, the Whites were not content to simply wait for the Red Army. On June 6 they made an amphibious assault at Kirilovka with 6,000 men which managed to push its way inland and capture the city of Melitopol. Wrangel's main force attacked the Red Army confronting the Perekop fortifications on June 7. Wherever the White forces attacked, the Red Army retreated. Even an attempted Red counterattack in the final days of June was beaten back. Yet the Volunteer Army was fighting long odds. The Bolshevik army by summer's end would number some five million men. Despite these numbers, the Red Army was concentrating most of its efforts on fighting a war with Poland in June and July. So successful were the military efforts of the Volunteer Army that, as the summer months turned into fall, it was still advancing. Its last success would come on October 8, when Wrangel got a force across the Dnieper river. While it held there for five days, Red Army counterattacks drove it back on October 13.

Having eliminated nearly all other serious threats, the Bolsheviks now set about to annihilate what remained of the Volunteer Army in the Crimea. The struggle was clearly an unequal one. An armistice with the Poles was signed on October 12, freeing the troops fighting on that front. Wrangel's front-line forces had been reduced to just above 34,000, of which 23,070 were infantry.[16] Yet, the Red Army, despite its overwhelming numbers, found resistance to be strong, and it advanced only slowly. Wrangel pinned his last hopes on what was known as the Turkish Wall, an old Turkish defensive position. The Wall had been reinforced and what remained of the Volunteer Army's heavy weapons and machine guns were incorporated into the defenses. As impressive and strong as the Turkish Wall had been made, it was a doomed line. As it readied for the final assault, the Red Army numbered 188,771 men as against 26,000 soldiers on the White side, supported by only 16,000 reservists. The Bolsheviks also had some 3,000 machine guns and 600 artillery pieces as against 200 field guns for the Whites.[17]

At 3:30 a.m. on November 9, 1920, infantry from the Fifty-first Division of the Red Army made what was the final assault against the Turkish Wall. Three earlier attacks had been beaten back by the defenders, but this attack succeeded. The collapse of the White defense at the Turkish Wall represented the final defeat for the Volunteer Army. In a way, it had not been the overwhelming numbers of the Red Army which determined the outcome. It was instead determined by the weather. The Volunteer Army had relied on the water of the Sivash salt marshes for their defense at one part of the Turkish Wall. Dry weather had exposed the marshes and cold weather had frozen the exposed mud sufficiently to allow the Red Army to send the Fifty-first Division across the flats. The division was fortunate that it made it across the marshes without being detected, perhaps more fortunate that its attacks ultimately were successful. Water had moved back in after the division had crossed, cutting off any possibility of retreat - or of reinforcements. In the end, it would not have mattered. The Volunteer Army had neither the economic resources nor the manpower to hold off the Red Army. Wrangel managed one final, albeit small, victory against the Reds. He was able to evacuate 145,693 people to Constantinople by November 16, 1920, thus avoiding a final humiliating surrender of the Volunteer Army.[18]

RED TRIUMPH/WHITE FAILURE

The story of the White armies, as told in this chapter, has focused more on the military and, to a lesser extent, the political side of the period between 1918 and 1921. Armed conflict is almost a purely political struggle, at least at the battlefield level. Soldiers motivated enough to risk their lives in a cause, or even to kill, represent the ultimate commitment to an ideology - the true believers in the political world of ideas. A focus on the military fortunes of the various White armies, as a result, may seem somewhat out of place in an economic analysis of the Soviet Union. It has been included in this discussion for two reasons. First, it is intended to contest the notion that the Bolshevik takeover in the October Revolution was totally without support - that the Bolsheviks somehow tricked people and were able to establish control with only a small group of fanatical supporters. The Bolsheviks, in reality, did not rely on a small group of fanatics. Instead they gained control through a much larger group of people who, while not fanatical followers of Bolshevism, were sufficiently committed to fight against the re-imposition of the Czarist regime or, conversely, not sufficiently committed to the White cause to concern themselves with its survival. Second, there is an economic element involved even in the military fortunes of the White and Red armies.

Economic forces made themselves felt in two ways in the Civil War. First, the Bolsheviks won, as a practical matter, because they controlled the most important industrial facilities, crucial to supplying their armies with weapons and ammunition. When both sides could find people equally willing to fight, victory would be determined by the side which could supply its troops with whatever was necessary. Economic strength, in the end, would determine the outcome on the battlefield, particularly when it was a protracted struggle, as the Russian Civil War became. Second, economic forces were, to a large extent, responsible for providing the Bolsheviks with volunteers for their armies. Life for both peasants and ordinary workers was difficult in Russia. Resource scarcity and economic conditions forced peasants off the land, made life hard for a factory labor force which had difficulty making ends meet, and created a large pool of people who resented those who were able to succeed where they could not. The focus of their resentment became the rich and their allies, the officials in the Czarist government who enforced what they considered to be unfair laws.

The White cause was, in the end, measured by its successes or defeats on the battlefield. Final defeat was not, however, simply a failure of soldiers or generals in combat. The Whites failed in other important areas. They offered no vision or solution to the problem of how to govern Russia. If their cause has been portrayed as an idealistic crusade defeated by a ruthless and evil enemy, they failed to live up to that image at the time. In fact, the Whites often proved to be corrupt and inept administrators in areas where they managed to establish control. While they thought of themselves as freedom fighters trying to save Russian democracy, the people they came into contact with often found them to be opportunists who were out for themselves.

The White armies and military strategy represent a significant part of the political story of the Russian Civil War period. Lenin's secret police, the Cheka, represent another aspect, the internal development of the government. The history of the Cheka as an institution provides some insight into the workings of the Bolshevik governmental structure.

THE BOLSHEVIK CHEKA IN THE CIVIL WAR

The Cheka, ironically, had its origins in banking. It may be recalled that Lenin had authorized the establishment of the Cheka in 1917 to deal with the State Bank and smaller banks which refused to cooperate with the new Bolshevik regime. The irony is that the Cheka, with its origins related to such a quiet field as banking, could be involved in some of the most horrendous acts associated with Bolshevik rule. The number of victims of the Cheka during the period of the Civil War has never been determined. The lowest figure is 12,733, while the highest is 1.7 million. Lincoln believes the most accurate figure to be around 100,000.[19] The numbers alone do not tell the entire story of the Cheka's operations. While there seemed to be the same obsession with secrecy, as in the killing of Fannie Kaplan, Lenin's would-be assassin, there also seemed to be a fascination with torture and pain and the use of unusual methods. In a return to Biblical methods of capital punishment, crucifixion was used in Ekaterinoslav and Kiev, while stoning was employed in other areas. Victims in Odessa, mostly White officers, were killed by being pushed into furnaces or into boiling water. Some victims were killed by physically twisting their heads off while, in other places, they were skinned alive. In Kiev, Cheka executioners used crowbars to kill victims - continually striking their skulls as the victim's heads were resting on a wooden block.[20]

During the French Revolution, Revolutionary officials sought to devise the most cruel and bizarre methods of execution. It was at Nantes that Loyalist captives were placed in boats, which were towed out into the middle of the Loire river, and sunk. In France political and societal pressure combined with force to bring the worst excesses to an end. Similar pressures, primarily from members of the Bolshevik party itself, in

Russia also eventually brought most of the excesses of the Cheka to an end. However, it took longer to reverse the operations of the Cheka and the number of victims far exceeded the numbers of the French Revolution. Why the discrepancy in numbers and such a slow administrative response? In part, the answer lies in the fact that Russia is a vast land. Many places were simply out-of-the- way places, from which little news was heard. Bolshevik officials were not even aware of what was going on. In addition, in a civil war where the Whites were themselves committing atrocities, any actions taken against the other side, however cruel or bizarre, would often be seen as acts justified by revenge or the need to survive.

Not only did Russia's geographical size create a different political situation than that of France, population figures were different. Russia had a larger population than that of France - and an ethnically more diverse population as well. France's cultural makeup was much more uniform. The length and vicious nature of the Russian Civil War itself may provide a partial answer as well. The Bolsheviks, in view of the existence of a number of White armies, felt themselves insecure. In France the forces of the monarchy were seen to have been defeated in a shorter period of time. Once that danger had passed, common social and cultural forces began to reassert themselves to put an end to the worst excesses of the most radical groups in French society. In Revolutionary Russia, the worst excesses of the Cheka, as in France, occurred when the Bolsheviks felt most threatened. The advance of the White armies on Moscow in 1919 resulted in an expansion of the Cheka's authority. White retreat tended to bring a relaxation of Cheka activities, although it did not bring total retreat.

December 7, 1917 was the date Lenin established the Cheka, although he did not rely on it for political control in the first few months of his regime. Opposition often took the form of large public demonstrations, and the Cheka was not suitable for large-scale military operations. To suppress demonstrations Lenin instead relied on regular troops. As with any governmental agency, it took time to develop an organizational structure and operational apparatus. In March 1918 it officially employed only 120 people. Many of its first recruits were, in fact, not Russians, but Latvians, Armenians, and Jews.[21] Created to deal with the revolt of the banks, the Cheka was actually slow to expand outside the financial area, nor did it show much aptitude in the general field of intelligence. Its first attempts at intelligence gathering and analysis proved disastrous. The Left SR revolt of July 6-7, 1918 was not only undiscovered by the Cheka, it was actually organized at the Cheka headquarters in Moscow. Just as embarrassing for Dzerzhinskii, the Cheka's head, was the fact that it had almost entirely ignored warnings about SR activities - SR leaders had openly called for an armed uprising only days before the attempted coup. It also had had no intelligence on Boris Savinkov's uprising in Iaroslavl, which occurred at about the same time.

The rebellion of the bankers provided a starting point for the first assignments given the Cheka, namely investigating economic crimes. The black market was one of the first targets, as were the "bagmen," so-named for the peasants who carried and sold individual sacks of grain in an attempt to profit from the agricultural segment of the black market trade. On February 22, 1918, the Cheka's power was theoretically expanded with Dzerzhinskii's decree authorizing summary executions. In April the Cheka enlarged its organization with the addition of military units which included machine gunners and armored cars.

In spite of the increased authority granted by Dzerzhinskii's February decree, the Cheka, at first, did not follow any uniform policy in its treatment of political opponents. Outside of Moscow and Petrograd, Cheka staff were quick to seize the initiative. In Vitebsk, two workers were executed merely for distributing posters in the spring of 1918. In Moscow and Petrograd, the Bolsheviks had made an agreement with the left SRs that political opponents were to be spared such treatment. Surprisingly, it was one of the few instances where the Bolshevik government honored an agreement. The protection provided by the agreement came to an end with the July 6 SR uprising, following which the Left SRs were removed from their positions within the Cheka. Even with the restraint exercised in Moscow and Petrograd, the local Chekas carried out 882 executions in the period from January to June of 1918. In July the number increased to 1,115.[22]

The Left SR revolt of July did not, in itself, bring about an immediate crackdown. The Bolsheviks, in fact, carried out few reprisal executions against those involved. While they publicly announced that 200 Left SRs had been shot, the report was false and most of the 650 arrested in Moscow were released.[23] The removal of the left SRs from the Cheka however, eliminated what few controls remained. There are indications that Lenin wished to implement a broader governmental terror campaign before Fannie Kaplan's attempt on his life. Yet it may have been the successful assassination of the Petrograd Cheka chief M. S. Uritskii on the morning of the 30th coupled with his own near-fatal shooting the same day which gave a strong impetus to Lenin's desire for more ruthless measures.

On September 4, the Commissar of the Interior, Grigorii Petrovskii, issued a decree authorizing the taking of hostages from among the bourgeoisie and (former) military class of officers. Coupled with this authorization was an order calling for mass executions. On September 5, the Sovnarkom issued a similar decree which provided for summary execution and the establishment of concentration camps.

The Cheka had not waited for these official decrees to go into effect to begin the Terror. In Nizhnii Novgorod, 41 victims were shot on August 30. Another 512 hostages were executed in Petrograd on the orders of Zinoviev. This was followed by the execution of several former officials of the Czarist regime. Although the Cheka may have had justification to punish those who actively worked against the government, the victims often were not killed for anti-Bolshevik activities. Many fell victim because they happened to be rich or had been members of the Czarist government.

What served to curb the Cheka's actions in January and February of 1919 was the realization, by Bolshevik Party members that the arbitrary methods used by the Cheka could easily be turned against them. In January 1919, the Moscow Committee of the Party defeated a motion to abolish the Cheka, but another motion would be passed limiting the Cheka's power. The Central Committee ordered a report which resulted in the transfer of some of the Cheka's power to Revolutionary Tribunals. The vote would not impress the members of the Cheka itself, which would largely ignore it. It did impress Lenin and other Party leaders to the extent that they at least backed off some of their pressure to expand the Terror - until the White armies again threatened Moscow in 1919.

While the internal opposition from Party members may have tempered the most extreme excesses of the Cheka, it was not enough to persuade Party leadership to totally curb the Cheka's power. In fact, the decision was to expand the powers of the Cheka, rather than to curtail them. That signal was given by the appointment of Dzerzhinskii, head of the Cheka, as Commissar of the Interior in March 1919, while he remained head of the Cheka. In addition, during 1919, the Cheka was given the authority to arrest preventively any citizen. The Cheka's powers of investigation were also expanded to cover all institutions; the Cheka's investigative powers were no longer limited to suspected economic crimes. Along with the formal authority and expanded power came an increase in the size of the Cheka. The Cheka's members were now organized into military units, more formally known as the Armies of the Internal Security of the Republic, with a strength of between 120,000 and 125,000 men in 1919. The numbers would increase to some 250,000 in 1920.[24]

The end of the Red Terror finally came in 1920 with the defeat of the White armies. It did not mean the end of repression. Political enemies were still summarily shot, but the Bolsheviks no longer needed the mass executions to eliminate their enemies - the most conspicuous and dangerous had already been eliminated by the Terror. The Cheka now had a sufficiently large military force to contend with what scattered resistance remained or would develop. Concentration camps, while inhuman, were not as liable to provoke the instinctive revulsion and political opposition that the large numbers of executions brought on. The killings or deaths which did occur in the camps were insignificant when compared to the numbers occurring at the height of the Terror. Party members, no longer alarmed at the prospect that they would themselves become victims, were content to leave the Cheka alone.

REASONS FOR THE WHITE FAILURE

The discussion in this chapter has focused primarily on two aspects of the political history of the Civil War. The victories and defeats of the White armies in the military struggle are one aspect of that political story. The development of the powers of the Cheka is the other. The final section of this chapter looks at the White side of the Civil War, specifically at the actual governmental rule of the Whites, and at some additional reasons for the Bolshevik victory.

In the final analysis the Bolsheviks did not win because they were willing to use force to overthrow the Provisional Government, while their democratic opponents were not. The soldiers of the White armies were highly motivated and fought ferociously, inflicting heavy casualties on the Red Army units they faced. The treatment of political prisoners and the mass executions carried out by the Cheka give the impression that atrocities were only practiced by the Red armies. In fact, the White soldiers were capable of practicing warfare at the same level. White soldiers once filled three box cars with the corpses of Red Guards killed in the fighting and sent them toward the Red lines together with the message - "fresh meat, destination Petrograd."[26] Petr Wrangel, the Volunteer Army's general, once had 400 Red prisoners shot in October 1918, before offering the remaining captives the option of serving in the White army to escape the same fate.[26]

One estimate of the number of deserters from the Red Army for the period from June 1919 to June 1920 is 2.6 million.[27] Pipes points out that, from July through December of 1919, more soldiers deserted from the Red Army each month than the Whites had in the Volunteer Army.[28] The figures clearly show that service in the Red Army was not a popular option with recruits. What should be noted however, is that, as unpopular as Bolshevik military service was, the Red Army desertions did not benefit the Volunteer Army or any of the other White forces. Committed supporters of the Bolshevik government may have been relatively small, but they appear to have been larger than those willing to commit to the White cause.

There were a number of factors at work in the Red victory, in addition to those discussed earlier. First, from a geographical standpoint, the Bolsheviks controlled the Russian land area in the geographical center of the fighting. They had shorter distances to transport troops and could move their forces more easily to deal with the movements of their opponents. Second, the Bolshevik armies were, for the most part, composed of ethnic Russians, whereas the White forces were a mix of ethnic groups - they lacked the ethnic cohesion helpful in providing an underlying motivation.[29] A related advantage was that the areas the Bolsheviks controlled contained a larger population base. Where the strength and size of armies depended, not so much on the motivation of the individual, but on the size of the service-age population in the areas "under control," the Bolsheviks benefitted from the larger population found within the areas they held. In fact, the population of Great Russia, the Bolshevik-controlled region, numbered around 70 million, which contrasted to the 8 to 9 million inhabitants residing in the White-controlled areas.[30]

In terms of weapons and armament, the Bolsheviks had two advantages. First, the majority of industries which produced weapons or ammunition were located in areas they controlled. Second, there had been large quantities of ammunition stored for use by the Czar's military forces. These too were located within the areas controlled by the Red forces.

While the population and weapons advantages held by the Bolsheviks were, to a certain extent, a matter of happenstance, the Red victory was not solely the result of one or two lucky breaks. The Whites, by their own actions, contributed to their own downfall. Had the Whites presented the Russian people with a clear choice between democracy and dictatorship, they might have provided a cause around which the Russian people would have rallied. Instead what they offered was a choice between a return to the rule of the Czar or, just as bad, an administrative operation which was itself as undemocratic as that of the Bolsheviks. In addition to such problems the Whites proved to be inefficient and corrupt administrators.

Corruption not only cost the Whites the support of the population they supposedly were fighting for, it worked against them on the battlefield. Supplies and armaments intended by the Allies for front line use disappeared into the hands of speculators. When Denikin was moving against Moscow in October 1919, tanks supplied by the British were not sent to the front because there were no freight cars to ship them. Yet there were freight cars available - for a price. Speculators had been in the habit of buying them.[31] Supplies which failed to reach the front were only part of the problem. Military officers or officials of the White regime were often accused of sanctioning illegal arrests, robbery, and murder.

A serious problem for the Whites was the inability to provide any clear political vision of what they intended. Often what they argued for was the concept of an anti-Bolshevik regime. In practice, what they offered was simply a return to Czarism. When Denikin's army pushed toward Moscow in October 1919, the administration he put in power in the regions behind the front did not just model itself after the Czarist regime, it often included the same officials who had worked in the Czarist government. On one occasion, a Czarist supporter is said to have nostalgically recognized the same police officials who had worked in the old government.[32] Royalists and ex-nobles may have been pleased by such events; peasants and those who had found the Czarist officials repressive, were not.

The White armies, apart from their placing officials of the old regime in power, did not conduct themselves in a way which would bring popular support. The peasants called the Volunteer Army the Looting Army and its members as well as the Cossacks were often guilty of terrorizing individuals or ethnic inhabitants of lands they gained control of. The support or opposition of individual ethnic groups was too small, in itself, to be a determining factor in the final outcome of the Civil War. At the same time, where power could depend on a coalition of smaller groups, the loss of support by seemingly inconsequential peoples came to add up.

Jewish inhabitants found White rule to be particularly oppressive. There were pogroms which were carried out against the Jews in Bolshevik territory. Yet the official Bolshevik policy was to work against pogroms and the number which occurred in Bolshevik-controlled territory were fewer. The Bolsheviks enforced stricter disciplinary measures to control potential problems. Those who participated in pogroms were shot and anti-Semitic writings were forbidden. The result was that the Red Army, even in retreat, found entire Jewish settlements seeking protection.

The viciousness of the pogroms which occurred, as well as the number of victims, in some ways rivaled those carried out by the Cheka. In September 1919, a five-day pogrom in Fastov, carried out by White forces, resulted in the murder of 2,000 Jews. Earlier, in August, White forces had raped 350 women at one Jewish settlement.[33] In May 1919 Ukrainian soldiers killed 400 in the district of Uman. In Kiev, the White forces bayoneted Jews, threw them from the upper stories of buildings, or drowned them in the river.[34]

The attacks against the Jewish population by the Whites largely went unpunished and they were able to act with impunity in certain regions. In other regions, it was dangerous to antagonize ethnic groups. Even without taking any overt action however, the antagonism often seemed to spring up from nowhere. The White cause could inspire a peculiar hatred. Nestor Makhno, a Ukrainian peasant leader, represented this type of opposition. It was Makhno's forces which caused such disruption in the rear of Denikin's advance in 1919 that troops had to be diverted from the push toward Moscow.

Makhno best illustrates the ethnic problems which faced the Whites, in addition to their general ineptitude. In some ways the Ukraine represented a unique situation. In other ways it was a "unique" situation which was duplicated elsewhere in the Civil War. Makhno provided the leadership for peasants who opposed any governmental authority imposed from outside. Ukrainian peasants did not like Russians nor the leadership provided by the Czar. Makhno fought, in turn, the Germans, the Whites, and the Bolsheviks. Makhno reserved his greatest hatred for the Whites, primarily because, from Makhno's perspective, their victory would bring a return to the rule of the Czar. What Makhno wanted, above all else, was an independent Ukraine. Perhaps because he had to concentrate all his energies against one enemy at a time, he tended to view the immediate threat as the greatest danger. The Whites, in 1919, seemed to represent that threat. The Bolsheviks had their hands full with the Whites and were content to leave him alone. That situation would change once the Whites had been defeated. In 1921 they turned their full attention to the Ukraine, defeated Makhno's armies, and forced him to flee to France. During the Civil War however, it was the Bolsheviks who benefitted the most from his anti-authority stance.

Makhno's success, in part, could be attributed to the geographical disadvantages the Whites were subject to. While Denikin had concentrated nearly all his forces in the assault on Moscow in October 1919, Makhno's forces captured the port of Berdiansk, on the Sea of Azov. They then moved north to capture Ekaterinoslav. They destroyed, at Azov, some 60,000 artillery shells, stored in reserve for Denikin's forces. At other cities they captured the Whites had reserves of guns and ammunition, which his forces either appropriated or destroyed. The disruption finally forced Denikin to divert troops from the front, a move which came at the time when he needed as many troops as possible in his assault on Moscow.

The Bolsheviks, for their part, showed little gratitude for Makhno's contribution to the defeat of the Volunteer Army. Shortly after Denikin's forces began their retreat, the Red Army attacked the cities of Kharkov and Kiev, then held by Makhno. Following their capture, he was declared an outlaw by the Ukrainian Communist Party. Too late he discovered that, like the Czarist regime and the Whites, the Bolsheviks were not going to tolerate a peasant army which could be turned against them if their policies proved unpopular.

CONCLUSION

The Bolsheviks emerged as victors in the Russian Civil War, not because they were more unscrupulous or unprincipled than their opponents, nor because they were fanatics who approached the Civil War with a religious fervor. In the end they won simply because they controlled the physical and human resources required in any war. They did not require any superhuman effort on the part of their followers, merely the normal commitment. The Whites lost, in large part, because they could offer no real alternative to Bolshevik rule.

In the context of this book's theory, perhaps the single biggest factor in the defeat of the White forces, was the presence of a large populace of discontented. Poor peasants and workers had borne the brunt of the economic problems which Czarist officials had been unable to solve. Insofar as the Whites came to symbolize a return to Czarist solutions, their cause held no appeal for the mass of Russian workers and peasants. Conversely, what the Bolsheviks offered was freedom from Czarist rule. The Bolsheviks were successful because the heart of their political message confirmed what the workers and peasants believed - their economic problems were the result of a "conspiracy" between the rich and the Czarist government. Without having to provide details of their own solution, the Bolsheviks benefitted from the "army of discontented." Their political message largely exploited the discontent. What they did not say was what they would do if their policies proved no more successful than those of the Czar. The next chapter looks beyond the Civil War, covering the political history of Russia from 1921 through 1938. As will be seen, the Bolsheviks, like their Greek and Roman counterparts, found the discontented to be a useful ally when used against others, but a dangerous and uncontrollable force when turned against them.

CHAPTER 12

THE COMMUNISTS IN POWER - 1921-1938

Petr Wrangel, the commanding general of the Volunteer Army, had not expected the Red Army attack at the Turkish Wall on November 9, 1920. His defenses had been reinforced at other positions along the line. Despite this unforeseen defeat, General Wrangel was able to conduct an organized evacuation of what remained of his army. The evacuation flotilla of 126 ships got 145,693 people safely away from the Crimean Peninsula.[1]

The White forces had been beaten long before November 9. Despite the difficulties the Red Army had in dislodging them, they had been bottled up in the peninsula and were no longer relevant to the political events in Russia. During much of 1920, the Volunteer Army had not even been the main priority of the Red Army. In April the Poles had invaded the Ukraine, causing the Bolsheviks to shift many of their forces to that front. The fighting would continue until an armistice was agreed to in October.

This chapter looks at the political history of the Communist regime following the end of the Civil War. In many ways it could be described as a period of disillusionment, both for the Bolsheviks and for the workers and peasants who supported them. The Bolsheviks, who, to some extent, believed that they had made the greatest sacrifices in overthrowing the oppressive regime of the Czar, now found themselves to be the object of the worker's hatred. The workers and peasants, rather than giving the Bolsheviks a chance to carry out their policies, turned on the new government.

They now called on the Bolsheviks to deliver on the promises they had made. It was not so much that the Bolsheviks had failed to deliver, but that they had failed to deliver on everything they had promised. Part of the problem was that they had promised more than one thing. The heart of their political message was that the rich, the aristocracy, and Czarist officials were the cause of all the economic ills of the poor. It was the one message which would be certain to appeal to the economically disadvantaged masses. Get rid of these groups and economic improvement for everyone would follow, according to the logic of the argument. The Bolsheviks had delivered on their promise to get rid of these groups, yet the economic distribution and prosperity which was expected to follow did not occur.

During the Civil War, when grain stocks had fallen, the Bolsheviks had sent armed parties into the countryside to take grain by force from peasants who were reluctant to sell or provide harvests voluntarily. Such actions were not popular with the peasants or with those in the armed forces who had been raised in the villages. While there were scattered protests in the villages, the first determined opposition came in early 1921, ironically, at a place far-removed from the grain growing regions of Russia, the Kronstadt fortress - the same military garrison which furnished the 5,000 sailors who had participated in the October 1917 attack on the Winter Palace.

At Kronstadt, the now-victorious Communist regime blundered into the same minefield the Czarist regime had encountered in the Petrograd garrison in February 1917 and the Provisional Government would discover in October of the same year. Many of the conscripts or recruits at Kronstadt or on the ships in the harbor there had come from the Ukraine or had peasant origins. Sympathetic to the plight of their villages and the workers, they began to brood about the wrongs committed by the new government. Disenchantment grew as a result of a shortage of clothing and food which the garrison was itself experiencing.

The Communist leadership misread the garrison and committed several blunders in dealing with the problem. Had it dealt with some of the more immediate complaints early, in a more tactful way, it could have diffused the situation and avoided the more dangerous confrontation which occurred. Instead, no doubt still in the confrontational mind-set of the Civil War, it goaded the garrison into a rigid position and then into open rebellion.

Although the shortages of food and clothing lay behind the complaints, it was the sufferings of others which initially moved the garrison to action. The city of Petrograd had had to endure shortages caused, in part, by a severe winter. The railway system, which carried coal, oil, and wood, fuel supplies crucial to the city, in December 1920 was disrupted by heavy snows. To provide wood for fuel, city officials authorized the destruction of 175 buildings from November through January, another 50 in February.[2] Fuel shortages impacted employment. A one-week factory and mill closure, from January 19 through 23, was ordered by the Executive Committee of the Petrograd Soviet. This was followed in February by the closure of 93 of Petrograd's largest factories coupled with a cut in wages. At the same time, food prices were rising. In January 1921, potato and rye bread prices tripled. In fact, during 1920, bread prices had risen 1,000 percent.[3]

Conditions in Petrograd provided authorities with few options. The decisions made however were a recipe for civil unrest. The growing number of unemployed now took to the streets, which resulted in police suppression of the protests. A street demonstration of 2,000 workers on February 24, 1921 was broken up by police. Petrograd authorities then forbade all public meetings and imposed a curfew. In addition, they closed all factories where demonstrations had taken place. Initially, these measures brought additional protesters into the streets. However, the physical condition of the workers provided them with little strength to mount continuing opposition. Many were brought back with the promise of extra holiday rations. For those not enticed by such offers, the heavy police patrols enforced the impression that the authorities would not be defied. Those who did return to work found themselves overseen by armed squads of "defense committees." The authorities, with a monopoly on arms and force within Petrograd, could physically control workers in the city. However, that control did not extend beyond the city. The Kronstadt garrison could more than match the authorities in arms and trained personnel.

The garrison sent a delegation to Petrograd to investigate the rumors it had heard. It reported back on February 28. Its members had been disturbed by what they found in the city. They also became concerned about stories told by those coming back from leave. In villages throughout Russia the actions of the authorities were viewed as oppressive. At a meeting aboard one of the ships, the sailors openly criticized the Communists and, in addition, passed a resolution calling for new elections. A delegation of government officials, led by Mikhail "Papa" Kalinin, tried to diffuse the situation the next day. The explanations offered did not satisfy the sailors who were assembled, particularly when contrasted with the reports of what was happening to the workers in Petrograd. Kalinin's speech was received coldly and the Party officials took a threatening tack. Though angered by Kalinin's explanations the sailors escorted him back to the city. The government, for its part, did not move in a conciliatory manner. Another delegation was sent from Kronstadt to look into the situation in Petrograd and the authorities had them arrested. In response to this action and the no-compromise stance taken by the government, the sailors became even more belligerent. While again calling for new elections for the Kronstadt Soviet, they also threatened to arrest Kuzman, the Commissar of the Baltic fleet as well as the chairman of the Soviet. Following the arrests the government sent truckloads of armed men to quell the growing revolt. The sailors were able to beat back the force and then voted to establish a Provisional Revolutionary Committee, on March 2, to assume authority until elections could be held.

The Bolsheviks could no longer prevent open rebellion. The only option was containment. Aware that discontent with their rule in Russia was not limited to Kronstadt, they now realized the need to move quickly. The arrest of the 30-member delegation on March 1 was their first decisive move. The sending of the armed contingent on March 2, though insufficient to stop the sailors, was another. These actions further galvanized the sailors, who now sent detachments to defend Kotlin Island. The authorities made one more attempt to end the revolt without full-scale military operations. Trotsky, in a speech before the sailors, ordered them to surrender unconditionally. Zinoviev, as head of the Petrograd Defense Committee, issued an order stating that those who did not surrender would be shot. The Defense Committee also had relatives of those at the fortress arrested and held as hostages. The threats served only to anger the sailors of the Kronstadt.

Tactically, with only a 15,000-man force, the garrison's real hope was not in mounting an offensive campaign into the Russian heartland, nor even a single battlefield victory over the Soviet army. Its real hope was more psychological. If it could defy the government and survive, it would provide a cause around which opposition could rally. Tactically, what was hoped for was an early spring thaw. During the winter, the ice which surrounded the island left it open to assault by land forces. If the defenders could somehow hold off attack until the ice was gone, they might be able to hold out indefinitely or at least through the summer. For their part, government military officials knew that the ice gave them the best opportunity to end the revolt. Aware that discontent was widespread, the longer the garrison held out, the greater the chance that it would come out into the open.

The battle began as an artillery duel on March 7. Mikhail Tukhachevskii, the commanding general of the government forces, ordered his heavy guns to begin firing. A heavy snowstorm began that evening and Tukhachevskii, believing it might provide sufficient cover, ordered an attack in the early morning hours of March 8. Though the advance had to be made over some five miles of ice, in some places, the attackers managed to reach the outer defenses before being discovered. The defenders beat back the attack, inflicting heavy losses - 500 of the assaulting force were killed and almost 2,000 wounded.[4] Signs of the coming spring thaw were even showing themselves in the attack. The attackers had spread out in an attempt to prevent the ice from giving way as they moved forward. Yet shells which exploded in the ranks of the advancing force often caused the ice to give way - giving the attackers some special terror - besides machine gun and artillery fire - to fear.

Tukhachevskii, in addition to the timetable set by nature and climactic conditions, had a political timetable as well. Lenin was presiding over the Tenth Party Congress in Moscow, which opened on March 8. Hoping to announce a successful conclusion to the events at Kronstadt, Lenin was embarrassed when he had to admit that the rebels still held out - and 320 of the delegates left after volunteering to go to the front to help in the fighting.[5]

The failure of the first assault and time itself seemed to work against Tukhachevskii. Other assaults were ordered - and beaten back. He faced the prospect of mutiny as troops became reluctant to attack other Bolsheviks - and to face the perils of attacks over thinning ice. Military leaders felt it necessary to reinforce army morale with Party believers. Young Communist volunteers were sent in. Lenin felt even this was not enough. Aware that the general discontent felt in the villages was contributing to morale problems in the attacking force, he made a political concession. He called, on March 15, for the elimination of forced governmental grain requisitions in the villages. Grain requisitions were one of the most odious - and hated - policies of the government. In view of Lenin's past actions, it may have been naive of the peasants to place much trust in his statements. Yet his political instincts proved correct and even the promise of an easing of the policy brought the government needed political support. Where the Kronstadt rebels had begun to gain sympathy as defenders of Bolshevik ideals, they were now seen as a threat to the goals of the Revolution.

With a force of 45,000 ready for a final assault, Lenin's political concession may have been unneeded. The Kronstadt garrison was being weakened by a shortage of rations. On the morning of March 17, 1921, Tukhachevskii ordered a final assault. Although the ice had continued to deteriorate, his troops managed to reach the lines of the fortress, despite losses to the cold water and mine fields. Beaten back several times, they regrouped and finally were able to capture Kronstadt. Despite the victory, some 8,000 of the defenders escaped to Finland. Those who surrendered were not so lucky. Several hundred were shot, while those who survived were sent to concentration camps.

The Kronstadt revolt represented the most politically embarrassing symbol of opposition to Communist rule. The regime had faced more serious opposition in other areas of Russia. Lenin's announced intention to end forced grain requisitions on March

15, while providing the needed political support against the Kronstadt rebels, in reality had been aimed at revolts in the rural areas of Russia. In August 1920, peasants in the city of Tambov, southeast of Moscow, killed members of a grain requisition team. The killings sparked a series of attacks and counterattacks between local villages and the Red Army. A peasant leader, Alexander Antonov, managed to bring some organization to the rebellious peasant groups. By the end of the year he had a force of 8,000. He increased this number to between 20,000 and 50,000 in early 1921.[6] Operating a guerilla war, with raids on government installations and killings of government officials, Antonov posed a serious threat to the Communist regime.

A force of 100,000 soldiers under the command of Tukhachevskii, the victor at Kronstadt, was sent into the area. Resorting to hostage-taking, mass executions, and relocation of villages, Tukhachevskii managed to defeat Antonov's army and bring the area under control. Unfortunately, just as the rebellion was brought under control, Russia had to endure a famine.

A drought, starting in 1920, proved disastrous to agricultural production in 1921. Dry weather in the fall of 1920 continued into winter and on into the spring of 1921. It is estimated that the drought impacted half of Russia's food-producing areas and that some 26 million Russians and 7.5 million Ukrainians were affected.[7] Peasants became so desperate that, during the summer, whole villages were abandoned, as their inhabitants left to find food in other regions. Hundreds of thousands died from typhus, cholera, typhoid fever, and smallpox. Conditions became so bad that the Communists, reluctant to even admit that famine was occurring, finally accepted American aid in August. Though denouncing the motives of President Hoover, Lenin allowed the American Relief Administration (ARA) to distribute food without interference from political officials - a requirement set down by Hoover.

In spite of these very real problems, the Party, coming out of 1921, seemed to focus on internal matters and side issues. As 1921 ended the Party began a purge of its ranks. The targets were primarily Mensheviks and former members of other parties who had been late converts to the Bolshevik cause. From a high of 659,000, membership was reduced to under 400,000.[8]

The church and religious belief, long a target of Bolshevik criticism, came under heavy attack in 1922. With around 100 million adherents, the church had escaped serious state criticism during the Revolution. Party attacks on the church varied in degree. Somewhat less severe were actions such as the elimination of state subsidies and the confiscation of church properties. At the other end of the spectrum lay imprisonment of church officials as well as executions. The actions taken against the Orthodox Church were not unwelcome in some areas. The clergy were often seen as being part of the hated nobility. Peasants in some areas even attacked priests as they expelled them from their villages. At the same time, while the Party had avoided public attacks on the church, the Cheka had not exempted church leaders or members from its activities. Tikhon, the Patriarch of the Orthodox Church, gave a figure of 322, as the number of bishops and priests executed between 1917 and 1920.[9]

Some of the Party actions gave rise to somewhat comical, as well as embarrassing, results for the Orthodox Church. The Church, in maintaining shrines where the bodies of saints were supposedly resting, reinforced the belief that, after death, decomposition did not occur. In March 1919 the Party decreed that coffins holding the supposed remains of the saints were to be opened. At many such shrines, the coffins contained either the skeletal remains of the sainted individuals, or, perhaps more embarrassing for the clergy, dummies.

The Party attack took a more serious - and deadly - tack in 1922, when Moscow placed Church officials and lay workers on trial in April and May. Five defendants would be executed as a result of the trials. While the Church could be characterized as conservative, even reactionary in some cases, it was not automatically the ally of the nobility. Patriarch Tikhon, in fact, was a moderate leader, not fanatically opposed to the new regime, but not uncaring about the plight of those suffering under the famine. Lenin was fully aware that the Church had not openly acted in opposition to Communist rule; it had, for the most part, stayed out of the political conflict. Nevertheless he had an instinctive, dogmatic mistrust of organized religion and was determined to eliminate its influence in Russian society.

The backdrop to the 1922 trials was Lenin's decision, in January, to force a confrontation with the Church, although Trotsky was likely involved in the decision. The attack came in the form of a request that the Church donate its "consecrated" vessels, i.e., those articles the church considered sacred, ostensibly to help in the relief of the poor. Created from precious and semiprecious metals, the works were valuable. The Church was not averse to using its wealth to aid in the relief. In 1921, Patriarch Tikhon had donated the "nonconsecrated" vessels for that purpose, when requested. Lenin knew that a request for consecrated vessels would meet with resistance. In fact, that was what he hoped for. Tikhon countered with an offer to raise funds equivalent to the value of the requested vessels. Lenin turned down the offer.

Lenin's inclination to force a confrontation was resisted by the Party; many members felt that recognition of the legitimacy of the Communist regime might be threatened by such an open strategy. Nevertheless, Lenin and Trotsky obtained a formal decree on February 26 - the sacred vessels and other precious objects of the Church were to be confiscated to help those suffering. Tikhon's response was to threaten excommunication of those laymen who helped, defrocking for any priests who also participated. Lenin had Tikhon arrested in May.

In many places, authorities met with resistance. Crowds gathered at churches in an effort to prevent removal. At Shuia, northeast of Moscow, officials on March 12 tried to carry out their assignment but were chased away by the crowd. They would return on March 15 with a detachment of soldiers. When the crowd became unruly, the soldiers opened fire, killing several people. These events caused Party officials to suspend further confiscations, but their decisions were made in the absence of Lenin and Trotsky. March 19, the same day instructions went out to the countryside to suspend further confiscations, Lenin decided to proceed. Perhaps irrationally convinced that resistance was part of an organized anti-government plot, Lenin specifically wanted those at Shuia punished and three people there would be executed. Shuia did not bring any sense of contrition on Lenin's part. Instead he saw events as an opportunity to be exploited, for they served as a pretext for expansion of the campaign. On March 22, Trotsky obtained a formal vote by the Commission for the Realization of Valuables - the confiscations were to resume.

By mid-April 32 people had been placed on trial. As in France, Revolutionary Tribunals began to conduct trials for counterrevolutionary activity. The most publicized proceedings were the Moscow show trials, beginning April 26 and ending May 6. A total of 54 were charged, primarily priests, 11 sentenced to death, and five actually executed.[10] In Petrograd, the Party charged 86, holding the trials through much of June and early July. Those found guilty were officially sentenced only to be defrocked. On the surface, the Party had dispensed justice leniently. Secretly, four were executed, including Benjamin, the Metropolitan of Petrograd. In the countryside, priests were often hung or arrested. One estimate put the number killed during 1922 as a result of the campaign at 8,000. Among these were 28 bishops and 1,215 priests.[11]

The show trials of the clergy were not the only political trials which would take place in Russia that year. Lenin had chosen to target the members of the SR party. Although the decision to hold trials had been made in December 1921, the announcement that trials would be held was not made until February 28, 1922. The state charged 34 SR members with counterrevolutionary activities and finally began the formal trials on June 6. Attempting to show how vile the defendants were, the trial organizers allowed spectators in to cheer the prosecution and jeer at the defendants. The authorities even went so far as to organize a mass demonstration on June 20, in which the judge and prosecutor participated and, in its final stages, the defendants had to appear on a balcony while the crowd harangued them. The trial came to an end on August 7, with the expected guilty verdict. While Party leaders, prior to the trial, had promised that the death penalty would not be applied, fourteen of those charged were given the death sentence. The executions were stayed temporarily by the judges and, in January 1924, would be commuted to five-year prison terms. The reason appears to have been Lenin's desire to use the condemned as hostages; Lenin was fearful of further attempts on his life and a retaliatory terrorist campaign by the SR, should the executions be carried out, seemed a possibility.

The range of punishment available to the Party, in dealing with opposition was unlimited. At the upper extreme, it could mete out the death penalty, as happened with the Church leadership and opposition parties. Lenin seemed to fear members of rival political parties the most, based on the actions taken against them and the severity of the sentences handed out. Intellectuals became a target for Lenin's wrath as well. In perspective, they were dealt with leniently. On August 10, 1922 the Party formally issued a decree which would exile those intellectuals who had proved troublesome. In some ways it is surprising that Lenin had largely left academic and intellectual writers, i.e., those outside the political parties, alone until that time. Prior to that time he appears to have viewed such critics as nothing more than a nuisance. The academics perhaps should have taken more notice of what was happening. A strong signal was sent on June 6, 1922. On that date Glavlit was established. Glavlit was short for Glavnoe Upravienie po delam Leteratury i Izdatel'stva (Main Administration for Literary Affairs and Publishing).[12] It was the official agency for state censorship. Publications which wanted to continue publishing would now need a license from Glavlit.

Following the August 10 decree, authorities began arresting those academics critical of the government. Hundreds had been taken into custody by the end of September. Most were sent to Germany. While the punishment itself was relatively mild, the Communists did ensure that those exiled understood the consequences of crossing the authorities again. Most had to sign a document which threatened them with death if they either refused to leave or if they tried to return to Russia in the future.

The confiscations of church property, the show trials, and the exile of the intellectuals represented the most prominent political activities of 1922. They also represented the last major policies in which Lenin played a major role. On May 25, 1922, he had suffered the first of several strokes which would ultimately lead to his death on January 2, 1924. The second would strike him in December, followed by a third on March 10, 1923, which would leave him paralyzed.

One last political struggle of significance would take place, prior to his death. In the last days of his life, Lenin seems to have worried about the permanence of his accomplishments. Joseph Stalin was also becoming the focus of Lenin's attention. In view of his own involvement in executions and killings, he might have felt some sense of admiration for Stalin's later activities. Yet, Lenin could have no inkling of that future. What gave Lenin pause were Stalin's activities within the Party. Paradoxically, for all Lenin's lack of concern for the suffering of the Russian masses or for the deaths he caused among the members of other political parties, he often seemed troubled by the hurt feelings or philosophical opposition within the Communist Party itself. This may have been at the heart of his misgivings about Stalin and the fear of leaving him in any position of prominence within the Party structure.

Lenin's dislike of Stalin may not have arisen from any high-minded concern about his deviation from communist ideals. It may have stemmed more from Lenin's basic political instincts and the envy of all rival political personalities. Seemingly immortal up to that time, Lenin's stroke in May 1922 may have suggested to potential claimants that his political power would soon decline as well. Partially paralyzed by the stroke, he was forced to rest for a two-month period. Since there was no single individual with the authority to displace him, three individuals assumed power: Stalin, Kamenev, and Zinoviev. There was no formal position they were elected to, but they operated as a "troika" or directory. Instead the three informally agreed to cooperate through their actual Party positions. Kamenev was chairman of the Politburo and the Sovnarkom, Stalin was chairman of the Secretariat and the Orgburo, and Zinoviev headed the Comintern and the Petrograd Party. Seeing Trotsky as their common political enemy, they courted Lenin's favor, while at the same time working to isolate, and ultimately, destroy Trotsky.

Stalin, who often allowed his rivals to control the public debate, was building his own power base. He was aware that power depended on the political support and votes of Party members rather than headline-grabbing speeches. Votes were more likely to be won with patronage - the positions which Stalin assumed allowed him to reward his supporters with jobs. Yet, though Stalin's political maneuverings were not obvious to Kamenev and Zinoviev, Lenin began to suspect that Stalin was working against him. Lenin did not suspect Stalin alone, for he came to view all three members of the troika as working against him. Their concerns about his health, welcomed at first, began to take on the form of orders. While eliminating much of his heavy workload, medical advice to reduce a heavy activities, no doubt went against Lenin's political desire to maintain power and control matters.

The troika, in their desire to take over from Lenin, made some premature moves to assume control. While Lenin had recovered sufficiently by October to return to work, he found that the troika was treating him as though he were no longer in control. Despite an ability to work 10 and 12 hour days following his return, he suffered the lingering effects of his illness and often was too tired to remain more than a few hours at meetings of the Politburo. The members of the troika simply waited until he had left to bring up important matters. He tried to stop such maneuverings by limiting Politburo meetings to three hours. That move came on December 8. Politically he was fighting back, but he now had two opponents: the members of the troika and the physical limitations of his own body. On December 15 he would suffer another stroke, which would be followed, on December 22, by still another one.

For Stalin, Lenin's illness was not a signal to display kindness to a failing leader, it was an excuse to move in for the kill. Perhaps, in a sense, it was a form of poetic justice. Lenin, who had shown little mercy when he ordered troops to fire on unarmed workers, now found himself at Stalin's mercy. Following the December 15 stroke, Stalin secured a Party vote which gave him responsibility for Lenin's medical regimen. Stalin took his authority to the extreme, even going so far as to telephone Lenin's wife on December 22 and threaten her with a Party investigation for having transcribed a congratulatory note to Trotsky dictated by Lenin. (Lenin's dictation fell outside the limited work schedule Lenin was to adhere to, according to Stalin.) Stalin was perhaps saved from political destruction by the stroke which Lenin suffered that night. Following the December 22 stroke, Lenin's dictation time was reduced to five to ten minutes a day.

It appears that one of Lenin's final battles with Stalin was over the state of Georgia. While Georgia was one of the non-Russian states which had fallen under Communist control in the course of the Russian Civil War, it was regarded as having special status by Lenin. Lenin, who cared little about the suffering imposed on Russians by Communist rule, was more deferential to the views of the republics having minority, or non-Russian, populations. For this reason, he was worried about the formal governmental ties between these republics and the central Russian state. He wanted republics, such as Georgia, given special treatment. Stalin felt that view was an unrealistic one. When he was given responsibility for the administration of Georgia, Stalin largely ignored the wishes of the

Georgians, even Georgians who were Party members. In October 1923, the Georgian Party members were so opposed to Stalin's actions that they resigned from the Party. Stalin saw this as an opportunity to obtain a more pliant political group and promptly had them replaced. Lenin however, had second thoughts in November and ordered an investigation of their grievances.

Whether Lenin was concerned about the Georgia question because of real underlying concerns for the Georgians or because of his dislike of Stalin, he ordered an investigation of their complaints in January 1923. While the reports exonerated Stalin, Lenin became mistrustful of the investigations, and still further mistrustful of Stalin. In March, Stalin was certain that Lenin intended to have him removed from the position of General Secretary. He expected Lenin to take such action at the Party Congress which had been scheduled for March. He was also aware that Lenin's health was failing badly. Without consultation, on March 9, he announced a postponement of the meeting until April 15. On March 10 Lenin had another stroke. He was no longer able to speak. One of his final wishes, that Stalin be removed from power, was frustrated by Trotsky, who agreed to support the reappointment of Stalin as General Secretary.

STALIN'S RISE TO POWER - 1924-1928

Unable to communicate following his stroke on March 10, Lenin nevertheless lived through the remainder of 1923. He would not die until January 21, 1924. Continually worried about the permanence of his achievements toward the end of his life, he did leave an ongoing, though somewhat temporary, legacy of relative calm. His policies during the Civil War and its immediate aftermath had largely eliminated the most open and dangerous groups opposing the Communist regime. The opposition which remained was reduced to such an extent that it could be controlled by the secret police. The Cheka, the secret police organization, had been formally abolished on February 6, 1922. Secret police operations were not done away with however. They were simply taken over by a renamed organization, the State Political Administration or GPU. The elimination of major political opposition, coupled with a bureaucracy of secret police, left the Party leadership free to focus on internal political rivalries.

Toward the end of the 1920s Stalin would ultimately emerge as the victor. In spite of the stated idealistic goals of communism, the world of Party politics involved more mundane struggles between ambitious individuals. Stalin possessed three traits, among others, which gave him an edge over more articulate and intelligent individuals. First, he had almost unlimited patience. He was willing to wait until he had secured his goal before acting. His ambition almost got the better of him in his dealings with Lenin, but the progressive decline of Lenin's health proved fortuitous for his political career. Second, Stalin had, if not an eagerness for paperwork, at least a stomach for it. He would volunteer for duties which other Party members disliked. Third, and most important, he seemed to intuitively grasp the realities of power far better than his opponents. Many among the early leadership had risen to positions of power through their writing or speaking ability. While speeches could often sway delegates, leaders such as Trotsky, Kamenev, or Zinoviev, deluded themselves into thinking that the accolades following successful speeches were a measure of real support and an indication of a strong following. Stalin, early on, found that patronage and the cultivation of a loyal group of supporters was a more reliable means of ensuring support. Perhaps Stalin realized, above all, that the problems facing the Communist government were unlikely to be solved by the seemingly brilliant, but theoretical, answers any of his political rivals came up with in their speeches. Stalin understood that it was the practical side of governmental operations where problems needed to be addressed.

Trotsky, as a confidant of Lenin, had seemed the likely successor to Party leadership. He had the ability to act decisively, one trait of successful leadership. At the same time, he was too much a loner; an intellectual, he failed to reach out to potential allies or to work toward long-term political alliances. Perhaps fatally, his decisiveness was not consistent. At times he would act almost impulsively. He had not hesitated to order soldiers of fleeing units shot during the Civil War. At other times he remained docile, even failing to act at all. At the time of Lenin's death, Trotsky had been at Tiflis, a three-days journey from Moscow, on his way to Sukhumi. He was told by Stalin to continue on his journey rather than return to Moscow for the funeral. Failing to grasp the political importance of attending the funeral, in view of the fact that he was going to Sukhumi for a vacation, he complied with Stalin's order. It did not mean the end of Trotsky's political career, but it did create a bad impression.

The Twelfth Party Congress, which could have proved Stalin's undoing, reelected him General Secretary in April 1923, and, at the Congress, also voted to approve his actions regarding the Georgia republic. While Stalin had perhaps learned the dangers of allowing ambition to come to the fore prematurely, he lost little time in laying the groundwork for the elimination of Trotsky. Playing on the ambitions and envy of others in the Party who sought to take Lenin's place, Stalin began assembling a coalition which could bring about that goal. He enlisted the other members of the troika, Kamenev and Zinoviev, together with Bukharin and others, against Trotsky. At the time of the Party Congress, Stalin was not in a position to assume Party leadership. He could not, in fact, have maintained his position as General Secretary without the support of Zinoviev and Kamenev. At the same time, they also needed his support. Of the three, Zinoviev appeared to be the most likely to come out on top.

Economic conditions in Russia remained relatively stable during much of 1923, although low wages resulted in strikes in many of the larger cities in July and August. Toward the end of 1923, Trotsky, perhaps sensing that he was losing out in the Party struggle, went on the offensive. He began with a letter to the Central Committee on October 8 which criticized the Party for becoming too bureaucratic. This was followed on October 15 by a "Letter of the Forty-Six," addressed to the Central Committee. Signed by 46 prominent party members, it again criticized the Party for bureaucratic tendencies and blamed it for failing to address economic problems and for a tendency to stifle democratic discussion within the Party. It was not formally published, but was circulated among

Party members. Trotsky's criticisms were sufficient to provoke debate, even the passage of a resolution by the Politburo and the Presidium of the Central Control Commission on December 5, 1923 urging greater democratic debate within the Party.

Trotsky determined to continue the fight, preparing another essay, called "The New Course," which was presented on December 8 to Party activists in Moscow. Trotsky called for a purge of the current leadership. The December 5 resolution proved the high point of Trotsky's battle. While the December 8 article was published in *Pravda*, the Party was not in a mood to compromise. It did have a report prepared on the subject on December 15. It also allowed *Pravda* to publish two more articles by Trotsky at the end of December. It was preparing a counterattack however.

One prong of the attack was the publication of a letter Trotsky had written in 1913 to the Menshevik Chkheidze. The letter had been highly critical of Lenin and had been written in rude terms. It was not simply the publication itself which undermined Trotsky, but the timing - it was published in the aftermath of Lenin's death. The other prong of the attack was taking place at the delegate level. Trotsky, due to a lengthy illness, found himself at a disadvantage.

Prior to the Thirteenth Party Congress, held in May 1924, the Party held the Thirteenth Party Conference. Trotsky allowed three of his supporters, Preobrazhensky, Osinsky, and Spronov to work for him at the Conference. Many important organizational changes made during the Conference were decided without any input from Trotsky himself. His supporters were so weak that a resolution was passed condemning the Left Opposition, Trotsky's group, as a "petty bourgeois deviation." When the Thirteenth Party Congress met in May, his participation was limited to a single speech.

The Party took no official action against him in May. He himself reignited the struggle in the fall of 1924. The Party, despite its internal dissension, could not resist the urge to publish a history of the Revolution. Trotsky, despite his current disfavor, was still recognized as having played a part in the Party's success. As a result, the State Publishing House included Trotsky's writings in its collected works publication. Trotsky, not content with inclusion in the publication, also published his writings as a separate volume. In addition, he wrote an introduction called "Lessons of October." It included a strong attack on the 1917 actions of Zinoviev and Kamenev.[13] The response to the attack was the publication of many of Trotsky's earlier writings and attacks on his earlier activities. This was followed by a Central Committee vote to discontinue publication of the "Lessons of October."

Trotsky was attacked in the press. There were discussions about expelling him from the Party and removing him as Commissar of War. Rather than respond to the press attacks or to fight to remain on as Commissar of War, Trotsky offered to resign. At the Central Committee plenum, held from January 17 to 20, 1925, he was removed as Commissar of War, but was not expelled. He remained a member of the Politburo.

He was kept on through the political maneuvering of Stalin. Having eliminated Trotsky as a political threat, Stalin now needed him to use against Kamenev and Zinoviev. They soon found themselves to be the targets of attack. Stalin was responsible for a report on the work of the Thirteenth Congress. When his report was issued, he used it to correct a statement attributed to Kamenev, suggesting that Kamenev was careless about Party doctrine.[14] He indirectly criticized Zinoviev as well. Unlike Trotsky, Kamenev and Zinoviev quickly fought back, demanding a Party conference. The vote went against Stalin, but the result was nothing more than a resolution urging reconciliation. In a public show of humiliation, Stalin offered to resign, but his offer was not accepted.

This public defeat did not have an effect on Stalin's behind-the-scenes political maneuverings. During 1924 he was placing political allies in positions of power, while removing the supporters of Kamenev and Zinoviev. The first real test of political strength came, ironically, over the removal of Trotsky. When the Central Committee discussed the expulsion of Trotsky, Stalin persuaded the membership with the argument that it would set a dangerous precedent to expel members. Seeking a way to get around Stalin, Kamenev and Zinoviev got the Komsomol, the Communist youth organization, to pass a resolution urging Trotsky's removal from the Politburo. In retaliation, the Politburo removed 15 members of the Komsomol Central Committee. The struggle would culminate at the Fourteenth Party Congress in December 1925 with the defeat of Kamenev and Zinoviev.

In continuing to focus on Trotsky after he had been defeated, Zinoviev and Kamenev displayed a lack of understanding of the political realities. However, the refusal of the Central Committee to back them was only the first of a series of reversals in 1925. Unlike Trotsky, they tried to fight back. Zinoviev had a strong following in Leningrad and both the Leningrad press and Party publicly backed his ideas there. Yet before the Fourteenth Party Congress, Zinoviev understood that Stalin's power on the Central Committee had become almost unassailable. While Stalin offered a compromise, Zinoviev would not agree to his demand that the Central Committee be allowed to take control of the Party in Leningrad. Yet, in what amounted to an admission of his weakening position, Zinoviev asked Stalin for guarantees that his Leningrad supporters would not be subject to repressive measures. Ominously, Stalin would not make such a promise. Stalin's only concession, in regard to the Party Congress, was that Zinoviev could present a minority report.

The voting formalities of the Fourteenth Congress gave Stalin a resounding victory - 559 delegates voted for his resolution as against 65 for the position of the "New Opposition," as the supporters of Zinoviev and Kamenev had become known.[15] Zinoviev's political position had so deteriorated, even in Leningrad, that he lost overwhelmingly in votes taken following the conference. When delegates were asked to vote on the decisions taken at the Fourteenth Congress, over 96 percent of the votes taken in Leningrad supported the majority resolution. Moreover, in the Leningrad elections to Party committees, Stalin got his supporters elected.[16] Having achieved victory in the very heart of Zinoviev's political base, Stalin now dealt with them as they had dealt with Trotsky. Kamenev lost his position on the Politburo - he became only a candidate member - and, in addition, lost the chairmanship of the Council of Labor and Defense. While Zinoviev remained a member of the Politburo, he lost the chairmanship of the Executive Committee of the Communist International (ECCI).

Zinoviev and Kamenev, despite their defeats, and the clear signs that Stalin was in control, deluded themselves into thinking that an alliance with Trotsky could reverse their political fortunes. Trotsky was persuaded to take up their cause. These efforts were short-lived. Zinoviev was removed from the Politburo in July 1926. Trotsky, despite joining the opposition, was nevertheless allowed to remain a member of that body. Perhaps hoping that they could somehow redeem themselves politically, the three formally admitted their mistakes in a letter to the Central Committee on October 16, 1926. For Stalin, their political usefulness was at an end. Far from resurrecting their political fortunes or bringing them back into the good graces of the Party, their admission only served as proof of what Stalin had accused them of. A week later Trotsky was expelled from the Politburo while Kamenev was removed even as a candidate member.

Stalin had not taken the final step of expelling Trotsky from the Party. In fact, Trotsky still remained a member of the Central Committee. He would himself provide Stalin with the excuse he needed to take the final steps. Trotsky was incautious enough to attempt to secretly organize opposition to the Party. He went so far as to allow his allies in the opposition to create small organizational groups which even collected dues from members. While opposition was on the increase, it was not strong enough to really take on the Party. Mistakenly believing that it could escape detection, the opposition set up an illegal print shop at one of the government printing shops. Stalin, aware of the activities the opposition was involved in, decided the existence of a secret press was sufficient to act against his opponents. Those operating the press were arrested, and Trotsky's involvement made public. Trotsky and Zinoviev were expelled from the Central Committee in October 1927. This was followed, on November 14, by a vote to expel them from the Party.

The expulsion of Trotsky and Zinoviev was the signal for a general purge. Beginning with the Central Committee and Central Control Commission, other individuals who had supported the opposition were removed from their ranks. Party organizations at the city level also expelled opposition members from the Party. The Fifteenth Congress, meeting in December 1927, confirmed the decision to expel Trotsky and Zinoviev. Kamenev's name was added to the list of those to be expelled, as were 74 others.[17] In hopes of salvaging their political careers, Zinoviev and Kamenev, after the Congress, publicly agreed to stop opposition work. They would be readmitted to the Party in 1928. Many of Trotsky's followers would not publicly acknowledge their mistakes. In fact, they vowed to continue the fight. The result was arrest, in many cases. Trotsky himself was to be deported. In January 1928 GPU agents escorted him from his home to a train which took him to Kazakhstan. Internal exile was not enough for Stalin however and in February 1929, Trotsky was sent to Turkey.

Stalin had removed his most dangerous opponents. He had one more obstacle to deal with - Nikolai Bukharin. Bukharin, not joining the revolt of Trotsky, Zinoviev, and Kamenev, moved into a leadership position following their downfall. His political authority came primarily from his ability to analyze and to present a logical explanation of Marxist theory. He threatened Stalin, because his attacks on Stalin's policies were based more on analysis of the policies themselves, rather than the politics of those supporting them. Stalin would not stand for any opposition, even that represented by Bukharin. As he had done with Zinoviev and Kamenev, Stalin sought to replace Bukharin's supporters with people loyal to him. Never a fully organized opposition group, the "right deviationists," as Bukharin and his allies, Rykov, Tomsky, and Uglanov, were called, they were also brought down by Stalin. In November 1929, despite a public statement repudiating his actions, Bukharin was removed from the Politburo.

AGRICULTURAL CRISIS - 1927-1929

In the period between Lenin's death and the exile of Trotsky, economic conditions in Russia had remained relatively stable and Stalin had been free to concentrate his energies on defeating his political opponents. In 1927, economic conditions would once again come to the fore. They were a two-edged sword for Stalin. While able to use the problems to his advantage in dealing with his opponents - the innovative solutions proposed as alternatives to his policies were subject to the criticism that they deviated from communist theory - Stalin's failed programs also gave his opponents plenty of ammunition when they wished to attack him.

In 1924 and 1925 a shift in governmental agricultural policy toward a free market had lifted many of the restrictions imposed in rural areas. Some private ownership was allowed and the tax on agricultural products was lowered. Combined with favorable weather conditions, these changes brought a good harvest for 1926. The harvest of 1927 was better than 1926. At the same time, government procurements in the fall of 1927 were down, not commensurate with the surplus indicated by the harvest. Although the Fifteenth Party Congress, in December 1927, hoped to limit any movement toward a free market in rural areas, it had not pushed for the implementation of emergency measures. The Party became alarmed at the severity of the shortage; grain reserves, important for the export market as well as the food supply for cities, were extremely low. One alternative would have been to offer higher grain prices. This was rejected. Instead, the Central Committee decided to change policy. It authorized the forcible taking of whatever reserves the peasants held. The normal procedure would have been to let local authorities carry out the new policy. To reinforce its determination however, the Central Committee also sent Party members into the countryside to help with requisitions. Stalin himself went to Siberia at the end of January. Forced requisitioning had the immediate effect of increasing governmental grain reserves. By April 1928 however, collections began to fall again.

When the Politburo reviewed the policies in July 1928, it was decided to put an end to the forced requisitions. Instead, the government would offer higher prices for grain. It was hoped that higher prices would increase the amount of grain the government could obtain. At the Central Committee meeting in July even Stalin, while arguing that the forced requisitions had been necessary, agreed with the governmental retreat on the issue.

Stalin however, qualified his position, stating, in essence, that extraordinary measures still remained an option, should a similar situation arise in the future. Stalin, at the same session, began to push for industrialization. While the agricultural and industrial sectors of the economy seemed to represent totally different questions, there was a reason why industrialization was tied closely to agricultural policy. Foreign grain sales provided a major source of the hard currency needed for capital investment in industry. Hard currency was thus tied to the availability of government grain reserves. The paradox in the policy was that, while grain reserves could be increased by offering to pay the peasants more, such payments came at the expense of scarce financial reserves. If the goal was to increase the funds available to the government, paying the peasants more in order to obtain grain tended to defeat that purpose.

By October 1928, it was becoming clear that the relaxation of emergency measures had not helped grain procurement. Stalin, still involved in his political fight with Bukharin, told him that he would back off his push for more capital investment. Since this would lessen the need for hard currency, the move should have reduced pressure to increase grain reserves. Stalin, not worried about the political promises made to Bukharin, reversed course in December. Directives were issued to again forcibly requisition. By February 1929 however, it was becoming apparent that, even with the renewed pressure, the results were disappointing. Collections were even below those of 1928. During the summer the Party would send some 100,000 Party members into the countryside in hopes that the large number would somehow ensure the maximum collections.[18]

Stalin was determined to continue his pressure on the agricultural sector and one factor contributing to his hard line was a desire to industrialize the Soviet Union. The first of Stalin's three five-year plans was officially put into place on October 1, 1928. It would be formally adopted in April-May of 1929. The shortages which occurred in 1929 could have been alleviated with grain purchases from abroad or an increase in government prices. Either step would have required using some of the monies allocated to industrial investment. Stalin, almost obsessed with the need to move the industrial sector ahead however, decided against any retreat from industrialization.

Aware that forced requisitions had failed and that they could provide no permanent solution to government shortages, Stalin moved toward a more permanent alternative. In April 1929 the Sixteenth Party Conference adopted a more aggressive policy of collectivization. Collectivization was itself not a new policy and the idea of a collective was not entirely negative either. Party leaders originally envisioned it as a way to modernize agriculture, by providing tractors and combines to peasants who could not afford to invest the capital needed for such purchases. The problem, in April 1929, was that the government lacked capital to support those who chose to join the collective. Nevertheless the number of peasant households which had joined collectives by June 30 was over a million, nearly twice the number - 564,299 - projected by government planners for the year.[19] By November 1929, the number of households participating had grown to 1,919,400, and the number of collectives stood at 70,000.[20] The weakness in the numbers, for the Party, was that most of those who had joined were poorer peasants. The middle or moderately successful peasant households were still reluctant to join, as were the kulaks, the most successful class of peasants. (The term kulak was loosely applied to any of the most successful of the peasant farmers, although it usually meant a peasant wealthy enough to hire laborers or peasants on a farm.)

Stalin, encouraged by the numbers, decided on a still more aggressive policy. Whether the kulaks were the real obstacle to collectivization or not, they had long been a target of the Party leadership. He initially decided the kulak question deserved study and a subcommission was appointed to prepare a report toward the end of 1929. Perhaps sensing that a campaign against the kulaks, hated by many of the poorer peasants, would have some popular support, Stalin went on the offensive on December 27 1929, even before the report had been issued. The kulaks, he said, were to be liquidated as a class. In a process known as "dekulakization," they were to be dispossessed of their landholdings. As carried out this often meant, not simply the elimination of kulak legal claims to their land, but deportation or resettlement.

Stalin's December 1929 pronouncement did not represent an abrupt change of course in governmental policy. It simply meant an intensification of the campaign begun in the spring. Local officials, under pressure to meet grain procurement quotas, in turn imposed quotas on kulak farms. Failure to meet the quotas meant the imposition of fines. It also meant that all or a portion of the kulak's landholdings could be sold. In 1928 and 1929 the kulaks may have lost as much as 30% to 40% of their lands.[21]

Had government policy been simply to transform the basis of agriculture from individual peasant or village farming to collectives, it could have required all peasants to join the cooperatives and collectives. Instead there was debate within the Party over whether the kulaks should be allowed to join. In fact, kulaks were treated differently depending on the region they lived in. Siberia would not allow them in while the Middle Volga was inclined to accept them.[22]

When the Politburo's subcommittee on the kulaks issued its preliminary recommendations for their treatment, they were found to be too lenient by Stalin. The subcommittee had decided that kulaks could be classified into one of three categories. The first category provided the most severe penalties. It included kulaks who, in opposing collectivization, engaged in terrorist acts. Such kulaks were to be arrested or exiled. Kulaks who merely opposed collectivization without resorting to terrorist acts fell into the second category. Their punishment was banishment, but only from the area of the governmental administrative unit they lived in. The third category, for kulaks who cooperated, allowed admission to the collective, but with the postponement of voting rights.

Stalin objected especially to the concessions granted to the third category. Instead of allowing the cooperative kulaks to join the collective, he wanted them to be resettled. They would be given separate plots of land, but would also be subject to separate production goals from those of the collective. Stalin's more punitive treatment was the one adopted when the Central Executive Committee issued instructions on February 4,

1930. Stalin, not content with targeting the head of a kulak household, had decided to include all the members of the kulak's family in the banishment orders.

Although the directives were aimed officially at those defined as kulaks, little distinction was made between real kulaks and peasants who were simply well-to-do. Stalin exerted as much pressure as he could on local Party officials in rural areas to carry out the directives, even sending out cadres of Party members from the cities to help in enforcement. Local officials, to show compliance, were obliged to come up with numbers of households which had been dekulakized. As a result, middle and even poor peasants were classified as kulaks and banished. The force of Stalin's personality was itself a strong incentive to local officials to carry his program to extremes. He also had incorporated an economic incentive into the directives - the property of all households which were dekulakized was transferred to the local collective. It was intended to provide the government with the investment funds needed to subsidize the collectives while ensuring that government resources would still be available for industrial development. Whether kulak or not, by October 1930, when the first stage of collectivization had come to an end, some 115,231 families, or between 500,000 and 800,000 people had been banished.[23]

While local Party officials were under pressure to report high numbers in the dekulakization campaign, Stalin also pressured them to report high numbers for peasants who agreed to join collectives. To reinforce the importance of the changes sought for the agricultural sector, Moscow trained a group of around 27,000 young Party members to aid local government officials in organizing villages. The 25-thousanders (25,000, rather than 27,000 had been the original Party estimate) often worked as managers of collective farms. Another 70,000 Party members, 13,000 accountants, and 50,000 soldiers or ex-soldiers were added to help the 25-thousanders.[24]

Stalin focused on two agricultural figures. One was that for collectivization. The other was agricultural production. Even if his overall goal was to ensure a stable governmental grain and food reserve, he needed something quantifiable. While the figures for collectivization were encouraging in themselves, the more significant measure of success was found in agricultural output figures. Local officials, interested in impressing their superiors, pressured for higher contributions. If it was easy for such officials to make claims about production goals, the difficulties in meeting quotas ultimately fell on the peasants. However, those 25-thousanders who dared to sympathize too openly with peasant conditions either resigned or were purged.

Communes, which differed from collectives by a form of pooling of resources, such as livestock, were an alternative form of village Party endeavor or were one of the ways in which a collective was formed. To finance communes, local officials relied on peasant contributions, rather than governmental funds. Yet the peasants resented the actions of local officials in obtaining contributions. The officials either made promises to provide advanced farm machinery - promises they could not, or never intended to keep - or simply forced the peasants to contribute. The peasants, even if they agreed to join a collective or commune, retaliated by slaughtering whatever animals they had, before joining. At the start of Stalin's collectivization campaign, in February and March of 1930, this resulted in the killing of some 14 million cattle in those two months.[25]

Stalin, perhaps surprised by the peasant opposition to his programs and warned by Party officials, decided to retreat from the most excessive aspects of his collectivization campaign. On March 2, 1930, he had *Pravda* publish an article entitled "Dizzy with Success." In the article Stalin criticized the use of force against the peasants by local Party officials. Stalin's conciliatory tone even went so far as to allow peasants who had joined, to leave the collective. Local officials, who had carried out the policy, now found themselves criticized by Stalin in the press. Stalin even had those guilty of what were termed "excesses," removed. While Stalin had backed down publicly, his retreat would only be temporary. One immediate result of the retreat was an exodus from the collective farm. Membership in the collective fell by 4,000,000 households; dropping from a high of 10 million to under 6 million by July 1, 1930.[26] Conquest states that 9 million households (40-50 million people) left the collective.[27]

Stalin's pronouncements were intended for public consumption. While local officials were punished for illegal actions, higher officials who had issued the orders were left alone. In fact, Stalin did not retreat far. If peasants were allowed to leave the collective, they were not allowed to take the cattle or animals they had contributed with them. In addition, while they might be given land, they did not receive the same parcel they had worked before joining the collective. Often, the new land was unproductive, swampy, or a great distance away.

While the pressure for dekulakization would continue into October, the pressure for collectivization eased somewhat over the summer of 1930 - but only temporarily. In September Stalin pressured local officials to renew efforts. Peasants who had left the collective were saddled with heavy grain quotas or had to pay additional taxes. Those who were members of collectives were exempt from certain taxes on their livestock. In addition to such on-going pressures, peasants still had the threat of dekulakization hanging over their heads, which officials used effectively as a threat. While pressure on the kulaks had also eased in the latter part of 1930, the Party decreed a second campaign in February 1931. This would result in the banishment of an additional 265,795 households by December of 1931.[28]

The harsh measures employed by the state, in turn, brought resistance from the peasant. Local officials were sometimes assassinated. Between January and June 1930, 150 acts of murder or arson were reported in the Ukraine.[29] Organized resistance by whole villages was widespread. The resistance was sufficient to require the use of regular army troops in some cases. Resistance had not suddenly sprung up in 1930. There had been resistance to government actions throughout the late 1920s. Some 300 government grain agents are reported to have been murdered between 1927 and 1929.[30] Peasants relied on less open means of resistance as well. Grain was often buried or, in the case of kulaks, sold at below market prices to poorer peasants. Sometimes what grain could not be stored was simply destroyed.

Stalin's response to such acts or even to the poor performance of the agricultural sector was the same - more repression. He had nine economists charged with sabotage on September 3, 1930. All nine disappeared. Another 48 officials of the People's Commissariat of Trade were indicted on September 22, 1930. The charge was again sabotage of food supplies. After signing confessions all 48 were shot.[31]

Though peasant resistance made life difficult for local officials, it was too disorganized and dispersed to defeat Stalin. With the renewal of the collectivization campaign in September 1930, the threat or actual use of force, combined with economic pressure simply proved too much for the peasant. The "collapse" of peasant resistance did not occur suddenly. In August 1931, the Central Committee officially declared that collectivization had been completed in several different regions, e.g., the North Caucasus, the Steppe, the Urals and the Volga. Over a year later, in December 1932, collectivized agricultural had reached 60 percent.[32] The collectivization figure would reach 90 percent by the end of 1934.[33]

The disruptions caused by dekulakization and forced collectivization contributed to another agricultural tragedy. As in 1921, Russia was struck by famine. It began in the fall of 1932. When it came to an end in 1933, between 5 million and 8 million people had died.[34] In some areas, as in 1921, large numbers of peasants sought to leave their villages; many dying as they attempted to reach areas where food was rumored to be plentiful; many dying who remained. The government, far from encouraging peasant movement, set up military roadblocks and checkpoints to prevent escape. The requirement that individuals possess ration cards in order to buy food prevented those peasants who managed to reach cities from buying what they needed. Despite these conditions, Stalin continued to export grain to the West, providing funds for his industrialization plans.

Partly in response to the famine, the government in early 1933 changed agricultural policies. There was a retreat from the most repressive measures and grain procurement targets were reduced. On January 19, 1933, a decree was passed which gave the central government final authority in setting procurement quotas. In one sense, the decree created a hardship on the rural administrator because Moscow would determine how much each region would contribute. In another sense, it eased the burden on the peasants by preventing local officials from arbitrarily raising the quota figure once met. One of the problems the decree tried to address was that of local officials changing the quotas in response to pressure from Moscow for higher procurement. To deal with the famine, the government took other steps. It reversed the policy of exporting grain, even importing small amounts of grain as well.

While the First Five-Year Plan was not officially to end until September 30, 1933, Stalin pronounced it a success in January 1933. Although its goals had, in fact, not been achieved, Stalin stated that it had been completed by December 31, 1932. A second Five-Year Plan was soon in place, with goals to be reached by 1937.

The year 1933 saw the end of the famine and an improving agricultural sector. At the beginning of 1934 Stalin found himself opposed by some members of the Party. Whether the opposition represented a real threat, it did urge a curbing of some of the worst excesses of industrialization and collectivization. The opposition had been somewhat active even in 1933. The disputes with Stalin had been over relatively minor incidents. The Politburo had, against Stalin's wishes, voted for lesser punishment for youthful distributors of literature which did not follow the Party line. At the Seventeenth Party Congress, held in January and February 1934, Stalin retaliated by replacing members of the Central Committee. Yet 1934 was largely a year of calm in governmental politics. It would remain calm until December 1, 1934, when Sergei Kirov was assassinated in Leningrad. Stalin, the same day, approved the emergency decree which signalled the beginning of the purge.

While a trial of some of Stalin's political opponents was held in January 1935, it would not be until August 1936 that the major political show trials would be held. Stalin first targeted individuals who had been members of the opposition. At the August 1936 trial, the defendants included the two members of Stalin's 1922 troika, Zinoviev and Kamenev. Another major trial was held in January 1937, again aimed at the political opposition of the 1920s. In March 1938, it was the turn of the "right" opposition members, represented by Bukharin and Rykov.

Having eliminated the former members of the opposition blocs, Stalin turned to current Party membership. During 1937 and 1938, he systematically eliminated members of the Central Committee. There were only 139 members of the Central Committee in 1937 and only 29 still remained by the end of 1938. Many of the 110 arrested were shot. In addition to the Central Committee, executives of the top government agencies were also purged. Thus the leadership and employees of many agencies were arrested and, often as not, shot. Purges included agencies such as the Presidium of the Central Executive Committee (CEC), the State Planning Commission (Gosplan), the Council of People's Commissars, the Russian Socialist Federated Soviet Republic (RSFSR), and the Commissariat of Foreign Affairs, among others.[35]

Having dealt with the central government, Stalin extended the purge down through the local ranks. Lesser Party officials in Russia or the republics were eliminated. During the collectivization drive and the campaign against the kulak, those who dared to publicly criticize or oppose the policies of Moscow, even those who expressed sympathy for the plight of the kulak, risked arrest. Now even those who had ordered or carried out the suppression of the kulaks fell victim. In the Ukraine, in Belorussia, in Azerbaijan, and in Georgia, the old Party leadership was decimated.[36] High-ranking officers of the army and navy were arrested and shot. The leadership of the secret police, the NKVD (People's Commissariat of Internal Affairs), became victims. Officials and individuals who had participated in the torture of political opponents, in the fabrication of evidence for the show trials, and in the actions against the peasants, were now arrested.

During 1938 Stalin decided to bring the terror to an end. He had either killed or forced many Party members out of active political life. Medvedev estimates that over a million Party members were expelled between 1936 and 1939.[37] Many of these were arrested. While some may have avoided death, those not executed remained in prison. Nevertheless, the number killed was high - officially 353,680 were executed in 1937 and between 200,000 and 300,000 were executed in 1938.[38] Stalin used a familiar theme to bring the purge to an end - he accused those involved of having carrying out excesses. He even formalized the investigation of such excesses with a special commission, appointed by the Central Committee.

Perhaps the first high-ranking official to fall victim to Stalin's about-face was Nikolai Yezhov, head of the NKVD. Appointed head of the NKVD in September 1936, Yezhov had conducted many of the purges of the Party leadership and had personally been involved in the trial of Zinoviev and Kamenev. In December 1938, Stalin had Yezhov replaced by Lavrenty Beria. While Yezhov himself was not arrested until a few months later (he would be shot in July 1940), Beria had many of Yezhov's associates arrested (and shot). Beria did not limit his own purge to Moscow. NKVD officials in the republics were also arrested. Beria went after, not just Party officials, but those in charge of the concentration camps. Stalin was now out to prove that the officials who had carried out his orders were the real culprits. Officials who had risen to power with Yezhov fell with his elimination.

In 1939 there was an easing of the repression. Some of the individuals imprisoned were released, although it was only about two of every 100 imprisoned.[39] The respite was only temporary. Some who were not released would be executed in 1939. However, NKVD activities would not continue at the pace set in the years 1936-1938. Stalin was still firmly in power and the war with Germany would force even his political gaze to focus on other more pressing problems.

CONCLUSION

This chapter has provided a brief overview of the political story of the Communist regime from 1921 through 1938. The next chapters focus more closely on the economic history. Chapters Thirteen and Fourteen deal with the history of Soviet agriculture, while Chapters Fifteen and Sixteen focus on the industrial side of the Soviet economy. Particularly under Stalin, agricultural and industrial difficulties proved difficult to solve. The government was forced to commit large amounts of political resources to the search for some permanent solution to economic problems.

CHAPTER 13

THE ECONOMICS OF THE RUSSIAN AGRICULTURAL SECTOR

This chapter and Chapter 14 discuss the history of Russian agriculture during Communist rule. Initially, they look at the state of Russian agriculture from the time of the Czar, then follow its development through 1939. To provide some frame of reference for a discussion, it may be helpful to focus on five questions. First, what was the structure of Russian agriculture during the time of the Czar and how did it differ from the system which existed after the Bolsheviks took power? Second, what were the problems the Bolsheviks, and later Stalin, faced in the agricultural sector? Third, if the ideological goal of communism was to eliminate private property, was Stalin's agricultural policy successful in that goal? Fourth, if private property, (and the accompanying profit motive), assumed to be a cornerstone for the success of the capitalist model, was eliminated, did that account for the loss of productivity in the Soviet economy? Fifth, where there were failures in the agricultural sector, were they caused by the introduction of central planning?

The five questions perhaps are too general to deal with the overall topic. A number of related questions are involved as well. Was the system existing at the time of the Czar a success and was the Soviet system which replaced it a failure? Did the decision to force collectivization bring about the collapse of Soviet agriculture? Did it solve the problems it was intended to address? In this connection, why did the system as it existed during Czarist times prove inadequate in Russia during the late 1920s or, at least, why did the Bolshevik leadership believe it to be inadequate? One final question relates to the topic of this book. Were agricultural resources scarce and, if so, did that scarcity contribute to violence and repression?

Questions regarding Stalin's collectivization policies are considered key to any analysis of the success or failure of Soviet agricultural policy. The Soviet agricultural system has been labeled a failure. In fact, the agricultural sector often is used to illustrate the overall failure of communist economic theory. Western economic thought argues that the ability to make a profit is the major driving force behind any productive economy and that one of the major causes for the productivity problem in Russia was the elimination of private property and the accompanying loss of motivation.

Before proceeding to an analysis of the Soviet agricultural sector, it may be helpful to look at economic productivity. Productivity is one way to measure the economic health of any country. Productivity is generally defined as the amount of output in relation to the amount of input in the production of a product, based on some unit of measurement. Productivity is often talked of in terms of labor productivity, e.g. how many feet of lumber at a mill are produced per hour of labor, although it can also be framed in terms of total factor productivity. Critics of the Soviet system have pointed to shortcomings in productivity as proof of the failure of the Soviet economy. Soviet consumers in Moscow don't have any goods because factories are inefficient, worker incentive is absent, and productivity is low. The premise is that shortages in Moscow are caused primarily by an overall low productivity. What if productivity or the lack of productivity were not uniform throughout an economy however? For example, what if the agricultural sector were productive, but the transportation sector were not? The consumer in Moscow would still suffer shortages even if there was a bumper wheat crop because the transportation system could not deliver it. Similarly, a highly productive transport system would not help the consumer if the agricultural system were not operating efficiently.

A related question is, what if there were other factors which contributed to shortages besides low productivity? Critics of the Soviet system point to low productivity at the source, i.e., the collective, as one of the major problems in Soviet agriculture. The collective is where grain or meat is produced. Critics have a valid point. Following collectivization, productivity did drop in many of Russia's richest agricultural regions. Productivity on collectivized farms was much lower than productivity on land held by independent peasants. Yet, productivity on the farm or collective itself provides only part of the economic picture. Low productivity may not be the only cause of a scarcity of consumer goods. What impact will competition for a product have on its availability? In the case of Russia, will the price or availability of wheat in Moscow be affected by the demand for wheat in Kiev or Leningrad? Throughout the discussion which follows, these questions may provide some frame of reference.

OVERVIEW OF THE HISTORY OF SOVIET AGRICULTURE

Russian agriculture, from the time of the Czar through communist rule, scored some impressive triumphs, but also suffered some tragic defeats. Some of these events were touched on in Chapter Twelve. The climate of Russia is one of extremes which, in some regions, provides an environment hostile to crops, people, and animals. At the same time, the lands of the former Soviet Union contain some very fertile regions, known for their ability to produce grain. On the positive side, Russia has long been a grain exporting country. In fact, the grain-producing regions were sufficiently resilient to produce bumper crops following recovery from the Russian Civil War in the mid-1920s - while the Communists were in power - although these harvests occurred before Stalin began his collectivization campaign.

In 1913, on the eve of the First World War, Russian peasants managed to produce a bumper crop. It was partly due to the weather, which was favorable that year. It was also the culmination of a series of good harvests. Harvests in the years between 1909 and 1913 had been good.[1] In fact, Russian grain production had been growing at a rate of 2.1 to 2.4 percent per year since 1895.[2] In 1926, after the Communist government had lowered taxes and removed the restrictions it had placed on private agricultural production, output increased. In 1926 it was 118 percent of the 1913 figure; it increased in 1927 to 121 percent.[3] Even in 1930, when collectivization was just beginning, the harvest proved good.[4] Following the completion of collectivization, with its disastrous short-term consequences, there was a good harvest in 1935 as well as a record harvest in 1937.[5]

Russian agriculture had experienced its share of bad harvests as well. The worst episodes occurred in 1891-92, in 1921, and in 1932-33. Famine was the result of the crop failures which occurred in those years. The number who died in the 1891-92 famine is estimated at between 375,000 and 400,000.[6] The 1921 famine is estimated to have killed some 5 million.[7] The number who died in the 1932-33 famine, according to Medvedev, is estimated at between 5 and 8 million, although Wheatcroft suggests it may have been 4 to 5 million.[8] Less catastrophic crop losses had occurred in 1906 and 1911.[9] It should also be noted that deaths from the 1921 famine would have been greater had Western countries, particularly the U.S., not provided aid. Another crop failure in the autumn of 1936 resulted in the "hunger" of 1936-37. The government was better prepared for the failure, having built up a fairly large reserve of grain and fodder. It also pursued a wiser political policy by reducing grain exports in the fall of 1936 and stopping them completely in the early part of 1937.[10]

Forced collectivization represents one of the most significant events in Soviet economic history. From a policy standpoint, it involved almost a total overhaul of the existing system of production. Its cost in human terms was extremely high. Robert Conquest estimates that some 14.5 million people died in the period from 1930 to 1937 as a result of Stalin's agricultural policies. Of this figure, he estimates that 6.5 million people died as a result of dekulakization, the policy aimed specifically at the middle and upper peasant.[11] Other authors dispute these figures, suggesting that the number of victims who died was not as great, perhaps around 10-11 million.[12] There clearly were a large number of people who died as a result of collectivization, whether the figure is 10 or 14.5 million.

In some ways dekulakization was part of Stalin's overall agricultural policy; in other ways it might be considered separate. It was part of collectivization in that it was intended to free up land for, as well as to force peasants onto, the collective. It was a separate policy in that its political goal was to break the peasants, both economically and psychologically. Officially the total number of kulak households which were dekulakized was 381,026 - 115,231 had been banished by October 1930, the first part of the dekulakization campaign, 265,795 would be banished in 1931. Medvedev asserts that the actual figure was probably closer to 1 million households (some 5 to 6 million individuals).[13] Conquest estimates that the number of individuals dekulakized was between 10 million and 12 million.[14]

The dekulakization campaign came to an end in May 1933, although the collectivization drive would continue through 1937. Officially, the collectivization campaign had begun with the adoption of the First Five-Year Plan at the April 1929 meeting of the Sixteenth Party Conference. (The plan, dated October 1, 1928, had already been in effect some six months by the time it was officially adopted. Drafting had begun much earlier, in 1925. While the plan had called for only 564,200 households to join collectives in its first year of operation, over 1 million had joined by July 1, 1929. (If the number seems high, it still represented only 4 percent of all peasant households.)[15] The number of collectives then in existence was 57,000.[16] When 1932 ended, 61 percent of Soviet farming had been collectivized.[17] There were 240,000 collective farms at the end of 1934, when collectivization had increased to 90 percent.[18] In 1937, the transformation was almost complete, when 99 percent of agricultural land had become part of the collective system.[19] Interestingly, the state made some concessions to free enterprise by allowing private ownership of livestock. Even peasants who were members of state collectives were granted this freedom. From 1934 to 1937 the livestock population, devastated in the years 1930 to 1933, recovered. The number of head of cattle, for example, which had stood at 33.5 million in January 1934, reached 50.9 million in January 1938. Nove attributes much of this increase to government policies which allowed or even encouraged private ownership.[20]

A discussion of Russian successes and failures in agriculture, as well as the figures for collectivization and banishment in the campaign against the kulak, provide only a brief glimpse of Russia's agricultural economy. For comparison, the next section looks at the rural economy during Czarist times.

RUSSIAN AGRICULTURE - PRE-1917

In 1897 Russia took a census of its population. Out of a total population of 124,649,000, some 106,213,000 people resided in rural areas, about 85 percent of the population. Around 1900 this population was included in 22 million households.[21] Even in 1914, when Russia's total population had increased to some 140 million, the proportion which was rural was still over 80 percent.[22]

Since private ownership was one of the first rights to be eliminated when the Bolsheviks took power, the perception is that the major agricultural change brought about by communism was the destruction of the free market. That perception is largely a myth. That the Communists tried to eliminate private ownership is not a myth. (On their second day in power, they would pass a decree ordering the confiscation of land owned by landlords.) The myth is that Russian agriculture, prior to the Revolution, had been a primitive version of the free market, based on private ownership of land. It was not. While there was private ownership, a large portion of Russia's agriculturally productive land was still held by the village or commune. In legal and practical terms, land was "owned" by the village or commune, not by the individual. Nor was the state collective farm a totally foreign concept, even if it was a new institution in 1929. Communal farming had been the general practice for much of the Nineteenth Century.

The commune was different from the village. The village was the place where the peasant lived; he "belonged" to the village. The commune, though closely associated with the village, was a formal legal entity. Peasants with land allotments were members of the commune (mir, or sel'skoe obshchestvo) and, as members, could vote in the village (not the commune) assembly.[23] The village assembly, the political organization recognized by the Czarist government, was responsible to the government for the payment of taxes owed by the village as well as for recruits for the military. At the local level, the commune, through the village assembly, had the authority to control land allotments. It had more authoritarian powers as well - members could be expelled and exiled to Siberia. Internal passports, required for travel, were issued - or not issued - by the village assembly.

The land around a village was distributed among the various landholders and, at periodic intervals, would be redistributed. The intervals between redistribution were fairly long - 10 to 15 years, in many cases. This was the officially sanctioned system up through 1906, when Stolypin, as Minister of the Interior, sought to reform it. Stolypin's reforms provided a degree of legal ownership sufficient to allow for the sale and acquisition of land by the peasants. Poorer peasants were able to get rid of, what for them, was unproductive land, while richer peasants were able to acquire more.[24]

The concept of private ownership was not totally unknown. There was land, outside the commune, held by landlords and peasants. Pipes estimates that, in 1910, some 14 million hectares of land in European Russia was privately owned - substantial, but small, compared to the 151 million hectares held by communes.[25] If a tradition of communal ownership was strong, it was not uniformly practiced throughout the Russian Empire. In the Cossack lands and in the Ukraine, peasants or individual households owned or rented land not subject to any communal rules. Property which was held by an individual, whether it was land or personal property, such as money or livestock, passed to his heirs.

Perhaps one other thing needs to be said about property rights in Russia. Private ownership, particularly ownership of land, under the Russian legal system was somewhat vague, yet utilitarian. The peasant normally had no absolute legal title to the land he might claim as his. The commune recognized the peasant's claim to the land he tilled, but only so long as he lived in or near the village. If he moved away, or if the entire household died out, the land reverted to the commune. The law was utilitarian in that it allowed the commune to benefit from continued production. If the tenant or landholder was absent, the land could still be put to productive use.

The legal status of peasant landholdings is one aspect of the Russian political and economic system. It provides some insight into the economic forces at work in Russia. Two events, or more accurately, policy initiatives, which took place under Czarist rule may shed further light on Russia's rural economy toward the end of the Nineteenth Century. First, Czar Alexander II legally freed the serfs with the Emancipation Statute of 1861. Second, Stolypin undertook his reforms in 1906.

Alexander II had announced his intent to free the serfs in a March 1856 speech. While he was more progressive than his predecessors, his reform involved less a concern for peasant welfare, than an attempt to modernize an inefficient system. Still smarting from the defeat Russia suffered in the Crimean War (1853-1856), and aware of peasant discontent, Alexander felt some overhaul was needed. Yet he also needed the support of the conservative aristocracy for his plan to succeed. The superficial advantage for individual serfs was that they were to be given a plot of land. (In operation, the Czar's plan did not formally give the peasant ownership of the land he worked. Ownership instead, was transferred from the landlord to the commune.) The disadvantage was that serfs were required to compensate their former landholders. They were to make payments over a forty-nine year period. There were other drawbacks for the peasant as well. While the landlords had to give up legal claims to arable land, they received more definite rights in return - such as legal ownership of pasture and woodland. Peasants now were charged for the right to graze their cattle or even for crossing the land now held by the former landlord, whereas before they had used such land for free.

The laws which Stolypin instituted in 1906 involved a variety of reform measures. One measure lifted restrictions on peasant movement - communes no longer could refuse to issue internal passports. Hoping to encourage private acquisition of land, Stolypin had the Peasant Land Bank provide peasants with easy credit terms. Crown lands and State lands, totaling some 6 million acres, were made available for private purchase. In conjunction with this measure, the government offered to resettle peasants to regions where there were fewer people. Around 3 million people decided to move, mostly to Siberia and Central Asia, between 1906 and 1916.[26] Perhaps the most far-reaching law, in theory at least, was that of November 9, 1906, which allowed peasants to take legal title to land then held by the commune. With legal title came the right to sell the land which had been cultivated for the commune. Stolypin further eased the financial burden on the peasants by an annulment of further redemption payments due under the 49-year plan of the Emancipation.

The Emancipation of 1861 and Stolypin's reforms represented dramatic changes in legal status and property rights. For some peasants the legal changes meant an opportunity to improve their economic status. Where this occurred, the agricultural economy benefitted from increased productivity. For other peasants, the changes made little difference - they continued to struggle - as did the economy of which they were a part. Both Alexander and Stolypin hoped that the changes would somehow invigorate the economy - and in some cases they did. The implementation of legal changes thus had an impact on the direction of economic forces. At the same time, while economic forces were given some direction by the legal changes, those same economic forces themselves served to shape the final legal and economic outcome. The economies of ancient Athens and Rome may serve to illustrate what was happening in the Russian economy following the implementation of the two legal and reform measures.

In Athens, it will be recalled, those who worked the land had often been sold into debt when they could not repay loans. One of the reforms which Solon had instituted in 594 B.C. was the *Seisactheia*, whereby debts incurred by farmers were cancelled and personal security was forbidden for a loan. The underlying economic problem which Solon tried to address was unproductive land, or at least land which could not economically sustain the individual farmer when the crop was grain. Athens' more long-term solution was to change to a different crop - olives - and to import grain. The economic solution for the Athenian agricultural worker was to leave the farm and become part of the work force of Athens. After 200 B.C., Rome experienced similar problems. Agricultural land proved unproductive, particularly for small farmers. The economic solution was a switch to raising cattle or producing grapes and olives, types of farming which were more efficiently done on larger holdings. As the Athenian worker had done, the small Italian landholder chose to abandon his holdings and move to Rome.

The economic histories of Athens and Rome suggest that small landholdings were unable to sustain the small farmer. The Russian agricultural producers of the Nineteenth Century were experiencing similar problems. Agricultural productivity did improve following Stolypin's reforms. Since Stolypin did advocate privatization and a greater role for the free market, there is some support for the argument that the free market would contribute to a more efficient rural economy. Yet that view provides only a limited analysis of what was taking place.

In ancient Athens, Solon's laws provided superficial relief from economic hardship, but they could not reverse the economic trends. Economic or market forces proved largely resistant to governmental action. In the case of Russia, what was the direction economic forces were moving in? Put another way, once legal restrictions were removed, what type of economy emerged? The Emancipation Edict of 1861 and Stolypin's reforms were intended to remove legal impediments to economic growth. Yet, the Emancipation decree did not free the peasant from the commune to any significant extent and did not bring any radical changes to the structure of the agricultural economy as a whole.

An overview of agricultural production shows that it was marginal at best. One indication of this fact is that, at the time of Stolypin's reforms, in 1906, peasants were still repaying the landlords for the land which they had received in 1861. (The payments actually were made to the government, which repaid the landlords.) Stolypin's solution was to forgive the remaining debt. On January 1, 1907, remaining payments under the 1861 repayment plan were cancelled. (Some evidence suggests that repayment difficulties experienced with the Emancipation loan were not the result of production problems, but were the result of a refusal to make payments. While failing to make payments under the forty-nine year plan, peasants were increasing their purchases of consumer goods.[27]

At least part of the reason for the lack of any real change in agriculture was that Alexander had not made a complete overhaul of Russian laws. Left intact was the mir's collective responsibility for government obligations, which now included the forty-nine year loan. The collective's power to deny passports to those desiring to leave had the effect of nullifying whatever freedom the Czar seemed to grant with Emancipation.

One of the major productivity problems of Russian agriculture was related to the way land was farmed. The communal method of partitioning provided some fairness by providing each peasant with access to land which was more productive. From a productivity standpoint, the disadvantage was that land was not distributed as a single plot. Instead each peasant was allotted several strips of land, often separated by moderate distances. A peasant, both in planting and at harvest time, thus had to spend part of the time moving equipment from one plot to another.[28] In addition to such inefficiencies, the individual peasant had to contend with a decrease in the overall size of allotments. A population increase caused the average size of an allotment to decline from 5.24 hectares in 1861 to 2.84 hectares by 1900.[29] In failing to bring about changes in the underlying rural economic structure or methods of farming, the 1861 Edict fell short if its goal was to free the serfs.

Whether the 1861 Edict was a major factor, it is clear that the rural economy was nevertheless undergoing change. The landed nobility, for their part, were getting out of farming. Between 1861 and 1900, the amount of land owned by the nobility declined by 40 percent.[30] The decline would continue up to the First World War.[31] By 1916, aristocratic holdings had dropped to a mere ten percent.[32] Some of the land sold by the former aristocracy went to the communes, some went to private owners. Agricultural production, in this respect, was being assumed by a more specialized producer, someone committed totally to agriculture.

The aristocracy was not the only group leaving. Peasants, as well, felt compelled to leave, seeking work in the cities, home to a small, but developing industrial sector. Urban population, around 6 million in 1861, had doubled by 1897. It would reach 18 million by 1914.[33] The communes would issue temporary permits which allowed an estimated 300,000 peasants to travel to the cities each year in search of work.[34] Even while industry was beginning to develop in the cities, localized cottage industries continued to exist, allowing peasants to manufacture needed goods close to their own villages.

The discontent expressed by the workers in the 1905 Revolution was an indication that industrialization was not without its problems. While the strikes and rioting suggested that governmental efforts should be focused on industry, they did not mean that problems in the agricultural sector could be ignored. One of those problems was seen to be the power of the commune. By allowing the administration of local agriculture to remain in the hands of the commune, the Czar had undermined the goals of the 1861 Emancipation. Stolypin was convinced that the agricultural system could only be reformed by eliminating the commune's control of land distribution; privatization was the key to a revitalized agricultural economy. The encouragement of the small, entrepreneurial producer was a necessity.[35]

The law of November 9, 1906, unlike the law of 1861, would grant title to land directly to the peasant, rather than to the commune. Peasants who wished to move away were entitled to a cash payment for their property. Stolypin provided more economic support for the peasant by cancelling arrears on the forty-nine-year loan and by direct loans from the Peasant Land Bank. The law was a success in freeing the peasant from the commune. Around 22 percent of the peasant households had taken title to their land by 1916.[36] The poorer peasants, in particular, were eager to get out of farming. On the other hand, the expectation that the law would eliminate the most inefficient aspect of strip farming, the parceling out of commune land in widely dispersed small strips, was not met. Under the law, peasants who withdrew were to be given a consolidated piece of land. The communes had sufficient authority to ignore this provision, the result being little change in agricultural practices. In 1916, 90 percent of peasant operations still involved strip farming.[37]

The bumper crop of 1913 was perhaps a tribute to Stolypin's reforms, although favorable climactic conditions that year were clearly involved. While Emancipation had not brought about an immediate revolutionary change, Russian agriculture had nevertheless changed in the years after 1861. The old landed gentry had been replaced by a more specialized ownership, more motivated and interested in agriculture. Many of the poorer peasants had left for the cities and the urban work force. Finally, a small, but substantial, class of entrepreneurial peasant had begun to develop. While these changes had contributed to a more efficient agricultural economy, some things had not changed. The commune, though in retreat, still remained a powerful force in the country. It effectively retained control of farming methods, acting as a brake on reform measures. If the changes had improved the rural economy, they also brought about some unintended political consequences. More peasants wanted to take advantage of the new opportunities than there were opportunities available. Those who could not benefit felt resentment for their more successful neighbors. As long as the government was able to maintain its authority, these political forces remained in check. When that authority was weakened however, the resentment would begin to express itself.

The Austrian Archduke Ferdinand was assassinated in Sarajevo on June 28, 1914. The First World War began shortly after, on August 1, 1914. For the first year of the war the Russian food situation remained relatively stable. In contrast to the hardships and heavy casualties suffered by those fighting at the front, those who remained behind benefitted from the war. The government largely met its military procurement needs through the market. It met its grain requirements by offering higher prices. Where horses or livestock were requisitioned, they were paid for. If the better-off peasants benefitted from higher grain prices, peasant laborers benefitted from higher wages. Since the draft had claimed many of the available farm laborers, there was now a shortage. Wages paid for farm labor increased as a result. Sending men for military service also made more land available. The village did not have to divide its land among as many inhabitants.

The benefits of the extraordinary war measures for the agricultural economy would continue through much of 1915. City inhabitants, in contrast, began to feel the downside of the war effort in the fall of 1915, when inflation set in and food shortages began to appear.[38] The shortages could be partly blamed on transport problems - when the war started one-third of railroad rolling stock had been requisitioned by the army.[39] Transport suffered as the war continued - breakdowns and a failure to replace worn-out equipment reduced shipments. Peasant hoarding added to shortage problems, as did a reduction in the amount of acreage cultivated - with a labor shortage, it was difficult to plant or harvest all available land. Shortages continued into 1916 and even worsened. Convinced that the government would pay even more for grain, peasants held off selling, even though the harvest had been good.

In spite of the continuing, even worsening, shortages in 1916, the government was reluctant to take any emergency efforts. Suggestions to fix grain prices or to requisition grain were brought up, then dropped. As winter approached, both Moscow and Petrograd were receiving a third of their needed food supply.[40] It was the continued shortages of food and fuel in Petrograd which contributed to the disturbances which occurred in February 1917, leading to the abdication by Nicholas and the formation of the Provisional Government in March.

The Czar's abdication had little immediate effect on the market. The Provisional

Government tried to require that sales could only be made to the government at fixed prices, but the law could not be enforced. While not changing market operations, the fall of the Czar did not go unnoticed in the village. Peasants who belonged to the communes, and felt a special hatred for those peasants who had left the commune, began a series of attacks on the holdings of their now-independent neighbors. While not physically attacking the peasants, they did cut down trees and take seed grain.[41] The communal peasants began to hope that the long-awaited Black Repartition, the great parcelling out (to the communes) of all privately-held lands, was about to take place. The peasants were persuaded to stop their attacks with the promise that their demands would be met, although it would not be until October that they heard anything specific from the government.

AGRICULTURE AND THE OCTOBER REVOLUTION

The Second Congress of Soviets, meeting on the evening of October 26, 1917, passed a Decree on Land, proposed by Lenin. It was one of the first measures enacted by the Bolshevik government; the Winter Palace had surrendered only that morning. When word of the measure reached the countryside, the peasants assumed that the Black Repartition had finally been authorized - and immediately took steps to implement it - insofar as they understood what it meant. Property still in the hands of landlords was taken over by the communes, then redistributed to members. In some cases property which had been purchased by peasants was taken over as well. There was a great deal of confusion about who actually was the owner of the newly acquired land. Many villages, seeking to model themselves after the new government, sought to set up local soviets, new bodies distinct from the old village assembly. In some cases, it was the new soviet which declared itself the owner; in other cases the assembly took ownership. In still other cases, the old assembly simply called itself a soviet, and continued control.[42]

The peasants managed to achieve their redistribution in a relatively short time - it was largely complete in the spring of 1918. Yet, for all the expectations raised, the results were disappointing. Overall, the newly acquired land amounted to some 21.15 million desiatiny, or 57.1 million acres, which averaged out to around 0.4 desiatina per adult peasant, or a little over an acre per peasant.[43] Theoretically, redistribution should have provided an equitable partition of lands which became available. In practice, it failed. For one thing, not all lands of the former Empire were under Bolshevik control. Much of the area where the Bolsheviks held power was already under communal ownership. Pipes estimates that around 53 percent of communes added no new land to their available holdings.[44] In addition, communal peasants viewed those who had left the village or who had elected to farm outside the commune, almost as outsiders. Those who had left the village and returned in hopes of obtaining land either received no allotment or received small or unproductive plots.[45]

What was the Land Decree and what was it intended to accomplish? Was it the Black Repartition, as understood by the peasants? Was it the first step toward the implementation of the communist grand scheme, as understood by Lenin? Bolshevik theory seemingly demanded some redistribution. In some respects, the Land Decree was the legal embodiment of what the peasants had hoped for - the Black Repartition. That it did not fulfill their expectations cannot be blamed entirely on the law itself. The peasants, believing in a myth, had failed to take any hard look at the overall availability of land and how much of what was available could be used for repartition. More dangerously, the peasants had never seriously questioned the underlying assumption, namely that the Black Repartition would mean increased yields and greater prosperity. For Lenin however, the Land Decree fell far short of a major ideological plan. It did not mean the taking of private property for state use.

The Land Decree, as passed, was a compromise. There were several things the law did (or did not do). First, it did not appropriate or nationalize private landholdings in the strict sense, i.e., the state or national government did not take over private land. The landholdings affected were, instead, to be given to the local commune. Private landholdings were "socialized" in that they were taken away from private owners and made part of the communally available land. Second, the Land Decree specifically exempted private land held by peasants and Cossacks. It did take land held by landlords (as well as land not being used by its owners), by the church, and even that land held by the state. Third, the Decree did not compensate those whose land was taken. (The Decree was similar to nationalization in this regard.) These three points provide the main elements of the law, expressing Lenin's views - at least the views he held in October 1917. The Decree did not necessarily represent the final form Lenin or the Bolsheviks expected or wanted. A new law, "On the Socialization of the Land," initially proposed in February 1918 was issued in final form in April. Revealing a split between the Left SRs and the Bolsheviks, the law as formulated by the Left SRs called for land to be farmed by collectives, although owned by the commune. Bolshevik amendments pushed for state ownership, with farm workers transformed from owners into wage earners on large state collectives.

The new decree provided the peasants with the first indication that the Bolsheviks were going back on their promises. Lenin did not mean to leave the communes in permanent control of their newly acquired land. The new decree characterized the previous grant of land to the communes as only temporary. While the Bolsheviks may have gone back on their promises in April, the law which Lenin formulated in October was the catalyst to undo much of what had been achieved by Stolypin's reforms. It served to revitalize the practice of strip farming, partially to blame for the inefficiencies present in Russian agriculture.

The Land Decree of October 1917 had exempted the private holdings of small peasants, but not those of landlords. By subjecting landlord holdings to communal seizure, Lenin hoped to gain political support for the Bolsheviks, playing off the supposed antagonism between the rich and poor in the village. At the least, the action temporarily neutralized peasant opposition to the Bolsheviks. The practical effect of the decree was to provide the peasants with some official-sounding excuse to take action. In many cases the communes acted, not only against the landlords, but also against former members of the communes, who had opted to work their own plots. Pipes asserts that the practice of forcing those who had left the commune to rejoin it was widespread.[46] Fitzpatrick suggests that, while some of these occurrences may have been spontaneous, Party members from the towns or in the Red Army may have been encouraging this form of class struggle.[47] In February 1918 Lenin spoke of a "ruthless war" against the kulak. The term dekulakization, made a formal government policy under Stalin, is first heard in this period.[48]

Whether communal farming practices made a comeback as a result of Bolshevik pressure or because peasant belief in the mir remained strong, they did revive. In the central Volga, for example, independent farming, representing about 16 percent of peasant households in 1916, had virtually disappeared by 1922.[49] During the 1920s, Fitzpatrick estimates that strip farming as part of communal operations reached nearly 100 percent in Russia's main agricultural regions.[50] Even with a new law in 1922 allowing withdrawal from the commune, communal farming would remain the dominant method. In January 1927, 95.3 percent of peasant land in the Russian Republic would be held communally.[51]

Whatever the long-term trend in Russian agriculture, Lenin's Land Decree of 1917 did have one immediate benefit. It freed the peasants from rent payments to their former landlords, an economic value of around 700 million rubles per year. In 1906 Stolypin had cancelled the forty-nine year loan payments, and encouraged the Peasants' Land Bank to lend peasants money. The Bolsheviks now cancelled peasant loans from the Land Bank, worth 1.4 billion rubles.[52]

WAR COMMUNISM

The Land Decree represented perhaps the most revolutionary aspect of the Bolshevik program in the agricultural sector. In the industrial sector, the Bolsheviks were attempting to nationalize many of the existing industries, such as transport and manufacturing. One of their most radical economic ideas was to eliminate money. In 1921 they would even offer free telephone and postal service to everyone. Perhaps most frustrating for communist economic planners was that the free goods offered by the state were found to have a market value, even in a supposedly moneyless economy, and would end up for sale on the black market. It is somewhat surprising then that in the early months of 1918, government planners still relied on market forces to obtain grain. Government grain stocks were maintained or replenished by purchasing grain from peasants.

Over half a year before the Bolsheviks seized power, on March 25, 1917, the Provisional Government had tried to create a state monopoly in the grain trade. Peasants were forbidden to sell grain on the open market. While they would be paid for the grain delivered to government purchasing agents, the prices were to be set by the government.

In 1918, the Sovnarkom officially continued the monopoly with its decree of May

13. Bolshevik leadership was coming to the realization that the monopoly created on paper was insufficient to deal with the shortages Petrograd, Moscow, and other major cities experienced in the winter of 1917-18. The bread ration in Petrograd was only two ounces per day in April. The one safety valve for the cities was the fact that many residents left for the countryside, in search of food. As a result, the Petrograd labor force in April 1918 had dropped to 40 percent of the January 1917 figure.[53] A diminished labor force, combined with shortages of fuel, led to factory closures and a drop in industrial production. The Bolsheviks were aware that the food shortages were contributing to dissatisfaction with their rule. They could have alleviated conditions by paying the peasants more for their grain. Instead they chose a more aggressive and repressive solution, which would come to be known as "War Communism." The term has been applied to the economic policy of the Bolsheviks in the period from 1918 to 1920, starting around the end of June 1918.

Agriculture was not necessarily the focus of the policy, but that sector received its share of attention. War communism might be described as the Bolshevik's greatest effort to put communist theory into actual practice. (The worst nightmare capitalists could imagine, it involved a full-scale attack on the market. Among its goals was the nationalization of industry and the elimination of private trade and money. At least those were its goals on paper.) While the Bolsheviks were not completely successful in the implementation of the plan, it was not all just on paper. It not only caused serious economic disruption, it also brought changes to the Soviet economy.

In 1921 Lenin defended Bolshevik actions by arguing that War Communism was a temporary response to conditions caused by the Civil War. Pipes disputes Lenin's interpretation, arguing that many of the actions taken were not intended to be temporary and that they were not mere responses to emergency situations. Pipes argues that the measures adopted were, in fact, taken as part of a systematic plan to impose communist theory on the market.[54] (In defense of Lenin, he argues that, while espousing communism, Lenin did not actually favor the more extreme economic program pushed by those under him.)[55]

The Bolsheviks began taking preliminary steps toward War Communism in the spring. On May 13, 1918, when they decreed the state monopoly on grain, they also included provisions in the law which were intended to give it more teeth. Peasants who failed to deliver their surplus grain to the state could be tried by Revolutionary Tribunals and imprisoned for ten years. Prior to this time, the Bolsheviks had authorized even harsher measures against "bagmen," the middlemen who got their name from selling small amounts of grain carried in bags on their backs. For them, the death penalty was authorized in February 1918. On May 20 the Sovnarkom created a police force for grain procurement by authorizing food supply detachments. Armed units were to be sent into villages to extract grain from the "kulaks" who were supposedly hoarding it, using force if necessary. The first unit was established by June 1. While it numbered only 400 men in the beginning, it would increase to 50,000. Even these numbers proved inadequate and the Sovnarkom ordered Red Army troops to participate in grain collection, providing another 75,000 soldiers. In addition to the food supply detachments, the Bolsheviks, on

June 11, 1918 had also authorized Committees of the Poor, which were to made up of poor peasants in the village.

Despite the use of force against the peasants the campaign initially brought in little grain. In July Lenin was complaining that Petrograd and Moscow still were short of food. The campaign instead brought revolt in the villages. Whether the figures can be considered reliable, some estimates place the number of government casualties as high as 15,000 killed between July and September 1918.[56] Official Cheka figures, cited by Pipes, indicate that 2,431 rebels were executed and another 1,821 were killed in fighting as against 875 on the government side, in connection with 245 separate rural uprisings during 1918.[57] The actions in the village beginning in June were followed by the institution of the Red Terror in September.

Ironically, where the Bolsheviks were reluctant to rely on the market to accomplish their larger economic goals, they tended to utilize profit incentives as a motivational tool for Party workers. They refused to pay the peasants more for grain, yet, to provide an incentive for grain collections, members of the food detachments were allowed to keep for their personal use around 20 pounds of food confiscated from the peasant "hoarders."[58] Peasants who joined the Committees of the Poor were also allowed a portion of grain or food taken from those hoarding food. In addition, they were to be allowed tools and implements taken from more well-to-do peasants.

One of the problems for the government was that a scarcity of grain had created such inflationary prices that wheat or rye were simply out-of-reach, given the budgetary constraints of wartime. The price for rye on the open market was some 20 to 30 times what the government would pay in August 1918.[59] With such low prices, the peasants were not tempted to part with much of their grain. In the end, the physical force used by the food supply detachments proved little more successful. At most the governmental units obtained around 570,000 tons of grain, which amounted to only one-hundredth of an estimated harvest of 49 million tons.[60] One estimate of the amount of grain collected in all of 1918 by the Commissariat of Food was 36 pounds per person in all of Russia.[61] The Bolsheviks slowly began to back away from some of their agricultural policies. In September they allowed peasants to sell small amounts of grain (25 kilograms) in the cities. In December they abolished the Committees of the Poor.

In January 1919, the Bolsheviks seemed to bring back Czarist methods of administration by imposing a tax in kind on the village, to be the collective responsibility of the districts and subdistricts where the villages were located. For the peasant it represented a slight improvement - at least in theory. The government would no longer demand all "surplus" grain. The term surplus, in practice, meant whatever grain or other foodstuffs the food supply detachments could find. While the amounts of grain demanded under the new system were set at high levels, the change replaced the requirement that the peasants surrender all their "surplus" grain. In spite of this change the government did not entirely abandon the policy of forced requisitions during the Civil War. Through 1919 and 1920 grain requisition teams continued to be used where quotas had not been met. As long as the White armies continued to exist, the Bolsheviks could justify the policies of

War Communism. In November 1920, when Wrangel's White army had been defeated, the justification for War Communism was largely gone. Only in March 1921 however, did Lenin publicly begin to retreat from official policy.

At the Tenth Party Congress on March 15, 1921, during the Kronstadt revolt, Lenin announced that there would be a new tax in kind requiring only about a fourth of the harvested grain. The peasants were once more to be given access to the free market and would not be subject to forced grain requisitions. With Lenin's about-face, the state thus relinquished its monopoly on the grain trade. The lifting of the ban on free trade in March 1921 might be considered to mark the end of War Communism.

What had been the peasant response to War Communism during 1919 and 1920? Peasant resistance to Bolshevik policy took two forms. First, peasants resorted to armed rebellion when government actions became too much to bear. Second, peasants used non-violent economic measures to show displeasure with official policy. Hoarding was one such measure, as was selling grain on the black market. Another method was to reduce the amount of land under cultivation. Resistance against the Bolsheviks in 1918 had required 75,000 Red Army troops to supplement the 50,000 members of the food supply units.[62] Officially, the Cheka recorded 245 uprisings in the countryside.[63]

In 1919 the Bolsheviks had to commit still more army troops to deal with the countryside - 180,000 were assigned to that task in the summer of 1919.[64] Where army units were unavailable, life could be dangerous for government officials. By 1920, Ukrainian peasants had reportedly killed 1,700 requisition officials.[65] Sometimes the resistance was isolated; at other times it took a more organized form. Peasant leaders who hated the Whites could turn that hatred against the Bolsheviks when their rule proved as distasteful. The Ukrainian peasant leader Nestor Makhno proved to be one such problem for the regime. Initially an ally against the Whites - he had captured Ekaterinoslav from them in December 1918, and been appointed a Red Army commander as a result - the Bolsheviks found him opposing their actions against the peasants. He threatened to execute Bolshevik officials in August 1919. In October 1919, just as Denikin's White army was moving on Moscow, Makhno's forces captured the port city of Berdiansk and had his army destroy White communication and supply lines. While such actions may have helped the Red Army turn back Denikin's advance, in January 1920 the Bolsheviks declared him an outlaw. Just as the Whites had, the Bolsheviks soon found themselves having to deal with attacks from Makhno's army on their rear supplies.

No sooner had the resistance of Makhno's force been suppressed than the Bolsheviks had to contend with a new peasant revolt. In June 1920 peasants in the Viatka province, northeast of Moscow, revolted. Unrest spread north into Siberia, south to Vladimir, closer to Moscow, and then into the richest grain growing regions - the Ukraine and the Don. The Cheka would report 121 revolts in February 1921.[66] In Siberia alone, it took 50,000 Red Army troops to deal with peasant opposition. The true seriousness of the peasant unrest can be gauged in terms of Red Army casualty figures for 1921-1922, which were 237,908.[67] Southeast of Moscow, the Tambov region had rebelled in August 1920. Members of a grain requisition team were killed and peasants from several villages tried to capture the city of Tambov. Though the Red Army was defeated in several encounters, it retaliated against rebel villages. The peasant army, which acquired a leader named Alexander Antonov, resorted to guerilla warfare, attacking railways and torturing and killing government officials. Over 1,000 Bolsheviks are said to have been killed.[68] The Bolsheviks, in turn, responded by taking hostages and executing villagers or deporting peasants. It would take until August 1921 for the Red Army to put down the Tambov revolt.

Armed resistance was only one response to Communist agricultural policy. Hoarding or even destruction of grain was a less open form of resistance. Peasants sometimes would bury grain or hide it in the forests or streams when requisition teams came through their villages. Since members of the food supply detachments were often from the cities, locating hidden food supplies proved difficult. The food units many times beat peasants to force them to reveal where grain was hidden. Hiding food was an immediate response of the peasant. Peasants, in the long run, realized that it would be difficult to win against regular forces, armed with machine guns and willing to resort to torture or to employ executions. Discouraged by the expected requisitioning of surplus grain, as well as by the prohibitions against market sales, the peasants simply planted and harvested less grain. They also took advantage of loopholes in the law. Foodstuffs such as potatoes, carrots, and beets, which were allowed to be sold on the market and which were not as likely to be confiscated, replaced grain in some places.

In March 1921 Lenin had to concede that a continuation of War Communism would not bring more food into the cities. Peasant opposition had not defeated the Bolsheviks, but had resulted in a temporary stalemate. Lenin conceded the field to the peasants and the economy to the free market. For the next several years, the Communists would experiment with what was called the New Economic Policy, or NEP, for short.

AGRICULTURE AT THE END OF THE CIVIL WAR

There were several factors at work in the production and productivity declines which occurred during the Civil War. Forcible requisitioning, in combination with the state monopoly on grain, was a major contributor. The Bolsheviks not only had to deal with active resistance, on the part of the peasants, but also with the inertia of the agricultural sector. The peasant response usually came in two forms: the hoarding of grain or the intentional reduction of the amount of land under cultivation. At the same time, peasant resistance was only part of the problem.

There were problems unique to the time period. The military's demand for recruits both during the First World War and during the Civil War had reduced the rural labor pool. The lack of workers made it difficult for landlords, and later, for village communes, to effectively plant and harvest the available land. By one estimate, the amount of acreage planted in 1914 had fallen by a third by the time the Russian Civil War came to an end. Another factor, unrelated to Bolshevik policy, was the lack of mechanization. Many peasants lacked modern equipment or fertilizers. In addition, the overall failure to deliver produce to the cities was often caused by difficulties unrelated to agricultural production. In February 1921 officials complained that they were unable to transport grain because there were insufficient sewing machines to make grain sacks.[69] Attempts to provide market incentives to the peasants, e.g. by making manufactured goods available, failed because Russian industry could not supply the needed goods.

What the Bolsheviks had failed to change was the underlying village structure and the agricultural methods employed during the times of the Czars. Strip farming, with all its inefficiencies, remained. Collective responsibility for grain requirements, and later, for taxes, the administrative mechanism of the Czar, was reinstated, only to be abandoned in April 1921. Apart from the disruptions caused by Bolshevik economic policy, the agricultural economy had to deal with the chaos caused by the numerous peasant revolts. (In one sense they can be blamed on Bolshevik policy and could have been foreseen by Lenin; in another sense they were something apart from the actual policy itself - unrelated to Bolshevik theory.) The continual series of revolts which took place reinforces the perception that the Russian peasant and village were extremely tough. Their recovery from the depredations of the food supply units and the Red Army serves as strong testimony to their resilience. The agricultural economy itself however, did not quite mirror the toughness of the peasant. Even during times of peace, crops fall victim to natural forces, such as hail, drought, or insects. Agricultural production requires planning. One of the major mistakes Lenin made, was not simply in trying to bring the rural economy under government control, but also in launching a war on the rural populace. Even as the Bolsheviks were winning the war against the peasant, the methods used were destroying the underlying ability to produce. The killings or deportations, necessary for political victory, were also eliminating the very peasant expertise necessary for future economic success, which was dependent on the planting and harvesting skills known to the peasant.

THE NEW ECONOMIC POLICY - AN OVERVIEW

On March 15, 1921, two days before the Red Army would make its final assault on the Kronstadt fortress, Lenin called for the abolition of forced grain requisitions. Speaking before the Tenth Party Congress, he advocated a tax in kind, fixed in amount, with the added incentive that the peasant would be allowed to sell any surplus after taxes on the open market. On March 21, the policy was adopted. Lenin's retreat in the agricultural sector was a preliminary signal for a general retreat from governmental economic controls in all sectors of the economy. By year-end the changes in economic policy would come to be called the New Economic Policy (NEP). The Party would allow the private sector greater freedom under NEP for a few brief years and then revert to measures mirroring War Communism. This section provides a brief overview of NEP for both the industrial and agricultural sectors and then provides a more detailed look at its impact on the agricultural sector.

The easing of economic controls in the agricultural sector was followed by the lifting of market restrictions on industry. Having nationalized industry during the Civil War, Lenin partially eased that policy by reversing the decree which had nationalized small-scale industry. The change occurred in May 1921. The Party would gradually expand the areas where it would allow market forces to operate. NEP would continue as government policy for only four years - through 1925. In 1926 the Party began moving toward greater government control. The government did not impose an outright ban on free trade or nationalize industry through decree. Instead, it began a gradual elimination of the private sector through fiscal and financial measures; it began charging more for government services and increasing tax rates for certain types of endeavors. One such area was that of rail transport. Private businesses used government rail services to transport many of their products. In 1926 however, the government began charging from 50 to 100 percent for such transportation services.[70] Taxes on private traders were raised as well. Financial controls were only the first step. In 1926, hoarding was made a criminal offense with the enactment of Article 107 of the legal code.

As the Party began to move against private business in the industrial sector, it also took more aggressive action in the agricultural sector. For the peasants, the practical end of NEP occurred in late 1927. (It would be continued for the rest of the economy through 1928. The amount of grain collected by the government had been dropping off and in December grain reserves were so low that they precipitated a "crisis." Stalin, in December, and again in January 1928, would decree that extraordinary measures were to be used against the kulaks.

Why had the Bolsheviks seemingly been so tolerant of NEP, a policy which ran counter to their ideological views? The implementation of NEP can perhaps be explained by the end of the Civil War and the need to stabilize the Soviet economy. If it worked so well however, then why did it come to an end? What changes occurred when it was in operation?

AGRICULTURAL RECOVERY UNDER NEP

In the months following the March 1921 decrees it was difficult to discern any real benefits from the policy changes. In agriculture, the raids of the requisition teams had deprived peasants of seed grain for the 1921 planting. At a larger level, the government economic program had been successful at reducing overall productivity. These two factors combined with drought, beginning in the fall of 1920, to reduce the size of the harvest and with it, the amount of grain collected in the fall of 1921. The grain harvest itself had been small in 1921 - only 37.6 million tons.[71] The amount of grain the government obtained that year was only 128 million poods (10 million tons).[72] Lenin had hoped that, under the new tax, the government would receive 240 million poods (18.8 million tons). While the figure was overly optimistic, in view of the harvest, it represented an easing of the amounts demanded. The amount of grain received in 1920 had been 300 million poods (23.5 million tons).[73]

Despite the disappointing collections, the Party did not immediately abandon the new policy. At the same time, while it could have resorted to extraordinary measures to deal with the famine, it nevertheless allowed its free market concessions to remain in force. (The government also could have purchased more grain abroad to ease the famine, but chose not to fully embrace such a policy.) Despite the hardships, the rural economy would recover in 1922, even producing a bumper crop, although still below that of the record 1913 harvest.

In March 1923 Leon Trotsky made a speech to the Twelfth Party Congress. Trotsky employed a graph during the speech to illustrate his talk. The graph compared prices for agricultural and industrial commodities beginning with the year 1913. Prices for both commodities had been increasing since 1913. However, the rate of increase for industrial goods prices was greater than that for agricultural products. The lines intersected, on the graph, in the autumn of 1922. The prices for industrial commodities continued to climb relative to agricultural prices into 1923. Trotsky pointed out that the lines on the graph looked like a pair of scissors and the phenomenon described by the graph came to be known as the "scissors crisis." At the time of the speech, agricultural prices were only three-fourths of their 1913 level, while industrial prices were one-and-a-half times what they had been in 1913. The "scissors" continued to widen until October 1923, when the crisis began to subside. At that time, agricultural prices stood at 89 per cent of their 1913 level, while industrial prices were at 276 per cent, an increase roughly three times that of agricultural goods.[74]

A combination of factors contributed to the narrowing of the scissors. Agricultural prices began to increase faster, in part, because of a seasonal demand for agricultural goods. Industrial prices began to fall as a result of price control measures instituted by the government combined with a drive for more efficient manufacturing, as well as by the industrial recovery which had been occurring following the end of the Civil War. In the months following the October peak, industrial prices continued to fall. By April 1924, they had been brought down to 131 on the 1913 index of 100; agricultural prices, as measured on the 1913 index, stood at 92.[75]

Governmental policy during 1923 and 1924 reflected an almost laissez-faire attitude. If forced food requisitioning always was an option, the Party chose instead to rely on rules of supply and demand to increase government grain stores. The problem, for the government, was not basic agricultural production - the agricultural sector, in fact, had recovered to such an extent that output stood at 75 per cent of pre-war output.[76] Instead, the problem was the government's inability to benefit financially from the resurrected agricultural economy. Put another way, the peasants and landholders simply would not sell grain or other agricultural products to government agents. Government food collections, primarily grain, remained low.

In relying solely on economic forces to bring in grain, the government had two obstacles to contend with. First, the prices it offered the peasants for grain were too low to provide an incentive to sell - to the government. Grain procurement agents, trying to save money, tried to obtain grain for the lowest price. Second, the shortage of manufactured goods meant that the peasants had no need for cash. Still largely self-sufficient, peasants did not have to participate in the economy. Manufactured goods were either unavailable or, if available, were extremely expensive. For the peasant, there were any number of markets available for his product - Russian consumers, Russian cities, and government grain agents always needed grain. Market forces, as a result, almost always worked in favor of the peasant. The reverse was not true for those who lived in the cities. For the manufacturer and the factory worker, market forces were too weak to create demand. To be sure, there was some need for the type of goods produced by factories, but peasants could make do if manufactured goods were unavailable or cost too much.

The inability to create a market for industrial goods in the countryside was one of the reasons grain procurement was low. Two basic factors were at work. First, Soviet industry was unable to produce enough goods to satisfy the market. Second, prices for the goods which were available were too high. One of the reasons for the shortage of goods was that basic equipment and manufacturing facilities had deteriorated or been destroyed as a result of the Civil War and there had been insufficient capital to invest in new equipment. In contrast to the agricultural sector, which required very little heavy equipment, or could manage with less intensive capital investment, industrial recovery required large outlays of funds. Changes in the agricultural sector contributed to production problems as well. The textile industry, which needed cotton for cloth, faced a cotton shortage. Russian peasants no longer grew cotton - only 70,000 hectares of land was sewn with cotton in 1922, where 688,000 hectares had been dedicated to that crop in 1913.[77]

There were a number of factors which contributed to the high prices of goods which were available. One factor in high prices was action taken by government-sponsored agencies, which monopolized sales of various manufactured products. While grain procurement agents were under pressure to buy grain at low prices, government disposal agencies were under pressure to sell goods at high prices. Where they controlled the supply for a particular manufactured good, they tried to charge as high a price as possible. A second factor was an increase in basic manufacturing costs, particularly labor costs. Labor productivity had fallen and factories, as a result, were required to hire more workers, adding to the costs of production. The third factor was an inefficient distribution system which added still more to the cost of those goods reaching the peasant.[78]

While government actions such as price controls and campaigns to reduce manufacturing costs helped to close the scissors, it may have been the gradual recovery of industry which played the most important role. In one sense, the "crisis" aspect of the scissors was in the minds of the Party leadership. Underlying the problems faced by the Communists in the overall economy was the fact that the agricultural economy had rather quickly recovered and was relatively strong. It was also independent. The problem for the Party was getting the peasant to participate in the larger economy. Short of resorting to force, the Party needed something to lure the peasants in. Manufactured goods were intended to provide the incentive. So long as they remained in short supply, or were very expensive, the peasants had no need to enter the market. Shortages of goods were not the only factor in peasant independence. Agricultural recovery had meant a recovery of economic strength.

Communist policy, in dealings with the agricultural sector, could be described as involving extremes. During the Civil War, it had been marked by the confiscation and distribution of land and the forced requisitioning of grain. During NEP the peasant was left alone. The Party had been successful in its war against the landlords and rich peasants - large landholdings had been eliminated during the Civil War. When the war ended, the Party focused its attention less on the rural economy and eased many of the restrictions it had used for control. Without controls, the number of peasant households increased. This increase took place within the confines of the size restrictions. In 1924 there were some 23 million peasant households, as compared to around 17 or 18 million before 1917. In 1925 the number of households increased to 25 million. At the same time, the amount of land devoted to farming remained the same. This meant that the average size of individual holdings was smaller.[79]

These small peasants demonstrated an independent spirit by avoiding membership in state farms and government collectives through much of the 1920s - 98.3 per cent of all acreage sown in 1927 was under the control of individual peasants.[80] Paradoxically, while the peasants superficially acted independently vis-a-vis the government, they demonstrated less of an independent spirit in their relationships with each other. As a result the village - and the inefficient farming methods which had been associated with it - began to rise again. Peasant willingness to support the village seemed almost to mirror the number who chose avoidance of government collectives. Where 98 per cent of the land was sown by peasants "independent" from government control, around 90 per cent of peasants in 1925 were members of village communities.[81] With the revival of the village, strip farming became accepted practice once more. In addition to the inefficient practices reintroduced by the village governmental structure, production was hampered by lack of machinery. The wooden plow (*sokha*) was still used by 5.5 million households in 1928 and the sickle or scythe was used for half the grain harvest.[82] Ironically, the low level of mechanization, while serving as an obstacle to efficient production, may have contributed to the peasant's independence. Where the wooden plough was the primary tool of the peasantry, the peasant would be indifferent to any shortage of manufactured agricultural implements.

The inefficiency of strip farming and shortage of equipment were only part of the reason for reduced grain collections by the government. Government agents were hampered by the refusal of peasants to sell grain which had been harvested. The refusal might be characterized as short-term. Governmental policy had also caused a long-term change in agricultural production. Before 1917 the landlords and kulaks accounted for 71 per cent of grain produced for the market.[83] For all the importance the Communists placed on grain collections, their political war against the entrepreneurial grain producers eliminated the one group they needed for success. Smaller peasants had concentrated on non-grain crops and production had often been geared to subsistence farming - production had been barely sufficient to sustain the peasants. With the rise of the small landholder, there was an increase in small landholding practices - and a general shift away from grain production. As a result there was less grain available in the economy as a whole.

The shift away from grain to other agricultural commodities was one change taking place in the Soviet economy. There was also the re-emergence of an upper class among the peasantry, a fact which dismayed Party officials. Peasant dreams seemingly realized by the Land Decree of October 1917 were coming up against the economic realities of 1925. In that year, some 1.7 million peasants were without land and hired themselves out to the more successful peasants.[84] The government had even given its blessing by making it legal for peasants to hire agricultural laborers. Depending on the source, the estimated percentage of households which were sufficiently well off to afford hired help was as low as 1.9 or as high 7.6.[85] The development of an upper class within the peasantry may have offended the political sensibilities of the Party; what worried Party leaders, at the local level, was the fact that the village political structure had more power than that of the Party. The council of elders, the village political unit, had greater authority than the local soviet among the peasantry. The threat to Communist rule brought on by the rise of a peasant upper class and the revival of the village was primarily felt by local Communist officials. There was, in fact, a split in the Party.

The economic division which was appearing in the ranks of the peasantry was being mirrored by divisions within the government. Party leaders in Moscow may have had difficulty reconciling the development of a peasant upper class with their concepts of class equality, but they were pleased with the increased productivity in rural areas. Local Party officials were concerned with the extent of the concessions Moscow seemed willing to make to capitalist ideas. Using profits as an incentive to the peasants was clearly at odds with communist theory. More importantly perhaps, it posed a threat to their political power. Stalin, still working his way to the top, publicly endorsed the then-current Moscow line. He was also aware that local officials, in dealing with the peasants, would be willing to support anyone willing to curb the rising political and economic power of the new peasant elite.

Rural officials perhaps drew conclusions about Moscow's views from other Party decisions. The village soviets were the governing unit in local areas, usually having administrative responsibility for six to eight villages. Party membership was not a requirement for the chairmanship of a soviet, although the Party had some 160,000 members it could call on in rural areas. In spite of their responsibility, the soviets generally had no budget and no resources. The chairmen received, on average, only 20 rubles per month, in spite of the fact that the national government collected taxes from the peasant. It was the village mir, not the soviet, which seemed to receive official recognition as the local governing body. The village mirs, as in Czarist times, could fine their members, could lease land to obtain revenues, and could enter into contracts and deal with governmental agencies. Local communist officials were also aware that the mir was viewed as the legitimate governmental authority by the peasantry.

Where officials in the rural areas worried about the threat from the mir in 1925, Party leaders paid more attention to the political struggles taking place in Moscow. Trotsky had been defeated by Stalin in April. At the Fourteenth Party Congress, which took place in December 1925, Stalin would decisively defeat his former allies, Kamenev and Zinoviev. In later years, he could deal with political opponents as he saw fit, but in 1925 he still was forced to rely on political argument and debate. On the surface, the debate involved communist theory; in reality it was a personal power struggle. Each side attempted to prove that their interpretation of communist thinking was correct. Stalin, often criticized for a lack of imagination, was actually quite skillful at putting together a logical argument. He was no less skillful at building a political base which would provide him with votes at crucial times. Rarely out front on issues, he appeared the moderate - his approach was simply common sense. That approach might be described as a form of camouflage. He was able to pick and choose different statements of Marxist political writers to support whatever argument he wanted to make. Unfortunately, any phrase from a prominent writer could be used to disguise true intentions. Yet, if there was a superficial aspect to the debate taking place, Stalin was not the only politician who was guilty.

One of the problems for the Soviet leadership in 1925 was that communist theory had never really addressed the specific economic situation facing the regime. It was hard-pressed to describe the economic forces at work, let alone find a solution to the problems which existed. Marxist theory had been obsessed with the problems associated with industrialization and the injustices visited on workers. If, in its broader sense, there was concern with the problems of the "masses," Marxist theory was less willing to deal with economic injustices occurring outside the context of the factory. The Civil War, with its accompanying food shortages in the cities, had brought this dilemma to the forefront. What good was a good wage or fair treatment by an employer, if it could not buy food?

Lenin's response to shortages during the Civil War was to reconcile economic argument so as to fit communist theory. All economic activity was somehow related to the struggle between capitalists and workers. Capitalists were behind all injustices, he argued; therefore, since peasant hoarding was causing food shortages in the cities, the peasants were part of a capitalist conspiracy aimed at the worker. While theory might worry about the injustices which peasant workers endured, Lenin rationalized that there was a class of peasantry which had allied itself with the capitalists, and which was therefore capitalist. He overlooked the fact that taking grain from the peasants was, in reality, little different than the treatment factory workers received from factory owners. Lenin may have justified his actions, in part, because of a bias toward the factory worker. Having to choose between the worker and the peasant, Lenin was willing to sacrifice the peasant.

NEP IN RETREAT (1925-1927)

The Fourteenth Party Congress, meeting in December 1925, formally adopted a resolution making industrialization state policy. It did not mark the beginning of a formal campaign to end NEP. That was a gradual process which had begun even before the Congress met. In mid-1925 steps were taken to reverse NEP policies and to reassert government control of the economy. The government chose to focus on industry, with relatively mild restrictions. It exercised more control over strategic resources and began charging more for private use of economic resources, such as rail transport. What was driving the changes was a debate within the Party over the economic direction of Russia, with a focus on the need for industrialization.

The debate in 1925 was really taking place at two levels. At one level, the debate involved an attempt to explain Russia's economic situation in terms of Marxist thought and to develop policies which would conform to communist theory. At another level, the debate involved industrialization. The need to industrialize the Soviet Union was perhaps becoming the more important of the two issues. There was, in fact, little argument over the need to industrialize. There was some disagreement over the pace of industrialization. The debate over industrialization would itself, take place at two levels, the theoretical and the practical. At the theoretical level, Party leaders were influenced by the Marxist bias toward the city and the factory worker. The communist goal of an egalitarian society and the fair treatment of workers which would come with the 'dictatorship of the proletariat' would not be realized, the argument went, until a country had become industrialized. On the practical level, Party leaders felt the need to make Russia into an industrial and military power. Allied intervention during the Civil War was sufficient reason to fear future action by foreign governments. Nationalist feelings and basic Russian pride in a strong state necessitated building up the industrial sector. The fact that the government had to use grain as a source of cash to buy foreign factory machinery was also a continuing reminder of the weakness in industry.

Much of the debate in 1925 seemed to revolve around the theoretical - was government policy following or deviating from accepted communist theory? The question of industrialization or, more specifically, the pace of industrialization and how to carry it out within the confines of communist theory, lurked in the background. While the debate about industrialization was not in the forefront, it may be helpful to look at the discussion which was taking place.

Industrialization, the ultimate goal, required investment capital - some form of cash or hard currency - to purchase equipment from abroad or to build factories. One source would have been Western capital, but continued antagonism toward capitalistic governments effectively cut off foreign investment. Communist leadership could disregard principles or Marxist doctrine when convenient - Lenin, after all, had accepted Western aid during the famine of 1921. However, as a long-term solution, Moscow could not, and would not, openly seek help in the West. The capital had to be found within the Soviet Union itself. Taxes were an obvious source of funds, but they were insufficient, especially for the type of large-scale industrialization being envisioned by Party leaders. Party identification with the urban labor force made the Party reluctant to impose greater burdens on workers. It had fewer qualms about treating peasants more harshly. Therefore, worker's earnings remained tax-free, while, after 1927, earnings of peasants did not.[86] Taxes, whether on workers, on peasants, or on industry, could be imposed at an extremely high level. Beyond a certain point however, high taxes amounted to government confiscation. Direct expropriation by the government was another option. The Bolsheviks had discovered during the Civil War that, while grain confiscations were inefficient and counter-productive, they did work.

Taxes and confiscation were one method of financing industrialization. Government investment was not the only alternative however. Industrialization could have been financed by private industry. Party leaders impatient with the pace of industrialization were undecided about whether financing should come from the public sector or from the government. There was not much disagreement over the need to accumulate some form of "capital" for investment. The debate was framed in terms of whether the state or the private sector should be in control. When the New Economic Policy had been implemented, the Party had temporarily conceded the argument to the public sector and the free market. Skeptics took a wait-and-see attitude initially. Their patience began to wane in 1923 and 1924 and they mounted an attack on the policy. Evgeni Preobrazhensky, one of the leading communist economic theorists, was one of the strongest critics. He favored state investment and charged that NEP had given away too much. In December 1924 and January 1925, debates about the views of Preobrazhensky and Trotsky resulted in official Party condemnation of the Left Opposition, and a major setback for Trotsky. Kamenev and Zinoviev, in trying to fight Stalin, took up the Left Opposition cause.

Kamenev and Zinoviev used Preobrazhensky's argument in criticizing the lenient agricultural policy of NEP. In allowing peasants to control the marketing of crops the government was granting them too much power over capital investment. Assuming peasants had any savings, they would not invest in the newly developing Soviet industry. State control was thus necessary to ensure that industrialization would take place. To this criticism was added a related argument, namely that the Party needed to adopt a much stronger industrialization policy - the pace was too slow. To their economic arguments Kamenev and Zinoviev added a political criticism - the market reforms under NEP were dangerous because they strengthened the kulaks and the kulaks still posed a threat to the Party. Though the attacks were directed against Party policy, they were aimed at Stalin and Bukharin.

Stalin was forced to defend NEP, as a policy, since he had been involved in its implementation. He had allied himself with Bukharin, the economic theorist responsible for the policy, but as strong as the attacks were, he perhaps needed all his persuasive powers to defend it. During the summer and fall of 1925, Zinoviev and Kamenev had strongly criticized NEP as encouraging capitalism. Allowing an elite class of peasants to exist in the countryside went against communist theory, they argued. Bukharin was on the other side of the argument, favoring a more lenient attitude toward the newly developing peasant class. Stalin did not commit himself fully to the debate. As a Party leader he had supported the free market changes and Bukharin's policies. Afraid of being criticized for advocating the most extreme of Bukharin's views, he backed away from fully endorsing everything Bukharin proposed. At the same time he would not allow criticism of Bukharin to be made public. Once Kamenev and Zinoviev had been eliminated, Stalin took steps to adopt their arguments - to be used against Bukharin at a future point.

It was not Bukharin's economic policies, as such, which concerned Stalin. Stalin could easily see the economic merits of much of what had been proposed. It was Bukharin's political sense which alarmed Stalin. Stalin was fully aware that his political power was maintained by espousing an "orthodox" image of communist philosophy. Bukharin's mistake was in publicly proposing solutions directly at odds with communist theory, as understood at the time. In April 1925, he came up with the slogan 'Get rich," as part of his agricultural program. Intended to motivate the peasants to increase production, it smacked of capitalism. Stalin had to publicly repudiate it almost as soon as Bukharin proposed it. At the Fourteenth Party Congress in April Stalin said that 'get rich' was clearly not Party policy. Supporting such an idea was a definite threat to Stalin's role as defender of communist orthodoxy.

Despite Stalin's repudiation of Bukharin's most extreme statements, Stalin did not call for any drastic policy changes for agriculture. As with industry, such changes were coming however. In 1926 taxes on the more prosperous peasants were increased. In April 1926 a decision was made to reduce the number of privately held flour mills. Despite these policy changes, the government had not yet launched a full-scale attack on the peasant or the agricultural sector. Both, in fact, remained relatively productive. The agricultural "crisis," as characterized by Stalin, would not occur until the end of 1927. Perhaps a major reason for the "laissez-faire" attitude toward agriculture was that the Party was still working out the implementation of its industrialization policy during the debates of 1925 and 1926. Stalin himself, over time, had changed his approach to the agricultural sector.

His changing views on agricultural policy were mirrored by his changing views on industrialization. In 1924 he, along with Bukharin, had argued for a gradual program of industrialization. Trotsky, at the time, argued for an increase in industrial investment. Stalin, however, favored a more moderate pace, which would not require severe economic sacrifices. Whatever position Stalin publicly took in dealing with his political enemies, he was beginning to formulate his own program. Much of it would incorporate the ideas of his opponents. Once his political enemies were eliminated, he felt free to adopt the very programs he had so vigorously opposed only a few years before.

Stalin had concluded that industrialization was necessary, whether he was convinced by his opponents' arguments or had come to that conclusion as a result of the Party debates. The major problem was financing. It could be found within Russia, but not without sacrifice. In addition it would require an overhaul of the Russian economy. The agricultural sector was to bear a major part of the burden, he had concluded. Agriculture however was a two-edged sword: if it held out hope as the greatest potential source of financing, its structure represented the greatest obstacle to exploitation.

By 1927 Stalin could draw on many year's experience in economic policy. He had seen the detrimental effects of War Communism as well as the benefits of a more relaxed economic approach. The government had tried market approaches to increase agricultural productivity. It had paid more for grain, had made efforts to increase the availability of manufactured goods, had granted tax concessions, and had allowed for increased private control of land and produce. Economic productivity had improved. The dilemma for Stalin was that, while such measures had strengthened the agricultural sector, they had also made it more independent. Free market policies clearly worked, but they also meant economic concessions on the part of the government. If the goal were simply increased grain collections, increased prices would bring in more grain. Increased prices however, meant that the government was investing more in agriculture. An economic policy which relied on market forces alone thus had its costs.

The alternative, for Stalin, was to reduce or eliminate market forces from the agricultural economy. War Communism, with forced requisitioning of grain, was an early government attempt to defy market forces. From Stalin's perspective, the problem was that it still left the peasant with some degree of control. Once the army left, the peasants would reassert their traditional control of the land and market forces would once more determine the course of the economy - frustrating the government. The solution was to destroy the peasantry, not just to bargain with it or to control it. The independent peasant was to be replaced by a wage earner, the village government by government managers. The collective was the solution Stalin turned to. When he actually made the decision is not clear. One of his first public statements came in February 1928 during his visit to the Urals and Siberia. He had in mind the formation of collective and state farms, he said.[87]

THE GRAIN CRISIS OF 1928

The change in agricultural policy can be dated to December 1927. The "crisis" aspect of the procurements crisis, or grain collections crisis, confronted the Party then, at the Fifteenth Party Congress. Stalin began warning the leadership that government grain collections were low and there was a crisis which needed to be dealt with. While not discussed in public speeches, it was sufficiently severe that Stalin was able to obtain support for the use of extraordinary measures to forcibly requisition grain, beginning in January 1928.

The news that grain collections were far below expectations came as a complete surprise to Party members attending the congress. Stalin had been making public assurances that collections were going well up to that time. Even in October he had given no hint that there were problems with collections. While it is true that government collections had fallen and that grain reserves were low, it is not clear that the "crisis" was all that Stalin said that it was.

There are some facts about events in 1927 which can be related with more certainty, yet certain aspects of the crisis are somewhat mysterious. The crisis did not result from a any catastrophic event impacting agricultural production. In fact, the harvest had been a normal one. Weather had caused some problems in the North Caucasus, but there was no drought or wholesale destruction of crops. State grain collections in July and August pointed to a good year for the government - they were running ahead of those for July and August of 1926. Although they fell off somewhat in September, collections for wheat and rye were still ahead of those of the previous year. Collections dropped sharply in October, then in November and December, were running at roughly half of those for the same months of 1926. The decline impacted grain reserves. Exports fell off and the emergency grain reserve for the use of the army and the cities during the winter months was threatened.

The Central Committee, in December 1927 and January 1928 ordered that "extraordinary measures" were to be taken by local officials. The measures, such as workers' brigades, and the forcible seizing of grain stocks did result in an increase in collections in January, February and March of 1928, even exceeding those for the same months in 1927. January's collections were 134 percent of the 1927 figure, while February's collections were 222 percent of the 1927 figure. If the numbers indicated success, the tactics were bound to renew peasant resentment of the government. Stalin was criticized by Bukharin, Rykov and Tomsky. In addition, the plenum of the central committee, meeting in April 1928, formally condemned the "excesses" and promised that such actions would not be repeated. Such public statements and Party actions suggest a lack of serious thought given to planning and a government caught unawares by the hostility of the peasantry and opposition to its policies. Public pronouncements however, shed only a partial light on what was happening behind the scenes.

Robert Tucker in *Stalin in Power: The Revolution from Above, 1928-1941*, suggests that Stalin may have contrived the crisis. Specific evidence supporting such an allegation is lacking however. The charge is that Stalin and some close associates intentionally worked to lower the price at which the government was buying grain from the peasants, while at the same time increasing the prices of manufactured goods being sold in the countryside. The peasants, in response, refused to sell grain. They either switched to different crops, sold other products on which the price was better, or simply held onto grain in anticipation of an increase in prices in the spring.[88]

Whether contrived or not, Stalin was all too aware that forced grain requisitioning was not the only option available. Neither Party dogma nor historical precedent demanded it. In 1925 the government had responded to a similar shortage by raising grain prices and attempting to make manufactured goods more available. That response had resulted in an increase in collections. One consequence of the 1925 decision was to divert budgetary resources away from the industrial sector, delaying the industrialization which the Party had planned for.[89]

Raising prices was a market tool the government could use to influence agricultural production. Forced requisitioning was a non-market policy, relying ultimately on military force for enforcement. It appears that Stalin had simply lost patience with the market. It was unwieldy and the results were often disappointing. He was not unaware of the impact a return to War Communism would have on the countryside, but he now viewed all economic problems in terms of industry and the need to finance industrialization. The peasants, with their stranglehold on the agricultural sector, came to be seen as the obstacle to modernization.

One of the problems the Soviet government had encountered in trying to use market forces was that its industrial sector was still relatively weak. There were really two market forces which played a significant role in the agricultural economy insofar as government collections were concerned. One was the price the government would pay for grain. The other was the availability of manufactured goods. Manufactured goods were the one commodity which motivated the peasant to convert his crops into cash. If industry could not produce sufficient goods, the peasant had little incentive to enter the market.

Beginning in 1925 the government had had to contend with what was called the 'goods famine,' or a shortage of goods. Manufactured goods were either unavailable in the countryside, or if available, were sold at prohibitively high prices. It was hoped that the recovery of industry would help with availability. The government, between 1925 and 1927, attempted to deal with high prices by instituting price controls. It was found that controls merely shifted money into the hands of private traders. Private individuals would simply buy up what goods were available and then resell them on the black market at higher prices.[90]

Part of the overall problem with Party economic policy was that it tried to combine idealism with the practical. Peasants were expected to respond to its good intentions. In 1924-1925 the Party had made concessions which, it was hoped, would bring in more grain in the 1925 harvest. Expectations were disappointed. The Party, anticipating increased grain collections, had hoped to use sales of exported grain to buy foreign manufactured goods. The import budget had to be cut when collections were lower than expected. This, in turn, made the 'goods famine' even worse. The Party was also naive in its calculation of the speed of market changes as well as the magnitude of the market. It expected an immediate market response to changes in Party "attitudes." Instead, while it found the market reacting quickly, that response tended to ignore Party intentions in favor of the faster-moving economic realities. Peasants, in other words, supplied the government with more grain when prices were increased; the mere announcement of a plan to aid the peasant brought little response. Peasant reaction no doubt reinforced the perception that the peasant could not be trusted. The extraordinary measures which Stalin employed in January and February 1928 resulted in Party condemnation in April, but many in the Party may have felt that the peasant was being justifiably punished for earlier betrayals.

THE 1928 INTERIM - PLANS FOR COLLECTIVIZATION TAKE SHAPE

Stalin, in the April 1928 plenum vote, had allowed a condemnation of Party 'excesses' to be passed. It was one of the last concessions he would allow Bukharin, Rykov and Tomsky. He was beginning to lay the groundwork for collectivization. At the July 1928 plenum, he supported a resolution which echoed the speeches made during his February tour of the Urals and Siberia: the formation of collectives would be beneficial. Bukharin, despite Stalin's moderate stance, suspected that Stalin was already planning a more forceful move toward collectivization. At the July meeting he warned that the use of force to collectivize agriculture risked a mass uprising by the peasant. With the outcome of the debate still in doubt, the Party had to retreat in the face of the economic realities of the time. In June the government would begin importing grain. In July procurement prices were raised. Even that was not enough to replenish the existing grain reserves. By August the amount of grain imported in the three-month period was 250,000 tons.[91]

Stalin would again bring up the suggestion of collectivization in a speech to the plenum of the Central Committee in November 1928. In September and October government grain collections had increased, then dropped off in November and December. The January 1929 collections were half those of January 1928. In February collections were less than a third of those of the same month in 1928. So low were grain reserves that rationing was introduced in February 1929. Despite assurances that the extraordinary measures of 1928 would not be used, the Party reversed itself and resorted to forced requisitioning. In contrast to 1928, the peasants put up a more determined resistance. Procurement agents were murdered. With all the turmoil in the countryside collections did not improve. By June collections for the year were less than 80 percent of 1928. Whether Stalin had actively manipulated economic events to bring about a crisis, the experience and collection results of 1928 and 1929 were sufficient justification for a change in policy. Official approval of Stalin's collectivization plans came at the Sixteenth Party Congress, held in April 1929.

CHAPTER 14

THE COLLECTIVIZATION OF AGRICULTURE: JUNE 1929 - 1933

THE PUSH FOR COLLECTIVIZATION - JUNE 1929

On June 1, 1929 there were some 57,000 collective farms in the Soviet Union. About one million peasant households were members of these collectives.[1] This figure was much better than Party projections for the first year of the five-year plan. (The First Five-Year Plan had begun in July 1928.) The original number of households expected to join by July 1929 had been set only at 564,200. The plan had provided for only a 0.5 percent increase in the amount of collectivization in the first year of the plan - from 1.7 percent, it would be increased to 2.2 percent. The ultimate goal for collectivization for the five years was 23 percent of peasant farms. It was estimated that this would place 43 percent of grain production within government control.[2]

By December 1929 there would be 4,311,000 households in collectives. To the one million households included in the membership on June 1, another 3,311,000 would be added between July and December. The number of collectives by that time had increased to 70,000.[3] In the first three months, July, August and September, some 911,000 households joined, while the remaining 2,400,000 would join between October and December. Whether the household statistics were exact, the figure represented some 25 million individual peasants, out of a total peasant population of 125 million.[4] In six months one-fifth of the peasantry had been collectivized. An even more startling figure would come in 1930. It would be claimed on February 20, 1930 that collectivization had reached 50 percent of all peasant households.[5]

While Stalin and Party leaders could exert pressure from above, it was local officials who were responsible for the high numbers. Why did the second half of 1929 see such dramatic results? The Party had been advocating collectivization for many years, yet little had been accomplished or even attempted. There are perhaps two reasons for the success. Perhaps the biggest reason was the single-minded focus of Stalin on collectivization. Party policy had been constantly shifting prior to 1929. As long as the peasants had not actively opposed the regime they had been pretty much left alone. In the second half of 1929 Stalin had already decided what needed to be done. The other reason was that Stalin maintained his focus over the long term. Stalin did not initiate the policy and then back off when he encountered difficulties. As with any bureaucracy, pressure for change needs to be sustained to accomplish results. Stalin, by *Pravda* editorials, Party directives, and exhortations by high-level officials, continually reminded local officials that collectivization remained a priority.

If Stalin was successful at increasing the number of collectives, his management mistake was in substituting a minor accomplishment for his real goal. His ultimate goal was industrialization, not collectivization. The agricultural sector was intended only as a tool to finance industrialization. To achieve that goal, agricultural productivity and output needed to be sustained. Rather than moving toward that goal, Stalin instead became sidetracked with collectivization statistics. Statistics are a useful tool for quantifying progress or success - but they need to be kept in perspective. The problem was that Stalin became obsessed with numbers, to the exclusion of all else. The result was that local officials found ways to increase the numbers. The methods used were of little concern to Moscow. They ranged from extravagant promises to threats. Peasants were promised easy credit and tractors, in some cases. In other cases, they were threatened with dekulakization and, if that were not enough, they were dekulakized. Where even these actions failed, local officials simply made up numbers. In some cases, the names of peasant households were added to the list of collective farm members without being told they had joined.[6]

ALL OUT WAR ON THE PEASANT - DECEMBER 1929

On December 27, 1929 Stalin met with a group of Marxist agricultural scholars. He chose the meeting to publicly announce an extreme change in agricultural policy. The kulaks were to be liquidated as a class, he said. While his policy to this point had been to force all peasants into collectives, he announced that kulaks would not be allowed to join. One of the unintended consequences of this policy was to increase the likelihood that farm animals would be killed. Peasants who owned two horses or cows ran the risk of being automatically classified as kulaks, providing officials the excuse needed to dekulakize them, seize their property, and deport them. That was not the only reason for the slaughter. Many peasants killed their animals rather than contribute the animals to the collectives. While these actions provided the state with meat, they also devastated the agricultural sector.

Stalin's speech was not necessarily an abrupt change in policy. He had begun waging war on the kulaks in July. What the speech signalled was that Stalin had no intention of calling off the attack. In hindsight, Stalin could have taken an alternative course in December 1929, relying on market forces to bring about collectivization. The market was already subtly changing the agricultural sector. Tradition-bound peasants were only too aware that mechanized equipment was an advantage and that farming was not the most efficient economic endeavor. In the 1920s many peasants were leaving the land in search of work in the growing number of factories.

Whether Stalin would have made different choices if he had known the costs can never be known. Two different statistics provide some indication of the terrible impact of the 1929 decisions. One relates to the number of animals destroyed; the other relates to the number of peasants deported and imprisoned. The figures for the collectivization drive were not made public until after Stalin had died. The number of animals killed was devastatingly high. Between 1928 and 1933, 46.6 percent of the Soviet Union's cattle, 47 percent of its horses and 65.1 percent of its sheep were slaughtered. In actual figures, the number of cattle killed was 26.6 million, the number of horses killed was 15.3 million, and the number of sheep killed was 63.4 million.[7] In terms of human cost, one estimate places the number of peasant households deported to labor camps or colonies at around 300,000, or around 1.5 million individuals.[8] Another estimate suggests an even higher number, around 3.5 million individual peasants.[9] The official number of deported households was given as 381,000.[10] Whether deported or not, dekulakization left some 15 million people homeless. If some two million escaped their fate by transferring skills to other enterprises, such as construction sites , around one million were placed in concentration camps.[11]

There are perhaps two interpretations of Stalin's decisions. Medvedev suggests that Stalin in December 1929 came to believe in the success of his efforts based on statistics for collectivization - the numbers had proved better than the projected figures. He deluded himself, not only about how successful his program had been up to that point, but also about how easy it would be to reach his final goals.[12] The other alternative is that Stalin was not blinded by the statistical evidence, but felt that the success of collectivization depended on speedy implementation of the program.

The statistics were very much at odds with the realities of the collectivization drive. The problem was not that the numbers were incorrect, although with inflated figures reported in some areas, there is reason to question their accuracy. A more basic problem was the type of peasant who was joining. The most productive peasants were avoiding the collectives. The majority of the households who joined were poor peasants who had been struggling in the agricultural economy. While the government had been able to entice over 7 percent of peasant households to join, it had not captured a corresponding percentage of agricultural productivity. Middle peasants and kulaks remained independent. Stalin would claim, in an article in *Pravda* appearing November 7, 1929, that middle peasants had joined the collectives. The statement was simply untrue.[13]

The problem, for agricultural productivity, was not just in the numbers or type of peasant joining the collective. The problem was also in the productive capabilities of the collective, once the peasants had joined. In theory, the collective was supposed to make Soviet agriculture more productive. It was not the mere organization of a group of peasants into a common work group which was to improve productivity. The organizational structure of the collective made it little different than the organization of the peasant village. The potential advantage of the collective was found in mechanization, i.e., in the increased use of tractors and combines. While the number of peasants entering the collective was growing, the number of tractors or combines provided to the collectives was not. There was not only a serious shortage of such equipment, but also a shortage of cattle sheds and silos as well.[14] Ironically, it was probably the lack of central planning which now contributed to the problem. Stalin's plans suffered, not from central planning, but from no planning at all.

Tucker has suggested a second interpretation of Stalin's December 1929 decisions. Under that interpretation, it was neither Stalin's ego which caused him to push harder, nor a lack of planning. A more basic reason was that the government hoped to use peasant resources to finance collectivization, which would then allow for industrial investment. Before the agricultural sector could finance industrialization, it had to be made more efficient. Collectivization, in other words, was a prerequisite to industrial development. The sooner collectivization goals were reached, the sooner industrialization could be achieved. December 1929 was chosen, not so much because Stalin was encouraged by the results of the past year, but because there was a limited window of time in which to put the plan into effect. There was a temporary grain reserve and to prolong the collectivization drive beyond March 1930 increased the risk that it would disrupt agricultural operations for the coming year.[15]

On November 10, 1929, a plenary session of the Central Committee began. While the proceedings have remained secret, there was one speech which was made public, that of Molotov. Acting as surrogate for Stalin, he argued for an increase in the pace of collectivization. His timetable did not call for a gradual increasing of the rate of collectivization, projected to take place over the five years of the five-year plan. His proposed speed-up was monumental. Collectivization needed to be complete by April of 1930. The months from November to March were called critical. He pointed to the 1.5 million ton grain reserve then-existing as contributing to the necessity for immediate action. If collectivization could be completed by March, it would not be as disruptive to spring plantings.[16]

Molotov's speech provided perhaps one other insight into Stalin's thinking. The industrial sector of the Soviet Union was then simply too weak to create the market incentives for collectivization. In practical terms, Soviet factories could not supply the tractors, combines, or other machinery which might entice the peasant into joining the collective while the state was in no position to invest in the agricultural sector. What Molotov was proposing was to force the peasantry to finance collectivization. He conceded that peasants had little cash and that any in-kind contributions by the poorer peasants would be small. He argued that, in the aggregate, the peasantry could generate the capital investment needed.[17]

A single speech by Molotov may not be conclusive proof that financing was the main motive for collectivization. There is other evidence which supports such an argument however. As far back as July 1929 Stalin had set up a system of forced grain requisitions. Forced requisitioning was nothing new. The difference was that it was no longer just an emergency measure but was to be operating continuously. The formal decree putting the plan into effect was issued on July 29. It had been preceded by similar decrees issued by the Russian Federation on June 28 and by the Ukraine on July 3. In a return almost to Czarist practices, the Party imposed grain delivery quotas on villages but also added quotas for individual peasants.

In November all Stalin wanted from the plenum of the Central Committee was formal approval of his proposal. While there was some cautious questioning about potential difficulties, the Central Committee voted for the plan. Following the session, Stalin quickly moved to implement his new strategy. On December 5, 1929 the Politburo set up a commission whose major task was to draft a decree implementing the decision.

The 21 members of the commission were divided among eight sub-commissions which dealt with different questions, such as how to deal with the kulaks. A draft decree was approved by the full commission on December 18. On December 22 the decree was submitted to the Politburo. Stalin did not like the draft. He objected particularly to the provisions allowing kulaks to join the collective, even if they were willing to submit to its authority. As he would make clear in his December 27 speech, the state was to go to war against the kulak. He also pushed for more extreme punishment, i.e., the death penalty, to be applied to kulaks who most actively fought collectivization.

What did Stalin find objectionable about the initial draft? In general he found it too lenient on the kulaks. In addition, while somewhat vague, it provided peasants with too many procedural protections against governmental seizures. The commission draft had divided the kulaks into three classes. The first consisted of kulaks who actively engaged in subversive activities. Essentially this meant peasants who organized revolts or committed terrorist acts. The second included kulaks who opposed collectivization, but whose activities fell short of strong opposition. The third involved kulaks who would submit to collectivization and to the government. Punishment varied for each group.

For the first group the commission proposed imprisonment or banishment, but not the death penalty, except in extreme cases. Around 60,000 households were estimated to belong to this group. The second group, estimated to be around 150,000 households, were to be banished from their own districts. The primary difference in severity between the first and second groups was that banishment for the first classification was to distant lands, whereas banishment for the second group meant banishment from the local district (oblast or krai). The punishment for the third group, estimated to be around 800,000 households, was not to be banishment or imprisonment. Members of this group were allowed to work in the collective, but would not be allowed to vote as members. Such kulaks could be admitted to the collective after a probationary period of three to five years.[18]

As made clear in his December 27 speech, Stalin had no intention of allowing even the third group of kulaks into the collective, whether they served a probationary period or not. He objected to the draft on three other grounds. First, he did not like the provisions which prevented officials from seizing small livestock, poultry, or implements. He wanted all peasant property or "instruments of production," subject to "socialization," or seizure by officials acting on behalf of the collective. Second, he did not like the timetable for collectivization. The commission proposed five-year period, but he wanted it to take place at a much faster pace. Third, he objected to a provision allowing the peasant to withdraw from the collective. Once members of the collective, he did not want them to be able to voluntarily leave.

To ensure that the committee's final decree was acceptable, Stalin personally edited the draft on January 4, 1930. The decree was adopted by the Central Committee the next day. The collectivization timetable was shortened - collectivization in the major grain-growing regions was to be completed by the fall of 1930. Other areas were given until the fall of 1931, still others the spring of 1932. The proposal allowing peasants to keep their small animals and implements had been eliminated as were most procedural protections related to confiscations. The provision allowing voluntary withdrawal from the collective had also been eliminated.

Stalin also made sure that his new kulak policy - total exclusion from the collective - was incorporated into the wording of the decree. While he left the three classifications of kulaks alone, he did increase the severity of the penalties attached to each. The estimated 60,000 households in the first classification could now be executed, in addition to being imprisoned. The 150,000 households of the second classification, which included the families of the first classification were to be sent to the distant regions (the North, Siberia, the Urals or Kazakhstan), not merely remote areas of their own districts. The 800,000 members of the third group would be allowed to remain in the district, allocated small plots of land and given separate quotas. While such peasants escaped the harshest penalties, they were subject to further deprivations by receiving poor, small plots of land in their allotments and, in addition, were often forced to work in labor detachments building roads or cutting timber.

The Central Committee called its January 5 decree "On the tempo of collectivization and measures to help the organization of collective farms." The decree gave the official signal to local officials to continue with (or to begin) radical measures to speed up the pace of collectivization. Many wanted to impress Moscow and Stalin and were so eager to achieve that goal quickly that they intended to complete collectivization by the spring of 1930, some six months ahead of the official timetable.

With the backing of Moscow and the official stamp-of-approval provided by the January 5 document, officials were more inclined to resort to physical terror to carry out the program. The OGPU was more actively involved now. What motivated local officials varied. Some, no doubt, wanted to impress Moscow, in hopes of furthering their careers. Others were motivated by fear. If they did not carry out the program with sufficient energy, there was the possibility that they would be accused of being 'right deviationists.'[19] They were only too aware that they could be the target of a Party arrest order, like the peasant.

THE TERROR CAMPAIGN

January 5, 1930 is important because the Party officially approved Stalin's new policy. At the least, the decree represented an official pronouncement of what official policy was. At the same time it contained no real bombshells which caught local officials totally unawares. They had begun implementing the policy before January 5. It may be wondered why Stalin put so much effort into the wording of the decree or why an official decree was important to him at all. With the administrative apparatus in place, Stalin already could get local officials to carry out his orders simply by issuing directives. He also could rely on the secret police and lesser officials to ensure that local administrators had a clear understanding of what he wanted. In addition, while Stalin wanted Central

Committee support, he was only too aware that many of them did not really believe in all aspects of his policy. Having packed the Committee with his supporters, he was also aware that it did not represent the feelings of most Party members.

There is a temptation to dismiss Stalin's actions as simply one more example of the sinister nature of his activities. The explanation probably lies, not so much in the realm of the sinister, but rather in his understanding of the workings of the Soviet administrative apparatus and bureaucracy. Instructions issued from Moscow tended to be interpreted, even changed, as they moved down the chain-of-command. Part of the problem was the fact that officials in Moscow failed to anticipate all problems which local officials might encounter in carrying out orders. What was meant by peasant opposition? Was a peasant resisting if he merely asked that his cow not be confiscated? In addition, official decrees did not always make sense - surely Moscow didn't intend to include something as inconsequential as a chicken in its collectivization order. Stalin would have encountered such normal bureaucratic problems even where Party instructions were clear. Unfortunately he often intentionally kept decrees vague.

For Stalin's goals, an official decree would serve two purposes. First, it would send an unambiguous signal to local officials that they were to proceed with collectivization. Second, it implied some standard against which to judge local performance. A clear signal was helpful for administration. Unlike the proddings of individual Moscow Party officials, which locals may have suspected were "interpretations" of what Moscow wanted, decrees had the official backing of the Central Committee and the Party. Where local officials might argue that they were slow at compliance because they were not sure what Moscow wanted - perhaps it was just some overzealous official - Stalin could always point to the decree as setting out policy. One could almost hear Stalin's answer to protestations from local officials - 'But comrades, was the decree not clear about what was to be done?' In fact, the decree was not clear. Stalin took pains to ensure that it was vague.

There was a third purpose which the decree accomplished. It provided Stalin with the cover of deniability. While seeming to give explicit instructions to proceed with collectivization, it was rather vague about specifics. If the Central Committee estimated that 60,000 households were subject to the death penalty, it did not order officials to come up with 60,000 peasants to execute. Instead, it created an atmosphere or situation designed to provoke peasant resistance, in turn giving officials an excuse to use extreme measures.

Above all, what the decree provided Stalin with was a political justification for his policy. While he engaged in many arbitrary actions, he took pains to link most with some greater political purpose. It was one thing to be feared, it was another to be viewed as a madman. With all the executions and imprisonments which occurred there was a danger that too many extreme actions would be viewed as irrational. In spite of his position as leader, Stalin depended on, even courted the favor of, lower Party officials. He was not worried that Party officials would fear him. In fact that was useful. As long as he was viewed as a rational, albeit strong, or even cruel, leader, he could maintain power. With the Central Committee publicly behind him, however reluctant their support, Stalin had a seemingly rational political justification for his actions.

Although Stalin had gone to great lengths to craft the decree, he did not wait until January 5 to begin implementation. The OGPU had begun mass arrests of designated "kulaks" in November 1929. Those arrested were shot. Most were former White Army soldiers. A second wave of arrests occurred in December, although those arrested were imprisoned, rather than executed. Their families, who had been left alone at the time, would be rounded up for deportation in January 1930.

The arrests, executions, and deportations of kulaks represented only one part of the collectivization campaign. It was intended both to remove the most active opposition and to scare the remaining peasants into joining the collectives. The January 5 decree made clear to local officials that, whatever it took, they were to increase the numbers of collective farm members. While peasants who were not considered kulaks might avoid execution or imprisonment, they would nevertheless come under pressure to enter the collective.

If Stalin could point to the growing number of peasant households joining the collectives as evidence of success, there was growing peasant resistance. Active resistance however came late and was to prove too disorganized. Stalin had gained two advantages. First, the peasants were not in a mood to rebel. The chaos of the Civil War, which had created an atmosphere of revolt and had prompted local peasants to actively join the fighting, had been over for some eight years. The peasants had been allowed to focus on farming and were less likely to get caught up in a mood of rebellion. Second, the eight years of peace had given Stalin the opportunity to consolidate power. The Party had been able to develop an effective military and police force in the countryside.

Despite these circumstances, peasant opposition to the government assumed violent forms. In 1929 there were 384 murders and more than 1,400 arsons related to the collectivization policy.[20] The violence was aimed, not only at government officials, but also at peasant activists who supported the government or those willing to inform on other peasants. Violence continued into 1930. Conquest reports that, in the Ukraine alone, there were more than 150 murders or acts of arson committed between January and June.[21] Peasant resistance was not confined to individual acts of violence but took on more organized forms in 1930. It was often necessary to call in the military to deal with disturbances on a wider scale. Whole villages rioted. In the period from December 17, 1929 to February 14, 1930, the Central Black Earth province reported 38 armed outbreaks.[22] Though sometimes violent, active peasant resistance was simply too weak and disorganized to stop or even to seriously threaten collectivization. Peasant action, in the form of livestock destruction, proved a more effective protest. Unfortunately, its very effectiveness also undermined the peasant's economic power. Stalin had hoped to use agricultural resources to finance industrialization. While peasant action effectively crippled agriculture, it also eliminated much of the economic leverage the peasant's productivity provided.

On January 16, 1930 Stalin issued a decree which allowed local authorities to confiscate the property of kulaks who destroyed livestock. In spite of the decree, or perhaps partly in response to it, peasants began slaughtering livestock. The government's own bureaucratic structure and incentive system contributed to the slaughter in its early stages. Government procurement agents worked on a quota system and were only too eager to buy. Peasants who had been reluctant to part with grain, now willingly sold their livestock to government slaughterhouses. Other animals were sold on the open market. Cattle which could not be sold were killed by the peasants themselves. The greatest losses for the entire period of collectivization (1928-33) were to take place in February and March of 1930. (The total number for the entire period would be 26.6 million.)[23] Some 14 million head of cattle would be killed in these two months. The slaughter in those months also took one-third of the pig population and one-fourth of sheep and goats.[24]

Stalin was no doubt aware that peasant opposition was coming from more than just the kulaks. However, it was politically expedient to continue focusing attention on kulak opposition. The January 5 decree had ostensibly concentrated on collectivization, although it did contain measures specifically aimed at the kulak. On February 4 the Party passed a decree which dealt almost exclusively with the kulaks. It had begun with a resolution passed on January 30 called 'On Measures for the Elimination of Kulak Households in Districts of Comprehensive Collectivization.'

The political aspect of the collectivization campaign had taken on a harsher tone and provided the Party with a needed, unifying enemy - the kulak. Some Party officials were becoming uneasy. While they publicly may have agreed with the political justification for what was taking place, they began to look at the underlying effect on agricultural productivity. They were only too aware that the wheat and rye harvesting depended on the spring agricultural timetable, not some political schedule. In February 1930 Party leaders paid visits to key rural areas to assess the agricultural situation. They found that, not only were the actual figures for the number of collectives far below official figures, but also that Party efforts to collectivize the peasant had totally disrupted the agricultural sector. They warned of a possible famine. It was decided that the mass collectivization policy needed to be reversed.

On February 20 the Central Committee called for an end to collectivization in the minority-nation republics. *Pravda* editorials called for an end to the confiscation of small animals, such as pigs and chickens. A special Central Committee meeting was called to deal with the situation. While no decree was adopted, the Committee had the backbone to stand up to Stalin. He was told he needed to issue some statement repudiating the then-existing policy. Stalin agreed. The statement he prepared, the March 2 *Pravda* article called "Dizzy with Success," emerged in a somewhat different form than the Committee intended, however.

Stalin, except for the article itself, ignored the Committee. The article was supposed to be cleared with other Politburo members before being published. Stalin submitted it to *Pravda* without bothering to let Committee members read it. In addition, the tone of the article, was not an admission of error on his part. He not only criticized officials for taking the very actions he had urged them to take, he also placed the entire blame for "mistakes" on those same officials. They had been overzealous. While Stalin had publicly given in to the Central Committee, the publication of the article created administrative problems for the Party. For example, were peasants to be given back their confiscated cattle, or their old plot of land? On the surface, the article made the Party look as though it were reversing its collectivization policy. How was such a reversal to be implemented? To many peasants at least, the article and a subsequent Party decree on March 14, signalled the end of collectivization. Some eight million peasants chose to withdraw from the collectives.[25]

What Stalin accomplished with "Dizzy with Success" was to temporarily restore a sense of normality for the peasant. Many would return to their fields in time for spring sowing, confident that they had permanently beaten the government. The governmental retreat was not complete however. In the grain growing regions the collectivization gains by the government remained. If Stalin may have mollified peasant resentment, he was also successful at angering local Party officials. Eager to impress Moscow by pushing collectivization, they now felt betrayed when Stalin not only acknowledged mistakes, but blamed them for having committed them.

In reality what Stalin did in March of 1930 was to settle for a more gradual approach to collectivization. He did not abandon force or terror as part of the campaign, but he did back away from the goal of immediate collectivization. Officially, the number of households collectivized by March 1, 1930, the day before "Dizzy with Success" appeared, was quite high - 14,264,300.[26] As the Party officials visiting the countryside had discovered, the numbers were inaccurate. There were two major problems with the statistics. First, they were inflated. (In spite of Stalin's optimistic reports, it is hard to believe that local officials could increase the number of households collectivized by some 10 million in just one month. In January 1930 4,393,100 households had been collectivized. By March 1 the number had increased to 14,264,300.)[27] Officials had simply invented numbers to be sent to Moscow, where actual collectivization had failed. Second, where peasants had been forced to join against their wishes, they had not only destroyed their cattle, they had left their productivity behind.

Having formally urged the Party to execute or deport kulaks, Stalin was hardly in a position to criticize local officials for "excesses." He may have been more embarrassed than disturbed by what was actually taking place. He had hoped for swift results, but continuing peasant resistance brought public reports and Party discussions of abuses. At least part of the problem may have been that, while Stalin had a clear vision of the final results - collectivization would modernize agriculture and finance industrialization - he had not really thought through the administrative steps it would take to reach that goal. He had not seriously analyzed the problems nor come up with a clear step-by-step plan for officials to follow. His job was to formulate a general plan - the details could be worked out later. His perception may have been that the advantages of collectivization were so obvious, even to the peasants, that they would be eager to join. If Stalin was willing to use a reward system to motivate people, he seemed to view physical force and intimidation as necessary partners in any motivational scheme.

It was not local Party officials, but the secret police, who began the push for collectivization in November 1929. If the mass arrests and executions of supposed kulaks were not viewed as having a direct link to collectivization, they did set a tone, reinforced by the new arrests in December. Initially these actions were handled by the OGPU itself. However, it did not have the manpower to deal with the increasing scale of the operation intended by Stalin. With his insistence on meeting collectivization goals local officials were soon given a greater role.

While local officials were aware that execution was available to enforce their decisions, they often hoped that less extreme measures would be effective. There was a belief that persuasive tactics would motivate peasants to join. The Party organized groups of workers to administer rural areas. In January 1930, a somewhat structured group called the "25,000-ers," (actually numbering about 27,000), was formed. Consisting of volunteer workers from the cities, the 25,000-ers were given a two-week training course and sent into the countryside to serve as managers of the collectives. Another 72,204 temporary workers were also sent, along with 50,000 soon-to-be ex-soldiers.[28] In many villages, meetings were held by these volunteers in which peasants were urged to join the collective.

If promises of tractors or easy credit worked to persuade the poorer peasants to join the collective, officials found that promises alone would not convince the more well-to-do village members. Some officials began making threats, either of arrest or dekulakization, which were sometimes sufficient to get peasants to sign up for kolkholz membership. Where they were not, officials began to carry out their threats. Fitzpatrick cites one instance, in the Urals, where the local chairman gave the peasants the option of joining the kolkholz or of being arrested by the police chief. Twelve peasants who did not join were immediately placed under arrest.[29] In other cases officials had peasants interrogated, beaten, or subjected to mock executions. If joining the kolkholz allowed peasants to escape such acts of official harassment, it did not prevent further abuse by local officials. Peasant livestock, grain or even money was immediately seized for the kolkholz, once peasants signed the papers agreeing to join.[30]

In some cases officials sought to avoid direct physical confrontations with hostile peasants. Instead they used the voting mechanism of the village mir (commune). Members of the mir accepted collectivization by simply voting to change the mir into a kolkholz.[31] If it was devious, it at least allowed local officials to report success to Moscow. Unfortunately, it encouraged Stalin in the belief that collectivization would come easily. It also did little to create a sense of trust among the peasantry. In some cases, not all the members eligible to vote were present when the vote was taken.[32]

The threat of dekulakization became perhaps the most commonly used ploy. While the Party pressured local officials to increase the number of households collectivized, it also pressured them to increase the number of peasants who were dekulakized and deported. The Party had decided in its December 1929 meetings that 60,000 kulaks should be imprisoned. Although the number was only an estimate, the orders which came from Moscow quickly turned it into a quota. Each district had so many kulaks to arrest. Included with the arrest orders were orders relating to quotas for the 150,000 households to be deported.[33] The OGPU contributed to an atmosphere of official coercion by providing kulak names from its own lists, then asking local leaders to make up the shortfall. Persuaded that terroristic threats were most effective if carried out, officials were more willing to dekulakize those who were otherwise unwilling to join the collectives.

Officials who were pressured to provide numbers for collectivization were now required to compile statistical proof of the success of their dekulakization campaign. They proved just as creative at this new mathematical game. In one sense, it was made easier by the state's concept of what a kulak was. A kulak was defined as much by the supposed attitude of the well-to-do peasant, as it was by his material possessions. In another sense the game was made more difficult by the very vagueness of what the kulak was supposed to be. The only advantage was that Stalin was indifferent to the truth or falsity of the charges. If people were added arbitrarily to the list of names of kulaks, the state was not inclined to question the figures. Teachers were sometimes the targets. In some cases those who became victims were chosen mainly because they were regarded as outsiders. Sometimes villages were allowed to vote. Ironically, villagers exacted revenge on the communists by naming former Red Army soldiers as kulaks.[34]

The combined collectivization drive and war against the kulak appeared to produce results. Officially 50 percent of peasant households had been collectivized by February 20, 1930.[35] Fighting a war on two fronts did give Stalin pause. If he reduced the pressure on the collectivization front when he published "Dizzy with Success," he was unrelenting in his war against the kulak. That he intended to continue. Even given Stalin's retreat, collectivization had made significant gains. Despite the disruptions, the kolkholz accounted for 26 percent of peasant households in the 1930 spring sowing.[36]

MARCH 1930 - COLLECTIVIZATION RESUMED

Despite the seeming retreat of "Dizzy with Success," Stalin had no intention of giving up the fight. He did have some officials dismissed and had others tried for mistakes, providing proof that he meant what he said. While the article and subsequent actions convinced peasants that the collectivization drive was over, Stalin sent different signals to local officials. The withdrawal of eight million to nine million households from the collectives (some 40-50 million people) wreaked havoc with the official statistics. On March 1, 1930 55 percent of peasant households were reported as being collectivized. By June 1, the percentage figure had dropped to 23.6 percent.[37] While Stalin's retreat may have been forced on him by officials, its timing before the spring sowing probably saved the harvest. In spite of the deportations and forced collectivizations the 1930 harvest was some 12 million tons better than that of 1929.[38]

The March 2, 1930 edition of *Pravda* contained significant concessions on the part of the Party - at least on the surface. "Dizzy with Success" emphasized the voluntary nature of membership in the collective. *Pravda*, in that day's edition, also published a lengthy version of the charter for the artel, one form of the collective farm. According to the charter, the peasants would be allowed to keep small farm implements, a milk cow, and smaller animals such as sheep, pigs, and poultry. To some peasants, leaving was the natural consequence of Stalin's article - he had now publicly said that membership was voluntary. They found however that leaving was no simple matter. If secret police or army units symbolized the most sinister and abusive elements of authority, they were only the most obvious tools available to the government. The Party had managed to establish a local bureaucratic structure which, if still seemingly fragile, was nevertheless tenacious. Peasants who managed to escape death or imprisonment, had to face continuous harassment from ambitious local leaders. The literal interpretation given Moscow's orders by local officials often made them seem, not just out of touch with reality, but even silly. The emphasis on communal property brought out a certain pettiness. In one district in the Urals, officials went so far as to include peasant clothing in their orders relating to the commune. They put all the peasant clothes in a pile and peasants had to chose what to wear from the pile before going to work for the day.[39]

Although such examples serve to illustrate the Bolshevik obsession with private property, they need to be kept in perspective. Peasant property rights had never been absolute, even before the communists came to power. The peasant commune (mir) had, to a large degree, controlled how individual peasants worked their land within the village. If the village mir had acted more democratically, out of concern for the well-being of the village, it was the mir, not the individual peasant, which effectively controlled use of the land.

In forcing Stalin to back down, even partially, the peasants temporarily could claim victory. The more obvious aspect of Stalin's program involved force and physical intimidation. It was this "public" side of the policy which Stalin chose to address in "Dizzy with Success." Behind the scenes he was working to change the administrative structure of the agricultural sector. What Stalin was attempting to do was to replace local control and administration with a centralized one. His fight was as much with the village council as it was with the individual peasant. Ironically, even as Stalin tried to establish centralized control, he had to rely on local Party leaders to carry out his orders. His public retreat did not stop the administrative revolution Stalin was pushing. Evidence of this change was the decree of July 10, 1930, passed by the Central Committee, which abolished the commune in areas which had been collectivized. In fact the Party had been at work on this aspect of the change in 1929. From an administrative perspective the Party had a major problem at the village level. It had to contend with two competing governmental bodies, the rural soviet and the village mir. Officially, the rural soviet had jurisdiction of the village mir. In fact the rural soviet normally had responsibility for six to eight village mirs.[40]

Although the rural soviet was the officially recognized governmental unit, it lacked credible authority with the peasants. The mir was regarded as the legitimate governing body. Part of the reason was that the Party had put very few resources into the rural soviets. When they had been formed in the early 1920s, their chairmen had no budget and were themselves paid very little. Another problem was that the Party continued to recognize many of the rights and powers the mir had traditionally exercised.[41] Perhaps a more basic problem was that the soviets were too closely tied to the village. On paper, the chairmen were part of the rural soviet. In reality, they voted as though they were still members of the village.

The administrative answers to such problems were not long in coming. The basic solution involved nothing more than focusing greater attention on the problem of rural administration. Two obvious solutions were to appoint officials more sympathetic to the Party and to eliminate the power of the mir. Beginning in 1929 the chairmen of the rural soviets were removed and replaced by more aggressive administrators. Conquest cites figures for the Central Volga indicating that, out of 370 village soviet chairmen, 300 had been replaced by March 1930.[42] The Party also moved away from a village elective system to a governmental system in which officials were appointed. The power of the mir was destroyed by frontal assault. Initially the Party had hoped that the mir would aid in collectivization. When the Party found that it got in the way, it simply did away with the July 1930 decree.

Stalin soon taught the peasants another lesson in power. The peasants believed that Stalin had confirmed their traditional property rights. At best, he was only willing to confer only vague and abstract rights and it was not enough to be given an abstract right. To be of any use a right had to be enforceable. Where rights related to some abstract concept, as they did where land "ownership" was concerned, power depended on the government's recognition of property claims. Similarly, where rights involved actions taken by officials, power stemmed from official recognition or approval of the actions taken. In such a case, recognition might come in the form of a legal claim of action. In other words, Stalin could have recognized peasant grievances against local Party officials by giving them a legal claim against officials or by granting a legal claim to the land they had given up.

Stalin had discovered that the ability to either recognize decisions or to deny them legitimacy, i.e., to approve or to disapprove of actions, was a great source of power. The village mirs had maintained their power because the central government continued to recognize their legal rights, such as the power to enforce contracts and initiate court actions. The decree abolishing the commune was a step toward consolidating power. The weakening of traditional power structures at the local level was only part of Stalin's plans. He also needed to strengthen the power of local officials. He did this by, not only granting them greater authority and more resources, but also by attacks aimed directly at the individual peasant.

One of the more powerful tools the government possessed was ironically, the power to decide property rights. Peasants who read "Dizzy with Success" believed that Stalin was returning things to the status quo. They believed that the article meant that they could simply resume farming on their original plot. Yet when they tried to leave, they found that local Party officials controlled land distribution. Officials claimed much of the land which had been worked by the peasants as the property of the collective. Where they allowed peasants to withdraw, they allotted them plots which were either further away from the village or of poor quality or both. Sometimes the plots were smaller than before or consisted of marsh or wasteland. Officials, in some cases, refused to grant some of the traditional privileges associated with farming, such as access to water or to pastureland.

The refusal to recognize peasant rights in their former landholdings was only one problem. Officials also ignored peasant claims to the cattle or animals confiscated by the collective. In some cases they claimed that the collective now owned the animals and refused to return them. In other cases, the animals had died or been slaughtered. Peasant implements were not returned. Officials offered no compensation in either case. Even in cases where peasants were permitted to withdraw, local officials were slow at deciding which land to allocate them or at distributing the seed necessary for spring sowing. The fact that eight to nine million households chose to leave, in spite of the obstacles officials placed in their path, represented a major defeat for the Party.

Official foot-dragging was only one governmental weapon, taxation was another. Taxes were both a source of revenue and a coercive measure. The Party provided tax incentives for the collective. In April 1930, fines levied for failure to pay taxes on livestock were cancelled for the peasant members of collectives. Collective members were also given a tax exemption for livestock for two years. More general taxes were imposed in the form of grain quotas, which were increased in the case of individual peasants. For a time, individual peasants seemed able to defy the government, managing to outproduce the collective farms in 1930. Yet the "free" peasant was losing the battle.

In the end it was probably not a single governmental action which defeated the peasant, but a combination of policies. Efforts to monopolize the most productive land did not prevent peasants from withdrawing from the collective. Its long-term effect however would eventually limit the individual's productivity. Ultimately, whatever the impact of individual effort, agricultural productivity depended on the productivity of the land. Even given the inefficiencies of collective farming, control of the most productive land would be an immense advantage.

While the Party was temporarily willing to rely on less confrontational economic pressure during 1930, it was planning a renewal of the campaign of force. The kulaks would be the targets again. In January 1931, the Party used failure to meet quotas as the excuse to begin deportations of kulaks who had been allowed to remain in their home districts. This was preliminary to a formal decision to act against the kulak taken in February 1931. In contrast to the dekulakization campaign of 1930, the 1931 campaign was more organized and more centrally run. Where local officials had been in charge, the OGPU assumed responsibility in 1931. Where the 1930 campaign involved a loosely administered quota system for dekulakization, the 1931 campaign involved a tightly controlled system targeting specific individuals. The OGPU used tax questionnaires to gain or confirm information about peasant households. From this information lists were compiled.[43] Before the start of the second dekulakization campaign, i.e., at the end of

1930, there had already been some 400,000 peasant households dekulakized.[44] The 1931 campaign, the so-called 'second-wave,' which officially ended in October 1931, would add another 381,000 households to that number - in individual numbers about 2.5 million people.[45] The end of the 'second wave' did not completely end the deportations. Conquest estimates that another 150,000 households would be deported between October 1931 and May 1933. It would only be in May 1933 that Stalin would formally decree the end of forced deportation.[46]

Although the war against the kulak served as the political rallying cry of Stalin's campaign, he had not let up in his campaign to collectivize. Peasant withdrawal from the collectives had quickly deflated the statistics for March 1, 1930 - 14,264,300 households collectivized.[47] A little over one year later however, on April 1, 1931, the figures showed that the collectivization campaign had been revived. Some 13 million households now were collectivized.[48] In July 1931 52.7 percent of all peasant households had been collectivized, more than double the 23.6 percent figure for July 1930. In terms of crop area collectivized, the July percentage was even higher - 67.8 percent of agricultural land was now farmed collectively.[49] The next twelve months would add another 1.9 million households, so that by July 1932 14.9 million households would be collectivized, or, in percentage terms, 61.5 percent.[50] This represented an increase of nearly nine percent. The next twelve-month period however revealed a slowing of the rate. Only 64.4 percent of peasant households were collectivized as of July 1933, or an increase of only 2.9 percent over the previous year.[51] Part of the reason for the slowdown may have been that problems within the collectives themselves forced Stalin to divert resources to deal with them. He was confronted by an internal revolt and it was necessary to consolidate the gains already made.

In 1933 Stalin chose to reply to a letter sent him by the Soviet writer Mikhail Sholokhov. Sholokhov had complained that some local officials were committing excesses against the peasants and that such practices appeared to be widespread. Stalin, in his reply, acknowledged that the excesses were taking place. While condemning such excesses, Stalin complained that peasants were sabotaging agricultural production. Even without committing acts of violence, the peasants were engaged in a 'quiet' war against the government.[52] What Stalin's letter referred to was general interference with government grain procurement. On other occasions he made reference to specific acts committed by peasants - the burning of storage depots or the breaking of machines or theft. This time, it was not outsiders, but individuals within the system who were to blame. Kulaks and kulak supporters were now causing problems as members of the collectives.[53]

There was some truth to what Stalin charged. Kulaks who had been allowed into the collectives, despite Stalin's efforts, were involved in acts of 'sabotage.' Yet the nature of Stalin's campaign had involved almost total war against the peasant and resistance was not limited to former kulaks. Even peasants who joined the collectives were treated as enemies, regardless of whether they fell under the classification of kulak or not. The extreme and strident tone of Stalin's campaign made new enemies among the peasant class, even among those who had been largely neutral. In some cases it was local officials who took extreme measures against the peasants. In other cases, Party leadership pushed such measures. In 1932, district officials in the Ukraine allowed collective farms to keep some of their grain for seed and as a reserve. An enraged Stalin accused the officials of deceit and called them crooks. In a circular, he called for the imprisonment of any officials who followed such a policy.[54]

The political tone of the campaign against the peasant was only partly to blame for the problems within the collective. There were two other, somewhat related, factors which contributed to internal problems. First, the government was squeezing the collectives, as well as individual peasants, for more grain. Second, its administrative methods, as in 1930, still measured performance in terms of short-term numbers.

The government, in 1931 and 1932, placed extraordinary demands on the agricultural sector in the area of grain procurements. In spite of all the disruption which was occurring, production in 1931 and 1932 was high, some 70 million tons in each year.[55] The governmental share, 22.8 million tons in 1931 and 18.5 million tons in 1932, was even sufficient to provide grain for export.[56] Unfortunately, the monetary value was lessened because the sales occurred during the Great Depression, when prices were substantially depressed. Stalin's focus on increased state grain procurements was part of the problem. It pressured local officials to increase current contributions at the expense of future harvests. Those officials who did try to plan for future harvests or disasters found Stalin unsympathetic. He wanted a maximum immediate return.

The heavy quotas demanded by the government began to take a physical toll on the peasants. They were hungry and the collectives had grain in storage, destined for procurement agencies. Where barns or storage facilities were left unguarded in the spring of 1932, collectivized peasants broke in to take grain or cows and horses. Some peasants found unexpected allies in the form of collective managers, who used the local grain to feed those working in the fields, or at least looked the other way when their own peasants took the grain. Peasants in the summer began raiding fields to harvest grain as it was ripening.

Often peasant women, seeing their children near starvation, were the culprits. Given the label 'hairdressers' or 'barbers' by the press, they would go out into the fields at night to clip stalks of grain with their scissors. Others would wait until the grain had been gathered. They would then stuff what grain they could into pockets or hide it inside their clothing. Stalin was unmoved. He did not want to lose any of the harvest, which in 1932, had reached 69.9 million tons.[57] As in 1930, he pressured local officials to crack down. The secret police were once more enlisted in the campaign. Peasants were the main targets, but sometimes it was local officials, those who were felt to be lax in carrying out a campaign against the peasant 'wreckers.' That officials were considered to be as much the problem as the peasant, is shown by the fact that between 25 and 30 percent of middle management on the collectives were arrested in five months during 1932.[58]

On August 7, 1932 a law was enacted which provided for the death penalty for the theft of state or collective-farm property. The law did not set any minimum value on the stolen property to which it would apply. Theft of as little as a stalk of grain could be considered a capital offense, giving the law the unofficial name of the "five stalks law." Stalin showed little mercy to those unlucky enough to get caught. There were 54,545 convicted within five months of the law's enactment and of this number, 2,110 were shot.[59] That resistance within the collective was a serious problem is indicated by the fact that kolkhoz members made up three-fifths of those convicted between January and March of 1933.[60]

Stalin, in January 1933, added a more effective policing organization to carry out his orders. Administratively, he had created what were called "political sections" or special police units assigned to the collectives and to the accompanying machine-tractor stations (MTS). By 1932 there were around five thousand of these special police units. Members were not locals but recruited by the Central Committee. They had the authority to dismiss even Party members from management positions in the collectives. Stalin did not rely entirely on the political sections. As in 1930 he mobilized Party members from the cities to work in the countryside.

Surprisingly, the harsh measures taken by Stalin in 1932 remained in effect for only a relatively brief period of time. In the spring of 1933 Stalin reversed policy and the mass deportations were stopped. The repressive measures, though brief, were severe. In some areas, the peasants gained little when Stalin eased the pressure. The hardships inflicted by the state were simply replaced by another merciless foe - famine.

The worst of the famine would come in 1933, but it was beginning to be felt in some areas in the summer of 1932. What made the famine worse was the fact that Stalin refused to help those who were starving. In fact, he seemed to view the famine as another means of dealing with the peasant. The state did not have to actively deport or shoot peasants, it could just let them starve. Whether Stalin deliberately planned the famine or simply saw it as another opportunity once it began, it does seem clear that it became a weapon. Many of the peasants came to that conclusion.[61] At the same time, dismissing the famine as government-caused leaves some questions unanswered. Was famine a specific goal of Stalin, intended to deal the fatal blow to the peasantry, or was it an unintended result of trying to reach another goal? Was it the result of the inefficiencies of the Soviet system or of an indecisive agricultural policy? Or was it case of Stalin's failure to fully analyze the situation before setting policy and, once committed, a refusal to admit a mistake and change policies?

There was clearly more than one factor at work. In addition, the significance of each factor changed over time, i.e., what caused the famine was different than what caused it to continue or factors which contributed to its severity. Fitzpatrick provides one of the more plausible summaries of the basic cause of the famine. Her argument relates to the administrative structure of the grain procurement system. A basic problem with the system was not that it was centrally planned, but that it lacked real planning. To be sure officials planned to the extent of preparing budgets. However they had little hard data and tended to be overly optimistic in the face of political pressures. The system was based too much on haggling and administrative bargaining between each level of administration. It was not simply that there was posturing about how much could be produced. The problem was more that there was a cynical view that the opposing side was assumed to be posturing. The administrative system, from Stalin on down, had built in the assumption that the other side was simply trying to get the upper hand in a bargaining arrangement.[62]

Each administrative level tried to bargain with the level above or below it. At the lowest level, the peasants complained that weather or other conditions would prevent them from fulfilling their quota. Their managers would pressure them to increase their production. At the same time the managers would adopt the peasant line in dealing with their superiors. Each administrative level pressured those below it to meet quotas while arguing with those higher up that the quotas could not be met. In theory, it was a manageable system. Whether it could have operated without Stalin's reliance on imprisonment or the death penalty to reinforce its operation is an open question. With such threats in the background however, the administrative structure responded in a cautious manner. Everyone had to assume or at least report the most optimistic figures to those above. Few dared to openly question the demands or the logic behind them. Stalin was quick to make object lessons of management failures, whatever their cause. In September 1930 he had 48 members of People's Commissariat of Trade arrested on charges of sabotaging food supplies. After confessing to their crimes all 48 were executed.[63]

Fitzpatrick points out a problem unique to 1932 and 1933. The collective system was too new to provide accurate data on what yields should be. Officials in Moscow did not know how much grain would be available. The peasants in the field did not know how much the state would demand.[64] The lack of data and the view that peasants and managers were probably lying about harvest problems to better their bargaining position was bad enough. An additional problem was that performance was measured by immediate results. The only quantifiable means of measuring performance was the amount of grain collected in the current season. The pressure to meet immediate quota demands, often meant that grain reserves for seed or for emergencies were sacrificed to satisfy demands made by higher officials. The government issued contradictory orders at times. Officials were ordered not to take seed grain. At the same time they were told to fill their quotas.[65]

In general Stalin's administrative structure relied heavily on intimidation and fear, rather than positive reinforcement or rewards for stronger performance. That same management philosophy often favored the collective, while coming down as hard as possible on the peasant. Yet, in some cases, Stalin viewed the collectives with the same disdain as he did the peasants. If the collective was favored over the individual peasant, the administrative structure disadvantaged the collective in dealings with the state. Individual collectives were often punished for poor performance. Such collectives risked being placed on a "black board" of dishonor. In such cases their seed grain could be confiscated and given to other collectives. In extreme cases a whole collective might be deported.[66]

In smaller ways, collectives were also treated little better than peasants. When collectives were paid by the government the prices were very low. Collectives were required to pay for services performed by other state organs. They had to make payments in kind to the Machine Tractor Stations (MTS), in return for the mechanized work done by the MTS and had to make payments in kind for having their grain ground. They were taxed for acreage sown and were fined for late deliveries of grain or for failing to meet their quotas.[67]

The famine which began in late 1932 had its causes in the philosophy and administrative structure of the agricultural system. Stalin intended to obtain as much grain as quickly as possible from the agricultural system. If the overall design and operation of the system should shoulder the blame for agricultural failure, a simple explanation for the famine was that grain quotas were too high, as Fitzpatrick points out.[68] It might be added that Stalin's refusal to lower the quotas made a bad situation worse. In January 1933, rather than easing up, Stalin tried to bring even more pressure to bear on the countryside.

The first deaths from starvation began to be reported in November 1932. Officially there was little sympathy. The focus was on obtaining grain deliveries. Villages were sanctioned for failing to meet quotas. Officials acted to prevent goods from reaching villages in the Ukraine, even setting up blockades until grain had been produced. Stores selling state goods were shut down. Officials refused to distribute grain in storage in local facilities. In some cases officials allowed grain or potatoes to rot rather than distributing them to peasants.[69]

Peasants in some areas tried to escape the famine by leaving their villages, although the government attempted to stop the migration as much as possible. It reintroduced the system of internal passports. Anyone needing to travel had to obtain a passport, but peasants were not allowed to even carry passports. Only industrial or office workers could be issued passports. Those caught without them were returned to their villages. While enforcement was initially somewhat lax, it was tightened in the spring of 1933. Railway workers were ordered not to transport peasants. Peasants encountered still another obstacle even if they managed to reach the cities. Without ration cards they could not buy bread in the stores. The residents and workers, while able to obtain food, were themselves living on short rations. Sometimes city residents tried to help, but the assistance was too little to do any good.

Many of the peasants managed to survive the months of January and February, but the death toll began to rise sharply in March 1933. Soldiers and railway workers were confronted by large numbers of peasants begging for food and starving. Cities were overwhelmed by peasants who, without help, died in large numbers. For a time in the city of Poltava, as many as 150 corpses were being collected each day. Poltava was not alone. The cities of Kiev, Kharkov, Dnipropetrovsk, and Odessa had to deal, on a daily basis with the corpses of peasants who had died during the night.[70]

While the campaign seemed to be aimed at all the peasants, there is some evidence that peasants in the Ukraine were specifically targeted. It was not simply that the state itself would not help, it also actively worked to prevent individuals from helping. Some

279

people tried to smuggle bread in from Russia, where it was still available. If officials found out about it, they acted to stop it. Police would confiscate any bread found on people they stopped and searched. To prevent peasants from even leaving the Ukraine to search for food, military units were stationed at railroad border checkpoints.[71]

Stalin had begun his new terror campaign with the "five stalks law" of August 1932. This was followed in January 1933 by an aggressive terror campaign in the countryside. It was decided to send another group of urban recruits into the countryside, an idea patterned after the '25,000-ers' campaign of late 1929 and early 1930. Rather than employ the recruits as managers of the collectives, they were to be organized into police units and assigned to the Machine Tractor Stations (MST).[72] The MST was intended to provide mechanized services, such as plowing, to the various collectives in its immediate vicinity. The number of party-police units grew to around 5,000.[73] Their primary job was to purge the kolkhoz, as opposed to trying to collectivize. As with other such operations, the measure of success was the number of kolkhoz members purged. The numbers from the Central Black Earth province provide some indication of the success of the campaign. There were 11,000 arrests and 20,000 firings. In addition, 3,677 kolkhoz administrators were purged. While it is not known how many total kolkhoz households were 'dekulakized' in this period of renewed repression, in the Leningrad district some 7,000 households were deported.[74]

Though severe, the repression of 1933 was relatively short-lived. Perhaps that was because Stalin's dream of collectivization was slowly being realized. By July 1933, some 15.2 million peasant households, or 64.4 percent of the total, had been collectivized. The percentage of crop area collectivized was even greater - around 83.1 percent.[75]

Stalin, despite the progress, may have felt that a renewed terror campaign was necessary in order to push his program through to completion. At the same time he was preparing to ease economic restrictions. Even as the party-political cadres were beginning their terror campaign, the Party began implementing administrative changes. A new law was passed on January 19, 1933 substituting a grain tax for grain collections. This was followed, on February 18, by an easing of restrictions on grain trading in certain provinces.[76] Perhaps more surprising, on February 25, a decree authorized the distribution of grain for seed for the spring sowing. The Ukraine was to receive 325,000 tons and the North Caucasus another 230,000. As if to publicly acknowledge the famine, the demand for grain from the Ukraine was officially lifted on March 15, 1933. There were even belated attempts to save those peasants still surviving. Army grain reserves were provided to starving villages in April and clinics were set up in May. Many peasants were too weak to respond and died despite the government efforts.[77]

In May 1933 Stalin ended the terror campaign with a secret instruction. Mass deportations and terrorist measures were to stop. If the instruction brought an end to the intense political campaign, the economic help did not completely end the famine, which would continue into 1934. The death toll from the famine was high, although the exact numbers are unknown. The lowest estimates place the number of dead at around three to four million, while the highest place the figure at between seven and eight million. Whatever the total number, most agree that some 3 million children died.[78]

The administrative restructuring of the agricultural system was marked by the January 19 decree eliminating compulsory grain requisitions. Yet, in one sense, compulsory requisitioning had been changed in name only. The zagotovki, or compulsory requisitioning was changed to a compulsory state tax, with the decree. However, the new tax was fixed by the central government, not subject to change and, despite its predictability, was still high. The fairness which seemed to be embodied in the tax changes was undercut by the creation of a new tax - a payment in kind which was to be made to the MTS - the naturplata. The prior system had involved payment of money based on the amount of acreage sown or harvested. In defense of the government, the old method had allowed the collectives to be paid for acreage harvested, whether the crop was suitable for eating or not. The collective could be paid for harvesting weeds as well as for harvesting wheat or rye.[79] Unfortunately, the new tax represented another burden which the struggling collectives had to shoulder.

The basic problem with the system was that the government still wanted to use the agricultural sector as a source of financing. That goal was at odds with the aspirations of the peasantry. Whatever face the government put on its system, the demand for more grain created an underlying weakness - the government would still need to "squeeze" the peasantry if it wanted money for investment and such a system could only be maintained by force. In the end, the only real hope for the peasantry lay in convincing Stalin that the system was providing the government with as much grain as possible. From Stalin's perspective, the solution was not necessarily to eliminate the haggling over quotas between each political unit. The solution was more basic - get an accurate estimate of the amount of grain the system could provide.

The change from the zagotovki to the state tax was one administrative change. Perhaps a more important change lay in a governmental restructuring which gave responsibility for agricultural planning to a single agency. The Committee for Procurements (Komzag) was created in December 1932. It was somewhat of a self-contained administrative unit. Organizationally, it was set up as a pyramid structure with Moscow at the top and regional and district administrators below. It was somewhat immune to local politics, because its members were outside the authority of the Party. It was also given emergency powers.[80]

To reinforce the authority of the Komzag, the special political or party-police units, mentioned previously, were formed. Attached to the machine-tractor stations (MTS) and collectives, they acted as an affiliate of the secret police - a representative of the OGPU was appointed as first deputy in every section.[81] (The OGPU deputy reported to officials in the OGPU, and could call on OGPU units for help as well.) While the OGPU presence added a sinister element to the political units, there was at least an attempt to raise the level of administrative competence. Those appointed to local posts had administrative experience. Some had even been in the military.[82]

Conceding the need for some incentive for the peasants, the government did allow private trade as early as the summer of 1932. Administrators were walking a fine line.

They were aware that profit would provide the peasants with an incentive to be more productive. At the same time, they knew that this incentive would cause peasants to concentrate on their personal production, rather than the government harvest. Both individuals and collectives were allowed to sell surpluses on the open market. Unfortunately, in the situations in which private markets were allowed, officials often found that government procurement suffered. The solution, for officials, was to move as quickly as possible to eliminate such private trade. Markets were ordered closed as soon as collections for the state tax began. In order to reopen, a special decree was required, and officials would only grant the decree after the state quotas had been reached.

The administrative and policy changes of 1933 eased the pressure on the peasants somewhat. However, in areas hit hard by the government campaign, such as the Ukraine, peasants were too weak to carry out their work. Working animals died or, in a weakened state, were in no better condition. Students and army troops were used to help with the harvest.

Stalin was prepared to continue, even to renew, a more ferocious campaign. If the Ukraine was suffering, Stalin seemed to view it with a special hatred. In June 1933, in a circular, he promised even more drastic measures. A chairman of one collective was publicly criticized by the press and then arrested for baking bread from the peasant's wheat on three occasions. Another was arrested for distributing wheat to his peasants.[83] Both actions occurred in the Ukraine.

While Stalin may have wanted to continue, there are signs that political pressure was building to force him to retreat. The pressure came from all levels, at the lowest, from peasants, at the top, from Party officials. The peasants found a voice in the newspapers. The press did not necessarily report peasant opposition directly. Instead it spoke of peasant distrust of the government.[84] It is difficult to imagine that the press would report such opinions without Stalin's knowledge or permission. It can be surmised that he, not only allowed the publication, but was aware of the background to the criticism. Party leaders also were publicly calling for a change. Though carefully wording what was said, in one speech Kirov suggested that it was time to stop 'squeezing' the peasantry. Other top officials were pressing for a more moderate policy.[85]

Pressure for moderating policy also came from the recently created political sections of the MTSs. Many questioned the grain quotas being set by Moscow. Some went so far as to defend the collectives against charges of mismanagement. Some refused to go along with prosecutions of collective managers. In creating the political sections, Moscow may have assumed that their predecessors at the local level had too many ties to the peasants. Replace them with more reliable Party outsiders and the Party would be able to defeat the countryside. The realization that dedicated Party people had turned against him no doubt aroused feelings of betrayal in Stalin. He also realized that his plans, in the end, depended on the support of lower echelon administrators. If he pushed too hard he risked losing the confidence so crucial to effective administration. The pressure from below probably helped convince Stalin to ease his policies. It did not appease him for the betrayal. He would dissolve the political sections in December 1934.[86]

The new atmosphere even gave the peasants outside the collective some peace. The number of households collectivized between July 1933 and July 1934 only increased by 500,000, going from 15.2 million to 15.7 million.[87] Nevertheless, in June 1934 Stalin renewed the campaign against the independent peasant, now reduced in numbers to only 9 million individuals.[88] The attack took the form of a tax increase. In October 1934 the remaining individual households were required to pay a tax in cash. This tax was followed by an increase in the grain delivery quota, which had been 10 percent, to 50 percent above that demanded of the collective.[89] As a result of the renewed drive, collectivized households increased to 17.3 million by July 1935.[90] In percentage terms this number represented some 83.2 percent of the peasantry. The amount of collectivized land had reached 94.1 percent by that time.[91] Between August 1935 and July 1936 another 1.1 million households were added. The following twelve months added just 100,000 households, although the total number of households collectivized had reached 18.5 million, or 93 percent by July 1937.[92] In 1938 the Party succeeded in eliminating the few remaining independent peasants. It did this by passing a special tax on horses, between 275 and 500 rubles, which most independents could not afford to pay. To avoid the tax, many decided to join.[93]

By 1937, life in the countryside for the peasant assumed some form of normality. Having resisted the collective for so long, they were beginning to accept it. The kolkhoz, apart from the terror, was attaining a form of legitimacy, in their eyes. The Party even felt secure enough to introduce a limited form of democracy at the local level. It did not give up the authority to appoint chairmen, but encouraged local leaders to participate. Peasants even began to see political gain by participating in the kolkhoz and competing for the leadership positions.[94]

One area in which the government tried to restore a sense of normality was that of land tenure. For all the energy the Party expended on forcing peasants to give up their private landholdings, the desire for legal recognition of land rights remained strong among the peasantry. At the same time, it seemed to express itself along collective lines - it often was the collective which pushed most strongly for some form of ownership. Surprisingly, the Party agreed to such a concession. In mid-1935 a law was passed which provided for "eternal use" by the collective of the land worked. It was estimated that 80,000 land surveyors would be needed to determine the boundaries and there were not that many which could be found in 1935. It would not be until 1937 that the surveying was completed.[95]

In some ways it is surprising that the traditional regard for land rights, even rights associated with the village, continued, even among Party officials. For all the efforts local officials put into forcing peasants to join collectives, they tended to respect property rights, once allocated. In one village, peasants began the spring sowing late because neither the members of the collective nor the independent peasants were certain what the new boundaries were.[96]

The countryside would endure one more political shock in 1937 - the Great Purges. Moscow was center stage for most of the trials, with Stalin's last major political rivals serving as the primary victims. Yet peasants found themselves victims as well, especially those who had been bold enough to enter the collective political arena in hopes of advancement. The victims of the purge often found that there was no systematic way to predict who would be targeted. Sometimes those indicted were charged simply because those who had hired them had fallen out of favor. Sometimes the trials involved those few collective chairmen who were not party members. In some cases charges related to general mismanagement, such as a failure to meet production quotas.[97] Charges were not limited to these categories. As if to appease the peasants, the Party seemed to encourage them to bring complaints against officials who had treated them badly. Stalin had been in the habit of encouraging his subordinates to take extreme action, then eliminating them later - often charging them with the very actions he had earlier encouraged them to take.

Where Stalin had acted indifferently to the wishes of the peasants, he now seemed interested in how they viewed the government - he wanted to win back their hearts. They were not only encouraged to make complaints, those complaints were taken seriously. Many of those put on trial in the rural areas were accused of having mistreated the peasants or of having violated the rights of collective members. Peasants, no doubt, felt some satisfaction when their complaints were actually acted on. In the Western oblast, for example, peasants had lodged nearly a thousand complaints about land titles, the poor quality of land assigned, and loss of forested land, in 1937. Such complaints provided the Party the excuse needed to purge those considered officially responsible.[98]

Officials may have been inclined to exercise some leniency in their treatment of the countryside because the 1937 harvest had been a bumper crop. Perhaps in an effort to give the appearance of being vigilant, local officials responded to the purges by expelling collective members from the kolkhoz. Those expelled were often charged with being kulaks. The Party allowed the expulsions for a time but then in April 1938, ordered that they come to an end.[99] Whether such actions saved those officials, the Great Purge was running out of steam. It was largely spent by the second half of 1938.

THE FINAL RESULTS OF COLLECTIVIZATION

In beginning the discussion of Soviet agriculture in Chapter Thirteen, five questions were posed. The first related to the structure of agriculture during Czarist times and its structure following the Bolshevik takeover. The second asked about the agricultural problems faced by the Bolsheviks and by Stalin. The discussion of the history of Russian and Soviet agriculture hopefully has answered both questions. The third question related to the specific goal of eliminating private property. Was Stalin successful at reducing private ownership? Assuming that he was successful at that goal, the fourth question asked whether the policy restricting private ownership also eliminated the incentives necessary for productivity. The fifth question, somewhat related to the issue of productivity, asked whether the failures of agriculture could be attributed to the introduction of central planning.

The right to own property and to accumulate wealth are considered core motivators where productivity is concerned, according to some capitalist proponents. The assumption, where Russia is concerned, is that the Bolsheviks were completely successful at eliminating private property. Because of the anti-property policies engaged in by the communists, there is a temptation to accept that assumption at face value. It is an inconsequential issue compared to the larger problem of productivity. Is the assumption borne out by the facts? Did the communists completely do away with the possibility of personal gain in running their new system? To what extent was private property or the free market actually eliminated in the agricultural sector? As shown by the discussion, the Soviet government did not entirely eliminate free trade, even after the agricultural economy had been converted to a collectivized system. If access to free markets was severely restricted, peasants were allowed to sell goods on the open market.

The ideological war against private property and profits is assumed to be the underlying explanation for the lackluster performance of the Soviet economy. A related assumption is that, because the Party sought to eliminate private property, it necessarily rejected all capitalist thinking about material rewards. The assumption is that the anti-profit, anti-private property crusade was so pervasive that it served as the motivational tool for everything from foreign policy to factory production. But, had the Bolsheviks really invented an alternative to the profit-driven system favored by the West? a method based entirely on idealism and an ideological appeal to the worker.

Superficially, the question of whether a profit-driven system was done away with under Stalin seems self-evident. The taking of peasant land and livestock, even down to the smallest chicken, is rather convincing proof. Yet, on closer examination, the evidence is not so clear cut, especially in the broader view of administration. While communist philosophy seemed to call for egalitarian treatment within the bureaucratic structure, in practice, the system operated on a basis which rewarded performance. The evidence shows that personal gain, even material reward, was a major motivator within the collective, particularly where leadership of the kolkhoz was concerned.

In contrast to its egalitarian philosophy, the Party clearly made a distinction between ordinary workers or peasants and managers. It conferred the greatest rewards on managers. The peasants were largely cut out of the system. Kolkhoz chairmen, on the other hand, could receive both a salary and credit for laptardays worked. A laborday was the method of calculating how much work had been done for the kolkhoz. Labordays allowed the worker to participate in the earnings of the kolkhoz, based on the number of labordays accumulated. Kolkhoz chairmen were 'paid' at the rate of 2 labordays on the bigger collectives. In addition, the chairman was considered to be permanently working, so he could earn 60 labordays per month by virtue of the fact that he served as the chairman.[100]

The question of regular salaries for officeholders in the collectives began appearing in the mid-1930s. Where the Party would not act to establish the practice, local districts decided to act on their own. Some, in 1937, passed resolutions to pay their chairmen regular salaries. (They were forced to reverse the resolutions in 1938 when Moscow objected.) The Party finally relented in 1940-41 when it allowed kolkhoz chairmen a monthly salary.[101]

The lack of a regular salary did not make the chairmanship unattractive. Kolkhoz chairmen soon discovered that the kolkhoz generated cash, which they had access to, even if they could not draw a salary. Each kolkhoz had a savings account and, just as helpful to the chairmen, a 2 percent portion of the account which was designated for "administrative-economic expenses." The main savings account was intended to be used for major kolkhoz expenditures, such as equipment or buildings, while the 2 percent was intended for personnel needs of the kolkhoz, such as payment of surveyors and craftsmen for services or payment of extra workers during the harvest.[102]

Chairmen found that both funds were useful. While they could not get official approval of a regular salary, they paid themselves, and sometimes other officers, out of the 2 percent portion anyway. Where the savings fund was supposed to be used to buy equipment for the collective, some chairmen used it to build themselves new houses.[103] More blatant illegalities were involved when chairmen simply appropriated kolkhoz property. In some cases they sold kolkhoz produce on the open market without turning over the proceeds. In other cases they used their position to take more land for their own use or used collective equipment as their own. The downside to these practices was that when the Party decided to conduct a purge of officials, investigators had little trouble finding evidence to support a charge of embezzlement or corruption. Access to kolkhoz money was one incentive; avoidance of field work was another. The then-current chairman of a kolkhoz was excused from field work. Some chairmen extended this privilege to members of their family as well as to the staff of the kolkhoz.[104]

The abuses found at the kolkhoz level, closest to the peasant, did not disappear at higher levels of governmental administration. The next administrative level above the collective was the rural soviet. It had responsibility for between three and ten collective farms, or roughly 2,000 individuals.[105] Above the soviet was the rural raion, which administered some 20 soviets. In terms of individuals, this meant a raion district of about 40,000 or 50,000 people.[106]

Like kolkhoz chairmen, officials of the soviet, which was primarily responsible for tax collection, found ways to milk the system for private gain. Sometimes it took the form of outright bribery. Where officials did not benefit personally they got some reward through the exercise of power. They arbitrarily seized peasant cattle or got the free use of peasant labor without paying the kolkhoz. Officials sometimes took kolkhoz property without paying or forced the kolkhoz to provide jobs for friends or relatives. Like kolkhoz chairmen, temptation proved too great for some raion officials in cases where they were given unrestricted access to kolkhoz funds.

MOTIVATING PEASANTS WITHOUT THE PROFIT INCENTIVE

The previous discussion has looked at the overall organizational or 'management' structure of Soviet rural administration. The peasant was still at the bottom. As noted, the Soviet system did not entirely eliminate material gain from all aspects of agricultural production. In fact, the Soviet management structure seemed to incorporate some very traditional motivational methods. Power, and the perks which came with it, seemed to be central to Soviet management. The rewards seemed unevenly divided however. Managers who were successful tended to accumulate a greater share of the rewards, while peasants, no matter how hard they tried, seemed to lose more and more. Given this circumstance, a key question is how management was able to motivate peasants to produce.

The collective system presented two major problems for management. The first problem was how peasant performance could even be measured. The second problem was how to motivate peasants when they received no benefit from increased productivity. In the new system peasant labor was divorced from the productivity of the collective. While the success of any collective was dependant on peasant productivity, the peasants, for the most part, did not get any personal benefit from the success of the collective. The advantage of a capitalist system is that performance, or productivity, can be measured by the success or failure of the product or the business. Peasant productivity, prior to collectivization, could be measured at the individual level by sales of wheat or rye crop, and at the business level, by whether the peasant farm could continue to operate profitably. Once peasants had been turned into nothing more than laborers, productivity became harder to determine. As the machine tractor stations discovered, peasant laborers, when reward was not tied to performance, could harvest weeds as easily as they could wheat.

Instead of adopting innovative management techniques, communist administration has been described as a return to serfdom.[107] It was expected that collectivization - with wider use of machinery and the introduction of scientific methods - would make life easier for the peasants. Instead it produced Soviet managers who treated the peasants as if they were serfs. The struggle between the peasant on the collective and his manager, in a way, mirrored the struggle between the free market and the Soviet regime in the overall economy. Were state production goals better served by tighter controls or by market forces? There was also an inherent conflict between increasing productivity and the proof of that productivity - demanded of every manager. Was it more important for the manager to improve the collective's output or more important for him to prove to his superiors that he was making the effort?

Agricultural production also created a unique dilemma for managers. There was no clear dividing line between what the peasant produced for the state and what he produced on his own, nor was there any easy way to quantify the difference. If the factory worker's productivity could be more easily judged by how much his factory produced, it was also simpler to separate what the worker did at the factory from what he did when he went home. The peasant, in contrast, worked for the collective to harvest grain, then worked on his own plot at night to produce vegetables. While what the collective produced might be a different crop than that of the peasant, both were agricultural products. If the communists brought improvements on the technical side by increasing mechanization, they had more difficulties coming up with an administrative alternative to the old Czarist system. The basic problem was in trying to convert to a purely performance-based system. The problem was not that they now demanded performance and higher output, whereas the Czarist system did not. The problem was more that the performance standard demanded of the collective would eventually bring it into conflict with the performance of the private peasant plot. If the productivity of the peasant plots was often greater than that of the collective, that private productivity was also competing against that of the state collective. One solution to this dilemma had been War Communism. In essence the peasant had been allowed to produce as much as he could, and then the state came in and confiscated it. However, it required the state to commit vast administrative resources and it was too disruptive.

If the communist system came to resemble serfdom, it was because the Party eventually gave up on hopes of finding an alternative solution. It chose instead to rely on past methods. Performance could be gauged by the amount of land held or by the amount of time worked. If land or time were not as exact as productivity when used as measuring tools, they had the advantage of being quantifiable. While the collective might not be as productive as the peasant, it had a better chance of success if it held more land. If it could not prevent the peasant from working his own plot, it could at least require him to work so many hours for the state. Where serfs had been forced to divide their time between the landlord's plot and their own, peasants found that they now divided their efforts between the collective and their own land.

In one sense, management did not worry particularly about motivating the peasants. Motivation was based ultimately on force or the threat of force. The government held a monopoly on food and control of the food supply was what the collective manager could use as a club. While peasants had been turned into little more than factory workers, they were not paid in the same way. Rather they were mostly paid in grain - a payment-in-kind system. In some cases, the payment was in cash. The unit of work was the 'labor-day' in which the peasant received credit for doing a certain amount of work. In exchange for each labor-day worked, the peasant was entitled to receive a certain amount of grain - his portion based on a certain proportion of the collective's production. Criticism of the communist system would suggest that the peasant merely had to show up in the field to receive his labor-day. In fact, the manager could exercise some discretion in crediting for labor-days. The manager could require that a certain amount of land be plowed before the award. The labor-day was not an informal development of collective management, but had been officially decreed by the Party to be the method of payment (March 17, 1931).

At the field level, work was organized in the form of brigades. The field manager, the brigade leader, who oversaw the brigade, was appointed by the kolkhoz board. In theory, the brigade leader had a number of sanctions available for peasants who were reluctant to work - anything from beatings to fines to arrest and imprisonment. Since the brigade leader was responsible for recording labor-days worked, that was the most practical sanction available. Fines were probably the most commonly used punishment, usually in the form of deductions of labor-days.[108]

The peasants adjusted to the work requirements of the collective, although they were a continuing source of tension. They would have preferred to put much of their energy into their private plots. In spite of the hostility expressed publicly by the government toward private agriculture, the governmental attitude toward the peasant's private plot was ambiguous. There was an understanding on the part of officials that the peasants relied on their private plots for subsistence. In fact, the government seemed to take a view similar to that taken toward the collective as a whole. Just as the collective had been expected to finance the modernization of Soviet agriculture, the peasant was expected to survive off what he produced himself.

In general, it might be said that the Soviet management structure attempted to control rather than to utilize individual motivation. Stalin wanted the peasants to produce and not prosper. Where motivation was part of the system it was limited to management. While Stalin could praise those who had produced, he almost seemed to favor force as a major motivator. For all the severity with which Stalin came down on the peasants he seemed forgiving of the excesses of lower-level managers. While they became the victims of purges from time-to-time, there seemed no systematic or long-term effort to control their dictatorial tendencies. If Stalin was intent on forcing the peasant to relinquish his livestock, he did not seem to mind the kolkhoz chairman who appropriated the livestock for personal use. Perhaps because their conduct, at times, was similar to his own, he was more forgiving of any excesses they committed.

FAILURES IN THE AGRICULTURAL SECTOR

The fifth question posed at the beginning of Chapter 13 related to central planning. Where there were failures in the agricultural sector, were they caused by the introduction of central planning? Central planning could be said to represent the ultimate limitation on personal freedom in an organizational setting. Individual initiative is discouraged and innovative ideas which conflict with the central plan are frowned upon. Since central planning emphasizes conformity and detailed planning, it necessarily will limit individual initiative. Such limits can impact productivity where individual motivation is based on the need to be recognized or rewarded for contributions to an organization's success. That criticism is mirrored at the market level. Just as the centrally planned organization ignores the contributions of its employees, central planning ignores the wishes of consumers and the forces of the market. Rather than letting consumers and the market decide what should be produced or which product is best, central planning rewards inefficiency. Companies or industries which would be eliminated by the market are allowed to continue operating.

Because the inefficiency at the market level resembles the inefficiencies within the central planning system itself, there is a tendency to treat all arguments about central planning the same, whether those arguments relate to production decisions or involve overall productivity. Central planning, according to the argument, not only ignores consumer wishes and the market, wasting resources in the process, (by producing products nobody wants), it also ignores the contributions of its own workers. Since central planning treats its workers badly, and since bad treatment will reduce productivity, the deficiencies of central planning are therefore the cause of, or equivalent to, a loss of productivity - or so the argument goes.

The loss of productivity is important for any discussion of the Soviet agricultural sector. There is no question that the Soviet system suffered serious problems with productivity. Before discussing those problems however, it may be helpful to look at one area considered crucial to productivity, the use of machinery. Machinery has long been known to bring about large gains in productivity. A tractor can easily outperform a horse when it comes to the number of acres plowed. Communist leaders had never questioned this. In fact, their hopes for agricultural production had been premised on increased mechanization. One of the partial goals of collectivization had been to upgrade Soviet agriculture by increasing the use of tractors and combines. This section looks at what was achieved in this area.

In 1929 Soviet industry only managed to produce 3,300 tractors.[109] By December 1932 there were nearly 75,000 tractors in use on the 2,446 MTSs.[110] The effort put into increased tractor production was Herculean, in view of the large increase in numbers. It was also Herculean from the perspective of the amount of resources consumed. Despite the increase, it was inadequate, given the size of the Soviet Union and the amount of land which needed to be worked. To gain some perspective on the shortage of tractors one can look ahead to more recent years for comparison. In 1976 the number of tractors in use was 2,400,000 and in 1980 the number was 2,600,000.[111] Whatever gains were made in tractor production, they could not offset the losses in horses, still crucial to an agriculture dependent on animal power. Some 17.2 million horses died or were slaughtered between 1929 and 1934.[112]

It would not be until 1938 that the agricultural sector would recover from the animal losses, even with the addition of new machinery. Horses and oxen had provided some 27 million horsepower in July 1928. By July 1933 the figure had fallen 11 million, to 16 million horsepower. Despite the increases in tractor numbers, tractor horsepower in July 1933 was only 3.6 to 5.4 million. Even in 1940 it was only 10.3 million horsepower. In 1938, the total horsepower available had barely recovered to the 1928 level. Where it had been 27 million in 1928, with animals alone, it was between 26 and 32 million horsepower in 1938 for the combination of machinery and animals. In 1938 Soviet agriculture had only 196,000 lorries, compared to some one million in the U.S..[113] Clearly, industrial production of farm machinery, even when supplemented by purchases from abroad, was not adequate to modernize the agricultural sector.

Productivity was clearly impacted by inadequacies in equipment. In addition, the government took steps clearly intended to destroy productivity in situations where peasant competition potentially threatened government programs. Forced grain requisitions, limitations on peasant sales through private markets, and high taxes were part of this campaign. Even in economic activities deemed important by the government, few steps were taken to encourage productivity. If Stalin focused on getting peasants to join the collective, his administrators seemed to care little about productivity once that objective had been achieved. There are countless examples of peasants, who, having joined the collective, lost a great deal of interest in work. In one Ukrainian village, a Party worker found only eight men working the harvest in 1930. The other members of the village were sitting and laying around, willing to let the grain go to waste.[114] The problem was not simply that the system discouraged productivity, it was more that it encouraged laziness. It seemed to create an atmosphere of lethargy among the peasants. In one case, the kolkhoz chairman became so exasperated by constant peasant requests for small items such as milk or boots that he jumped out a window one day and ran away.[115]

Waste was another result of the system. In many cases, high-quality equipment purchased from foreign countries was left in the open and rusted.[116] Peasants who were entrusted with animals on the collectives often failed to care for them and many of the animals died. Central planning clearly was a source of inefficiency. Conquest speaks of problems with the implementation of the Machine Tractor Station idea. In one province in September 1933, it is estimated that some 7,300 hours were wasted in driving time alone because the MTS was located so far from the fields to be plowed.[117]

That the market was a great motivator can be shown by one statistic from 1938. It is estimated that the private peasant plots, which totaled only 3.9 percent of sown acreage, provided as much as 45 percent of total farm output. For specific products, private plots accounted for an even higher percentage - 71.4 percent of milk and 70.9 percent of meat.[118] The difference between collective and private plot production provides strong evidence that restrictions on the free market contributed to a loss of productivity. The argument is supported by countless stories illustrating the problems associated with state control and central planning. Establishing a loss of productivity, however strong the case may be, does not prove that productivity losses were the sole cause of failures in the Soviet agricultural system. The stories used to illustrate productivity loss, also contain elements pointing to shortages as a major problem.

Conquest relates a story about an MTS in Polyvyanka which occurred in February 1933. The whole staff was arrested on a charge of sabotage. The charge was based on the fact that the machinery had not been maintained. The reason for the lack of maintenance was an inability to obtain spare parts. In addition, there was no way to manufacture needed parts because there was no fuel for the forges and no materials such as iron or wood. Another MTS in Krasnovershk in 1933 also could obtain no spare parts for its tractors and thrashing machines and had had to borrow a forge and anvil from another kolkhoz.[119]

Problems with shortages in Russia can be seen, not just in grocery store lines, but in nearly every facet of Soviet society. In a larger sense, scarcity can be seen in the attempt to finance industrialization through the agricultural sector. But it can also be seen in operations at the local level. It would not be until 1940-41 that kolkhoz chairmen would be given a regular salary.[120] Other evidence of shortage can be seen in some of the examples cited earlier. Over half of the quality rolled steel production in 1931 had to be committed to the manufacture of farm machinery.[121] The collectives suffered from a lack of even the most basic equipment, such as cattle sheds or silos.[122]

WAS COLLECTIVIZATION NECESSARY?

Stalin had two major goals in collectivizing agriculture. The specific goal was to change from a system of private production to the state-run system of collectives. The second goal was to finance industrialization. While the goal of collectivization was achieved, it did not bring spectacular changes in agricultural productivity. It was not a total failure, since there were modest improvements in productivity. In 1928 the grain harvest amounted to 73.3 million tons. In 1935 it had increased 1.7 million tons to 75 million tons. The years in between had seen fluctuations, from a low of 67.5 million tons in 1934 to a high of 83.5 million tons in 1930.[123]

While the Soviet Union could not match the West in industrial productivity, under Stalin it did move forward. He managed to create industries which had not existed prior to his plans, with new manufacturing capabilities for tractors, automobiles, and aircraft. Russia had also significantly strengthened production in coal and oil as well as steel and textiles. Overall productivity of the industrial sector was improved. The manufacturing sector had made up only 48 percent of total economic output in 1928, while agriculture produced the other 52 percent. By 1932 industry accounted for 70 percent of output versus 30 percent for agriculture.[124] Apart from Stalin's often exaggerated claims for the success of his Five-Year plan, it is estimated that industrial output expanded by 50 percent.[125]

Were the successes in industrialization the result of forced investment by the agricultural sector? The question may never be answered, although it is one of the major areas of debate over Soviet economic policy. Some argue that it was the urban economy which provided the capital investment needed.[126] Those who support that view would argue that Stalin could have achieved as much by relying on the "normal" economic growth and increase in productivity, rather than trying to forcefully extract resources from the agricultural sector.[127]

CONCLUSION

This section has provided a history and analysis of the changes which took place in the Soviet agricultural sector. It went from a village-oriented system, which largely relied on animal power, to a government controlled system which attempted to introduce mechanization. Stalin was partly successful in converting Russian agriculture to a more modern system. In other ways he had left the village system intact. Perhaps one of the major changes was to involve the government more directly in administration than had been the case under the Czar. Yet, for all the administrative resources applied, there were limits to what even Stalin could do. While he used the secret police more, in some ways he left the rural areas alone.

Stalin's obsession with peasant influence over the grain market and his determination to bring that market under government control was what caused him to pursue forced collectivization. He was successful in achieving that goal. At the same time, the successes in collectivization were offset by the resulting loss of productivity among the peasantry. There is little doubt that the system Stalin established severely restricted initiative and destroyed much of the productivity of the peasants. Conventional wisdom is that communist policy, in eliminating the free market, is the cause of Soviet economic problems. The purpose of this chapter has been to show that scarcity, not restrictions on the market, was the real reason for the Soviet Union's economic problems. The next section looks at the industrial sector. Like the agricultural sector, it had to endure constantly changing goals and policies. Communist policy changed from moderately liberal concessions to the free market to strict government control.

CHAPTER 15

RUSSIAN INDUSTRY AND THE REVOLUTION

The forced collectivization of agriculture, for whatever it accomplished or whatever hardships it visited on the peasantry, will likely remain the major economic policy for which Joseph Stalin is remembered - at least in the realm of agricultural policy. If his name has any other association with economic policy it is with his five-year plans. They may be ridiculed in the West for their shortcomings, but they are nevertheless remembered. There were clearly shortcomings between what Stalin hoped the plans would achieve and what was actually accomplished, (or what he would publicly admit to and what he actually knew). At the same time there is no question that they transformed the Soviet Union from a largely agricultural nation into an industrial power. If the five-year plans represent something of significance, they really only tell part of the economic story, important though they are.

This chapter is intended to provide an overview of Russian industry, as it existed prior to the Revolution and how it was transformed immediately after the communists came to power. It then looks at the policy impact of War Communism, the major economic program carried out during the Civil War. The period which followed in the mid-1920s is covered in more detail in the next chapter (16). Chapter 16 also looks at what happened under Stalin's five-year plans and discusses what was accomplished.

HISTORICAL OVERVIEW OF THE INDUSTRIAL SECTOR - 1860 - 1939

The history of industrial growth in Russia can be dated to around 1860, with the coming of the railroad. Over the next 50 years, large-scale industry would expand to eleven times its 1860 level. Yet, for all its growth, industry still produced less than half of the national income in 1913 and employed only one-fourth of the work force. Heavy industry in 1913 - mainly mining and large-scale manufacturing - employed only 2.5 million people.[1] At that time the population was around 140 million people.[2] Small-scale industry, consisting of workshops and artisans, accounted for the majority of industrial employment - 5.2 million workers in 1915, or 67 percent. Heavy industry, while employing fewer people, still accounted for 67 percent of industrial output. (Heavy industry represented 67 percent of output while small-scale enterprises employed 67 percent of workers.)[3]

The government played a larger role in industrial development than in Europe or the U.S. It had been responsible for the development of the railway system and largely owned the railroads by 1913. It also provided the largest market for industrial goods and was more involved in managing the capital goods industries. In contrast to the U.S., where anti-trust legislation, such as the Sherman act, limited monopolistic activities, Russia allowed a small number of companies to control the markets with sales quotas and price-setting. This oligopolistic behavior was largely limited to the capital goods sector. Consumer goods producers operated in a more open market.

While Russia was developing a capital goods industry, there are indications of some underlying weaknesses - one technological, the other financial. On the technological side, Russia still relied on foreign manufacturers for industrial equipment. The reliance on German manufacturers in particular created difficulties during the War. On the financial side, Russia was heavily dependent on foreign investors, primarily from Germany, France and England. (It is possible to see signs of resource scarcity in the inability of Russian business people to generate sufficient surplus to invest.) At the same time, Russian investment was increasing. Between 1900 and 1913 it increased by some 60 percent. In the same period foreign investment increased by 85 percent. Overall foreign ownership in private companies went from 28.5 percent in 1900 to 33 percent in 1933.[4] All this was taking place in the private sector. The Russian government, like its private counterparts, found itself "under siege" from foreigners. It was heavily reliant on foreign investors for financing - particularly for its railroad building.

Borrowing money was one thing; paying it back was another. To repay investors, the Russian government looked to the agricultural sector. The idea that peasant farmers could provide a solution to Russia's financial woes seems almost laughable in light of the collectivization experience. Yet, if Stalin can be criticized for his overly optimistic expectations and for his methods, the basic idea of an agricultural solution did not originate with him. The Czarist policy largely escapes criticism, because it pales when compared to the scale of Stalin's efforts. Nevertheless, it provided a primitive model, both in its methods and in its goals. Its method of squeezing the peasants through higher taxes was thought necessary because Czarist policy-makers sought to finance industrialization through agricultural surpluses. In hopes of forcing peasants to sell grain (and to consume less themselves), the government kept agricultural taxes high. The surplus could then be re-sold abroad by the government, allowing it to repay investors.

Despite its shortcomings, the general policy had provided Russia with a measure of success. Unfortunately, World War I would measure success or failure by a much stricter standard. Although industrial development had been substantial, Russian industry was too fragile to withstand the strains which the War imposed. The level of fighting was such, in the first six months of the war alone, that weapons and ammunition were nearly exhausted. The government shifted industrial production from civilian manufacture to war-related armaments. This in turn disrupted normal manufacture and resulted in shortages of spare parts, particularly in the rail industry. Industrial expansion did not stop completely, but was greatly slowed.

The Czarist government did make some organizational changes in the governmental structure to deal with the war. It set up a Special Council for Defense, which oversaw other agencies dealing with such as areas as food and metal supplies. It was this war-created structure which the Bolsheviks inherited and used as the organizational model for their regime. Ironically, it was the democratically-oriented Provisional Government which came up with the idea of a state grain monopoly, later almost the cornerstone of communist agricultural planning.

When Czar Nicholas abdicated on March 2, 1917, the Provisional Government inherited a number of problems in the industrial sector. The railroads were suffering from a lack of maintenance and the transportation breakdown caused shortages of both food and industrial supplies. Inflation accompanied other problems. The workers, egged on by the communists and similar radical groups, began to assert a vague 'democratic' power at the factory level. Strikes became more frequent, as did the number of lockouts.

The Bolsheviks, following their takeover in October 1917, initially felt that power in the hands of the workers was a good thing. On November 27 they even passed a decree which strengthened the factory committees. They soon discovered that the worker control which had been an effective weapon against the Provisional Government, was not so desirable when used against them. They began to assert control of the various labor groups which were seen as interfering with their programs. The railroad union was forcibly taken over in March 1918.

From unions, they expanded the policy to cover all aspects of production. Major industries were systematically nationalized. They found the war-time governmental structure, with its newly created agencies, to be suitable for their plans. The Special Council for Defense was turned into the Supreme Council of the National Economy (Vysshyi Sovet Narodnogo Khoziaistva or VSNKh) as decreed by the new government in December 1917. Economically it had very broad goals - it was to oversee organization of the national economy while being responsible for state finances. The most significant power it was given was the authority to nationalize just about everything economic - production, distribution and finance.

The government did not formally decree the nationalization of industry until June 28, 1918. However, nationalization had begun almost from the Bolshevik takeover. Much of it was done on local initiative and was limited to individual factories. The two exceptions were the railways and the merchant fleet, which were nationalized in total in January 1918. The central government found itself in a power struggle with local authorities. While going ahead with nationalization plans for the railroads and merchant fleet itself, it was also attempting to prevent local authorities from nationalizing factories on their own. It threatened agencies with a loss of funds if they acted without central approval. The threat may have had some effect. By June only 487 enterprises had been nationalized.[5] (The number is small when compared to the number which would be reported in the fall of 1920 when 37,226 enterprises would be under government control.)[6]

The June decree, most significantly, did not compensate business owners for the loss of their businesses. Although the decree was a radical change on paper, the government did not have the administrative resources to manage all the businesses which were taken over. Of the 37,226 enterprises nationalized by 1920, it is estimated that the Economic Council could only administer 4,547.[7] Ironically, while the Economic Council was criticized for minimal management of nationalized enterprises, it employed almost 25,000 people.[8]

Nationalization was only one economic policy pursued in 1919, 1920, and 1921.

The Bolsheviks also tried to put some of their most theoretical ideas into practice. The most innovative was an attempt to eliminate money as a medium of exchange. More along the lines of nationalization, the Bolsheviks also tried to eliminate all private trade. In keeping with their theories, they did experiment with providing free services to people. Housing, utilities, and transport were services which did not have to be paid for.

The problem was that the Bolsheviks were relying on a system not really self-contained or self-sustaining - they were freeloading off the capitalist production system they despised. If they decried the exploitation of workers, they saw nothing wrong with using the products which "exploited" workers had produced or built during Czarist times. They were financing their operations from monies which had been saved by the Czar and with infrastructure created before they came to power. They were also dealing with physical structures, which were subject to physical limitations rather than economic rules. Buildings could be used for nothing only until they physically wore out. So long as accounting and depreciation calculations held an association with capitalism they were to be avoided. Once it became clear however that they were valuable tools in measuring physical deterioration of structures they once more were useful.

While Party theorists could experiment, those in charge had to contend with serious shortages of food and goods and a decline in industrial production. In the countryside the peasants had to endure the forced grain requisitions of "War Communism." For workers, "War Communism" in late 1919 meant forced membership in factory brigades. Civilians were essentially "drafted" to perform service in factories or public utilities. Soldiers, instead of being demobilized, were assigned to work details, primarily repairing railroad tracks and agricultural equipment or transporting fuel.

With the defeat of Petr Wrangel's White Army in the Crimea in November 1920, the economic strains caused by the demands of war were significantly eased. However, shortages did not immediately end. They even contributed to the revolt at Kronstadt in February 1921. With the mutiny put down in March, Lenin announced a change in economic policy. The New Economic Policy (NEP), (as it became known sometime in the winter of 1921-1922) represented a liberalization of government policy. Lenin, worried about the food supply, initially wanted to win over the peasants. So, on March 15, 1921, the Politburo voted the end of the forced grain requisitions of "War Communism." Lenin only intended to lift restrictions for agriculture, not for industrial goods. Having changed policy in one area, it was difficult to hold the line in others. On May 17, 1921, the Party reversed the decree which had nationalized small businesses. Where the government did not totally give up control, it was willing to lease facilities back to their former owners. Leasing of enterprises controlled by the VSNKh was formally decreed on July 5, 1921. The mobilization of labor was formally abandoned in October. Lenin still wanted state control of large-scale industry and this remained in state hands.

During the second half of 1921, even the communists had to concede that a moneyless economy was causing problems for production. While the elimination of money had been good for employment, it also meant that factories had more workers and bureaucracy than they could afford. The experiment in free services was abandoned. Bookkeeping and standard accounting were reintroduced and, in general, governmental fiscal practices were tightened. By the decree of August 9, 1921 a form of market economy was introduced requiring manufacturers, even state manufacturers, to sell their products and to pay suppliers and workers. The government even allowed state goods to be sold to private traders rather than government enterprises, if the private traders were willing to pay more.[9]

Despite these changes industrial production took some time to recover and goods shortages existed through much of 1923. In 1924 however, industrial production significantly improved. In addition, the currency, which had been unstable for several years, was showing signs of stability, helped by the successful balancing of the government budget in 1923-24.

While many enterprises reverted to private ownership, the government had not completely surrendered to free market forces. It still maintained the system of trusts. It encouraged individual enterprises within production units to be competitive, but maintained control overall. In 1922 there were 430 trusts and VSNKh controlled 172 of these.[10] The effect of state control varied. In heavy industry, central planning dictated production goals. In consumer-oriented enterprises, the government allowed production to be determined largely by market demand. Private enterprise, such as it was, did fairly well in 1924 and 1925. It accounted for 77 percent of total output in 1924-25.[11] It had one Achilles heel - it was heavily dependent on state industry for materials. In addition, the state acted as landlord for many smaller shops.

VSNKh was not the only agency created to deal with the economy. (VSNKh, while involving the government in the control of the general economy, was not as involved with formal government activities.) In February 1921, Lenin had set up Gosplan. In contrast to VSNKh, it dealt with large-scale infrastructure projects, such as programs to provide electricity. A subdivision of the Council of Labor and Defence (STO), its goals were related to war or heavy industry endeavors.

Lenin had only reluctantly agreed to NEP. He had made concessions to the market in hopes of bringing some stability to the economy. The policy proved successful at reviving the economy. However, it bothered the most ideological of the communist leaders and they argued that it should be ended as soon as possible. It survived nearly intact during 1925, but the government did begin to set limits. While private trade was not outlawed, the government began using economic measures to make it more difficult. State and cooperative organizations were given priority in deliveries of scarce materials. Those who relied on the government-owned railroads for transport had to pay increasingly higher rates. In June 1926, a new tax was decreed on Nepmen (private traders who dealt primarily in small quantities of grain or other goods and who were so-named because of their association with the free trade of NEP - NEPmen). Article 107 of the criminal code was adopted. It made hoarding or refusal to sell goods a criminal offense.

The change in policy was only partly the result of ideological opposition to the market. Another factor was a general agreement among Party members about the need to industrialize. Efforts in the industrial sector until 1925 had been concentrated on recovering from the effects of the Civil War. The Nepmen, it was felt, were taking some of the resources which the state needed for an expanding industrial program. Where the Nepmen did not deny goods to state projects, their activities drove prices up.

At the time there was no formal government plan to guide industrialization. In June 1927, the Council of People's Commissars decreed the creation of an overall economic plan under government auspices. It would be over a year before a plan could be developed and implemented. So eager were planners to put a five-year plan in place that the plan was operating before it had even been submitted to the Party. The first five-year plan was implemented in October 1928. Six months later, in April 1929, it was submitted to the Sixteenth Party Congress for approval. Despite the competition involved in using different agencies, it was a joint effort of the staffs of VSNKh and Gosplan. Financing was to be done with industrialization loans and the forced investment of the agricultural sector.

Stalin was encouraged by the results of the first year. He revised the plan, confident that the plan would achieve its stated goals in four years. The original target date had been September 30, 1933. The date was moved ahead to December 31, 1932. Unfortunately for planners and workers, it was not just the date which was changed. The achievement of projected goals caused Stalin and planners to continually revise and increase the goals for production.

While government claims of success for the plan were often exaggerated, there were some areas in which the plan had achieved substantial results. There may have been an overemphasis on major projects, yet infrastructure necessary for industrial expansion was created. The Dnieper dam was constructed, providing electrical power needed for expanding industries. Industries crucial to industrial expansion were created or developed. Factories turned out greater numbers of turbines and machine tools while production of coal, oil and iron was greatly increased.

With prodding from Stalin, the First Five-Year Plan had officially ended on December 31, 1932, ahead of schedule. Publicly Stalin pointed to the plan's success. Privately, he made a more sober assessment of the results. In developing the Second Five-Year Plan Stalin decided to scale back the budgetary estimates for growth. The Plan covering the years 1933 to 1937, was formally adopted in February 1934. Instead of trying to expand into new areas of economic development he chose to consolidate in those areas where industries had only gained a foothold. The new theme, disclosed in January 1933 when Stalin spoke to the Central Committee, was to make things work. The facilities which had been built during the First Five-Year plan were to be placed in operation.

The first year of the Second Five-Year Plan saw a reduction in the pace of growth. Gross industrial production grew only 5 percent in 1933 whereas it had been growing by 20 percent annually during the First Five-Year Plan. The slowdown may have been part of an overall re-evaluation of economic priorities by Stalin or it may have been forced on him by the economic problems of 1933. The famine which began in 1932, was only one problem. The country also experienced serious transport problems and a goods shortage.

The years 1934 through 1936 were more productive. In addition, there was a shift in emphasis from heavy industrial output to consumer-oriented production, which eased shortages for ordinary citizens. That change was only temporary however. As the industrial sector began to recover, the government began to shift more resources into military production. Ironically, while Stalin eased the pressures under the Second Five-Year Plan, its success was due in part to the extraordinary efforts of the First Five-Year Plan. Many of the projects which had been started during the First Five-Year Plan were placed into full operation and began to show results. One important achievement of the Second Five-Year Plan was an increase in self-sufficiency in key industrial areas. There was less need to rely on foreign imports.

In 1937, despite the gains, there was an industrial slowdown. Production of consumer goods fell and shortages were widespread. It was not just consumer production which was disrupted. There was also a decline in basic industries, such as iron and steel. Nove attributes the decline to two factors: First, a decline in investment in these areas, in part due to the shift to military production and second, the Great Purge, which was aimed, not only at the Party leadership, but also at the management of many of the factories.[12]

In 1939, the Third Five-Year Plan was adopted by the Eighteenth Party Congress. Begun in 1938, it seemed patterned after the First Five-Year Plan, characterized by renewed energy and more ambitious goals. To its ambitious production goals were added non-industrial goals such as improved education among Soviet children. Initial planning involved an increase in overall productive capability. The threat of war with Germany caused a greater concern with the inadequacy of military production and a shift to armaments manufacture. While that shift would prove fortuitous for the coming war effort, it also resulted in shortages of consumer goods. For the worker, war preparations were a two-edged sword. They were subject to stricter work rules with longer hours. At the same time, the increased needs of industrial output created a demand for labor and a labor shortage. The Third Five-Year Plan was interrupted by the German invasion of June 1941.

The Soviet economy had undergone tremendous turmoil in the years following the Civil War. While it still had problems as Russia entered the war, it had gained enough strength to withstand the German assault. The period just prior to the beginning of the war provides the end point of this overview. The remaining discussion in this chapter focuses on War Communism, the major economic policy associated with the Civil War. The New Economic Policy (NEP) and the five-year plans are left for the next chapter. The discussion in both chapters follows a chronological order, although it is organized within a framework of "significant" economic events, namely War Communism (June 1918-March 1921), NEP (1922-1927), the First Five-Year Plan (1928-1932), the Second Five-Year Plan (1933-7), and the Third Five-Year Plan (1938-42).

WAR COMMUNISM (June 1918 - March 1921)

War communism will always be remembered for two major economic policies: the first, the nationalization of industry; the second, the forced requisitioning of grain. While one policy impacted industry and the other impacted agriculture, both involved a direct attack on the free market. War communism was extremely disruptive and was difficult to sustain for long periods of time. At heart, it involved a direct challenge to the direction of economic forces. If the government found itself swimming against the current, it also found the current extremely strong. War communism could only be sustained through a huge commitment of resources and a regular reliance on force. Where possible the force used involved the secret police, which was less costly than the army. Where the secret police proved inadequate, the government called in regular army troops.

When the Bolsheviks took power in October 1917, they inherited a work force and business community which had become accustomed to confrontation and disruption. The Bolsheviks themselves had encouraged workers to strike and march. The resulting unrest had contributed to the Czar's decision to abdicate in March 1917. When the Provisional Government took over, they encouraged a rebellious attitude among soldiers. Unjust authority needed to be confronted. While they had liked the idea of worker disruption when it was aimed at the Czar and the Provisional Government, they were less pleased when it was directed at them. Worker confrontation with the government began sooner than even they could have expected. The Winter Palace fell on October 26, 1917 and private banks began to close that day. The government workers union in Petrograd called for a work stoppage on October 29 to protest the Bolshevik action. Then telegraph and telegraph workers walked out in Petrograd and other cities. By November 7, pharmacists, water transport workers, and even schoolteachers had struck.

The Bolsheviks, through the Council of People's Commissars (Sovnarkom, the temporary governmental organization decreed by the Bolsheviks on October 26) on October 30, ordered the banks to reopen. Some did. However, getting the banks to open their doors was one thing, getting them to cash Sovnarkom checks was another. Even the State Bank joined the opposition in refusing to cash checks. The Commissar of Finance, V. R. Menzhinskii, tried to intimidate officials by personally leading a contingent of troops into the Bank's building on November 7 and 11. (Officials may have been less than impressed on November 7 because the troops consisted of armed sailors and a military band.) Not only did bank officials defy the new Commissar, State Bank employees voted to continue their participation in the government strike on November 14. The vote and the resulting walk-out of employees may have helped the Bolsheviks. On November 17, Menzhinskii tried again. With the Bank virtually empty he and his armed contingent forced Bank officers to open the vaults. He took what cash was on hand - around 5 million rubles - and personally delivered it to Lenin, carried in a sack.

The revolt among the normally conservative banks was only part of the problem. (Ironically, it was the banking revolt and not an aroused populace which was the reason for the establishment of the Cheka, the security police, in December 1917.) The other major headache for Lenin was the government, or more specifically, the government employees. Not only were the employees of the various government agencies, such as Foreign Affairs and Justice engaged in work stoppages, the general service agencies, with their municipal workers, went on strike. The goal of this quiet revolt was to pressure the Bolsheviks to move toward democratic government. The expectation among many workers was that their actions would paralyze the government and force some accommodation, just as the workers in 1905 had done. The difference was that the Czar had been more receptive to compromise. Lenin was not.

Perhaps a major difference was that the Czar and his ministers, in contrast to Lenin, were not totally immune to what was perceived to be the "public" opinion of Russians. The deaths of 200 workers on Bloody Sunday (January 9, 1905) could have been ignored if the Czar had decided to act in a more ruthless manner. One circumstance perhaps worked in Lenin's favor. The Czar, with hundreds of years of tradition behind his authority and power - had presented a single target for opposition groups - and a rallying cry for workers. The Bolsheviks, with as yet no recognized claim to power, were too new to provide a clear target and no cause around which an opposition could rally. More critical however was Lenin's single-minded determination and ruthlessness. He had few qualms about the use of force.

Between November and January 1918 Lenin acted to bring the governmental strike to an end. Force and physical coercion were major ingredients in his success, but these factors were not all that was involved. Success came from the use of a carrot and stick policy - force combined with appeals to ambition. Strategically, Lenin's forces won by taking over all the agencies in revolt. While they physically occupied buildings and dismissed uncooperative workers, they also promised (and gave) promotions to those in lower positions if they would continue to work.

Despite Lenin's actions, the strike did not come to an immediate end. No doubt many workers still believed that the strike would have an impact on policy. Lenin's leadership would, like the Czar's, be sensitive to public opinion, the Bolshevik government would collapse, and the strike would be all the pressure that was needed. They received a rude awakening on January 5, when Lenin ordered troops to fire on the demonstrators in Petrograd. This was almost immediately followed by the dissolving of the Constituent Assembly on January 6. It was these decisive actions which finally brought the strike to an end. Workers began returning to their jobs. Apart from the actions of the Bolsheviks, what caused the strike to lose steam was the lack of any public response. The Czar in 1905 had sensed some form of general outrage over the killings. This time public outrage was absent.

The first few months of the new regime were an indication of future Bolshevik labor policy. Workers, in the future, would not receive preferential treatment. The deep-seated philosophical concerns over worker well-being, when the Bolsheviks were fighting the capitalist factory-owners, disappeared when the Bolsheviks themselves came to power and needed work done. Labor relations were only one aspect of the industrial side of the economy. The Bolsheviks also had to decide on a policy toward business owners as well. Business policy, by necessity, involves a number of related issues - everything from taxation to surcharges for transporting goods on government railroads. The most radical or far-reaching decree was that of June 28, 1918, which called for the nationalization of industry.

In retrospect, nationalization seems to be an inevitable result of the Bolshevik takeover. That conclusion seems justified, particularly in view of the philosophical antagonism toward business, supported by the later actions of Stalin. Pipes argues however that, while Lenin would have exercised greater government control, he did not intend to completely take over all private businesses.[13] According to Pipes, Lenin received pressure from the more extreme factions within the Bolshevik party to clamp down on business. In one sense, his opponents had a point. Where he had once used the Factory Committees to sow discord and create dissatisfaction with the Provisional Government, he now proposed that they be dissolved and factories be returned to professional management. What he proposed was almost bourgeois and a return to the status quo for business operations.[14]

The Bolshevik factions which favored worker control at the factory level seemingly had communist theory on their side. Yet their opposition to the return of "capitalist" factory managers was not entirely due to ideology. Party officials, appointed to head the Factory Committees, were now afraid of losing their jobs. Power, even at the factory level, held temptations few could resist once they had experienced it. (One irony of the industrial situation was that, while the Bolsheviks railed against the evils of capitalist management, they kept many of the managers on to actually run the factories. Many were in awe of the capabilities of factory managers. The minor Party officials, though nominally in power at the factory level, lacked the experience necessary to operate the production line and had to rely on the managers they despised.) In his efforts to bring down the Provisional Government Lenin had unintentionally created a bureaucratic structure at the factory level. Communist managers, like their capitalist counterparts, were not only subject to office politics, but were interested in using those politics to promote their own interests. Lenin's opposition however, was not limited to lesser officials. There were 'true believers' among the Bolsheviks who felt that communist theory, carried to its logical conclusion, did call for the elimination of the private capitalist. Chief among the proponents of this philosophy was Iurii Larin.

Larin was not the only "left theoretician," but the article he wrote in April 1918 came at an opportune time for Lenin's opponents. On March 3, 1918, Russia had agreed to the terms of the Brest-Litovsk Treaty, which ended hostilities with Germany. Agreeing to the treaty may have saved Russia from German armies but it had cost Lenin political capital and not just in Moscow. Many Party members were not pleased with the treaty. Following the signing of the treaty, votes in the soviets went against the Bolsheviks. There were accusations that Lenin was compromising with German industrialists. If not total surrender to capitalism or outright betrayal of communist beliefs, it was an unprincipled compromise. Perhaps he was not as committed to the Revolution as believed - at least that was the argument that worried Lenin. To prove his commitment, Lenin felt compelled to retreat on his economic program. If nationalization of industry was the heart of the Left program, he would now support it, if only to prove his loyalty.

The battle over economic policy was largely over by the middle of the spring of 1918, but any new policy would not be implemented until June. The decree of June 28, 1918 initially was aimed at the nationalization of larger enterprises - those having capital greater than 1 million rubles (or those set up as corporations or partnerships.) It was intended to formalize what was already taking place. By the time of the decree local officials had already nationalized some 487 factories.

The important thing to local Party leaders was to put communist theory into practice immediately - at least as they understood the theory. Unfortunately they had given little thought to actually running the factories or industries they were taking over. What exactly did that theory say about takeovers or about day-to-day management? The assumption was that factories were to be run by the "Factory Committees" which were set up. Lenin may have had more than a few doubts about the workability of such an arrangement. If the nationalization decree sanctioned the takeover of industry, it also required the now-former managers to stay on the job. Forcing the former managers to remain was a concession that Bolshevism had no revolutionary answer to the problems of running a factory. The titles of those in charge may have changed, but the management system was not that different than its capitalist counterpart.

In a little over a year, the number of nationalized enterprises had increased to 3,300. Yet, while that was the figure given in September 1919, it was a deceptive statistic. Of the 3,300, there were only 1,375 which were actually viable. Shortages of supplies and serious transport problems had led to a decline in operations.[15]

In 1919 the Soviet economy was in total disarray. The problems did not cause a re-thinking of Bolshevik economic policy. The response instead, was to push even harder for nationalization, although there was one concession which even the Left communists were willing to make. Small industrial enterprises were to be left alone. At least that was what was said publicly. That sentiment was even enacted into law by the decree of April 26, 1919. Enterprises with five or fewer employees were not to be nationalized. In practice the decree was ignored and even businesses with a single employee were taken over. By August 1920 an estimated 37,000 enterprises had been nationalized, including 5,000 which only employed one worker.[16] On November 1, the Supreme Council (VSNKh) would only claim "active" management of around 4,500.[17] That month it was decided to formally extend nationalization to small enterprises. Ironically the decree came just on the eve of a retreat from the policy. That specific decree was reversed on May 17, 1921.

When Lenin proposed, in March 1921, the economic changes heralding the arrival of NEP, he was primarily concerned with agriculture. He once again had to retreat before political pressure. The May 17 decree lifting small-enterprise nationalization was one of the first concessions. It was followed on July 7 by a decree encouraging individuals to organize new businesses. While these decrees represented major policy changes, the Party did not repudiate completely the idea of government ownership. In many cases, it reached a partial accommodation with the private sector by holding onto legal ownership of an enterprise, but leasing it back to new or former owners. Although compromise with the market was possible in the case of small to medium-sized enterprises, Lenin now stood firm with respect to large-scale businesses. The state would not relinquish control of major mining and factory operations.

The immediate cause of Lenin's policy reversal was peasant unrest. Peasant resistance during 1920 and 1921 was not confined to a single area or limited to a few small riots. The extent of the problem can be seen in the casualty figures for the Red Army in its campaign against the peasants. The army suffered 237,908 casualties, according to Pipes.[18] The unrest contributed to shortages of food in the cities. Yet, food shortages were only one of the economic problems confronting the government. There were also shortages of fuel caused, in part, by the breakdown of the transport system. In Petrograd the shortage was so severe that wooden houses were destroyed so their wood could be used for fuel. In addition, the shortages, of both fuel and material, led to factory closures.

Whether Lenin had planned to totally change economic policy at the time of his speech in March 1921, the positive results encouraged, or forced, him to adopt the other changes. The relinquishment of government control over small businesses was only one change. In those enterprises which the government still controlled, he instituted a policy almost identical to capitalist operations - state operations were to adopt business accounting methods and were required to be profitable enough to pay their own way. Those managers who failed to comply found that they could lose their jobs - Lenin was willing to lease unprofitable government businesses to their former owners. Just as significantly, Lenin overhauled the state fiscal system. The State Bank (Gosbank) was created in October 1921 and one of its first assignments was to stabilize the currency. Lenin may not have liked foreign capitalists, but he recognized the importance of attracting foreign investment. A related policy change was the requirement that the state move toward a balanced budget.

In moving back toward a market-oriented economy Lenin had some help from the Left Communists. They had discredited themselves by the policies they adopted. Lenin, after allowing them to experiment, regained the political initiative. Whether those policies had been the only reason for the economic problems of 1920 and 1921, the failures and the policies were closely linked in people's minds. Whether the policies were actually based on Marxist theory, they seemed to fit the anti-capitalist "spirit" of communist thought. One problem was that Larin and the other Left Communists who implemented the program had little experience in economics. The result was that some of the most outrageous proposals were actually put into practice. Perhaps the most extreme was the idea of a moneyless economy.

The Bolsheviks did not decree that money was no longer to be used as a medium of exchange, but they came close. In March 1919 the Party stated as one of its objectives the abolition of money. The idea never got beyond the proposal stage, despite repeated attempts. In spite of these setbacks, the Left implemented policies which minimized the use of money. Government institutions were the first to benefit, in October 1921, when they were offered free use of telephone, telegraph and postal services. The policy was extended to all citizens the next year. Transportation and municipal services were also provided for free. Part of the reason may have been that workers were paid in kind. Those who lived in government-owned housing did not have to pay rent. (The downside for tenants was that the government didn't spend money making repairs either.)

For business enterprises, the idea of a moneyless economy might have had a certain appeal. Since businesses were not charged for materials or services obtained from other enterprises, their recorded costs were zero. The other side of the coin was that they had to provide their own goods or services for free. While they thus appeared to have no expenses, they also received no income. Rudimentary bookkeeping was done to track the various inflows and outflows. By instituting a moneyless society, Bolshevik theorists assumed that they could mitigate what they considered the worst aspects of the money-oriented economies of the West. Money requirements served as a barrier to those who were poor. Even without money, the poor should be able to obtain food and basic services, or so the argument went.

The problems caused by a lack of money are an unfortunate, (even bad) aspect of money's function in any society. However, the societal need for money, was not based, even in ancient societies, simply on the need to separate the rich from the poor. In a general economic sense, it has been needed to provide an accurate measure of the value of an economic unit. There was a flaw in the logic. Since the proposed solution involved eliminating both the good and bad aspects of money, (and eliminating money altogether had that effect), they needed to come up with alternatives to replace the useful (or good) functions, such as the measurement of economic value. They offered solutions, such as labor units. Unfortunately, labor units did not represent an alternative to money, just an alternative name for it. In the end, they were forced to concede that, if economic value must be measured, money is the most efficient means of accomplishing that goal.

The idea that eliminating money would solve a great many economic problems was only one of the ideas which proved false when actually tested. Another idea was that the evils of the market could be partially eliminated by controlling the banks. A related idea was that the banking function could be captured by simply taking over a bank. Western financiers and bankers were believed to be part of a "conspiracy" which effectively controlled the world's markets. The Bolsheviks moved relatively quickly to nationalize the banks - the job was complete by the spring of 1918. The Party took an additional step and liquidated bank assets. Only the People's Bank (formerly the State Bank) remained. Although it was believed that banks possessed unlimited wealth, the cash, securities, and gold bullion were far below expectations. It was also discovered that the economic function and value of banking was not in the liquid assets held. The banking "function" involved the banking system's ability to both provide funds and to continually generate revenue through lending. A practical result of the bank takeover and liquidation was not an increase in government coffers, but an inability to obtain loans. The repudiation of foreign debt, which accompanied the bank nationalization, caused foreign investment to decline.

While Lenin did not return the banks to private ownership under NEP, he did resurrect the State Bank in October 1921. His decision was part of an overall plan to stabilize the ruble. Thinking that the private banks were the implacable foe of communism, he found that his own People's Bank was not much more inclined to be helpful. Banking and finance were completely foreign to most of Lenin's associates. In May 1919, both the people in charge of the People's Bank as well as Party officials thought that they had found a new solution to the country's economic problems. Rather than trying to eliminate money, they decided to print as much of it as they could. Like the idea of a moneyless economy, this idea was dashed by economic reality. The amount of money in circulation went from 61.3 billion rubles in January 1919 to 2.3 trillion rubles by June 1921. Inflation accompanied, (or followed), the increased money supply. By October 1919, prices were 923 times higher than their 1913 level. The only seeming advantage was that payments to the peasants for grain were in currency that was virtually worthless.[19] Lenin recognized that, in addition to alienating the peasants, already angry over the forced requisitions, the Bolshevik government could not sustain itself with such irresponsible policies.

VSNKh AND THE 'TRUST' SYSTEM

The nationalization decree of June 28, 1918 had been issued by the Council of People's Commissars (Sovnarkom), but the administration of the newly nationalized firms was to be done by the Supreme Economic Council or Supreme Council of the National Economy (VSNKh or Vesenkha), which was part of Sovnarkom. VSNKh, like the Party, had its regional subdivisions, the local Councils of the National Economy (SNKh) or Sovnarkhozy. Where the local soviets were concerned with general political matters, the Sovnarkhozy focused on economic matters. The Sovnarkhozy, along with the local Soviets, had been responsible for the factory "nationalizations" which occurred prior to the decree of June 28, 1918. Despite the seemingly narrow economic focus of the SNKh, their number was not inconsequential - in 1920 there were almost 1,400.[20]

In attempting to organize its operations, Vesenkha assigned the newly nationalized enterprises to departments or divisions, or 'trusts,' known as *glavki*, based on the type of production the firm had specialized in. Each *glavki* focused on the production, (and production needs), of its particular industry. There were departments worried about timber, paint, oil, and textiles. Even seemingly small industries, such as matches and soap, received their own departments. Initially there were only 18 departments. The number had increased to 42 by December 1920.[21]

Such a system made sense from the perspective of specialization. Managers could gain experience and concentrate on the specific needs of a particular type of industry. A major defect was that it allowed for too much politics in the decision-making process. Apart from the political impact of the Bolshevik involvement, there were the more mundane office politics involved. It was too easy for the Party comrade who wielded personal power to persuade others that his particular department was deserving of more resources. Without the reality which market forces brought to the decision process, the head of a particular department could focus on making his own industry sector look good at the expense of other sectors.

Another problem was that the system involved duplication and waste. Each *glavki* was somewhat self-contained. For example, the department which produced matches required its own suppliers and its own machinery for every stage of production, from timber cutting to final output. Rather than buying wood from a general supplier, who could also service the timber or paper industries, the match agency got its own supplier. A department benefitted if its own agents showed initiative and obtained quality supplies, but other agencies and the economy as a whole suffered because the various departments were not out to help competing agencies. The difficulties of supply caused the staff to turn to the market to obtain materials which could not be supplied by the other departments.

The idea of the trust continued beyond the end of War Communism. The number of trust departments actually grew - it was 430 in 1922.[22] After mid-1921 however, the policy goals and administrative structure changed. Lenin emphasized fiscal responsibility, profitability and the idea that enterprises were to pay their own way. The policy change got results, but it might have been better planned. Combined with Lenin's tighter budgetary controls, the new policy forced enterprises to both cut costs and to increase sales. They bought supplies from private suppliers where cheaper or if the private suppliers had materials unavailable from other trust members. Trusts sold assets to raise cash. So desperate were the individual businesses that they even resorted to street sales in the bazaars. The budget-cutting also led to unemployment, as the various enterprises cut their staff. The changes were overdue, since many of the enterprises had been little more than make-work projects. The combined staff of the VSNKh and the SNKh was an illustration of how much excess there could be. In 1920, it was around 25,000 people.[23]

Lenin's new policy brought an overall restructuring of the trust system. While the change took place in 1922, after the end of War Communism, it illustrates how Vesenkha had been structured during between 1918 and 1921. In 1922 the 430 trust departments were divided between national and regional control, i.e., between the VSNKh and the SNKh. The majority of trusts, some 258 were administered by the SNKh, while 172 were still controlled by the VSNKh in Moscow.[24]

COMPULSORY LABOR UNDER WAR COMMUNISM

Lenin in 1918 had moved quickly to put down labor unrest. Earlier, he supported the various factory committees when they served to undermine the Provisional Government. When their existence threatened his government, his policy changed however. The factory committees, for their labor agitation, seemed to be a source only of problems for whatever regime was in power. Yet, that charge is somewhat unfair. There were dedicated leaders who, while seeming to be single-minded in their demands for higher wages, also fought for increased factory productivity. Leaders of the factory committees sometimes took on management roles. Their workers did not get paid if they did not work, which many conceded to the system. However, where factory committee members felt that the lack of work was caused by management failures, they tried to take on or take over management duties. For example, when scarcity prevailed, factories closed due to fuel or raw material shortages. At times, the shortages could not be helped. At other times, the workers felt that management was not particularly interested in solving the problem and could do more. In such situations the factory committees began to take an interest in running the factories themselves.

A discussion of the factory committees and worker initiative may seem out of place, particularly when much of it happened prior to the October Revolution. It is intended to provide a backdrop for a discussion of one of the more bizarre or stranger ideas to come out of War Communism. During a period when shortages caused unemployment among a willing labor force, Lenin and Trotsky endorsed the idea of forced labor. On October 29, 1918 a decree was passed intended to set up the organizational structure for managing a force of workers. This was followed on December 10 by the enactment of a "Labor Code" which required some form of labor service. Those who were not already working had to sign up for service. These enactments were a civilian version of the military draft.

Officials acted quickly to use the new laws, calling up railroad workers in November 1918. Normally workers, particularly professionals, were called up to work in their particular professional specialty. A significant aspect of the policy was that those who refused to comply were subject to military court-martial. Trotsky came up with an alternative policy in December 1919. He wanted to use military personnel to perform civilian jobs. He managed to persuade Lenin that the policy was workable and many army units had been shifted to construction and transport by 1921. Trotsky wanted to continue the system even as the Civil War was coming to an end. At the Ninth Party Congress, which was held in March 1920, he urged its continued use as part of an ongoing economic policy. It was not out of character for a regime which had forbidden workers from striking, but Trotsky had trouble convincing the delegates, with the end of the War in sight, that as a non-emergency measure it was necessary.

The forced labor policy of 1918 provides a partial picture of the labor situation during the period of the Civil War. At the same time there was a contradictory set of circumstances between the government labor policy and the labor situation in 1918. While authorities wanted legislation requiring labor service in October 1918, the labor market in July had been so poor that there were 1.5 million registered unemployed at that time. The incongruity can be partially explained by the fact that many of the unemployed were unskilled workers, who were the first to be laid off. In addition, the shortage of supplies had led to factory closures and a loss of wages while a shortage of food had led to an exodus of workers from cities and towns to the countryside where food and work could be obtained. Although all able-bodied between 16 and 50 could be called up, the workers most likely to be called for service had special skills or were employed in crucial sectors, such as defense. Thus medical personnel, workers in the water transport sector, coal miners, metalworkers, and electricians received compulsory work orders between

1918 and 1920.

The end of the Civil War brought a calmer analysis of the economic necessity of compulsory labor. Most had concluded by late in 1921 that it was not a very efficient utilization of the labor force. The military work units which Trotsky had pushed for were found to be inefficient, although their work mostly involved construction or transport. He tried to argue that forced labor was a necessary part of a long-term communist plan. His argument that Red Army units were well-suited for civilian projects was no doubt undercut by the fact that he was Commissar of War at the time, as interested in finding work for himself as in furthering the goals of the Revolution. He was discredited. On October 12, 1921 the Party decreed the end of compulsory labor for the civilian sector. In November the use of army units for civilian labor was also ended.

GENERAL ECONOMIC CONDITIONS UNDER WAR COMMUNISM

War Communism could be defined by five major characteristics: 1) the nationalization of industry; 2) the organization of industry into trusts or syndicates; 3) the suppression of strikes and the elimination of labor unions; 4) the introduction of compulsory labor; and 5) in the agricultural sector, the forced requisitioning of food reserves. War Communism was noted, more generally, as a period of economic difficulty for both peasants and workers. The historical debate has centered on the specific cause-and-effect relationship between conditions and communist policy. Were economic problems caused by the Civil War the reason for War Communism or was War Communism to blame for the economic conditions during the Civil War? Lenin would claim that the Civil War had forced the communists to adopt many of the policies of War Communism. (Most authors view Lenin's later explanations as an attempt to deflect criticism for bad policy decisions.)

Tied to the debate about the policy are questions involving the decision to bring it to an end. Did Lenin end War Communism because he was convinced the policies had been wrong or did he recognize that the state lacked the will and political resources to remain such extensive controls? The Russian economy in March 1921 was a shambles and Lenin probably had doubts about the government's ability to deal with growing peasant dissatisfaction. Indications are that he intended no policy change up to that time. Did he feel that privatization was needed to revitalize the economy? Prior to the peasant revolts, he would not concede the economy to the private sector. When he did retreat, his primary goal appears not to have been to return the economy to its natural free-market state, but to salvage enough of the economy to keep the Revolution alive.[25]

An almost continuous theme in the Russian economy during the period of the Civil War was a shortage of food, made worse by other shortages. The severity of the food and fuel shortages in Petrograd in January and February 1921 were the major cause of the Kronstadt revolt. Industrial workers there had to get by on food rations which provided only 1,000 calories per day.[26] Those living in the cities not only had to contend with food and fuel shortages, but also factory shutdowns and unemployment. In February 1917, a shortage of fuel had prevented bakeries from baking bread and had idled factories in

Petrograd. Marches and rioting by the unemployed had led to the abdication of the Czar. While Lenin moved relatively quickly to consolidate power, fuel shortages in May 1918 led to unemployment, (as high as 87 percent in Petrograd) which, combined with food shortages, resulted in strikes, riots, and violent confrontations with the government. The new communist government may have been partly saved during the winter of 1917-18 by the fact that many workers left the city to seek work and food in the countryside. During the winter of 1918-19 the cities were fed, although forced requisitioning was involved. The communists managed to procure more grain than the prior winter. Again the situation was eased somewhat by the fact that many city-dwellers left for the country.

In 1919 and 1920, the government's experiments at doing away with money were put into practice, so far as possible. Workers were no longer paid in wages. Municipal services were free in major cities. While the government sought to help its citizens with free services, it was uncertain what to do about industrial production, which fell. In spite of efforts to increase production, there was a shortage of consumer goods. One of the problems was that the workers needed to run the factories were no longer in the cities. The number of workers in 1920 had dropped to under half of its 1917 level. There were 1.2 million workers in 1920, while before the revolution, in 1917, there had been 2.6 million.[27]

The communists, by December 1920, were almost successful at creating a moneyless economy, but not in the way they had intended. Inflation was doing for them what they thought could only be done by decree. Prices were some 16,800 times the level they had been in 1914.[28] Accompanying the inflation were severe shortages during the winter of 1920-21 in the large cities, which led once again to an exodus from the cities. The government did not help matters with its fiscal policies. While the Party advocated a moneyless economy, many communists were clearly fascinated by the phenomenon of being able to pay for expenditures by printing money. The inflation which was the result of shortages was not cured by this practice. By June 1921, the supply of money had reached 2.3 trillion rubles, compared to the 61.3 billion of 1919.[29] While the policies which accompanied NEP after March 1921 would eventually bring the inflation rate to more reasonable levels, prices continued to rise during 1922 and 1923.

Lenin's concession on the agricultural tax in March 1921 marks the end of War Communism. The agricultural economy, while free now of government pressure, was devastated by the famine which followed. The industrial sector began slowly to recover. The conservative fiscal measures which Lenin would adopt also aided economic recovery. The privatization of industry also contributed to recovery under NEP. The next chapter looks at the Soviet economy under NEP. While NEP represented a major policy change from War Communism, it was only allowed to operate for some four years. It did not abruptly end on a certain date. In fact, it would not be officially reversed until 1930. However, it did not survive in any meaningful form after 1926.

CHAPTER 16

THE NEW ECONOMIC POLICY AND THE FIVE-YEAR PLANS

This chapter looks at two time periods during which two separate policies were pursued: the first, the New Economic Policy (NEP), which was in effect from March 1921 until roughly 1928; the second, the five-year plans, which represented the major economic policy between 1928 and 1942.

THE RISE AND FALL OF NEP (1921-1928)

NEP did not begin as a comprehensive plan to overhaul the Russian economy. In that regard, it was a contrast to such later ideas as Stalin's First Five-Year Plan, which involved a great deal of deliberation. Lenin did not even call his policy change a New Economic Policy when it was put into effect. The policy got the label NEP sometime in December 1921. It started with a change in the agricultural tax. While that concession may seem small, it let loose more political pressure than the government could control. The easing of government restrictions on the peasants was soon extended to industry. NEP revitalized the economy and brought renewed growth. Unfortunately, NEP represented a challenge to the government and it was doomed as an economic policy once the decision was made to push for industrialization. It was a slow death. The government, in 1926, would not so much decree NEP at an end, it simply demanded a greater share of the economic resources. NEP was squeezed out of existence.

While the government may have eased economic restrictions during NEP, it was not prepared for a political conversion to Western democratic practices. In fact, it added more concentration camps. At the end of 1920, there were only 84 camps. The number grew to 315 by October 1923. Nor was the government overly concerned about the prisoners' well-being. The number of reported deaths in the camps was 18,350 in 1925.[1]

NEP began on March 15, 1921, when Lenin got the Politburo to vote for a change in the method of taxing peasants. The vote was taken on March 15, while the policy was announced on March 23. The vote had less to do with fiscal reform than it did with the need to make concessions to the peasant, and the workers in the cities. The government policy of forcibly taking grain, called *prodrazvërstka*, had driven the peasants to open revolt. In western Siberia, the government needed 50,000 regular army troops to put down the revolt in February 1921.[2] There was also a sense that the uprising at the Kronstadt, which occurred in February, was fueled by peasant grievances learned from peasant relatives in the villages. The forcible takings had also been partly responsible for food shortages in the cities. The peasants had either hidden grain or reduced the amount of acreage sown. While confiscation could be effective on an emergency basis, as a long-term measure it was an inefficient method of bringing goods to market. Resources either had to be concentrated on administration, in the form of additional staff, or on armed force, in the form of additional army units or police forces.

In place of the *prodrazvërstka*, Lenin wanted a tax in kind, the *prodnalog*. Along with the change in taxation method, Lenin proposed that peasants be allowed to sell whatever surplus left over on the open market. In some ways it is difficult to tell the difference between the old tax and the new, for there was a good deal of coercion involved in both. The central government, through the Commissariat of Supply, still determined the total amount of grain and other foodstuffs the peasants were required to produce. It changed the method of administering the tax somewhat. Administration was transferred to the local soviet and the tax was determined based on individual peasant households. Under the grain requisitioning system of War Communism, the villages had been collectively responsible to the districts, which were, in turn, responsible to the provinces. With that administrative structure, managers could be as hard or as lenient on individual peasant households as they chose.

What may have been of most benefit to the peasant was the method of calculating the tax. Under the old system, the Commissariat of Supply used total consumer demand to determine how much grain was needed in any year. That base included both city-dwellers and members of the armed forces. The new system reduced the "consumer base" by factoring out the number of city dwellers when calculating demand. Demand for foodstuffs was now reduced to the minimal needs of the Army and the needs of industrial workers, along with some nonagricultural groups.[3]

Perhaps as important for the peasant was the change in attitude toward collection of the tax. The old system had encouraged a short-term focus on numbers - collect more grain, whatever the cost. Provincial officials had continually been pressured from Moscow to increase collections. They, in turn, pressured districts, which themselves pressured villages to increase grain confiscation. To be sure, the new system did not have any more safeguards to prevent upper management from pressuring lower management and staff. However, the new system, by providing for a more systematic calculation and lower overall goals, gave lower officials more guidance and served as a signal to higher officials that government policy had changed.

If the government seemed willing to ease the peasant's burden, nature proved unrelenting. Drought led to crop failures and famine in the summer of 1921. Lenin's announcement however changed the political climate in two ways. First, it convinced the peasants that the government would now leave them alone and they began to lose interest in revolt. Second, the policy change weakened the Party's justification for total economic control. In one sense, the public concession to the peasantry was really just a symptom of an underlying weakness. The Bolsheviks, though they could intimidate whole villages with army and police units, were still reliant, almost fatally reliant, on agricultural production for political survival.

The political problem was that the cities were suffering from food shortages. While grain might not go to the government, it would at least help to relieve the shortages there. The government was thus interested in trade, even free trade, if it meant that more grain was put on the market. If increasing the availability of grain would further one goal - easing the plight of the cities - access to the market was only one aspect of that problem. Lenin realized that it was not just access the peasants wanted, but more manufactured goods. The assumption was that the peasants would sell grain if they had something to buy. As a result, any policy which furthered the flow of goods from the factory to the village was to be encouraged. A major problem was that few manufactured goods were available and production was inadequate. It was recognized that so long as government control remained, goods production was likely to continue to fall short. Within two months of Lenin's March speech, small enterprises were returned to private hands. The nationalization decree which applied to small enterprises was formally reversed on May 17, 1921. This was followed on July 5, by a decree which allowed the VSNKh to lease enterprises to their former or new owners. The Party also tried to encourage the formation of new businesses with a decree of July 7 which legalized private ownership of small enterprises (under 20 workers).

NEP DURING 1923 - RECOVERY, CRISIS AND ECONOMIC STABILIZATION

The sudden turn to privatization in 1921 caused severe economic turmoil during 1922. The state trusts, forced to operate on a cash basis, had to begin laying off workers. (Even the secret police were not immune. The OGPU had trimmed 38,000 staff members from its payrolls by May 1922, leaving a force of 105,000 people.)[4] Many of the layoffs were justified, in terms of production. The Bolshevik policy of not requiring state-owned enterprises to pay for materials or labor, had encouraged the hiring of large numbers of unnecessary, if not unqualified, workers. These workers were among the first to be hit, but they were not the only workers unemployed. The unemployment came amid conflicting economic signals. On the one hand, there was a strong demand for manufactured goods, which contributed to a steadily increasing inflation rate. On the other hand, the inflated cost of goods made them hard to sell, which somewhat weakened the market. Workers, dependent on strong markets for employment, found that there was less work. Workers themselves were in no position to contribute to market demand. Not only had the labor force declined in numbers, but the wages paid workers had dropped as well. The total number of workers in 1921-22 was only 6.5 million, compared to the 1913 figure of 11 million. In 1922 the real value of wages the typical worker earned was less than 40 percent of its 1913 level.[5]

The weakened markets were one factor in the growing problem of unemployment. Just before the First World War, it is estimated that unemployment may have been around 500,000, out of a total work force of around 11 million.[6] With the cost-cutting measures and the general decline in demand during 1922 and 1923, unemployment at the end of 1923 was 1.24 million, when the total work force was around 7 million. With an improving economy in 1924, unemployment was down to 950,000.[7] If these figures suggest serious problems, they might be viewed in a wider context. While part of the unemployment figures can be attributed to weak markets and problems at the factory, another factor was the migration of large numbers of able-bodied from the villages.

314

People were leaving for the cities at the rate of 300,000 per year in 1923.[8] Industry may have been having its problems but there were increasing opportunities which villagers found attractive.

As if unemployment were not enough of a problem, the Party had to deal with another economic "crisis" in 1923. It came to be known as the scissors crisis. In March 1923 Trotsky gave a speech to the Twelfth Party Congress in which he warned of the problems related to the "scissors." The crisis was related to falling grain collections and the availability of manufactured goods. The scissors was Trotsky's description of prices. To make his point, Trotsky brought a graph with him to the speech. On the graph, Trotsky plotted the increases in prices for industrial products against the drop in prices for agricultural products, using 1913 prices as a starting point. Industrial prices, which had been low relative to agricultural prices in 1913, had been steadily increasing. They intersected in the autumn of 1922, but continued to climb above agricultural prices. As Trotsky pointed out, the graph looked like a pair of scissors. At the time of the speech, March 1923, industrial prices were one-and-a-half times the 1913 prices. Agricultural prices were only three-fourths of their 1913 level.

As an economic phenomenon, the scissors did nothing more than illustrate the increased demand for industrial goods and the relative decline in demand for agricultural products. Agricultural prices were only in decline in relation to industrial prices. Agricultural prices were in fact still increasing. Scarcity was not the only reason for the increase in industrial prices. The new emphasis on profitability had forced government-controlled enterprises to now include costs that they had left out of prices when they had not been required to pay cash. Salary costs for unneeded employees, also had to be passed on to the consumer, at least until layoffs could take effect.

What turned the situation into a crisis was the need for peasant grain and the policy of using market forces, rather than force, to obtain it. What Trotsky feared was that the peasants would no longer sell grain. The Party's policy, under NEP, was to avoid the forced requisitioning of War Communism. The government was instead to rely on market forces to persuade the peasant to give up his grain. While the new fixed tax would bring in some grain, it was hoped that the availability of manufactured goods would serve as the primary incentive. The fear was that, if the price of manufactured goods were not brought down, the peasants would refuse to sell.

The 'crisis' lasted until October 1923, when the cost of manufactured goods finally began to fall relative to agricultural prices. It is difficult to tell whether the crisis was as serious as Trotsky warned. His warnings probably lent support to the cost-cutting campaign and government enterprises were moved to reduce unneeded staff more quickly. Cost reductions would eventually be reflected in prices, but Trotsky's warnings may have pushed the government to act more directly against high prices. New price controls were imposed. The experience of government cooperatives seemed to provide an economic justification for such controls. Goods, even those offered by cooperatives, simply did not sell when the price was too high. What may have been just as effective at reducing prices were the new credit policies imposed by state lending agencies. By refusing to grant additional credit, state enterprises could only come up with cash for operations by reducing prices when goods were offered on the open market. The government benefitted from a more general economic trend - the economy was finally recovering from the effects of the Civil War. Both agriculture and industry were doing better in overall terms.

INFRASTRUCTURE AND THE CREATION OF AN INDUSTRIAL BASE

The same Twelfth Party Congress which listened so attentively to Trotsky's scissors speech did not limit its economic concerns to manufacturing. The delegates were also enchanted with electricity. While there was always a concern about the welfare of the worker, the Party often was fascinated by the possibilities of technology. The result was a resolution encouraging the development of electrical power. It was not that they were wrong. (The West had been quick to see the advantages which electricity could bring.) It was more that they were premature, given the relative backwardness of the Russian economy.

Lenin was one of the true believers when it came to electricity. He had hoped to create a huge power system, using hydroelectric dams, to bring electricity to even remote rural areas. For that purpose the State Commission for the Electrification of Russia (GOELRO) had been created in 1920. Unfortunately, once the costs were calculated, the idea was dropped. The electrification plan was ambitious. The estimate of annual expenditures was one billion rubles (500 million dollars) and the time estimate was 10 to 15 years.[9] Perhaps the major technical difficulty was that any electrification project required high-quality equipment. Russian industry, in the early 1920s, did not have the expertise or facilities to manufacture such equipment, nor did the government did not have the economic resources to make purchases abroad. Grain exports were still the major source of government funds. The change in the agricultural tax system, which came with NEP, cost the government in grain receipts and potential income from foreign grain sales. The other problem was that, with Trotsky's push for improved manufacture to overcome the scissors crisis, the government had to commit resources to improve the manufacturing sector which might otherwise have been used for electrification.

Electrification would have to wait for Stalin's time. Whether totally successful, Stalin went a long way toward achieving Lenin's goals. When completed the Dnieper dam project provided industry with electricity for its expansion. In 1921 Russia produced only 520 million kilowatts of electricity. By 1937, it would be producing some 36.2 billion kilowatts.[10]

Problems in the development of an electrical system were only part of the infrastructure picture. The government also needed to improve transport. Some traffic moved by roads, but there was a heavier reliance on railroads, particularly where industry was concerned. Czarist governments, since the 1860s had committed resources to the development of the railway system. At the same time, the shortcomings became apparent when the First World War broke out. Russia had roughly one-tenth the rail mileage of Germany. Germany's rail system contained 10.6 kilometers of track for each 100 square kilometers of territory compared to only 1.1 for Russia. In addition, the Russian system was hampered by the fact that it had only a single track for 75 percent of its network.[11] It suffered from a shortage of cars, a lack of fuel, and equipment and rolling stock which was deteriorating. Forced to shift industrial production to armaments, the Czarist government had had to try to maintain its rolling stock and locomotives with fewer and fewer spare parts. The Bolsheviks fared little better. In 1919, not only was their equipment in need of repair, but wood for fuel was difficult to obtain - this at a time when the trains were needed to supply food to major cities.

While Lenin may have been publicly worried about peasant revolt in 1921, the government was also trying to deal with another fuel shortage impacting the railways. The lack of repair or replacement of locomotives was so bad that there were serious mechanical problems with over half the stock. The situation had finally become bad enough to force government action and steps were taken to obtain the needed fuel. Replacement stock which could not be manufactured in Russia, was purchased abroad, together with spare parts. The changes were sufficient to allow for an increase in 1922-23 of 59 percent over the previous year of goods traffic.[12] At the same time, traffic remained substantially below that of 1913 in the following year - just over half of the 1913 level. A continued government commitment however allowed railroad traffic to finally overtake the 1913 level by 1926-27.[13]

The transport system, as represented by the railroads, was not the only sector of the Soviet economy to show improvement during the period of NEP. The industrial sector, as a whole, also expanded. The expansion, with growth continuing year after year, surprised the Party planners. The rate of growth for individual sectors was phenomenal. In 1924-25, large-scale industry grew between 53 and 61 percent, while overall growth for industry in 1925-26 was between 34 and 39 percent.[14] In perspective, much of the improvement involved regaining ground lost in the aftermath of the Civil War. Industrial production had taken a major hit in 1920-21, when it fell to 18 percent of its 1913 level.[15] Predictions about 1926-27 industrial production, made in 1923, were that it would still be half of the 1913 level. Actual industrial production in 1926-27 was 104 percent of the 1913 level.[16]

1924-1925 - HIGH NEP AND THE BEGINNING OF THE END

The government's attention to some of the more serious infrastructure problems, particularly those in the railroad industry, no doubt contributed to the industrial recovery and expansion taking place during the mid-1920s. Efforts to deal with the scissors crisis of 1923 represented perhaps the last major active economic intervention of that time period. After the crisis was met, an almost laissez-faire attitude set in. Few committed Bolsheviks were won over to the advantages of a free market, but the government was not inclined to any radical reversal of policy. The liberal policy would last for two years, 1924 and 1925, labeled by some as 'high' NEP.

317

Despite the obvious economic benefits which had accompanied NEP, there were Party members who were convinced that it should be brought to an end. Even if they conceded that it had brought about economic recovery, it was now an obstacle to the creation of a socialist and just society. To allow the private sector to gain the upper hand was to invite all the problems associated with capitalist economies. That was the general philosophical argument. More importantly, the Bolsheviks were now more focused on the need to industrialize. If they conceded that NEP had furthered industrialization, the pace of industrialization was now too slow. When it came down to a choice between the government or the private sector, the government, not the private sector, was in a better position to carry out industrialization. Perhaps NEP survived through 1926, because Party leadership was still divided. Stalin, once his enemies had been eliminated, would be the driving force behind industrialization. He did not have the patience to allow the private sector to create an industrialized society. If he moved quickly to end NEP, he had to concede publicly that it was a popular idea, maintaining in 1929 that it remained in effect.

It is somewhat ironic that, what are considered the two best economic years for NEP, 1924 and 1925, came at times when government tolerance of NEP was coming to an end. The private sector continued to grow, at the expense of the governmental sector, but the first steps were taken to brake that growth in 1924. With one exception, the government did not outlaw trade, but made it more expensive for private traders to operate. (The single exception was the 1,000 Nepmen, small private grain traders, who were charged with 'speculation' in February 1924 and forced to leave Moscow.)

Where the state did not directly confiscate privately produced products, it moved to take private property through higher taxes. It also began to reserve materials for its use or for the use of state cooperatives in late 1925 while officially allowing private traders to buy materials. In 1926 railroads began raising transport rates charged to independent businesses - between 50 and 100 percent, while Nepmen had to pay a super-profits tax after June 18, 1926.[17] The super-profits taxes and the transport charges, though significant, were merely preliminary moves, and largely uncoordinated. The comprehensive scheme would begin to take shape as the Party began formulating its First Five-Year Plan in 1927. The Plan did not change the methods of confiscation, it merely intensified them. Nepmen and kulaks were forced to pay even higher taxes. Where private transport charges had only been 100 percent in 1926, the state raised them as high as 400 percent.[18] While the state tried to increase production of metals, it also enacted measures which further restricted availability. Only state-controlled enterprises could obtain metal supplies.

THE END OF NEP - 1928

The formal end of NEP came in 1928. While it had come to be associated with a liberal industrial policy, the catalyst, as in 1921, was a change in policy on agriculture. Just as the peasants in March 1921 were the first to obtain relief from government policies, so in early 1928 were they the first to suffer under the changed policy. The "grain crisis" which Stalin announced in December 1927, allowed him to bring back the confiscatory measures of War Communism in early 1928. The forced grain requisitions were aimed directly at the peasant. Other measures which accompanied the takings were aimed at the NEP itself. The NEP policy, which relied on market forces to provide the incentive to market goods, was reversed. In its place, a policy of force and threats was used. The markets, where peasants had been allowed to sell their surplus, were ordered closed. Peasants were threatened with prosecution as speculators, if they were found to be hiding grain. Article 107 of the criminal code, passed in 1926, provided for a three-year prison term for those hoarding grain or even refusing to place it on the market.

The concessions Lenin made to the peasants on the agricultural tax in March 1921 led to an easing of economic restrictions in other economic sectors. In 1928, a similar situation developed - in reverse. Economic restrictions first applied to the peasants were expanded to the entire economy. There was a change in the economic climate which favored state control in every facet of economic life. There is one interesting aspect to the end of NEP and it involves speculation about Stalin's role. Just as he is suspected of involvement in the creation of a grain crisis in December 1927, there is a suspicion that he may have also deliberately manipulated the availability of goods in order to provide an excuse to end NEP. What he did was to keep price controls on manufactured goods while refusing to raise the prices paid to peasants for their grain.[19]

In theory, price controls should have meant that consumers, including peasants, could buy goods at reasonable prices. In reality, goods would either be totally unavailable or obtainable only at exorbitantly high prices. It had to do with the distribution system. Private traders bought goods in government cooperatives at lower prices and resold them in the villages - but at prices marked up by 100 or even 200 percent.[20] The result was that more peasant money was going to the private sector. If that situation could be viewed favorably as an example of entrepreneurial capitalism at work, it also worked a hardship on government enterprises. Not only did private traders receive the cash for the mark-ups, but government factories had to absorb costs which could have been recovered with higher prices. Another consequence of price controls was what was called a 'goods famine' which hit in 1925-26. The distribution system favored those with immediate access to goods, i.e., those who lived closest to the factories or outlets. If high prices acted as a brake on consumer demand, lower prices served as an incentive to buy. Private traders as well as consumers in the towns were quick to snap up any goods offered. Consumers, even if they could not use the goods themselves could always resell them. The result was that products which were intended to be provided to rural areas at reasonable prices were not available at all.

The resulting goods famine made grain procurement difficult. Since the market failed to make manufactured goods available, cash did the peasant little good. The government compounded this problem by setting grain prices too low. Even if there were manufactured goods available, the cash which would come from sales to govern-

319

ment agencies was hardly worth the effort.

Stalin, depending on the policy desired, had two arguments he could rely on. If he wanted to eliminate price controls, he could cite the actual results. Price controls, despite good intentions, did not make cheap goods available to peasants. They actually brought shortages and higher prices. If he favored price controls he emphasized the intent of the policy. Price controls were intended to make cheap goods available to the consumer. The government, in enforcing controls, had at least made an effort to accomplish that goal, whatever happened late. He adopted what sounded like the orthodox approach. Lower prices for goods benefitted the consumer; lower grain prices were helpful in keeping the state budget under control. His arguments, as usual, sounded very orthodox, and were sufficient to defeat his then-political opponents. At the same time, the profits made by the private traders, as well as the peasant reluctance to deliver grain, would provide him with the political ammunition needed when he chose to attack both the traders and the peasants.

The measures taken against the peasant in 1928 may have ended NEP, but they did not bring an end to the private sector. That would take another two years. Nevertheless, even in 1928, Stalin had already significantly reduced it. In 1924-25, private trade had been as high as 42.5 percent of all trade within the Soviet Union. By 1928, that percentage had been reduced to 22.5 percent. In 1930 it was reduced further to just 5.6 percent. Without specifically outlawing private trade, the government had used its taxing power and economic monopolies to accomplish much of the task. Stalin finally took measures to outlaw private trade specifically. Private trade, in 1930 was classified as crime, being defined as speculation. It was also made illegal to hire workers for the private sector.[21]

The New Economic Policy and its history can be viewed from several perspectives. In one sense, it was a concession by the Bolsheviks to the strength of the market. The government found that the resources needed to control economic forces were beyond its capabilities. In another sense, NEP was simply a period of recovery from the economic devastation caused by the Civil War. The Bolsheviks agreed to a temporary retreat, so as to regain their strength for a renewed offensive against the market and the evils which accompanied the capitalist system. From still another perspective, it was a time in which consumers were allowed to invest in the private sector rather than the government. The next section deals with the five-year plans. Stalin, having eliminated private trade, took steps to see that it did not rise to the level it reached under NEP. The imposition of economic controls and the loss of economic freedom can be viewed from a purely political perspective. In that sense, Stalin's actions are linked to the political terror and loss of political freedoms associated with dictatorship. In analyzing the five-year plans, it may be helpful to view what took place from an investment perspective as well.

THE FIVE-YEAR PLANS

It might be said of Stalin that his life revolved around a single idea - getting power and keeping it. To the extent that he dealt with lesser ideas, they involved the mechanics of eliminating opposition. His obsession with power involved both the grandiose and the mundane. At one extreme, he had few qualms about using the power provided by the state to have enemies killed. At the other extreme, he took on the most monotonous tasks for the most mundane projects the Bolshevik bureaucracy could dream up. Everyday reports and paperwork seemed his obsession. If there was one grand vision which consumed him, apart from the acquisition of personal power, it was the idea of making the Soviet Union a major industrial and military power. In a sense, it was nothing more than an extension of his ambition for personal power. What greater achievement could there be - to not only be the leader of Russia, but the leader of a Russia which was a major player on the world stage.

Stalin, the practical politician, probably cared little about the success or failure of NEP. Its very existence was an irritation to many Party economic theorists however. He probably cared even less what those 'intellectual' theorists thought. He became fascinated, or obsessed, with one of their ideas however - the idea of industrialization. Industrialization, during the mid-1920s was taking place, but the pace was too slow for Stalin. NEP, to be sure, had been responsible for economic recovery and industrial growth. But it was beginning to be seen as a hindrance.

The idea of a five-year plan did not really originate with Stalin. In February 1921 a newly created body, the State Planning Commission (Gosplan) was instructed to come up with a state economic plan which would include a budget and some means to implement the plan. Gosplan did not have the dictatorial powers needed to exercise any form of central control of the economy. It was nevertheless to develop some form of five-year budget projections for 1925-26. If the Party had entertained notions of using Gosplan to exercise control, they were soon dashed by the concessions made under NEP.

The First Five-Year Plan officially began in October 1928, although it would not be formally adopted by the Sixteenth Party Conference until the following April. The fact that the plan was only adopted after it had begun creates the impression that the government was haphazard and indecisive. In fact, the plan had been over a year in development before the October start. The Council of People's Commissars (Sovnarkom) had decreed, as early as June 8, 1927, that there was to be a plan for economic development of the Soviet Union. In contrast to the five-year plan of 1921, Gosplan was not simply to prepare five-year budgetary figures and economic predictions. It was to be given whatever powers were necessary to carry out the plan.

The push for industrialization can be dated to the June 1927 decree. The Party had long discussed its advantages. In fact there had been drafts of an implementation plan as early as 1925. It may be asked why it finally decided to go ahead in 1927. The answer may lie in developments on the political scene. By June 1927 Stalin had all but eliminated his political opponents. Zinoviev had been removed from the Politburo in July

1926 and Trotsky had been expelled from the Politburo in October. Stalin also had had Kamenev's name taken off the candidate's list as well. While Trotsky and Zinoviev were not ex-pelled from the Party until November 1927, they were both through as politicians in 1926.

There may be a number of reasons why serious industrial planning began in June 1927, depending on whether that date is considered a delay or an early start. If it is considered a late start, then the reason may be that Stalin, and the Party, was pre-occupied with the political struggle. If it can be described as an early start, it is early considering the state of the economy. While the Soviet economy had made a significant recovery from the Civil War, it was not really in a robust state.

Whether the Soviet economy had reached the optimum point for industrialization is an academic question. The results of the First Five-Year Plan suggest that it was at least in a better condition to withstand a crash program than it had been five or six years earlier. Lenin had been forced to abandon his electrification project because the cost was simply too much and government resources too little in 1921. Under the First Five-Year Plan construction would begin on the Dnieper Dam project and the project would be pushed through to completion. Total electrical output would increase from 5.05 billion kilowatts in 1927-28 to 13.4 billion kilowatts by 1932.[22]

The work of developing the figures for the First Five-Year Plan was assigned to the staffs of Gosplan and VSNKh. Actually there were two plans prepared, one with more conservative goals, the "starting point" plan, the other with more ambitious objectives, the "optimal" variant. Perhaps the lessons of War Communism had been learned and the staff were more aware of the dangers of providing political leaders with any figures. The danger for planners was that, while politicians might praise them for a "can-do" spirit when the planners set optimistic goals, the politicians also would damn them later when those goals were not achieved. The planners, with that caution in mind, may have dreaded the actions of the Sixteenth Party Conference in April 1929. The Conference opted for the more ambitious plan. The 'damned if you do, damned if you don't' situation would not allow the planners to escape by providing politicians with an option. Just presenting the less optimistic plan left planners open to the charge of "wrecking" and some received prison sentences.

At the end of the year, they must have been both relieved and alarmed - relieved because the goals had been fulfilled, alarmed because the achievement encouraged many in the Party to call for a revision to the Plan - upwards. On December 1, 1929 a decree was voted which raised the goals for 1929-30. As if that wasn't bad enough, there was pressure to speed up the overall timetable. When the Sixteenth Party Congress met in June 1930, Stalin came up with the slogan "The Five-Year Plan in Four." He was success-ful at moving the timetable for ahead. When the First Five-Year Plan was officially com-pleted, on December 31, 1932, it had only taken four years and three months to accom-plish. Changing the date of completion was relatively easy to accomplish, but Stalin's public pronouncements about having accomplished the goals were untrue. The plan had fallen far short of its economic goals. Few however, were willing to argue with him.

Even as Stalin was addressing the Sixteenth Congress, economic problems were causing a slow-down in growth. The Plan's goals were in jeopardy. The Plan, which relied heavily on foreign expertise and purchases of foreign equipment, was premised on strong economic performance by the Soviet economy during the five years it was to be in effect. There were four assumptions for success. The first was related to agricultural output - there had to be good harvests for all five years. The second was related to raw materials, as well as to agricultural output - there had to be an increase in external trade. The third related to an overall improvement in quality and the fourth, a decrease in the military budget. Unfortunately, the Great Depression depressed prices for all commodities. Even where production was maintained, the government saw a drop in revenue from foreign sales because goods and produce were selling at a lower price.[23]

While Stalin was aware of the difficulties, he would not publicly concede them. He refused to back away from the Plan's budget figures. Perhaps it was his political sense which told him that he needed to maintain administrative pressure on the Party bureaucracy to keep the momentum going. The result was a demand for an increase in the figures. The Sixteenth Party Congress complied and voted to double the Plan's figures.

Stalin's method of dealing with local officials, where the peasantry was concerned, had been to focus on a policy and to continually pressure them to work toward a specific goal. For reinforcement he could also threaten arrest. His methods did not change in dealing with those in charge of industrialization. According to one report, around 7,000 engineers, out of a total of 35,000, had been arrested by the spring of 1931.[24] The Party also put on a show trial of technical specialists in November and December 1930. The eight defendants were accused of being members of the "Industrial Party," whose members were guilty of wrecking and sabotage. After being found guilty, the defendants were sentenced to death, the sentences later being commuted to prison terms. This trial was followed by the "Union Bureau" trial, in March 1931. Fourteen defendants involved in the planning agencies, were accused of trying to hinder industrialization by altering planning figures. They were sentenced to prison following the finding of guilt.

What Stalin felt was needed was total commitment. Motivating managers and workers was only one aspect of that problem. Motivational factors aside, Stalin also needed a monetary commitment. While his main strategy may have been to finance industrialization from the agricultural sector, he was not about to let workers off the hook. Workers, like their peasant counterparts, were forced to invest in the industrialization campaign.

FINANCING THE FIVE-YEAR PLANS

Investment, apart from the agricultural sector, came from two conventional sources - taxes and loans. Workers were required to pay a tax, although it was not a major source of revenue for the government. Workers were also "requested" to buy government bonds. It was turnover taxes, i.e., taxes imposed where there was turnover of goods, which hit workers and consumers the hardest. This was in addition to the taxes imposed on peasants. There was an implied tax in forced procurements, at the village level. The government kept grain prices low, thus sparing the budget from outlays for grain. Government agencies did not pass on these savings to consumers. In fact, the government placed an additional burden on consumers by charging and passing on taxes to the final purchaser. In 1933, for example, the government tax for wheat amounted to 195.5 rubles per centner (commercial weight of about 50 kilograms). The 195.5 ruble cost was the major part of the 216 ruble price the consumer paid.[25]

Where taxes were insufficient to fund industrialization, Stalin was not averse to borrowing. The government raised 200 million rubles in June 1927 by issuing industrialization bonds which paid 12 percent interest.[26] Stalin even turned to Western sources for short-term credits for purchases. For Russia, there was one benefit of the Depression. Western governments were willing to go to great lengths to obtain sales and adopted a liberal credit policy. Nove estimates that Russia had obtained $721 million in credits in 1931.[27] Stalin also resorted to printing more money. Reversing Lenin's conservative fiscal policies, Stalin allowed the money in circulation to increase, from 1.7 billion rubles in January 1928 to 8.4 billion rubles by January 1933.[28]

GENERAL ECONOMIC CONDITIONS DURING THE FIVE-YEAR PLANS

Stalin's obsession with industrialization had one benefit for the average citizen. In spite of continuing unemployment, there was a demand for labor, particularly skilled labor. Managers found that higher wages were a motivating factor for workers. Stalin was inclined to overlook the discrepancy between communist theory and the realities of the market where labor was concerned, if it furthered industrialization.

While the upward pressure on wages benefitted the worker, its long-term effect was to create hardship for the average consumer. With higher wages, workers had more money to spend. Unfortunately, consumer goods production was far behind consumer demand. Stalin's interest in the development of heavy industry meant that government efforts were concentrated on industrial production rather than greater consumer output. The result was inflation coupled with severe shortages of food and consumer goods. To deal with the shortages, the government introduced food rationing in early 1929, beginning with bread. By December 1929, all food was being rationed. Consumer goods also became subject to the rationing system in early 1930.

Shortages led to the growth of a black market. The government tried to suppress it by resorting to the criminal laws regarding speculation. There were continuing attempts to deal with inflation by imposing price controls in 1930. However, the government modified its policy on price controls on October 1, 1930 with a change in tax policy. On that date a turnover tax went into effect. The Party maintained the official line that low prices were important to the average consumer. However, the Party saw a golden opportunity to obtain additional revenue. Rather than suppressing trade, why not use market forces to get workers to provide the investment needed by the government?

The turnover tax was one method of getting consumers to invest. Another method was to set up a separate system of stores which would sell goods to consumers who were willing to pay more then the official prices. While the government had done everything to suppress private trade, in July and October 1929 it placed 16 tons of sugar on the market - at prices well above official prices.[29] In addition to different types of stores, there were different types of pricing systems. The less well off could continue purchasing food or consumer goods with ration cards. Those with more money had a number of stores with goods available at higher prices. Specialty stores even catered to those who had gold or foreign currency. By 1932 the policy had proved so successful that the government established 'commercial' shops to sell consumer goods. While the government was able to tap into the market with its commercial shops, it hardly controlled it. A free market continued to exist outside official channels, with prices even higher than those of the government establishments.

RESULTS OF THE FIRST FIVE-YEAR PLAN

The First Five-Year Plan officially ended on December 31, 1932, although there had been another nine months left according to the original timetable. (The Plan was supposed to end on September 30, 1933.) What were the results of the plan? Perhaps one way of gauging what had been accomplished comes from a story related by Tucker. It seems that one of Russia's leading metallurgical engineers, named Avraam Zaveniagin, was taken to see Stalin in January 1933. (Apparently Stalin did not feel threatened by Zaveniagin or what he said, because he would later offer him as a candidate for the Central Committee.) What Zaveniagin said, however, carried an implied criticism of the results of the First Five-Year Plan, (and the leadership which drove it - Stalin). He was asked by Stalin what was most important for industry. The thrust of what he said was that while the Plan had been successful at creating many new facilities, many did not work or were working at less than full capacity. What was needed now was some way to make the system actually work.[30]

The examples provided by Zaveniagin, which pointed to serious problems, were clearly at odds with the results implied by the official statistics. Stalin, whatever his public proclamations, was aware that there were serious deficiencies in the program. While touting accomplishments was a helpful way to focus the bureaucracy and to motivate staff and officials, to overlook problems was unrealistic. Politically, Stalin also recognized that, if an engineer was not only seeing problems, but was openly discussing them (if only in the privacy of Stalin's office), his political opponents were capable of the same analysis. It might be prudent to retreat. In speaking before the Central Committee that January, he sounded a more conciliatory tone. In the resulting resolution adopted by the plenum of the Central Committee, the goal for the Second Five-Year Plan was to make the facilities constructed during the first five years operational. As if to reinforce his new tone, he agreed to a reduction of the projections for industrial growth, down to 13-14 percent.

325

The story of Zaveniagin's meeting with Stalin, and Stalin's subsequent actions, suggest that the First Five-Year Plan was almost a total failure. There is little question that it fell short in many areas. Metal production was well below the planned figures at the end of 1932. Despite its shortcomings, the Plan had allowed the Soviet Union to make significant strides toward the goal of industrialization. Russia was not as dependent on foreign manufacture as before. Foreign equipment purchases, required because the Soviet Union lacked its own production facilities, had taken huge outlays of cash. Between 1928 and 1933, some 1.5 billion rubles were spent on foreign purchases of heavy industrial equipment.[31]

While many of the industries, even in 1933, were still in their infancy, development was far ahead of where it had been before the start of the plan. The creation of three industries would prove particularly important for future years: armaments, agricultural machinery, and motor-vehicles. There was no combine-harvester production at all in the Soviet Union before 1931 and the number of tractors produced had been relatively insignificant, even in 1928 - a total of 1300 were produced that year. While the development of production did not take place entirely during the First Five-Year Plan, by 1936, tractor production had reached an annual level of 112,900 and combine-harvester output was 43,900 in 1937.[32]

Crucial to the output of finished goods was the development of an industry capable of supplying other industries with the equipment, tools, and raw materials needed in manufacturing. An example was the machine-tool industry, which supplied metal-cutting equipment. Metal-cutting tool production went from 2,000 in 1928 to 20,000 by 1932. Another example was quality steel production, which increased from 90,000 tons in 1927/28 to 165,000 tons in 1936. Steps were taken to begin domestic production of turbines, boilers and other equipment necessary for generating plants - steps necessary to end the heavy reliance on foreign imports of such equipment. In spite of the inefficiencies of the Soviet system, industries such as iron or steel production, benefitted, not only from the increased scale of construction, but also from the incorporation of some of the newest technologies.[33]

THE SECOND FIVE-YEAR PLAN

Like the First Five-Year Plan, the Second Five-Year Plan was in operation before it was even presented to the Party. It began in 1933. Stalin, at the Central Committee session of January 1933 had set the tone for the new plan. It was one of consolidation - the structure developed during the First Plan was to be made to work. The Plan was adopted in February 1934 by the Seventeenth Party Congress.

The First Five-Year Plan had ended in 1932 at a time when the agricultural sector was in turmoil. The Soviet Union was exporting grain, but the famine which would kill so many had begun to take hold that year. In August Stalin would order the implementation of the Draconian "five stalks law" under which 2,110 peasants were shot and some 54,000 were sentenced to prison for some form of grain taking.[34] The famine would continue through "hungry thirty-three," and 1934 and take anywhere from 3 million to 10 million victims.[35]

Stalin, in 1933, was willing to reduce exports of food, but his goal was not to relieve the suffering of the peasants. He was concerned about the inhabitants of the cities, the places where workers lived. City dwellers benefitted, in 1933, from increased availability of food. For all the difficulties of collectivization and peasant distress, the harvest of 1933 was good, providing vindication for Stalin's tough policy. Agricultural production in 1934 showed continuing improvement and, by 1935, rationing was no longer needed.

In the early stages of the Second Five-Year Plan, Stalin gave every indication that consumer interests were to be taken into account. He promised an improved living standard, higher wages, more housing, and more consumer goods. He quickly backtracked, committing more resources to heavy industry and armaments. In that regard the Second Five-Year Plan resembled the First. It differed in a significant respect. The Second Five-Year Plan came closer to achieving projected goals. In part this was due to the decision to scale back. In part it was due to the completion of some of the large-scale projects begun during the First Five-Year Plan. Gross industrial production for 1937 had been expected to reach 92,712 million rubles (in 1926-27 prices). The actual figure was higher - 95,500 million rubles. Electrical production, while projected at 38 billion kilowatts, was actually only 36.2, however that figure was a phenomenal increase over the 13.4 billion figure of 1932. Coal production had gone from 64.3 million tons in 1932 to 128 million tons in 1937. The reliance on imports of foreign machinery had been significantly reduced as well. In 1932 the Soviet Union had imported some 78 percent of its machine tool needs. The percentage had dropped below 10 percent by 1936-37.[36]

The successes of the Second Plan suggest a steady movement toward the goals. While there was steady economic growth during much of the Plan, there was a slow-down which hit the economy in 1936. The economic problems which affected the economy have been blamed in part, on the Great Purges, which took place during the years 1936-38. Leading economists, engineers, and factory managers were among the many victims. Any problem, from an accident to low production, could lead to a charge of 'wrecking' or sabotage. Morale suffered and fear of becoming a victim led to a drop in initiative. The Great Purges however, were not the only reason for the slow-down. Economic problems made their appearance in the first half of 1936, before the purges began. (Sergei Kirov was assassinated on December 1, 1934. That assassination provided Stalin with the excuse to impose tighter political controls. The Great Purge however, can be dated to the arrest of Kamenev and Zinoviev in June 1936.)[37]

Agriculture was one of the areas which impacted productivity negatively, since output sometimes fell below expectations. Agricultural results were not consistently good or bad. The harvest for 1935 had been a good one, in contrast to the disaster of 1933. However 1936 proved to be a poor harvest. A severe drought wreaked havoc with crops. While the figures contributed to a poor showing overall, it is difficult to point to the 1936 harvest as the major culprit in the economic slowdown. The problems which the industrial sector experienced in early 1936 were appearing before the peasants went into the fields for the fall harvest.

In the industrial sector, the problem was not just shortages, but shortages in areas which were important to other production activities. Coal and oil, crucial for both transportation and industry, could not be produced fast enough. Production problems were compounded by transport difficulties. Shipments of iron, other industrial metals, and cement were slowed by problems with rail and river transport. Rail transport, both crucial for fuel deliveries and dependent on fuel supplies, was disrupted, while river transport was impacted by the drought. Shipments of fuel by barge were nearly impossible. Timber production also lagged. These shortages in turn, contributed to problems with the harvest. The shortage of fuel meant that tractors and combines could not operate at full capacity. Livestock shelters were either not built at all or were left incomplete because of the shortage of timber. Animals which were not left unsheltered were sometimes housed with sick animals, spreading disease among the herds still recovering from the slaughters associated with collectivization.[38]

If logistical problems weren't enough, the Great Purge, which began with the June arrest of Kemenev and Zinoviev, finally visited the production lines in August and September. It took some of the most experienced engineers and severely impacted the morale of those who remained. The economic problems worsened in 1937 when the Second Five-Year Plan ended, while the arrests of the Great Purge continued into 1938 and 1939. The economy was slow to recover, even as the Third Five-Year Plan began in 1938.

1935 - TIGHTENING THE REIGNS ON THE BUDGET

While the last years of the Second Five-Year Plan were a disappointment for industry, the successes of the early years seemed to benefit consumers despite Stalin's continued focus on industrial development. For the Russian consumer, 1935 was a year of change. Rationing of food items was lifted, beginning with bread on January 1. Later in the year rationing for meat, fish, fat, sugar, and potatoes was lifted. (October 1, 1935) The lifting of rationing signalled a change in economic thinking which would lead to the abandonment of price controls for basic industries in 1936.

In 1922 Lenin had pushed the government to adopt a more conservative approach to budgeting. The enterprises within the trusts, which had been allowed to operate as though a moneyless economy existed, suddenly had to make themselves profitable. They could no longer count on government subsidies or the goodwill of other enterprises. The peasant revolt and chaotic economic conditions had been the reason for the change. In 1935 it was economic problems which served as the impetus for another policy review. The problem this time was neither peasant revolt nor a devastated industrial sector. Stalin's collectivization program had effectively ended the political power of the peasantry. For all the difficulties caused by industrialization, industry was in a much stronger position. The problem in 1935 was that economic policy and the bureaucratic structure were too cumbersome to be manageable. The policies which were designed to advance industrialization were now seen to be hindering it.

Government economic policy created a number of problems. One example perhaps illustrates part of what was wrong. While Stalin was unlikely to admit it, the Party had encouraged, even adopted, capitalist factory practices to encourage industrial productivity. As long as those practices furthered industrial development and increased output, Stalin allowed them. One area where this occurred was that of wages. The Party found that workers were more productive when they were paid on a piece-work basis. The "discovery" probably had more to do with a public relations ploy, than it did with some new insight into worker productivity.

Stalin was looking for heroes as part of his campaign to increase productivity. He found one in a coal miner named Alexei Stakhanov. In August 1935 he, together with his co-workers, had mined 102 tons of coal in one night, which was nearly 14 times the normal 7.3 tons. Stalin wanted him to serve as the model for other workers, in fact, for all industry. He hoped to promote a certain management style. The whole program came to be known as the "Stakhanov (or Stakhanovite) movement."

The Stakhanov movement was a public relations bonanza. However, managers found that there was an economic aspect of the program which made implementation more difficult. Increased productivity often required new and improved equipment and there were budgetary restraints which limited that option. At the same time there was one benefit for the factory manager - it was possible to argue that, while equipment would cost more, it would also improve productivity. Upgrading equipment was not the only way to improve productivity. Productivity, whatever the level of equipment, had a labor component as well. One way to increase productivity was to pay higher wages. Piece-work, where pay was based on the number of units produced, was one of the methods employed. Factory managers also added as many workers as possible to increase output.

Why did the Stakhanov movement and emphasis on labor productivity contribute to the economic policy changes of 1935? Before answering that question, it may be helpful to state just what some of the major policy changes were. First, in addition to the elimination of rationing, price controls were lifted for many items at the wholesale, or factory level. (Prices for manufactured goods at the retail level had been allowed to rise even before 1933. Second, the government decided to end the subsidies it provided to many enterprises. This second item was in large part related to the lifting of price controls. Enterprises which had been forced to keep prices low, had been operating at substantial losses. The government, to maintain operations, had covered these losses by subsiding them.

Labor, for all its importance, had created problems for the government in two ways. First, it increased costs for industries at a time when they were under pressure to keep costs low. Second, labor incentives, in the form of higher wages, were less effective when there were no goods to buy. Soviet industry had two conflicting goals. It was directed to increase productivity while at the same time it was expected to cut its costs.

329

Stalin, in pushing for growth, had emphasized expansion, while ignoring costs. The demands for industrial expansion required an increase in the number of workers. Even if wages per worker remained the same, additional workers increased overall labor costs and factory budgets. Individual wages however, did not remain the same. The Stakanhov movement, which resulted in a piece-work incentive system, drove labor costs per worker even higher. Between 1932 and 1937, wages increased from 1,427 rubles per year to 3,047 rubles per year.[39] While the factory manager had to contend with increased labor costs to maintain productivity, he was unable to increase revenues because of the price control system.

Increased labor costs were a concern for the government as well. As long as the it kept a lid on prices, it felt compelled to subsidize industries for the losses they suffered. Formal action to limit subsidies would come in April 1937, when a decree totally eliminated state subsidies to the MTSs and some industries. The 1937 budget had reduced subsidies to half the 1936 level.[40] There was also a recognition that while price controls were intended to make goods affordable for the average person, they had the effect of creating shortages. In addition, if goods were unavailable, the incentives provided by higher wages would be lost, because the worker would have nothing to buy. Nove indicates that there were two other reasons why the government would want to move away from continued control. First, maintaining a separate pricing structure required complex calculations and a bureaucracy which was costly to maintain. Second, both consumers and state enterprises, were willing to resell controlled items. Consumers, rather than using the items themselves, wanted the cash. The state enterprises, simply used the outside sales to cover their costs or to make money.[41] The result of artificially low prices was not to help consumers, but to forfeit revenues. The private trader was obtaining the investment which could have gone to the state. Not only did the state have to absorb the loss of potential revenues, it also had to pay out subsidies to cover the losses resulting from price controls.

Consumer goods did become more available in late 1935 and 1936, following the end of the rationing system. If the government was expecting even greater productivity from the end of rationing and the use of wage incentives, its hopes were soon dashed. The Stakhanov movement did not last much beyond 1937. Expectations were probably unrealistic on both sides. The workers, who had made extraordinary efforts to improve output, began to suspect that the economic incentives and awards received were merely a ploy to get more work. Additional increases in productivity were rewarded, not with additional pay, but with ever-higher work standards. Officials and managers believed that long-term productivity growth could be sustained by an incentive system alone. An additional element was the loss of productivity by non-Stakhanovite workers, who resented both the awards given to more productive workers and the managers who gave them. The resentment led to real acts of sabotage directed toward the favored workers.

The downturn of 1936-7 was not solely related to worker morale. Stalin had become concerned with the state of the Soviet military and the industries which produced armaments. While industries, such as iron and steel or electricity, produced materials which were interchangeable in any industrial setting, other industries could only make specific products and required specific manufacture. Machining tools for rifle production were not the same as those required for electrical turbines. Designating funds and resources for military use, which increased after 1935, meant that other sectors of the economy suffered.

THE THIRD FIVE-YEAR PLAN

Despite the slowdown of 1937, Soviet planners started working on the Third Five-Year Plan, which was to begin in 1938. In contrast to the retreat of the Second Plan, which had emphasized consolidation and getting things to work, the Third Plan called for increases in output. Formal adoption by the Eighteenth Party Congress in 1939, would again take place with the plan already in operation.

When the plan began the Great Purge had not yet run its course. The mass arrests of the Purge would only come to an end in early 1939. It was clear that war was close and economic efforts were focused on armaments. It is not surprising that a shortage of consumer goods developed. While the shortage of goods represented the downside of the economic situation, there was an increasing demand for workers. By one estimate some 1.5 million workers were needed in 1939 in industry, construction, and transport.[42] This shortage led to an increase in wages. By 1940 wages were as high as 4,054 rubles per annum compared to the 3,047 they had been in 1937.[43]

In one sense it is difficult to gauge the economic effects of the Third Plan. The preparations for war had a disruptive effect on overall economic planning and results. Where the government focused its efforts, there were significant gains. Where it ignored sectors, there was a decline. Machinery and engineering, by 1940, had already fulfilled 59 percent of their five-year goal, but this was where armaments production was heavily concentrated. Steel production, at the same point in time, had only increased by 5.8 percent.[44]

On June 22, 1941, a German army of over three million men, began carrying out Operation Barbarossa, Hitler's planned invasion of Russia. Though Stalin had been preparing Russia for war, the retreat of the Russian army suggested that his preparations were inadequate. Initial German gains were deceptive indicators of relative strengths. It was German technology which would be proved inadequate, if not against the Russian armies, at least against the monumental nature of the task assigned.

In attempting to analyze the economic results of the three five-year plans, the war effort perhaps provides a good analogy. The three five-year plans were neither total successes, nor total failures. There were major achievements in some areas which contrasted with serious deficiencies in others. The Russian army, similarly, took tremendous casualties and gave up large areas of land, before finally achieving victory. The focus of this book is not economic success or failure, in an absolute sense. That the Russian armies in World War II beat back the German invasion, does not validate Stalin's economic policies and says nothing about the success or failure of his plans. The Russian economy was at least adequate to the challenge. At the same time Stalin could have made other economic choices. Some may have been better; others may have been worse. The next chapter returns to a discussion of the theme of this book and the key question: Was political repression and centralized economic control caused by communism or was it caused by a scarcity of resources?

CHAPTER 17

THE ROLE OF SCARCITY IN POLITICAL AND ECONOMIC CONTROLS

The question often discussed, following the fall of the Berlin wall in 1989, was 'what caused the collapse of the Soviet Union?' The larger question was 'why did communism fail?' The shortcomings of the Soviet system have been so obvious that the debate has not been about 'whether' communism is a failure. It has focused instead, on the question of 'why' it failed. As if failure was not enough, it has come on two fronts: one economic, the other political. On the economic front, the debate was pretty much over when it was seen that central planning could not even supply the Russian people with the goods they needed. The long lines at stores and the absence of goods was strong evidence that Russian factories and the entire Soviet system did not work. On the political front, the failures were shown by the existence of a secret police and widespread repression. The problem was not simply that there were failures, the problem was that they took place on a grand scale. Stalin did not just execute a few hundred people, he caused the deaths of millions. There were not just occasional shortages, those shortages continued to exist years after the communists had come to power.

Critics of the Soviet political system have often been able to summarize (and win) their argument by pointing to the existence of a secret police and the suppression of political dissent as the most obvious indications of failure. There is a general standard by which all governments are judged, and any government which uses a secret police clearly violates that standard. Yet, in the context of the Soviet Union, the debate over failure has often involved a more complex argument. It was not simply that the Bolsheviks were repressive by some generally recognized democratic standard, it was also that they violated the standards they set for themselves. While they professed a commitment to help workers, they outlawed labor unions and strikes. If they decried the inhumanity of the capitalist factory owner and professed a determination to do better by providing opportunities for laboring people, they themselves killed and imprisoned workers and peasants in pursuit of their idealist goals. They were no better, in practice, than the capitalist system they despised. In their idealism, it was said, they had dreamed of creating a utopian society for workers. Instead they had created a nightmare.

Criticism of the economic system took place on too levels, one simple, the other more sophisticated. The simple argument was straightforward. The communist economic system was unequal to the task of feeding or clothing its own people. The complex argument focused less on failure, which was assumed, and more on the reasons for that failure. The fundamental flaw in the Soviet system, said critics, was that it did away with profit and private property, crucial ingredients in productivity. The ability to accumulate wealth, they argued, was key. Profit is an incentive for individuals to produce and when individuals produce, the market as a whole will be productive. This was compounded by an emphasis on central planning rather than the market for economic decisions. The market, which was more efficient at allocating resources, based as it was on consumer demand, was relegated to a back seat to government planners.

Collectivization was offered as damning proof of their argument. Stalin took the land away from the peasants, confiscated their grain, and forced them to join collectives. On the collectives, the peasants did all the work, but the state received what 'profit' there was. Since the peasant could not make a profit, and received little compensation for his labor, there was little incentive to produce. Productivity for the individual peasant fell, and the loss of productivity impacted the whole economy. The result was that there were continual shortages of food. Similar limitations impacted industrial production, creating shortages of goods.

ECONOMIC CONTROLS AND THE LOSS OF PRODUCTIVITY

Free market critics have made a case for the impact which economic controls have had on productivity. There are examples of what happened when economic controls were either tightened or eased. The lifting of economic controls, following the Civil War in March 1921, led to NEP and recovery for the economy during the next few years. When economic freedoms were granted the peasants there was increased production and an easing of the food shortages. The economic freedoms which were allowed during NEP helped in the overall recovery of the Russian economy.

Stalin would make concessions to private peasant trade in 1932 and 1933, even defending the use of the private plot. Productivity figures suggest that private ownership was a strong incentive. Lewin cites one statistic for 1938. The privately-held plots, which made up only 3.9 percent of sown acreage, accounted for 45 percent of total output.[1] The Stakhanov movement represented another illustration of how economic incentives contributed to increased productivity. Once the incentives were eliminated productivity fell.

There are also numerous individual stories about the effect of taking away economic incentives. Peasants, who were turned into wage earners with no stake in the economic output of the collective or enterprise lost much of their initiative. Fitzpatrick's story of the kolkhoz chairman who jumped out the window to escape peasant demands for small items such as milk, butter, boots, and flour is one such example.[2] In another case a team leader assigned weed-filled plots to Stakahnov agricultural workers to frustrate efforts to improve sugar beet production.[3] These stories are just two of a large number of instances in which productivity was stifled in some way. In the face of such evidence, proving that resource scarcity was the major cause of economic problems seems somewhat daunting. There is a case to be made however.

RESOURCE SCARCITY AND COMMUNIST ECONOMIC PROBLEMS

Following the end of World War II, the Cold War brought fears of an expansion of communism and the Soviet "Empire." What is often forgotten is that the Soviet Union, even before the Cold War, covered one of the largest geographical areas of any nation on earth. It extends through eleven time zones, in contrast to the United States, which, with the exception of Alaska and Hawaii, is divided into only four time zones. In addition, Russia contained a population which was greater in size than that of the U.S.. In the context of the Soviet Union, neither geographical size nor population statistics, in and of themselves, are sufficient to prove a scarcity of resources, since scarcity is an inexact term. However, it is possible to make a preliminary argument that resources were scarce in Russia. Per capita output of agricultural products and industrial materials is a good starting point.

In 1930 the population of the U.S. was estimated to be 122,923,000, the population of Russia 159,551,760, and the population of Germany 64,506,631.[4] (Statistics for Germany are included here, even though Nazi Germany will be more fully discussed in the following chapters. Economic output in fascist countries, such as Nazi Germany, falls between the extremely low output of communist economies, such as Russia, and the extremely high output of democratic economies, such as the U.S..) The table below provides data on per capita agricultural production of the three countries. The figures reflect the strength of Russia's ability to grow grain, which had provided the chief source of exports, even in Czarist times.

TABLE I
AGRICULTURAL PRODUCTION PER CAPITA[5]

PRODUCT		1926	1927	1928	1929	1930
Wheat	U.S.	7.08	7.35	7.58	6.57	7.21
(bushels)	Russia	5.57	4.99	5.26	4.43	4.31
	Germany	1.53	1.90	2.22	1.92	2.15
Rye	U.S.	.29	.43	.31	.28	.36
(bushels)	Russia	6.13	6.45	4.95	5.12	5.82
	Germany	4.02	4.25	5.27	5.01	4.68
Corn	U.S.	21.69	21.97	22.12	17.50	16.92
(bushels)	Russia	.97	.99	.84	.75	.65
	Germany	-0-	-0-	-0-	-0-	-0-
Oats	U.S.	9.81	9.18	10.88	8.15	10.36
(bushels)	Russia	6.71	5.96	7.40	6.93	7.17
	Germany	6.07	6.91	7.57	-0-	-0-

Barley (bushels)	U.S.	1.41	2.01	2.72	2.16	2.45
	Russia	1.72	1.43	1.69	2.11	1.94
	Germany	1.67	1.98	2.41	2.28	2.03
Sugar Beets (bls)	U.S.	122.00	130.20	117.80	120.0	149.60
	Russia	90.38	143.30	145.50	85.98	191.80
	Germany	354.94	376.99	38.30	381.30	507.46

Russia was behind the U.S., but ahead of Germany, for most products except sugar beets and rye. Table II shows the comparison in per capital output of industrial raw materials. In contrast to agricultural output, the relative rankings of the three countries remain the same over the entire five-year period. The U.S. led in all areas from 1926 through 1930, while Germany ranked second, and Russia came in third.

TABLE II
INDUSTRIAL RAW MATERIAL PRODUCTION PER CAPITA
(IN POUNDS)

PRODUCT		1926	1927	1928	1929	1930
Iron Ore[6]	U.S.	1290.24	1160.32	1155.84	1341.76	1064.00
	Germany	168.21	231.04	224.20	219.35	195.99
	Russia	48.38	70.32	86.64	109.79	143.52
Pig Iron[7]	U.S.	728.00	654.00	710.00	763.84	544.32
	Germany	337.30	456.35	407.85	454.15	330.69
	Russia	30.86	41.88	46.95	59.52	69.00
Steel[8] (Ingots & Castings)	U.S.	681.00	844.00	945.00	1023.00	732.00
	Germany	427.00	566.00	501.00	557.00	394.00
	Russia	41.00	61.00	61.00	68.00	77.00
Coal[9]	U.S.	11,206	10,045	9,560	9,998	8,734
	Germany	5,097	5,355	5,244	5,621	4,761
	Russia	379	469	507	586	650
Copper[10]	U.S.	14.60	13.80	15.00	16.20	11.40
	Germany	.95	.96	.91	.99	.92
	Russia	.15	.19	.28	.52	.66

Lead[11]						
	U.S.	11.64	11.18	10.40	10.64	9.00
	Germany	1.89	2.91	2.99	3.35	3.76
	Russia	-0-	-0-	-0-	-0-	-0-

While Germany was ahead of the Soviet Union in nearly all industrial raw materials, she was almost entirely lacking in petroleum reserves. Russia did have oil reserves, but even in this area she lagged behind the U.S., as the following figures indicate.

OIL PRODUCTION (BARRELS PER CAPITA)

PRODUCT		1926	1927	1928	1929	1930
Oil[12]	U.S.	6.56	7.57	7.48	8.27	7.3
	Russia	.41	.50	.56	.68	.85

Resource production per capita is only one measure of availability. To provide a different perspective, it may be helpful to look at resource production in relation to geographical size. Coal was a major fuel relied on by both the railroads, for transportation, and by industry, for production. Output in relation to the amount of track was woefully short. Germany, within its 1932 boundaries, was measured at 180,986 square miles. Russia, in contrast, had an area of 8,244,288 square miles. Germany had 33,466 miles of railroad track, while Russia, despite her enormous size, had only 20,000 more miles of track, or 50,269 in total.[13] As the following figures show, Germany's coal production was far ahead of Russia's when based on the amount of tonnage per mile of track.

COAL PRODUCTION (TONS PER MILE OF RAILROAD TRACK)

	1926	1927	1928	1929	1930
Germany	4,341	4,589	4,507	4,883	4,176
Russia	505	638	704	829	936

The difference in coal production is even greater if the comparison is done using the total geographical area of each country.

COAL PRODUCTION (TONS PER SQUARE MILE)

	1926	1927	1928	1929	1930
Germany	802.69	848.55	833.39	902.91	772.18
Russia	3.08	3.89	4.29	5.05	5.71

The examples used, while not extensive, do indicate shortages in materials crucial to industrial output. Other evidence of scarcity can be seen in the actual shortages which occurred during the period of time discussed. Having "established" the fact of shortages, the question remains - what caused them? Were they caused by Bolshevik economic policies, as suggested by conventional wisdom, or were shortages actually caused by "shortage." If communist policy was to blame, then economic problems should have been absent before the communists took over or should have disappeared once communism was eliminated. Similarly, was productivity, strongly associated with economic well-being, destroyed by the Bolsheviks? If that were the case, central planning, viewed as the ultimate "damper" on economic activity, should have generated a continual downward economic trend. It did not. Economic productivity, even during various periods of communist control, was not uniformly good or bad. There were periods in which the Soviet economy experienced growth and periods in which it experienced slowdown. The reverse argument might be applied to capitalist economies. If the free market is the engine behind economic growth, then why would Western economies experience downturns at all?

The argument of this book is that scarcity was the reason the Soviet government imposed controls on the market. The counter-argument is that communist restrictions on the market were the cause of scarcity. Evidence of scarcity in the Soviet Union is not hard to find. Since that is the case, scarcity can be used to support either argument. In fact, the argument that restrictions caused scarcity is strengthened by the fact that some of the periods of the most extreme scarcity occurred after the Bolsheviks had taken power. The problem, in making the case for either argument, is that there must be some causal relationship established.

Those who argue that Bolshevik policy caused scarcity point to the serious economic problems which Russia and the Soviet Union encountered following the October Revolution. There is at least a prime facie case which can be made to support that argument. Russia experienced two severe famines following the Bolshevik takeover: the first in 1921, which may have killed some 5 million people; the second, from 1932-34, which may have killed as many as 10 million. Government policy clearly contributed to both famines, and government policy, be it Lenin's reluctance to accept aid, or Stalin's deliberate decision to cut off aid to the starving regions, clearly made it worse.

There is, in addition, some "internal" evidence associated with the changes which occurred following an easing of government controls. Goods became more available and the Russian economy generally improved when Lenin lifted the restrictions which the

338

Bolsheviks had imposed under War Communism. Private property was restored in a limited way under NEP - nationalized businesses were returned and free enterprise was encouraged. A similar improvement occurred in the mid-1930s. Peasants were allowed the use of private plots and greater access to the market. Similar free-market policies seemed to improve the industrial sector of the Soviet economy as well. There was an increase in worker productivity when the piece-work incentives associated with the Stakhanov movement were initiated. There was an increase in the availability of food and consumer goods following these changes.

The examples cited support the argument that communist market controls were the reason the Soviet Union experienced scarcity. There is an argument to be made on the other side however. It can be made along two lines, the first historic (or external, the second contemporaneous, or internal). The historic relates to events which were "external" to, or occurred before the communists took power. The contemporaneous involves evidence provided by events occurring within Russia or during the period of communist rule.

THE HISTORIC (EXTERNAL) ARGUMENT

In arguing the relationship between political policy and scarcity, there are really two areas which are likely to provide evidence. The first area involves obvious examples of scarcity, such as food shortages or shortages of consumer goods. The second relates to the indirect evidence, such as the inability of Russia's capitalists to finance their own industrial expansion, the general lack of surplus capital, or the formation of industrial trusts. When critics point to the shortcomings of the communist system, they most often bring up the obvious shortcomings, such as the long lines to buy goods or the empty store shelves. While these examples serve as object lessons in the failures of communism, they tend to ignore indirect evidence, which can be just as telling. The evidence does not clearly point the finger of blame at the Soviet system. It reveals instead, some underlying weaknesses in the Russian economy. They were present long before the Bolsheviks took power, and they did not disappear following the fall of the Berlin Wall in 1989. Had these weaknesses suddenly appeared following the Bolshevik takeover, that would suggest that communism was the cause. That is not the case.

The communists, in their nationalization decree of June 28, 1918, confirmed critics' suspicions that they intended to put their theories into effect. While the decree seemed a revolutionary change in policy, the decree itself was strikingly similar to the policies of Czarist governments which had directly owned or financed many industries. This was particularly true of the railroads, which had either been built by the state, or, had proved so unprofitable that the state had taken over. The 'trust' system, the method of organizing industries under VSNKh, did not differ significantly from the syndicates which had been formed to control industry after 1903. In the U.S. the Sherman Anti-Trust Act had been enacted to deal with the abuses of various cartels. Such abuses involved price-fixing and agreements on sales territories or quotas. In Russia syndicates controlled the market for industries such as iron and steel, coal and oil.

The existence of cartels or trusts, as such, does not prove scarcity. U.S. companies saw advantages in being members of cartels, and the U.S. certainly is not a poor country. Based on the diversity of the economic climate of the U.S. and Russia, any similarity in result can be blamed on the manufacturing culture. One difference however, is that in Russia the practice was continued, even encouraged by the Bolsheviks, whereas in the U.S. it was controlled. The Sherman Act, in some ways, judged cartels as morally wrong, in the context of free trade and the consumer's interests.

If cartels have been condemned on moral grounds, do they have a practical purpose which makes them attractive to those involved? Cartels do benefit the enterprises who are participants. Since competition is limited manufacturers can charge higher prices for goods. A major argument against cartels is that, because there is no competition, consumers will pay more for goods. That argument would suggest that the economic climate would be less favorable to cartels in poorer countries. If consumers are poor, they will be less able to afford goods which cost more. The market, which can barely support production when prices are low, will not support artificially high prices. The experience in Russia suggests the opposite situation. There is an economic explanation, but it is not related directly to the benefit consumers would receive in the form of low prices. The economic "benefit" is that an enterprise is being subsidized for unprofitable activities with the higher prices it charges. If this subsidy is not allowed, production will stop altogether. Higher prices, in other words, represent a form of a loan or investment in the enterprise by the purchaser.

There are other indications that industry in Russia was not as robust as its counterparts in the West. The military disaster of the Crimean War in 1854 had convinced the Czar that the manufacturing and transport sectors of the Russian economy were inadequate. His efforts brought results and key industries were strengthened. Oil output by 1900 was the highest in the world.[14] By 1913 Russia was producing at a rate more than 13 times that of 1860.[15] At the same time, even in 1910, she was still behind most European countries in industrial development. According to one study, Russia ranked around 10th among the European countries, behind even Italy and Spain.[16] The Russian consumer may have been subsidizing industry by paying higher prices, but the state provided subsidies in other ways. Through the railroads and the army and navy, it represented the biggest market for manufactured goods in Russia.

The level of investment in Russian industry by Russians suggests that there was a chronic shortage of capital. A substantial portion came from foreign investors - 28.5 percent in 1900; 33 percent by 1913.[17] Capital goods industries were owned largely by foreigners and capitalists from Britain, France and Germany had provided most of the funds for heavy industry. The Russian government itself relied heavily on foreign loans. The French government was probably the major lender. If borrowing is not conclusive proof of scarcity it does imply that the Russian economy was struggling to generate an investing surplus. Problems with surplus income were not confined to the industrial sector. The agricultural sector was struggling as well. It will be recalled that Russian peasants, who had been freed with the 1861 Emancipation decree, had also been saddled with a forty-nine year repayment plan to compensate the landlords. It had been a struggle for many villages to pay off this debt, and the Czar, to quell the disturbances of 1905, had agreed to abolish the remaining payments by 1907.

The circumstances surrounding the loans suggest underlying economic problems. The Czarist government was able to repay the loans, but only at the expense of the market for domestic goods. The principle method of repayment was agricultural exports. Taxes were raised on the villages in the hopes of forcing grain on the market. While more grain was exported as a result, the lowering of peasant discretionary income also lowered market demand for industrial goods. The extent of Russian reliance on foreign debt was a function of the general state of her economy. Agricultural output in 1913 had been particularly high and in 1914 there was decrease in the amount of foreign debt. Some loans were completely paid off.

While the Bolsheviks could eliminate debt by decree, they could not cure the underlying need for credit. In January 1918, they repudiated all foreign and domestic debt. This was followed by the nationalization of Russian banks. By repudiating debt the government reduced its outstanding obligations; by nationalizing the banks, it obtained cash. Yet, if current loans could be eliminated by decree, the underlying problem -the need for credit - was hardly solved. The problem was underscored in 1922, when the government took steps to reduce the amount of debt. The trusts, which had been allowed to finance operations with the credit system, suddenly had to sell raw materials at street bazaars to raise cash.

Stalin's policy was to keep foreign borrowing to a minimum. While that would suggest that he had moved the economy forward, there are indications that the economy was struggling. If less debt was incurred, repaying it involved immense sacrifices. Peasants were sacrificed, either through starvation, deportation, or imprisonment, in order to increase the grain available for exports. On a somewhat less tragic scale, the same economic need forced the sale of art treasures and the confiscation of private gold or currency holdings.

The slowness of economic development and a reliance on debt are symptoms of underlying economic problems. Such problems were present before the communists took over and created problems for them once they took power. If communism was the cause then these problems should have disappeared with the elimination of communism. The evidence suggests that they have continued and that Russian business and industry continues to struggle. One of the more commonly-heard complaints of Russian businessmen today is that they have difficulty collecting receivables.

EXPERIMENTAL CONTROLS AND VARIABLES

In conducting any experiment to prove or disprove a theory, it is necessary to have a variable and a control group. The control group provides the standard against which the results of the variable group are compared. Russia has come to be viewed as the great experiment in communism. In that experiment, it has long been assumed that communism itself was the variable and the period of Czarist rule represented the control. This comparison involves two different time periods. When the experiment was viewed from an economic perspective, the variables and controls changed. The restrictions on private property and central planning were said to be the variables which the communists introduced into the economy, while the free market conditions assumed to exist under the Czarist government were considered to be the controls. An underlying assumption was that, just as the policies were different, the results of Czarist and Bolshevik economic practices could be clearly seen to be different.

There are four problems in analyzing the results. The first is that most of the debate has focused on the problems associated with communism, without really examining the difficulties of Czarist times. The results of communism were so bad; how could they have been any worse under the Czar? The second problem involves a sleight of hand comparison between Russian and Western output, while avoiding a more direct comparison between communist and Czarist economic productivity. Since Stalin's five-year plans fell short of Western capitalist standards, what is the point of even drawing comparisons to Czarist times? The third problem involves the assumption that communist policy represented a radical contrast to industrial practices under the Czar. For example, how could the continued use of industrial syndicates under the Bolsheviks represent a true 'experimental variable' if it largely followed the Czarist pattern? The fourth problem is that communism is judged, not against the actual standard set by Czarist Russia, but by a more evasive standard - what Russia would have been like if it had been allowed to become a democracy. As elusive as such a standard is, the problem is compounded by its seeming ability to travel back and forth in time. Not only are communist productivity figures under the five-year plans viewed as dismal, in comparison to what they would have been, the Czarist government and its economy are seen as the industrial ideal, leading a robust economy while producing an abundance of goods. Without attempting to determine actual pre-Bolshevik industrial output, the natural assumption is that the communists stepped in and destroyed what was there.

There is some justification for questioning the basic assumptions about the validity of the communist "experiment," as an experiment. First, it is not clear that communist economic policies constituted a true experimental "variable." They were not significantly different than those of the Czar. A "variable," by definition, cannot be the same thing as the "control." Second, it is not clear that the results of either the control or variable experiments were significantly different. The Czarist economy, while going through good and bad periods, did not perform significantly better than the communist economy. It almost crumbled when confronted by significant external pressures, such as the Crimean War or World War I. In addition, the Russian economy since the fall of communism has not performed significantly better. Third, it is not clear that there was only one variable introduced into the Soviet economy. It has long been assumed that the economic policy changes introduced by the communists could be grouped together and defined as a single variable. There were a number of variables present, in fact, a number of different results, depending on the year looked at. For example, were the shortages experienced between 1938 and 1941 the result of a generally bad communist economic policy or were they the result of a specific decision to devote scarce resources to heavy industry and armaments? In addition to changes in government policy other variables were the movement of peasants to the cities, the increase in the number of workers, and the overall conversion of Russia from a rural society to a more urbanized one.

In any experiment there is a certain time element involved. The results are looked at before and after the point in time when the variable has been introduced. In the case of Russia, there may have been too much focus on the time element and not enough attention paid to the variables introduced. It has long been assumed that everything associated with the October Revolution was part of the variable. October 1917 almost became the variable.

The problem, in trying to judge the results of the communist experiment is that the economic variables which the Bolsheviks supposedly represented have become too closely identified with a point in time. Thus, the variables have not been defined by specific policy changes or events, but by everything that happened under communist rule after October 1917. For Russia, the control has been assumed to be the economic policies for the period of time before the experimental variable, communism, was introduced, i.e., the October Revolution. The variable has been assumed to be the economic changes made by the communists after October 1917. (The result of the experiment being looked at is the economic output for both periods.) The experiment could be said to be related to time. If the experimental results are related to time, then proof of the experiment's validity could be found in Russia - what happened before can be compared to what happened after. It may be however, that the experiment is not related to time but to a condition.

The thesis of this book is that a lack of industrial productivity is caused by a condition - scarcity, or lack of resources - and not by the inefficiencies of a governmental economic system. If the experimental variable involves a condition such as poverty, then the experiment cannot be validated by data obtained within Russia alone. (The evidence suggests that Russia was poor before the communists took over and remained poor during the time they have been in power.) It can only be validated by data from other countries. The variable, poverty or wealth, would have to differ significantly.

This discussion of experimental controls and variables is intended to highlight the problems of causation where resources and economic productivity are concerned. The next section discusses the conditions of scarcity which existed in Russia during communist rule. By themselves the economic hardships faced by Russians do not establish the cause of the scarcities which occurred. If the inefficiency of the Soviet system is believed to be the cause of Russia's economic problems, then the shortages can support that argument. If resource scarcity is believed to be the cause of the problems, then the shortages can provide proof to support that argument as well.

EVIDENCE OF SCARCITY DURING COMMUNIST RULE

The Bolsheviks, in spite of their rhetoric about a classless society, often displayed an admiration for the capitalist reward system. Rewards for Party service were quite material. One incentive was an increased ration. However much workers or Party members deserved rewards, they caused friction and gave dissatisfied workers an obvious focal point for any grievances felt toward the government. That was the case in January and February 1921. Food was in short supply in most of the major cities. When Moscow metallurgical workers met at a conference in early February they denounced the special rations which Party officials received. Dissatisfaction felt in Moscow caused strikes there and in Petrograd.

It was not the food shortages alone which caused resentment, but the Draconian governmental policies which accompanied them. There were two problems with the policy. First, the government had reduced the official rations allowed under their rationing system. A January order reduced the bread ration by one-third for ten days and workers in Petrograd had to survive on 1,000 calories a day. More importantly, government officials would not allow workers to obtain food outside the ration system. When some workers had gone into the countryside to barter for food, government units confiscated any produce they tried to bring back.[18]

The food shortage of 1921 was one of the few shortages to spark open revolt against the Bolsheviks. It was only one of many such occurrences. In the months immediately after October 1917, the cities had been forced to go on a rationing system. The bread ration had been as low as 2 ounces per day in Petrograd.[19] Despite the ending of the Kronstadt revolt, the 1921 food shortages continued into May and June, forcing Lenin to buy food abroad. (The worst hardships were suffered by the peasants, but the food purchases were mainly to ease the shortages in the cities.) The food situation had eased sufficiently by the end of 1921 that rationing was no longer needed, the system being abolished on November 10, 1921. Food remained in short supply through the winter of 1921-22, although conditions had improved over the previous year. Owing to the agricultural recovery, the supply situation continued to improve in 1923, although food was still short.

While government policy during the NEP years allowed for private food purchases, food was not abundant. The inflationary prices charged by the Nepmen were an indication of this. Economic difficulties were not serious enough to attract the political attention of Party leaders until late 1927, when Stalin sounded the alarm about grain reserves. The grain crisis of early 1928 led to Stalin's Siberian trip and forced grain confiscations. The slowness of collections caused bread shortages in the cities, although they were not critical at the time. By June, the shortage of grain was felt serious enough to begin importing grain. This was followed in February 1929 by the introduction of bread rationing. After 1929 nearly all food was rationed. There was some easing of the situation in 1931 and 1932 and rationing after April 1932 was limited to major food items such as bread, meat, and sugar. Food prices would climb despite the rationing, particularly in 1933. Nevertheless rationing remained in effect until 1935. Bread was no longer rationed after January 1, 1935. Rationing was abolished for meats and fish on October 1, 1935.

The shortages for the years 1930 to 1934 can be attributed to government policy, not just to the famine which hit in 1932 and lasted into 1934. It was also that the government continued to export grain during this time period. While the peasants were being deliberately starved to death, city-dwellers were forced to continue on short rations. It can be argued that the policy was linked to Stalin's malicious nature, although an economic rationale can be found in Stalin's obsession with industrialization. If cash was needed to purchase foreign equipment the normal output of the Soviet economy would not provide it. The shortages after 1938 can be traced to government decisions regarding industrial investment. (The relatively greater availability of foodstuffs, which followed the ending of rationing in 1935, lasted until 1938.) Rather than a broad push for industrialization, Stalin concentrated most of his efforts on armaments and deficiencies in war-related industries.

There have been two questions involving food shortages and communism. One relates to the existence of shortages - would they have been avoided if Russia had had a more democratic government? The other relates to the severity of the shortages which did occur - when they did occur, were they worse under the communists than they would have been under other leadership? The occurrence of shortages, from a historical perspective, had little to do with the form of government. Severe shortages had occurred during Czarist times, as evidenced by the famine of 1891 or the unrest of February 1917 - which would lead to the Czar's abdication in March. It was empty store shelves, long lines, and rumors of bread rationing, when mixed with labor grievances, which had agitated the crowds. The evidence suggests that shortages were made more severe as a result of communist rule, however the unknown variable is the impact of policy decisions. For example, what if a Czarist government had pursued a policy of industrialization with the same single-minded determination as Stalin?

Shortages of goods were the other major problem for Russian consumers. They often occurred at the same time as food shortages and while they were a cause for complaint, they were not life-threatening in the way that food shortages were. Shortages of consumer goods were apparent almost from the start of the Revolution and continued through 1921. Much of this shortage can be blamed on the nationalization decree of June 1918, state attempts to suppress private trade, and by the diversion of scarce raw materials to favored industries. In May 1921, when the decree was revoked, the goods situation began to improve.

In 1925 state efforts to keep prices low began to cause shortages. The ensuing 'goods famine' provided opportunities for private traders who were able to charge significantly higher prices for goods. Rationing would finally go into effect in 1930 for manufactured consumer goods. Rationing did not play as key a role in supply and demand where goods were concerned. The state found that its price differential system rationed goods more effectively than formal rationing. If the differential pricing system resembled the capitalist market, the similarities were officially ignored. In 1933 the state allowed prices to increase for goods and like food, goods were more available through

1937. In the remaining years before the war, goods once more became scarce and difficult for consumers to obtain. If these examples serve to illustrate the fact of shortage for certain time periods, what were its causes?

The transport system had proved to be one of the major bottlenecks for industrial development. One of the often-encountered problems for transport, particularly rail transport, was a shortage of fuel. Lack of fuel was both a part of the general transport problem, when trains could not run, and part of a larger problem for industry, which was dependent on delivered fuel to keep factories running. Factory fuel shortages had often led to unemployment and labor unrest, while train fuel shortages had prevented deliveries of factory fuel as well as food supplies, contributing to shortages in the cities.

The spark for the Kronstadt mutiny had been government efforts to further ration food in January 1921. A major cause of the food difficulties was a fuel crisis which hit the railroad system, causing the shutdown of rail lines. Fuel had been a problem, not only for the railroads, but also for city inhabitants. Residents of Moscow had torn down houses to use the wood to keep warm that winter. For the communists, 1921 had not been the first year in which fuel shortages had caused problems with the food supply. In 1919 a fuel shortage, mainly of the primary locomotive fuel, wood, had forced the railroads to curtail passenger service so that they could concentrate on carrying food shipments to the cities.

With the coming of NEP, the railroads seemed to obtain some respite and by 1926, they seemed to have recovered to their 1913 level, in terms of the amount of traffic carried. To achieve these results however, the government had been forced to allocate resources to new equipment purchases and fuel, in order to maintain fuel reserves. The First Five-Year Plan taxed the railroad system beyond its capabilities. Industries, which depended on railroad deliveries for supplies, found that they could not maintain production because of non-deliveries in 1929. The oil industry, for example, could not obtain enough pipes or cement. To compound matters, industries which were successful at production, found the railroads lacked the capacity to deliver finished products.

The situation did not improve in 1930. The railroads were able to carry more freight, but it was far below what industry was producing. This contributed to additional losses. Two million tons of grain, which had been forcibly taken from the peasants, was unshipped and unprotected from the winter weather. Much of the problem was a shortage of rolling stock and a lack of repair and maintenance. It would not be until 1935 that the Party would agree to make the additional investments needed to improve railroad capabilities. The railroads had to endure a fuel shortage, primarily coal, in 1937-38. The coal was desperately needed by factories, but the railroads were themselves so short of fuel that they were forced to use the coal to keep the locomotives operating.[20]

The railroad system had been both a cause of fuel shortages and a victim of them. Yet the railroads had not been the only victim. Various industries and workers had had to contend with shortages, not only of fuel, but also of raw materials. Even the unrest which led to the Kronstadt mutiny was driven, to some extent, by the lack of fuel. Factories in Petrograd had been forced to close because they lacked the fuel to continue operations in January 1921. Workers who were laid off, as a result, had one more grievance to air. The situation had been similar to that of February 1917, when fuel shortages led to factory closures in Petrograd and thousands of unemployed workers ready to vent their anger.

Were the shortages caused by the inefficiencies of the Soviet system or were they caused by an underlying shortage of resources? The fact that shortages existed does not, of itself, establish causation. If system-wide "inefficiency" is another term for a loss of productivity at the individual level, was the absence of material reward a major factor in the loss of motivation? Where Stalin could not motivate with material rewards, he substituted threats. If the threat of imprisonment or death would not motivate people, is it possible that motivation was not the real reason for the lack of productivity? There were instances where the lack of productivity was due to a lack of resources. Conquest tells the story of an MTS in 1933 in which the administrators were tried for sabotage because the equipment had not been kept in repair. The reason for the lack of repairs was the unavailability, not only of spare parts, but also of fuel, iron, or wood for the forges. Another MTS, which was supposed to repair 25 tractors and 25 threshing machines, also had no spare parts to make the repairs and the forge and anvil it was using had been borrowed from another collective.[21]

The question of whether productivity failure was the key player in shortages is one of many questions related to the Soviet economy. Another question relates to the cause of tighter state economic controls at the end of NEP. Was this related to resource scarcity? It has long been assumed that the communists eliminated the freedoms associated with the private sector because of their fanatical hatred of anything associated with capitalism. That hatred did seem to play a significant role in the nationalization decree of 1918. Yet, however reluctantly, the Bolsheviks did back off some of their most anti-market policies after 1921. Why did they return to their anti-market policies after 1926? It was not entirely due to their belief in communist theory, although for some, that belief did play a part in the policy debates. The evidence suggests that the reason for the ending of NEP was related to the competition for resources between the government and the private sectors of the market. The immediate goal was to speed the pace of industrialization, not to bring about a socialist state - at least not in the short run. It appears that Party leaders saw the private sector, not so much as opposing development, but as less committed to industrialization and something which stood in their way.

The Party did not immediately outlaw the private sector. Instead it began to crowd the private sector out of the market, first, by reserving raw materials for state industry in late 1925, later by taxing private enterprises for the use of the railways. Resources, in the form of raw materials, were insufficient for the needs of the governmental and the private sector. Resources, in the form of transport services, were also scarce.

One final argument can be made to support the thesis that resource scarcity was the cause of many economic problems and not the result of communist policies. That argument relates to the economic disruptions which occurred when resources were committed to any single sector of the economy. One of the problems which both Lenin and Stalin encountered was the chaos which occurred whenever they focused on one economic goal, to the exclusion of all others. The problem was not so much in pursuing more than one goal. The problem was more that, when investments were made in one sector, the necessary resources were obtained somewhere else. By committing economic resources to one particular sector, any gains came at the expense of other sectors. Russian consumers had to put up with shortages after 1938, when Stalin committed the state to strengthening the armaments industry.

The railroad system provides a telling example of what happened when the government committed large amounts of resources to a single goal. The Russian army, at the beginning of World War I, requisitioned one-third of the rail cars for transport. (That the army could take one-third of the rolling stock indicates either the inadequacy of the railroad inventory or the tremendous transport requirements of the army.) It was this requisitionment which was a major cause of the disruption of food supplies and raw material deliveries which occurred. If governmental economic goals and resources conflicted with those of the private sector, potential conflict was not limited to the economic sphere. There was a geographical, even regional, aspect to conflict as well. This seemed to be especially true of the food supply. Lenin, in trying to ensure grain supplies for the cities, resorted to forced grain requisitions in the countryside. The cities were fed, but only at the expense of the peasants and the rural areas, both at the time and in the ensuing famine of 1921.

The conflict between the cities and the countryside was reflected in the larger economy, but it was only symptomatic of a wider problem. No matter how things were divided up, whether economically, geographically, or otherwise, there was a potential conflict. The inability to accommodate both the public and private sectors - illustrated by the Party's favoring industrial production over private enterprise in 1926 - was only one problem experienced. There was a conflict between the wishes of consumers and the demands of industry. Still another confrontation loomed between the industrial and the agricultural sector. Industrial growth came at the expense of the agricultural sector. Stalin managed to squeeze the peasants for investment, but his efforts wreaked havoc with the agricultural economy and contributed to the famine of 1932-34. Government planning and economic results fell into a familiar pattern: if one sector or industry received attention and improved, others were neglected and fell into disrepair. The Five-Year Plan focused so much of its efforts on industrial production that the railroad system was largely ignored until 1935, when it became clear that transport problems were frustrating industrial production goals. When Stalin concentrated on heavy industry, consumer manufacturing suffered. When he changed his focus to armaments, certain sectors of heavy industry suffered along with those sectors devoted to consumer goods manufacturing.

The government's seeming inability to take on more than one task at a time only suggests that resources were scarce in Russia. An alternative explanation might be that communist or totalitarian regimes, just to remain in power, demand such a large portion of governmental resources, that they cannot devote the time or effort necessary for multiple endeavors. Such a circumstance, if it does not prove that scarcity was the cause of Russia's problems, at least provides additional evidence for a scarcity theory.

SCARCITY AND OPPRESSION

This chapter has been devoted primarily to the relationship between resource scarcity and government controls in the Soviet Union. The thesis of this book deals with the overall issue of the relationship between scarcity and dictatorship. The facts and arguments presented in this chapter, regardless of whether they have settled the debate over economic controls, have at least provided a picture of a society in which resources were in short supply, if not scarce. The question, in relation to dictatorship, is - did scarcity lead to repression? It may be difficult to fully prove or disprove that question. A major problem with causation and proof, in this case, is that the periods of greatest repression do not necessarily coincide with the periods of time in which shortages were the most severe. Repression can be measured at times by numbers, e.g., how many troops were required to quell a revolt, how many people were executed during a given period of time, or how many people were placed in concentration camps. At other times, repression is present but with few outward signs which can be quantified. For example, an interrogation by the secret police may not result in imprisonment or show up as a statistic. Yet, it serves to remind those who must endure it that the secret police are present and can arrest or execute the suspect in the future. It is the same problem encountered in the data for ancient Sparta. In Sparta there were long periods in which there was no open rebellion. Yet when rebellion occurred, the severity of the fighting suggests that the hatred was intense and the grievances felt were long-standing.

Another problem with proving a causal relationship between scarcity and repression is that repression is carried out by an administrative arm of the government. While the employees of a governmental agency may be aware of the outside world, they do not carry out their functions based on perceptions of what the outside world wants - for all practical purposes their reality is the organization. Those who carry out governmental activities, such as arrests or executions, carry them out on the orders of their superiors. Administrative agencies often operate independently of outside circumstances. If there is a connection between scarcity and repression, the point of connection will be the point in time when the agency is set up. In other words, resource scarcity may cause violence, which will convince a government to set up a police force to deal with the violence. Once that force is set up, its operations may not seem to have any connection with resources or with the reason the organization was originally created. It will follow its own rules.

The actions of the secret police during Stalin's time provide an example of the operational independence of any agency. In one sense Stalin was justified in using the police to protect the government from real threats. Stalin also used the police to eliminate "enemies," such as Bukharin, who no longer posed any real danger. The state police apparatus did not bother to sort out the difference. It was a bureaucracy which had grown accustomed to carrying out orders.

It is possible to draw a direct connection between the opposition of the peasants to collectivization and the repressive measures used against them. However, the causal relation between scarcity and resources is somewhat remote in that case. Officially, the

349

scarcity which caused Stalin to push for collectivization was the shortage of grain, or at least the low collections. That shortfall seems to have been contrived. The scarcity at the heart of Stalin's policy has a more indirect connection with agriculture. It was the capital required for industrialization. Neither the government nor the economy as a whole had sufficient funds to finance industrial growth. However, the scarcity of investment resources was itself only symptomatic of a more basic scarcity, that of material resources.

It would probably be accurate to say that the repression which existed, while at times more severe than at others, never went away. It did not necessarily appear to be that closely associated with severe shortages. The period known as the Red Terror which began in September 1918, and lasted through 1920, claimed between 50,000 and 140,000 lives.[22] This period of time was roughly the entire Civil War period and the war was a time of shortage. While the end of the Civil War should have brought an end to many of the economic disruptions, the number of concentration camps continued to increase, along with the number of prisoners. In October 1923 there were 70,000 prisoners in 315 camps, where there had only been 84 camps and 50,000 prisoners in December 1920.[23] It is true that recovery did not begin immediately at the end of the war and so the scarcities which existed were not immediately cured. In fact, the economy had to deal with the problems of the famine, which hit in 1921.

There is some debate over whether the repression which occurred during the Great Purge was caused by economic problems or whether it caused them. It clearly contributed to economic disruption. The purges which took place in the factories caused a precipitous drop in productivity. Roberta Manning argues however that productivity had been dropping off before the Purge even began and that there was a severe shortage of food and goods in 1936 and 1937.[24] While there may have been a connection between shortages and the repression, the mechanism was only indirectly related to Stalin's fears of the Soviet masses. It more likely had a closer connection to Stalin's worries about his political opponents in the Party.

According to Tucker, there is evidence that many in the Party were ready to replace Stalin in January 1934, when the Seventeenth Party Congress met. There was some dissatisfaction with his leadership, which may be indirectly traced to economic problems. Kirov, who would be targeted for assassination by year's end, was approached about leading a move to oust Stalin from the post of general secretary. There are conflicting stories about whether he informed Stalin about meetings or whether Stalin was told by someone else. The mere fact that Kirov had been asked was sufficient to mark him for elimination, in Stalin's eyes. Much of the dissatisfaction centered on Stalin's mistakes and style of leadership. His tendency to blame others when his policies had gone wrong was one of the grievances.[25] Yet it is possible to read into the complaints about leadership an underlying dissatisfaction with the overall results of Stalin's programs. The development of a political faction willing to oppose Stalin may have only a remote connection with economics. However, the cause of the shortcomings of the programs which contributed to that dissatisfaction, can be traced more directly to the economic problems - among them scarcity - which existed.

This chapter has provided a summary of the discussion of Russia, in particular those aspects of the economic situation which are related to the thesis of this book - resource scarcity and political repression. The next chapter begins a discussion of Nazi Germany. Germany under Adolf Hitler was, like the Soviet Union, a dictatorship. At the same time, the reasons for Hitler's rise and the forces which served as his power base were different than those present in Russia. Economically Germany was more developed than Russia, yet not developed enough to cope with the economic problems which confronted it. Similarly the political system proved inadequate in its dealings with the problems which spilled over from the economy.

CHAPTER 18

BACKGROUND TO FASCISM AND AN OVERVIEW OF NAZI GERMANY

June 30, 1934 would come to be known as the "Night of the Long Knives." Adolf Hitler, fearful of losing power and convinced that rivals within his party were ready to betray him, ordered the murder of many of the people who had helped bring him to power. When the SS was through, perhaps as many as 100 people had been killed, some executed after being arrested and tortured, others assassinated in their homes.

It was something of an irony that many of the victims were leaders of Hitler's own SA (Sturmabteilung or Storm Detachment). The irony was that Hitler would destroy the very groups which had contributed so much to his political power. A lesser irony was that Hitler should draw his strength from working-class groups and the economic problems of workers, while being vehemently opposed to the labor movement. Unemployment, which increased in severity after the Great Depression began, caused many workers to join the SA. With increasing economic problems and unemployment, the political power of the SA and of Hitler, had grown. Yet Hitler would take decisive steps to eliminate the trade unions, even using the SA to carry out his directives. In March 1933 the SA and police began a campaign designed to destroy labor organizations, attacking and arresting union members and taking over their buildings.

Hitler's moves against the unions were only one example of the political repression which occurred under the Nazis. In its suppression of the unions, Nazi German differed little from the Soviet Union. It was a dictatorship complete with a secret police. Where Germany did differ from Russia was in the economic sphere. Nazi Germany had more resources than Russia. At the same time, its resource wealth was not at a level comparable to that of democracies, such as the U.S. or Britain. Fascist governments, if they represent a different form of dictatorship than communism, arise under resource conditions somewhere between the resource-starved economies conducive to communism and the resource-rich environment where democracies thrive.

WHAT IS NAZISM OR FASCISM?

Those who study fascism have found it difficult to come up with a clear definition of what of fascism is. Although Germany represents the most prominent example, the fascist "phenomenon" was not confined to Germany. The reason for the focus on Germany has primarily been related to the scale of the destruction which followed in the wake of Hitler's rule - the war which he began caused the deaths of nearly 40 million people and some six million people are believed to have died in the Nazi death camps. Perhaps it is the deliberate and grotesque way in which people were killed - in gas chambers - which focuses our attention, (although Russian secret police methods of execution could be just as diabolical). Perhaps it is simply the way in which the victims -

Jews or gypsies - were chosen.

There were fascist movements in many of the countries of Western Europe. They did not achieve the same notoriety as Germany; some because they were unable to seize power, others because they did not possess Hitler's single-minded obsession with a goal far beyond merely staying in power. Where they did succeed however, they employed dictatorial methods similar to those of Hitler - opposing political parties were outlawed and political dissent was suppressed. Italy, not Germany, was in fact the first fascist regime. There were also fascist governments in Spain, Hungary, Romania, and Austria.

There is a temptation to approach fascism as a single event or unique phenomenon. Everything which occurred in the political and governmental realm can be explained by the personality of the individuals who led the movements. Fascism may be better analyzed however, by treating the political and governmental aspects separately. In other words, the political forces which brought fascist leaders to power were not identical to the bureaucratic mechanisms they used once they had taken over. Clearly Hitler put his own 'Nazi' stamp on the German government, once in power. At the same time, despite the strength of his personality and the scale of devastation which followed in his wake, his actual impact on the governmental bureaucracy may be somewhat exaggerated. If Hitler took pains to inspire the Gestapo and SS with a fanatical devotion, he was largely unconcerned with the routine activities of governmental file-clerks. Explaining fascist governments, in the context of day-to-day operations, may be an easier task than understanding the political motivations and beliefs behind the movements.

The one idea which fascists were identified with (or by), in every country, was a hatred of communism. What they were for seemed to depend on the country. There was a certain nationalism involved in most cases, which combined with an expansionist foreign policy. However, dreams of military conquest were often tailored to military capabilities. If Mussolini had wanted to truly resurrect the Roman Empire he so admired, he would have looked north to challenge Germany or England. Instead he settled on North Africa where desert tribes would be no match for his tanks or machine guns. Hitler, with a fully mechanized army, could dream of conquering Europe. Franco, although an army general, recognized that Spain lacked the military resources of either Germany or Italy. Military conquest was left off his agenda.

In very basic ways, fascism, like communism or any other political movement, depended on 'great' ideas to inspire a mass of people. Communism was more universal in its appeal - its goal was to help the masses in their struggle against capitalist oppression. It provided workers with a sense of belonging to a larger movement. If fascism provided a similar sense of belonging, the appeal was couched in terms of the individual country involved. Hitler's group was the mystical Nordic race to which all true Germans belonged while Mussolini rallied Italians to the ancient Roman Empire created by their ancestors.[1]

Those who have wrestled with the definitional problems surrounding fascism have tended to focus on the "crowd mentality," summarized bluntly by the question "Why did so many Germans blindly follow Hitler?" If the question suggests some trance-like crowd mentality, it is misleading in its factual assumptions. Not all Germans blindly followed Hitler or believed in his programs. Although Josef Goebbels' films of mass rallies gave the impression of fanatical adherents, behind the scenes it was the secret police who maintained order. If Hitler found mass support helpful on the road to power, he did not find it necessary once power had been achieved. A democratic majority was not necessary to the exercise of political power.

While the makeup of Hitler's followers gave him a powerful political base, the Nazi phenomenon cannot be explained in purely psychological terms. There were economic forces at work as well. Hitler came to power against a backdrop of hardship and unemployment. These conditions were not unique to Germany. In fact democracies, such as England and the United States, had to endure them.

There was one ingredient in the political equation which was present in greater amounts in the 'fascist' countries - violence. Whether it was caused by unemployment, the worst periods of violence seemed to coincide with some of the highest periods of unemployment. In Germany in 1932, there were some 5,575,000 unemployed, out of a total work force of 18,093,000, or a 30.8 percent unemployment rate. In the two months leading up to the Reichstag elections in July, there were 461 political riots reported by the Prussian police. In these riots 82 people were killed and 400 seriously injured. The number of deaths in 1932 was 84 Nazis and 52 communists. It is believed that the number of injured in 1932 totaled 9,715.[2]

Italy had gone through similar economic problems and a similar period of violence some ten years before. Mussolini made his famed March on Rome on October 28, 1922. During the two years which preceded the march as many as 300 fascists and 3,000 antifascists were killed in political fighting. Italy's unemployment rate was not as high as Germany's would be, but it was substantial. In the early part of 1922, it stood at 602,000, out of a total industrial work force of 4 million, or an unemployment rate of 15 percent. For those who were working, particularly agricultural laborers, the wages were just a little above subsistence levels.

In Italy the violence had an almost comical aspect. Rather than throwing stones or engaging in fist fights, the fascists brought in artillery and tanks. In some cases they threatened towns with these weapons to force elected officials out. In the autumn of 1922, political assaults occurred at the rate of 12 a day. In one incident in 1921, a group of fascists invaded the house of a local co-operative and forced the workers to run a gauntlet of knives and clubs. Thirty-eight people were stabbed, including old men, disabled soldiers, and a 14-year old. In February 1921 fascists murdered a communist leader in Florence after their afternoon procession was the object of a bomb attack. In one battle at Scandicci, the police and fascist squadistri attempted to storm positions held by workers. After being driven back they returned with artillery and armored cars, broke down the barricades and demolished the People's House. Workers in the town of Empoli became so nervous, that they fired on a lorrie containing naval mechanics, simply on the rumor that it was a force of fascists. Eight were killed and ten were wounded. In August 1922, the fascists captured the city of Milan after three hours of fighting, burned the socialist presses and buildings, and threw the socialist government out. At Fiume they not only attacked the city but captured a destroyer, in retaliation for the killing of a fascist.

Spain experienced a period of violence not unlike that in Italy. In October 1934, the Socialists had tried to overthrow the government. By the time the revolt was put down over 1,000 people were dead. In the next eighteen months there were violent street demonstrations and strikes which culminated in the actual outbreak of Civil War in July 1936.

On the other side of the world, Japan, with its seemingly docile and conformist society, was rocked by political violence in the 1930s. Right-wing radicals killed the prime minister in 1931, along with other government officials. Still dissatisfied with official policy in 1932 they again targeted the prime minister for assassination, and were successful. In what was called the February 26 Incident in 1936, army officers went on a murder spree in which they killed the Lord Privy Seal, the Finance Minister, a Naval Admiral, the Inspector General of Military Training, the brother-in-law of the Prime Minister, as well as guards and servants.

ECONOMIC TRANSFORMATION AND THE EMERGENCE OF FASCISM

The violence associated with the fascist period represented the extremes to which political expression would go, although it was symptomatic of deeper societal problems. On the economic side, unemployment, itself a serious problem, was also a symptom of a more serious problem underneath - the basic economic structure was undergoing change. Small businesses and merchants were losing wealth and power to large banks and industrialists. Small artisans and workers were losing out to large factories, with their increasingly automated methods of production. The strength of the labor movement and the level of unrest may have been different in each country, but labor problems existed, in one form or another, in each country where fascism made an appearance, whether in Germany or Italy, or in Spain or Japan.

Labor unrest could be attributed, in part, to increasing industrialization. With an increase in the size of the labor force there would be an expected increase in the number of problems. Ancient Rome and Revolutionary France were proof of that. At the same time the turmoil surrounding the fascist period is not totally explained by the growth in the labor force, or a market economy increasingly dominated by industry. There was something else - an economic circumstance which made the labor market unstable. It was all in the timing. The problem for workers was, not so much that they would enter the labor market, but that they would enter it at a time when the markets for goods the produced were growing weaker. Specifically, markets were at the saturation point. If workers had come to rely on the market for survival, the level of dependence was out of all proportion to what the market could sustain. Employment, at a level desired by workers, in other words, was becoming a burden which the market could not support.

Whether the term instability could be accurately applied to the overall economic situation is not clear. Market saturation is simply an economic phenomenon, not in every case an indication of economic turmoil. However, when one particular sector of an economy experiences radical swings which make it unreliable as a predictor, it could be considered unstable. That would clearly be the case with labor markets when workers could not depend on them to provide employment from one day to the next. In the case of the fascist period, economic instability had the potential to spill over into the political realm, creating instability there.

Germany, in modern eyes, has been seen to be a model for mechanization and industrialization. Perhaps part of the reason is that the superiority of its technology was self-evident as German armies marched across Europe in the Second World War. Yet, technological advancement was a relatively recent development. In the 1800s Germany was still a largely rural society. In 1849 sixty-four percent of the population of Prussia lived in rural areas.[3] At the same time it was growing more difficult to survive by working the land. Peasants, as well as land owners, were struggling.

The growing market for industrial goods seemed to offer a solution. If weaker agricultural markets were eliminating the need for agricultural workers, those displaced were welcome to work in the factories. The urban working class began to grow in numbers. If the newly emerging markets of the industrial revolution seemed invincible at the time, it was only by comparison to weakening agricultural markets. Markets, which were strong in 1860, could weaken over time, creating problems which would appear in the 1930s. The problem was neither unique to Germany nor limited to a particular time period. Italy experienced similar problems in the 1920s. Both the German and Italian economies had the capability to physically produce enough to sustain their populations but neither economy could sustain the market demand necessary to keep workers fully employed.

In Italy, weakness in the market for goods and for labor evidenced itself, not so much in the lack of jobs, but in low wages. Factory owners would have argued that there were plenty of jobs available for those willing to work - suggesting that market demand for manufactured goods was, in fact, quite strong. Yet, if demand was strong and people could find jobs, why was there so much dissatisfaction among workers? Over a million industrial workers participated in 1,663 strikes in 1919 and their agricultural counterparts, some 500,000 laborers, participated in another 208 strikes. In 1920, the number of farm laborers who participated in strikes had grown to around a million, although there were only 189 agrarian strikes. The number of industrial workers who struck in 1920 remained the same, about a million, but the number of strikes had increased to 1,881.[4]

Why would strikes be an indication of market weakness? The large number of workers involved suggests just the opposite. If demand for goods had not been strong, why would factories have hired so many people in the first place? That fact alone would normally settle the argument. Unfortunately, it must be reconciled with the high level of discontent, which was related to low wages. How can strong market demand be reconciled with low wages? There was clearly some basic demand for manufactured goods or they would not have sold at all. Yet demand was only there so long as prices remained low. When prices were raised demand disappeared or was seriously weakened. Can demand really be described as "strong" if the market places price conditions on demand?

A political movement, such as fascism, is not explained away by suggestions that labor unrest was the cause. At the same time, fascist movements seemed to draw strength from a worsening economic situation. In Germany, the Nazis benefitted directly from unemployment. As the number of unemployed grew, membership in the SA increased. In Italy sluggish economic conditions contributed to an increase in fascist ranks. Ironically, it was defections from labor which contributed to fascist support. Labor had proved to be an early and formidable opponent of Musollini.

If labor unrest served as the backdrop to the fascist movement, there was a certain paradox in its operation. Hitler was openly antagonistic to labor, focusing particularly on its hated communist associations, while appealing to industrialists and large landowners. Musollini adopted a more conciliatory stance toward, even forming his own organization of trade unions, which claimed some 500,000 members in 1922.[5] If he was less openly antagonistic he eventually took steps to curb their power. Hitler developed a strong following among the middle class - small shopkeepers, teachers and professionals - not necessarily unemployed, but threatened by economic circumstances.

If fascism grew out of economic difficulties, what was at its center? Was it primarily a belief system with economic origins? It has been said that people were seeking an answer to the chaos and destruction of the Twentieth Century. The technological advances which had promised to better mankind had instead produced massive battlefield deaths in the First World War and widespread unemployment and depression in the period after. Whether Hitler was right or wrong, he at least provided his followers with a sense of purpose. Certainty was one defense against a chaotic world. On the other hand, was fascism, at heart, an economic program which adopted certain beliefs to lend legitimacy to its goals. That view suggests it was just another political program, whose success could be attributed more to leadership skills, than to real problem-solving. Hitler, the consummate politician, was simply adept at tailoring his message to a particular audience. That may better explain why he could attract support from groups with potentially conflicting views. Workers and industrialists, traditionally at war with each other, found common ground in Hitler's message. They were joined by individuals from the middle class.

Did the answer come down to only two choices - between fascism, the belief system, and fascism, the economic program - or was the answer even simpler? Was fascism simply a political luxury which urban societies could afford to indulge from time to time? Why did Russia, which experienced economic difficulties, labor unrest, and political turmoil, not evolve into a fascist dictatorship? If Stalin's Russia has been classified as a dictatorship, what emerged in Russia has never been confused with the dictatorship of Hitler's Germany. In fact, the political concept of fascism is somehow foreign to Russia. What made the Soviet dictatorship different? The basic answer is Joseph Stalin. He looked to a bureaucratic solution rather than an uncontrollable mass movement, when it came to a political base of support.

Joseph Stalin aside, there are other obvious differences between Russia and Germany. Where Hitler had drawn support from both the middle class and industrialists in Germany, their power was inconsequential in Russia, for two reasons: first, there was no middle class to speak of in Russia and second, if the industrialists had once held any power, it was now in the hands of the state. Another difference was in the need for popular support. It played a smaller role in political decision-making in Russia. Where Hitler made an effort to enlist popular support through public rallies, Stalin focused more on maintaining Party support, while ignoring public opinion. Finally, unemployment or uncertainty about the job market, was the least of economic worries for the typical Russian worker. Russia did not avoid all problems with unemployment. In 1924 there were 1.46 million unemployed out of an urban labor force of about 8.5 million workers, or 17 percent. In 1929 there were 1.6 million unemployed.[6]

Russia, for all the industrial development which the Five-Year plans imply, remained largely rural. Even in 1939, the urban population of Russia was only 33 percent of the total. In 1926, the urban labor force in Russia was 22.6 million, out of a total population of around 147 million, or 15 percent of the population.[7] Germany, in 1932, had a total labor force of around 18 million, out of a total population of around 65 million people or roughly 27 percent of its population. The fact that Russia's work force was smaller did not prevent labor problems. Strikes had been a serious problem during the 1905 Revolution and in the February Revolution of 1917.

Russia seemed disadvantaged in nearly every way, when it came to industrialization. For all its problems however, Russia's weakness gave it one clear advantage. Because industry was incapable of producing enough it was unlikely that market demand could ever be satisfied. Market saturation was an unlikely possibility, given the fact that resources were scarce and industrial capacity limited. The same could not be said of the industrialized economies of the West. Market saturation was the problem for German industry. One other factor combined with market saturation to threaten the worker - in a word, automation. Even as German factories came close to achieving market saturation, that "goal" could be accomplished with fewer and fewer workers.

If there was a spiritual dimension to these economic circumstances, one that might tempt people to follow a Hitler, it lay in the psychological impact on those most vulnerable to economic pressures, the workers and middle class. German workers not only faced unemployment, but a society which provided them no alternative means of survival. By implication, those who were unemployed and ignored by the economy, were unneeded by society as a whole. If the Russian worker risked starvation in hard economic times, if he risked death or imprisonment at the hands of the secret police, he at least was needed by the Soviet economy. So long as that economic need existed his place in Russian society was secure.

Surprisingly, there was one area in which the economic policies of Nazism and communism was similar, that of industrial syndicates or trusts. Following the nationalization of industry in Russia in June 1918, production had been organized into trusts, based on the type of industry involved. Nazi Germany stopped short of nationalization, but it did authorize the government to create industrial cartels in July 1933. Some 30 existing cartels were reorganized under the law and 28 new cartels had been formed by November.[8] The government set production quotas, determined prices, and controlled wages. Italy, in September 1926, organized industry into twelve national syndicates, which were converted into 22 national corporations in 1934.[9]

THE POLITICAL BACKGROUND TO NATIONAL SOCIALISM

Adolf Hitler was appointed chancellor of Germany on January 30, 1933. He had not been elected to the post, since it was an appointive office, but he had not seized power either. It would take eighteen months for Hitler to turn what had been the Weimar Republic into a dictatorship. In the July 1932 elections he received substantial support - 37.3 percent of the vote - but not a majority. However, dictatorships are not based on popular support. As Lenin had demonstrated, the secret to power was control of an apparatus of repression, such as the police or the military. At the same time, even dictatorships demanded some minimal level of support, if only within the governmental apparatus. Hitler could not have become a dictator by himself. What allowed Hitler to take power was a curious combination of circumstances. He was able to build up a following due to the economic conditions which existed in the late 1920s and early 1930s and he was able to take advantage of weaknesses in the German governmental structure. Like Lenin, Hitler found that it was relatively easy to frustrate attempts by a government to govern.

The next section looks at four things: 1) the historical development of Germany; 2) the form of government which was in place at the time Hitler was appointed chancellor; 3) the circumstances which surrounded his appointment; and 4) the early history of the Nazi Party and how it had developed by 1933.

GERMAN UNIFICATION AND THE GOVERNMENTAL STRUCTURE
(1814 - 1871)

While Hitler tried to inspire Germans with his visions of a great Nordic or Teutonic state, the historic reality was that Germany as a nation or country had very little history at all. Prior to 1814, 'Germany' had been nothing more than a group of principalities whose princes were interested in control of their own geographical domains. The state of Prussia claimed part of Poland, while Austria was part of the Austro-Hungarian Empire.

The decision to try to organize the various principalities into a larger German state was taken, in large part, to control France. Napoleon's successes had convinced many in Europe that an additional military power would be helpful. Even before Napoleon was defeated at Waterloo in 1815, delegates to the Congress of Vienna were in the process of creating a 'German Confederation.' The result was the German Confederation of 1815, which loosely allied some of the major principalities such as Austria, Prussia and Bavaria with some minor states, and managed to provide the group of 39 states with a constitution, in the form of the Federal Act.

While the Confederation had a constitution, it resembled a government only in form. Its members would not agree to set up a court system. It had a 'legislative' branch in the form of the Federal Diet or Bundestag but the individual states had been given sufficient power to veto most of its proposals. The defence of the Confederation members was perhaps the one area where there was agreement, although in reality Austria and Prussia provided most of the military muscle.

The Confederation, whose primary goal had been the military containment of France, could only serve as an idealistic model for a unifying German government. In 1848 and 1849 Germany was rocked by civil disorder which came to be known as the Revolution of 1848-1849. The Revolution would produce the first serious attempt to create a German government. In contrast to the Confederation, the new government was not to be a defensive alliance, but a governing body with real powers.

While the Revolution is dated from 1848, the states which were part of the Confederation had been experiencing severe economic distress prior to that time. The market for industrial goods had entered a downturn in 1846. Factories were closed and large numbers of people were thrown out of work. Much of agriculture still was dominated by laws which favored the landlord and continued the feudal system of dues. Where the feudal system was being ended the peasants had to compensate the landlords. In addition, blight and drought struck the harvests of 1845 and 1846 which brought famine in 1847.[10] The economic unrest brought violence to some of the towns in the winter of 1846-47.

When the citizens of Paris revolted in February 1848, the immediate result was a series of meetings in the German cities. In many of the states the princes were quick to surrender to demands for constitutional government. These independent actions were followed on March 1 by an attempt to revise the 1815 Confederation constitution. While labor disagreements to this time had been largely peaceful, the trend was toward more violence and the number of workers involved was growing. King Frederick William IV of Prussia, strengthened the Confederation by calling for constitutional changes in all the German states on March 18. On March 21, he called for the creation of a German parliament. The king was hoping his moves would both appease the crowds, while placing him in a position to lead the growing movement. Instead violence increased in March and April. Cities suffered through rioting, while workers destroyed machinery in factories. In the countryside peasants turned their anger on the castles of their landlords.

The civil unrest no doubt contributed to the relatively quick movement toward democratic government. A Pre-Parliament met on March 31 and set a date for National Assembly elections of May 1, 1848. By May 18 the new Parliament was meeting in Frankfurt. The 585 members of the Frankfurt Parliament soon encountered the problem which had baffled the 1815 Confederation - the interests of each state differed. There was even a reluctance to elect an imperial administrator or Reichsverweser. Finally Archduke John, the brother of the Austrian Emperor Ferdinand, was offered the job. His government, administratively, was comprised of several ministerial posts. While there had been internal disagreement, the Frankfurt Parliament had gained enough prestige to be considered legitimate. The Federal Diet, the governing body of the Confederation, transferred its functions to Archduke John in July 1848.

The stalemate over the election of the Reichsverweser represented a minor squabble. In March 1848 Denmark had undergone a revolution and when a new government emerged it claimed the state of Schleswig as part of Denmark. This angered Germans who claimed that it was so closely tied to the state of Holstein that it should be part of the new Germany. Prussia sent in troops in April, which angered Austria and other major European states. Prussia, aware of the political problems created, withdrew its troops. The Frankfurt Parliament however, was fired up over the issue, and demanded a continuation of the war. When Prussia concluded an armistice in August, the Parliament rejected it. Then, on September 16, 1848, it accepted it. While the September 16 action may have been realistic, the crowds in Frankfurt were outraged. Having avoided civil unrest since March, the city erupted, all of its anger being directed at the Parliament. In contrast to the disturbances of early 1848, the authorities did not make concessions. Instead, Austrian and Prussian troops, using artillery, suppressed disturbances in Berlin and other cities where they occurred.

The Frankfurt Parliament was not totally discredited. It even managed to produce a plan for a constitutional monarchy in March 1849. Unfortunately the king of Prussia turned down the offer of the crown and states, such as Austria and Prussia, ordered their delegates home. The Revolution would see one more wave of urban violence between May and July 1849. As in September, troops were called in, and it was suppressed.

While the rulers of the German states were pleased with the demise of the Frankfurt Parliament, they did not want to reinstate the monarchy. Instead they resurrected the Confederation as a symbol of authority. The Federal Diet was assumed to have governmental authority. It moved to nullify many of the actions of the Frankfurt Parliament and revoked many of the freedoms, such as freedom of the press, which had been approved by the Parliament's members. While the governmental moves would be considered conservative and even reactionary, there were attempts to deal with the grievances which existed. The Prussian government, for example, set up a banking system to loan peasants money to pay off their feudal obligations.[11]

The purpose of a united Germany in 1815 had been that of a military buffer against France. After 1850, the goal of uniting Germany was to establish Germany as a power in its own right. It turned into a struggle between Austria and Prussia. There was a great deal of political maneuvering, but in June 1866 Bismarck maneuvered Prussia into a war with Austria which was over in seven weeks. A Prussian army of 280,000 scored a complete victory over an Austrian and Saxon force of 270,000 at Sadowa on July 3, 1866. Bismarck did not win territorial control of all of Germany by the war, but he did add Saxony, Hanover, and Hesse-Cassel. In addition, the northern part now controlled by Prussia was completely dominated by her. What emerged from the war was the North German Confederation in 1867, complete with a constitution. The constitution established a federal council, or Bundesrat, with representatives from each of the 24 member states. These representatives formed committees to supervise the government. The federal chancellor was charged with overall administration. To give the appearance of democracy, Bismarck created a parliament, the Reichstag, whose members were elected by popular vote. The Bundesrat could veto any legislation passed by the Reichstag, so it had little real power.[12]

With the north under Prussian control, Bismarck's next goal was to add the south. He believed the union would eventually take place, but did not know whether war would be necessary. When elections were held in the south in 1868 the returns went against unification. Only after Prussia had gone to war with France in 1870 would the southern states agree to join Bismarck's German state.

The Franco-Prussian War was short, although it lasted a little longer than the Austro-Prussian War of 1866. The French declared war on July 15, 1870. On September 2, not only was the French army defeated at Sedan, but their Emperor was taken prisoner. On January 28, 1871, following a siege of Paris, France agreed to an armistice. Bismarck had not waited for the French surrender before formally uniting Germany. King William of Prussia accepted the title of Emperor on January 1, 1871.

The governmental structure of the German Empire was not significantly different from that of the 1867 North German Confederation. The Bundesrat, or Federal council, was expanded to 58 seats to accommodate the new members, although Prussia held more votes. The Reichstag still was without real power, although it was elected by universal suffrage. The chancellor was the chief executive officer, appointed by the Emperor. While the individual states theoretically, and sometimes actually, were independent political bodies, the political tendency, as Europe moved closer to the First World War, was toward a unified German state.

THE CREATION OF THE WEIMAR REPUBLIC

Emperor William died in March 1888. He was succeeded by Crown Prince Frederick, who himself would live only three more months. Crown Prince William became Emperor in July 1888, as William II. In one sense governmental power was exercised by the chancellor, yet William, managed to gain control of Germany's foreign policy. That involvement would ultimately lead to an alliance with Austria-Hungary, and involvement in World War I. Whether war could have been avoided, in view of the inherent rivalries and conflict between the European powers, William's assertive personality and belligerent attitude was not much help.

The First World War both reinforced the legendary status of German military prowess while undermining it. If the leadership drew optimistic conclusions about military capabilities from Bismarck's tactics in the 1860s, they had overlooked some crucial facts. Bismarck, in spite of using Prussia's armies, had used them sparingly. Prussia fought her enemies separately. Austria had been defeated in 1866 and Prussia had four years of peace before the Franco-Prussian War began in 1870. A protracted war on two fronts, even with Germany's superbly organized military, proved too much. In 1918 her military machine collapsed.

Hitler would look back on the end of the First World War with bitterness. Blinded by a British poison gas attack in October 1918, he was in a hospital in November 1918 when the war ended. On November 9, Kaiser William agreed to abdicate as Emperor and went into exile in Holland. This was followed on November 11 by the signing of the armistice. Hitler would always believe that the army had not been beaten but was in a position to continue fighting. The army and Germany had not lost the war; they had been betrayed by the "November Criminals," who had agreed to an onerous peace when Germany was still able to fight.

Hitler's belief about the army's condition at war's end was far different from the reality. He would have been horrified to learn that the German soldiers, not only refused to fight, but began setting up revolutionary soldiers' councils, roughly modeled on those of their Russian counterparts. The mutiny had begun among the naval forces on October 28, when crews on two cruisers at Wilhelmshaven refused to put to sea for a raid. While naval authorities tried to quell the mutiny by arrests, it soon spread. Even the German people were not as eager to continue the war as Hitler would come to believe.

Soon after the naval forces had mutinied, the Independent Socialist party in Bavaria proclaimed itself the head of a new government (November 8, 1918). On November 9 Berlin workers took to the streets. One of the socialist leaders, Philipp Scheidemann, in speaking before the crowds, almost as an afterthought, ended his speech with the words 'long live the great German republic.' The statement was at least enough to create the impression that a government had been formed. Friedrich Ebert, another socialist leader, acted as if there was a government in existence, and assumed control, calling himself 'imperial chancellor.'[13] Without a formal government, Ebert on November 10, got the co-operation of the army leadership, now fearful of the soviet-styled soldier's councils.

In January 1919 the Communist Party decided to openly challenge Ebert and proclaimed its own revolutionary government. While some viewed such action as premature, communist workers managed to take over government buildings in Berlin. Regular army units were called in, although the officers were unsure of how far the soldier's councils had undermined discipline. To supplement the army, 'Free Corps' volunteers, members of civilian paramilitary organizations were asked to help. (Some of the Free Corps members would later evolve into Hitler's SA.) The combined army and Free Corps units had quashed the communist revolt by January 13.

Despite the street unrest, elections for a constituent assembly were held on January 19, 1919. Ebert was elected president and Scheidemann became chancellor. The assembly's primary job was not to govern, but to create a new constitution. In some ways the form of the new government resembled that created by Bismarck. The kaiser was replaced by a president who was elected every seven years. There were still the two legislative bodies, the upper Reichsrat and the parliamentary Reichstag. The Reichsrat, while still representative of the various states (renamed Länder), no longer could veto legislation of the Reichstag. (It technically could veto legislation, but the Reichstag could override with a two-thirds vote.) The position of chancellor was filled by the president. The president was also given the authority to suspend civil liberties in an emergency. The

Reichstag members were elected to four-year terms and anyone over 20 was eligible to vote. While Bismarck's government had seemed to move toward a unified German state, the new Reich went even further. Elections to the Reichstag were direct elections which tended to create a feeling of German unity. At the same time the Reichsrat, which emphasized the sovereignty of the separate states was diminished in power. Another important change was the imposition of direct taxes by the new Reich government. It did not have to rely on the individual states for its budget.[14]

The new government quickly ran into trouble when the Allies presented the final peace terms. On June 19, the cabinet refused to agree to the terms and resigned. A new government voted to accept the treaty. Even the army recognized that it was in no state to fight the Allies. On June 28, 1919 a German delegation signed the Treaty of Versailles. The territorial concessions, such as the surrender of Alsace-Lorraine to France and the transfer of West Prussia to Poland, would provide Hitler with a very specific excuse to attack the new government and the injustices of Germany's treatment under the Treaty.

The Treaty itself was only one topic about which Hitler would brood. The army would give him another. The military leadership, in the immediate aftermath of the war, wanted to avoid blame for Germany's loss. Whether they truly believed it, they publicly stated that the German army had been betrayed. Hindenburg, in an appearance before a commission investigating the war in November 1919, stated that the German army had been 'stabbed in the back.'[15] Ebert, the Social Democrat, reinforced that impression with a statement that the German army had not been defeated on the battlefield. Those who had agitated for peace had been responsible for the betrayal. The fact that Hindenburg would publicly state such ideas confirmed Hitler's own perceptions about the war.

Despite Hindenburg's later assertions, the military leadership had urged that the Versailles Treaty be signed. While they recognized the concessions Germany was making, they also understood that the German army was in no position to defend her and risked total humiliation and elimination. Hindenburg's statements cost the government in prestige and support. Despite these problems the basic form of the government had been established in 1919. It would come to be known as the Weimar Republic because its first meetings had been held in the city of Weimar, rather than Berlin.

THE WEIMAR REPUBLIC AND HITLER'S RISE (1919 - 1923)

Hindenburg's charges that the army had been betrayed may have given many ex-soldiers an official-sounding reason to dislike the Socialist-led government. It was not the only reason they opposed it. Many held anti-communist or anti-socialist views and, apart from the harsh terms of Versailles, they had an instinctive hatred of government policies. It did not take long for this resentment to be translated into action. On March 13, 1920, a group of Free Corps units, led by Wolfgang Kapp, attempted to take over Berlin and establish a new government. The Kapp Putsch, as it was known, fell apart soon after it began. While Kapp was able to seize some buildings in Berlin, a general strike by trade unionists shut the city down and Kapp left after four days. No sooner had Kapp's right-wing coup attempt failed than the government faced a threat from the left. Communists in the Ruhr, protesting Kapp's action, managed to create a 50,000 man Red Army which seized power there. The army welcomed the help of Free Corps volunteers in suppressing the revolt. A year later, in March 1921, communists tried to organize another rising in Prussia, which also was suppressed. Between 1919 and 1923, the revolts and suppression which followed would kill over 2,000 people.[16] These deaths were primarily associated with mass uprisings. There were an additional 376 political murders between 1919 and 1922.[17]

For Hitler and the ultra-right, the terms of the Versailles Treaty had been a humiliation. They created other problems, particularly in the economic sphere. Where Germany, under Bismarck, had engaged in power politics against France, the French now turned the tables. The German economy was extremely weak following the war, yet France insisted on compliance with Treaty reparation terms. In addition, France continually tried to annex German territory, such as the Rhineland. Whether French actions were motivated by revenge or by fear of a revitalized Germany, she found that Britain was less inclined to push Germany. If France saw economic opportunity in Germany's territorial possessions, England saw greater opportunity in a market for goods. Britain had economic problems of her own which motivated her to revive Germany as a potential market.[18] While Britain acted as a check, France was still able to maintain pressure for reparations.

The government was hit on several fronts. The Versailles reparations were only one burden created by the war. There was also the debt which Germany had accumulated itself during the war. At war's end the government needed to pay off 144 billion marks in war appropriations. In April 1921 the Allies demanded that she make reparation installment payments of two billion marks annually against a total payment amount of 132 billion marks plus annual payments of one-quarter of her exports.[19] The armistice agreement had taken the industrially productive Saarland and Upper Silesia. In January 1923 France moved troops into the Ruhr after Germany was declared in default on her payments. In September, Stresemann, the German chancellor, agreed to resume them.

What may have saved Germany from further economic hardship, insofar as the reparations were concerned, were some economic realities. The Allies realized that continued economic pressure was causing severe hardship. The consequence for international trade, particularly for Britain, was the continued loss of potential German markets. France was the major obstacle to a reduction of the pressure. France had two reasons for opposing leniency: first, as long Germany remained economically weak, she posed little military threat to France; second, German intransigence gave France an excuse to exploit German material resources, such as those of the Ruhr. Yet, even France found that her economic fortunes were tied to German recovery and that exploitation based on military force had an economic price. Following the occupation of the Ruhr, the value of the franc fell 25 percent in 1923.[20] This drop may have contributed to the fall of the French government the following May, which paved the way for the acceptance of the American-backed Dawes Plan in the summer of 1924. The plan substantially eased the burden on Germany by reducing the annual payments to a level Germany could afford.

With the acceptance of the Dawes Plan, Germany received an 800 million mark loan. She was helped by the withdrawal of foreign troops from her important industrial states. French troops left the Ruhr in August 1925 and part of the Rhineland in 1926. In 1925 Germany was able to enter a period of relative economic boom. It was a contrast to the economic chaos of the years which preceded it.

The turmoil of the period between 1919 and 1924 was not limited to the economic sphere. Economic problems had been bad enough to seriously impact the political system. There was widespread dissatisfaction among workers resulting in a large number of strikes. Severe inflation in 1923 ruined a majority of the middle class. Although economic problems may not have been the explanation, the Nazi movement gained strength during this time period.

Inflation was one of the problems and the war, with its debt financing, was partly to blame. Deficit financing however, did not stop with the end of the war. The government continued the policy to fund programs. The inflation which struck in 1923 was, in some ways, simply an offshoot of governmental spending policy. However, it had a very specific cause - the occupation of the Ruhr by a French and Belgian army. The occupation, which included taking over production at mining facilities, was economically disruptive. However the inflation had another cause related to German government policy. The government, not only encouraged worker resistance to the occupation by paying unemployment, it also financed that policy by printing money.

On June 24, 1922, Walter Rathenau, Germany's foreign minister, was assassinated by right-wing terrorists. If the assassination was an indication of political turmoil, economic problems became evident in July and August when there was a request for a moratorium on reparations payments. France's prime minister, Raymond Poincaré, was reluctant to grant such a concession unless France was allowed direct access to the Ruhr coal fields. In November 1922, Josef Wirth, the German chancellor, resigned. His replacement, Wilhelm Cuno, renewed the request for a moratorium. The Reparations Commission however, in December 1922, declared Germany in default. The official reason was that Germany had failed to make required timber deliveries. This was followed in January 1923 by a declaration that Germany was also in default on coal deliveries.

French and Belgian troops marched into the Ruhr on January 11, 1923 and physically seized mines and industrial facilities. The German reaction was to call for passive resistance. The government decided back this request with subsidies. When miners and workers went out on strike, the government paid them unemployment. Since it did not have the funds available to cover these expenditures, it began printing money. Inflation inevitably followed. By the end of 1923 the exchange rate for the dollar was four billion marks.[21] Internally, prices were unreal - a single egg cost 80 million marks.[22]

When the Cuno government fell in August 1923, Gustav Stresemann took over as chancellor. He announced, on September 26, that Germany would resume making reparations payments. In addition, the passive resistance campaign was ended. To bring inflation under control, Stresemann resorted to other measures. He drastically cut back on government spending, while taking steps to withdraw the inflated currency from circulation. One of the biggest drains had been the subsidies paid to keep passive resistance going. With the ending of the campaign, a major cause of inflation was brought to an end. The German government was also aided by the fact that the 1924 Dawes Plan provided her with external loans and a reduction, of her reparation obligations, in the short-term. Politically, Stresemann's offer to resume reparations, undercut the French argument for continued occupation of the Ruhr. French troops would leave in August 1925. Stresemann had help from the French electorate in May 1924, when Poincaré's party was defeated in the elections.

While Stresemann took decisive measures, any economic action takes time to work. Political events can move much more quickly. On the night of November 8-9, 1923, Adolf Hitler would stage his beerhall putsch in Munich. The ultimate goal of the putsch was to overthrow the Weimar Republic. The immediate goal was to take over the government of Bavaria. Hitler's SA units, armed with machine-guns and pistols, invaded a Bavarian political social at the Bürgerbräukeller on the evening of November 8. Even though he got the crowd's attention by standing on a chair and firing a shot into the ceiling, Bavarian government officials present would not support him and the putsch fell apart. Hitler received a show of support the next day when some 2,000 of his followers marched through Munich. Unfortunately, the Bavarian "Green Police" had blocked one of the streets and when a shot was heard, the confrontation turned into a battle. Sixteen of Hitler's Nazis died. Hitler was arrested later. He was tried in February 1924 for high treason, convicted, and sentenced to five years in prison on April 1, 1924. He would be free by the end of December. While the beerhall putsch was a failure, what Hitler had accomplished in even making the attempt, was an extraordinary feat - the Nazi Party had been in existence for less than five years at the time.

THE NAZI PARTY TO THE BEERHALL PUTSCH (1919 - 1923)

Under the terms of the Versailles Treaty, the size of the German army could be no more than 100,000 men. Adolf Hitler was among those who were still employed by the army following the reduction. As a "political observer" Hitler's job was to report on the activities of some of the new groups forming in the wake of the war. One of these groups was the German Workers' Party (DAP, short for Deutsche Arbeiterpartei) In September 1919 he attended one of their meetings. While he was supposed to be gathering intelligence on the group, he found its ideas so seductive that he soon became a member and also took a place on its board. It was Hitler's speaking abilities which would propel him into the leadership position. His skills were such that he was able to earn a living as a speaker. The irony was that he gained his wealth by decrying the economic conditions while those who suffered the most from unemployment financed him. The beerhall putsch may provide some indication of just how persuasive Hitler was and how lucrative that talent could prove. When he arrived at the beer garden in 1923, he was riding in a Mercedes Benz. He had only attended his first DAP meeting in September 1919. When

367

the DAP held a meeting in February 1920, Hitler attracted a crowd of 2,000.

Despite Hitler's hatred of the left, when the name of the DAP was changed shortly after the February meeting, the word "socialist" was added to the title. The party was now to be known as the National Socialist German Workers' Party (NSDAP). For Hitler there were career changes around this time. He felt secure enough in the new party setting that he retired from the army at the end of March 1920.

While Hitler's oratorical skills attracted converts to the NSDAP, the right-wing message itself was attractive to a larger audience. The National Socialists were not the only right-wing group in Germany with a following. At the core of the right-wing ideology was a nationalistic belief in the German state and a closeness to the military. Hitler's ideology focused the Party's hatred on Jews and foreigners and emphasized the ideal of the pure German race.

During 1920 the Party expanded into other regions. The expansion required it to incorporate, so it once again changed its name. In October 1920 it became the Nationalsozialistischer Deutscher Arbeiterverein (NSDAV). Its membership in January 1921 was around 3,000. As instrumental as Hitler had been in the growth of the Party, he abruptly resigned in July 1921. The reason was a proposal to merge the Party with the German Socialist Party. While it would have increased the Party's base, he felt that it would also dilute his own power. Aware that his efforts had been the major reason for its growth, the Party quickly moved to bring him back in. If he wanted back in he also set a price. He demanded, and received, the chairmanship and control of appointments. In addition to the administrative changes on Hitler's rejoining, he took steps to turn the Party into a more military organization. The organization which furnished the Nazi storm troopers, the Sturmabteilung (SA) was created, although the SA did not receive its name until October 1921.

From the 3,000 members of January 1921, the Party increased in size to 6,000 in January 1922. By November the number had again increased, to 41,000.[23] In November 1923, the time of the beerhall putsch, membership had reached 55,000.[24] Some 15,000 members were also storm troopers in the SA.[25]

There is a temptation to label everything Hitler did as the actions of a fanatic. Many actions clearly were. Yet Hitler had a calculating side, concerned as much with personal ambition as with beliefs or Party principles. Like other demagogues, Hitler had the capacity to rationalize actions to fit immediate and practical political needs. His resignation from the Party in 1921, couched in the language of principle, was intended to neutralize his political opponents while increasing his own power. That is not to say that he was totally insincere or was merely acting when expressing moral outrage. When he addressed the crowd in the beer garden he had worked himself into a frenzy. Yet, the beerhall putsch was hardly a spontaneous outburst. It had been planned, even if its failure indicated a miscalculation of the level of popular support or the capabilities of the storm troopers.

In the fall of 1923, Stresemann had called off the passive resistance campaign over the Ruhr and was trying to bring inflation under control. His actions, if they represented a practical solution, infuriated the ultra-right and provided Hitler with one more "grievance" against the Weimar government. With 55,000 Party members in November 1923, Hitler felt that he was in a position to attempt a takeover of the Bavarian government. Having secured that base, he could move against Berlin. However, even as he was finalizing plans for the coup in November, he was already too late. Stresemann had already struck politically. In October he had used the army to put down communist governments in Saxony and Thuringia. It was considered an illegal move since the communists had legally come to power. Yet it gave Stresemann some conservative credentials, while undermining the Nazi political platform. No longer could Hitler accuse Stresemann of allying himself with the communists. While many in the army may have remained sympathetic to Hitler's ideas, they were less inclined to action against the government.

Hitler's mistake was in going through with his plan once political support for action was eroding. There was a flaw in the plan itself, as well. It relied too much on the support of members of the Bavarian government, who listened to their own constituencies. As Hitler was making final preparations they were beginning to pull back. Hitler might have done better the night of the coup, if he had maintained tighter control of the operation. While his storm troopers were beating up political opponents in Munich that night, government officials were allowed to escape and the operating units of government, such as the police, were largely left alone. The police units assembled the next day were enough to stop Hitler's 2,000 supporters when they marched, still hoping to seize control. When the police opened fire sixteen Nazis died.

Hitler slipped away from the confrontation unwounded, but he did not escape all consequences. He was tried in April 1924. He used the trial to promote his political views and those of his Party. Although he received a five-year sentence, he would serve only one year. In addition, prison conditions made his stay seem almost resort-like. He would use the time to write *Mein Kampf* (My battle), which would bring him wealth - he earned over eight million marks between 1925 and 1945.[26]

THE WEIMAR REPUBLIC AND HITLER'S RISE (1924 - 1933)

On December 20, 1924, Hitler was released from Landsberg prison. In his absence, not only had membership fallen, but the Party had been officially banned throughout Germany. He had tried to provide some guidance while in prison, but found that various factions within the Party were tending to pull it apart. Tired of being asked to mediate, in the summer of 1924 he informed members that he was withdrawing from active participation.

He had no intention of abandoning the Party. His first task, on his release, was to get the ban lifted in Bavaria. He visited with the Bavarian prime minister, Dr. Heinrich Held, in January 1925. While Held may not have been convinced of Hitler's peaceful intentions he lifted the ban. Hitler almost lost even this concession when he held a rally in February at the same beerhall where he had staged the putsch. The fact that 4,000 people showed up alarmed the Bavarian authorities, who banned him from further public speaking. The ban would remain in effect through March 1927.

Hitler was still able to build his organization. Party membership, once as high as 55,000, had fallen to 27,000 in 1925. Hitler was able to increase it to 35,000 in 1926, then to 75,000 in 1927. When the Great Depression hit in 1929, membership had reached 108,000.[27] The growth experienced by the Party as a whole was reflected in the SA, which had over 30,000 members in 1929. While growth was important to Hitler he also wanted a more committed membership and he began to rid the Party of political opponents. The Party which would emerge at the end of the 1920s was one more dedicated and more personally loyal to Hitler.

Considering its tiny beginnings, only 2,000 members in 1920, the fact that it received 810,000 votes in the May 1928 elections was also a major feat. Yet, that showing represented only 2.6 percent of the total vote and gave the Nazis only 12 seats in the Reichstag, which had 491 members.[28] The poor showing convinced Hitler that a tactical change was needed. Between 1926 and 1928 Hitler had been trying to cultivate support among city dwellers. While the growth in SA membership suggests that there was a mob of urban unemployed waiting to join the Nazis, that impression is deceptive. Workers were found to strongly favor either the socialists or the communists. After the 1928 elections Hitler sought to cultivate rural voters.[29]

Both urban and rural voters had reason to worry about economic conditions. At the time of the New York stock market crash of October 1929 1.3 million Germans were unemployed.[30] The unemployment was a symptom of Germany's internal problems. It was foreseeable that a crash in New York would have some impact on the German economy. The severity of that impact however, came as something of a shock. It was not so much that the German economy was necessarily tied closely to the economic fortunes of another country, such as the United States. A more basic problem was that Germany's markets were inherently weak. As a result, German industry had come to rely on artificial measures, such as abnormally high borrowing, to sustain markets. When American investors began calling in German loans in the weeks following the Crash, German businesses began to go under or were forced to cut back on operations. A second problem was that German industry was dependent on the U.S. as a market for its products. When the U.S. market began to shrink, German manufacturers quickly saw sales fall off.[31]

In December 1929 the number of unemployed was 1,892,000, out of a work force of 19,761,000 or an unemployment rate of 9.5 percent. In December 1930 the number of unemployed had grown to 3,076,000 or 15.7 percent.[32] The increase in unemployment caused the collapse of the government in March 1930. The major issue was an increase in the unemployment benefit. The battle essentially pitted the employers against the employees. The Social Democratic Party (SPD) and the People's Party (DVP) had jointly ruled in what was known as the "Great Coalition." The SPD not only wanted to increase the unemployment fund, but also favored greater employer contributions. The DVP, representing the employers, opposed the plan.[33] To form a new government Hindenburg appointed Heinrich Brüning chancellor. Brüning dissolved the Reichstag and called for new elections. The date for the elections was September 14, 1930.

The Nazi Party was in a much better position to exploit this opportunity than it had been in May 1928. Hitler's major advantage, in one sense, was that he had not changed his basic message. The message still evoked images of a greater Germany, while blaming the Jews, the communists, and the government leaders who had sold out in 1919, for Germany's problems.[34] At the same, Hitler had changed strategies. The strategy did not involve a workers' program patterned after a communist model. In fact Otto Strasser was expelled from the Party in the spring of 1930 for advocating such an economic solution. The strategy instead was based on an appeal to empathy - Hitler "understood" the problems of the little man.[35] While he offered sympathy, he seemed unwilling to compromise on his basic program - the solution to all economic problems was to follow the Nazi plan. Where he did compromise was on tactics. He tailored his message somewhat to different audiences and targeted the part of the electorate which would provide votes. The urban strategy had failed in 1928. The Party now sought support in rural areas and among the middle class.

In January 1930 the Nazi Party had 178,000 members. When the elections were held on September 14, it was clear that the increase in Nazi support was not limited to those who had joined the Party. Where they had only received 810,000 votes in the May 1928 elections, they now received 6.4 million, which was about 18 percent (compared to the 2.6 percent of 1928). This gave them nearly one-fifth of the Reichstag seats (107 out of 577).[36] The publicity which followed caused another 100,000 people to join the Party before the end of 1930.

With 107 seats the Nazis were unable to pass legislation of their own, but they did obstruct the Reichstag as much as possible. Despite their actions, the Brüning government was able to avoid total collapse through much of 1931. Brüning, despite his inability to control the Reichstag and Hitler's attempt to oust him in October, would not be asked to resign as chancellor until May of 1932.

Hindenburg's term as president expired on May 5, 1932. In February Hitler announced that he would seek the office, even though he had doubts about running against Hindenburg. In December 1931, he had behind him a membership of 800,000, with an accompanying SA membership of 225,000. Unemployment had increased to 4,520,000 or 24 percent.[37] The election was held on March 13. While Hitler's chances of defeating Hindenburg were slim, the winner needed over 50 percent of the vote to claim the office. Hindenburg's total, 18,651,497, was 49.7 percent, just short of the majority required. If Hitler was far short of that figure, with 11,339,446 votes, or 30.2 percent, he had received enough votes to force a runoff. In the runoff election between Hindenburg and Hitler, held on April 10, Hindenburg gained almost a million votes, while Hitler added two million to his total. The final vote gave Hindenburg 53 percent to Hitler's 36.8 percent, or in raw numbers, 19,359,983 to 13,418,547.[38]

By the end of 1932 unemployment would reach 5,575,000, or 30.8 percent.[39] Nazi Party membership had gone above a million members in July, when 1932 was only half over. Brüning had resigned in May and Hindenburg replaced him with Franz von Papen. Papen moved quickly to create a new government. The Reichstag was dissolved and new elections were set for July 31. The Nazis did even better than they had done in the April presidential runoff, receiving some 13,700,000 votes and increasing the number of Reichstag seats to 230.[40] Hitler believed the election results were sufficient to allow him to take over the government. If he was inclined to interpret the results as a form of popular mandate, he forgot that governmental power was still one step removed from popular elections. Hindenburg still controlled the government, if only because he decided who to appoint. Hitler was reminded of this fact in August. At a meeting with Papen he threw a fit and threatened a takeover if not given complete control. He was not only rebuked by Hindenburg the same afternoon, but Hindenburg's office followed up with a press release detailing Hitler's actions.[41] If Hindenburg was prepared to stand up to Hitler, he was not willing to commit totally to Papen. Papen was expected to find a way to end the political stalemate. When the new Reichstag met in September, he had already decided to dismiss it. After meeting only a few hours, the Reichstag was again dissolved. The new elections were scheduled for November 6, 1932.

Based on the still serious unemployment and the growth in Party membership, the Nazis should have gained even more seats in the new elections. Yet Hitler's now-public August tantrum had cost his Party support. In addition, the Nazis gave the impression of wavering over long-standing principles. Despite their instinctive opposition to communism, they joined with the communists in a transport strike in Berlin just four days before the election. When the election results were tallied they had received two million fewer votes. They now had only 196 seats in the Reichstag, a loss of 34.[42]

In spite of this setback, they remained a powerful political force. Papen, who had only served as chancellor since June, resigned on November 17. Hitler once again approached Hindenburg about taking over the government. Again Hindenburg refused to appoint him and requested the recently-resigned Papen to take over again. Papen's new appointment lasted less than a day. What he proposed was considered extreme. He wanted to suppress all political parties and assume dictatorial powers until a new constitution could be approved. When he could not find support among the cabinet members, Hindenburg felt compelled to replace him with General Kurt von Schleicher.

In many ways the advantage now lay with Hitler. Schleicher, although initially a supporter of Papen, had schemed to oust him. Yet Schleicher, like Papen, assumed that he could use political tricks to manipulate the government. The problem was that neither Papen nor Schleicher had a political base to use in negotiations. Each had to rely on some other source of power, such as the army. While Hitler's popular support might rise or fall, he could count on the committed support of Party members. In addition, Hitler's SA provided a physical force which, in numbers, could rival the army.

Hitler's political opportunity came in January 1933. Papen, betrayed by Schleicher, now decided to use Hitler to get revenge. In a series of meetings with Hitler Papen negotiated a joint government which would replace that of Schleicher. Schleicher, who found that he had no better success than Papen at governing, resigned on January 28.

Papen had persuaded Hindenburg that he should once more take over. Unfortunately he also had persuaded him that Hitler should be given the chancellory. On January 30, 1933, Hindenburg appointed Hitler to the post. At the time unemployment stood at 6,013,612. SA membership would continue to grow through 1933 and 1934. By May 1933 it had reached two million and by September 1933 2.5 million. Whether that growth was related to unemployment is not clear. Unemployment began to fall during 1933, dropping to 4,804,000 by the end of 1933, while SA membership reached three million in 1934.[43] It seems more likely that membership by this time was seen as a way to career advancement or job security.

If Hitler's appointment to the chancellory was a personal milestone, it also represented a radical change in political operations. He had used the political power of the masses to gain control of the government. Once in power the governmental apparatus provided a more effective method of control. Hitler still used the Party, but he was able to dispense with many of the people who had helped him on the way up. In eighteen months he was able to advance from the position of chancellor to absolute dictator of Germany. The next chapter looks at how he transformed his political victory in January 1933 into the Nazi dictatorship.

CHAPTER 19

THE NAZI DICTATORSHIP (1933 - 1939)

CONSOLIDATION OF POWER - JANUARY 30 - MARCH 1933

On January 30, 1933 Hitler had achieved part of his dream. His goal was not simply to become chancellor, nor even leader of Germany. His goal was to make Germany into a nation with power. Unlike Papen or Schleicher, Hitler bargained from a position of strength. They had little power themselves and, relying on others, were tempted to engage in behind-the-scenes maneuvering. Papen contributed to his own problems by entering into a pact with the Nazis in the summer of 1932. In return for their support he would lift the ban on SA rallies. The ban had been imposed because of SA disruptions and, once lifted, allowed SA units to resume their practices. Hitler was not above political intrigue where it was to his advantage, but it was not central to his power.

In contrast to his failed beerhall putsch of 1923, he had come to power legally - if the use of his storm troopers to intimidate his opponents was not counted or the obstructionist tactics of the Nazi members of the Reichstag. To his opponents Hitler had only a toehold in government - from their perspective a relatively weak position. He controlled only two cabinet positions, in addition to the chancellory. There were nine other positions. The Nazis still held the same number of seats in the Reichstag and they were in the minority there. Nevertheless, within two months he would eliminate the Reichstag and gain enough power to render his opponents powerless.

This section looks at the actions Hitler took immediately after becoming chancellor. While the economic situation had not changed appreciably, economic forces played a very small role in what had become a totally political game. Hitler's transformation of the political process involved the manipulation of the political and governmental structure which controlled Germany.

THE HITLER CABINET

The structure of Hitler's new cabinet was either the most fitting symbol of Papen's understanding of politics or a symptom of the problem with Papen's logic where power was concerned. Papen, who had played politics to oust Schleicher and whose dream was to provide Germany with decisive leadership under his direction, had chosen the position of vice-chancellor as his means of exercising authority.

Papen's reasoning was that, even if Hitler was chancellor, the real power still lay with Hindenburg, who could dismiss him at any time, and Papen could control Hindenburg. The flaw in his logic was that traditional governmental controls, such as the prestige accorded to governmental office, might or might not work against Hitler. If they did not, Papen had no other means of controlling him. He should have known that Hitler would be willing to test his limits. In the negotiations leading to his appointment, he had asked for, even demanded, four positions in the new government - at a time when Papen was unsure whether Hindenburg would even agree to Hitler's participation at all. Papen had also ignored the lessons of the summer of 1932. It was Papen who had ordered the ban against the SA lifted, ushering in one of the bloodiest periods of political campaigning - 82 people died in June in Prussia in the 461 confrontations which occurred at that time.[1]

The reason for Hitler's appointment as chancellor may have had little to do with Papen's influence with Hindenburg. There is a suggestion that Hitler, in a private meeting with Hindenburg's son, Oskar, on January 22, 1933, may have threatened to reveal the Hindenburg family's involvement in the *Osthilfe* scandals. Certain Prussian landowners had been accused of accepting subsidies from the government. Oskar may also have been offered other inducements, since he became a general after Hitler came to power and the Hindenburg estate was enlarged as well.[2]

When it met on January 31, Hitler's cabinet included only two other Nazis, Wilhelm Frick, minister of the interior, and Hermann Göring. Göring however, held two positions - minister without portfolio and minister of the interior for Prussia. In theory, Göring served under Papen where Prussian affairs were concerned, since Papen was minister president of Prussia. Yet Göring had effective control of the Prussian police. He soon began to purge the police of non-Nazis. The transformation of the Prussian police was one of the initial organizational changes in the governmental structure. There were even more dramatic changes to come.

THE ENABLING ACT

On February 1, Hitler dissolved the Reichstag and set new elections for March 5, 1933. While he intended to hold the election, he did not want to make it easy for his opponents. Under Article 48 of the Weimar Constitution, the President could issue emergency decrees. One of the first such decrees restricted freedom of the press and outlawed public meetings. The decree gave Hitler an excuse to attack the communists. He also intended to use the powers Göring held in Prussia to their fullest. He first ordered the police, on February 17, to support patriotic associations, meaning the SA. Feeling that this did not go far enough, Göring incorporated the SA and SS into the police as auxiliaries on February 22. In Prussia, 25,000 SA and 15,000 SS troops were officially armed as a result.

On February 27, 1933, the Reichstag, the building which housed the German parliament, was destroyed by fire. It was never clear who set the fire, although a young Dutch communist was arrested by police at the scene. He would later be executed for the crime, following a three-month trial. There are suspicions that the Nazis set the blaze themselves. The fact that a communist had been apprehended at the scene gave Hitler sufficient reason to publicly blame the communist movement. He persuaded Hindenburg to issue another emergency decree. The 'Decree for the Protection of the People and State,' issued on February 28, suspended some important civil liberties, such as freedom of the press and freedom of assembly. The decree did more than that however. It also gave the federal authorities the right, not only to restore order in the individual states, but also to take over their governments. The Nazis began using this provision even before the election.

They did well at the polls on March 5, receiving 43.9 percent of the vote. In the June 1932 elections they had received 37 percent. This meant they picked up additional seats in the Reichstag, for a total of 288. If they were interested in passing legislation, they could get a majority by joining forces with the German Nationalists, who controlled another 52 seats.

Many politicians would have been satisfied with what Hitler had already accomplished. He had been appointed to the chancellorship and, with a working majority, could realistically expect to pass any political program. Even if he fell out of favor, he was likely to remain an influential figure in German politics for the foreseeable future. Yet for Hitler, the outward trappings of power, even a political title such as the chancellorship, may have appeared hollow. While he drew political strength from celebrity and the adulation of the masses, he may have concluded that following the crowd's expectations would prove unfulfilling for him. What he may have seen, following the elections, was a life limited to drafting legislation or making speeches before the Reichstag. He was a restless individual and his political vision of leadership would not be content with such a passive role. His views of political leadership, even his overall goals, were similar to those of Stalin. Both had goals beyond mere leadership of a political movement. However, if Hitler was inspired by a vision of Germany's greater role on the world stage, he may also have been taking cues from lesser political events. Papen, his recent political rival, could serve as an object lesson.

As Hitler saw it, Papen's problem had not been the lack of a popular base of support, nor even his opposition to Hitler. His real problem was that he had been forced to work within the confines of popular government. Rather than acting, he had wasted his time trying to find political support for a program. What may also have bothered Hitler was the lack of permanence. What was accomplished by one Reichstag session could be easily undone with the next election. In addition, lawmaking was a slow process which required agreement among a large group, difficult enough in less turbulent times. The problem was that the political chaos outside was reflected in the Reichstag's proceedings. In Russia, the Bolsheviks had exploited a weakness in the political system which allowed the revolutionary worker's committee to obstruct plans of the Provisional Government. In Germany, the Nazis found a similar opportunity in the Reichstag. If their goal was simply to prevent the passage of meaningful legislation, it was easy to disrupt legislative proceedings. As tools in the quest for power, Hitler found such actions useful. When it came to his overall understanding of the political process however, he drew other conclusions about them. They represented a weakness, if it was that easy to disrupt the political process. Facing the prospect of a combative legislature or unfavorable election results, Hitler's goal became the elimination of the Reichstag.

To accomplish that he proposed an Enabling Act. Legislative power was to be transferred from the Reichstag to the government, meaning himself. In essence, he wanted the Reichstag to vote itself out of existence. For that he needed a two-thirds vote, since it involved a constitutional change. He did want additional powers before such a drastic step was taken however. The power of the chancellory was to be increased - the chancellor could issue laws directly. The Enabling Act went further by allowing the enactment of laws which violated the constitution. Perhaps to blunt some of the criticism, the law was to be in effect only for four years.

The vote on the Enabling Act took place on March 23, 1933. Even with the German Nationalists, the Nazis were short of having the two-thirds majority necessary for passage. They found the Center Party willing to deal. With a large Catholic constituency, its particular worry was the February 28 emergency decree, issued in the wake of the Reichstag fire. If the Nazis would rescind the act and leave them alone, they would vote for the Enabling Act. Believing they had an agreement the Act was passed 444 to 94.

The Reichstag vote on March 23 might be considered the formal date of the Nazi takeover. Certainly Nazi activities intensified after that date. However, they had been mobilizing the SA and seizing local governments before that date. While Hitler put enormous effort into passage of the Enabling Act, it is not clear that it was crucial, or at least that its passage was crucial in March. The Center Party has been criticized for caving in to Hitler's demands. Yet his strength was almost to the point that he did not need to bargain. He had not bargained with the 81 Communist members, most of whom had been arrested.

CREATING THE POLICE STATE

Hitler, like Stalin, found elections and lawmakers useful for establishing legitimacy. They were not necessary when it came to day-to-day governmental operations, but they tended to reassure the public. Adherence to constitutional procedures was also reassuring to officials, such as Hindenburg. Securing passage of the Enabling Act by the Reichstag gave every appearance that Hitler was following the letter of the law, even as he did away with it.

For all the public attention the Reichstag proceedings received, Hitler may have been more concerned with the battle for control of the police. What was remembered of the beerhall putsch was a wild-eyed Hitler firing a pistol into the ceiling. What was conveniently overlooked was the accompanying force of storm troopers, armed with machine guns. In the ten years since the putsch Hitler had overhauled his radical image and become a convert to democracy. Whatever the current image, the beerhall putsch hinted at a more primitive understanding of political power. The real source of power was force, not speechmaking or persuasion. If that was the case, the key to power somehow lay with police and military units, the governmental arm entrusted by the state with the physical power to enforce laws. It was a view held by many governments, who reserved to themselves the exclusive right to military power.

Against such a tradition, Hitler had managed to create his own private military, perhaps the greatest testament to the turbulence of the times. In size, the SA rivaled the German military, the Reichswehr, although the Reichswehr, with its discipline and training, was more than a match in any direct confrontation. Whether the SA would do better in a comparison with the various police forces is another matter. If the police had greater discipline, their smaller size and the nature of their training left them vulnerable in large military-style confrontations. On the other hand, the Nazis had come out second best in one of the few organized confrontations to occur, that following the Munich beerhall putsch.

If Hitler coveted the power held by the police or the military, his goal was not to destroy them. He saw them as useful tools, which, if given proper direction, could serve his purposes. His plan, this time, was to avoid outright conflict. The danger posed by the Reichswehr, for Hitler, was military intervention in civil affairs. Once the army chose to involve itself he had little doubt it would win. To prevent that he needed to keep civil disturbances below a certain level. So long as the army remained convinced that German society was not on the verge of total breakdown the army was unlikely to act.

If Hitler's political calculations told him that the power held by the military needed to be taken into account, he probably did not view the matter entirely in political terms. He maintained a sentimental attachment to the army. It was not surrender he was looking for, but approval. His political opponents, in his eyes, were contemptuous. If they were taken away at night to be beaten or shot, they deserved it. If his idealized view of the military made him reluctant to act, there were practical considerations which presented obstacles. The Reichswehr was a closely-knit structure, not easily penetrated by outsiders, and potentially more difficult to defeat than the Reichstag. He had been able to defeat the Reichstag, in part, because his status as a politician guaranteed him acceptance. What gave him an advantage over the army was its mind-set. It was not inclined to get involved in the civil government and saw its job primarily in terms of preparing for international conflicts. Hitler was only too willing to leave the military alone so long as it agreed not to get involved in the civil side.

The police forces were a different matter. Unlike the military, they were not a single organization, but separate agencies with individual command structures. While they were smaller, there were more of them. Taking control of one did not mean control of all. If that gave them a certain advantage, it was offset by the fact that, individually, they were weaker than the army. More importantly, their command structure was linked to local government. To bring the police forces under control, Hitler had any number of options available. He could have publicly challenged them, ordering his storm troopers to start attacking police stations. As it was, the police were kept busy trying to quell the street brawls started by the SA. Yet, the street demonstrations, if they invited police intervention, were now more of a diversionary tactic. Hitler had opted for a less obvious strategy which targeted the state government, rather than the police. He had concluded that it was not the physical capabilities of the police which made them vulnerable, but their political ties to the state. If the Nazis could control the state governments they could replace those in the police organizations who would not cooperate. Göring's reorganization of the Prussian police proved that such a plan was feasible.

By the time the Enabling Act was passed, the Nazis had gone a long way toward implementing their plans for a dictatorship. The process of transformation, starting with Hitler's appointment as Chancellor, on January 30, was a continual one, although it may be better understood by dividing it into three phases. The first phase was the period of time between Hitler's appointment as chancellor on January 30 and the Reichstag fire, on February 27; the second was the time from the February 28 decree until the passage of the Enabling Act on March 23; and the third was the period following passage of the Enabling Act.

The first phase of the Nazi takeover involved the transformation of the Prussian police. Göring's appointment as Prussian minister of the interior allowed him to eliminate its top management. Fourteen presidents within the organization were retired and lesser officials were fired. In addition, Göring began setting up a special secret police, which would become the Gestapo. (The name was a shortened version of GEheime StAatsPOlizei.)[3] The SS (Schutzstaffeln or guard squadrons), the other organization associated with terror, had been created in 1925 as a contingent of bodyguards for Hitler. Under Heinrich Himmler, its membership had increased to 52,000 by January 1933. It would become responsible for carrying out assassinations and for running the concentration camps.[4] When Göring authorized the formation of auxiliaries on February 22, 25,000 SA and 15,000 SS troops in Prussia were added to his forces.

If the first phase had allowed the Nazis to secure a foothold, in the second phase they used that base to move against their opponents. With the Reichstag fire and February 28 decree, they became more aggressive. They used the street disorders, which they usually instigated, as an excuse to call for federal intervention. Frick, as minister of the interior, would appoint a Nazi as police commissioner. Instead of suppressing the SA, those usually responsible for the violence, the Nazis would use the federal orders to attack communists or other opponents. It was in this period that the Nazis began to set up concentration camps. Initially, they used army barracks or factories to house the people they arrested.[5] With the police organizations in Nazi hands there was no one to appeal to. Some arrested ended up in concentration camps, others were tortured and murdered. The takeovers of local and state governments continued following the March 5 elections and by the end of March most state and local officials had been forced out of office and replaced by Nazis.

In the third phase, the period following passage of the Enabling Act, the Nazis attempted to bring a more regimented structure to state and local governments with their policy of Gleichschaltung, or coordination. On March 31 a law was decreed by the new central government which allowed Reich officials in the states to issue laws. The state parliaments, like the Reichstag, were thus eliminated from the law-making process. The Nazis were sufficiently in control in the states, that they no longer needed to use a pretext to call in help. On April 7, another law was issued which provided that the central government would appoint governors in all the states.

With state and local governments in Nazi hands Hitler had virtual control of the machinery of government. What opposition remained was less organized. Nevertheless, Hitler wanted all opposition eliminated. He ordered a purge of the civil service on April 7. Those targeted were primarily Jews and leftists. Considering the trade unions another source of potential problems, he had union leaders arrested on May 2. A German Labor Front was established by law on May 10. It was intended to be a governmental union which would replace the formerly free trade unions. Only one source of opposition now remained - the rival political parties. On July 14, 1933 the government formally outlawed all opposition parties. In fact, by that date most parties had either been banned or had disbanded. The Communists had been outlawed in March; the SPD had been banned in June.

With opposition parties banned, Hitler had made the transformation to dictatorship nearly complete. Technically, he could have been removed from office by Hindenburg, but Hindenburg had become senile. The worst of the Nazi activities were taking place out of public view and any news he received was superficial and allowed him to maintain a favorable opinion of what was happening. He would survive another year, until August 1934. When he died, Hitler removed the last technical hurdle to power by eliminating the presidency as a separate office. Presidential duties were merged into those of chancellor and assumed by Hitler. Hitler would be both Führer and Reich chancellor.

While the period between January and June 1933 was noteworthy for its public legislative activities, such as the Enabling Act, the organizational development of the Gestapo and SS was perhaps even more significant. With increased prestige and additional powers they were becoming more efficient. Their development spelled the end for the SA. It had played an important role in bringing the Nazis to power. Once power had been achieved however, the SA became just one more potential threat to worry about.

The Nazi government began cutting back on the activities of the storm troopers. The street brawls, which had been the excuse for the national takeovers of the state governments, were to be curtailed - they were too disruptive of government operations. Göring, who had turned the 25,000 SA members into Prussian auxiliary police in February, dismissed them in August. Despite such measures, the SA continued to grow, reaching 2.5 million members in January 1934. While the army may have been better organized, it was still limited by the Versailles Treaty to 100,000 men. Röhm suggested that the two groups be merged, but the army did not view any association favorably.

Whether Hitler ever seriously considered the SA an equal to the army, he was not ready to dismiss it as totally irrelevant. At the same time, he was beginning to take the side of the military more. In February 1934 he decided that the SA was to be disarmed - only the army would be allowed to carry weapons. Even on June 30, 1934, the 'Night of the Long Knives,' Hitler was still undecided about eliminating the SA. Manipulative subordinates, such as Himmler, convinced him that Röhm was plotting against him, going so far as to concoct a false report of a putsch in Munich.[6] The purge eliminated the top leadership of the SA and virtually ended any threat it might pose. Many of its duties were assumed by the SS.

What emerged following the SA purge was a leaner terror apparatus - more efficient and stronger, but not as much of a 'loose cannon' from Hitler's perspective. The SS, in May 1933, had numbered around 100,000. Although it was similar to the Gestapo, it was a Party unit, whereas the Gestapo was formed from the Prussian police force. In 1934 Himmler took over the leadership of both organizations. While technically under Himmler, the organizations remained separate. The Gestapo tended to deal more with the 'actual' political opponents of the regime, those foolish enough to openly criticize or act against the government. The SS, in contrast, was concerned more with ideological opponents. It focused its efforts primarily on Jews, political opponents, such as communists, or moral enemies, such as pornographers. It would thus be responsible for operating the concentration camps.

THE STRUCTURE OF THE NAZI GOVERNMENT

One of the supreme ironies of the Nazi takeover was that Hitler, for all the effort he put into seizing power, had almost no interest in the day-to-day operations of government. While he seemed to enjoy the explosive confrontation involved in the dismissal of a cabinet minister, he quickly lost interest in the meetings themselves. In 1936, he met with his full cabinet only four times; in 1938 only once.[7] He tended to focus on particular goals. Unfortunately, when it came to carrying out programs, he tended to assign projects to individuals, rather than to departments. It was not that the individuals were incompetent, it was more that there was a potential for duplication of effort. When construction of the autobahn was started in 1933 Hitler assigned Fritz Todt the project and gave him a budget from Reich Chancellory funds. Normally highway construction would be under the ministry of transport. If the use of special deputies was intended to streamline the process by going around existing bureaucratic structures, its real effect was shift to shift inefficiencies from one area to another. Hitler allowed the various ministries to survive, but he created an atmosphere in which personal politics increased in importance.

As a manager Hitler had the luxury of delegating details to subordinates. It may have allowed him to escape the problem, but the escape was only temporary. He was often called upon to arbitrate disputes, once projects were underway, which meant that the details he had avoided at the start, had to be revisited to resolve problems. The dislike of detail was really just symptomatic of a larger problem - a reluctance to confront difficult problems coupled with an inability to make decisions. While he projected a public image of decisiveness, he often avoided decision-making, either by postponement or by shifting responsibility to others. One illustration of this was his solution to the problem of providing jobs for supporters. He found himself torn between loyalty to those who had supported him and his general sense of duty. Those who had brought him to power wanted jobs, but did not have the competence to fill them. He thought he had found a solution. The professional civil servants would actually run the government, while his followers would be appointed to Special Reich Authorities. If it did not solve the problem it had two advantages. First, it bought him additional time before a decision had to be made. Second, it shed light on the obvious solution. If his appointments were incompetent, that incompetence would soon become apparent. At the same time he had satisfied his political debt by giving them a chance.

From an efficiency standpoint, Hitler's management of government operations showed mixed results. How would the elimination of the Reichstag be judged, using a similar standard? The administrative effect of the elimination of the Reichstag was an increase in the size of the Reich Chancellory. There were some savings on the political side - Hitler did not have to waste energy on legislators or legislation. Eliminating the Reichstag however, had not entirely done away with the legislative function - or political fighting. Instead, it had transferred it to the various ministries. If Hitler believed he had created an all-powerful office in the Chancellory, his practical achievement may have been to downgrade its importance. It became nothing more than that a go-between for the various ministries. With the power to decide the fate of individual ministries, it had to rely on them for the details. The Chancellory often had to gather information from the various ministries to assess the potential impact of Chancellory laws.[8] Whatever problems existed, the government did have some successes it could point to, or at least take credit for. Whether Nazi policy was actually the cause, Hitler's activist approach allowed him to claim his first major victory. His campaign to reduce unemployment was having results.

HITLER'S ECONOMIC PLAN - SOLVING THE UNEMPLOYMENT PROBLEM

Hitler had begun to attack the unemployment problem in 1933, even as he was eliminating his political opponents. He initiated a giant public-works program during the summer, the centerpiece of which was the construction of the autobahn, or state highway system. The project was not limited to highway construction. It also built bridges and canals and renovated buildings. The number of unemployed slowly began to drop from its January 1933 high of 6,013,612. At the end of 1933, it had fallen to 4,804,000.[9]

Unemployment would continue to fall during 1934 and by the end of the year was only 2.6 million, a decline of 2.2 million.[10] The public works projects were responsible for more jobs, but they were playing a smaller role. In reality the increased demand for labor was being fueled by Hitler's decision to rearm Germany. He would not go public with his plan until March 1935, when he announced the reinstitution of universal military service, but he began quietly seeking military contractors for synthetic materials. By June of 1935 unemployment had dropped to 1.7 million. It would fall another 700,000 in 1936. By 1937 unemployment, now below 500,000, was no longer the economic problem it had been when Hitler took power. Yet it was only one of several economic problems. In mid-1934 Germany ran short of reserves for foreign exchange. In 1935 she was short of foodstuffs.

ECONOMIC PLANNING, SHORTAGES, AND REARMAMENT

Managing the German economy between 1933 and 1939 was a juggling act. Economic difficulties were partly related to general economic conditions, but they were compounded by government policy. The most persistent of the general problems was the chronic shortage of raw materials. Planners were constantly on a search for synthetic substitutes. If the problem created headaches for military planners, it found its way into the civilian sector as well, where there were shortages of consumer goods, accompanied by inflationary pressures. As if general economic problems weren't enough, planners had to contend with inherent contradictions in Hitler's policy. His determination to increase the defense budget was at odds with conventional wisdom about spending policy. It was not possible to have both 'guns and butter,' according to most. Achieving rearmament through deficit financing would be self-defeating politically, since it would lead to inflation. The events of 1923 were a recent reminder of that fact.

Between the obvious problems created by shortages and the more theoretical problems related to spending policy, planners may have preferred dealing with shortages. If they were difficult to solve, they at least were taking place in the real world, and more importantly, they could be measured. Being part of the real world, they had one other advantage, particularly for politicians. They could be attacked with a plan. The idea of a plan was almost as important as its success or failure, since a failed plan could always be changed.

There were two prominent economic "plans" created to deal with shortages, the New Plan and the Four Year Plan. Both were related to Germany's dependence on imported raw materials. The New Plan was created in September 1934 specifically to deal with a foreign exchange shortage. Germany's balance of payments was at a crisis stage. It was not a general economic plan, but primarily involved foreign trade. It also represented a stronger government presence in the trade arena. The major policy change was a requirement that importers had to obtain prior approval by the German government before shipping goods. With the New Plan, the government could decide what food or raw materials could be imported, as well as which countries they would be imported from.

The Four Year Plan was the result of another balance of payments crisis which occurred in 1936. A major problem was that the demand for imported goods had increased, both because more people were employed and because the rearmament program was demanding more foreign raw materials. Added to the increased demand was the fact that import costs had risen.[11] Hitler was persuaded that Germany was too dependent on foreign imports, especially in the event of war. He decided that Germany must embark on a program of autarchy, or self-sufficiency. In the fall of 1936, he decided to formalize a program to overcome her deficiencies. A major goal of the plan was to develop a group of synthetic fuels and raw materials which would allow Germany to escape her dependence on foreign suppliers. Göring was put in charge of the program.

In the final analysis, the Plan did not achieve the self-sufficiency hoped for. The hoped-for breakthrough in synthetic fuels never occurred and one-third of raw materials were still supplied by foreign countries in 1939. It was not a total failure, since there were some areas in which goals had been achieved. At the same time, successes, where they had been achieved, had demanded a heavy budgetary commitment.

NAZI JEWISH POLICY

Although the number of Jews killed in the concentration camps is not known, it is believed that it was between five and six million. There were an additional nine to ten million non-Jews who died as a result of Nazi policies. Despite the use of concentration camps by the Nazis as early as 1933, it was not until 1942 that the "Final Solution" was implemented as official policy. In fact, the majority of the five to six million Jewish deaths would take place between 1942 and 1944. In spite of the fact that Hitler took every opportunity to blame Germany's problems on the Jews, he appears to have been undecided about how to incorporate his anti-Jewish policy into a specific legal program. The vacillation which marked other policies could be seen in his policy here as well. Between 1938 and 1941, official government policy had been to encourage Jews to emigrate from Germany.

While Hitler did not immediately try to implement the "Final Solution," when he came to power in 1933, he did not wait long to put his rhetoric into practice. On April 1, 1933 the Nazis organized a boycott of Jewish businesses and professionals. This was followed by a series of laws in 1933 excluding Jews from the Civil Service and from the professions of law and medicine. During 1935, the government and lower Party members encouraged public displays of anti-Jewish sentiment and in September the so-called Nuremburg Laws were decreed, which tried to define who Jews were and to implement a policy which would protect the 'Aryan' race.

The summer Olympics of 1936 forced the Nazis to tone down the most obvious excesses of their policy. It would be 1938 before they resumed their campaign with any vigor. In April of that year Jews were required to register their wealth if it was greater than 5,000 marks. This was followed in July by a requirement that they carry personal identification. The SA, which had been kept quiet, was once again allowed to resume its activities. The Munich synagogue was destroyed in June and the Nuremburg synagogue in August. The concentration camps, which had been reserved for political opponents of the regime, were now used to house Jews.

On November 7 1938 a young Polish Jew assassinated a secretary in the German embassy in Paris. On November 9 and 10, the SA and anti-Jewish mobs took part in what was called the 'Crystal Night,' which involved the wholesale destruction of Jewish synagogues and businesses throughout Germany. In the rampage 100 Jews died, some 7,000 Jewish businesses were destroyed, and between 20,000 and 30,000 Jews were sent to concentration camps. In the aftermath of the riots, the Reich imposed a 1 billion mark collective fine on the Jews and decreed the expulsion of Jewish children from schools. The government intensified its campaign of deportations.[12]

The invasions of Poland and Russia brought a change to the policy. Special SS groups were charged with hunting down and killing all Jews they could find.[13] As German forces advanced into Russia, there were mass executions. At Kiev, some 33,000 Jewish inhabitants were shot to death in a mass execution. The formal plans for the Final Solution were decided on at a meeting at Wannsee on January 20, 1942. The use of gas chambers at Auschwitz would not begin until June, but would continue until October 1944. With the gassings coming to an end, the Nazis took pains to cover up what had happened. Just as units had been formed to hunt down and execute Jews when the Final Solution was implemented, new teams were formed to destroy any evidence of what had been going on. The crematoria at Auschwitz were blown up in November 1944.[14]

THE RESULTS OF NAZI POLICY BY 1939

This chapter has provided an overview of the major economic and political policies of Nazi Germany following Hitler's takeover. When war finally came in 1939, economic conditions in Germany had greatly changed since 1933. Unemployment had been eliminated. In fact there was a need for an additional 500,000 workers.[15] The rearmament plan, which had helped bring unemployment down, did contribute to shortages of consumer goods and food, but consumers were at least comfortable. Based on the early successes of the German army, Hitler's planning had prepared her well for war. The next chapter provides a more detailed look at her economic circumstances and history.

CHAPTER 20

GERMAN ECONOMIC RESOURCES AND THE GERMAN ECONOMY

The last chapter provided a brief overview of the Nazi regime and some of the economic programs instituted by Hitler. This chapter takes a more detailed look at three aspects of Nazi Germany's economic history. First, it discusses the general state of the German economy from two perspectives: one involving resources; the other focusing on the market. Nazi Germany, in economic terms, is a prime example of two economic phenomena: a relative lack of resources coupled with the development of an economy geared almost exclusively to the market. Second, this chapter looks at the economic solutions tried by Hitler. Third, it takes a more detailed look at the economic history of Germany. Within the discussion is an analysis of the industrial and agricultural sectors of the German economy.

RESOURCE WEALTH AND THE CONSEQUENCES OF A MARKET ECONOMY

Fascist governments, according to the thesis of this book, develop in countries in which resource availability is greater than that of communist countries, such as Russia, but is not as great as that of democratic countries, such as the U.S.. In Chapter Seventeen there was a comparison of resource availability in the U.S., Germany, and Russia. Germany's major weakness was in agricultural productivity. It even lagged behind Russia where production of major grains was concerned. The thesis would predict that production should have fallen in the middle. If agricultural production figures are somewhat at odds with the thesis, those for the industrial sector fall neatly into place. It may be helpful to look at those figures again.

INDUSTRIAL RAW MATERIAL PRODUCTION PER CAPITA
(IN POUNDS)

PRODUCT		1926	1927	1928	1929	1930
Iron Ore[1]	U.S.	1290	1160	1156	1342	1064
	Germany	168	231	224	219	196
	Russia	48	70	87	110	144
Pig Iron[2]	U.S.	728	654	710	764	544
	Germany	337	456	408	454	331
	Russia	31	42	47	60	69

Steel[3]	U.S.	681	844	945	1023	732
(Ingots &	Germany	427	566	501	557	394
Castings)	Russia	41	61	61	68	77
Coal[4]	U.S.	11,206	10,045	9,560	9,998	8,734
	Germany	5,097	5,355	5,244	5,621	4,761
	Russia	379	468	507	586	650
Copper[5]	U.S.	14.60	13.80	15.00	16.20	11.40
	Germany	.95	.96	.91	.99	.92
	Russia	.15	.19	.28	.52	.66
Lead[6]	U.S.	11.64	11.18	10.40	10.64	9.00
	Germany	1.89	2.91	2.99	3.35	3.76
	Russia	-0-	-0-	-0-	-0-	-0-

The figures suggest a more generous resource base than existed in fact. The output of refined products such as steel and pig iron may have been high, but the statistics do not reveal the extent of dependence on imported raw materials. Two-thirds of iron and lead, nine-tenths of copper and 100 percent of oil and gasoline were imported. Germany was almost totally lacking in fuel oils and India rubber. On the eve of the Second World War, she still had to import one-third of her raw material needs.[7] Shortages of industrial raw materials were compounded by shortages in agricultural output. Some 45 percent of German consumer expenditures went to food as Germany approached the Second World War. In the United Kingdom, the percentage was 41.[8] The severity of the shortages make it somewhat difficult to classify Germany as a country with even medium resource availability. The extent of the shortages almost placed it closer to Russia on an availability scale.

Resource scarcity represented one of the major economic factors at work in Germany. The other factor, at a more basic level, was the development of a market economy. If any country seemed destined for the market, it was Germany, with its industrial capabilities. Yet, the ability to physically manufacture goods was only part of the equation, when it came to market suitability. The other part was the market itself, or more specifically, the strength or weakness of the market where goods were sold. The problem, in Germany's case, was a weak domestic market. Had that been the only problem, it could have been overcome by finding other markets. Unfortunately, alternative international markets proved just as weak.

So long as the market provided the framework for most political and economic discussion, solutions to such problems as unemployment were likely to involve the market in some way. If the autobahn construction project could be criticized for the "artificial" jobs it provided, it at least reinforced the idea of a job, a concept central to the market system. With a job being a key concept, economics came to revolve around the job-related problem of unemployment. Make-work projects, if they seemed artificial by conventional standards, at least solved the most pressing economic problem politicians had to deal with. Having solved that problem, the underlying problem of weak markets could be put off.

The problem, for the German economy, was not that the autobahn solution was a make-work project or represented an artificial stimulus. The real problem was that the problem was long-term in nature. The autobahn project stirred the public's imagination because it seemed dynamic and new, suggesting, in the economic realm, that unemployment was a rare occurrence for a market economy. However, Hitler was not the first leader to resort to public works to deal with unemployment. That had also been the solution in 1924, when the government received foreign assistance under the Dawes Plan. In the late 1920s the various governments, both state and federal, had subsidized public works projects involving the construction of schools, hospitals and sports facilities. Government expenditures for unemployment and social services were 26 percent of GNP by 1929.[9]

The private sector was fighting its own war in its own way. Its only advantage was that whatever it did would not carry the stigma associated with government programs, such as the make-work nature of the autobahn construction program. Make-work projects were suspect, not simply because of their government association, but because they represented a major violation of economic principles. If the sins of the private sector seemed less serious, by comparison, they were sins nonetheless. The one temptation which would prove irresistible for business was easy credit. The German government had fallen into that trap in 1923, with its deficit financing of the Ruhr strike. But the government had paid a heavy price when it was blamed for the inflation which followed. The economic lessons of 1923 were lost on the business world of the late 1920s. Businesses, rather than avoiding credit, had become heavily reliant on it by the time of the 1929 Crash.

A moralistic interpretation of the Depression suggests that the market has a way of punishing those who violate its principles. When American investors called in their loans in the weeks following the Crash, German businesses failed and workers lost their jobs. Explaining the Depression in terms of punishment has a certain appeal, but it may be shifting the focus away from some important considerations. The real lesson may not be that businesses failed, but that the failure was so widespread and occurred so quickly, in the wake of the Crash. Was it in such a fragile state that events in New York could bring it to its knees in a matter of a few months? Another lesson may involve the connection between business borrowing prior to the Crash and government efforts to provide work for the unemployed. If they seem to exist in totally different worlds, they have one thing in common. Both represent "artificial" methods of coping with weak markets. Borrowing is artificial because it allows a business to temporarily avoid costs and keep prices competitively low. Make-work projects are artificial because the employment created is outside normal market channels. The rearmament campaign, if it allowed the government to avoid the appearance of interfering with the private sector, did not demonstrate economic self-reliance. It represented instead an artificially-created market.   The 1934 New Plan of Hjalmar Schacht, if it illustrated the need for raw materials, also pointed to the inability to overcome market weaknesses. Germany bought raw materials on credit from foreign countries but required those governments to redeem their credits by purchasing goods from German manufacturers.

LOAVES AND LAMPS

Market weakness, if it sounds like an absolute concept, is really a relative term. The problem for German companies, in fact for most businesses, in the late 1920s, was not the disappearance of consumer demand. Russia, with its shortages, suggests that there was a certain demand level existing in all economies. The weakness instead, was related to the market saturation point of a given country. The irony was that the very things which the capitalist economies prided themselves on, their manufacturing abilities and technological skills, contributed to their difficulties. Automation, in a word, destroyed markets, even as it came closer to its goal of satisfying consumer demand. If business wanted workers to be more productive, that very productivity was undermining the market on which their jobs depended.

A simple example, with four variations, may be helpful to explain the problems caused by a dependence on weak markets as well as the relationship between productivity and employment. In this example there are 1,000 farmers and 1,000 factory workers. The farmers produce three loaves of bread each for a total of 3,000 loaves. Each farmer needs to keep only one loaf of bread to live and can trade the other two. (For simplicity's sake, it will be assumed that one loaf is sufficient food to live on.) Each worker makes one lamp for a total of 1,000 lamps. In a normal market a lamp can be traded for a loaf of bread. The farmers only need one lamp, so they will exchange one loaf for each lamp produced. In this situation the thousand workers will be able to satisfy their basic food needs with the bread and their economic needs through their jobs.

In the second variation, the facts remain the same except that there are only 500 factory workers. There is now a shortage of lamps since only 500 can be produced. From the perspective of the farmer it is an inflationary situation. The cost of a lamp will go up, based on scarcity. Depending on how badly a farmer wants a lamp, he may be willing to offer two loaves of bread for each lamp. There is no problem with unemployment since there is a strong demand for lamps.

The facts will be changed again for the third variation. The factory process has been automated so that each worker can produce two lamps. As long as there are only 500 workers, this increase in productivity will benefit the worker. The farmer benefits because the portion of inflation caused by a scarcity of lamps has been alleviated. Each worker benefits because they can now earn two loaves of bread for the same amount of

389

work.

For the fourth variation, it will be assumed that worker productivity has been increased even more, so that each worker can now produce 10 lamps. It only takes 100 workers to manufacture 1,000 lamps, the number demanded by the original market. Productivity has now become something of a two-edged sword. Viewed from a technological perspective, productivity gains have either freed up 900 workers, who are now available to produce other products or it has increased factory capacity. Viewed from a market perspective however, the advantages are not so clear-cut. What happens, for example, if the manufacturer takes a purely technological approach and utilizes the new capacity to produce more lamps. If 100 workers can produce 1,000 lamps, 500 workers can produce 5,000 lamps, and 1,000 workers can produce 10,000 lamps. An output of 10,000 lamps is ideal for the farmer but a disaster both for the manufacturer and for the worker. The normal market will absorb 1,000 lamps, but there are 9,000 lamps which cannot be sold. To move this inventory, prices will have to be reduced. Since the lamps are bartered for loaves of bread, the price reduction will appear in the form of additional lamps for each loaf of bread. In the most extreme situation a farmer could buy 10 lamps for a single loaf of bread. The manufacturer, with 10,000 lamps on hand, also has the option of keeping them to sell at a later time. In this case the market seems to dictate a layoff. There is no point in continuing to pay workers to produce more lamps when the current inventory cannot be sold. The manufacturer, instead of operating at full capacity, could have opted for a more market-oriented approach at the beginning. With 100 workers able to satisfy the market demand for 1,000 lamps, the 900 excess workers could be let go.

The equation can be changed, of course, by varying market demand. What if the manufacturer seeks new lamp markets? For example, it is possible that there is a demand for 9,000 lamps in foreign countries. In this case, the manufacturer can operate at full capacity and the 900 workers will keep their jobs. Finding new markets for old products is only one alternative. Another possibility is to find or create markets for new products. What if the manufacturer, or the workers, discover that the demand for milk pails among farmers is just as great as that for lamps? The 900 workers displaced by lamp-producing technology can now find jobs manufacturing milk pails. There is a potential problem. The belief that new markets offer a solution rests on the assumption that market demand can be infinitely expanded. Unfortunately, it appears to have limits.

The four variations in the loaves and lamps example are intended to emphasize some lessons about market operations. It may be helpful to summarize the points they are intended to illustrate. First, productivity increases, up to a point, are helpful in meeting market demand and in reducing inflation which is caused by a scarcity of goods. This was the case where only 500 lamps were produced and the market demanded 1,000. Second, productivity increases, beyond a certain point, create problems in employment. If the ability to produce 1,000 lamps with only 100 workers represented an improvement, from a technological standpoint, the downside was that it created an excess of 900 workers. The larger lesson perhaps is that a particular market, at a given technological level, will sustain only a certain number of workers (or manufacturers). In Germany efforts to increase productivity had worked, in terms of physical output, but they had also resulted in an unemployment rate of over 30 percent by 1932. Third, if improved productivity is the goal, it is incompatible with the goal of full employment. If both are pursued at the same time, the market offers only one solution - new markets.

Market economists would take serious exception to this third point. Improved productivity, they would argue, is not incompatible with full employment; it, in fact, promotes employment. By satisfying consumer demand in one area, it creates consumer demand in other areas - once consumers have purchased all the pots they want, they will start buying pans. On the production side, it allows one worker to produce more and frees up other workers to move on to other jobs where they can produce more products. The problem is that it assumes a continually expanding market.

Improved productivity has been a long-cherished economic goal. The specialization of labor, which accounted for increased factory output, fascinated Adam Smith. Economists today emphasize comparative advantage, the concept that one nation should focus its productive efforts on areas where it has superior technology or resources and allow other nations and economies to put their energy into areas where they excel. Specialization has a certain logical appeal, in its own right. That appeal explains the importance attached to the goal of productivity. Explaining why a goal may be important however, is not the same thing as saying that no conflict exists with other goals. The fact that increased productivity has been a long-standing goal, does not mean that there is no conflict with the goal of full employment.

What does a discussion of Adam Smith and specialization have to do with the specific problems facing Germany in 1930? If comparative advantage is the subject, a more appropriate setting would seem to be in a discussion of Russia and Germany. The two countries, in fact, provide a classic illustration of comparative advantage. Germany, with a weak agricultural system and strong manufacturing capabilities, was better off trading for grain than producing it itself. Russia's most efficient use of its resources was as a grain producer, not as a manufacturer.

When comparative advantage serves merely to teach the benefits of trade between Germany and Russia, it has little relevance to this discussion. However, in a broader context, comparative advantage, with its emphasis on efficiency, offers another lesson. That lesson does not involve the calculations intended to prove foreign trade superior to domestic manufacture nor does it involve the mathematics of job creation or factory output. The lesson is related to the philosophical approach or outlook assumed by its advocates. Comparative advantage and specialization are active, production-oriented philosophies, which take as their starting point the idea that market problems are related to production. Failure can be explained in terms of production and, if solutions exist, they will be found in production. In other words, a company or nation fails because it has either chosen the wrong product to make or the wrong method of production, not because production is lacking altogether.

How would events in Germany be interpreted, given such a view? The argument would be that German industry, in spite of appearances, had become comparatively less efficient. Germany needed to either become even more efficient at production or to find an entirely new line of activity which would restore its trade advantages. Since the U.S. economy was experiencing similar problems, it too was at a stage where industrial manufacturing was not its most productive endeavor.

It may be helpful to return to the loaves and lamps example to better understand Germany's situation. It needs to be changed somewhat to more closely fit what was happening. What needs to be changed is the productivity of the farmers. Instead of producing three loaves of bread, they only produce two. Since they keep one for themselves, this means that they now only have 1,000 loaves available to barter on the market. While agricultural productivity has decreased, manufacturing capabilities will remain high - only 100 workers will be needed to produce the 1,000 lamps. From a market perspective, the situation is ideal for lamp manufacturing, since the 100 workers will be able to satisfy the demand for lamps. The problem is the market for milk pails, which will impact the labor market for the 900 excess lamp workers. When the farmers produced three loaves of bread, they had enough bread to buy milk pails (1,000 loaves of bread left after trading 1,000 for lamps and keeping 1,000 for themselves). The example can be made even more extreme. What happens if the farmers can only produce one loaf of bread? Their total production is only 1,000 loaves, which means that they have no excess loaves to trade. Now even the 100 workers find their jobs in jeopardy.

For purposes of illustration, the example has used the most extreme conditions of scarcity to explain Germany's economic situation. Because it uses the farmer as the market, it suggests that the only weakness encountered was in the agricultural sector. There was an overall weakness in demand, not one confined to the agricultural sector. In the final variation of the example, farmers are reduced to producing only one loaf of bread each. In some ways that is not a totally inaccurate picture of German agricultural production. Germany was continually short of food. In fact, it cost twice as much in Germany during the Depression as elsewhere.

INDUSTRIAL AND AGRICULTURAL SECTORS

Unemployment in Germany was only one symptom of economic weakness and workers were only one group which had difficulty coping with the economy. Business owners, whether in the industrial sector or the agricultural sector, also faced economic hardship. They were in a somewhat better position to weather poor conditions than workers, but they found the economic seas to be rough and sailing difficult nevertheless.

The small business was no more immune to economic problems than the large manufacturer. If size was what defined small business, it was nevertheless a diverse group. Small retailers, who in 1925 had numbered 847,900, represented just one category.[10] Another was the artisans, who in 1936 were counted at 1,650,000.[11] If numbers alone were the measure, a figure of over two million suggests that success had been achieved. Being able to claim success by virtue of membership in an entrepreneurial class fell somewhat short of total victory. Most of the artisans and small retailers, in economic terms, were living on the margins.

The size of this groupwould attract the notice of any politician; their economic circumstances would make them ripe for political exploitation - as Hitler discovered. If they were a receptive audience, their very zeal could sometimes turn them into a political liability. Hitler clearly struck a responsive chord when he framed his appeal in terms of the threat posed by the large department stores and cooperatives to small businesses. He went on to link this appeal to his anti-Jewish theme, since many of the large department stores were under Jewish ownership. If the message sounded logical, he had not thought through the logical consequences of its implementation. The department stores, Jewish-owned or not, were major employers. In the spring of 1933 the Nazis organized a boycott of the department stores in hopes of forcing them out of business. The problem for Hitler, still facing an unemployment problem, was that the stores employed some 90,000 people.[12] The problem for the boycott organizers was that Hitler was a pragmatist who seldom followed principle where political ambitions were concerned. He moved quickly to suppress the boycott.

The manufacturing and heavy industry side of the industrial sector also exhibited signs of struggle. Where economics and politics met, German industrialists presented something of a paradox. If they exhibited a surprising political strength, when it came to favorable legislation, that strength seemed to contrast sharply with their economic weakness. As far back as the 1870s, industrialists had pressured the government for tariffs to shield German industry from foreign competition. They obtained this protection in July 1879 when a tariff bill passed. If they opposed unions and pressured workers to keep wages low, they sought market favors which would allow them to increase the prices they could charge for their own goods. They embodied the conservative spirit for which capitalism was condemned.

Yet, conservative attitudes aside, an economic analysis provides some insight into the underlying economic problems facing industrialists. Like workers, they were captive to market forces. They had to contend with weaknesses in foreign markets, where competition and government policy kept them out, and with weaknesses in the German domestic market, where high prices served to dampen consumer demand. A major roadblock in the development of any domestic market was the poor buying power of the German worker. Ironically, the goal of keeping wages low, important to immediate profits, was a self-defeating policy, when it came to creating markets, since it limited the aggregate purchasing power of the German population. Conservative wage policies, if they provide an easy target, do not entirely explain the lack of purchasing power. The high cost of food was a big factor. That too can be blamed on the conservatives, who lobbied for higher tariffs on imported grain, (although it was the large landowners, rather than the industrialists, who favored grain tariffs). Yet, blaming food costs on tariff policies may also be too simplistic. If tariff legislation made certain foods cost more, the basic problem was not tariff policy but Germany's inability to produce sufficient food.

Pressure to keep wages low was one indication of economic weakness. A scarcity of capital was another, as evidenced by a concentration of ownership. In 1925 two percent of industry accounted for 55 percent of employment. (Industrial concentration alone is a somewhat ambiguous proof of weakness and also requires some understanding of lending practices. Grunberger argues that scarce capital causes lenders to charge higher interest rates. Because smaller businesses cannot afford loans, lending is restricted to larger customers who are involved in massive factory projects.)[13] There is another problem, if scarcity of capital is intended to show a long-term weakness in the German economy. Part of the scarcity could be attributed to the war and government policy. The war had clearly taken its toll on capital reserves and efforts to replenish them had been slowed by government taxes imposed in the 1920s, used to pay for welfare benefits and for reparation payments. The cartelization of industry, was another trend suggesting weakness, although, like lending practices, it was an ambiguous proof. If there was a natural tendency in that direction, it was encouraged by the Nazis after their takeover.

German industry, to compensate for the underlying scarcity of raw materials, had concentrated on finished products. Those efforts were so successful that Germany ranked first in the export of finished products in 1930 and only the U.S. was ahead of her in total exports.[14] If the pursuit of an export strategy represented a workable solution, its success depended on the continued existence of a strong market. One potential downside was that the market would come to dominate all production decisions, to the exclusion of all other factors. To a certain extent that is what happened. Market demand, not factory capacity, dictated the level of production, and demand proved so weak that industry was only utilizing 50 to 80 percent of capacity during much of the 1920s.[15]

The agricultural sector was a study in contrasts. There was clearly a demand for agricultural products. Consumers had faced a chronic shortage of food, both before Hitler came to power and during much of the Nazi regime. In fact, it was the shortages of food which had contributed to a weak domestic market for manufactured goods - consumers had to spend so much money on food that they had little discretionary income. Despite the existence of such a strong market, small farmers and large landowners had difficulty surviving economically. High consumer demand should have brought a strengthened agricultural sector, yet agricultural workers were leaving the country for higher paying factory jobs. In 1882 some 42 percent of the German population was part of the agricultural sector. By 1933 the percent had dropped to 29.[16]

The problems experienced by German farmers in the 1920s were not a new phenomenon. There were indications, in the 1840s, that the agricultural economy was marginal. Politicians, in response to the Revolution of 1848-1850, had made concessions to the peasants by abolishing feudal dues or at least making dues payable in money. Even these concessions were not enough - German peasants, like their Russian counterparts, experienced problems making payments. Many abandoned their farms to seek work in the cities, while those who stayed behind remained poor. Other evidence, from the 1870s, supports the idea that German land was not well-suited to agricultural production. She had imported two million tons of wheat from Russia in 1874.[17] Large landowners, despite their weak economic position, held substantial political power. In July 1879, they formed a coalition with industrialists to secure passage of a tariff bill. If it was successful at keeping foreign agricultural products out of Germany, and giving landowners some economic breathing room, it also had the effect of forcing up food prices for the German consumer.

As Germany moved into the Twentieth Century, agriculture experienced some changes. Yet the basic economic problems remained largely unchanged, even into the 1920s. German farmers had difficulty with loan payments. The Nazi government paid off 650 million RM in farm loans between 1933 and 1936. The Weimar government had provided a similar bail-out between 1926 and 1931. The amount then had been smaller, but it was still substantial - 453.6 million RM.[18] The peasant struggle to pay off debts to landlords had not been eliminated, it had just changed forms. Instead of dues owed to landlords, peasants had to contend with mortgages held by banks. The government offered some protection by making the property of small farmers immune from fore-closure in September 1933. The result was not economic relief, but economic hardship. If the law was intended to protect the peasant by granting him ownership, it also prevented him from getting cash. Since the law would not allow peasants to mortgage property, banks would no longer lend money.[19]

As an additional prop, the Nazis resorted to import tariffs to protect German farmers. While it did prevent farms from going under, its overall effect was to continue an inefficient system while making consumers pay more for food. At the other extreme, when the regime sought to bring down the price of food for consumers with the institution of price controls in 1935, a side-effect was to restrict capital availability. Farmers, unable to recover costs, had difficulty accumulating sufficient money for needed capital investment. German agriculture, like its Russian counterpart, needed capital if it was ever to increase the level of mechanization and productivity.

Despite help from the government the agricultural sector showed only marginal improvement toward the end of the 1930s. Its production was at least adequate for the needs of the population. Germany did not suffer the extreme privations of Russia. However, 45 percent of income was spent on food and not all foods were available in sufficient quantities. Adjustments were made in diet to compensate in certain areas; potato flour and maize were substituted for wheat and rye in bread.[20] Apart from the import protections and legal changes designed to protect peasants, the Nazi government did not attempt any massive overhaul of the agricultural economy. Hitler wanted to include agricultural production in his policy of autarchy, yet he did not adopt the radical program of collectivization employed by Stalin in the Soviet Union.

NAZI ECONOMIC PROGRAMS

In one sense the discussion of Germany and her economic history in this book differs from the discussion of Russia. In Russia the focus was, not so much on the Bolshevik takeover, but on the communist political response to economic conditions and the development of economic policy over time. As a result it was more of a history of communism once power had been achieved. Here the focus is more on the seizure of power and the economic conditions contributing to political discontent and less on the economic policies once power had been attained. Nazi policy is helpful, not so much to explain Hitler's economic philosophy, but for the light it sheds on economic conditions which existed in Germany, both before 1933 and during his regime. If it provides additional support for the thesis that Germany was short of resources, it also provides insight into the workings of a market economy generally.

Hitler was successful at solving the problem of unemployment. Yet severe unemployment was the type of problem which cried out for an immediate political solution and, in many ways, was more easily solved. Resource scarcity, by its nature, was obscure, easily overlooked as a problem, and presented no obvious, quick solutions. Autarchy was Hitler's attempted solution, but he clearly underestimated the extent of the problem. What he attempted, with autarchy, was a leap into the future; what he settled on had a stronger resemblance to the past, particularly the days of the Roman Empire. His solution to scarcity was war and geographical expansion.

"Guns and butter," describes an economic policy where governments increase military expenditures while allowing growth in the civilian sector. A major danger is inflation, which the U. S. economy experienced when Lyndon Johnson increased expenditures during the Vietnam War. Joseph Stalin's attempt to bolster his military created similar problems in the Russian economy, or at least made the existing ones much worse. One of the long-standing debates has concerned Hitler's seeming success with both guns and butter. Yet that success exists only if the evidence is looked at selectively. Inflation was under control, only in the sense that it had not reached the 1923 level. If Hitler had increased the military budget, the government was not yet printing money at the pace set by the Weimar government following the French invasion of the Ruhr in 1923. Unemployment, a likely result of inflation, was avoided, not because inflation was absent, but because the labor market was determined by markets subject to military needs, not civilian economic demand.

While Hitler managed to reduce unemployment substantially between 1933 and 1935, his measures largely involved "artificial" stimulation, i.e., creating demand outside normal market operations and therefore not governed by rules of consumer demand. Between 1933 and 1935 these measures often involved either public works projects, such as the autobahn construction, or tax incentives for private construction projects. The Nazis appropriated 5000 million marks for public works through 1935.[21] Despite the size of the expenditure in money terms, it appears that it was more of a public relations ploy. For all the attention focused on the autobahn project there were, during much of 1934, only around 84,000 workers employed on the roads.[22] According to some, it was not the road projects which aided recovery so much as the rearmament program which began in 1934. In its early phase, rearmament almost resembled the autobahn project, with an emphasis on military infrastructure needs, such as barracks, docks or manufacturing facilities.[23]

In one sense arms production does not represent an artificial stimulus or an imaginary market. The number of rifles or artillery pieces can be calculated and budgeted for, just like any other commodity. At the same time there is a difference in the nature of the market. A "normal" market, such as the market for food commodities like potatoes, is finite or limited by the ability of buyers to consume the product. Bullets or artillery shells may be "consumed," or used up, in the same way as a potato. What makes them different is that demand is unconnected to human needs. If the number of hungry people in the world suggests an unlimited demand for food, agricultural demand has practical limits which do not apply to military products. One individual can only eat so many potatoes. Soldiers, in contrast, can never have enough bullets in a battle. It is not so much that they actually need an infinite supply of bullets, it is more that, in practical terms, the demand far exceeds the ability to produce.

The extent of government investment in armaments, and its effect on employment, can be gauged by the figure for 1935. In that year the government spent 5400 million marks on armaments, in contrast to the 5000 million marks it had spent in the previous three years for make-work projects. In 1938, the government was spending 44 percent of its budget on armaments, or 17,200 million marks.[24] In 1938 unemployment had dropped to 429,000 and in 1939 was only 70,000.

Military service, while not intended as an employment program, nevertheless contributed to the reduction in unemployment. In March 1935 Hitler defied the Allies by reinstating compulsory military service. He intended to increase the size of the army from the 100,000 allowed under the Versailles Treaty to 550,000 men. The German army which invaded Poland in September 1939 numbered 1.5 million men, while the Russian invasion force used in Operation Barbarossa in June 1941, numbered more than three million. In the summer of 1935 Hitler also instituted compulsory labor service. Males between the ages of 18 and 25 had to provide six months of service.

Just as public works projects and rearmament represented a form of gimmickry related to unemployment, government efforts to fund such projects represented a sleight-of-hand related to financing. The Nazis were unable to come up with an alternative to deficit financing, but they were creative in disguising it. One method was the use of 'mefo' bills, which hid expenditures for armaments. The secrecy was not totally related to fiscal policy. Hitler wanted to keep the fact that Germany was rearming a secret as long as possible since it represented a violation of the Versailles Treaty.

The 'mefo' bill was short for 'mefo-wechsel' or Mefo Exchange. The name was an acronym for a fictitious company, the Metallurgische Forschungsgesellschaft G.m.b.H., which had been created by four armament firms. Its purpose was to discount bills presented by defense contractors who had taken work from the government. The Reichsbank, by law, was not allowed to discount such bills, but got around the law by using the company as a front. The bills were short-term notes, with a primary term of six months. Apart from the secrecy, the main advantage of 'mefo' bills was that they remained outside the governmental budgetary process, i.e., they were not officially an appropriation or expenditure of the regime. In fact, the four defense contractors had provided an underwriting of one billion marks. The advantage for the defense contractor was that it had a strong guarantee of payment, even though the front company was engaging in illegal conduct. There was an economic advantage for the government, apart from the fact that the extent of government spending was covered up. The advantage was that the contractor was relying on its own capital to pay workers until the time the bill was discounted. It was, in other words, an artificial means of financing market demand which, without involving a formal government appropriation, nevertheless served to create employment. It was not an inconsequential amount. Between 1934 and 1936 the government financed half of total arms expenditures with 'mefo' bills. In March 1938, when the program was discontinued, the government owed defense contractors some 12 billion marks in 'mefo' bills.[25]

'Mefo' bills were only one artificial means of financing. In 1938, another financial trick was to get banks to lend the government money. While the Nazis gave the banks treasury bills in exchange, the government would not allow the redemption of the bills. The government also forced businesses to lend money to finance the Second Four-Year Plan or to invest in plant facilities they otherwise would not have. Germany consumers did not escape the gimmickry. In 1938 the government announced that it would produce a "people's car," the Volkswagen, which would sell for only 990 Reichsmark. The financial gimmick relating to the car was that the it would not be delivered until the final payment had been made. Despite this drawback, the government had received 300,000 orders by November 1940. Unfortunately for consumers, the only models ever produced were the show models used in 1938. Before large-scale production began the factory had been converted to arms manufacture.

The artificial aspect of government policy was not confined to the areas of employment or financing. There was an economically unreal aspect as well about the methods used to increase the availability of raw materials. The Second Four-Year Plan, with its goal of economic self-sufficiency, represented the extreme in government efforts to alter or even to defy market forces. The problem was that the Four-Year Plan was not a one-time solution to an unexpected problem. Germany was confronted with a series of emergency shortfalls. The New Plan in 1934 had been an extraordinary response to a foreign exchange shortfall. In 1939 she was on the verge of another economic crisis and was saved only by the beginning of the Second World War. While shortage problems were aggravated by Hitler's determination to rearm, Germany would have faced problems in these areas because she was reliant on foreign sources for raw materials and food.

The exchange crisis of 1934 did not catch the government totally unawares. Almost from the start Nazi economic policy had been directed toward securing supplies of foreign raw materials. In the Balkans the situation was ripe for exploitation. While it was a productive agricultural region, selling prices were relatively high and marketing difficult as a result. Germany agreed to serve as a market, but in return, it wanted Balkan producers to buy German products. Rather than transferring funds via the government exchange mechanism in the Balkan country, the Nazis set up special accounts in Germany from which funds would only be released when goods were purchased from German manufacturers.[26] Similar arrangements were made with Latin American countries for purchases of raw materials. Forcing the countries to buy German goods was only part of the economic gimmickry involved; the other was the increased price the Germans would sell their goods for to compensate for the high cost of the agricultural purchases. For a time the Balkan countries went along with this exploitation, but eventually most would decide to receive cash payments or require Germany to use the normal foreign exchange mechanism. From their perspective, whatever advantage had been gained by finding a market for their agricultural products was offset by the disadvantages of buying German goods at inflated prices.

The foreign exchange crisis of 1934 occurred in June. The still-secret rearmament program and the increased factory production meant a welcomed revival of the market generally but had also created an unexpected demand for more raw materials. Any changes in the volume of imports and exports, whether related to raw materials or not, would eventually be registered in the accounts of a country's central bank. Banking authorities in 1934 could have expected an increased level of exchange activity from the increased demand. However the Reichsbank was particularly sensitive to changes in raw materials demand. It was not so much that the raw materials market was, by nature, an international market which would necessitate greater bank involvement. It was more that Germany's heavy dependence on foreign raw materials was not offset by any compensating markets for her products. If Germany needed raw materials, the countries she bought them from did not need anything Germany produced.

After paying off foreign creditors, the Reichsbank found itself in June, with only had 100 million RM in gold and foreign exchange reserves. The situation contrasted with that of 1933, at least where foreign exchange was concerned. Germany's trade balance then had been a positive 667 million RM. In one year it dropped by nearly 1000 million RM to a deficit of 284 million RM. The surplus of 1933 was related to agricultural imports, which had declined, the result of a curious contradiction in Nazi economic policy. While the government went to great lengths to import agricultural products from the Balkans, it also increased tariffs on foreign agricultural products to protect its own farmers.[27]

The government moved relatively quickly to deal with the crisis. A moratorium on government debt payments was ordered and the 'New Plan' was put into effect in September 1934. Its main goal was to slow the drain on Reichsbank foreign exchange reserves. As a result, it left barter type of arrangements alone. It had a secondary purpose of limiting imports to those commodities considered crucial by the government, namely food and raw materials. The main mechanism for enforcement was the government's ability to determine which import agreements would be honored for payment. The major change in the law was the requirement that importers obtain government approval prior to bringing in goods. With the New Plan the government not only expanded its control over the types of products imported, but also determined the countries which importers would deal with. In conjunction with the New Plan, the German government concluded some 25 agreements with trading partners in South America and the Balkans. While the government now had asserted more control over trade, the result in 1935 was a 19 percent increase in exports and a trade surplus.[28]

THE SECOND FOUR-YEAR PLAN

In 1935, the rearmament program created a dilemma for the Nazi government and its finance minister, Dr. Hjalmar Schacht. Rearmament provided employment for those who had been unable to find work. Unfortunately the defense industry and the worker were both consumers - the defense industry consumed raw materials and the worker consumed food. Schacht, despite the New Plan, had not been able to solve the basic problem of shortage. Germany still had to import large quantities of both food and raw materials and both required foreign exchange. It appeared that the time had come to choose between guns and butter. One option was to introduce rationing, but the Nazis did not want to damage their image, so that idea was shelved. Within the government the battle lines were drawn between Schacht, who favored the continued use of foreign exchange for raw materials (for armaments) and the head of the Reich Food Estate, Walter Darré, who wanted an increase in the allocation of foreign exchange for agricultural products such as butter and vegetable oil. Darré won the battle in 1935, although it was a temporary victory. The military was pressuring the government for more raw materials for defense and Hitler, who's goal was rearmament, was unlikely to put defense needs on the back burner. Hitler, ever the politician, was aware that he could not totally ignore consumer needs, in spite of his desire to prepare Germany for war. He was however, open to any solution which would free Germany from her dependence on foreign imports.

The Second Four-Year Plan was announced in the fall of 1936. Apart from the overall goal of autarchy, or German self-sufficiency, Hitler wanted both the army and the economy to be ready for war in four years. When Germany finally did go to war in 1939 she was better prepared than in 1936, but the economic goals set by Hitler had not been achieved. Some were clearly unrealistic. Setting impossible goals was perhaps not unexpected, given his political outlook and background. He projected confidence in the face of seemingly impossible odds. Yet he was basing economic growth on, not just one, but a wide range of unproven, even undiscovered, processes. In the area of synthetic fuels his hopes were pinned on the possibility of scientific breakthroughs, not on the exploitation of an existing technology. At the same time, it appears that he looked to the Four-Year Plan only as a temporary measure. He more probably believed that military conquest was the real answer. It was the acquisition of new territory where he more realistically expected to acquire the resources necessary to solve Germany's shortages.

Perhaps the major criticism of the Plan is not that it totally failed, but that, from a cost-benefit standpoint, the successes were achieved at high cost. Göring, who had been placed in charge of the Plan, made budget decisions based more on wishful thinking than on economic analysis. Because the centerpiece of the Plan was autarchy, large portions of the budget were allocated to synthetic fuels production. Similar thinking went into his decision to set up an ore-processing plant, which came to be known as the Reich-Works-Hermann-Göring, at Salzgitter. Aware that Germany possessed large quantities of iron ore, his thinking was that the only obstacle to development was the lack of a production facility. The problem was that it was such low-grade ore that it was prohibitively expensive to process. Experienced industry leaders were aware of the technical problems and shied away from participation. Göring went ahead with the project anyway. In the end, the plant was neither a technical triumph nor an economic success. Something of an economic 'black hole,' it cost 400 million marks to build and the private sector, which had opposed the project, was forced to absorb a large portion of the costs.[29] The major steel firms were forced to invest 130 million marks. To add insult to injury, it began to actively compete with them by using high-grade Swedish-ore.[30] They might take some comfort from the fact that their position had been vindicated.

The Four-Year Plan absorbed some 50 percent of industrial investment between 1936 and 1942, yet Germany still imported one-third of her raw materials when the war began.[31] Of the money the Plan received, half was invested in the development of synthetic fuels. For all that investment, Germany still had to import 82 percent of its fuel needs.[32] There were plan targets which were met in some areas, such as explosives and brown coal, and some which, even falling short, represented substantial accomplishments. The Plan target for aluminum for 1942 was 273,000 tons and actual output was close to that figure, 260,000 tons. In 1936 only 98,000 tons had been produced. The 1942 output of iron ore was 4,137,000 tons, short of the targeted 5,549,000 tons, but greater than the 1936 output of 2,255,000 tons.[33] The question is whether the money would have been better spent building up reserves through imports.

This section has looked at some of the major economic policies pursued by the Nazis. Their first major problem was unemployment, addressed with public works projects and a rearmament program. They also had to deal with a shortage of foreign exchange reserves, which Schacht attempted to solve with the New Plan of 1934. The foreign exchange crisis of 1934 was related to Germany's chronic shortage of raw materials, which the government attempted to solve with the Second Four-Year Plan in 1936. The next section takes a more detailed look at the history of the German economy. Its primary focus is on what might be called the 'business' sector. Hitler took an almost 'big business' attitude toward the economy. He suppressed the labor unions, imposed wage controls, and encouraged cartels. Yet this solicitous attitude was not unique to the Nazis. Earlier German governments had also favored business interests, as the tariff act of 1879 suggests.

BUSINESS DEVELOPMENT IN A RESOURCE-SCARCE ENVIRONMENT

The climate for big business under Hitler was mixed. It had to put up with high taxes and the government extortion represented by projects such as the Reich-Works-Hermann-Göring. What it got in return was almost total victory on the labor front. Workers could no longer strike and had no right to collective bargaining. The government intervened further by imposing wage controls. The defeat of labor represented an important victory, if only because labor problems had become the all-consuming obsession of business. There was only one thing which business wanted more and that was greater profits. It got that as well. In spite of being taxed at a rate of between 60 and 70 percent, in spite of being forced to invest money in government-ordered expansion, its undistributed profits stood at 5.0 billion RM in 1939, compared to 1.3 billion RM in 1928.[34]

There were elements of both views in the policies of Hitler. Because some of the larger firms received favorable treatment from the government, the policy gave the appearance of a generally pro-business stance. In fact, Nazi policy toward business was somewhat arbitrary. While public pronouncements suggested a free market stance, actual policy was quite intrusive. Even the bigger firms, viewed as the darlings of the government, were told what to do, although they found that Nazi attitudes could be changed by making contributions to the Party. Treatment depended on the type of business involved as well. Export firms, who favored a free trade policy, found their interests taking a back seat to the interests of firms involved in armaments.

From a communist perspective Nazi economic policy epitomized the very worst aspects of the capitalist system. The huge profits, coupled with the suppression of the unions, provided confirmation of a capitalist conspiracy which extended beyond big business to the government itself. If Germany demonstrated, not just the existence of a capitalist conspiracy, but proof of its strength as well, Russia served as a cautionary note. The government in Russia was not above exploitation, since it had also eliminated the unions and forbidden workers to strike. Unlike Germany however, "big business" in Russia had not been made a partner with the government, but had fallen victim to it.

The suppression of the unions coupled with the encouragement of big business, was enough to give the Nazi government a pro-business reputation. That reputation was deserved in the case of the armaments industry, but was less applicable where other types of businesses were involved. The Russian government had found that its taxing authority was an effective weapon against private business. When it wanted to assume control of a sector, it increased tax or tariff rates, as it did in the case of railroad transport charges in the mid-1920s. German methods may have appeared more sophisticated, but authorities were not about to overlook such a tool. In some ways what they did was more intrusive. Russian policy, in the case of the railroads, was to tax businesses only after they entered the market, for example, at the point where goods were shipped. The German authorities took a more aggressive approach which involved them in business at an earlier stage.

While taxing authority was still used to collect taxes, it also used it to monitor the overall viability of a business. The policy began in 1935 with a requirement that businesses keep records. Ostensibly the record-keeping requirements were for purposes of accuracy in tax collections. They also provided a useful tool if the government wanted to close uneconomical businesses down. (The OGPU in Russia, it will be recalled, had compiled its list of kulaks for the deportation campaign of 1931, by using tax questionnaires.) The government had two options if it decided to put someone out of business. It could either raise taxes or it could enforce regulations which many businesses could not meet. Raising taxes was often enough since the tax itself was a particularly heavy burden. Marginal businesses struggling with ordinary business costs found the tax burden too much. If that was not enough the government could use its licensing authority to add other burdens. One very effective measure was a minimum unencumbered capital requirement of 30,000 marks for wholesalers. As a result of this requirement they lost one third of their number. If Nazi ideology temporarily took a back seat to economic considerations, authorities made up for that in their enforcement zeal. With economic viability the standard, they hounded those on the economic margins. Radio retailers had dropped below 30,000 by 1939, half of their 1933 level.[35]

Was there an economic justification for such extensive interference in the market? It can be argued that nonproductive businesses would have been eliminated by the market anyway. It is likely that the 60,000 radio retailers would have declined in number over time without any government action. Small business owners, like the unemployed farm workers attracted to cities, would quite likely have been drawn to the higher paying defense jobs. The government, to enforce its bookkeeping requirements, had to increase the amount of bureaucracy. Someone, after all, had to look at the books and make a decision about how well the business was doing. From a cost-benefit standpoint, the extra effort hardly seems justified. The government's argument would have been that it was more efficient to weed out marginal businesses early. To allow them to continue when they would never be profitable represented a drain on the economy, since they siphoned off resources from businesses which were likely to succeed. Government policy was intended to accelerate market processes, not necessarily to defy economic trends.

If government involvement in the market was only intended to weed out marginal businesses, its other economic consequence was cartelization and an anti-competitive atmosphere. In fact, the 1933 law had specifically given the government the authority to force firms into cartels.[36] Businesses, tempted to eliminate competition through secret agreements, found that the government was doing the job for them. Nor was it confined to the retail trade. In 1932, for example, there were 9,634 joint stock corporations. By 1941 the number had fallen to 5,418. Where monopolies had controlled 40 percent of industrial production in 1933, by 1937 they had increased control to 70 percent.[37] For those businesses which survived, cartelization meant increased profits.

There was a downside to Nazi planning even for industry giants. To do well, they had to learn to live with politicians with little experience in economic planning. For those firms savvy enough to understand Nazi thinking there were monetary rewards. I. G. Farben was almost fanatical in its support of Nazi policy, (even producing Zyklon B, the poison gas used in the death camps), and was rewarded with one of the contracts for the development of synthetic fuel. If its experience in chemicals made it a logical choice, its owners hedged their bets with contributions to the Nazi Party. In 1936 it donated nearly 5 million marks to the Party and increased the figure to over 8 million in 1938.[38] In 1943 it employed 330,000 workers and recorded a profit of 822 million RM.[39] Farben's profitability was particularly remarkable, given the "success" of the synthetic fuels program itself - the program was, in fact, one of the real failures of the Four-Year Plan.

The sometimes arbitrary nature of government contract awards was only one of the difficulties business had to endure. The government became a substitute for the market in decision-making, in areas other than general business viability. If the government controlled wages, a form of interference welcomed by most business, it also controlled how much was produced and the prices which could be charged. It controlled the allocation of raw materials. What had been internal business decisions, such as the amount of investment in facilities, were more and more made by the government. Businesses also had to contend with the governmental gimmickry related to financing. Where the government did not formally tax firms or appropriate government funds, it demanded that businesses invest in facilities, even told firms where new plants were to be built. Nazi planners often imposed such severe restrictions on investment - sometimes firms were told to reinvest funds, at other times they were directed to buy government bonds - that profits not taken by high taxes were eliminated through government controls.[40]

COMMUNISM VS. NAZISM - DEFINING THE ECONOMIC DIFFERENCE

Government policy, at times, amounted to serious market manipulation, even tampering. Yet, for all their bullying, the Nazis were unwilling to take the final step - having the government take over all aspects of the economy. They were content with industry management of factory operations. That may have been, in the final analysis, what separated them from the Soviet Union. Hitler saw such clear differences between Nazism and communism that when he ordered the Russian invasion in 1941 he fully intended to destroy the Soviet Union. It was not always clear just how he distinguished Nazism from Bolshevism however. Given the opportunity he was willing to adopt their policies. The fact that the Bolsheviks had come up with the idea of outlawing unions in Russia did not deter him from embracing a similar policy himself when he came to power.

If industry did not come under total government control, as in the Soviet Union, it still had to endure a great deal of government interference and remained heavily reliant on government contracts for its existence. The interference practiced by the Nazis in Germany was different than that engaged in by the communists in Russia. However, what was the difference? Was it simply a matter of quantity? - the Nazis did the same thing as the communists, but they did less of it. Or, was it more an apples and oranges comparison? Was there something qualitatively unique about communism? - the communist outlook was so different that whatever the Nazis did, it could not be compared to Russia. In Western eyes, of course, Soviet communism, with its avowed goal the elimination of private property, will always set the standard and nothing done in Germany could come remotely close to that level. That argument suggests that the key difference could be found in a mental outlook, rather than in economic operations themselves. The Nazi attitude toward profits represented a major contrast between the two systems. The Nazis were not philosophically opposed to profits; they were all too willing to indulge the wishes of their favorite firms for higher profits. If they took steps to eliminate firms, the standard they used to judge them was profitability.

Making a distinction based solely on a philosophical attitude lets the German regime too easily off the hook, and overlooks a more important puzzle. Conventional wisdom holds that greater governmental involvement in an economy is inconsistent with

404

the idea of a free market. A government can choose either one system or the other, but cannot have not both. The puzzle is that Germany somehow managed to combine the two. If at times it seemed willing to eliminate marginal businesses or to dictate how profits were to be used, something similar to the experience of Russia, it was, at other times, willing to let firms keep those profits they had made. While that may be debated for some time, the more basic question remains - was there a qualitative difference between Nazi and communist controls?

It might be argued that the difference lay, not only in the fanaticism displayed by the communists in their determination to eliminate private property, but also in their success. That fact is hard to argue with. By 1930 private trade in Russia had been reduced to only 5.6 percent of all trade, (and that was before it was formally made illegal).[41] In contrast, it took the Nazis six years, from 1933 to 1939, to eliminate the 30,000 retailers involved in the radio trade, which left 50 percent still operating. Some differences might be seen in the methods employed. Russian administrators had often used military or Cheka units to threaten or take action against peasants, while German authorities, in the case of businesses, resorted more to the courts.

In the end, what distinguishes the two regimes is largely a matter of degree. Attempts to separate them based on their administrative methods, even their comparative ruthlessness, fail. If the Soviet government eliminated businesses by raising railroad freight charges, German authorities forced them out with regulations tied to their profitability. If communist officials came off looking more ruthless, as in their treatment of the peasants, German authorities appeared benign only because the financial enforcement tools at their disposal were more effective and the results not particularly dramatic. They didn't need to bring in the Gestapo against business owners because they could enforce tax decrees in courts. In the realm which judges economic rights and wrongs, Soviet officials were condemned, not just for the actions themselves, but also for the way in which those actions were portrayed to the world. Nazi officials may have been relentless in their pursuit of a business, but the end result, a court order closing down operations, attracted little attention. When Soviet officials deprived the peasants of their lands, the images were of people being driven from their homes and shipped off to distant lands in box cars. The power of this image was all the proof needed that what was happening in Russia was incomparably worse than what was taking place in Germany.

Where the communists sought to eliminate private property altogether, the Nazis were at least willing to treat property rights with some respect. They did not go so far as to make rights to private property absolute however. They freely trampled on the rights of those businesses they had decided to eliminate. In that regard there was little difference between Russia and Germany - private property and businesses were taken away by the state in both cases. Where they differed was in the way they disposed of the confiscated property. In Russia the actions were taken on behalf of the state with the intent that the state would assume control completely. The goal was state control of all sectors of the economy. In Germany the state kept its role to a minimum. Its goal was not to replace the private sector with the state, but to strengthen the private sector as it existed.

Given their track record, it might be asked whether the Nazis were sincere in their beliefs, where profits were concerned. Perhaps the firms which were allowed huge profits, like I. G. Farben, were intended only as showpieces; like Goebbels' mass rallies, they served as public relations tools, creating a false image of Nazi beliefs. The evidence suggests that sincerity was not the issue. Hitler actually believed in the capitalist system and admired those who were successful. While the number of profitable firms may have been small, their profits were quite real. A more fundamental problem is the difference between what the Nazis believed in and how their beliefs played out in practice. If there was a belief in capitalism, the regime was rather selective in its recognition of the accompanying property rights. Property rights were fully recognized only if firms were able to demonstrate their success. Businesses which the government decided were marginal found such rights to be meaningless.

Whatever its shortcomings, Nazi economic policy seems to avoid the ultimate condemnation - being placed in the same category as communism. If failing businesses suffered at the hands of Nazi financial planners, policy-makers can be forgiven because their "hearts were in the right place." That they failed to live up to some ideal is not for lack of trying. The problem with that justification is that it undercuts the often-heard criticism of communism - the idea may sound good in theory, but doesn't seem to work well in practice.

If Germany's attitude toward profits contrasted with that of Russia, the attitude toward cartelization was remarkably similar. In fact, Nazi efforts to encourage business concentration among enterprises in Germany might have taken their cue from Bolshevik planners. If not copied from Russia, the pattern was certainly a familiar one. While there might be a temptation to blame cartelization on the Bolsheviks or even the Nazis, Germany had exhibited a tendency toward concentration, in the absence of Bolshevism, and even before the Nazi takeover. In addition to cartelization, both Germany and Russia had one other thing in common. Cartelization, in both countries, took place against a backdrop of scarcity.

INDUSTRIAL EXPANSION AND THE MARKET - GERMANY FROM 1850

The discussion, to this point, has focused on the economic history of the Nazi period. It is clear that Nazi Germany had serious economic problems and that among them was a scarcity of resources. Schacht's 1934 New Plan, intended to rescue Germany's foreign exchange reserves, and the 1936 Four-Year Plan, with its emphasis on autarchy, underscore the crucial shortages of resources faced by Germany. Yet, focusing on the problems of the Nazi era provides a very limited perspective. The fact that Germany, almost single-handedly, was able to sustain a major war effort in two world wars seems to contradict almost all evidence of economic weakness.

In this book's introduction it was pointed out that resources are based on human needs and that needs change over time. Raw materials do not become resources until economic use creates a demand. Germany provides one of the better illustrations of the dynamic nature of resources. Despite its lack of oil, Germany had not been permanently disadvantaged, because oil had not always been a resource of consequence. Similarly, Germany could not be described as suffering from "scarcity" until oil became a resource. In one sense Germany's economic problem was not so much that she had created a demand for resources, rather it was that the areas of strongest demand were areas where resources were deficient. In other words, she had created a market which played, not to her strengths, but to her weaknesses.

The Industrial Revolution arrived late in Germany. Starting in England in the 1760s, it had involved advances in industrial technology which transformed craft industries into models of mass production. The steam engine patented by James Watt in 1769 provided a more powerful source of power than simple water alone. During the 1700s there had also been improvements in iron production which involved the use of coke, derived from coal, instead of charcoal, which was normally produced from wood.[42] The technological changes meant a transformation in the resource base of industrial economies. Where water power and wood had been the basic resources of industrial economies, coal and iron began to take on a greater importance.

The Industrial Revolution, when it finally came to Germany, may have been driven by technological change, but it was also shaped by accidents of geology and geography. Not all of the German states possessed coal or iron, but there were areas where these materials could be found in quantities - among them the Ruhr (the territory occupied by the French army in 1923), Silesia, and the Saarland. The geographical location of the ore deposits, if they aided industrial development, almost doomed Germany to a military conflict with France, since the Ruhr and Saar basins were not far from the French border. Following the end of the Franco-Prussian War in 1871, Germany would add the mineral-rich region of Alsace-Lorraine to its territory. Almost as soon as industrial development began the Prussian government had to struggle with one major policy question - Should economic development be left to private industry or was it the responsibility of government? With governmental institutions still in their infancy, the government approach represented something of a compromise. In the Ruhr the government took a free market approach and eliminated government controls on coal production in the period between 1851 and 1865. That policy paid off in accelerated development. In the Saarbrücken and Upper Silesia state control of coal mining operations wasn't enough. It sought to use the monopolistic powers gained there to control industry.[43]

German industry quickly moved to the forefront. Between 1850 and 1870 industrial output grew at an astonishing pace. In 1871, for example, German coal production was greater than that of France and Belgium put together. The 1871 output, 29.4 million tons, represented a ninefold increase over the 1846 figure of 3.2 million tons. She also moved ahead of France in pig iron output. In 1875 France produced 1.4 million tons while Germany produced 2 million tons.[44] If industrial advance brought increased output, the ability to mass produce goods spelled the end of the trade guilds. Craftsmen could simply not compete against manufacturers offering a wider variety of goods at much cheaper prices. The market for manufactured goods, if it spelled the end of craft production, fueled a demand for workers. However much productive capacity had been increased, it could not keep pace with the demand for goods. Industry would benefit from an expanding market for nearly 30 years. Part of this was related to a population increase of some five million people between 1850 and 1870.

What did these changes mean for the agricultural sector? Did they represent a timely rescue of a faltering economy, coming at a time when peasants and laborers were struggling to survive? If they seemed to offer that promise, the reality was that the agricultural economy was largely left behind. What progress there was was confined to the manufacturing sector. Since factories required more workers there was an improved labor market. Despite that impact, strength in the industrial sector was not enough to compensate for fundamental weaknesses in agricultural production. Advances in industrial productivity were never matched by agriculture and output remained too inefficient to compete with that of other countries. The inability of peasants to pay their feudal dues, which had led to the dismantling of the feudal system in the 1850s, was one symptom of economic weakness. Some 640,000 Prussian peasants obtained government loans to pay off their feudal debts between 1850 and 1865.[45] Another symptom was the inability of grain-growers to supply domestic markets, despite a strong market. Germany imported two million tons of wheat from Russia in 1874.[46]

Where the problem for industry between 1850 and 1870 was an inability to keep up with demand, there were signs, in the mid-1870s, that the market was reaching the saturation point. In 1876 demand for pig iron was so low that German iron producers were only operating at 50 percent of capacity.[47] What accounted for the sudden turn-around? If the Industrial Revolution offered the promise of revolutionary advances in technology, it was just in its infancy. Whatever discoveries were to be made, they lay far in the future, or so it seemed. Yet, it was also undeniable that a market, which had seemed so infinitely large in 1850, had suddenly become finite.

It has been said that great military leaders, such as Napoleon, have emerged at times when there have been revolutionary changes in military tactics or technology. The same might be said of business leaders. Those who are quick to recognize the market potential of new technology will rise to the top. The fact that German industry made such rapid gains in productivity after 1850 suggests that it was adept at recognizing opportunities in changing environments. Unfortunately history often teaches more than one lesson. If Napoleon represented the height of military genius, his name is more often associated with a major defeat, the battle of Waterloo. How could German companies, so shrewd at recognizing opportunities after 1850, experience setback in 1873, when over 160 companies failed? - or, like pig iron producers, find themselves in 1876 with a productive capacity twice that demanded by the market?[48] The answer was that they had benefitted, not just from advances in technology, but from unique market circumstances.

Conventional wisdom holds that creative genius is rewarded for the newness of an idea. Thomas Edison, for example, was successful in part because electricity was a fascinating and novel discovery. The reality is that economic rewards are tied more to the strength of the market in which an idea emerges, rather than to the fact that the discovery is new. German industrialists had been successful, not so much because they were the first to recognize the potential of factory mass production, but because of the strength of the market they were producing for. They had come on the scene at a time when the potential market was extremely strong, so strong, in fact, that the guilds or craftsmen were unable to fulfill it.

Unfortunately for German industry, the Industrial Revolution and mass production were not a German monopoly. French and British manufacturers were also straining to produce as much as possible for the market. By the end of the 1870s manufacturers in most countries had begun to bump up against market limits. German companies sought to maintain their markets through higher tariffs on foreign competitors. Siding with the large landowners, they supported the 1879 tariff bill, which increased tariffs on both agricultural and industrial products.

Bismarck needed a strong army to conduct his foreign policy and military needs provided a partial solution to the problem of weakening markets. While weapons production provided a new market for industry and a means of employing workers, the protectionist policies which allowed German industry and agriculture to survive also kept consumer prices high.

Protectionist policies worked a hardship on workers, however the state tried to compensate through the creation of a welfare system. Legislation in 1883 set up a medical services program which covered three million workers and, in 1886, seven million agricultural workers were granted accident and health insurance. In 1889 a pension system was created. While such measures were a clear social benefit for workers, they created an additional financial burden for both employers and the state. The medical programs involved contributions from both employers and workers; the pension plan involved an additional contribution from the state.[49] The existence of protective tariffs and an employer-funded welfare system was something of a paradox. Manufacturers and landowners had pressed for protective legislation because their costs of production prevented them from lowering prices to meet foreign competition. The irony was that, at the same time they required tariff protection to survive, they were asked to take on an additional cost to support a welfare system. The state contribution was also a potential financial problem for the government. (It was the state expenditures for unemployment benefits in the Ruhr in 1923 that would cause a loss of confidence in the mark and lead to hyper-inflation.)

In 1890 General Leo von Caprivi became chancellor following Bismarck's retirement. Caprivi, despite his military background, sought to reconcile the various political ideologies. Rather than suppressing the Socialists and radical parties, he made concessions to bring them into the government. Caprivi also signaled a change in trade policy with the introduction of a bill to lower tariffs. Although he was clearly a forward-thinking leader, his goal was not to promote a radical agenda or even to defy the conservative financial or business community. In fact, he had the support of manufacturers. Why would the industrial leadership suddenly decide to follow a more liberal trading policy in 1891?

There are indications that economic conditions were changing for industry. If it still desired protection against foreign competition, it had concluded that foreign markets offered greater opportunities. In addition, the bill represented a breakdown of the normally unified "conservative coalition" of agricultural and industrial interests, since it was not an across-the-board reduction. It focused instead on reducing tariffs on agricultural products, particularly cattle and grain. In the aftermath of the bill's passage Caprivi negotiated trade deals with neighboring countries, including Russia, Italy, and Austria-Hungary.

The policy certainly represented a change of heart on the part of industry. Were second thoughts about the 1879 tariff bill related to an enlightened view of foreign trade or was the reversal better explained in terms of base self-interest? -industry had 'sold out' the Junker landowners. The change did not come about from any questioning of fundamental assumptions about the market. German industry since 1850 had demon-strated the success of its mass-producing methods, even if there had been ups and downs. What was different in 1891 was the market. The problem confronting industry in the 1870s was market saturation. Markets were unable to absorb all the products industry could produce. So long as industry remained focused on those markets, there was little hope of any change. In the 1860s however a new power source, electricity, would emerge. In one sense it represented a dynamic change, a totally unexpected transformation of the resource equation. In another sense it was just one more market opportunity, new in concept, but somewhat ordinary in effect.

For a world accustomed to setting its clock by the sun, electricity was a wonder. For manufacturers, it promised new opportunities and new markets, the unlooked-for solution to the problem of saturation. It solved the immediate problem for industry by creating new markets. As miraculous as that seemed, it did not really deal with the more fundamental problem of market limitations. Even with that drawback, it was not something to be overlooked. Electrical technology gave Germany an advantage in the field, which was quickly exploited. The electrical generator invented by Werner Siemens in 1866 provided such an edge that Germany was still dominant in 1913 when it supplied half the total market in electrical products.[50]

Industry benefitted from technological advances in other fields which could exploit the raw materials available in Germany. It was discovered that synthetic dyes could be made from coal by-products in the 1860s. The iron and steel industries benefitted from the Gilchrist process which used the phosphoric ores found in the Lorraine region and Germany became a major producer of pig iron and steel. In 1910 steel production would be 13,149,000 tons, greater than that of Britain.[51] The domestic market remained Germany's Achilles' heel, however the overwhelming technological advantage held by Germany suggested that foreign markets were a reliable substitute. The nature of the export market changed as well, with a shift from raw materials to finished products, which would account for 63 percent of German exports by 1913.[52]

Caprivi's tariff reform of 1891 may have heralded an era of free trade, but that era was rather short-lived. Agricultural tariffs were restored in 1902. If that political victory suggested the landowners were making gains at the expense of industry, long-term indicators suggested otherwise. The cities and industries still held an attraction for rural residents. In 1870, the rural population accounted for 63.7 percent of the total population. In 1910 it had dropped to 40 percent.[53] Not all the opposition to free trade could be blamed on the Junkers. For all its support of liberal trading policies, where foreign markets were concerned, industry was operating in an environment almost hostile to the market at home. The number of cartels grew from eight in 1875 to 366 in 1905 and would continue growing to around 3,000 in the 1920s. The Rhenish-Westphalian Coal Syndicate, one of the more prominent cartels, controlled 95 percent of coal production in the Ruhr. German industrial cartels, in some ways came to resemble those which existed in Russia. Just as the Bolsheviks would form vertical trusts to control everything from raw materials to final product, German industries also grouped themselves into vertical cartels. Other cartels formed around control of a single product.[54]

Despite these weaknesses, Germany did well as Europe approached the First World War. On the other hand, once hostilities began, her resource needs proved greater than her available supplies. She gained crucial supplies of coal and iron ore when her armies occupied France and Belgium, but still had to import copper and tin. The need to import raw materials put a strain on foreign exchange reserves. Military production was a two-edged sword. The army's needs created a demand for products and for labor, partially offsetting the loss of foreign markets. On the other hand, military production competed with civilian industries for raw materials. Price controls were put in place, followed by food rationing in January 1915.

THE AFTERMATH OF WAR

To outward appearances Germany escaped the worst of the First World War. Although her soldiers had suffered hundreds of thousands of casualties, the war itself had been fought outside of Germany. If her spirit remained unbroken, the violence and political unrest which followed the war's end suggested a society under strain. Yet, compared to the front-line casualty figures, the number of deaths from assassination or street unrest were relatively small. She also got off relatively lightly in terms of physical destruction. Fighting the war in French and Belgian territory meant that her industrial capacity was largely intact.

Whatever territorial or economic advantage Germany hoped to gain by the war was undone by the Treaty of Versailles, signed in June 1919. Although Hitler later tried to excuse Germany's conduct based on the injustice of the Treaty, it was, in reality, the logical conclusion of the realpolitik game played by the European powers. The game had been a long-standing one. Perhaps Hitler's real success lay, not so much in his ability to raise the issue of right or wrong, but in his ability to narrow the time frame in which the debate took place. Actions were unjust, not because of their particular burdens, but because they were most recent in time. Of all the injustices which had occurred in history,

411

he suggested, the Versailles Treaty foisted on Germany was the worst. France then, was justified in focusing on the injustice perpetrated on her in 1871. Under the terms of the Frankfurt treaty concluding the Franco-Prussian War she lost Alsace-Lorraine. Hitler's argument allowed France to conveniently ignore whatever wrongs Napoleon might have been guilty of.

Whether the Versailles Treaty represented the ultimate injustice or was merely one more move in the European game of power politics, it did change the territorial landscape for Germany. France, clearly the motivating force behind the most onerous terms of the treaty, had two goals in mind, one economic, the other military. Economically, she not only wanted to regain the Alsace-Lorraine region lost in the Franco-Prussian War, but also to acquire or exploit additional resources. Militarily, she wanted to weaken Germany's capacity to make war. That case was the easier one to make with the allies. Germany's ability to fight a major war on two fronts for four years was convincing proof of her potential. The economic case however was a more difficult one. Even though the suffering of the French people provided some moral justification for punishing Germany, the allies were less willing to threaten war over economic gains which would primarily benefit France.

Some of the provisions of the Treaty allowed France to combine her military and economic strategies. She got Alsace-Lorraine back and, in addition, was given control of mines in the Saar basin - compensation for the deliberate destruction of French mines by German troops. (In 1923 France would temporarily acquire the coal fields of the Ruhr as well.) Other provisions, if not benefitting France, at least weakened Germany. Germany not only lost territory to the newly created Polish state, but also suffered economically because of the geographical losses. Upper Silesia, for example, was a major coal-producing area. France benefitted economically from the reparations provisions of the Treaty, even without additional territory. An annual payment was tied to the amount of exports. Since it was a percentage payment it was tied to economic recovery. On the other hand, it was a substantial amount - 25 percent. This was in addition to the total liability fixed at 132 billion marks. (Under the 1929 Young Plan, which represented a compromise, reparation payments were to continue until 1988.)[55]

In terms of economic strategy, France viewed the Treaty as an opportunity to acquire additional resources at the expense of Germany. Because iron or coal deposits were the most obvious evidence of economic wealth, there was a temptation to view economic impact solely in resource terms. Overlooked was the impact of the Treaty on markets and employment. What may have made the loss of iron or coal supplies so critical was not the losses themselves, but the impact those losses had on the market for German goods. If German factories had escaped destruction in the war, industrial capacity alone could not create demand. Markets would experience a recovery in the period between 1919 and 1924. Unfortunately the recovery was not a sign of economic health, but could be traced to economic problems. The inflation which followed the end of the war caused the mark to fall, which made German goods cheaper in foreign markets. The increased sales caused a decline in unemployment between 1919 and 1924.[56]

The German economy throughout the 1920s would send out conflicting signals. Whatever the overall message was, it hinted at the importance of market forces. With a continual supply of labor available for her factories, German industry had a seemingly infinite capacity to produce. However, the slow recovery suggests that markets, not technical capabilities, were the major limiting factor. Industry emerged from the war with little physical damage, yet industrial leaders, such as iron and steel, coal, or chemicals, did not even reach their 1913 output and export levels until 1929.[57] As the 1920s came to an end, the German economy, in basic structure, remained the same. Heavy industry had continued its trend toward cartelization, with a few major firms controlling major segments of economic production.

Tied to the problem of markets was the problem of resource scarcity. In limited areas she was able to compensate, yet her overall resource needs were so great that success in a limited number of areas could not offset her major weaknesses. She had not solved the problem of food scarcity. Agriculture was not productive enough to supply Germany's domestic market, while producers remained economically weak.

The next chapter deals with the United States. With its democratic institutions and great resource reserves, the U.S. provides some of the strongest evidence for the existence of a relationship between resource abundance and democracy. It also poses some interesting economic and political questions. Given the amount of resources available, an economic catastrophe such as the Great Depression seems inconceivable. Why did it occur? On the other hand, once the U.S. did encounter economic problems, why did they not lead to the extreme unrest experienced by Germany? The unemployment level in the U.S. was approaching that seen in 1930 Germany, yet it remained relatively free of the violence seen there.

America was not just different from Germany, but unique in history as well. Democracy has been a relatively rare occurrence on the historical stage. If Athens and the U.S. are the two examples of democracy chosen for this book, they make up a large proportion of the total number ever existing. The total number of democratic governments over time has been small. If democracy has been rare, resource reserves on the scale found in America are equally hard to find. America, like Athens, was blessed with vast resources. While its economy has gone through numerous business cycles, those reserves have proved amazingly durable. Even as the resource base has changed to accommodate new discoveries, such as electricity or atomic energy, immense supplies of new resources were discovered to meet those needs.

PART V

MODERN DEMOCRACY

CHAPTER 21

THE UNITED STATES AND THE GREAT DEPRESSION: TOO MUCH CREDIT, TOO LITTLE CASH

There is no economic event in the United States which has been etched into memory as deeply as the Great Depression. Black Tuesday, October 29, 1929, the day the New York Stock Exchange crashed, is perhaps the most famous economic date in history. There have been other economically dismal days. There was a Black Monday on October 19, 1987, when the Exchange collapsed again and the London Exchange dropped 500 points, as well as a Black Thursday, which occurred the week before the Great Crash. There was even another Black Tuesday, on October 19, 1937. The U.S. has endured other depressions, or severe recessions. Some have been labeled as panics, such as the Panics of 1819 and 1837, (which lasted for three to four years), another lengthy "panic" of five years beginning in 1873, and panics in 1893 and 1907. The Panic of 1893 put some 4.6 million people out of work in 1894, 18.4 percent of the work force, and lasted until 1897.[1] In its first year, some 8,000 businesses failed, along with 360 banks.[2] Panics got their names, not from their length, but from the almost hysterical fear of system-wide financial collapse which accompanied them. The sudden desire to turn everything into cash led to bank runs and "fire sales." Recession brought unemployment of nearly 12 percent in 1921.

The Great Depression was different however. It would last almost 10 years and, in terms of unemployment, was much more severe. Where unemployment had been high - 18 percent - in the depression of 1893, it would go even higher during the Great Depression, 24.9 percent in 1933. It was not quite as severe as unemployment in Germany, although in the spring of 1933, with 15 million out of work, the percentage was 29.1. The Great Depression involved the near-total collapse of the market, not the productive capabilities of industry. There had been no war to destroy machinery or factories and the physical ability to produce goods was undiminished.

This chapter looks at the United States during the Great Depression. The Depression, as an economic phenomenon, provides an interesting area of economic study in its own right, since it contains major contradictions. How could people experience deprivation and want in an economy with an abundance of resources? Why, given the need for jobs and the large labor pool, did labor stop being a resource, (as evidenced by the severity of unemployment)? That being said, what does the Depression have to do with the relationship between democracy and resource availability? This book proposed a "resource mechanism" in Chapter 3, which suggests that unemployment is tied to resource scarcity because scarcity contributes to higher product costs and reduced demand. If anything the resource mechanism predicts that vast resource reserves would ensure a permanent demand for labor, since product costs would remain low. That the opposite occurred during the Depression suggests that the thesis is wrong. Whether the facts are enough to disprove the theory, what occurred during the Depression does need to be reconciled with the resource mechanism.

Do the contradictions of the Depression threaten to completely undermine this book's thesis, before the evidence is actually presented? Probably not. At a basic level, the Depression was the product of a market economy which, in itself suggests adequate resource reserves. Market economies do not come into existence unless they pass a certain resource threshold and a market could not have developed in the U.S. unless resources had been available in more than minimal amounts.

If the Depression is important because it raises doubts about this book's thesis, it is important for one other reason. It serves to emphasize the difference between the physical ability to manufacture and the market's ability to sustain demand, i.e., the difference between potential capacity (what factories can produce) and actual capacity (what factories actually produce given market limitations). In 1932 what was known as the Technocracy movement swept the U.S.. It would last just six months: receiving press attention in August 1932, it was being condemned by January 1933, and quickly faded. The name combined the term "technology" with "democracy" and was intended to signify an era in which technologists would rule. Although the word had been coined in 1919 by an inventor and engineer named William H. Smyth, it was another engineer, Howard Scott, who popularized it.[3]

Technocracy had, as a central theme, the importance of energy. In 1932 Scott was able to get the attention of the press, not just by assembling a "committee" dealing with energy, but also by naming his group the Energy Survey of North America. The Energy Survey intended to produce 3,000 separate reports on America's energy reserves. What gave Technocracy its popular appeal was not its focus on energy nor its predictions about technology and the industrial use of machinery. What made it popular was the way it combined a message of hope with a fascination with technology. If its message was an optimistic one, some of its underlying assertions were unsettling and even a little suspect. For one thing, it took a decidedly anti-capitalist and anti-profits tack. The capitalists, if they had all the newest technology at their disposal, had chosen to use it for their own benefit rather than for mankind. Given the hard times, that accusation almost sounded plausible.[4]

What should have alarmed people even more, given the unemployment levels in 1932, were the implications of the technological arguments. Automation, taken to its logical conclusion, was not going to make the unemployment situation better, it was going to make it worse. It was not that the facts were necessarily wrong. In fact the conclusions reached by the Technocrats merely confirmed what people already suspected about factory modernization. One example was the brick industry. What had taken 2,730 plants to produce in 1929 could be done in 1932 with five plants run by only 100 men. Another example was the auto plant in Milwaukee which could produce 10,000 auto frames a day with only 208 men.[5] If the employment picture looked bleak, the overall message was one of optimism. History was on the verge of a technological revolution which knew no limits. Machines may have been replacing workers, but the ability to turn out goods meant that human needs could be met without the need for work. Poverty might even be eliminated.

What condemned Technocracy to its status as a six-month fad was probably political ambition. Even if it contained some important economic observations, it sounded more and more like a political campaign for the technocrats. Forecasting the outcome of factory improvements was one thing, putting Howard Scott in charge of the details was another. Another problem was that Technocracy offered no quick solution to America's economic problems. If it offered hope of a permanent solution to want, the fulfillment of that promise lay 10 or 20 years in the future. There were also practical obstacles which needed to be considered. Was technology really capable of production at the levels assumed by Technocracy, particularly when it came to different products? Producing a million more automobiles was infinitely more difficult than adding a million more units of output, when the product was bricks.

There was a flaw in the logic used by the Technocrats. They looked narrowly at the automation process and the trend toward fewer workers and drew broad conclusions about a related area, production capabilities. If they were wrong in concluding that technological advances would wipe out poverty, they were not incorrect in identifying the potential conflict between employment and automation. This had tremendous significance for the market. Not only was the labor market beginning to separate from the larger market, but it was being reduced in importance as the demand for workers diminished.

That this factory trend was occurring does not explain the Depression. In a sense however, it was representative of a wider problem. It was not just that the labor market was becoming separated from the general market, a problem for workers, it was more that the market side as a whole was operating independently of the production side. If the demand for products would always dictate some connection, the market seemed to distance itself from some of its more traditional activities, such as manufacturing. Demand was no longer associated with output but was sustained artificially, often through loans or credit or through competitive measures such as discounts or price reductions.

THE GREAT CRASH

While the stock market crash is generally recognized as the start of the Great Depression, there is some debate about whether it caused it. Some argue that, while the crash may have triggered events, there were other factors at work which turned the Crash into the Depression. Some believe the Depression was simply a more severe version of the normal business cycle. Others believe that the U.S. government made wrong decisions about monetary policy (the policy relating to the money supply) or failed to act at all when it should have. According to that argument, if the Crash was unavoidable, the Depression might not have been as severe or lasted as long if different policies had been adopted.[6]

Signs of a downturn appeared in the spring of 1929. The number of contracts for building construction fell and the decline was significant enough to be noticed when official federal statistics appeared in March. Orders for new automobiles also fell, from a high of 622,000 in March, to 416,000 by September.[7] Although the figures hinted at disaster, independent of economic happenings in New York, October clearly had an impact, if nothing else accelerating the downward trend.

In analyzing the relationship between the Crash and a general slowdown there is a fundamental question involved. Why would the fortunes of the stock market have any impact at all on markets or events in the outside world? The stock market after all is a limited market. Whatever its importance as a business barometer, its prestige is still a form of reflected glory. Unlike businesses which manufacture products its profits are generated by selling paper. It participates in the market no more than gamblers participate in sporting events. If that was the theory, something had happened in the 1920s which transformed the relationship. The stock market, for business and industry was not just a passing interest, but a full-blown addiction. Where an occasional increase in stock value had been an added bonus in past years, businesses came to increasingly rely on stock for profits.

Compounding this problem was the increasing reliance on credit. Lenders had extended credit to stock market investors in greater amounts than was wise, depositors had placed too much faith in banks, and both were fatally attracted to credit. Homes could be purchased on credit, along with automobiles and other consumer goods. Businesses could finance expansion on credit. Even stock could be purchased on credit. Lending money for stock investment was not in itself a problem, unless potentially risky loans began to outnumber the good loans held by a particular institution. In addition, risky credit policies normally threatened only the institution involved, unless the number of shaky institutions began to outnumber the sound ones. What tied the fortunes of the general economy so closely to that of the lending institutions was not just the extensive involvement of the institutions in the market, not just the heavy consumer reliance on credit, but the fact that both shared a common lending pool. Investors used the same banks and mortgage companies which manufacturers and homeowners did. When investors could not come up with the cash, it was manufacturers and homeowners who were pressured to pay.

In hindsight, 1920s investors are condemned not only for their greed, but also for their failure to notice clear signs of trouble. Some of that criticism has more to do with the severity of the Depression which followed than with anything investors did. If they were naive, they were certainly not unique in history. "Unrealistically high expectations" might be a symptom of the 1920s but it also is a characteristic of "gold fever," which infected, not only the Spanish Conquistadors, but also the settlers at Jamestown in 1606, and the Forty-niners who rushed to California gold fields in the mid-1800s. What was different was the economic impact.

To suggest that 1920s attitudes differed little from earlier times, is not to deny that expectations played a role in the Crash. There was a loss of judgment about the returns which were possible and the number of investors who speculated had grown increasingly large. It was not just investors, but banks and lenders who were infected with the bug. They saw potentially high returns without assessing the real risks involved.

THE BLACK TUESDAY CATALYST

In one sense credit did for demand what automation and the production line had done for manufacturing. It got around the traditional limits set by the market. A worker's ability to turn out products had often been limited by the production capabilities of the machinery involved. Automation had overcome those limits and goods could be produced in almost unlimited quantities. On the market side, trade had been hampered by the inability of consumers to accumulate large amounts of money (or goods, if it was a barter economy). Credit enabled the producer to get around this restriction since consumers could now buy products whether they had cash or not. Its Achilles' heel is that the stimulation is an artificial one. Sometimes credit serves to create new markets; at other times it merely serves to shift them around in time. Sales in the current year may come at the expense of next year's operations, since the consumer who buys a car now on credit may not be interested in buying one in the future.

If overreliance on credit posed a threat for manufacturers in the 1920s, that threat lay in the future. The U.S. economy, by most standards, had been performing well during much of the decade following the end of the First World War. The war itself had provided a boost for business and for workers. Although most trade had been with England and France, the needs of their armies alone had demanded large quantities of weapons and explosives. Business profits were high and factory workers were in demand. In 1917 unemployment had been 4.6 percent. In 1918, it was down to 1.4 percent and remained at that level during 1919.[8]

When the war ended, the unending market opportunity represented by Europe abruptly came to an end. Economic problems did not immediately come with the November 1918 Armistice, but when they came they were serious. The recession began in late 1920. Unemployment at that time was 5.2 percent with 2.1 million out of work. In 1921 it had increased to 4,918,000 or 11.7 percent of the work force.[9] The toll on businesses was severe - there were 100,000 bankruptcies.[10] Congress, in an effort to shore up those businesses which survived, decided that they needed protection from foreign competitors.

The European companies which had been seen as the ideal market for U.S. goods during the war, were now viewed as a threat. In the 1920 elections, Warren G. Harding won the presidency and the Republicans won the Congress. Even before the election the Republicans had handed President Wilson a stunning defeat by rejecting the Versailles Treaty and his proposal for a League of Nations. The U.S. was becoming isolationist, and not just in foreign policy. Economic matters were included as well. In 1921 the Congress passed the Fordney-McCumber tariff, which raised tariff rates sufficiently high that nearly all European goods were kept out of the U.S. market. The Europeans responded with their own tariffs.

In 1922 the U.S. economy began to show signs of recovery. Unemployment was reduced to 6.7 percent. It would fall still further in 1923, to 2.4 percent.[11] In spite of the difficulties in 1921, the economy grew between 1919 and 1929. The increase in the gross national product for the period was an inflation-adjusted 39 percent. There were six million new homes built between 1922 and 1929. Industry was able to increase productivity without adding significantly to the number of workers. Output nearly doubled between 1921 and 1929. The automobile industry, in particular, did well, representing some 13 percent of the value of economic output in 1929.[12]

While the economy appeared robust during the 1920s, there were some underlying problems. Close to the top was the heavy reliance on credit. Most families had used mort-gage financing to buy their homes. The amount borrowed for home purchases would triple during the 1920s. The use of credit was not limited to large items like houses. Credit purchases accounted for 75 percent of sales of smaller items such as radios, and cars and furniture as well were bought on installment - around 60 percent were estimated to be credit sales.[13] The amount of unpaid installment debt was 1.375 billion in 1925, but reached $3 billion by 1929.[14] A related problem was that employment in the U.S. economy was too heavily concentrated in the automobile and construction industries, where credit played a major role in sustaining demand.

Credit promised a single solution to two different problems. On the one hand it could resurrect weak markets for business. On the other hand it allowed consumers to acquire things they could not afford. If it seemed to address two problems, the problems could be traced to a single source - poverty. The inability to afford things was what defined poverty while the inability of a large number of workers to buy was what undermined markets. One third of personal income in 1929 was earned by the top 5 percent of the population, while some 40 percent of the population earned only 12 percent. Put another way, some 36,000 of the wealthiest families in 1929 earned as much as the 12 million poorest families.[15]

Despite the income disparity between rich and poor, there had been enough excess cash available for investment, or at least there seemed to be. Private American investors would loan $10 to $12 billion in markets outside the U.S. during the 1920s. By comparison the U.S. government had leant some $10 billion to the Allies during the war.[16] Serious and widespread interest in stocks and investing began around 1924. In 1925 there were two days when trading volume reached three million shares on the New York Stock Exchange. While 1925 brought a growing sense of excitement, it still paid to be cautious. Investors who believed that Florida land speculation was the road to riches saw the market collapse. The collapse would drag down banks which had been caught up in the frenzy.

Whether involvement in risky ventures typified investors in the 1920s, they were constantly seeking better opportunities. Europe provided one such opportunity in the immediate aftermath of the war. However European companies were hurt by U.S. trade policy. The Fordney-McCumber tariff effectively eliminated the U.S. market, cutting down on potential income. At the same time, U.S. demands for repayment of war debt by European governments represented a budgetary drain. With industrial revenues down, European governments received less in taxes, had less money to budget, and less money to spend to create work. From 1925 on the stock market in the U.S. began to look more appealing. One long-term impact of the Florida collapse may have been to give the New York Stock Exchange more prestige and credibility. It was the only legitimate place to safely put money. While the stock market had not yet reached the point where stock investments had become a substitute for selling products, stock returns were looking more promising and unfortunately, very secure.

The U.S. government, far from being worried about the downside of investing, seemed to encourage it. In mid-1927, the U.S. economy suffered a "recession," or so it seemed to the members of the Federal Reserve Board. What they saw was a decline in the index for industrial production which occurred between May and November. (The decline coincided with Henry Ford's six-month factory shutdown as he re-tooled his factories from Model T to Model A production.) The recession was only one economic problem. There was also a worldwide fall in commodity prices.[17]

In July 1927, Ogden Mills, the U.S. Treasury Secretary, invited the government financial representatives of some of the major European countries to his Long Island home. There is some debate about whether this "Long Island conference" fueled the rise in the stock market or not.[18] The actions resulting from the conference at least gave the appearance of the government's blessing for investment activities. Mills was concerned about European economic problems, in addition to those in the U.S. It was decided that the U.S. Federal Reserve System would lower interest rates, which in turn, would ease pressure on European currencies. The Federal Reserve also put an additional $200 million into the banking system with open market purchases. In 1928 the Federal Reserve would reverse course and try to restrict credit. It would raise the rediscount rate three times in that year. The problem was that, while the government was having second thoughts about the overuse of credit, investors were beginning to see it as their salvation. On March 1, 1928 the number of shares traded reached four million.[19]

The credit mechanism for stock investment was not that different than other business activities, but it was subject to its own peculiar rules. Stock investments involved less reliance on collateral for loans, a significant difference from the home mortgage market. When a homeowner defaulted on a loan the mortgage gave the lender the right to take back the house. Stock investors did use stock as collateral for their loans, but the value of the stock could vary and it became more common to loan amounts far in excess of value. Stocks were normally purchased on margin. The margin was the amount which an investor paid in cash to the broker when purchasing stock. It was common for the broker to accept as little as 10 percent of the cost of stock, while being promised payment of the remaining 90 percent only when the stocks were sold. Call money loans were another financing device. They were not the same thing as buying on margin, although they were similar. Margin involved primarily an uncollateralized advance or loan from a broker. Call loans could be granted by anyone, whether the lender was a broker or not, who was willing to accept stock as collateral. Technically, the lender could demand repayment at any time, although the call usually came only if the stock which secured the loan began to fall in value.

As 1928 began there was a good deal of money being lent to investors. Call money loans at that time amounted to some $4 billion. Those who did not want to invest in the stock market themselves could earn money from the loans. Financial intermediaries, such as savings and loans institutions, insurance companies, and finance houses, legally prohibited from buying stocks, nevertheless profited from the market with their lending activities. The high returns attracted the attention of non-financial companies. Railroads and manufacturers began to rely on call loan portfolios for income. By December 1928 call loans had increased from the $4 billion of January to $6.4 billion.[20] Investor confidence remained high in the early part of 1929 and the market through much of the year did better than it had done in the previous year. Where March 1, 1928 had been recorded as the first day in which 4 million shares had been traded, the average number of shares traded daily was now well above that figure at 4,277,000.[21]

Part of the growing fascination with stock could be attributed to easy credit and the "gold fever" mentality which was infecting investors. Yet if the glamour of the market was what was attracting investors in 1929, they were also being pushed by more mundane economic forces. Normal investment returns were starting to decline toward the end of the 1920s. Easy credit had temporarily increased consumer demand, but manufacturers were again finding their markets saturated. Costs were rising and profits were falling. The fact that the market had defied these trends perhaps suggested that the danger signals of 1929 - the decline in building starts in March and the fall in auto sales in September - could be ignored as well.

What accounted for the sudden and total loss of confidence on October 29, when investors had optimistically ignored danger signals for much of 1929? The simple answer is that investor confidence collapsed at nearly the same time as the financial support which was behind the investment. It was lenders who had really made the dream possible, since they provided the means for investors to get involved in the market. Unfortunately, while lenders had the financial strength to make loans, they found themselves too weak to escape the problems encountered by investors. When the investment world collapsed the world of finance collapsed with it.

There is some disagreement about the exact chain of events leading up to October. The market had actually peaked on September 19, and began a decline on October 3. Foreign investors were beginning to have doubts fairly early. Well before the October 24 panic a substantial number took steps to reduce their stock portfolios. Instead of asking for additional credit to buy stock, they began selling. Around October 10, the amount of broker's loans fell by $120 million. Recent events in London had caused them to question the assumptions about market risks. They also had to face economic pressures from their governments now more suspicious about the overextended European security markets.[22]

The event which caused Europeans to seriously rethink investment policy was the collapse, on September 20, of what was known as the Hatry empire, a mixture of companies owned by Clarence Hatry. Hatry had enough credibility in financial circles to attempt a purchase of United Steel, but was in reality so short of funds that his empire was close to failure. He attempted to cover his financial shortcomings with fraudulent securities and was forced into bankruptcy once his actions became known. Whether the scandal was the reason the Bank of England sought to reduce the British reliance on credit, and raised its rates on September 26. Ironically, while the European investors may have saved themselves from disaster, their actions brought misfortune on their countries. In the aftermath of the Great Crash, American investors withdrew funds from Europe in a desperate attempt to find cash, contributing to the failure of many companies and the loss of employment for many European workers. Not all foreign investors acted in time. Between October 29 and March 31 1930, they would withdraw another $450 million, an action which did not help to restore confidence.[23]

The drop in borrowing by foreign investors in early October 1929 took two weeks to have any real impact. There was more selling as prices declined during October, although the volume was too low to cause widespread margin calls or to demand payment of call loans. Many investors still held out hope that prices would recover. That situation changed on "Black Thursday," October 24, when investors in large numbers began to liquidate their positions. In hopes that the mass sell-off represented something temporary, a syndicate of bankers bought stock, but confidence had been shaken badly. When the price trend continued down on Monday, October 28, investors decided in larger numbers to get out. The volume of trades on Tuesday was phenomenal. Where average daily volume during 1929 had only been 4,277,000, it was nearly four times that, some 16.4 million shares, on "Black Tuesday."[24] The loss in stock value was around $31 billion. Before the Crash, the value had been $87 billion. Afterwards it was only $56 billion.[25]

Although the losses were severe they were still confined largely to the investment community on the day after Black Tuesday. It soon became apparent that they would not stop there. In the wake of the Crash there was an almost immediate jump in unemployment. In October unemployment had been under 500,000. By the end of December it had reached 4 million.[26] That unemployment would follow so closely on the heels of the Crash suggests that the business community was in some way uniquely connected to the stock market. Perhaps the Crash came as such a shock that businesses laid off workers in anticipation of certain hard times. Any connection between the Crash and the onset of economic difficulties however, had less to do with business attitudes and more to do with the availability of cash. Business could adjust psychologically to the fall of a seemingly infallible institution. It could not continue operating without cash - or credit. The Crash created a severe shortage of both.

There were those who realized that cash was a serious problem, although they may not have realized how extensive the problem was. Following the Crash New York banks assumed over $1 billion in call money loans and did not demand payment for stocks bought on margin. Both the New York banks and the Federal Reserve Bank of New York also attempted to restore confidence by purchasing stock. By the end of November $370 million in stock purchases had been made. In addition the Federal Reserve tried to ease credit by lowering the rediscount rate. The combined actions did have some effect. The Dow-Jones industrial average, which had fallen to 198 in the aftermath of the crash recovered by year-end to 250.[27] Yet these efforts were not enough.

Except for the New York banks, those who held margins now decided that the cash value of what was owed them was greater than the stock value. Clients were requested to pay, regardless of whether stock had been sold. Holders of call money loans demanded payment. While some investors had the cash, many did not. Some had to liquidate portions of investment portfolios. Loans to European firms were called, creating a particular hardship in countries such as Germany, where lenient credit policies had enabled marginal businesses to stay afloat.

Whether calling European loans represented a last act of desperation or was merely the first sign that lenders were serious, they were not overlooking domestic loans. Lender demands soon overwhelmed borrowers in the U.S. as well. Those involved in borrowing for stock speculation were logical first targets, but lenders were in such need of cash that they went after mortgage holders. Unfortunately, whatever they hoped to gain through foreclosure was offset by the depressed market for home sales.

The cash shortage was the most immediate result of the Crash. A more long-term effect had to do with credit availability and a change in the attitude toward credit. Both problems would impact business. Lenders called in business loans, forcing cost-cuts and lay-offs. In addition, there was a reluctance to make new loans. Adopting a more conservative approach meant that markets were likely to remain flat, since demand could not be stimulated with credit. In a broader sense, faith in the overall monetary system had been destroyed, particularly among lenders. There had been an assumption, prior to 1929, that businesses would be prosperous and that loan repayment would be automatic. There was felt to be little need to employ safeguards, such as collateral or even basic analysis. The Crash caused a serious rethinking of assumptions within the financial community. Creditworthiness now became the watchword for lenders.

A connection between Black Tuesday and the Depression becomes more understandable when two additional factors are considered: first, the extent to which business in the U.S. had come to rely on the returns generated by the stock market and second, the degree to which business was overextended. More and more firms either invested in stock or made money off loans made to investors. Unfortunately business had also been operating so close to the edge. Credit had been used to prop up weak markets and businesses had relied too much on credit to expand operations.

ECONOMIC ACTIVITY DURING THE GREAT DEPRESSION

Depressions are marked by high unemployment levels and business failures. They are more formally defined as a fall in output. A recession has been defined as a decline in real GNP for two or more consecutive calendar quarters. Describing a depression or recession as a "fall" in output or a decline in GNP seems somewhat misleading. It suggests a passive response, as if factories gave up trying to produce. In reality, a fall in output has less to do with physical production capabilities and more to do with market conditions. Output falls because the market does not require as many goods or products and manufacturers cut back. If a fall in output means a reduction in the number of units manufactured, it can also be accompanied by an aggressive program of price reduction, cost-cutting, and layoffs.

The Great Depression was also marked by deflation, a fall in the general price level.

Falling prices normally are welcomed as a sign that inflation is under control, a good thing for consumers. Below a certain point however, price reductions are unhealthy for business because companies can no longer operate profitably. Even if businesses survive, deflation is likely to lead to layoffs. As a result, what consumers gain in terms of lower prices can be offset by losses workers suffer in employment.

Industrial output and prices are two ways in which market strength is measured. In the wake of the Great Crash, it was industrial output which gave the first indication of a drop-off in demand. The index of industrial output for 1929 fell off ten points between October and December, dropping from 110 to 100. Auto production, a large part of the index, had been 440,000 units in August, but was down to 92,500 units by December. Commodity prices, another measure of market strength, began to register signs of weakness, by falling. Markets which had only been able to maintain their strength through credit were the first to show obvious signs of weakening. Imports fell and prices quickly followed. Countries which had relied on the U.S. as an export market found that market disappearing; they, in turn, began to cut back on purchases from U.S. companies. Prices were lowered in an attempt to increase sales.[28]

What turned the 1929 declines in output and prices into a full-blown Depression? In statistical terms, it was their failure to recover. They continued a downward trend. There was some hope in early 1930. Industrial output increased and unemployment was not as great. Unfortunately prices continued down. The price decline was not as great as in 1929, but it was still a downward trend. Credit was part of the reason for the recovery. Lenders had regained some confidence. The reason why the recovery was only partial and only temporary was also credit-related. Despite some loosening of credit policies, most lenders were now skeptical of borrowers and there was a reluctance to finance purchases. Commercial loans declined after 1929 and would not begin to increase until March 1936. They were likely to lend only in circumstances where a business could guarantee a cash return. The decline in prices meant, for cash-starved businesses, that they could neither maintain cash-flows with sales nor provide sufficient guarantees of profitability to qualify for loans.

In early 1932 wholesale prices began to increase along with industrial output. Hopes for the end of the Depression proved premature. In the fall banks in many states were forced to close to keep depositors from withdrawing funds. Fears of continued decline led to a panic in February-March 1933, culminating in now-President Roosevelt's decision to close all banks on March 4. Statistically, actual recovery began in 1933. Industrial output began to rise generally between 1993 and 1935. While the increase was not continuous, when industrial production declined, it did not fall to the March 1933 low of 59 (on the 1923-25 scale of 100). Commodity prices similarly exhibited an upward, though unsteady, trend.[29]

While the fall in commodity prices and the decline in industrial output are statistics which help to define the Depression, they provide only an outline of economic trends. Yet, it is difficult to comprehend the severity of the decline from these figures alone. The change in national income is perhaps a more revealing figure. In 1933 it had fallen to less than half of what it had been in 1929. In that same period employees had to face a drop in income of 42 percent.[30] Investment declined by 98 percent. Stock value for all investment, which had been as high as $87 billion prior to the 1929 Crash, dropped to $18 billion in 1933. There were 5,000 bank failures by 1931 and 9 million savings accounts were lost as a result. As one indication of how industry suffered, in the summer of 1932 the steel industry could only operate at 12 percent of its total capacity.[31]

AGRICULTURE

While the worst problems of the Depression are associated with industrial production, agricultural producers were severely hit as well. Just as commodity prices for industrial raw materials fell off, so too did prices for agricultural products. While the price decline was the most severe following the Crash, there were problems in agriculture even before that time.

Agricultural production, in market terms, does have certain similarities to manufacturing. For the manufacturer the ideal market is one in which prices are rising. The response, in such circumstances, is to increase output. Selling more of a product at a higher price will increase profits. When prices begin to fall, on the other hand, the manufacturer is likely to cut back production. If the manufacturing facility were able to switch to another product, particularly one where prices were rising, the producer might be tempted to shift production to the new product.

Cutting back production may be helpful when prices are falling. In fact, the economic result of increasing production during periods of falling prices is to make prices fall even further. There are situations however, in which a producer may continue, or even increase output, when prices are falling. In some situations selling a product at a lower price may be preferable to not selling the product at all, particularly if the producer needs cash. The producer may need to repay loans or may want to hold onto workers that will be needed once prices move back up. He may even continue manufacturing just to maintain cash flow if prices fall even further. While any manufacturer faces a dilemma when prices are falling, how big a problem it is may depend on the size of the firm. Larger companies may have the resources, such as cash savings, to afford to cut back. They may not worry about laying off workers or may have other product lines to fall back on. Small companies, on the other hand, may have no cash reserves to fall back on and can obtain cash only by increasing output even if sales take place in a declining market.

Agricultural producers face the same dilemma, although market decisions are complicated by some unique problems. Like manufacturers, farmers have to repay loans. In contrast to other producers they have to worry about spoilage. A product like coal demands little in the way of storage requirements. A product like milk or fruit is more demanding, and therefore more costly. The longer milk is held off the market, the greater the chances it will spoil. American farmers, following the Crash, saw agricultural prices plummet. Yet, they had few options except to continue selling, which almost ensured that prices would continue to decline. One of the real ironies of the Depression, for agriculture, was that while output fell in economic terms, in real terms physical production and reserve stocks remained high. Such a circumstance presents a seeming contradiction between the definition of a depression - a fall in output, as discussed previously - and the actual production results.

This inconsistency can be cleared up by examining the "fall in output." Normally output is measured in terms of gross national product (GNP), or more recently, gross domestic product (GDP). GNP and GDP have become synonymous with national output. (Technically what they measure is the total cost of physical output at any given point in time, rather than the physical quantities produced.) When speaking of the fall in output which occurs during depressions and recessions, it is common to refer to a fall or decline in GNP. GNP is defined as Consumption + Investment + Government purchases + Net exports.[32] Consumption refers to spending by households. The measurement of both consumption and investment involves a quantity and a price element. As a result, GNP can decline when either the physical amount of purchases decreases or the price of goods declines. Thus it would be possible to see a fall in output, as measured by GNP, even when physical production is increasing.

Investment, similarly, involves a cost element which can be related to the price of goods. Production of goods for inventories, even if not sold, are included in GNP as inventory investment. If the cost of inventory items declines, output will be said to decline, even as physical production stays the same or increases. For example, if 10 cars are produced in January and valued at $100,000, January output will be considered to be $100,000. If in February 10 cars are produced, but the cost has declined to $90,000, February output will be considered to be $90,000. Although physical production has remained the same in each month - 10 cars - output has fallen, in terms of how output is measured economically.

The agricultural depression can be understood more easily from the perspective of physical output and prices. Starting in the mid-1920s, physical output in many agricultural products increased, causing prices to fall. It was not confined to a single product. Wheat producers in the U.S., Canada, Australia, and Argentina had the same problems with overproduction and falling prices as sugar producers in Cuba, Java, and Europe, coffee producers in Brazil, and rubber producers in Asia.[33]

If agriculture was in economic difficulty long before the Crash, the Crash did have an impact on borrowing. Creditors, rather than granting additional credit, pressed farmers for repayment. The need for cash forced farmers to unload harvests, causing prices to decline even further. The economic solution to the problem of low prices would have been to reduce output. That was the thrust of the government program adopted. Although intervention would not come until the end of the 1930s, it finally brought about an increase in prices.

Congress passed the Agricultural Adjustment Act in 1933, then was forced to pass a new bill in 1936, when the 1933 Act was voided by the Supreme Court. The thrust of both acts was to subsidize farmers for taking land out of production. Until farm prices increased, farmers would simply be paid directly, based on a certain amount of acreage which was left unplanted.[34] Some of the actions were more aggressive. In 1934 six million baby pigs were ordered killed by the Agricultural Adjustment Administration (AAA) in order to reduce the supply. Some 10 million acres of cotton already planted was ordered destroyed as well. While such actions created controversy, the overall results were successful. Gross farm income had increased by half in 1936 and in 1939, was double its 1932 level.[35]

The agricultural depression was ended through government intervention and support. The response of the U.S. government was completely different than that of the Soviet Union. The problem in the U.S. was that too many producers were placing their produce on the market; the problem in Russia was the opposite - not enough produce was reaching the market. The U.S. government intervened, not to bring grain to market, but to withdraw it from production. The Soviet government intervened to force grain into the market. What was ironic was that the Russian peasant, surrounded by poverty and lacking in modern equipment, proved so resistant to government policies that Stalin could only defeat him through the use of armed force.

What made the peasant so resilient? The answer probably had less to do with the peasant's character and more to do with the market environment. The U.S., in comparison to Russia, had a strong and well-developed market system. In spite of the difficulties encountered by farmers in the 1920s and 1930s, there were monetary rewards which the system offered. Goods which the farmer wanted to buy were readily available. In Russia the peasant had little difficulty finding a market for produce, but goods were so scarce that there was little incentive to convert harvests into cash. This was the problem in 1925 when communist officials had to deal with the goods famine. Peasants, with few manufactured goods to buy, refused to sell grain to the government.

Part of the answer could also be found in the more sophisticated economic and legal structure of the U.S., particularly in the area of property rights. The one continuing criticism of the communist system has been that it took away individual property rights. Perhaps the irony of that argument is that the very weakness of property rights in Russia represented an advantage when it came to resisting the market. The opposite side of the coin is that the strength of the individual's property claims in the U.S. made them more vulnerable to the demands of the market.

Traditionally land in Russia had been held or "owned" by the village. The peasant had some claim to his plot, but formal legal claims were vague and were related to the peasant's willingness to remain in the village. There was a utilitarian relationship between the peasant and land ownership - so long as the peasant or his family worked the land, the village recognized his claims to it. When he or his family left, the village gave the land to someone else. The system contrasted with Western concepts of individual ownership. While its disadvantage was that individual peasants had only a vague claim to ownership, its advantage was that it was more difficult to take away what they had. In fact, in general, the legal system in Russia was more vague. While that made it difficult for individuals to establish rights, it also was more difficult for the system to impose sanctions. How was this related to the market? It meant that Russian officials had one less tool available to encourage production. They could not threaten to take away a peasant's land because the peasant didn't own any land.

Czarist officials and later, Party leaders, by-and-large negotiated at the village level, not at the level of the individual peasant. While clearly less formal than most legal systems found in the West, the Russian system did recognize some formalities. The peasants, under the 1861 Emancipation, had been required to make redemption payments for forty-nine years. There were also the continuing demands by the state for the payment of various taxes. Officials pressured villages for payment, but had few legal sanctions if the payments weren't made. They couldn't force the peasants off the land because they needed them to work it. They couldn't seize the land because the peasants technically didn't own it. Had there been a large private sector, it might have taken over some of these functions. Yet the private sector would have had similar problems in enforcement. A common financial practice in the West is the granting of rights in property in return for a loan. In Russia the absence of property rights posed a special problem for lenders. Without property rights how could contracts be enforced? A bank could not take title to land through foreclosure when private property was not recognized. Without the threat of foreclosure, how could a bank force an unwilling peasant to pay back a loan? The situation which existed in Russia contrasted with that existing in America.

The U.S. legal system has a strong tradition where individual property rights are concerned. Unlike Russia, where rights were vague, rights provided in the U.S. were quite specific. Whether technically part of the market, these rights do serve to reinforce the market structure and market forces. Property and contract rights, as related to creditors and debtors, are probably the most obvious example of how the legal system supports the market. If farmers found the benefits of credit attractive, they also knew that mortgage holders could foreclose on their farms. Farm mortgages, which totaled $6.7 billion in 1920 and $9.4 billion in 1925, have traditionally been used to illustrate the economic difficulties encountered by farmers.[36] If they are an economic indicator, they also suggest a possible motivation for continuous production. Farmers needed cash to cover loan payments or risk foreclosure and their cash requirements did not change, even if the price of grain did.

CONCLUSION

Despite the difficulties of the Depression, the market system as a whole remained largely intact, if the urban population is any indication. In 1920, for the first time, more of the U.S. population was living in cities than in the countryside - some 51.2 percent. In 1930 the percentage had increased to 56.2 percent. Clearly the Depression slowed the process of urbanization, since the 1930 percentage had increased only slightly, to 56.5 percent, by 1940.[37] At the same time, despite this slowing, the Depression did not reverse the trend.

While the agricultural sector was going through problems, they had existed long before the Crash. Economic problems for farmers were of a different nature than those encountered by manufacturers. Farmers maintained close ties to the market, even when price drops made it advantageous to get out. Their loan obligations may have provided the motivation to sell, even when the market did not. Manufacturers faced a somewhat different problem. The market for products did not totally disappear, but in some areas it approached collapse. For those who had thrown in their lot with the market system, the future held unemployment or a struggle to find work.

There were some who did choose to leave the system totally or partially. Many people began growing food in their gardens or left the cities to rejoin relatives on family farms. To many local and state governments, such decisions were a relief. Trying to help those without work or homeless was more than many cities could afford. In perspective, the number of those who chose to opt out of the market system was relatively small, particularly when compared to Russia. The government there felt compelled to intervene because so many peasants remained outside the market system.

The next chapter returns to the central theme of this book, the relationship between resource availability and the political system. It looks at the political system as it has operated for much of the history of America. If not totally free of violence, for much of its history the U.S. has been marked by relative calm. The next chapter looks at that violence, but also looks at some of the broader economic trends which influenced American political history.

CHAPTER 22

AMERICAN DEMOCRACY AND PATTERNS IN ECONOMIC DEVELOPMENT

Where this book's thesis is concerned, democracies are notable for two main characteristics - an abundance of resources and an absence of violence. There have been recent complaints about the increasing level of violence in American cities and current difficulties in the U.S. economy. Yet few would seriously question that it is both a rich country and a country which has avoided extreme political unrest. Nor would few argue with the classification of America as a democratic nation.

The U.S. presents something of a problem in attempting to prove a relationship between resource availability and democratic government - it is difficult to find a period in which democracy was not present. Democracy has existed for such a long period of time and is so deeply embedded in America's culture that it is difficult to limit the discussion to any particular period of time. In the area of theories and causal connection, proof is more convincing when differences are extreme rather than subtle. The problem is that the U.S. has not experienced any wide swings between democratic government and dictatorial rule. Since there have been few periods of total repression, there is little data for comparison.

A similar problem exists in the economic arena. In attempting to show that democracy has been the result of an abundance of resources, it might be helpful to have examples of scarcity to compare against periods of abundance. Yet, in spite of sluggish periods of economic growth, the U.S. economy has not deviated significantly from an overall ability to produce. The U.S. has experienced few periods of scarcity. Even during the Depression, when jobs were hard to find, overproduction was a major problem. The overall history of the U.S. would probably be described in terms of gradual changes, rather than drastic swings in political or economic circumstances. The last chapter used the Great Depression to highlight certain aspects of the market economy as it exists in America. This chapter takes a broader look at the U.S., from both a political and economic perspective. The discussion begins with a brief look at Colonial origins and governmental structure. Changes in government in some countries have only come about through revolution. In the U.S. the transfer of power from one administration to the next has been marked by regularity and peacefulness. Violence, though minimal, has played a part in the political process and this chapter looks at that role. Finally this chapter looks at the history of the economy in the U.S. The discussion in the last chapter focused primarily on the role played by market forces in the economy. The discussion in this chapter deals with economic development from the perspective of resource availability.

THE ORIGIN AND STRUCTURE OF AMERICAN GOVERNMENT

When the Thirteen Colonies went to war against England in 1776 they did so without a true government or constitution. The Constitutional Convention, the body organized to draft a formal constitution, would not even meet until May of 1787. It would be another two years before the new government and Constitution, with its three branches of government, would go into effect. George Washington would take the oath of office on April 30, 1789.

The government of what would become the United States really began almost as a grievance committee. On September 5, 1774, representatives of twelve of the colonies met as a Continental Congress in Philadelphia. The 51 delegates had no power to pass laws. Their primary purpose was in fact not to legislate, but to discuss a common course of action. The results were a number of resolutions opposing recent acts of the British Parliament. The delegates even went so far as to propose a boycott of English goods and the stoppage of all trade with England. What gave the Congress an air of legitimacy was that eleven of the colonies gave some formal approval to the proposed boycott and in all thirteen colonies there were committees willing to implement the proposals. With such approval, what had been mere proposals began to take on the form of law. Legitimacy for the Continental Congress had been attained largely by the common recognition. It contrasted with the legitimacy of the colonial governments established in the early 1600s, which had been conferred by some formal recognition from the Crown.

The second Continental Congress, which met in May 1775, still had no formal powers. It began to stake a claim to legitimacy largely by taking action. Fighting had already begun on April 18 at Lexington and the Americans had decided to besiege the British troops stationed in Boston. The Congress declared the Americans the "American continental army" and appointed George Washington commander. The Declaration of Independence would be proclaimed on July 4, 1776 and seemed to strengthen the Congress' claim that it was a government. Those who signed the Declaration had committed themselves sufficiently to the revolt, in the eyes of the British government, that they could be hung for treason. However, even that commitment was not enough for complete recognition by the colonists, a handicap when it came to financing the war. The Congress could not levy any taxes and had to ask the individual colonies for money. Most of the war effort was financed with loans. The Congress did issue notes, but because they had little real backing, they became worthless. In 1781 the Continental Congress became the Congress of the Confederation. If its powers were not much greater, when the British government agreed to peace in 1783, the body it dealt with was the Congress of the Confederation.

The new Congress, and its predecessor, were viewed by the colonies as almost figurehead governments, convenient for organizing a war effort and defending the colonies, but not suitable when it came to general matters. With the British government out of the picture, the colonies were not sure they wanted the Congress as a real government. They were not opposed to all cooperation, since they had agreed to the Articles of Confederation, yet the Articles did not set up a presidency or a court system, as the Constitution later would. The colonists also would not authorize any national tax system.

In going to war with England the colonists had become obsessed with the oppressive aspects of British rule, particularly the hated taxes imposed by Parliament. In the aftermath of the war they discovered that the English system had provided many commercial advantages which had been largely overlooked. For one thing, it had provided a uniform currency, recognized in all the colonies. The states now began issuing their own paper money, which rapidly depreciated. The system of English rule had also been relatively successful at keeping the commercial competition between the various colonies in check. The former colonists soon discovered that the individual states were only too willing to take over Parliament's job of levying taxes. Many states now began to impose their own duties and taxes on merchants from out of state. The basic economies of each region created differing responses to foreign trade as well. In the New England states, where manufacturing firms were afraid of competition from Europe, tariffs on foreign goods were imposed. The southern states and some of the non-manufacturing northern states wanted tariffs eliminated to bring in more European manufactures. The differing tariff policies of individual states caused the states, in turn, to take retaliatory measures against each other.

The eagerness with which the states were willing to tax out-of-state residents was only one problem. In 1785 and 1786 there was a depression. The new nation may have been in its infancy, but its market economy was fully developed. When the markets for agricultural products collapsed, crops were left in the fields to rot. Not only had farmers switched from a purely subsistence-level production, they had become addicted to credit. Fully 130 years before the credit-related problems of the Great Crash, farmers and merchants found that credit served to stimulate demand. The colonial debtors however found a novel solution to their problems. They got their representatives to pass legislation requiring creditors to accept payment in state notes. Unfortunately, the debtors also got the state printing presses to print money as fast as possible. Armed with a rapidly depreciating currency, the debtors sought out creditors to pay off their debts. It was not long before the debtor-creditor battle contributed to the already bitter state rivalry. When debtors used their own state's laws to pay off out-of-state creditors, those creditors pressured their states to retaliate.[1] (The debtors of 1929 might have found the idea appealing, but by that time state legislatures were out of the business of printing money and the U.S. government was fully committed to a national currency.)

While the debtor-creditor battle contributed to the interstate rivalry and forced states apart, it tended to unite the wealthy and propertied classes. In 1786 farmers were having trouble meeting their mortgage obligations. To add to their problems the Massachusetts legislature raised taxes to repay debt from the war. The focal point of the battle was the court system, since both mortgagors and the state sought to enforce their rights to the land. Confronted by a weak market, on the one hand, which made it difficult to raise cash, and an unsympathetic legislature, on the other, farmers felt their only alternative was to somehow stop the courts. Crowds began disrupting lower court proceedings in August. Then in September the Massachusetts Supreme Court became the target when Daniel Shays organized 500 men for a march on Springfield. The court was forced the court to adjourn. By January Shays' forces had increased to 1,200 and the goal had become the arsenal in Springfield. It took 4,000 militia and the personal intervention of General Washington to bring the rebellion to an end. While not a serious threat to the nation, it did help to convince many that the economic problems and squabbles between the states could only be solved with some national government.

The idea of a constitutional convention was a gradual process. Oddly enough the Convention had its origins in a more mundane, but nevertheless related, economic issue, navigation rights to the Potomac River and Chesapeake Bay. Maryland claimed sovereignty over the entire river, a potential problem for Virginians. In 1785 and again in 1786 there were discussions over the question. At the 1786 meeting Alexander Hamilton convinced the attending members that it would be wise to convene a meeting of all the states to discuss, not just the commercial problems of Maryland and Virginia, but the problems which all thirteen states were having with each other. The Continental Congress, gave the proposal legitimacy by not only approving a meeting but also setting a date, May 1787, when it would convene.

It was thus against a background of commercial rivalry that the Constitutional Convention began its deliberations. What would emerge in September 1787 was a governmental structure which has survived in its basic form for some 200 years. Anyone who has taken an introductory political science course is familiar with that form. The Constitution divided the government into three branches, the legislative, executive, and judicial, and divided governmental power among the three branches. The legislative branch was charged with passing laws and consisted of elected representatives chosen by the electors in each state. The Senate, or upper house, consisted of two representatives from each state. The House of Representatives consisted of representatives from each state, with representation based on population. The executive branch, as represented by the Presidency, had responsibility for carrying out the laws.

Discussions of American democracy have often focused on the structure of the federal government as outlined by the Constitution. In perspective, the division of power among three branches at the federal level was only one way in which power was divided. There was also a division of power between the federal government and the state governments. State governments were, in large part left alone, and retained many of the powers they held prior to the ratification of the Constitution. While their power to discriminate against other states in commercial areas was drastically curtailed, they retained the power to levy taxes. Related to the division of power between the federal and state governments was the growth of large city governments, with the authority to legislate independently. The development of local government is notable, in an economic sense, for the ability of cities to sustain themselves through taxation.

If the governmental structure created by the Constitutional Convention was unique, the operation of American democracy has also been remarkable. Where other countries have suffered losses in the area of civil liberties, Americans have remained relatively free. The United States has managed to avoid the creation of a secret police force. Perhaps a major reason is that the American government has not had to contend with serious or violent challenges to its authority.

THE INFLUENCE OF VIOLENCE ON AMERICAN DEMOCRACY

To claim that the United States has been a country free of violence seems laughable. It conveniently overlooks some disturbing figures. The number of dead from the Civil War has been estimated at over 600,000. Four Presidents have been assassinated: Abraham Lincoln in 1865, James A. Garfield in 1881, William McKinley in 1901, and John F. Kennedy in 1963. The struggles between labor and management have contributed their share of violence as well. In the Haymarket riot of May 1886 a bomb was thrown, killing a policeman, and in the return fire the police killed a participant. Four labor leaders were executed as a result. The year 1887 saw the "Great Uprising," a two-week period of unrest which left over 100 people dead across the U.S. It began in Pittsburgh on July 21, when state militia members killed 21 people in a confrontation with striking railroad workers. Another 20 died the next day, along with five of the militia. Strikers were killed in Chicago and strikers in San Francisco, rather than confront police, killed residents of a Chinese neighborhood. A fight between strikers and Pinkerton detectives at the Homestead iron works in July 1892 left nine strikers and seven detectives dead. Thirteen workers participating in the Pullman strike died in July 1894 clashes with federal troops near Chicago, while another 34 were killed in other parts of the country in confrontations. Militia opened fire with machine guns on a camp of strikers in Ludlow, Colorado in 1914, killing 14 people, mostly children. In July 1916 a bomb exploded during a parade held in San Francisco. The explosion killed 10 people and injured 40. The parade had been sponsored by the local chamber of commerce which had also been promoting an anti-union open-shop campaign. Apart from the violent confrontations, there is other evidence of unrest associated with the labor movement. There were some 37,000 strikes which occurred between 1881 and 1905.[2]

The violence which has occurred has not generally been organized and has not had as its goal the overthrow of the government. The presidential assassinations may have been politically motivated, but they were not part of a larger movement to replace the government in power. Most of the assassins acted alone. The Civil War, which involved the most carnage, was not technically fought to overthrow or to replace the government in power. It was instead a war fought to separate one section of the country from another. In that sense it differs from the Russian civil war, where the goal was to replace the government in power while keeping the Russian Empire intact.

That argument has some credibility in light of the government response. In much of the labor strife the most extreme governmental response was to send in troops, either federal troops, as happened in the Pullman strike, or state militia, in the case of the coal miners' strike in Colorado. While government, at the federal or state level, may have felt sufficiently threatened to send in troops, it did not feel the threat serious enough to warrant the creation of a permanent secret police apparatus. Part of the reason is that the strikes were not directed at the government but at the private businesses involved. Part of the reason is that, in many cases, the local police or private security forces were sufficiently strong to deal with the situation.

Shays' Rebellion, the abortive 1786 uprising, was probably more representative of the type of unrest which was aimed at the government itself. Its specific goal may only have been to change government policy. Nevertheless it represented a form of challenge which the government could not easily ignore. The immediate response was indeed a military one - the state sent troops in.

Like claims about an absence of violence, the claim that America has remained free is subject to some glaring exceptions. During the Civil War Lincoln suspended certain rights, such as habeas corpus, where opponents of the war were concerned. Over 100,000 Japanese, whether American citizens or not, were relocated to concentration camps during World War II. During the red scare of 1919 and 1920, the Attorney General of the United States, A. Mitchell Palmer, had suspected communists arrested and detained. Some were beaten, some deported, but many were not charged with any crime. In January 1920 there were 6,000 arrests across the country. Basic rights were ignored since warrants were sometimes not obtained and those accused were not allowed contact with lawyers. While the Justice Department in the 1920s may not have set up a secret police apparatus, it did use private detective agencies to track radicals.[3]

Senator Joseph McCarthy resurrected Palmer's anti-communist program in the 1950s. The House Un-American Activities Committee (HUAC), as part of the campaign, provided data it had gathered on some 60,000 people to private employers. Over 15,000 federal employees lost their jobs from investigations and as many as 13.5 million Americans may have been subject to federal, state, or private loyalty programs.[4] Although these happenings represent a deviation from the freedoms allowed in the U.S., they are notable as much for the fact that they occurred as for their infrequency. In perspective they represent a handful of occurrences over a 200-year political history.

Does the existence of any violence totally negate this book's thesis, if the argument is that the high levels of resources present in the U.S. would serve to limit the level of violence? Possibly - although a case can be made that the United States, by and large, has escaped, if not all violence, at least the politically-focused violence which topples governments. The discussion here has left the question of resource availability for last, even though a condition of abundance or scarcity must be established before the thesis can even be tested. Partly this is because a detailed discussion is unnecessary. It is clear, to even the casual reader, that the United States has long been able to meet its resource needs. The next section is intended to fill in some of the details.

RESOURCE RESERVES AND ECONOMIC PATTERNS OF DEVELOPMENT

American society, in its history, has undergone dynamic economic change. It began as a largely agricultural economy, at the time of the American Revolution, but then was transformed into the leading industrial power of the world. It started out behind countries such as England, but then began to overtake them. In one sense the transformation involved improvements in the basic level of technology. In another sense the transformation involved the pace at which new technology was being implemented. In 1769

James Watt had obtained a patent on his rotary steam-engine, an invention of special importance to rail transport. A little over 60 years later, in 1830, the Liverpool and Manchester railroad line would be opened in England. Just 39 years later, the Union Pacific and Central Pacific railroads would link the continental United States by rail. Meeting at Promontory Point, Utah in May 1869, they had laid 1700 miles of track.

The changes which took place in England between 1760 and 1830 are generally referred to as the Industrial Revolution, although there are other periods which have been given that label. Any period in which technological advances have brought economic growth has been called an industrial revolution. In fact the Industrial Revolution in England has sometimes been divided into more than one industrial revolution. In the 1780s the revolutionary advances involved primarily textile technology. The railway boom of the 1830s and 1840s has been designated as a separate "industrial revolution." A third, according to Walt Rostow, involved the overall transformation of industrial economies to the use of steel and automobiles, lasted until the 1970s. Rostow suggests that there is a fourth taking place, involving robots, electronics, and biology.[5]

The period between 1840 and 1970 is a long one and it may be wondered how so many technological advances, even if "revolutionary," can be included in one "revolution." What is remarkable is that the United States, despite these changes, has figured prominently in the changes, from both a technological and economic standpoint. American inventors have been at the forefront of development, as for example, the Wright brothers and the invention of the airplane. Not all societies which endure technological change have the resources to adjust. Ancient Egypt, for example, lost its dominance once weapons technology shifted from copper to iron. In contrast, the U.S. made the adjustment rather easily, even though some of the shifts represented radical resource changes. Transport and manufacturing were two areas where this occurred.

In foreign trade American shipbuilders had access to large quantities of softwood during the mid-1800s, which provided them with economic advantages in the construction of clipper ships and in the shipping trade.[6] When the economic base changed from wood to steel, manufacturers had access to large quantities of iron ore, coal and coke. Automobiles created a demand for gasoline as a fuel after 1900 and America was able to call on its large oil reserves to satisfy that demand.

If the building of the Transcontinental Railroad was one of the more obvious signs of the technological advances associated with the industrial revolution, the Depression of 1893 provided indications of how pervasive that revolution was - and how quickly it had taken place. Not only were workers becoming more dependent on the market, but the market was shifting away from an agricultural orientation to industrial production. The 1893 Depression was perhaps the first truly national depression, at least geographically. Employers from California to Chicago to New York laid off workers. The number of unemployed in San Francisco was 7,000, out of a California total of 50,000, while in New York the number was between 100,000 and 200,000.[7] The makings of truly national market and an accompanying increase in the work force had been tied to the geographical increases in the size of the U.S.. The transformation to a more industrial economy had also coincided with the discovery or acquisition of large resource reserves. The reserves had spurred growth, but they had also become available at a particularly fortuitous time, in economic terms, i.e., at a time when manufacturing industries were creating new demand.

The face of industrialization changed almost exactly at the mid-century point in America. It was not that there was a sudden interest in manufacturing. There had been a strong manufacturing environment, even at the time of the Revolutionary War. What happened around 1850 however, was the discovery of larger reserves than ever before. The Marquette Range in Upper Michigan was discovered in 1845 and other deposits of copper and iron were prospected in the next few years. The Vermillion iron range of Minnesota would be discovered in the 1870s, followed by the Mesabi range in 1890. The Mesabi was an unusually pure and extremely large lode. It was close to the surface and required little processing.[8] The copper reserves of Montana and Arizona were added to those of Michigan in the 1880s.

The size of these reserves and their value for manufacturing can be better understood by comparing the iron ore output of 1900 with that of 1850. In 1900, after just ten years of operation, the Mesabi range alone had produced 40 million tons of iron ore. In 1892 ore production from the first mine had been a million tons, double the total production of pig iron some forty years before. In 1850, the output of pig iron for the entire United States had been only a half-million tons per year. In 1900 steel output was greater than that of the combined outputs of Germany and Britain.[9]

In 1890 the U.S. began its first commercial production of aluminum and American bauxite reserves were second only to those of France.[10] Five years after oil was discovered in Pennsylvania in 1859, annual production amounted to two million barrels, largely driven by the demand for kerosene.[11] An even stronger market was created with the gasoline-powered automobile, invented in 1903. If two million barrels per year had seemed phenomenal in 1864, it hardly compared with the 9.5 billion barrels per day produced in 1972.[12] Coal was everywhere. Pennsylvania and West Virginia had coal and more was added when Illinois, Kansas, Texas, and Colorado became states. In 1913 world production of coal and lignite was 1,342,000 thousand metric tons and 38.5 percent, 517,057 thousand tons, was produced by the U.S..[13]

Resources were not evenly distributed throughout the U.S.. This had resulted in regional differences in economic development, starting long before the American Revolution. The most obvious difference was between the North and the South. The South, by-and-large was lacking in industrial raw materials. It tended to focus on agricultural production. Where the market was concerned, it found that the greatest return came from tobacco, cotton, and sugar. The invention of the cotton gin by Eli Whitney in 1793 had turned cotton into a potentially profitable crop. Yet, agricultural operations were marginal at best, even though slavery kept labor costs to a minimum. When the share-cropping system replaced the plantation in the aftermath of the Civil War, small farmers ran up huge debts without significant economic advancement.

While many in the North could smugly point to the evils of slavery, the track record of factory owners was not much better than that of their southern counterparts. The growing number and increasingly violent nature of strikes in the second half of the 1800s suggests that workers were not happy with their situation. The North's reputation as the industrial "region" of the U.S. was gained more by accident of nature, than by deliberate planning. Raw materials may not have been found in one place, but they were relatively more accessible. Development had always been a compromise between access to raw materials, the related convenience and/or cost of transporting them, and the availability of labor. Pittsburgh, the center of iron production which developed around 1800, was one such rare combination of nature. The land in the area contained nearly all the ingredients for iron production - iron ore, coal, wood (for charcoal) and limestone.[14] The later discoveries of iron and copper in Michigan, Wisconsin, and Minnesota, served, not to totally eliminate the North as an industrial sector, but to move production west.

Although the U.S. had established itself as the leading industrial power in the world by 1900, it had retained its rural character. Only 39.6 percent of its population of 76 million lived in large cities at that time. It would not be until 1920 that the urban population would finally break the 50 percent barrier.[15] Manufacturing, despite its dramatic achievements by 1900, had taken a long time to overtake agriculture. Only in the 1880s did manufacturing output equal, in dollar output, the output of the agricultural sector.[16]

The rise of the manufacturing sector may have suggested great strength, but there were other signs which indicated underlying weaknesses. The ever more violent confrontations with labor were one such sign. The tendency toward monopoly was another. The last twenty years of the Nineteenth Century saw the establishment of large trusts. Standard Oil was only the first monopoly to emerge in 1882. A sugar trust was formed in 1887, a tobacco trust in 1889, and a rubber trust in 1892. The economic weak-ness of the trusts was not apparent by looking at the winners, such as Standard Oil, but at the losers. Before 1904, according to one survey, some 5,300 businesses had been sacrificed in the formation of 319 trusts, while another 2,400 businesses had been absorbed into 127 utilities.[17] While the federal government responded to the rise of the trusts with the Sherman Antitrust Act of 1890, government efforts to restrict trust activities met with limited success. One of the biggest mergers took place in 1901 when 150 corporations agreed to form U.S. Steel.

In 1899 unemployment dropped, from the 12.4 percent of the previous year, to 6.5 percent, signalling the end of the Depression. It had showed signs of ending by June 1898 when the U.S. had gone to war with Spain. The $400 million spent on the war may have provided an economic stimulus. The war itself was brief, lasting from April to August, and cost only 4,108 American lives, of which 385 were on the battlefield.[18] The government would spend another $600 million fighting a six-year insurrection in the Philippines, resulting in casualty figures of 4,234 killed on the American side and 16,000 among the Filipinos.[19] Some in the business community had supported the war in hopes of opening new markets. Despite the military resources dedicated to the Philippines, it was in Latin America where new markets were actually found. Latin America not only provided markets for U.S. exports, but also served as a cheap source of raw materials. Until 1914 the U.S. economy enjoyed a relative period of prosperity with a low unemployment rate. If there were potential problems with markets, the advent of war limited their effect. Unemployment reached a high of 8.5 percent in 1915, but then dropped to 5.1 percent in 1916. In 1918 and 1919, it was down to 1.4 percent.[20]

The discussion of the Depression in Chapter 21 focused on the problem of credit. There were two aspects to the problem. One was the fact that it had been allowed to grow to such high levels, without any accompanying safeguards. The other aspect was that a heavy reliance on credit was symptomatic of an otherwise weak market. It represented an artificial stimulus, since it allowed producers and consumers to get around traditional market limits set on purchases. Credit was not the only artificial stimulus, although it was one of the more popular ones. There was something artificial about the radio and auto markets. In some ways they were examples of how innovation served to expand markets. In other ways they were examples of niche or novelty markets which tended to decline as the novelty wore off. The market for radios was approaching the saturation point by the end of the 1920s. Automobiles did not really lose their appeal as more were produced, but their higher cost would restrict their marketability. Henry Ford had demonstrated the connection between low cost and demand. The price of a model T in 1916 was $360 and sales went from 600,000 to two million by the 1920s.[21] On the other hand, their relatively higher cost tended to limit the market.

Credit had been given a bad name as a result of the Depression. The "moral of the story" in many eyes was about morality. If credit didn't cover a multitude of sins, it seemed to combine two the Seven Deadly ones: covetousness, an inordinate desire for possessions, and sloth, the avoidance of work. Yet, the temptation to use credit, if it symbolized human failing, really only hinted at the market's problem. The real problem was an inability to sustain demand, within the constraints of the market. Given the relationship between demand and employment, whatever workers were paid would never be enough to both sustain demand and keep them employed. If credit had fallen out of favor as a stimulus, the market demanded a substitute. Whether defense spending was the only option, it could create demand.

What probably contributed more to the end of the Depression than any other factor was rearmament. Hitler had been the first to rearm in 1935, but Britain was not far behind, appropriating 1.5 billion pounds for a five-year program beginning in 1937.[22] While Roosevelt was becoming aware of the dangers of a new European war, the threat did not result in any immediate economic changes - Congress would not appropriate new funds for defense until 1939. Congress even wanted to discourage trade with warring countries by passing the Neutrality Act of 1935. The Act would be repealed in 1939. Not only would trade see an increase after that, but direct appropriations for defense began to increase. Unemployment, following the recession of 1937 only gradually came down. In 1938 it was at 19.0 percent, fell to 17.2 percent in 1939, and was at 14.6 percent in 1940. In 1941 it was finally under 10 percent.[23]

The dramatic fall in employment suggests the significant impact which the war effort had on the U.S. economy. In terms of American resources, the Second World War provides some of the most dramatic evidence of resource abundance and productive capability. Between July 1940 and August 1945, American factories produced 300,000 military planes, 86,000 tanks, and 71,000 naval ships. Some 100,000 trucks and jeeps were produced for the British, while another 400,000 trucks and 50,000 jeeps were produced for the Russian effort, along with 7,000 tanks.[24]

The major economic problem facing America in 1946 was converting to a peacetime economy. Returning soldiers had to be assimilated into a civilian work force and the factories which had been geared to military output had to be either converted to peacetime use or closed. Workers had to confront two problems. First, the market created by a nearly fully employed work force was contributing to an inflationary shortage of goods. Second, the workers, who wanted to continue their spending, wanted an increase in wages. An increase in wages would only serve to fuel inflation by making goods more expensive. It was unacceptable to management because it would both increase labor costs and reduce profits, in addition to reducing sales by adding to the sales price of goods. The result of these contradictory stands was to make 1946 a year of strikes, almost as bad as 1919, although the strikes resulted in few gains for labor.[25]

If business did have to convert from war to a peacetime economy, it got some help from the government. Investment in military plant facilities, particularly in the steel industry, had been paid for by the government. It was sold to private manufactures at extremely low prices. The advantage, for the market, was that it freed up private funds for other uses. One of the problems of the 1920s had been that firms had tied up resources by building new facilities.

The threat from the Axis powers was soon replaced by a threat from the communist world. Russia was seen as the immediate threat following the war. The first confrontation took place over Greece in 1947. President Truman got Congress to appropriate funds to turn back the communist threat. The Cold War began to take a more tangible form with the formation of the North Atlantic Treaty Organization (NATO) in 1949. Two events reinforced the hardening of battle lines between Washington and the communist world in 1949. One was the takeover of China by communist forces under Mao Tse Tung. The other was Russia's explosion of an atomic bomb in September 1949. This was followed by the North Korean invasion of South Korea in June 1950, which prompted Truman to send in American troops. While the Cold War represented a dangerous confrontation once nuclear weapons became part of the arsenal, it justified the continuation of military appropriations which, in turn, pumped money into the economy. In 1950 the military accounted for 50 percent of the federal budget and 10 percent of total consumption.[26]

For some 25 years, from 1947 into the 1970s, the economy grew at an annual rate of just under 4 percent, inflation remained below 5 percent and unemployment remained low. The damage done by the war to the European and Japanese economies accounted for part of the economic growth. American manufacturers found that they had no competition in some of the markets. European and Japanese factories and infrastructure had been so devastated by the war that recovery would not take place until the 1950s.[27] The American domestic market had also improved considerably. In contrast to the years preceding the

1929 Crash, there was less reliance on credit to sustain demand. Part of the reason was that incomes had increased. Between 1941 and 1969 average family income almost doubled.[28]

The automobile still played an important part in the economy. Five million cars were sold in 1949, more than in 1929.[29] The auto industry however, was not the only sector of the economy to benefit from the improving economy. Three years later, $255 million was spent on chewing gum. Where the cost of cars in the 1920s had restricted the market to one car per family, in the 1970s there were two cars owned for every three people.[30] While the U.S. automobile industry was a strong force in the economy, it would receive a shock in 1974. An oil embargo by Arab countries caused American consumers to consider buying smaller non-American cars. The embargo, begun in October 1973, did not just affect consumer car choices. It triggered a price increase which, in turn, headed the economy into a recession which would last through 1975. The oil embargo of 1973 was only the first oil shock.

In September 1979 the Chrysler Corporation had to ask for government help to prevent bankruptcy. Chrysler's insolvency was not simply the result of higher gas prices. There had been marketing mistakes by the American auto industry which allowed Japanese auto manufacturers to gain a foothold in the market. Part of the problem was that total U.S. car sales would drop from 11.3 million in 1978 to 8.0 million in 1982. The other part was that foreign manufacturers were increasing sales at the expense of American companies. American car sales in 1978 were 9.3 million; in 1982 they had dropped to 5.8 million.[31] Chrysler was not the only manufacturer to suffer losses. Both Ford and General Motors also lost money. The problem was related to inertia in marketing - the auto makers not only failed to look at buyer needs but also failed to adjust marketing to changing consumer patterns. The auto makers were certain that consumers viewed cars more as a status symbol than a mode of transport. They bought cars because of the prestige associated with high price and sporty design, not because cars were dependable or saved on gas.[32]

The humbling of the auto makers had an element of arrogance and the lessons learned came with a high price tag. Marketing mistakes were not the only factor at work however. There was an element which was related to resources. Oil was becoming a scarce commodity. America was still a major producer of oil. The discovery of large reserves in the Prudhoe Bay area of Alaska in the late 1960s had ensured a source of oil far into the future. Yet, Alaska aside, oil production was moving away from America to the Middle East.

In February 1979 the Ayatollah Khoumeini returned to Iran from exile in France. Even before his arrival the interim Iranian government had stopped the export of oil. The decision was not insignificant in economic terms. Iran was the next largest producer behind Saudi Arabia. Iranian prices increased 30 percent between December 1978 and February 1979. OPEC prices had increased 24 percent by June. This, in turn, led to a 52 percent increase in gasoline prices in the U.S. by September (over the September 1978 prices) and an even larger increase in heating oil prices - they increased by 73 percent.[33]

The inflation rate, which had been at 7.0 percent in May of 1978, rose to 9.3 percent in January 1979, and continued climbing to 11.3 percent by July of 1979.[34]

Oil prices came down again in response to decontrol. In July 1981 Congress adopted Ronald Reagan's Budget, which included some $64 billion in budget cuts combined with a 30 percent tax cut. Whatever savings had been made were soon offset by an increase in defense spending, projected in 1982 at $200 billion. Despite the long-term problems associated with deficit spending, Reagan's image as a conservative, pro-business politician may have contributed to a strengthened dollar. Foreign importers now saw the price of their goods fall sufficiently to be competitive in the American market. As consumers began buying foreign goods, the market which sustained American companies fell. The result in 1982 was a loss of 1.25 million jobs from some 2,700 layoffs or shutdowns and all the statistical indications of a recession. Unemployment reached nearly 11 percent.[35] Not all the fall in prices could be attributed to a strong dollar. The Japanese had geared their auto production for price competition, regardless of the strength of the dollar. That planning was one reason foreign auto manufacturers were successful at capturing some 25 percent of the market.

The end of the recession brought some startling results. Normally increased government spending would bring inflation, yet the rate of inflation began to decline steeply after 1982. Between 1981 and 1986 it would average only 3.3 percent. The unemployment rate came down, from 10.7 percent at the end of 1982, to 5.3 percent in 1989, but the fall was not dramatic. To these somewhat contradictory results was added the stock market crash of October 19, 1987. The total loss in stock value was over $500 million dollars as the result of a 508 point drop in the market.[36] Yet, in contrast to the Crash of 1929, there was not the corresponding fall in output or cutbacks in the work force.

If the 1987 crash did not trigger a 1929-like Depression, there were other ways in which the economy of the 1980s was beginning to resemble that of the 1920s. The 1980s economy was becoming stratified and wealth concentrated. The income after taxes of the richest 2.5 million people almost equaled that of the 100 million people at the bottom. One-third of those working had incomes below the poverty level.[37]

Chrysler may have survived the Japanese auto onslaught in 1979, but it did not eliminate the competition coming from Japanese auto makers. The American economy under George Bush and Bill Clinton has witnessed "globalization," with its emphasis on competition in a world market. McDonald's hamburgers, for example, has tried to develop markets in Russia. If American companies have opportunities in foreign markets they must also defend their home market against foreign competitors. Globalization, on its positive side, has made it easier for companies to enter new markets and compete worldwide. Computer technology has created new job opportunities in many fields. The downside is that the traditional market for U.S. manufacturers has provided fewer employment opportunities for unskilled workers. Layoffs and downsizing, if not as dramatic in scale as the Great Depression, have become almost daily newspaper headlines. Globalization, while opening potentially new markets, has also created new competitive pressures. Profitability emphasizes efficiency and low costs. The pressure to keep costs down has made low-wage regions of the U.S. or low-wage countries attractive. If the North American Free Trade Agreement (NAFTA), implemented on January 1, 1994, symbolized the benefits of global free trade, it also embodied the fears of workers that their jobs would be shipped overseas.

Globalization provides a convenient stopping point for the discussion. In some ways, it has made the U.S., even the world economy, completely different than the economies which have come before. Advances in the field of telecommunications have made instant worldwide communication feasible. Computers have revolutionized services such as accounting. Such advances have also given businesses a broader perspective on markets. In other ways, globalization has created no revolutionary market concepts. It involves the same principles of trade employed by the ancient Egyptians and Athenians, it just applies them on a larger scale and at a much accelerated pace.

Before ending the discussion it may be helpful to look at two limited areas of American economic development. The first is transportation and technological resources. The second is agriculture. When resources are mentioned, it is usually mineral resources such as iron or copper, which first come to mind, not trains or ships. Yet the physical means of transporting goods and the technology that comes with it is very much a resource. Defined in terms of what a resource is, rail transport was something that America possessed and could "use to advantage." Agriculture merits a separate discussion, not so much because food is unique as a commodity of trade, but because the availability or lack of food plays a much more crucial role in the political arena. In ancient Rome it was the food dole that kept the Roman mobs from becoming unmanageable and the French authorities in the 1790s were always conscious of the need to supply Paris with food.

TRANSPORTATION AND TECHNOLOGICAL RESOURCES

The state of transport in the 1600s and 1700s may have had something to do with the geographical location of the original thirteen colonies - along the Atlantic coast of America. The pattern of colonial settlement, if early maps are to be believed, was in a north-south direction along the coast. Newly arriving immigrants did not all remain in the coastal cities of Boston, New York or Charleston, to be sure. Many began moving inland. The British, even at the time of the American Revolution, had stationed troops as far west as what are now the states of Michigan, Indiana and Illinois.

Transport, particularly where cheap, bulk commodities are concerned, has been one of the eternal problems for merchants. Power is one of the chief limitations. Neither humans nor animals are normally able to supply sufficient power to transport large quantities of goods - or at least not in a cost-effective manner. The Egyptians are believed to have used animals or humans to move the limestone blocks used in the construction of the pyramids. The pyramids however, might be considered extraordinary projects. If they proved that bulk transport was possible, the cost involved did not make the system easily adopted for general commerce.

Water transport, while sometimes hazardous, was an early solution. It required some form of power, yet the energy requirements were far less than land transport demanded. Whether power was supplied by wind or oars, it represented a significant improvement over land transport in terms of cost and bulk transport capabilities. So successful and universal was the idea that, once adopted, it would continue in use over thousands of years.

Why was land transport so expensive? The simple answer was friction - the resistance to motion by surfaces which are touching. As elemental as it may seem, it was friction which created the extraordinarily large power requirements involved in land transport. It was the relative lack of friction which gave water transport the advantage. The ancient discovery of the wheel had overcome some of the problems of land transport. Even though the wheel was incorporated into the cart however, the cart had structural limitations which prevented its use for bulk loads. Its power requirements still were far greater than those of water. While land transport was not competitive with water where bulk goods were concerned, it was useful for smaller items or communications. (Meat was perhaps the only commodity for which land transport was competitive. Cattle and sheep could be driven to market.) Even if a horse and rider could not compete with a barge or sailing ship in the carriage of heavy loads, they had the advantage of speed for smaller items, such as letters.

The problem with water transport was not with the carrying capacity of vessels. The problem was location. Transport was restricted to rivers, lakes or oceans. Factories could be located near rivers, partially solving this problem. Yet, factory location did not solve all problems related to raw materials, not always conveniently located near water. Agricultural production was an accommodation to climate and growing conditions, not transport. An early solution was the canal. An artificial waterway could substitute where rivers were scarce. In Britain the era of canal building occurred in the 1760s. It would come later to the United States. The Erie Canal, finished in 1825, was the most famous of the American projects.

Even while canal building was in its heyday, the technology to replace the canal was being developed. Oddly enough, it began with an attack on the universal problem of friction. If the wheeled cart had not made land transport cheap, a slight modification began to make it feasible. The operation of wheels on a highway or road still required too much power. However when rails were substituted for the highway, the reduction in friction reduced the amount of power required to pull a heavy load. Horses could even pull heavy loads in mining work. The first iron railroad track was constructed in England in 1767 to transport coal. In 1801 the first railway track would be constructed for public transport (as opposed to strictly mine-related operations).[38] While the steam engine had been patented by Watt in 1769 and model locomotives had been built in 1784 the idea of using the steam engine to power locomotives would not come into use until 1821.[39]

The problem, until 1812, was friction. It had taken some time to comprehend that iron rails could reduce friction enough to transport heavy commodities efficiently. The opposite belief, that friction had been almost eliminated, led to the assumption that wheels would not "bite" on a smooth track. William Hedley proved in 1812 that smooth wheels had enough traction to drive cars without the aid of animals. All that was needed was a powerful enough engine. That came with the discovery by George Stephenson that more air supplied to the engine could make it hotter. In 1821 Stephenson demonstrated both the "bite" and the new engine, although his train still relied on horses for power. Finally in 1829 the steam engine had been sufficiently improved to power locomotives unassisted.[40]

There was now an alternative to water transport. For overland shipment, the railroad's convenience and speed would put the canals out of business. Almost as soon as British engineers constructed their first rail lines in the 1830s, the Americans began setting up a rail system. By 1850 almost 10,000 miles of track had been laid. Between 1850 and 1860 another 21,000 miles of track had been laid. On the eve of the Civil War, shipping time between New York and Chicago had been reduced to three days, where in 1830 it had taken three weeks. The 1,700 miles of track laid in the completion of the Transcontinental Railroad in 1869 represented only a small portion of the 60,000 miles which would be laid in the 1870s. Another 75,000 miles would be added in the 1880s.[41] Such an extensive network not only reduced transport costs but also helped to reduce overall commodity costs. Where a bushel of wheat had cost 37 cents to ship between Chicago and New York, it only cost a penny in 1890.[42]

To gain some perspective on American railroad capabilities, it may be helpful to compare the United States with Russia. The Soviet Union, even by 1930, had laid only 50,269 miles of railroad. Germany at that time had 33,466 miles of track. The U.S. had 260,440 miles.[43] America in 1880 had a total of 90,000 miles and had reached 240,000 miles in 1914.[44] Part of the rail capacity can be attributed to steel-making capabilities. In 1913 the United States produced 31,301,000 tons of raw steel, or 41.9 percent of world production. In 1920 production had increased to 42,133,000 tons, for 59.3 percent of the world total. Russian production of iron ore in 1913 was only 4,181,000 tons or 5.5 percent.[45]

The transport industry was fortunate in having available the specific resources needed for expansion - iron and timber. The ability to transport these resources cheaply - made possible by the very technology they were exploiting - gave them an added advantage. This, in turn, contributed to lower investment costs, although financing did not come totally from the private sector. The federal government provided some sixty-five million dollars in loans for the Transcontinental Railroad, as well as a grant of twenty-four million acres of land to the two railroad companies. While the railroads provided the means for economic expansion and development of the West, they did not totally displace water as a means of transport. Ocean transport, like its land counterpart, the railroad, benefitted from the resources, particularly wood, which were abundant in America.

Foreign trade had been profitable for New England. In the early 1700s, what is sometimes known as the Triangle Trade developed. Merchants in the Northern colonies shipped wheat, meat and lumber to the West Indies. In return they would get molasses, which was then made into rum, used to buy slaves in Africa. The slaves would then be sold in the West Indies or in Southern colonies. In the 1840s the abundance of softwood allowed American shipbuilders to reduce costs and build ships competitively. The speedy clipper ships, for a time, provided the edge to take over the China tea trade. Yet, speed alone was not enough to ensure profitability. Other transport methods, if slower, could carry more cargo at cheaper cost. By the Civil War Britain had regained the lead in ocean trade.[46] If it was a serious blow to American pride, there was little time to brood over the loss. Construction was about to begin on the Transcontinental Railroad in 1862 and America would be preoccupied with internal trade for the next 40 years or so.

The railroads seemed the answer to a 6,000-year old problem in transport - how to physically carry large heavy items from point A to point B. If they delivered on that promise, they fell short of solving the whole transport puzzle. What happened before the goods got to point A or after they had been left at point B? The Kansas wheat farmer had access to a transport system which could deliver wheat anywhere in the world, if only he could get the grain to the railroad station. Having solved one problem, the railroads could have been asked to solve another. Yet building a railroad line to every single farm or every single home was somewhat beyond the physical capabilities of even the most ambitious railway man. Even Carnegie Steel could not have turned out enough rails to supply such an undertaking. Being confined to railroad tracks limited transport flexibility, but it was related to a larger technical problem. Power, especially the amount needed to pull heavier loads, could only be obtained by increasing weight. As efficient as the steam engine had been over what had come before, power gains could only come with additional weight. The internal combustion engine would provide the answer. Not only could it deliver more power, but it could deliver it without the additional weight requirements of steam.

In August 1859 "Colonel" Edwin Drake, with a derrick and a drill powered by a steam engine, struck oil just 69 feet below the surface at a site near Titusville, Pennsylvania.[47] Even in 1859 there was a demand for oil. The actual demand was for kerosene, a by-product of oil, and it was artificial light, not transportation, which created the market. If the market for artificial light remained strong, the market for oil was threatened by the invention of the light bulb and the use of electricity. Although that demand was irrelevant in the context of transportation, kerosene production did serve one important purpose. When the automobile was invented there was already a refining industry in place ready to produce gasoline.

Auto transport would likely have taken off, whether refining capacity had existed at the turn of the century or not. What was phenomenal about the auto industry was not simply the technical expertise required to design the car, which in itself was a remarkable achievement. The real phenomenon was the fact that it could serve traditional transport needs while enjoying extraordinary market success. Success depended, not simply on the ability to manufacture cars cheaply, but also on a cheap source of fuel and a good system of roads and highways.

In 1900 there were 8,000 automobile registrations and U.S. oil output was 63.6 million barrels. In 1927, auto registrations had reached 20,193,300 and oil output had increased to 901,129,000 barrels, which was 71.4 percent of world output. Pig iron production was 36,289,000 tons, or 42.4 percent of world output. In 1930 auto registrations were up to 23,034,000. Oil output had dropped to 898,011,000 barrels, although that still was 63.8 percent of world output. Pig iron production had dropped as well, to 31,441,000 tons, although that still was 40.1 percent of world output. Iron and oil only represent part of the cost equation where auto transport is concerned, however the figures do suggest that, as a resource, auto transport ranked high in the U.S.[48] If auto transport had made an impressive showing, it had not totally displaced the railroads. In 1930 some 1,220,134,000 tons of freight were hauled by rail, an increase over the 1,072,796,000 tons hauled in 1913.[49]

Technological resources clearly exist, yet they are often such an integral part of the production process that they cannot be easily identified, apart from the process itself. The number of patents issued by the U.S. Patent Office might be one way to measure technology. In 1901 there were 25,546 patents issued. The number had risen to 42,238 in 1940, and had reached 68,406 in 1966.[50] Another measure might be hydroelectric power. In 1901, the U.S. produced 264 trillion British thermal units (BTUs) of electricity from water power. In 1970 the figure had increased to 2,659 trillion BTUs.[51] Technological resources might be calculated based on the number of engineers or chemists. In 1910 there were 77,000 engineers and 16,000 chemists. By 1970, engineers had increased in number to 1,230,000 while chemists had grown to 110,000.[52] Still another measure might be the types of products associated with technology, such as telephones. In 1929 Americans spent 569 million dollars on telephone service. In 1950 the amount had increased to 1,942 million and in 1970 it totaled 9,879 million. In 1950 2,421 million dollars was spent on radios and television sets, records, and musical instruments. In 1970 the amount had grown to 9,439 million.[53] These figures do not reflect the technological resources which are incorporated into manufacturing processes, such as steel production, but they do suggest the level of resources present.

AMERICAN AGRICULTURAL DEVELOPMENT

Farmers in America have suffered through lean times, yet agricultural production has rarely reflected such problems. Agricultural output has remained high, even if individual farmers struggled financially. The problem which Congress sought to address in 1933, with the Agricultural Adjustment Act, was the profitability of farming, not its physical output. That Act, and the 1936 Act, were intended to subsidize farmers, either directly, by making payments for taking products off the market, or indirectly, by increasing the market price - the result of holding crops off the market. There were other concessions on the economic side as well. The farm program expanded agricultural loans and provided crop insurance. In 1925 farm mortgages had totalled $9.4 billion, some three times the 1910 figure of $3.3 billion.[54]

Even while the world economy was entering the first years of the Great Depression, agriculture production seemed to defy the downward trend. Wheat output may provide some indication of production trends. Between 1921 and 1925, wheat production in the United States had averaged 787 million bushels or 21.2 percent of world output. By 1929 production had been increased to 813 million bushels, or 19.1 percent, and in 1930 output was 858 million bushels, or 17.9 percent of output.[55] There are perhaps two curious aspects to these figures. First, U.S. production increased, even as the economy was entering the Depression. Second, while U.S. production was increasing, it was falling in relation to the rest of the world, suggesting that the U.S. response was not unique. Producers in other countries were increasing output as well. The demand for potatoes, while exhibiting some ups and downs, by and large remained strong. In 1928 Irish potato production had reached 256,349,000 cwt (hundredweight = 100 pounds) In 1929 production fell to 200,035,000 cwt, but recovered to 206,290,000 cwt in 1930. Its low point in the Depression years came in 1936, when it dropped to 194,373,000 cwt. In 1937 it was back to 225,869,000 cwt.[56] While beef production fluctuated as well during the Depression years, it also remained high. In 1928 some 5,771 million pounds of beef was produced. By 1937 the amount had increased to 6,798 million pounds. Production had not dropped below the 1928 level during any of the nine years in between. The closest it came was in 1932, when production had fallen to 5,789 million pounds. Even as farmers increased output, they were seeing prices fall, from a high of $13.91 per cwt in 1928 to $5.42 in 1933. They did recover somewhat in 1937, reaching $11.47 per cwt.[57]

The tension between agricultural output and financial survival is not something new historically, if Athens and Rome are any indication. If the phenomenon was not something new, it did serve as a major economic theme of American agriculture. Within that framework there were certain other trends at work. One was the migration of farming production from the East to the West. The other was the technological transformation of agriculture.

In American agriculture there was almost a regional operation of comparative advantage, the idea that a country should specialize in producing those goods it can produce most efficiently and trade for those goods it cannot. As newer farm regions opened up in the West, Eastern farmers could no longer compete. In 1860 the states of Virginia, Pennsylvania, Ohio, Indiana, Illinois, and Wisconsin were the leading wheat producers. Only Ohio would rank among the top wheat producers by 1900. Between 1865 and 1915 the amount of land under cultivation in New England fell by half.[58]

Westward expansion accounted for part of the increased productivity, although the mechanization of agriculture had an impact as well. John Deere would invent the steel plow in 1837 in Illinois. Other inventions would increase the productivity of wheat farming. In 1800 the average output in wheat amounted to about half an acre a day with the handle sickle. The cradle in 1830 would increase the rate to two acres. The mechanical reaper developed by Obed Hussey and Cyrus McCormick would allow the harvesting of five to six acres a day. The advantages of the reaper were so obvious to farmers that there was almost an immediate demand for the invention. Between 1847, when he established his plant in Chicago, and 1860, McCormick sold 250,000 machines. In the 1880s, the combine, a combination reaper and thresher was invented. Although it used horses for power - teams of 20 to 40 were required - it increased productivity immensely. Where a single farmer could only harvest half an acre in 1800, the new combine could harvest seventy to eighty acres in a day. In terms of workers, manpower requirements were reduced from 300 men to only four. The combine not only cut the grain, but threshed and bagged it as well. Steam and gasoline engines eventually replaced animals, with demands for pasturage, and lowered the number of workers even further.[59]

Wheat farming was not the only agricultural activity to benefit from mechanization. The mechanical corn husker allowed one man to do what had required eight before. Machines took over potato planting, corn shelling, and manure spreading. There were economic trade-offs. Machinery required a large capital investment and was thus better suited to the large-scale farming of the West. In 1920 the capital investment in farm machinery in Iowa was as great as the combined investment of New England and the Middle Atlantic states. That fact tended to encourage specialization - large farms devoted to a single crop such as wheat.[60]

The low prices which continually plagued farmers might be attributed to market saturation. Market saturation, in turn, can be explained by the westward migration of agricultural production and the technological advances which aided productivity. Yet market saturation alone does not entirely explain the economic difficulties farmers experienced. In one sense saturated markets related more to the production side of farming, i.e., the physical ability to grow and harvest more bushels of wheat than the market required. It did have financial consequences. More wheat production tended to lower prices. Yet the financial plight of the farmer was only partially related to low prices. There were other economic factors at work as well.

Low prices represented only one part of the financial difficulties farmers found themselves in. Expenses represented the other part of the problem. Labor-saving devices may have increased productivity but they were extremely expensive. If machines reduced labor costs by eliminating workers, such savings were offset by the increased investment costs for the new machinery. Machinery may have meant savings in labor costs, but it had to be paid for year after year whether the harvest was good or bad. Human workers normally were only paid if they worked. When crops were destroyed by hail, workers did not need to be hired for harvesting. If farmers were going further into debt, part of the reason was their greater reliance on equipment. From $250 million in 1860, the value of farm equipment had increased to $3.5 billion by 1920.[61]

While machinery investment costs hit Western farmers the hardest, farmers in general had to contend with a steadily declining soil productivity. Erosion from rains and from wind caused deterioration of the soil in the West. To compensate, farmers had to increase the use of fertilizers, which increased costs. In the South, tobacco and cotton farming took a heavy toll on the soil, in addition to losses from erosion. Whatever economic problems farmers were experiencing, American consumers benefited. The total value of agricultural output continued to increase after 1900. In 1900 net production was $13,041 million (in 1967 constant dollars). In 1960 production had reached $30,793 million. Meat consumption, which in 1900 had been $7,056 million, increased to $18,762 million by 1960, while the value of crop consumption went from $4,451 million to $10,843 million.[62]

The New Deal farm program of the 1930s used a market mechanism to help farmers financially. Subsidies were paid to withdraw land from cultivation and, as a result, to reduce the amount of produce on the market. It was an artificial means of creating scarcity which, in turn, led to an increase in the market price. Although production may have decreased slightly as a result, overall productive capabilities were never seriously threatened.

AGRICULTURAL GROWTH AND THE MARKET ECONOMY

The division of labor, with its emphasis on specialization, was a major explanation of factory success, according to Adam Smith. Agricultural productivity, even in Colonial times, suggests that a form of specialization had occurred at a larger level as well. Not only were factories increasing output by giving their workers specialized tasks, but the manufacturing and agricultural sectors were increasing their output by concentrating on their specialties. Just as the division of labor aids productivity at the factory level, in a broader sense the economic specialization which developed within the agricultural and manufacturing sectors tended to accelerate overall economic growth and to reinforce the growing commitment to the market system. While it has been argued that the free market is the driving force behind economic development, there is an argument to be made that a market economy cannot come into existence without a substantial agricultural surplus.

Perhaps the first real proof that a market economy had fully taken hold is the depression of 1785-1786. It was not just that the Colonial economy was geared to the market, it was also that the agricultural sector in particular had been converted. Crops were left unharvested because they could not be sold. The market for meat had virtually collapsed - the price of cattle in 1786 was half of what it had been. There are also indications that, like the Great Crash, some 140 years later, the markets had been artificially stimulated with credit. Other indications are that the market was reinforced by the associated legal and business system. Farmers were bound to the market, not by the promise of wealth, but by the need for cash. They either had to pay off creditors or had to pay their state tax obligations. While the state had given farmers title to their property, it could take back the land through foreclosure. It was the undeclared war between creditors and debtors which finally led to Daniel Shays' rebellion in July 1786.[63]

In spite of the Depression of 1785-86, many among the former Colonists were doing well. They wanted to facilitate trade and accommodate expansion and found the old methods of conducting transactions cumbersome and inefficient. If many of the coming changes were beneficial for economic expansion, they had a downside as well. Those changes would provide the backdrop for the first real economic depression the country would experience, the Panic of 1819.

There were two trends in particular which aided economic development. The first was the increasing use of the corporation as the preferred form of business enterprise.

The second was the development of a formal banking system. The idea of several people pooling money to increase the capital available for investment was not new. Colonial investors had frequently employed the partnership or the joint-stock company to finance business ventures, but they were cumbersome to use. They often ended once the particular venture came to an end, then had to be reformed for a new venture. The corporation continued in existence forever. It was not so much the idea of using the corporation which was new but the idea of using it for private business. Before the Revolutionary War there had been only seven private corporations; by the end of the 1790s more than 300 had been chartered.[64] Perhaps symbolic of the change was the formation of the New York Stock Exchange in 1792.

If the use of the corporation for private business was new, so too was the idea of applying corporate forms to banking. The first bank to be incorporated was the Bank of North America. It was a national bank, granted its charter by the Confederation Congress in 1781. It was successful enough to pay annual dividends of nearly ten percent until 1821. In 1791 the first Bank of the United States was chartered. It differed from the Bank of North America in that it was a semi-public, rather than a private, bank. (The fact that British shareholders had acquired a controlling interest no doubt contributed to Congress' refusal to renew its charter in 1811.) The states were determined not to leave all the banking business to the national government and by 1815 had chartered over 200 banks. It was not the mere existence of so many state banks that would create problems in 1819, it was the way in which they operated.[65]

What occurred before 1819 was a change in the way people viewed money. Initially silver and gold coins were regarded as the only true measure of the value of money. There was really a two-step process involved in changing their minds. In the first step, banks convinced their customers that bank notes, i.e., printed paper containing a promise to pay in gold or silver, were as valuable as the coins themselves. Since the notes promised gold or silver if redeemed, the assumption was that the banks would not issue notes exceeding the silver and gold reserves they actually held. Having gotten customers to accept the notes as money, the next step was to ignore the actual reserves and to issue notes exceeding the reserves held by the bank. The real trick was to do it without losing the confidence of the public.[66]

In 1816 the second Bank of the United States was chartered by Congress. Just as state interference in commerce and differing state currencies had contributed to the push for a national government, the problems created by state banks convinced some that a national banking system was needed. The notes issued by state banks had taken on a life of their own. Since each note offered to redeem a specific amount of gold or silver, they should have been interchangeable. Yet there were regional differences in value. The refusal by state banks to honor demands for silver or gold led to a loss of confidence, which only differed in degree for individual banks.[67]

The newly chartered federal bank at least offered hope for those seeking an orderly system. It was however too late either to slow the expansion of the system or to reverse the drive for greater credit availability. By 1818 the states had added another 198 banks to the 200 existing in 1815. The problem was not so much that the number of banks was expanding. The real problem was that the new system had become dangerously removed from the old specie (gold and silver coin) base, which, even if conservative, provided some basis for confidence in the system. The specie-based system had, realistically or not, tied credit to more tangible collateral. The new system allowed bank notes and stock to serve as collateral, and there were fewer safeguards. In addition, the system began to operate more on speculation. Like the investors of 1929, gain was to come from resale of stock, not from the actual earnings of the company it represented.[68]

The only way in which 1819 differed from 1929 was the credit mechanism. In the 1920s investors were able to find banks or businesses with the actual money to lend. In the world of 1819, new banks created credit by simply printing more notes. The banks did have some gold and silver reserves, but they largely ignored them when making loans. For the American economy as a whole, the continued issuance of new notes created an inflationary situation. The state banks did not help the situation by refusing to redeem their notes with silver and gold. The federal government did have one mechanism available to at least slow down the state banks. It served as a clearinghouse for state bank notes and could, like any citizen, ask a state bank to redeem its notes for silver or gold. Congress had hoped that the second Bank of the United States would begin forcing the state banks to resume specie redemption.[69]

Unfortunately in 1817 the majority of the bank's directors defied Congress. They did begin specie redemption from the state banks, but not sufficiently to reverse the system. In addition, the various branches of the federal bank, particularly Baltimore, began making loans themselves. The new federal notes added to the country's inflationary problems. Unlike the state banks, the federal bank could not easily refuse redemption of its own notes and the demand began to drain its reserves.[70]

The Panic of 1819 hit in the spring. One cause was the change in federal bank policy in the summer and fall of 1818. To rebuild its own specie reserves the Bank began calling in its own outstanding loans. It also began to pressure state banks for redemption of their notes. While the federal bank's policies led to a loss of confidence by forcing the state banks to publicly face their lack of hard reserves, the Panic did not come about simply because of the new banking policies. The other factor was the sudden collapse of commodity prices. Though speculative agricultural prices were contributing to inflation, they also were making businesses profitable. The inflated prices were well above those for normal demand. They collapsed in the spring, triggered by an English market collapse. Cotton prices were cut in half, from 33 cents a pound to 14 cents a pound. There was no sudden recovery and cotton prices would continue falling through 1923, when they hit 11 cents a pound. In South Carolina cotton planters left their plantations and moved west because they could no longer survive economically at the then-current cotton prices. Wheat fell from $2.41 a bushel in 1817 to 88 cents in 1821.[71]

While the economy may still have been largely geared to agriculture, the unemployment figures suggest that an urban work force was beginning to take hold. Some 500,000 workers are estimated to have been idled by the Panic. New York, Philadelphia, and Baltimore accounted for 50,000.[72] The agricultural nature of the economy may have helped ease the unemployment problem as many left the cities to find work in the countryside. While the exodus may have solved the unemployment problem, it did not help the economy to recover.

The Bank of the United States perhaps could have helped recovery by easing pressure on state banks. At the same time the overreliance on credit clearly needed to be reversed. The problem in 1819 was that the new hard-line policy of the federal bank came at a time when commodity prices were falling. The lower returns meant that loans could not be repaid. Businesses which might have survived were forced under. Farmers, unable to repay their loans, had their property foreclosed. Many banks failed along with businesses.[73]

Discussion of the Panic of 1819 seems more appropriate to a general discussion of the market and economic conditions in the United States. It is included in a discussion of agriculture to reinforce the idea that agricultural production in America was high. The argument is that, without strong agricultural productivity, farming cannot get beyond subsistence level and farmers will be committed to the land rather than to the market itself. Conversely, a strong commitment to the market suggests that the level of productivity is so high that crops become just another economic commodity, no more crucial to survival than a piece of coal or iron ore. The Panic of 1819 is useful for the insights it provides about the market generally, about the impact of credit on markets, and about the rise of an industrial class of workers. However, in the area of agriculture, it also illustrates the level to which farming had been converted from mere subsistence production to market orientation.

Land, as much as stock, was one of the major commodities of speculation. Land speculation had been practiced almost from the pre-Revolutionary War Colonial beginnings.[74] One of the paradoxes of speculation was that land, which had often been available for nothing, often played a central role in profit-making enterprises. Whether from speculation or other economic factors, the transformation of land into a market commodity with increasing value had tax consequences. Tax valuations increased, bringing into play the state's legal enforcement apparatus, and with that pressure, the motivation to enter the market.[75]

The belief that the Bank of the United States had been to blame for the economic problems in the Panic of 1819 contributed to an anti-bank sentiment which Andrew Jackson exploited in the 1832 election campaign to defeat Henry Clay. Although the Bank's charter would not expire until March 1836 Jackson vetoed its renewal in 1832. In September 1833, he ordered that U.S. Treasury funds were to be withdrawn and deposited in state banks - the so-called "pet" banks (pets of the administration, they were called). As in 1819, there was pressure to expand credit, and the Bank War over the Bank of the United States represented only the more visible signs of the opposing forces. Once again, land would be viewed, not as a crucial element in agricultural productivity, but as another commodity.

Whether the expiration of the charter of the Bank of the United States in 1836 was seen as a signal for making credit more available or whether economic conditions were favorable, there was a boom with an accompanying increase in inflation. Credit was again a major culprit, although easy credit was not the direct result of the use of pet banks by the federal government. The Treasury Secretary, Levi Woodbury, had imposed severe restrictions on the pet banks which he could enforce by threatening to withdraw funds. A major problem was that silver, the less expensive specie reserve, suddenly became widely available due to Mexican mining output and fewer demands for silver payments. State banks began buying as much silver as possible. Unfortunately, while they were increasing silver reserves, they were also granting more and more credit. State legislatures responded to the demand for more credit by chartering more banks. By 1836 there were over 600 state banks. Government land sales, which had been around $5 million in 1834, increased to $25 million in 1836.[76]

Jackson's war against the Bank of the United States in 1833 had exploited the popular sentiment that the national bank was primarily a tool of the rich. As his second term was nearing its end in 1836, Jackson began to have misgivings about the uncontrolled activities of the state banks and the dangerous increase in land speculation. He began espousing a hard money policy, and in late 1836 got the Treasury Secretary to issue a Specie Circular to the federal land offices. Federal lands could only be purchased with gold or silver coin. Congress tried to pass a law nullifying the Circular in December. Although it had the votes to override a veto, the December adjournment meant that it would not meet again for a vote. Jackson refused to sign the bill and the Circular remained in effect. The pocket veto came too late to prevent the economic downturn. It had begun some six months before in England.[77]

While Western American banks were busy extending credit to land speculators in the summer of 1836, the Bank of England had an unusually high number of demands for payment of silver and gold on its notes. It began restricting credit by raising interest rates and, where American businesses were concerned, by denying any credit to firms involved in American trade. Cotton prices would eventually fall 25 percent. By the spring of 1847 the fall in cotton destroyed 93 New York firms whose capital values had totaled $60 million. The collapse of the cotton market was not the only economic disaster of 1836. The wheat crop had also failed.[78]

To add to the problem of business failures and unemployment there were also food shortages, which led to a flour riot in New York city in February 1837. President Jackson's Specie Circular not only slowed federal land sales but also caused the credit-inflated land prices to fall. The state banks had been encouraged to grant loans by the silver glut. Note holders now began demanding silver and the banks found their actual reserves inadequate. On May 9, 1837 depositors withdrew $652,000 in coins from Manhattan banks. Although bank closures, first in New York and New Orleans, then in the rest of the country, prevented further customer raids, they could not prevent failures caused by widespread loss of confidence.[79] The economy appeared to recover in late 1838. Bank confidence had been sufficiently restored by August that most agreed to resume specie payments on demand. The recovery was only temporary and when specie demands once again overwhelmed them in 1839, the banks closed their doors. The depression would last until 1843. It represented the second longest U.S. depression in U.S. history.[80]

The Panics of 1819 and 1837 have been included for discussion to illustrate, in part, that the transformation from subsistence-level to market-oriented production in agriculture was complete. More importantly, they have been included to bolster the argument that agricultural resources were abundant. Subsistence-level production is designed to fend off starvation. Almost by definition, it is insufficient to generate a surplus, let alone a surplus large enough to market. American agriculture in 1819 and in 1837, not only seemed unconcerned about basic survival, but concentrated nearly all its energies on making a profit. Survival was virtually assured, profitability was the next step. Agricultural production, even the basic components of production, such as land, had been turned into commodities.

That agriculture had adapted itself so completely to the market was not news to New York's unemployed in 1837. Those who participated in the flour riot in February were only too aware that flour had become a commodity. At eight dollars a barrel, it was not only a commodity but a commodity which was unobtainable by those who were unemployed. The Panic of 1837 was not the last economic downturn of the Nineteenth Century. Another panic would hit in 1857, a more severe one in 1873. The worst would hit in 1893. Apart from the business failures and unemployment which marked all three, there was continuing commitment by farmers to the market. Completely divorced from their role as components of survival, crops were just products which commanded a price. In all three depressions, hardship for the farmer was defined in terms of falling prices rather than in terms of an inability to grow things. In fact the fall in commodity prices used to measure the Depression included agricultural commodities, indicating that overall productivity was still high - as were agricultural resources.

CONCLUSION

This chapter's discussion was intended to establish the relative availability of resources in the United States. Production figures provide the primary evidence. Yet, the market itself may serve as additional evidence of resource abundance. For markets to exist, there must be some minimal level of resources available. For markets to thrive, there must be a correspondingly greater pool of resources available.

The next chapter deals with recent economic trends in the U.S. economy. While economic figures suggest that the economy has done well, there are signs of underlying economic weakness. Large corporations seem to be continually announcing layoffs in an effort to streamline operations. U.S. firms have been able to meet the new market demands for competitiveness, yet the need to compete has come as a shock. If the fact of competition has caught many businesses by surprise; what has made it difficult to accept is the extraordinary effort involved.

A discussion of recent economic difficulties encountered by Americans may seem unrelated to this book's main theme. Like the discussion of the Great Depression however, such a discussion may be important - if only for clues it provides about the market mechanism. The market mechanism does have an impact on employment, which itself often impacts political events. There are some basic questions which need to be asked about economic trends. Even if resource scarcity is not "the cause" of American problems, have there been recent changes in resource allocations? As important as oil has become, is the American reliance on oil causing a net loss of resources or can resource loss be blamed on specific events or trends? It has been said that the American economy is being transformed into a service-based economy and revolutionized by computers. Does that mean that traditional resources, such as iron or coal, are now irrelevant or that an abundance of technological resources will make up for the loss of traditional mineral resource wealth? Whether there is enough data available to answer such questions, they at least provide a starting point for any analysis.

PART VI

THE GLOBAL MARKETPLACE

CHAPTER 23

THE GLOBAL MARKET
MORE PROFITS, LESS EMPLOYMENT, NEVER-ENDING COMPETITION

American companies once dominated the world - or at least they seemed to until recently. In fact it wasn't that long ago. Then they began to fall off the pinnacle. Some of the falls were dramatic and quite public. The Chrysler Corporation went broke and had to be rescued with a government loan in 1979. Despite Chrysler's problems, Americans still had confidence in the superiority of their system over that of foreign competitors and they still took pride in their manufacturing capabilities - even as they resented the companies which did well. (Chrysler's failure, from that perspective, didn't prove that American industry was in trouble, it was more an object lesson to a managerial class which had became arrogant and complacent.) If Americans resented the success of American corporations, they also found reassurance in the job security that success provided. That confidence began to erode in the 1980s and 1990s. Familiar names such as Sears, AT&T, Xerox, and Eastman Kodak laid off workers, not just in small groups, but in large numbers and not just for a short time, but permanently. People began to wonder if it was more than a temporary thing. Did the layoffs signal more than just business slowdown? or were they something even more serious - an industrial decline?

Jeffrey Madrick, in his book, *The End of Affluence*, identifies 1973 as the year in which the American economy began to slow down. He argues that current economic problems can be traced to the slowdown in the rate of growth. Where the average annual rate of growth had been 3.4 percent before 1973, it fell to 2.3 percent after that. He argues that that slowdown in growth is the underlying cause of many of the current economic problems in the U.S.. While using the term "decline," Madrick labels the phenomenon of slow growth America's "economic dilemma," a less ominous sounding term.[1] Other authors provide support for the idea that something occurred in 1973, or at least in the early 1970s.[2] Real wages and income levels peaked in 1973 and would not reach the same level until the late 1980s.[3] Did something actually happen in 1973 or was 1973 just the year the changes were noticed? There was the Arab oil embargo.

In October 1973 Arab oil producers placed an embargo on oil shipments to the U.S. and Europe in retaliation for support of Israel. It was ended in March 1974. If it caused problems, they should have disappeared once it was over. Yet the American economy did not quickly recover. Factory output fell 10 percent in 1974. The Consumer Price Index had increased 12 percent by September 1974 over the previous year and unemployment in November 1974 was 6.5 percent.[4] Did the embargo fundamentally change something about the American economy? - or, just as frightening, was the American economy so close to the edge in 1973 that the smallest economic event would prove enough to send it over the precipice to economic ruin?

Today, with globalization in full swing, some question the very fact of decline. In fact there are conflicting signals. The Dow-Jones average keeps going up at a time when many are warning that the sales price of stock is far above its actual value. Firms are showing profits when massive layoffs are occurring. If unemployment has remained fairly low, those who have found work complain about lower wages and salaries. Even optimists will concede that many have had problems adjusting to the new economy and that the globalization of the market has been hard on both American workers and companies. They counter with the argument that U.S. companies had become complacent and that competition has forced them to become leaner and more productive. Americans have always loved to compete anyway. Those who take that position would also question the use of such terms as decline to describe recent trends. Even if there is a downward trend, how does that trend turn into a decline?

Decline, historically, has meant something more ominous than a simple downturn. Whether recent economic changes indicate a decline on a scale equal to that experienced by the Roman Empire, and whether that decline is permanent, there does seem to have been a transformation of the American economy. When did the American economy begin to decline? - probably sometime in the 1970s - probably in 1973. The exact date may never be known and may or may not be important. If 1973 marks a turning point, it is not because of some specific event, such as the oil embargo. It is more likely that 1973 was simply the time when changes in the economy began to be reflected in economic statistics.

GLOBALIZATION

Globalization has been defined as the worldwide integration of economic systems. One of the more obvious changes associated with globalization has been termed the global shift of industry - the worldwide relocation of industrial activities and production that began in the 1970s.[5] In one sense globalization is a little overblown. Merchants from different countries after all have been involved in exporting and importing since ancient times. Is globalization just a new name for that trade? - a label given to explain a new awareness of the outside world.   Or is it something associated with the communications revolution and the ability to communicate over the Internet?

Globalization is partly hype - a new name for traditional world market operations, enhanced perhaps by sophisticated, electronic systems - partly substance. There are differences between the old world market and the global one. In one sense, the economic rules which used to apply within a single country have been extended to the world market. Workers in the coal fields and steel mills of America found that their unemployed neighbors were their competitors in the job market in the 1800s. Now the same battle is taking place, but on a worldwide scale. Where before corporations could threaten to hire people locally or from across the country, now they can threaten to move entire manufacturing operations to foreign countries or outsource specific production. Nor is the battle only between companies and their workers. It now takes place between companies and governments, particularly in the realm of taxes. Corporations have not only pitted American cities or states against each other in an attempt to gain favorable tax status, they have also forced countries to compete against each other. Cleveland is no longer competing against Nashville or St. Louis, but against Paris, London, Singapore, and Glasgow.

Globalization, in its broadest sense, is a global awareness of worldwide opportunities. In its more technical sense it involves multinational corporations. A local importer or exporter may deal in the global market, but cannot have the economic resources or influence which true globalization requires. Leaders in the global marketplace do more than just import or export. Most are involved in actual manufacturing or other activities in more than one country. McDonald's hamburgers, for example, has locations worldwide. That may be the key distinction between a small firm which imports goods and the active participants. Active participants conduct operations in foreign countries.

Advances in telecommunications technology and computerization might be considered as trends apart from globalization. Yet, while separate they seem to be an integral part of the change. Telecommunications provide instant information from around the world. Advances in personal computers have allowed that information to be, not just recorded, but analyzed, seemingly instantaneously. While the physical movement of facilities has attracted much of the recent attention, the movement of money between countries has also been on the increase. In 1994 the total amount of foreign direct investment (FDI), i.e., investment in companies in other countries, was $204 billion.[6]

OVERPRODUCTION AND WAGE COMPETITION

Globalization for the world has meant increased competition, which is partly to blame for the loss of confidence in America's economic abilities. To Americans, the most obvious signs of economic problems are the increasing number of layoffs and a growing sense of job insecurity. If layoffs and unemployed workers have grabbed most of the headlines, workers are not the only victims. Businesses as well, are struggling to be competitive, and are falling victim in ever greater numbers. Conventional wisdom holds that if competition is the problem, then even more competition must be the solution.

While competition may be the cause of many economic problems, it may not be the solution. In fact it may make things worse. William Greider in his book *One World, Ready or Not*, deals with the twin problems of corporate downsizing and unemployment. He has identified two problems associated with globalization. The first problem, the pressure to reduce wages (or to lay off workers), is caused by competition and the need to reduce costs. The immediate solution, the ability to reduce wages, is related to what he calls arbitrage. Arbitrage is the business practice of shopping for the cheapest market in which to buy something. In this case that market happens to be labor. Globalization has allowed companies to shop for the cheapest market anywhere in the world. The second problem is overproduction - producing more than the market can absorb.[7] According to his theory, while companies are producing more in hopes of increasing market share and profits, the opposite is occurring. Markets are becoming saturated and prices are going down, resulting in a decline in profits. In some ways overproduction is the single cause of falling wages and falling prices because it exerts a downward pressure on both wages and prices. To compete in the market, they must keep prices down and to keep prices down they must cut costs, which forces them to reduce wages.[8]

Greider also identifies the dilemma facing both companies and workers in the new competitive arena: either do whatever it takes to compete in the market or get out of the market altogether. Competition will require cost-cutting and job elimination, yet refusing to compete does not guarantee a different outcome. Increased production not only contributes to oversupply and falling prices, fatal to business, but also reduces the need for workers, destructive of employment. While new technology has tended to increase productivity, it has also reduced the number of workers needed to manufacture products. If a company does upgrade its equipment, the upgrades are likely to involve the latest automated technology, which can function well with minimal human input. The dilemma is that, if a company chooses not to invest in the equipment, its competitors will be able to produce the same product at a cheaper price. The result is that it will lose out on orders.[9]

Streamlining production and expanding capacity go hand-in-hand with the desire to compete - a proven formula for success. Why does this belief remain strong, even in the face of market saturation? It is probably found in the deeply-rooted belief in American know-how, the faith that Yankee ingenuity will come to the rescue. There is an economic assumption that a product can be developed which is so much better, in terms of quality, and so much cheaper, in terms of price, that no product and no foreign company can hope to compete against it. In practical terms this means that American companies have joined the race to develop new manufacturing technologies.

There are two problems with this assumption. The first relates to the probability that an overwhelming advantage can be secured in any technology. If globalization has meant increased competition, it has also brought increased access to information. Companies are not only quick to find out about new information, they are quick to implement it. Industrial espionage has replaced conventional spying. The second problem relates to the assumption itself, which is that lack of competitiveness is a technical problem, which can be solved by applying more energy to development. Germany, in 1936, was convinced that there was a technical solution to its shortage of fuel, yet found itself no closer to an answer after four years of effort. It may also be asked whether competitive problems represent a single problem which can be solved by a single technology. Would a revolutionary manufacturing process help to solve transportation problems, for example?

The world auto industry was betting on better factories to win the competitive game. Between 1985 and 1995, it increased its factory capacity by 25 percent, even though demand for autos during that time only increased by 20 percent. Eventually such planning was overtaken by the realities of the market. Between 1980 and 1994, 32 car and truck assembly plants in North America were shut down and 180,000 jobs eliminated. Plants in Europe were closed as well. Mercedes laid off 25,000 workers and Volkswagen another 28,000. Even in Japan automakers had to close plants in 1995, where overcapacity was estimated at 50 percent.[10]

Belief in the invention of an ultimate product was only part of the logic behind overproduction. There was also the hope that a company might get the edge on the competition by underpricing everyone else. There was even the possibility of finding a totally unexploited market. Perhaps in the back of the marketing mind was the faint dream of the monopolist - keep early prices so low that competitors either keep out altogether or go broke trying to stay in the market - then raise prices. The problem in relying on such a strategy over the long-run is that it increases risk, particularly in markets where new businesses are willing to step in and compete even as old ones drop out. If the global market's ability to depress prices has been a new phenomenon, it has only been new to the manufacturing sector. The agricultural sector in America has long faced the same problem. If the goal of the individual farmer was to outproduce and outlast the competition, it often worked. Prices fell, more grain or corn was sold, and farms went under. Yet, as a financial strategy, it would never succeed in the long run. New farmers were willing to step in to replace those who failed, ensuring that production would remain high and prices low. Globalization might encourage the hope that competition was the answer, yet it provided no guarantees that the market would reward those who competed the hardest.

THE COMPETITION BEGINS

While Jeffrey Madrick has identified 1973 as a watershed year, American companies began experiencing difficulties before that. In the late 1960s they began to experience a decline in profitability. Some attribute this partly to increased wages and accompanying benefit costs (health and unemployment).[11] Problems caused by increased labor costs were compounded by increased oil prices, the first coming with the Arab oil embargo in 1973, the second coming with the Iranian embargo in 1979. Although the trend was observed by economists and business writers, it largely escaped public notice.

It was the mass layoffs, which began in the late 1970s, which began to attract public attention. While the numbers were shocking enough, it was also the names of the companies involved which began to make the public uneasy. General Motors, between 1976 and 1996, eliminated some 185,000 jobs. Between 1990 and 1995 Sears would reduce its work force by 50,000, AT&T by 123,000 and Eastman Kodak by 16,800.[12] Layoffs were only part of the problem. There was a growing public awareness that replacement work seemed to involve a fall in wages or salaries. In 1996 the percentage of those who moved to higher paying jobs following a layoff was only 35 percent. In 1971 the percentage had been closer to 100. Median wages have also declined by three percent since 1979.[13] While elected officials try to reassure people that the replacement jobs are good ones and not just jobs flipping hamburgers, such claims are greeted with skepticism.

If the layoffs were terrible news to those involved, the response of Wall Street was enthusiastic - stock prices of firms which cut jobs often went up in the wake of the downsizing announcements. Sears' stock increased 4 percent with the announcement of job cuts of 50,000 workers. It was one of the many contradictions related to the American economy. Another was that layoffs were occurring at a time when the economy was doing well. When large layoffs were occurring in the 1990s the country was said to be in an economic recovery. While workers were losing jobs companies were returning to profitability. There was also a seeming contradiction between the publicly announced layoffs and job availability. If Labor Department figures showed that 36 million jobs had been lost between 1979 and 1993, it also showed that there were 63 million added - a net gain of 27 million jobs.[14] There was also a basic contradiction between labor productivity, which declined, and technological advances which enabled fewer workers to physically produce more goods.

PRODUCTIVITY GAINS AND EMPLOYMENT LOSSES

In June 1812 authorities in England executed 10 men. Eight of the hangings were carried out in Manchester and two in Chester. This was followed, in January 1813, by the execution of 14 more individuals in York. The executions brought the Luddite Rebellion to an end. For fifteen months, from November 1811 until January 1813, the Luddites, (who supposedly followed a mythical leader named Ned Ludd), broke into factories and destroyed machinery. Their goal was to destroy the steam-driven textile looms which were taking jobs away from skilled wool-cloth finishers known as croppers.

Fully 100 years before Howard Scott would formulate his ideas about the ascendancy of machines and Technocracy, they had tried to warn of the dangers posed by technology. History treated them little better than the authorities of the time. They became symbols - not of foresight or progressive thinking - but of futility. Their cause was so hopeless that it would not even grant them the status of martyrdom. In the modern world they became symbolic of a hopeless struggle against progress. For all that, they were not necessarily wrong in their analysis. Machines were eliminating their jobs and reducing their pay. Five people in 1828 could do what it had taken 27 croppers to do in 1800. In the city of Leeds there were 1,733 croppers working in 1814. By the 1930s the number would fall to less than 100. Wages, which had been 36 to 40 shillings a week, fell to 10 to 14 shillings.[15] Howard Scott would make similar observations about factory output in the 1930s.

The ability of machinery to outperform the croppers meant, in economic terms, that their productivity was declining, relative to that of the steam-driven looms. Rather than destroying equipment, they would have been better off to concede that fight and seek work in some other activity. Machinery was taking over the cropper's job because it was, in a real sense, more productive. It could physically produce more finished wool than the cropper could. At the same time there is a definitional problem with productivity, because productivity is limited by the market, not just determined by the output capabilities of equipment. Under normal circumstances, it is defined as the amount of output produced per unit of input, which can be increased if a worker works harder or with additional machinery. Unfortunately when market forces come into play, productivity is no longer determined by production capabilities alone. What the Luddites and Howard Scott observed, was not a function captive to productivity. It was almost an independent phenomenon. Workers were being forced out of the labor market, not because machinery was more productive than they were. They were being forced out because the market could not accommodate that much productive activity.

Economists have tended to judge the U.S. economy in terms of growth. Because productivity is related to growth, there has been a tendency to judge increased productivity as "good," while falling productivity is considered "bad." Increased productivity has generally been helpful where overall industrial output is concerned, but its relationship to employment is somewhat more complex. Whether it helps employment seems to depend on whether there is unlimited market demand or has become saturated.

How much the market will accommodate employment may be understood if the market is seen as something tangible. Conceptually, it may be viewed as a large cube, 100 feet on each side, which can be divided into a million smaller cubes of one foot each. Each cube represents the market demand for a single unit of output. When labor productivity is low each worker can produce only one cube of output, but the entire cube will accommodate one million workers. If labor productivity is increased to the point where each worker can produce 10 cubes of output, the entire cube will accommodate 100,000 workers. If productivity is increased again and each worker can produce 100 cubes, the number that can be accommodated will be reduced to 10,000. With each productivity gain individual workers can carve out larger shares of the market faster, but only at the expense of employment for other workers. There is a time factor as well. Increases in productivity mean that market fragmentation occurs at a faster pace.

THE STEEL INDUSTRY - LOCATION CHOICES AND OVERPRODUCTION

The struggle to control labor costs is not new to business. Neither is the tendency to shop for the cheapest labor market. Globalization just expanded the geographical area in which the game could be played. Why did corporations suddenly begin to exploit the labor pools of Asia and Third World countries? There is almost the suggestion that American corporations were not even aware of the existence of workers outside the U.S. until the global marketplace emerged. Possibly labor arbitrage on a worldwide scale required satellite communications or a more educated populace in Third World countries. In fact the explanation is much simpler. Cheaper labor markets have only recently been exploited, not because they required a hi-tech communications breakthrough, but because there were basic transportation obstacles involved, as well as physical and capital requirements for factory location.

The ability to shop for labor depends on where production can be located. The steel industry provides one of the better examples of the problems involved. For many years iron and steel production demanded huge facilities and transportation systems which could handle heavy, bulky raw materials such as iron ore and coal. One of the reasons Pittsburgh survived for so long as a steel producing center was its location close to water and the costs involved in setting up facilities in other locations.

In 1901 the giant U.S. Steel Corporation was formed in a merger of 150 smaller corporations. Some 85 years late, in 1986, U.S. Steel would change its name to USX Corporation and would also close the Homestead steel plant. The name change was intended to signify a change in the nature of U.S. Steel's business. By 1986, steel accounted for only 25 percent of its revenues. If the name change signified a change in direction for the company, the shutdown of the Homestead plant symbolized the decline of an entire U.S. industry. It was certainly symbolic of the changing fortunes of labor and of the region around Pittsburgh.[16]

Homestead was gone. The place where 300 Pinkerton agents had tried to break a strike on July 6, 1892 using two floating barges - only to be confronted by workers armed with rifles, dynamite, and a single cannon. While seven Pinkertons were killed, as well as nine workers, the strike had been broken after the state militia had been called in. If the battle - and its final outcome - mirrored the history of the labor movement, Homestead seemed to symbolize the steel industry as well. It had been part of Pittsburgh's steel production and history almost from the start. Built in 1881, it had been acquired by Andrew Carnegie in 1883, eventually becoming the largest plant in the Monongahela Valley. If Homestead was gone, it was just one of many steel producing plants which were now history.[17]

The region around Pittsburgh had iron ore deposits when early settlers began arriving. If few would have guessed that its economy would revolve around iron, even fewer would have expected that an iron-based economy would survive for a hundred years - long after the iron ore had been depleted. The Monongahela Valley probably was more attractive to early settlers for its potential transport advantages - near the confluence of the Ohio, Allegheny, and Monongahela rivers. What Pittsburgh had, in terms of resources, was large quantities of coal and limestone. In fact, coal was probably the first major industry to develop, even supplying markets as far away as New Orleans. If iron ore was not its most abundant resource, the Pittsburgh region nevertheless began to develop into a metals center. Its first iron rolling mill would be located at McKeesport, south of Pittsburgh, in 1851.[18]

In 1875 Andrew Carnegie's Edgar Thomson Works, eight miles from Pittsburgh, began turning out steel, using two Bessemer furnaces. Steel production required a fuel which both burned intensely and was relatively free of impurities. Coke was produced by baking coal, and in Carnegie's time, the baking was done in beehive ovens. In 1889, Carnegie's firm would use some 10,000 beehive ovens to meet its factory coke requirements while controlling some 35,000 acres of coal land.[19]

Location is always a compromise based on competing costs or offsetting benefits.[20] That Carnegie's factories would have access to large coal and coke supplies, together with limestone, explains why steel production would remain in Pittsburgh. The exhaustion of iron ore deposits in the area suggests one reason why it should have moved. Pittsburgh remained the location choice for steel manufacturing, even though ore deposits seemed to move further away from the Monongahela Valley - iron ore had to be shipped, first from Missouri mines, then from mines in northern Michigan and Minnesota.[21] If Pittsburgh seemed disadvantaged by location as ore deposits were discovered farther west, that disadvantage was offset by the reduced costs of water transport. In addition, shortages were felt mostly in iron ore, and iron was just one of the many ingredients required in steelmaking. If transportation costs for iron ore were higher, those for coal and coke were much less. In 1900 steel production required 1.85 tons of coal and 1.83 tons of iron ore for each ton of finished steel. Chicago iron and steel producers saved on iron ore costs because of their proximity to the mines of Minnesota and northern Michigan, but paid more for coal and coke - the shipments came from the Pittsburgh region. The net transportation costs were thus lower for Pittsburgh - in the early part of the Twentieth Century. By 1960 the amount of coal for each ton of steel had dropped to 0.79 ton but the amount of iron ore had increased to 1.10 ton.[22] The relative shift in ingredient use may have explained the fact that Bethlehem Steel built the last U.S. integrated steel mill in Chicago rather than Pittsburgh in 1960.[23]

The Mesabi range of Minnesota, by 1902, had supplied 40 million tons of iron to the plants in Pittsburgh and Chicago.[24] If it had done nothing else, the discovery had shifted the geographical center of iron resources west. While the location formula for resources had changed - giving greater weight to transportation costs for iron - the formula for plant location had not. In that formula - the equation which weighs raw material costs against transport costs against investment costs - Pittsburgh was still the winner. The new discoveries may have weakened her while making Chicago competitive, but they had not destroyed her. Pittsburgh was "saved," in a sense, not by any transportation advantages, but by industrial inertia - it simply cost too much to invest in new steel plants. Rather than set up new sites at geographical locations which reflected more exactly the formula balance, companies upgraded old facilities. There was another alternative - invest in something other than steel. Investment in new steel facilities by U.S. companies declined between 1960 and 1980.[25]

In the larger battle for dominance of the world market, the formula was different. The elements of the equation - raw materials, transport, labor, and investment - remained the same, but the relative weight given the numbers was different. For a long time, the numbers favored the United States, even Pittsburgh. If Pittsburgh's claim on location had lost some ground with the Mesabi range, America's claim to leadership had been strengthened. By 1986, when US Steel changed its name and the Homestead plant closed, it was clear that the numbers had changed.

In 1986 the Monongahela Valley was the victim of two trends. Pittsburgh was no longer the location choice for steel production in the United States and America had lost its overwhelming dominance of the steel industry in the world. Between 1950 and 1986 Pittsburgh's steel industry suffered the loss of around 75,000 jobs. In the 12 years between 1974 and 1986, the American steel industry lost 337,552 jobs.[26] In 1980 the

United States' share of world steel production was only 14 percent, behind even the Japanese. Pittsburgh was the victim of the overall decline in steel demand suffered by the American industry as a whole. It was also the victim of new technology. Not only had a more efficient production technique, the basic oxygen furnace (BOF), been developed in Germany, but a much smaller minimill had been developed which could reprocess scrap into steel.[27] In reducing size and costs the minimill altered the equation once again. Reductions in facility size did not explain all the difficulties. Some of the new facilities in Asia have been immense. The Pohang plant in South Korea is the largest in the non-communist world, and Shanghai's No. 5 plant boasts a capacity of eight million tons a year.[28]

The minimills, in a sense, represented the more complex, technological reasons for Pittsburgh's decline. There was a more basic, resource-related reason for the decline of American steel. The Mesabi Range stopped producing high-grade ore in the 1950s. There were two practical effects. The first had to do with price. High-grade ore was available farther north in Canada, but development costs increased its price. It thus became cheaper to import high-grade ores from Australia or Brazil. Although the second effect was related to price, it also had an impact on location. In terms of worldwide production, the location equation began to shift toward Asia. Japan was able to import ore from Australia at half the price U.S. steelmakers paid to bring ore down from Canada. That shift could be seen in the production figures for steel. In 1946, the U.S. had produced 54.1 percent of the world's steel. The percentage fell to 20.1 percent in 1970, to 14 percent in 1980, and to 11.8 percent in 1984. In addition imports made up a growing percentage of the U.S. domestic market - 18 percent in 1971.[29]

There were other market-related forces at work as well. At a time when iron prices were going up, the market for steel was going down. The auto industry began to turn to substitute products such as aluminum, plastics, and ceramics. Between 1976 and 1986, steel demand by the auto industry dropped by 11 million tons.[30] Although the steel content had been reduced, the auto makers were unable to benefit from cost savings. Many of the new synthetics were petroleum-based and if the price of oil would stabilize following the embargo, that stabilization would not bring prices down. Plastic prices would increase after 1973. By 1980 they were double what they had been in 1973. (The increase in plastic prices made the switch to alternative products seem a mistake. Yet going back to steel would not necessarily have saved costs - steel and metal prices also doubled in price during the same period.)[31]

In some ways the movement toward petroleum-based products and away from steel represented a transformation of the resource base of the economy. Oil had been something of a demand constant, but its nature had changed over time - from illumination to heating to transportation. Between 1850 and 1900, kerosene had been the primary product and the desire for artificial light the driving force. Edison's invention of the electric light bulb would lessen demand for kerosene as a light source, but the invention of the automobile would resurrect the demand for oil by creating a market for gasoline. Steel would undergo a similar transformation. The miles of railroad track laid in the late

1800s had ensured a demand for steel rails. If transportation trends began to favor road transport, the steel industry found that there was still a demand for steel in automobiles. Now the steel industry became the victim of still another change in demand. If transportation still favored the automobile and there was a need for a structurally strong auto body, steel was not the only material available to fill that need.

The loss of the Mesabi's high-grade ores in the 1950s and the auto industry's switch to plastics in the 1970s were two phenomena which changed the operating environment for American steel producers. Lean production was another. The Toyota Motor Co. began experimenting with a production technique known as lean production or flexible manufacturing technology following World War II.[32] Lean production involved an attempt to reduce times in auto assembly, for example in die changing, and to eliminate raw materials waste in mass production. "Just-in-time" or JIT, was one of the methods employed, a technique which reduced inventories, relying instead on deliveries of materials only as needed.[33] Lean production was one of the reasons U.S. auto makers had had difficulty competing with the Japanese, a contributing factor in the Chrysler insolvency in 1979.

The success of the Japanese with lean production techniques led to a re-evaluation of American production systems. Many in business felt that American companies were losing out to foreign competitors because they were not interested in the quality of their products. There was an emphasis on total quality management(TQM), which involved focusing a company's efforts on improving the quality of products.[34] Various terms were used to describe specific aspects of a TQM program. "Zero defects" was one such term, meaning that a production process should be designed to eliminate all defects. Another concept was that of employee empowerment, which was intended to give employees greater responsibility and encouraging greater participation by employees in decisions.[35]

An inattention to quality was not seen as the primary cause of the downfall of the steel industry. Nevertheless, in the post-mortem analysis there was a temptation to cite the steel industry as another example of America's decline in manufacturing. There was some evidence that U.S. steelmakers focused less on quality in the 1960s and 1970s, that they rated supervisors on the quantity of steel output, and that customers began to complain about the products they were receiving. The steel industry similarly could be criticized for failing to empower employees. The employees of one plant of the National Steel Company had suggested cost improvements which saved $10.6 million in 1986 alone.[36] The commitment to empowerment had come, but it had come too late.

If the market for steel products after 1960 was more and more determined by price, American manufacturers were more and more disadvantaged by contractual obligations. Managers were quick to point to the high cost of worker benefits as a major obstacle to cost cutting. In 1982 U.S. workers were paid around $22 an hour (wages and benefits), Japanese workers were paid $11, and Korean workers $2.[37] If management blamed the unions for saddling them with such obligations, it was often silent about the costs associated with its mistakes. The decision to develop Canadian ore deposits and to modify plants to process the lower-grade Mesabi Range ore was made by management.

It was finally recognized that the cost of the Canadian and Mesabi Range mines was too high in the 1980s and they were shut down. The costs did not suddenly end, for the companies now had to pay off the loans they had taken to finance the ventures.[38]

The economic problems after 1960 were the problems which now plague the global economy, namely oversupply and overcapacity. There were three factors which would lead to oversupply in steel between 1960 and 1980. First, foreign producers were now tempted to enter the market in greater numbers. The Second World War had destroyed the industrial infrastructure of Europe and Japan and by 1960 both regions were beginning to recover. Second, the new market was being driven more and more by prices, and the productivity level of the new producers gave them an edge. The Mesabi Range's high-grade iron ore had long given the American firms an advantage, if only in price. Now that was gone. Foreign firms could offer steel at a lower price than American firms. While European and Japanese industry had been crippled in 1945, that very destructiveness of the war gave them one unique advantage. When they did rebuild, they invested in newer technology, such as the basic oxygen furnace (BOF). Labor costs were lower because productivity was higher and fewer workers were needed. Third, a strategy driven primarily by prices encouraged maximum output by all firms. Like farming, the hope in steel was that an individual firm might capture a large enough share of the market if it kept producing. If Pittsburgh and Chicago lacked the efficiency of European or Japanese producers they were still capable of turning out large quantities of steel. Older firms believed that they could produce their way to profitability, while newer firms were encouraged their relatively lower production costs.

Unaccustomed to any competition, American firms were startled by the success of the Japanese. Because firms, such as Toyota, had suddenly developed a reputation for quality in manufactured goods, there was the suspicion that their "secret" involved some high-tech gadgetry. Find out what the Japanese had done and America would once again become the world's leader in competition. The Japanese system was analyzed, quantified and adopted. The assumption was that the formula for success was actually a formula, something which could be designed like a machine.

If Americans were convinced that the Japanese had found some long lost secret, Japanese steel firms by 1986 must have wondered whether that secret was slipping away. For 11 years, starting in 1975, they had been forced to close down plants and lay off workers - the number of steelworkers in Japan had been reduced by 23 percent. The Japanese looked successful only by comparison with the U.S., which cut steel employment by 48 percent - a drop of 265,000 jobs. Japan may have gained some advantage when it combined German BOF technology with Japanese innovations, or when it bought low-cost Australian iron ore. Yet there were indications that the difference between success or failure was not the competitive advantage provided by a secret technology. The enemy was overproduction, not a specific country, such as Japan, or company. Other steel producing countries had been forced to cut back. West Germany had cut its steel work force by 32 percent in the same period while France had reduced its force by 41 percent.[39] Modern facilities began to emerge in Brazil, South Korea,

Taiwan, Mexico, and Argentina. They used the latest technology, to be sure, but their competitive advantage lay in offering steel at low prices.

At the turn of the century American steel producers were justifiably proud of the their abilities to turn out steel. In 1900 the United States had produced 11,227,000 tons of raw steel. In 1913 the figure had grown to 31,301,000.[40] It was really just the beginning. By 1985 producers worldwide supplied almost 100 million tons. What they actually produced and what they could have produced were two different things. If they only produced 100 million tons in 1985, they had the ability to produce three times that amount. In 1986 excess capacity worldwide was 200 million tons. In 1986, the steel industry's problem had become overcapacity, not production.[41]

In 1950 U.S. steel mills had a capacity of 100 million tons. By 1960 they had increased capacity to 148 million tons. In addition, 35 of the 48 million tons consisted of open hearth technology, which, because of its inefficiency, would need to be replaced later by BOF technology. The failure to install BOF technology early cost double. First, expenditures for open hearth operations had been wasted - the cost of BOFs included the unnecessary cost of the open heart operations. Second, when BOFs were purchased, the steelmakers had to pay additional amounts in interest on loans. In 1980 capacity had reached 154 million tons. The growth in capacity had been fueled by optimistic projections from both government and industry analysts.[42]

It was the 1982 Recession which dampened the optimism. Steel mills operated at less than 50 percent capacity.[43] In 1983 capacity had been reduced to 151 tons. By 1987 it was down to 112 million tons, although even that figure represented some 20 million tons of overcapacity. World overcapacity led to a price war between 1983 and 1985. The problem was that the more efficient new producers could afford to make cuts, the American producers could not. Imported steel, by 1985, made up 25.2 percent of the market. U.S. steel producers sought government help in the form of tariffs and quotas, but these measures proved ineffective.[44] While U.S. producers were battling foreign producers for market share, that battle was part of the larger war against the decline in the use of steel. Steel output for the Western countries (the U.S., Western Europe, and Japan), which had been 494 million metric tons in 1974, was 368 million metric tons in 1986.[45]

Looking back from 1986, the steel industry had provided a number of lessons in a remarkably short period of time. One lesson was the general difficulty of developing a competitive strategy in the face of a saturated market. Another lesson was the relative speed with which technology could change the location equation. If American producers had been able to rely on the daunting capital and investment requirements to shield them from competition, they discovered that new developments could quickly eliminate that advantage. There were lessons about how costly mistakes could be. The industry spent money on old open hearth technology, then spent still more replacing it with BOF technology. It even provided an example of how the economic theory of comparative advantage works in the real world. Investors, who watched profits fall, concluded that American steel was losing whatever advantage it had held in productivity and began to look for other opportunities. Even companies, such as U.S. Steel, which had formed the core of the industry, began diversifying.

THE TECHNOLOGICAL REVOLUTION IN INDUSTRIAL PRODUCTION

In 1980 Japanese auto makers accounted for 30 percent of world auto production.[46] They had only been in the auto business for some 25 years, beginning around 1955, yet they had made serious inroads, even in the American domestic market. The Chrysler Corporation had suffered the most damage, avoiding bankruptcy only with a government-guaranteed loan in 1979. American auto workers had taken a terrible beating as well. Between 1979 and 1982 some 250,000 jobs were lost in the auto industry.[47]

There were two reasons the Japanese were successful. The first was that they were better able to read the American market for cars. Whether the Big Three auto makers actually believed that Americans bought cars solely for their prestige value, there was a sense among consumers that cars weren't built as well as they had been and that the auto makers routinely ignored complaints when things went wrong. The Japanese saw a market opportunity for a well-built car and one that was affordable. The second reason was that they had developed a superior method of producing cars. Not only did their factory assembly methods provide the quality Americans were seeking, they were able to do it at a lower cost. The production method used by the Japanese was given the name flexible manufacturing or lean production.[48] Their assembly lines were able to turn out large numbers of cars, implying that lean production was nothing more than an improved form of mass production. In other ways lean production differed from mass production to that time.

Mass production, as its name implied, involved the manufacture of large quantities of a product. While the concept was easy to understand, implementation involved a fairly sophisticated level of technology. Henry Ford took several years to perfect his system for manufacturing cars. One of its advantages comes from economies of scale, the idea that the cost of producing a single unit is reduced as more units are produced.[49] The technical obstacle to mass production was the inability to turn out large numbers of standardized parts in a relatively short period of time. The craftsman of the Nineteenth Century could create parts which could be assembled, but only one part at a time and not at a particularly fast rate. The breakthrough for mass production was when machine tools could accurately cut hardened steel and turn out uniform parts. Apart from the development of a method of producing standardized parts, Ford's contribution was determining the proper speed of the assembly line.[50]

Ford's system represented a tremendous advance over prior production methods, but it had its shortcomings. While standardization had reduced the differences in parts from different production runs, it did not eliminate all defects and it did not allow for early discovery of problems. Defects might not be discovered until the auto had gone through the assembly line and the cost to correct them had been increased. One of the technical problems for Ford's early plants was the difficulty and time involved in changing dies. As a result the system was rigid and encouraged long production runs.

There was a reluctance to alter production quotas because of the time and costs involved in any such changes. The advantage of economies of scale was that costs could be allocated among the large number of units produced. The key to profitability however, lay not simply in the ability to produce mass quantities, but in the ability to sell what had been produced. Producing more cars than the market would buy could cost more than any savings gained from cheaper parts.

Lean production did not attempt to do away with the benefits provided by economies of scale. Instead, its goal was to correct some of the weaknesses resulting from the rigid nature of mass production. The mass production answer to defective parts was to order large quantities of raw materials and to manufacture more parts than would be needed in assembly. Lean production's answer was to order smaller quantities of raw materials and to produce just enough parts to meet assembly needs. The defects which did occur were immediately corrected. The rigidity of mass production was partly caused by the time and expense of changing dies. Lean production's answer was to design a press which shortened the time in which dies could be changed. The Japanese added another innovation when they reduced the total number of die presses required at individual plants. This lowered investment costs.[51] Flexible manufacturing systems (FMS) were another innovative development. If the mass production system took advantage of economies of scale, its limitation was that it could only produce a single product or product line. FMS can produce multiple products with one system, have the added advantage of being able to change product output without significantly increasing unit costs.[52]

The invention of the silicon chip in 1958-1959 resulted in a technological revolution in computer technology. It significantly changed everything dealing with numbers. If the microprocessor's most dramatic impact would be seen in personal computer technology, its real legacy may be its impact on the manufacturing process. For all that computers can do however, manufacturing is still bound to the earth. Fac-tories can produce more goods with greater precision because of computers, but they cannot avoid the rules of physics. Computers will not eliminate the need for raw ma-terials or a physical location for a factory. They cannot yet totally eliminate labor costs, even as they can calculate differences in wages in Detroit or Singapore. That being said, computers did allow for a reduction in factory size, even if they could not eliminate the need for factories.

Die press modifications represented a specialized area of technology although that did not make its contribution insignificant, since auto manufacturing was an important component of many economies. However technological developments were not limited to auto manufacturing. Between 1960 and 1980 manufacturing technology across a wide spectrum saw advances. There were really two trends taking place. The first was a general improvement in manufacturing technology. Precision equipment became smaller, more accurate, and able to perform additional functions. The second trend was the increasing use of robots, accompanied by an improving robot technology.

Both trends were helped by the microprocessor, which allowed manufacturing directions to be programmed into equipment. The advantage for foreign competitors was not that computer-guided robots could perform tasks better than people, (although they could in many cases). The major advantage was that they could be programmed to perform identical tasks anywhere in the world.[53] If the internal workings of the new manufacturing tools had become more complex with computer technology, the equipment had become simpler to operate. Where Third World workers were perceived as being unskilled, the new equipment eliminated the need for highly skilled workers.

The ability to manufacture virtually anywhere in the world was not without its costs. If the Japanese were able to buy high-grade ore from Australia, they had to ship it to Japan to be refined and, if the final product was a car, had to ship it again to the U.S. for its final sale. What lowered shipping costs in water travel was the development of superfreighters following World War II. There were innovations which also made transport operations more efficient, containerization, for example.[54] In addition to enlarged capacity represented by the new freighters, producers had the advantage of an abundant supply of fuel, which meant fuel costs were minimized.

The advances in automated manufacturing and transportation and the modernization of Japanese and European plants suggests that it was superior technology which weakened American industry. That was partly true. Yet the mode of attack may not have been the frontal assault represented by European and Japanese manufacturers. It was true that, when they finally recovered from the war, they had more modern equipment and were the most obvious rivals. Yet, if American producers were in danger of being overwhelmed, the attack was being made across a broad front. The technological problem was that, even as technology became more advanced, it was becoming cheaper and more dispersed. The real problem with technology was that it encouraged more competitors to enter the game, not that it provided a single company or country with a competitive edge.

THE ROLE OF RESOURCES

Overproduction and overcapacity are two ways of saying that the market has become saturated and that demand has fallen. Overall demand may remain constant even as individual firms find demand for their particular product dropping off. Whether oversupply is just another word for competition, it does create a more competitive environment. If they want to remain in the market, they will be forced to lower prices, under normal circumstances. If they wish to remain profitable, lowering prices will force them to cut costs. Workers, in such an environment, find that the demand for labor is related more to the demand for their company's product and their willingness to work for less. In the 1960s American producers had to confront an increasingly saturated market, brought on by a growing number of producers and technologies which increased the productive capabilities of all firms. Workers had to cope with the fact that those new technologies reduced the need for workers. This was occurring at a time when basic resources, such as iron ore and petroleum, were becoming scarce or less available to American firms.

The resource question, in the context of this book, is whether resources actually were becoming scarce in the United States. The evidence presented in the discussion of the steel and auto industries suggests that at least some resources were. High-grade iron ore, the industry preference, was disappearing in the U.S., as was oil. There is a question which relates to technology in this context. If scarcity was contributing to profitability problems for U.S. firms what was the nature of the scarcity? Was the crucial scarcity that of the traditional raw materials, such as iron and oil, or was it a scarcity of technology? It might be argued, for example, that what prevented European steelmakers from being competitive prior to 1960 was not the lack of high-grade Mesabi iron ore, but the lack of a technological alternative to Pittsburgh's open hearth furnaces. The crucial resource was thus technology. The counter-argument is that the Mesabi iron ore provided such an ideal ingredient for steel that whatever technological advances were made were never sufficient to offset the cost advantages provided by the ore. The crucial resource was thus raw material.

Where general manufacturing is involved the question of technology wealth versus raw material wealth is not as clear cut. Steelmaking technology is a very specialized area of manufacture. While it may have spread worldwide, it cannot escape its dependence on specific ingredients. An argument can be made that, in the general area of technological resources, whatever advantage U.S. manufacturers had had in manufacturing technology was lost as that technology was dispersed. It might be said that American producers once held a monopoly on technological resources. Once other countries began adopting it the amount held by U.S. firms was diluted. Technological resources were not really scarce, but compared to the rest of the world, they were no longer abundant either. The problem with proving or disproving the availability of technological resources is that they are difficult to quantify and are closely bound to the resources they interact with.

Whether technological resources have become scarce, even in relative terms, is difficult to determine. Raw material resources clearly have. Resources, such as oil, may have received more attention because of a noticeable or spectacular recent decline, but a comparative decline may have started as long ago as 1940, when U.S. industrial dominance was coming to an end. A major problem, from the resource standpoint, was that manufacturing dominance was not based on anything other than natural resources. During the rise of the U.S. as an industrial power between 1890 and 1940, the major characteristic of U.S. exports was their raw material component, as opposed to some special labor skill or capital ingredient.[55]

CONCLUSION

This chapter has looked at problems the U.S. economy has experienced with profitability and employment in the context of the global market. The discussion has tried to link recent economic problems with the question of resource availability. The problem is an important one, although it is not central to this book's theme. This book's hypothesis deals with the larger question of the relationship between resource availability and governmental development. There are indications that, apart from the role resources play in government, resource availability also plays a strong role in economic development.

The Achilles' heel of the global economy is overproduction. Companies, in entering the world market, have committed themselves to an endless world of competition, which demands price cuts, investment in technology, downsizing, layoffs and cutbacks. If technology has played a role in global manufacturing and wage arbitrage, it is not the only villain. The evidence suggests that resources and scarcity have played a role as well. Resources may have begun to decline as early as 1940 and began to be noticeably short during the 1950s and 1960s. Signs of economic difficulties began to appear shortly after that. It was not a sudden or dramatic happening - but crucial resources did not disappear overnight either.

The global economy has presented one seeming paradox. Even as it becomes more competitive, the market has signalled to many that demand is strong. While workers endure massive layoffs and many companies fail, the market still seems to encourage others to enter. There has been a tendency to explain the arrival of new economies, such as the city-state of Singapore, in terms of computers, telecommunications, and the spread of the capitalist spirit. Computers and high-technology played their part, but at the heart of the changes was a more basic resource shift which moved resources away from the U.S., and caused a realignment of prices and profits. In one sense it was an example of how market forces efficiently allocate resources. If, in the context of the U.S., recent changes have been an indication of economic decline, they are in the larger context more a symptom of the migration of resources.

CHAPTER 24

THE NEW WORLD ECONOMIC ORDER

In 1099 A.D., a contingent of crusaders battered down the gates to the city of Jerusalem and hacked their way to the city center. It was the triumphant end of the First Crusade. Pope Urban II had electrified the European world in 1096 with his call to all men of arms to rescue the city from the Infidel. Accustomed to fighting among themselves for feudal domains, the Pope's idea of some-greater-than-life, all-consuming purpose, clearly struck a chord, which probably surprised even Urban. Yet the response suggests a deeply-felt human need for some extraordinary goal, a purpose which transcends life itself.

The capture of Jerusalem, while marking the end of the First Crusade, proved an ephemeral victory. The city would be lost in 1187 and, despite several new crusades, would not be recaptured. However, the Catholic Church had not ended its wars with the Moslem world. It would score a decisive victory, using Spanish galleys, against a Turkish navy at Lepanto in 1571. Lepanto is barely remembered today, while the crusades are remembered more for the idea of a grand undertaking, than for the specifics of the campaigns. Even Spain, which had managed the victory at Lepanto, was more interested in the New World than in the Mediterranean. History and economics had moved on.

When Russia exploded its first atomic bomb in 1949, what had been largely a war of words and ideas threatened to become something else. The West had clearly been irked by the communist takeover of Russia in 1917. What was even more irritating about the communists was the fact that the more they failed the stronger their hold on power became. With Stalin in possession of the bomb, the fight against communism took on a greater urgency. The Soviet Union was no longer just an example of bad government and failure, it was something diabolically evil. It was now the type of idea which could inspire a crusade.

Does globalization and the triumph of markets signify the victorious end of a modern-day crusade? - and if it does, what is the nature of the victory?[1] Given the collapse of the Soviet Union, globalization suggests victory on an unprecedented scale. Not only has democracy triumphed over communism but the free market has been vindicated in the economic realm. Yet, is its significance the fact that victory has been achieved, or like the Crusades, is its real meaning found in participation? It may not even be possible to judge the significance of any event at the time of its occurrence. The overwhelming victories at Jerusalem and Lepanto, so significant in 1099 and 1571, faded with time.

If the defeat of communism was welcomed in the West, it seemed to bring little real satisfaction. Perhaps that was partly due to the lack of a conclusive final battle. Communism had gone out with a whimper. Tearing down the Berlin Wall had been the leading news story on the day it happened, but it was not the anticipated nuclear Armageddon many had predicted. In addition, American workers were worried about their own economic futures. If the collapse of communism represented one less threat to them, that threat had now been replaced by the immediate threat of lay-offs and unemployment.

Victory had both advantages and disadvantages. On the plus side, the collapse of the Soviet Union provided market advocates with absolute proof of the market's superiority. The free enterprise system had been totally vindicated. On the minus side, they had lost the perfect foil to any criticism of the market. The Soviet Union had served as the ultimate example of bad economic policy. If capitalism had its faults, the communist alternative was clearly much worse. With communism discredited and capitalism becoming the only game in town, the free market would have to argue its case on the merits.

When the free market has been criticized, the attack has generally been along moral lines. Capitalism, in its desire for material rewards and profits, treated workers badly and was indifferent to the problems of the poor. While such charges were not insignificant, they were more easily dismissed since they were not based on economics. At the same time, the evidence made the economic logic of capitalism seem unassailable. The productive capacity and economic output of the capitalist countries was all the proof needed, and if that wasn't sufficient, one only had to look at Russia. Yet, economic difficulties which suggested underlying problems were often rationalized away - which meant that they were excused without being explained. The job losses which occurred in a depression or recession were just part of a business cycle, something that came with the territory in any market economy.

Depending on how the pie is sliced, historic evidence suggests that the market is inherently weak in six areas. (Six is an arbitrary number since the categories overlap somewhat.) First, agricultural production, for all societies, has shown signs of a continuing economic weakness. Second, labor is vulnerable because of its peculiar relationship to the market. If the market seemingly invites labor in, i.e., into the market, by providing jobs, it also exerts pressure to force labor out (of the market). While providing jobs, it exerts continuing downward pressure on labor costs. Third, although it is claimed that the market is the most efficient method of allocating scarce resources, (at least compared to centrally planned economies), it is not clear that individual components within the market system exhibit the same level of efficiency. The technological side of the market can operate at a much more efficient level than the financial. That may help to explain why workers are losing out to automation in ever greater numbers. Fourth, the competitive environment itself may be contributing to a permanently unstable economic condition. Businesses attracted to the market find themselves subject to competitive pressures seemingly intended to drive them out. Like the laborer, they are attracted to a force intent on destroying them. Fifth, the competitive pressures to cut costs can undermine the demand which sustains markets, particularly where labor is concerned. The weakness stems from the interdependence of labor and the market. The business which views labor as nothing more than a cost which needs to be cut, forgets that the money which workers spend on purchases helps to sustain the demand which businesses need for survival. Sixth, demand is subject to distortion and is not always determined by cost. The market, in other words, is not always logical.

THE PROBLEM WITH AGRICULTURE

Agricultural production, for ancient Athens, represented a permanent source of economic instability. When it made the decision to import grain it all but conceded the production battle. Attica could not compete with the more fertile soils of Egypt, the Black Sea, and Italy. In one sense, importing was the only logical solution, since Athens was clearly not the most efficient grain producer. In another sense it meant that Athens had been unwilling to risk failure when faced with a really serious problem. There is a temptation to forgive economic shortcomings, where Athens is concerned. Given the success of Athenian democracy, there is almost the presumption that Athens was success-ful in everything it pursued, even in the economic arena. Yet, Athens did not really solve problems with its agricultural economy, it just avoided them. That it was unable to find a comprehensive economic solution was not fatal to democratic government. Democracy did not depend on economic perfection for success, only on a stable supply of grain. The crucial ingredient for democracy was calm, or the absence of violence, not a smoothly-operating economic machine.

Athenian problems with grain production had everything to do with conditions unique to Athens' soil, climate, and hilly terrain. Those conditions made it difficult for farmers to survive economically. Yet the cause of economic failure was something deeper - something apart from poor soil, something not limited to Athens, something not even confined to the fifth century, B.C. - it was something connected in some way to the mar-ket. Agriculture, some 25 centuries after Athenian farmers had conceded defeat, was still struggling. French peasants struggled in 1789, as did German peasants in the 1850s. Russian peasants in 1900 had not paid off their Emancipation debts after 39 years. Despite the advantages of mechanization and the quantum gains in agricultural productivity, American farmers had accumulated $9.4 billion in debt in 1925.[2] After 2,500 years the economic viability of agriculture still remained in doubt.

For all the solutions tried by governments, few tackled the central problem of economic viability. Even the programs put in place by the U.S. Congress in the 1930s did not address such problems. If they were generous packages, they were designed to avoid normal market operations. Farmers were paid to take land out of production and to plow crops under. Where market prices were too low, the government stepped in with price supports.

LABOR, TECHNOLOGICAL EFFICIENCY, AND COMPETITION

Globalization has made Americans more aware of just how fragile labor markets can be. They have always been fragile. Once workers have accepted the rules of the market, they are at its mercy. Although labor can blame its problems on a poor manage-ment "attitude," its greater problem is the nature of the competitive market, which exerts a continual downward pressure on all costs. The problem is not limited to the labor market. Competition is also behind the drive for technological efficiency as well as the more general struggle of businesses to survive. Following the Homestead strike in 1892 Henry Clay Frick broke the union by firing and blacklisting the leadership. If there was any sympathy for the workers, it came more from the fact that the battle at Homestead gave the struggle a human face. If anything gave Andrew Carnegie a black eye, it was the public exposure of the Pinkerton battle, not public outrage over industry practices. Workers, over the next 20 years would lose jobs to modernization, but such technological changes would attract little notice. Behind Carnegie's treatment of his workers and his drive to modernize was the need to reduce costs to stay competitive.

If terms such as downsizing, re-sizing, right sizing, and mass layoffs are new, the problem of unemployment is not. Nor is it a problem which can be laid at the feet of globalization or even the global market's drive for more automated and efficient production. The Athenians went through cycles of unemployment, as did the Romans. France, just before the Revolution, was plagued by terrible levels of unemployment, as was Germany in the early 1930s. In focusing on the current wave of downsizings, Americans have forgotten examples from their own past. The Great Depression was more severe and other depressions, such as that of 1893, were also long and difficult.

The problem for labor was not an Andrew Carnegie determined to cut wages or push for technological improvements. The problem was not necessarily one of saturated markets. At a more basic level, the problem was that labor was embracing a system which, by nature, was committed to the destruction of labor. The problem was competition. The problem was not that competition was present as a side-effect or an ideal which had been adopted to make the market better. The problem was that it was something central to the market system. If it seemed beneficial because it brought cheaper products or better service, competition also dictated the reduction of all costs. The Homestead strikers, if they hated Henry Clay Frick and Andrew Carnegie, maintained a basic belief in the market system. They were not out to destroy the steel mills at Homestead, but to participate in the market by producing steel. Their belief was that the market could be expanded enough to allow for fair treatment. However strongly labor disagreed with management, it nevertheless conferred a kind of legitimacy on management goals by its commitment to the market system.

Progress in the industrial sphere has always been associated with automation and improvements in machine output. While it is unlikely that human activity will be totally eliminated from production - someone will be needed to run equipment or to repair a broken piece of machinery - it can be minimized. With the introduction of robots and automated assembly lines, that need can be reduced to virtually zero. One person pushing a button can now complete what used to require thousands of workers to produce. While people desperately need jobs to survive in a market economy, the market has no real need for people - market demand can be satisfied without the use of human workers.

Tied to the problem of technology pushing aside labor is the problem of technology itself. One of the claims made on behalf of the free enterprise system is that it is more efficient than the central planning of communist economies when it comes to allocating scarce resources. Yet, there is an assumption that efficiency is a term which can be ap-

478

plied to an entire economic system or that any given economy is uniformly efficient across all its various components. In the agricultural sector alone, there are geographical differences in efficiency based on soil or climate. One of the areas where efficiency differences are pronounced is that between technology and economics. The downsizing and layoff problems which seem to be following the global market may have more to do with the attributes of technology than with the new competitive environment of world trade. However efficient free markets are on the financial side, technology has shown the capacity to quickly overtake economic forces. If the global ability to transfer funds anywhere in the world instantaneously suggests that markets now move more quickly, the market world moves almost at a snail's pace in comparison to technology. The increasing overcapacity in the auto industry and in many other industry segments suggests that technological innovations have now allowed manufacturers to easily saturate most markets.

LABOR AND MARKET INTERDEPENDENCE

If competitive pressures forced management to lay off workers or to cut wages, it would need to worry about new markets. The wages which represent just another cost to management inside a company, contribute to market demand in the wider market. Workers who lose their jobs or have their pay cut are unlikely to be making purchases. Weak demand cannot be blamed entirely on low wages, but the impact of this relationship should not be discounted entirely either. Whether weak demand is enough of an ongoing problem to be counted as a weakness, its cyclical nature at least implies an inherent problem. The fact that markets all too often require some artificial stimulus suggests that weakness in demand may be something more than a minor problem. Credit is not a recent innovation. It was being used by the Athenians in 600 B.C. - and by Americans in 1996 - to the tune of $1.4 trillion in consumer debt alone. Prior to the Great Crash of 1929, sellers had induced people to buy everything from stocks to cars using credit. Easy credit in 1836 had fueled the the boom market prior to the Panic of 1837. The French government at the time of the Revolution had become accustomed to financing endeavors with credit. Credit-driven markets, far from being the exception, have been the rule throughout history.

THE NEED FOR ENERGY AND EFFICIENCY

Man's battle with the forces of nature has been going on for such a long time that there is a reluctance to concede anything to the natural world. In fact, one of the few times this occurred was when Darwin's 'survival of the fittest' was used to justify John D. Rockefeller's practices at Standard Oil. The theory appealed to capitalists, not because they suddenly believed in nature, but because nature confirmed their faith in competition. (The problem with the "Rockefeller" interpretation of Darwin's theory is that it suggests that nature judges species solely on physical strength. Better to be the lion chasing the prey than the antelope failing to escape. Yet, Darwin's notion of survival was not intended to explain the survival of individuals, but of species, and survival did not always depend on strength. Fitness was often determined by speed or the ability to avoid a physical confrontation. Camouflage could be just as effective a defense mechanism as size or strength. If predators, such as bears or lions, have the advantage in strength over their prey, they are at a disadvantage when it comes to energy requirements. A hunting lifestyle demands energy. The elephant, zebra, water buffalo and antelope, have successfully combined large size with an energy-efficient diet. Even if they occasionally fall victim to predators, they may be better adapted for survival. In addition, the lion's survival depended as much on the continuing survival of its prey as on its physical strength and hunting skills. If the lion had to kill to survive on a daily basis, the equation for long-term success dictated that more prey survive than were eaten.) Survival of the fittest may be an appropriate metaphor for competition, but if nature is to serve as an example, other lessons may have more to offer. Ecology, for example, has broader implications for economics than survival of the fittest.

Ecology may seem to be a strange word to use in the context of economics, given the political nature of the environmental debate. It normally is defined as the relationship between living organisms and their environment. How is survival of the fittest related to ecology and how do both concepts apply to the world of economics? The biological world in which organisms live may be described as a hostile environment. Organisms must expend a great deal of energy just to survive. At the microscopic level, bacteria have to use chemical reactions to break down food and convert it into energy. Warm-blooded animals require more energy to maintain body temperature, in addition to the energy demands which come with greater mobility.

Energy demands in the wild come in many forms. If the battle between predator and prey represents the most spectacular, there is a more low-level struggle going on. Something as simple as nest construction for birds may present difficulties. Whether resistance involves gravity or the energy needed to gather nesting materials, a form of 'ecological inertia,' the natural resistance to change, sets in. Nest location may itself represent a compromise between safety and proximity to food and water. The ability to survive in desert regions depends, not only on adapting to the heat, but also on finding the energy to extract water. One of the ironies of the natural world is that bacteria seem to be the organisms most successful at solving the energy dilemma posed by a hostile environment. They solve "transport" problems by setting up house on whatever energy source they need for survival.

Economic activity has similar energy restrictions. Coal and iron may be buried under hundreds of feet of rock, requiring explosives and heavy equipment for removal. Once extracted, they have to be transported, requiring additional energy output. While energy requirements can be roughly measured in terms of fuel consumption, the market normally translates all activity into costs. Just as gravity and distance place energy demands on the nest-building bird, costs accumulate to discourage activity, a form of 'ecological inertia.' The complexity of the global economy suggests that the economic equivalent of the bacteria's solution exists only in the distant past. The tribal village or clan, by living close to its food sources, was able to exist at a relatively low economic "energy" level. Transport was not necessary where someone could eat berries as they were gathered. As civilizations developed however, energy requirements increased and solutions became more complex. The price of greater productivity was an increased demand for energy.

To the extent that the market's 'energy' needs mirror those of the natural world, the analogy is an accurate one. Just as more complex life forms will require more energy, more complex economies can be expected to have greater energy needs. However, the analogy begins to run into problems when large discrepancies are unexplained. One of those discrepancies involves the seeming ability of markets to defy economic odds. The world market in oil is an obvious example. Since it costs money to both extract and transport oil, it seems inconceivable that U.S. demand could support a market whose raw materials are located half-way around the world. In nature, serious imbalances are redressed over time. Perhaps the dinosaurs went extinct, not because of an asteroid strike, but because they had grown too large or too specialized in diet to adapt easily to changed conditions. In a world which favored the average and eliminated extremes, they were doomed.

An 'ecological' analogy may be important, if only to explain the existence of a market such as oil. It is not the first market where large distances separated resources from their primary market. The Spanish demand for New World gold is an example of an earlier market. Neither market made sense, when measured against an ecological standard. As if mining and basic transport problems weren't enough, Spain had to contend with hurricanes and buccaneers. The problem was not that either market was illogical. They were logical, although their logic was not found where it would be expected - among the costs. (A quick answer to the puzzle of the oil market is that oil flows freely to the U.S. market because its prices are competitively low.) The logic of an ecologically improbable market was related to demand, something independent of the underlying costs.

To suggest that the market for oil is somehow illogical, is to fly in the face of what we know about markets. If natural conditions make gold more difficult to extract; if the location of oil means an increase in the distance it is transported, such variables will be reflected in higher prices. All physical activity, no matter how difficult, can be valued. The more demanding the physical environment, the greater the costs involved. That assertion seems to hold true in the case of the U.S. steel industry, which found prices increasing after the 1950s because the Mesabi Range had been depleted and Canadian ore was more difficult to extract. The argument might end there, if prices themselves were solidly grounded in logic. Unfortunately, prices are not always an accurate reflection of economic costs. Gold has been known to increase in value, without regard to its extraction or transportation costs, whenever there is the threat of war. Even as the Dow approaches the magic 10000 figure, there are warnings about the over-valuation of stock. Similar warnings were taking place prior to 1929. When commodity prices fell, in the wake of the Crash, the decline had more to do with the then-current stock market conditions than with the underlying value of the companies involved. Andrew Jackson in 1836 issued his Specie Circular, requiring gold and silver payments for public lands, because the prices for land were not related to the land's underlying economic value.

The argument for price rationality does not improve with age, particularly if the Spanish period is examined. Gold was not unknown to the Indian civilizations. In fact, Aztec and Inca artisans were as familiar with gold's superior properties as their European counterparts. European and Indian rulers, as well as their goldsmiths, had independently come to view gold as a precious metal. Yet the Indians, while valuing gold, were puzzled by the extraordinary obsession with it. The Spaniards were not the only Europeans who prized gold. Early English settlers at Jamestown nearly starved to death because they chose to search for gold rather than to harvest crops. It was English buccaneers, such as Francis Drake, who decided to contest Spain for the gold.

Demand, as New World gold illustrates, can be a function of society and culture, is subject to distortion, and is not always determined by cost. Economic costs do not explain the traffic in hard drugs, such as heroin, nor the strength of the demand for tobacco products. While the market may appear to be some form of universally objective standard, it is anything but. Demand can be so strong, in some cases, that it will override cost considerations.

Market 'distortions' associated with varying levels of demand may help to explain why a market such as oil can, at times, seemingly defy the physical limits imposed by an 'ecological' world. (Demand distortion, it will be recalled, was one of the six weaknesses inherently found in a market economy.) Discussion of an 'ecological standard,' to this point, has served only to highlight the problem of demand distortion. Unfortunately such a standard suggests another inherent problem with market economies. Whether it is only a problem from an ecological standpoint or should be added to the other six (for a total of seven) is unclear. (Perhaps the last thing the market needs is some new 'ecological' standard against which it will be measured, in view of the problems with current environmental standards.) The problem has to do with waste. Contrary to what is claimed, the market does not always promote the efficient use of resources. What it is designed to do is use cheap resources efficiently. Cheap resources, in other words, are often wasted. A propensity for cheap resources only hints at two other possible problems One is that markets, rather than creating wealth, may be the products of it. Capitalist economies place such heavy demands on economic resources that only countries rich in resources can support them. To that extent markets are luxuries. The other problem is that there may be physical limits to economic efficiency, in the context of a global world. The world places such overwhelming physical obstacles in the path of economic output that no economic system can hope to produce efficiently. For every Andrew Carnegie able to wring extraordinarily high levels of profits from a business, there are thousands which fail. It may also help to explain the continued existence of poverty and a large lower class. What is strange is not that societies of today seem to have divided themselves into upper, middle, and lower classes, but the fact that modern structures differ little from those existing several thousand years ago.

THE COST OF SUCCESS

Among the Seven Wonders of the World were the Pyramids of Egypt and the Colossus of Rhodes, a bronze statue which straddled Rhodes' harbor. If the technology used has been lost (the Colossus itself has never been found), the ambitiousness of the ancient engineers can be gauged by the size and number of limestone blocks used in just one of the Pyramids. Some 2,500,000 limestone blocks, weighing 2 1/2 tons each, went into the Great Pyramid of Cheops.[3] If such achievements were showcases for the human spirit, they suggest a certain stubbornness, almost a defiance of natural forces. While they demanded advanced engineering and technical skills, they were not the most utilitarian of projects. There were ancient projects which, if less ambitious, were more useful. The cities of Sumer found growing conditions in Mesopotamia ideal, but were forced to create a system of canals for irrigation because rainfall and rivers provided little in the way of a reliable water source. Petra, the ancient city in Arabia, enjoyed the advantages of location along a desert trade route, yet had to expend resources on the maintenance of a reservoir.

Were the Egyptians wasting their time building the Pyramids, or worse yet, wasting their economic resources on something frivolous? As economic projects go, they had little logical connection to more traditional markets, such as foodstuffs. That demand was not tied to the market did not make it illogical, since the Pharaohs believed that there was some connection between the demand for a magnificent tomb and eternal life. When it comes to efficiency, there might be two standards against which to judge the Egyptians. It might be asked in the first place whether the projects themselves represented an efficient use of resources. It might be asked in the second place whether the engineering or construction methods used were the most efficient way to build the Pyramids.

It has long been the claim that the market mechanism is the most efficient method of allocating scarce resources. Competition promotes efficient use of resources, according to the theory. The claim is true in the context of competing firms. If five firms are competing for a market, the firm which can cut costs and use its resources most efficiently is likely to prevail in any competition. Firms with no competition can waste resources since they have little incentive to improve their products or cut costs. If competition promotes efficiency between firms, the implication is that the market as a whole will operate more efficiently. Since cost reductions are associated with efficiency, the market argument is valid - but only to a point. It would be more accurate however, to say that competition exerts pressure to use cheaper sources. What the market is geared to is not the efficient use of resources nor the conservation of scarce commodities. Markets, more accurately, operate to quickly use up cheap resources. They could be said to function efficiently when resources are cheap. That does not mean that markets provide for the most efficient use of resources.

Competition does provide an incentive to cut costs. The problem is that competitors, while exerting pressures to cut prices, will be using the same resource pool to produce their products. As more competitors enter the market, resource use will increase.

If one business, for example, uses one ton of iron ore, five can be expected to use five tons. The practical effect will be to increase the price of iron ore. Even as the resulting price increase will motivate firms to reduce individual iron ore use, their combined use will accelerate the depletion of iron ore reserves.

Resources which are cheap because they are abundant exert a stronger attraction because they promise larger profits. The problem is not that they reduce costs and encourage efficiency. The problem instead is that they encourage the creation of new markets. Rather than fighting for current market share through efficiency and price, the temptation is to use cheap resources to avoid competition by entering entirely new markets. Like credit, cheap resources represent an "artificial" means of stimulating demand. They encourage unnecessary creativity in an attempt to get around market rules. Market advocates would argue that the point of the market system is to create new markets - that is the very genius of such a system. Unfortunately that goal conflicts with the efficient use of resources in many cases.

Oil may be the best illustration of this point. The development of the glass-chimneyed kerosene lamp in the 1850s is an example of how the market brings more efficient products to consumers. Older lamp design had produced too much smoke and had an acrid smell. There is a great deal of evidence however, more suggestive of waste than efficiency. In recent years, there have been complaints from the trucking industry that increasing fuel costs are forcing many truckers out of business. Because petroleum products are important to transportation, to home heating and to agricultural production, the conservation of oil products would seem a high priority for any society. Yet, there are any number of industries which depend on the recreational use of oil products. The auto industry markets off-road vehicles which consume large quantities of fuel, the boat industry markets a variety of motor-boats for recreational purposes, and there are any number of assorted water and winter products, such as snowmobiles or power snow-blowers, which are marketed. Complaints heard about being buried in "junk-mail," and the amount of paper and packaging which goes into the garbage, suggest, not the market's efficiency, but the market's encouragement of waste when resources are abundant and cheap.

Over time the market can be expected to correct such abuses through a form of cost-benefit analysis. Even great civilizations are not immune to such rules. We may remember the Pyramids of Egypt more than the canals of Sumer, yet great achievements and difficult victories can exact a terrible price. In the physical world the often-asked question is not whether victory can be achieved, but how much will have to be paid to achieve it. Survival in the wild often has involved trade-offs. If the Arctic is a harsh environment, the extreme conditions tend to discourage predators. The tropics may have the advantage of milder conditions and greater food availability, but animals living there are more likely to be eaten by predators. People and economic systems have had similar trade-offs to deal with. Pre-historic peoples attracted to regions for their plentiful game or rich soil were likely to come into conflict with neighboring tribes attracted for the same reasons. Competition was not as great in regions of extreme, but survival could be more difficult.

The central issue, in any cost-benefit approach, is not whether success or failure is the likely outcome. The focus instead is on the cost of whatever outcome is desired. The technological achievements of the great civilizations, when viewed in that light, take on a different perspective and the nature of the questions change. The initial reaction to the Pyramids is universal - how was it possible to construct them, given the level of ancient technology? Cost-benefit analysis shifts the focus away from engineering to the economic - and the question of the costs. What were the costs of the pyramids, in the context of the Egyptian economy and culture and why was a society willing to commit resources on such a grand scale? Apart from what was unique about Egyptian culture, there is a nagging question about the economic logic behind projects such as the Pyramids or even the Colossus of Rhodes. If we do not understand the 'how' and 'why' of Egypt because the answers have been lost to time, we confront similar questions today.

The Grand Coulee Dam on the Columbia River in the state of Washington was completed in 1941. It required nearly 12 million cubic yards (9 million cubic meters) of concrete. The Hoover Dam on the Colorado River required 3.25 million cubic yards (2.48 million cubic meters) of concrete. That they serve as a testimony to the potential of modern engineering does not logically explain their existence. The increasing demand for hydroelectric power provided some justification, yet power needs alone did not necessarily require these specific projects, nor projects of such size. The city of Las Vegas, with its desert location (not far from Hoover Dam in fact), may serve as an example of man's ability to overcome the forces of nature. It is not the first desert city able to survive in the face of seemingly insurmountable odds. Petra managed to thrive for some five centuries in the Arabian desert, even if the price of desert existence was a commitment to maintain its reservoir.

Is it fair to characterize the market's use of resources as waste, based on some ecological standard, or is it really a question of semantics? A willingness to go to the ends of the earth to extract precious resources would seem to demonstrate the human spirit at its best, not a desire to promote waste. In defense of the market it might be said that there are no right or wrong decisions, only consequences. There is also the problem of gray areas. Can the market be expected to step in at the first sign of wasteful use? Knowing very little about Petra, should its inhabitants be condemned for the waste and futility of a struggle with the desert? or were they making the best of a bad situation?

Wasteful or not, resource output and usage in market economies is high. It may be that that high output is a prerequisite to productivity and market development. Are capitalist markets then, a form of luxury, and does that make the global economy the equivalent of a high-energy sports car, or, in ecological terms, the lion? If their dynamic and extraordinary capabilities suggest a comparison to the lion, it should be kept in mind that the lion represents a highly specialized life-form. While it possesses a dynamic strength, it occupies a fragile ecological niche, at the mercy of the same climactic conditions which eliminate its prey.

If the Pyramids are any indication, man-made structures can last for a very long time. The major Pyramid projects of Egypt were undertaken between 2600 and 2130 B.C., which makes them about 4,000 years old. The Parthenon in Athens stands after some 2,400 years. Any project which involves moving parts has a considerably shorter life-span. It was once thought possible to design a perpetual motion machine which would operate indefinitely off its own energy. It was found that, however tiny physical forces, such as gravity, were, they were enough to slow and eventually stop the device. There was an upper limit to efficiency, where machinery was concerned. The end of that particular concept did not put an end to all faith in technology. Advances in manufacturing somehow reinforced the belief that ever greater efficiency levels could be achieved. Evidence suggests however that technological advances, however great, do not always translate easily into economic productivity or advancement.

Whether steel making technology was comparable to that of Pyramid building, Andrew Carnegie's accomplishments rivaled those of the Pharaohs. Both he and these ancient rulers were successful at concentrating enormous amounts of wealth. At the same time Carnegie, with all his technical accomplishments, had made no fundamental changes to a societal structure which was 4,000 years old. Oddly enough, with a few of the rich at the top, a smaller number of middle class people in between, and a large number of poor at the bottom, in 1890 it even resembled a pyramid. Its real significance may lie, not in the universally bad treatment of the poor, but in the fact that economic advancement had failed to keep pace with technology. It was as if, with all the exciting scientific discoveries and technological breakthroughs, humanity was barely ahead of where it had been in 2300 B.C.. It was as if an invisible economic force had resisted or absorbed technological activity or had simply allowed energy to leak into space.

MARKETS AND THE ROLE OF GOVERNMENTS

Whether free markets are more efficient than centrally-planned ones, they certainly have proved themselves more productive. Yet, if this chapter has seemed to focus extensively on comparisons of market efficiencies, that discussion may be irrelevant to government. Democracy does not require a market system, only a lot of resources. Resources and the political calm which comes with their possession are the crucial ingredients for democracy, not the delivery system represented by the market.   It is also not clear whether extensive government involvement negatively impacts economic prosperity. Athens did extremely well under Pericles and yet the economy was an Athenian government operation from start to finish.

The supreme irony of the resource-government equation is that governments which have the fewest resources must take on the greatest administrative burdens. If governments have come under increasing criticism for their bureaucratic inefficiency and waste, they have been forced to take on the projects no one else wanted. Caesar Augustus didn't take charge of the grain dole in Rome because it was a valuable prize; he did it because the market had proved unequal to the task of feeding people. Perhaps much of the criticism of 'big government' today comes, not from its inefficiencies, but from its ability turn a profit in areas which the private sector had given up on.

Administrative costs of government operations can be expensive. Even the GPU in Russia had been forced to trim its staff in 1922. Government mismanagement has often led to costly mistakes. Crassus lost 30,000 men fighting against the Parthians at Carrhae in 54 B.C.. Mark Antony lost another 22,000 men in a second invasion of Parthia in 36 B.C.. Napoleon Bonaparte had taken an army of 700,000 into Russia and left 500,000 of them behind when he retreated in 1812 - 400,000 were casualties and 100,000 were prisoners.[4] Yet government bureaucrats had no monopoly on mistakes. The Chrysler Corporation was only rescued from bankruptcy by a government loan in 1979.

Resources did not necessarily bring more efficiency to government or prevent bureaucratic mistakes. Instead they eased the administrative burden. With food or other resources available in abundance, governments had one less problem to worry about. The Committee of Public Safety in 1794 could have focused on other problems if the French economy had been able to supply Paris with food. In that context, efficiency was simply irrelevant.

THE MORE THINGS CHANGE....

Athenian democracy was, in many ways a myth, as was her commitment to free trade, although she probably represents the first example of the "triumph of markets." She treated her own citizens well, to be sure, but she was ruthless toward the city-states which fell under her control. Her democratic reputation has survived largely because there are few critical references to her activities and because discussions of her democracy focus on what took place in Athens itself.

In 432 B.C. the Athenians placed a ban on merchants from the city of Megara. They would not be allowed to trade in Athens or at any of the cities within the Athenian empire. Megara was being punished for helping the Corinthians, rivals of Athens, in a sea-battle the year before. Athens was not afraid of the economic threat represented by tiny Megara. She was afraid that any sign of weakness on her part would encourage other states to resist Athenian demands. Megara and Corinth used the ban as an excuse to involve Sparta. Sparta would eventually agree to war, not because she viewed the Athenian actions against Megara as unjust but because her existence added weight to a Spartan alliance. War was a policy matter related to economic and political goals. Unjust actions by one city-state against another were not a justification for war, only an official excuse.

Perhaps what makes the Athenian market period different than that of today's global market is that the Athenians did not try to elevate economic thinking to the level of a philosophical debate. They tended to act without philosophizing. They needed no moral justification for their conduct and offered few apologies. Military and economic power were the same thing - policy options which were to be used to weaken or eliminate potential rivals.

With the collapse of communism, it may be tempting for the market to assume the moral leadership role. Even the communists have conceded the bankruptcy of their philosophy. Before taking over however, the market might want to look at some of the problems involved. Perhaps a hypothetical case may explain how a proposed "capitalist" moral code would operate - a choice of laws question. The clash between Spanish and Indian cultures in the New World should present a fairly clear case, although there are some interesting moral questions involved. To begin with, who did the gold belong to? Did the Aztecs or Incas own it because they owned the land? (They at least seemed to own the land, since they lived on it.) Or, did the Spaniards own the gold by virtue of having "discovered" the lands they discovered. They claimed sovereignty based on the authority of the Spanish king, who, in turn, derived his authority from the Pope.

Who would have won if the standard had been based on the free market concept of private property? Did the Aztecs or Incas hold a superior claim, because they had first mined or used the gold? or, were they automatically disqualified because their society did not seem to value private property rights or the gold itself? Did the Spaniards have a superior claim because they had a more formal system of ownership? - or because they had a greater need for gold? If the Indians really didn't care that much about gold, then shouldn't the Spaniards be able to claim it by virtue of their economic demand? - or their hard work?

In the end, the debate over ownership of New World gold was determined by force. Spanish activities clearly illustrate how the desire to accumulate personal wealth can be a motivating force for productivity. In a broader sense, the Spanish experience is an extreme example of the free market, patterned, not on some moral code of conduct, but after the earliest market model available, the Athenian state. If anything, the activities of Athens and Spain suggest that the origin and guiding principles of the market are closely related to raw force. Because Spain's claim to the New World was based on military control, her claims lost legitimacy when military resources began to fail. While market needs served to justify the conquest, the market offered little sympathy when Spain was ousted from power. The Spaniards had a custom, when confronting new Indian tribes, of reading from an official order which commanded that the Indians immediately submit to Spanish rule. Since the order was read in Spanish, the Indians had no idea what was being said and normally said and did nothing. When they made no response, Spanish soldiers set about killing or capturing them. The official reading was intended to fulfill Spain's official duties. In their eyes it may have relieved them of any responsibility for inhumane treatment of the peoples they found, yet it served only as cover for a multitude of sins. In the eyes of the market, Spain's real sin was that she was too weak to defend what she had gained.

A major problem in trying to create a moral code patterned after the market is that the market sets few moral boundaries on conduct. Markets are governed by rules of force or power. The Athenian market boundary was set more by its naval resources or by the economic costs of transport outside a certain geographical area, than by democratic notions of fairness. Others would make a virtue out of necessity. Better to use market forces to accomplish some good than to totally ignore them. If the market for African ivory is too strong to prevent poaching, then perhaps the only workable solution is to offer another market which offers poachers greater economic rewards for keeping elephants alive. In addition, the market at least provides something to believe in. Where the world appears a dangerous place, any system which provides some sense of certainty - even a remote connection to something permanent - will always be welcomed. When the Cold War was at its height, the battle between East and West brought some sense of order.

THE MARKET'S FUTURE

Whether globalization represents just a trend or the wave of the future, the future is likely to be dominated by the market. Its success has little to do with the much-heralded triumph of the market or the collapse of communism. The market, even the free market, was never seriously challenged by the Bolsheviks in 1917. Market forces have an existence of their own, independent of ideology which, in a way, makes them resistant to change. Stalin proved that change was possible, but the effort required a monumental commitment of resources and took a toll on Russian society.

Market forces are little more than figures on a piece of paper. They are not something which can be enlisted in a crusade, or something which can be easily destroyed. The ideological battle between capitalism and communism was not crucial to the future of the market. The market has been seeking dominance of the world for some 6,000 years, but that battle was taking place well outside the confines of capitalist and communist ideologies. The greater struggle was between the markets and more traditional institutions in society. Communism, if it represented an alternative to capitalism, never really was an alternative to the market. For all their criticism of capitalism, the Bolsheviks patterned much of their economy on Western production techniques. The primitive level of economic development was not proof that the market had been eliminated, only suggestive that market economies could not run efficiently without resources.

A basic problem for the global market is that globalization emphasizes the importance of attitude at the expense of economic analysis. So long as there is a healthy attitude toward profits, anything is possible. Yet, market strength has more to do with economic factors such as resource distribution or transportation, than with the pursuit of profits. The desire to get rich may be universal, but some countries are better suited to the market than others. Just as demand within a country can vary from region to region or between products, market strength can vary as well.

NOTES

Chapter 1
Introduction

1. J.B. Bury and Russell Meiggs, *A History of Greece to the Death of Alexander the Great*. 4th ed., (Macmillan: London 1989), pp. 173-174.
2. Thucydides IV 80.
3. Robert Ingpen & Philip Wilkinson, *Encyclopedia of Mysterious Places The life and legends of ancient sites around the world*. (New York: Viking Studio Books, 1990), pp. 89-92.
4. Ibid, pp. 213-217.
5. Ibid, pp. 184-187; Paul Johnson, *Civilizations of the Holy Land*. (New York: Atheneum, 1979), p. 136.

Chapter 2
Resources and a Theory

1. Mead L. Jensen and Alan M. Bateman, *Economic Mineral Deposits*, 3rd ed. (New York: John Wiley & Sons, 1979), p. 386.
2. Göran Burenhult, ed., *Old World Civilizations: The Rise of Cities and States*, Vol. 3 of *The Illustrated History of Mankind*. (San Francisco: Harper, 1994), p. 137.
3. John A. Wolfe, *Mineral Resources: A World Review* (New York: Chapman and Hall, 1984), p. 129.
4. Jensen and Bateman, *Economic Mineral Deposits*, p. 386; Burenhult, *Old World Civilizations: The Rise of Cities and States*, p. 137.
5. Wolfe, *Mineral Resources: A World Review*, p. 10.
6. Jensen and Bateman, *Economic Mineral Deposits*, p. 386.
7. Wolfe, *Mineral Resources: A World Review*, p. 10.
8. Burenhult, *Old World Civilizations: The Rise of Cities and States*, p. 137.
9. Wolfe, *Mineral Resources: A World Review*, p. 130.
10. Burenhult, *Old World Civilizations: The Rise of Cities and States*, p. 137.
11. Jensen and Bateman, *Economic Mineral Deposits*, p. 374.
12. Jensen and Bateman, *Economic Mineral Deposits*, pp. 373-374.
13. Sir Dudley Stamp, *Chisholm's Handbook of Commercial Geography*, 19th ed., G. Noel Blake and Audrey N. Clark, ed. (New York: Longman, 1975), p. 1.

Chapter 3
The Resource Mechanism

1. Eugene H. Methvin, "Hitler & Stalin - Twentieth-Century Superkillers," *National Review*, Vol. XXXVII, No. 10 (May 31, 1985), p. 24.
2. William Doyle, *The Oxford History of the French Revolution*, (New York: Oxford University Press, Inc., 1989), p. 253.
3. W.G. Forrest, *A History of Sparta 950-192 B.C.*, (New York: W.W. Norton & Company, 1969), p. 101.
4. Richard Pipes, *Russia Under the Bolshevik Regime*, (New York: Alfred A. Knopf, 1993), p. 400, from Andrzej Kaminski, *Konzentransionlager 1896 bis heute: eine Analyse* (Stuttgart, 1982), p. 87.
5. William S. Allen, *The Nazi Seizure of Power - The Experience of a Single German Town 1930-1935*, (New York: New Viewpoints, 1973), Tables 1, 2 and 3, Table 7 in the Appendix; Peter H. Merkl, *Political Violence Under the Swastika - 581 Early Nazis*, (Princeton:Princeton University Press, 1975), pp. 66-67.
6. Paul A. Samuelson and William D. Norhaus, *Macro-Economics*. 14th Ed. (New York, McGraw-Hill, Inc., 1992), pp. 214, 240-242, 234, 237.

7.   Sir Dudley Stamp, Chisholm's Handbook of Commercial Geography, 19th ed., G. Noel Blake and Audrey N. Clark, ed. (New York: Longman, 1975), p. 79.

8.   Eric Foner and Alfred Young, consulting eds. *Who Built America, Vol. One From Conquest and Colonization Through Reconstruction and the Great Uprising of 1877.* (New York: Pantheon Books, 1989), p. 550.

9.   Allan Nevins and Henry Steele Commager, *A Pocket History of the United States*, (New York: Pocket Books, 1992), p. 281.

10.   Nell Irvin Painter, *Standing At Armageddon: The United States 1877 - 1919*, (New York: W.W. Norton & Company, 1987), p. 114.

Chapter 4
Athens: Silver, Ships, and Grain

1.   Plutarch *Themistocles* 4.
2.   Plutarch *Solon* 13.
3.   Plutarch *Solon* 14.
4.   Plutarch *Solon* 15, 16.
5.   Plutarch *Solon* 18. The four classes were 1) *Pentacosiomedimni* or 500-bushel men; 2) Knights; 3) *Zeugitai* or teamsters; and 4) *Thetes*.
6.   Bury, J.B. and Russell Meiggs, *A History of Greece to the Death of Alexander the Great*. 4th ed. (London: Macmillan, 1975), p. 124; Plutarch *Solon* 18.
7.   Plutarch *Solon* 19.
8.   Plutarch *Solon* 29; Bury & Meiggs, supra, pp. 125-6.
9.   Bury & Meiggs, p. 127; Plutarch *Solon* 29.
10.   Bury & Meiggs, ibid, p. 127; Plutarch *Solon* 30.
11.   Bury & Meiggs, p. 128.
12.   Bury & Meiggs, pp. 134-135.
13.   Bury & Meiggs, p. 136.
14.   Bury & Meiggs, pp. 136-138.
15.   Plutarch *Aristides* 24.
16.   Plutarch *Themistocles* 14.
17.   Bury & Meiggs, p. 211.
18.   Bury & Meiggs, pp. 215-217.
19.   Plutarch *Alcibiades* 37.
20.   Plutarch *Aristides* 7.
21.   Plutarch *Pericles* 12.
22.   Plutarch *Solon* 22.
23.   Plutarch *Solon* 22.
24.   Bury & Meiggs, p. 122.
25.   Plutarch *Solon* 24.
26.   Bury & Meiggs, p. 122.
27.   Plutarch *Solon* 29.
28.   Plutarch *Pericles* 12.
29.   Plutarch *Solon* 13.
30.   Plutarch *Solon* 30.

Chapter 5
Sparta: Dictatorial Democracy and a Society Under Siege

1.   Leslie J. Worley, *Hippeis: The Cavalry of Ancient Greece* (San Francisco: Westview Press, 1994), p. 142-145.

2. Xenophon *Hellenica*, VI, 4, 15.
3. Bury & Meiggs, *A History of Greece*, p. 274.
4. Arnold Toynbee, *Some Problems of Greek History*, (London: Oxford University Press, 1969), p. 171.
5. Toynbee, *Some Problems of Greek History*, p. 180.
6. Toynbee, *Some Problems of Greek History*, pp. 184-185.
7. Toynbee, *Some Problems of Greek History*, p. 183.
8. Bury & Meiggs, *A History of Greece*, p. 162.
9. Anton Powell, *Athens and Sparta: Constructing Greek Political and Social History from 478 B.C.* (Portland: Areopagitica Press, 1988), p. 107.
10. Powell, *Athens and Sparta: Constructing Greek Political and Social History from 478 B.C.*, p. 109; Herodotus IX 64.
11. Powell, *Athens and Sparta: Constructing Greek Political and Social History from 478 B.C.*, p. 110.
12. Thucydides IV 80.
13. Arnold Toynbee, *Some Problems of Greek History*, pp. 228-229.
14. Arnold Toynbee, *Some Problems of Greek History*, pp. 204-206.
15. Arnold Toynbee, *Some Problems of Greek History*, p. 202.
16. Arnold Toynbee, *Some Problems of Greek History*, pp. 153, 218-219.
17. Arnold Toynbee, *Some Problems of Greek History*, pp. 222-223.
18. Arnold Toynbee, *Some Problems of Greek History*, pp. 217-218, 221.
19. Arnold Toynbee, *Some Problems of Greek History*, p. 221.
20. John V.A. Fine, *The Ancient Greeks: A Critical History*. (Cambridge, Mass: Harvard University Press, 1983), pp. 159-160.
21. Plutarch, *Lycurgus* 28.
22. Plutarch, *Lycurgus*, 28.
23. Xenophon, *Hellenica*, III, 3, 4.
24. Xenophon *Hellenica*, III, 3, 8.
25. Xenophon, *Hellenica*, III, 3, 11.

Chapter 6
Rome: Out of Work, Out of Bread, Out of Control

1. Plutarch *Tiberius Gracchus* 17.
2. Plutarch, *Tiberius Gracchus*, 19-20.
3. Michael Grant. *History of Rome*. (New York: Charles Scribner's Sons, 1978), p. 10.
4. Michael Grant, *History of Rome*, p. 36.
5. Michael Grant, *History of Rome*, p. 45.
6. Michael Grant, *History of Rome*, p. 82.
7. Michael Grant, *History of Rome*, pp. 87-89.
8. Michael Grant, *History of Rome*, p. 187.
9. Lesley Adkins and Roy A. Adkins. *Handbook to Life in Ancient Rome*. (New York: Facts On File, 1994), p. 40.
10. Lesley Adkins, *Handbook to Life in Ancient Rome*, p. 39.
11. Michael Grant, *History of Rome*, p. 67.
12. Lesley Adkins, *Handbook to Life in Ancient Rome*, p. 41.
13. Michael Grant, *History of Rome*, pp. 199-201.
14. Michael Grant, *History of Rome*, p. 68.
15. Lesley Adkins, *Handbook to Life in Ancient Rome*, p. 40.
16. Michael Grant, *History of Rome*, p. 68.
17. Lesley Adkins, *Handbook to Life in Ancient Rome*, pp. 41, 43.
18. Michael Grant, *History of Rome*, pp. 68-69.
19. Lesley Adkins, *Handbook to Life in Ancient Rome*. p. 39.

20. Lesley Adkins, *Handbook to Life in Ancient Rome*, p. 41.
21. Lesley Adkins, *Handbook to Life in Ancient Rome*, p. 39.
22. Lesley Adkins, *Handbook to Life in Ancient Rome*, p. 38.
23. Lesley Adkins, *Handbook to Life in Ancient Rome*, p. 43.
24. Lesley Adkins, *Handbook to Life in Ancient Rome*, p. 43.
25. Lesley Adkins, *Handbook to Life in Ancient Rome*, p. 39.
26. Lesley Adkins, *Handbook to Life in Ancient Rome*, p. 38.
27. Lesley Adkins, *Handbook to Life in Ancient Rome*, p. 38.
28. Michael Grant, *History of Rome*, p. 73.
29. Michael Grant, *History of Rome*, p. 73.
30. Michael Grant, *History of Rome*, p. 74.
31. Michael Grant, *History of Rome*, p. 75.
32. Michael Grant, *History of Rome*, p. 49.
33. Michael Grant, *History of Rome*, pp. 78-79.
34. Michael Grant, *History of Rome*, pp. 80-81.
35. Michael Grant, *History of Rome*, p. 82.
36. Michael Grant, *History of Rome*, pp. 107-110.
37. Michael Grant, *History of Rome*, p. 162.
38. Michael Grant, *History of Rome*, pp. 162-163.
39. Michael Grant, *History of Rome*, pp. 162-163.
40. Georgine Masson. *Ancient Rome: From Romulus to Augustus.* (New York: The Viking Press, 1974), p. 70.
41. Hammond, N.G.L., and H.H. Scullard, ed. *The Oxford Classical Dictionary.* (Oxford: Oxford University Press, 1978), p. 89.
42. N.G.L. Hammond and H.H. Scullard, *The Oxford Classical Dictionary*, p.576.
43. Fritz M. Heichelheim. *Wirtschaftliche Schwankungen der Zeit von Alexander bis Augustus* (Jena, 1930), p. 77.
44. Fritz M. Heichelheim, "Romische Sozial-Und Wirtschaftsgeschichte," *Historia Mundi* (Bern 1956) IV, 412.
45. Hammond, N.G.L. and H.H. Scullard, ed., *The Oxford Classical Dictionary*, p. 928.
46. Michael Grant, *History of Rome*, p. 169. Plutarch, *Tiberius Gracchus*, 8.
47. Plutarch *Tiberius Gracchus*, 8.
48. Plutarch, *Gaius Gracchus*, 5.
49. Plutarch, *Gaius Gracchus*, 6.
50. Plutarch, *Gaius Gracchus*, 5, 6.
51. Michael Grant, *History of Rome*, p. 179.
52. N.G.L. Hammond and H.H. Scullard, *The Oxford Classical Dictionary*, 2d. ed., p. 365.
53. Michael Grant, *History of Rome*, p. 186.
54. Michael Grant, *History of Rome*, p. 187.
55. Michael Grant, *History of Rome*, p. 189.
56. Michael Grant, *History of Rome*, p. 199.
57. Michael Grant, *History of Rome*, p. 206.
58. Michael Grant, *History of Rome*, p. 218.
59. Suetonius, *Julius Caesar*, 42.
60. Michael Grant, *History of Rome*, p. 234.
61. Suetonius, *Julius Caesar*, 44.
62. Suetonius, *Julius Caesar*, 42.
63. Frank, Tenney. *An Economic Survey of Ancient Rome*, Vol. I. (Paterson, New Jersey: Pageant Books, Inc., 1959), pp. 227, 329-330.
64. Suetonius, *Julius Caesar*, 41.
65. Tenney Frank, *An Economic Survey of Ancient Rome*, pp. 221, 316.

66. Suetonius, *Julius Caesar*, 42.
67. Plutarch, *Tiberius Gracchus*, 19, 20.
68. Plutarch, *Gaius Gracchus*, 18.
69. Michael Grant, *History of Rome*, p. 187.
70. Plutarch, *Sulla*, 32.
71. Michael Grant, *History of Rome*, p. 242.
72. Michael Grant, *History of Rome*, pp. 174-175.
73. Plutarch, *Tiberius Gracchus*, 10.
74. Plutarch, *Tiberius Gracchus*, 11-12.
75. Michael Grant, *History of Rome*, p. 70-71; Plutarch, *Tiberius Gracchus*, 18.
76. Plutarch, *Tiberius Gracchus*, 19-20.
77. Plutarch, *Gaius Gracchus*, 13-14.
78. Plutarch, *Gaius Gracchus*, 17.
79. Michael Grant, *History of Rome*, p. 179.
80. Isaac Asimov. *The Roman Republic*. (Boston: Houghton Mifflin Company, 1966), p. 152.
81. Plutarch, *Gaius Marius*, 30.
82. Plutarch, *Gaius Marius* 35; *Sulla* 8.
83. Plutarch, *Sulla*, 8.
84. Plutarch, *Gaius Marius*, 35; *Sulla*, 9, 10.
85. Plutarch, *Sertorius*, 4.
86. Plutarch, *Sertorius*, 5.
87. Plutarch, *Sertorius*, 26-27.
88. Plutarch, *Caesar*, 8.
89. Plutarch, *Caesar* 14, *Pompey* 48.
90. Plutarch, *Cicero* 30, 31.
91. Plutarch, *Cicero*, 33; *Pompey*, 48, 49.
92. Plutarch, *Cicero*, 33.
93. Plutarch, *Cicero* 33; *Pompey* 49.
94. Plutarch, *Pompey*, 49.
95. Plutarch, *Cicero*, 34.
96. Plutarch, *Pompey*, 51.
97. Plutarch, *Crassus*, 40; *Pompey* 52.
98. Plutarch, *Caesar*, 28.
99. Plutarch, *Pompey* 54; *Cicero* 35.
100. N.G.L. Hammond, *The Oxford Classical Dictionary*, 2nd ed., p. 687.
101. Suetonius, *Augustus*, 32.
102. N.G.L. Hammond, ed., 2nd ed., *The Oxford Classical Dictionary*, p. 975.

Chapter 7
France and the French Revolution: The Political History

1. Simon Schama. *Citizens: A Chronicle of the French Revolution*. (New York: Vintage Books, 1989), p. 622.
2. Simon Schama, *Citizens: A Chronicle of the French Revolution*, p. 837.
3. George Rudé. *The Crowd in the French Revolution*. (New York: Oxford University Press, 1959), p. 55.
4. George Rudé, *The Crowd in the French Revolution*, p. 54.
5. Simon Schama, *Citizens: A Chronicle of the French Revolution*, p. 390.
6. Simon Schama, *Citizens: A Chronicle of the French Revolution*, p. 399.
7. William Doyle. *The Oxford History of the French Revolution*. (New York: Oxford University Press, Inc., 1989) p. 72.

8. George Rudé. *The French Revolution*. (New York: Grove Weidenfeld, 1988), p. 40.
9. William Doyle, *The Oxford History of the French Revolution*, p. 106.
10. George Rudé, *The Crowd in the French Revolution*, p. 45.
11. Simon Schama, *Citizens: A Chronicle of the French Revolution*, pp. 327-328.
12. Simon Schama, *Citizens: A Chronicle of the French Revolution*, pp. 328-329.
13. George Rudé, *The Crowd in the French Revolution*, p. 48.
14. George Rudé, *The Crowd in the French Revolution*, pp. 47-49.
15. Simon Schama, *Citizens: A Chronicle of the French Revolution*, p. 382.
16. Simon Schama, *Citizens: A Chronicle of the French Revolution*, p. 384.
17. Simon Schama, *Citizens: A Chronicle of the French Revolution*, p. 388.
18. Simon Schama, *Citizens: A Chronicle of the French Revolution*, pp. 404-405.
19. William Doyle, *The Oxford History of the French Revolution*, pp. 112-115.
20. William Doyle, *The Oxford History of the French Revolution*, pp. 115-116.
21. William Doyle, *The Oxford History of the French Revolution*, p. 138.
22. William Doyle, *The Oxford History of the French Revolution*, pp. 185-186.
23. William Doyle, *The Oxford History of the French Revolution*, p. 188.
24. William Doyle, *The Oxford History of the French Revolution*, p. 189.
25. William Doyle, *The Oxford History of the French Revolution*, p. 190.
26. Simon Schama, *Citizens: A Chronicle of the French Revolution*, pp. 631-632.
27. William Doyle, *The Oxford History of the French Revolution*, p. 193.
28. Simon Schama, *Citizens: A Chronicle of the French Revolution*, pp. 690-693.
29. William Doyle, *The Oxford History of the French Revolution*, pp. 256-257.
30. William Doyle, *The Oxford History of the French Revolution*, pp. 234-235.
31. Simon Schama, *Citizens: A Chronicle of the French Revolution*, p. 758.
32. William Doyle, *The Oxford History of the French Revolution*, p. 253.
33. Simon Schama, *Citizens: A Chronicle of the French Revolution*, p. 783.
34. Simon Schama, *Citizens: A Chronicle of the French Revolution*, p. 789.
35. Simon Schama, *Citizens: A Chronicle of the French Revolution*, p. 766.
36. Simon Schama, *Citizens: A Chronicle of the French Revolution*, p. 817.
37. Simon Schama, *Citizens: A Chronicle of the French Revolution*, p. 837.
38. William Doyle, *The Oxford History of the French Revolution*, pp. 281-282.
39. Simon Schama, *Citizens: A Chronicle of the French Revolution*, p. 837.
40. William Doyle, *The Oxford History of the French Revolution*, pp. 282-285.
41. William Doyle, *The Oxford History of the French Revolution*, pp. 291-292.
42. William Doyle, *The Oxford History of the French Revolution*, pp. 293-294.
43. William Doyle, *The Oxford History of the French Revolution*, pp. 294-295.
44. William Doyle, *The Oxford History of the French Revolution*, p. 322.
45. William Doyle, *The Oxford History of the French Revolution*, pp. 330-331.
46. Martyn Lyons, *Napoleon Bonaparte and the Legacy of the French Revolution*, (New York: St. Martin's Press, 1994) pp. 61-64.
47. Martyn Lyons, *Napoleon Bonaparte and the Legacy of the French Revolution*, pp. 118-120.

Chapter 8
France and the French Revolution: The Economic History

1. William Doyle, *The Oxford History of the French Revolution*, pp. 293-294.
2. William Doyle, *The Oxford History of the French Revolution*, p. 22.
3. William Doyle, *Origins of the French Revolution*, 2d ed., (New York: Oxford University Press, 1990), p. 194.
4. George Rudé. *The Crowd in the French Revolution*, pp. 23-24.
5. William Doyle, *The Oxford History of the French Revolution*, p. 66.

6.   William Doyle, *The Oxford History of the French Revolution*, p. 62.
7.   William Doyle, *The Oxford History of the French Revolution*, p. 67.
8.   William Doyle, *The Oxford History of the French Revolution*, p. 80.
9.   William Doyle, *The Oxford History of the French Revolution*, p. 86.
10.   Simon Schama, *Citizens: A Chronicle of the French Revolution*, p. 325.
11.   William Doyle, *The Oxford History of the French Revolution*, p. 87.
12.   William Doyle, *The Oxford History of the French Revolution*, p. 87.
13.   Simon Schama, *Citizens: A Chronicle of the French Revolution*, p. 307.
14.   Simon Schama, *Citizens: A Chronicle of the French Revolution*, p. 306.
15.   George Rudé, *The Crowd in the French Revolution*, p. 11.
16.   Simon Schama, *Citizens: A Chronicle of the French Revolution*, p. 307.
17.   William Doyle, *The Oxford History of the French Revolution*, p. 109.
18.   Simon Schama, *Citizens: A Chronicle of the French Revolution*, pp. 325-326.
19.   Simon Schama, *Citizens: A Chronicle of the French Revolution*, p. 328.
20.   William Doyle, *The Oxford History of the French Revolution*, p. 121.
21.   William Doyle, *The Oxford History of the French Revolution*, pp. 181-182.
22.   William Doyle, *The Oxford History of the French Revolution*, p. 134.
23.   William Doyle, *The Oxford History of the French Revolution*, p. 223.
24.   William Doyle, *The Oxford History of the French Revolution*, p. 229.
25.   William Doyle, *The Oxford History of the French Revolution*, p. 246.
26.   Morris Slavin, *The Hébertistes to the Guillotine: Anatomy of a "Conspiracy" in Revolutionary France*, (Baton Rouge: Louisiana State University Press 1994), p. 180.
27.   William Doyle, *The Oxford History of the French Revolution*, p. 265.
28.   Morris Slavin. *The Hébertistes to the Guillotine*, p. 180.
29.   Morris Slavin, *The Hébertistes to the Guillotine*, p. 220.
30.   Morris Slavin, *The Hébertistes to the Guillotine*, pp. 36-37.
31.   Morris Slavin, *The Hébertistes to the Guillotine*, p. 41.
32.   Simon Schama, *Citizens A Chronicle of the French Revolution*, p. 844.
33.   William Doyle, *The Oxford History of the French Revolution*, p. 286.
34.   William Doyle, *The Oxford History of the French Revolution*, p. 286.
35.   William Doyle, *The Oxford History of the French Revolution*, pp. 290-291.
36.   William Doyle, *The Oxford History of the French Revolution*, pp. 290-291.
37.   William Doyle, *The Oxford History of the French Revolution*, p. 295.
38.   William Doyle, *The Oxford History of the French Revolution*, p. 253.
39.   Simon Schama, *Citizens A Chronicle of the French Revolution*, pp. 758-760.
40.   Morris Slavin, *The Hébertistes to the Guillotine*, p. 180.
41.   Walter Laqueur, *The Dream That Failed: Reflections on the Soviet Union*, (New York: Oxford University Press 1994), p. 5.

Chapter 9
Russia and the October Revolution

1.   Roy Medvedev. *Let History Judge: The Origins and Consequences of Stalinism*, (New York: Columbia University Press 1989), pp. 337-339; J. Arch Getty and Roberta T. Manning, ed. *Stalinist Terror: New Perspectives*, (New York: Cambridge University Press 1993), pp. 42-49.
2.   J. Arch Getty, *Stalinist Terror*, pp. 46-49.
3.   Roy Medvedev, *Let History Judge*, p. 341.
4.   Roy Medvedev, *Let History Judge*, pp. 341-342.
5.   J. Arch Getty & Roberta T. Manning, ed., *Stalinist Terror*, p. 270, from G. Kurman in *Pravda*, June 22, 1989.
6.   Roy Medvedev, *Let History Judge*, p. 455.

7. J. Arch Getty, *Stalinist Terror*, p. 270.
8. J. Arch Getty, *Stalinist Terror*, p. 270.
9. Roy Medvedev, *Let History Judge*, p. 455.
10. J. Arch Getty, *Stalinist Terror*, p. 271, from A. Dugin, "Stalinizm: legendy i fakty," *Slovo* no. 7, 1990.
11. J. Arch Getty, *Stalinist Terror*, p. 270, from *Moskovskie novosti*, March 4, 1990.
12. Alec Nove, "Victims of Stalinism: How Many?" *Stalinist Terror*, pp. 269-271.
    Roy Medvedev, *Let History Judge*, p. 455.
13. J. Arch Getty, *Stalinist Terror*, p. 271, citing A. Dugin, "Stalinizm: legendy i fakty," *Slovo* no. 7, 1990, p. 44.
14. J. Arch Getty, *Stalinist Terror*, p. 13.
15. James D. White, *The Russian Revolution 1917-1921: A Short History* (London: Edward Arnold, 1994), p. 174.
16. James D. White, *The Russian Revolution 1917-1921*, p. 175.
17. Richard Pipes, *The Russian Revolution* (New York: Vintage Books, 1990), p. 552.
18. Richard Pipes, *The Russian Revolution*, p. 557.

Chapter 10
1917 - Background to Revolt

1. Richard Pipes, *The Russian Revolution* (New York: Vintage Books, 1990), pp. 24-25.
2. Richard Pipes, *The Russian Revolution*, p. 26.
3. Richard Pipes, *The Russian Revolution*, p. 29.
4. Richard Pipes, *The Russian Revolution*, p. 41.
5. Richard Pipes, *The Russian Revolution*, p. 237.
6. Richard Pipes, *The Russian Revolution*, pp. 274-275.
7. Richard Pipes, *The Russian Revolution*, p. 277.
8. Richard Pipes, *The Russian Revolution*, p. 278.
9. Richard Pipes, *The Russian Revolution*, p. 434.
10. Richard Pipes, *The Russian Revolution*, p. 448.
11. Richard Pipes, *The Russian Revolution*, p. 486.
12. James D. White, *The Russian Revolution 1917-1921: A Short History*, (New York: Edward Arnold, 1994), p. 175.
13. Richard Pipes, *The Russian Revolution*, p. 147.
14. Richard Pipes, *The Russian Revolution*, p. 466.
15. Richard Pipes, *The Russian Revolution*, p. 40, from Oscar Anweiler, *The Soviets* (New York, 1974), pp. 40-42.
16. Richard Pipes, *The Russian Revolution*, p. 49.
17. Richard Pipes, *The Russian Revolution*, p. 293.

Chapter 11
The Russian Civil War - 1918-1921

1. Richard Pipes, *The Russian Revolution*, p. 558.
2. Richard Pipes, *The Russian Revolution*, p. 559.
3. Richard Pipes, *The Russian Revolution*, p. 652.
4. Richard Pipes, *The Russian Revolution*, p. 816.
5. Richard Pipes, *The Russian Revolution*, pp. 837-838.
6. Richard Pipes, *The Russian Revolution*, p. 836.
7. Richard Pipes, *Russia Under the Bolshevik Regime* (New York: Alfred A. Knopf, 1993), p. 11.
8. W. Bruce Lincoln, *Red Victory: A History of the Russian Civil War* (New York: Touchstone, Simon & Schuster, Inc., 1989), p. 78.

9.   Richard Pipes, *Russia Under the Bolshevik Regime*, p. 19.
10.   W. Bruce Lincoln, *Red Victory*, p. 81.
11.   W. Bruce Lincoln, *Red Victory*, p. 85.
12.   Richard Pipes, *The Russian Revolution*, pp. 627-628.
13.   W. Bruce Lincoln, *Red Victory*, p. 189.
14.   W. Bruce Lincoln, *Red Victory*, p. 214.
15.   W. Bruce Lincoln, *Red Victory*, p. 226.
16.   W. Bruce Lincoln, *Red Victory*, p. 441.
17.   W. Bruce Lincoln, *Red Victory*, pp. 444-445.
18.   W. Bruce Lincoln, *Red Victory*, p. 449.
19.   W. Bruce Lincoln, *Red Victory*, p. 384.
20.   W. Bruce Lincoln, *Red Victory*, pp. 384-385.
21.   Richard Pipes, *The Russian Revolution*, p. 802.
22.   Richard Pipes, *The Russian Revolution*, p. 816.
23.   Richard Pipes, *The Russian Revolution*, p. 644.
24.   Richard Pipes, *The Russian Revolution*, p. 832.
25.   W. Bruce Lincoln, *Red Victory*, pp. 48-49.
26.   W. Bruce Lincoln, *Red Victory*, p. 217.
27.   Richard Pipes, *Russia Under the Bolshevik Regime*, p. 59, from Orlando Figes in *Past and Present*, No. 129 (November 1990), 200.
28.   Richard Pipes, *Russia Under the Bolshevik Regime*, pp. 59-60.
29.   Richard Pipes, *Russia Under the Bolshevik Regime*, p. 11.
30.   Richard Pipes, *Russia Under the Bolshevik Regime*, p. 11.
31.   W. Bruce Lincoln, *Red Victory*, p. 220.
32.   W. Bruce Lincoln, *Red Victory*, p. 226.
33.   W. Bruce Lincoln, *Red Victory*, pp. 322-323.
34.   W. Bruce Lincoln, *Red Victory*, p. 323.

Chapter 12
The Communists in Power - 1921-1938

1.   W. Bruce Lincoln, *Red Victory*, p. 449.
2.   W. Bruce Lincoln, *Red Victory*, p. 493.
3.   W. Bruce Lincoln, *Red Victory*, p. 493.
4.   W. Bruce Lincoln, *Red Victory*, p. 504.
5.   W. Bruce Lincoln, *Red Victory*, p. 505.
6.   Richard Pipes, *Russia Under the Bolshevik Regime*, p. 377.
7.   Richard Pipes, *Russia Under the Bolshevik Regime*, p. 411.
8.   Richard Pipes, *Russia Under the Bolshevik Regime*, p. 441.
9.   Richard Pipes, *Russia Under the Bolshevik Regime*, p. 355.
10.   Richard Pipes, *Russia Under the Bolshevik Regime*, p. 354.
11.   Richard Pipes, *Russia Under the Bolshevik Regime*, p. 356, from A. I. Vvedenskii, *Tserkov' i gosudarstvo* (Moscow, 1923), 230; Szczesniak, *Russian Revolution*, 156-157; McCallagh, *Persecution*, p. ix.
12.   Richard Pipes, *Russia Under the Bolshevik Regime*, p. 296.
13.   Roy Medvedev, *Let History Judge*, p. 131.
14.   Roy Medvedev, *Let History Judge*, p. 144.
15.   Roy Medvedev, *Let History Judge*, p. 154.
16.   Roy Medvedev, *Let History Judge*, p. 155.
17.   Roy Medvedev, *Let History Judge*, p. 174.
18.   Robert Conquest, *The Harvest of Sorrow* (New York: Oxford University Press, 1986), p. 105.

19. Roy Medvedev, *Let History Judge*, p. 222.
20. Roy Medvedev, *Let History Judge*, p. 223.
21. Robert Conquest, *The Harvest of Sorrow*, p. 101, from Dorothy Atkinson, *The End of the Russian Land Commune: 1905-1930* (Stanford, 1984), p. 334.
22. Roy Medvedev, *Let History Judge*, p. 231.
23. Roy Medvedev, *Let History Judge*, p. 233.
24. Robert Conquest, *The Harvest of Sorrow*, pp. 146-147.
25. Roy Medvedev, *Let History Judge*, p. 225.
26. Roy Medvedev, *Let History Judge*, p. 227.
27. Robert Conquest, *The Harvest of Sorrow*, p. 166.
28. Roy Medvedev, *Let History Judge*, p. 233.
29. Robert Conquest, *The Harvest of Sorrow*, p. 154.
30. Robert Conquest, *The Harvest of Sorrow*, p. 102.
31. Robert Conquest, *The Harvest of Sorrow*, p. 185.
32. Sheila Fitzpatrick, *Stalin's Peasants: Resistance & Survival in the Russian Village After Collectivization* (New York: Oxford University Press, 1994), p. 62.
33. Robert Conquest, *The Harvest of Sorrow*, p. 182.
34. Roy Medvedev, *Let History Judge*, p. 244.
35. Roy Medvedev, *Let History Judge*, pp. 397-399.
36. Roy Medvedev, *Let History Judge*, pp. 411-413.
37. Roy Medvedev, *Let History Judge*, p. 449.
38. Roy Medvedev, *Let History Judge*, p. 455.
39. Roy Medvedev, *Let History Judge*, p. 466.

Chapter 13
The Economics of the Russian Agricultural Sector

1. R. W. Davies, Mark Harrison, and S. G. Wheatcroft, ed., *The economic transformation of the Soviet Union, 1913-1945* (New York, Cambridge University Press: 1994) p. 125.
2. R. W. Davies, ed., *The economic transformation of the Soviet Union, 1913-1945*, p. 108.
3. Roy Medvedev, *Let History Judge*, p. 146, from *Narodnoe khoziaistvo SSSR, 1922-1972. Iubileinyi statisticheskii spravochnik* (Moscow, 1972), p. 119.
4. R. W. Davies, *The Economic Transformation of the Soviet Union*, p. 125.
5. J. Arch Getty, *Stalinist Terror*, p. 118; Alec Nove, *An Economic History of the USSR*, p. 242.
6. Richard Pipes, *Russia Under the Bolshevik Regime*, p. 413.
7. Richard Pipes, *Russia Under the Bolshevik Regime*, pp. 413, 419.
8. Roy Medvedev, *Let History Judge*, p. 244; J. Arch Getty, *Stalinist Terror*, p. 290.
9. Roy Medvedev, *Let History Judge*, p. 410.
10. J. Arch Getty, *Stalinist Terror*, pp. 122-123.
11. Robert Conquest, *The Harvest of Sorrow*, p. 306.
12. J. Arch Getty, *Stalinist Terror*, p. 268.
13. Roy Medvedev, *Let History Judge*, pp. 233-234.
14. Robert Conquest, *The Harvest of Sorrow*, p. 127.
15. Roy Medvedev, *Let History Judge*, p. 222.
16. Robert C. Tucker, *Stalin In Power: The Revolution from Above, 1928-1941* (New York: W. W. Norton & Company, 1992), p. 130.
17. Sheila Fitzpatrick, *Stalin's Peasants*, p. 62.
18. Robert Conquest, *The Harvest of Sorrow*, p. 182.
19. Alec Nove, *An Economic History of the USSR*, p. 241.
20. Alec Nove, *An Economic History of the USSR*, pp. 241-242.
21. Richard Pipes, *The Russian Revolution*, p. 92.

22. Sheila Fitzpatrick, *Stalin's Peasants*, p. 19.
23. Sheila Fitzpatrick, *Stalin's Peasants*, p. 19.
24. Sheila Fitzpatrick, *Stalin's Peasants*, pp. 23-23.
25. Richard Pipes, *The Russian Revolution*, p. 98.
26. Richard Pipes, *The Russian Revolution*, p. 171.
27. Richard Pipes, The Russian Revolution, p. 106, from James Y. Simms, Jr., in *SR*, XXXVI, No. 3 (1977), 377-98.
28. Richard Pipes, *The Russian Revolution*, p. 96.
29. Richard Pipes, *The Russian Revolution*, p. 104.
30. Richard Pipes, *The Russian Revolution*, p. 86.
31. Richard Pipes, *The Russian Revolution*, p. 176.
32. Richard Pipes, *The Russian Revolution*, p. 100.
33. Richard Pipes, *The Russian Revolution*, p. 105.
34. Richard Pipes, *The Russian Revolution*, p. 105.
35. Richard Pipes, *The Russian Revolution*, p. 173.
36. Richard Pipes, *The Russian Revolution*, p. 175.
37. Richard Pipes, *The Russian Revolution*, p. 176.
38. Richard Pipes, *The Russian Revolution*, p. 237.
39. Richard Pipes, *The Russian Revolution*, p. 207.
40. Richard Pipes, *The Russian Revolution*, p. 245.
41. Richard Pipes, *The Russian Revolution*, p. 327.
42. James D. White, *The Russian Revolution 1917-1921: A Short History* (New York: Edward Arnold, 1994), p. 190.
43. Richard Pipes, *The Russian Revolution*, p. 718.
44. Richard Pipes, *The Russian Revolution*, p. 718.
45. Richard Pipes, *The Russian Revolution*, p. 721.
46. Richard Pipes, *The Russian Revolution*, p. 720.
47. Sheila Fitzpatrick, *Stalin's Peasants*, p. 23.
48. Sheila Fitzpatrick, *Stalin's Peasants*, p. 23.
49. Sheila Fitzpatrick, *Stalin's Peasants*, p. 23.
50. Sheila Fitzpatrick, *Stalin's Peasants*, p. 25.
51. Richard Pipes, *The Russian Revolution*, p. 720.
52. Richard Pipes, *The Russian Revolution*, p. 718.
53. Richard Pipes, *The Russian Revolution*, p. 724.
54. Richard Pipes, *The Russian Revolution*, pp. 671-672.
55. Richard Pipes, *The Russian Revolution*, p. 679.
56. Richard Pipes, *The Russian Revolution*, p. 736.
57. Richard Pipes, *The Russian Revolution*, p. 736, citing M. Ia. Latsis, *Dva goda bor'by na vnutrennem fronte* (Moscow, 1920), 75.
58. Richard Pipes, *The Russian Revolution*, p. 734.
59. Richard Pipes, *The Russian Revolution*, p. 723.
60. Richard Pipes, *The Russian Revolution*, p. 742.
61. W. Bruce Lincoln, *Red Victory*, p. 71.
62. Richard Pipes, *The Russian Revolution*, p. 734.
63. Richard Pipes, *The Russian Revolution*, p. 736.
64. Richard Pipes, *Russia Under the Bolshevik Regime*, p. 96.
65. Richard Pipes, *Russia Under the Bolshevik Regime*, p. 390, from Tsiurupa, *Desiatyi S"ezd*, 422.
66. W. Bruce Lincoln, *Red Victory*, p. 467.
67. Richard Pipes, *Russia Under the Bolshevik Regime*, p. 373.
68. Richard Pipes, *Russia Under the Bolshevik Regime*, p. 377.
69. W. Bruce Lincoln, *Red Victory*, p. 466.

70.	Alec Nove, *An Economic History of the USSR: 1917-1991*, 3rd ed. (New York: Penguin Books, 1992), p. 135.
71.	Alec Nove, *An Economic History of the USSR*, p. 81.
72.	Richard Pipes, *Russia Under the Bolshevik Regime*, p. 392.
73.	Richard Pipes, *Russia Under the Bolshevik Regime*, p. 391.
74.	Alec Nove, *An Economic History of the USSR*, p. 90.
75.	Alec Nove, *An Economic History of the USSR*, p. 91.
76.	Alec Nove, *An Economic History of the USSR*, p. 89.
77.	Alec Nove, *An Economic History of the USSR*, p. 88.
78.	Alec Nove, *An Economic History of the USSR*, pp. 89-90.
79.	Alec Nove, *An Economic History of the USSR*, pp. 101-102.
80.	Alec Nove, *An Economic History of the USSR*, p. 101, from *Etapy ekonomicheskoi politiki SSSR*, ed P. Vaisberg (Moscow, 1934), p. 35.
81.	Alec Nove, *An Economic History of the USSR*, p. 102.
82.	Alec Nove, *An Economic History of the USSR*, p. 102.
83.	Alec Nove, *An Economic History of the USSR*, p. 106.
84.	Alec Nove, *An Economic History of the USSR*, p. 108.
85.	Alec Nove, *An Economic History of the USSR*, p. 108.
86.	Sheila Fitzpatrick, *Stalin's Peasants*, p. 28.
87.	Alec Nove, *An Economic History of the USSR*, p. 153, from J. Stalin, *Works*, Vol II, p. 7.
88.	Robert C. Tucker, *Stalin In Power*, pp. 80-81.
89.	R. W. Davies, *The Economic Transformation of the Soviet Union*, pp. 13-14.
90.	Alec Nove, *An Economic History of the USSR*, pp. 136-139.
91.	Robert C. Tucker, *Stalin In Power*, p. 82.

Chapter 14
The Collectivization of Agriculture - June 1929-1933

1.	Robert C. Tucker, *Stalin In Power*, p. 130.
2.	Roy Medvedev, *Let History Judge*, p. 222.
3.	Roy Medvedev, *Let History Judge*, p. 223.
4.	Robert C. Tucker, *Stalin In Power*, p. 130.
5.	Sheila Fitzpatrick, *Stalin's Peasants*, p. 53.
6.	Robert C. Tucker, *Stalin In Power*, p. 130.
7.	Robert C. Tucker, *Stalin In Power*, p. 182.
8.	Alec Nove, *An Economic History of the USSR*, p. 166.
9.	Robert C. Tucker, *Stalin In Power*, p. 180.
10.	Roy Medvedev, *Let History Judge*, p. 233.
11.	Robert C. Tucker, *Stalin In Power*, p. 181.
12.	Roy Medvedev, *Let History Judge*, p. 222.
13.	Robert C. Tucker, *Stalin In Power*, p. 133.
14.	Roy Medvedev, *Let History Judge*, p. 222.
15.	Robert C. Tucker, *Stalin In Power*, pp. 134-135.
16.	Robert C. Tucker, *Stalin In Power*, pp. 134-135.
17.	Robert C. Tucker, *Stalin In Power*, p. 135.
18.	Roy Medvedev, *Let History Judge*, pp. 232-233.
19.	Robert C. Tucker, *Stalin In Power*, p. 179.
20.	Sheila Fitzpatrick, *Stalin's Peasants*, p. 42.
21.	Robert Conquest, *The Harvest of Sorrow*, p. 154.
22.	Robert C. Tucker, *Stalin In Power*, p. 182.
23.	Robert C. Tucker, *Stalin In Power*, p. 182.

24. Roy Medvedev, *Let History Judge*, p. 225.
25. Robert C. Tucker, *Stalin In Power*, p. 186.
26. Robert Conquest, *The Harvest of Sorrow*, p. 159, from Alexander Baykov, *The Development of the Soviet Economic System*, Cambridge, 1946, p. 196.
27. Robert Conquest, *The Harvest of Sorrow*, p. 159.
28. Robert Conquest, *The Harvest of Sorrow*, pp. 146-147.
29. Sheila Fitzpatrick, *Stalin's Peasants*, p. 52.
30. Sheila Fitzpatrick, *Stalin's Peasants*, p. 53.
31. Sheila Fitzpatrick, *Stalin's Peasants*, p. 44.
32. Robert Conquest, *The Harvest of Sorrow*, p. 151.
33. Sheila Fitzpatrick, *Stalin's Peasants*, pp. 54-55.
34. Sheila Fitzpatrick, *Stalin's Peasants*, p. 55.
35. Sheila Fitzpatrick, *Stalin's Peasants*, p. 53.
36. Sheila Fitzpatrick, *Stalin's Peasants*, p. 65.
37. Alec Nove, *An Economic History of the USSR*, pp. 170-171.
38. Alec Nove, *An Economic History of the USSR*, pp. 172, 186.
39. Sheila Fitzpatrick, *Stalin's Peasants*, p. 50.
40. Sheila Fitzpatrick, *Stalin's Peasants*, p. 27.
41. Sheila Fitzpatrick, *Stalin's Peasants*, p. 27.
42. Robert Conquest, *The Harvest of Sorrow*, p. 150.
43. Robert Conquest, *The Harvest of Sorrow*, p. 123.
44. Robert Conquest, *The Harvest of Sorrow*, p. 125.
45. Robert Conquest, *The Harvest of Sorrow*, p. 126.
46. Robert Conquest, *The Harvest of Sorrow*, p. 126.
47. Robert Conquest, *The Harvest of Sorrow*, p. 159.
48. Robert Tucker, *Stalin In Power*, p. 187.
49. Alec Nove, *An Economic History of the USSR*, p. 173.
50. Robert C. Tucker, *Stalin In Power*, p. 187; Alec Nove, *An Economic History of the USSR*, p. 173.
51. Alec Nove, *An Economic History of the USSR*, p. 173.
52. Robert C. Tucker, *Stalin In Power*, p. 194.
53. Robert C. Tucker, *Stalin In Power*, p. 187.
54. Robert C. Tucker, *Stalin In Power*, p. 191.
55. Robert C. Tucker, *Stalin In Power*, p. 190.
56. Alec Nove, *An Economic History of the USSR*, p. 180.
57. Robert C. Tucker, *Stalin In Power*, p. 190.
58. Robert Conquest, *The Harvest of Sorrow*, p. 229.
59. Robert C. Tucker, *Stalin In Power*, p. 191.
60. Sheila Fitzpatrick, *Stalin's Peasants*, p. 73.
61. Robert C. Tucker, *Stalin In Power*, p. 194.
62. Sheila Fitzpatrick, *Stalin's Peasants*, p. 70.
63. Robert Conquest, *The Harvest of Sorrow*, p. 185.
64. Sheila Fitzpatrick, *Stalin's Peasants*, p. 70.
65. Sheila Fitzpatrick, *Stalin's Peasants*, p. 74.
66. Sheila Fitzpatrick, *Stalin's Peasants*, pp. 76-77.
67. Robert Conquest, *The Harvest of Sorrow*, pp. 175-176.
68. Sheila Fitzpatrick, *Stalin's Peasants*, p. 70.
69. Robert Conquest, *The Harvest of Sorrow*, p. 236.
70. Robert Conquest, *The Harvest of Sorrow*, pp. 248-249.
71. Robert Conquest, *The Harvest of Sorrow*, p. 327.
72. Sheila Fitzpatrick, *Stalin's Peasants*, p. 76.
73. Robert C. Tucker, *Stalin In Power*, p. 188.

74.   Sheila Fitzpatrick, *Stalin's Peasants*, p. 78.
75.   Robert C. Tucker, *Stalin In Power*, p. 187; Alec Nove, *An Economic History of the USSR*, p. 173.
76.   Robert Conquest, *The Harvest of Sorrow*, p. 261.
77.   Robert Conquest, *The Harvest of Sorrow*, pp. 241, 262.
78.   Roy Medvedev, *Let History Judge*, p. 244; Robert Conquest, *The Harvest of Sorrow*, p. 303; Robert C. Tucker, *Stalin In Power*, p. 195.
79.   Moshe Lewin, *The Making of the Soviet System*, pp. 157-158.
80.   Moshe Lewin, *The Making of the Soviet System*, pp. 156-157.
81.   Robert C. Tucker, *Stalin In Power*, p. 188.
82.   Moshe Lewin, *The Making of the Soviet System*, p. 157.
83.   Robert Conquest, *The Harvest of Sorrow*, p. 264.
84.   Moshe Lewin, *The Making of the Soviet System*, p. 160.
85.   Moshe Lewin, *The Making of the Soviet System*, p. 160-161.
86.   Moshe Lewin, *The Making of the Soviet System*, p. 162.
87.   Robert C. Tucker, *Stalin In Power*, p. 187.
88.   Alec Nove, *An Economic History of the USSR*, p. 181.
89.   Moshe Lewin, *The Making of the Soviet System*, p. 164.
90.   Robert C. Tucker, *Stalin In Power*, p. 187.
91.   Alec Nove, *An Economic History of the USSR*, p. 173.
92.   Robert C. Tucker, *Stalin In Power*, p. 187.
93.   Sheila Fitzpatrick, *Stalin's Peasants*, p. 158.
94.   Sheila Fitzpatrick, *Stalin's Peasants*, p. 194.
95.   Sheila Fitzpatrick, *Stalin's Peasants*, p. 109-110.
96.   Sheila Fitzpatrick, *Stalin's Peasants*, p. 110.
97.   Sheila Fitzpatrick, *Stalin's Peasants*, p. 199.
98.   Sheila Fitzpatrick, *Stalin's Peasants*, p. 110.
99.   Sheila Fitzpatrick, *Stalin's Peasants*, p. 201.
100.   Sheila Fitzpatrick, *Stalin's Peasants*, p. 190.
101.   Sheila Fitzpatrick, *Stalin's Peasants*, p. 191-192.
102.   Sheila Fitzpatrick, *Stalin's Peasants*, p. 192.
103.   Sheila Fitzpatrick, *Stalin's Peasants*, p. 192.
104.   Sheila Fitzpatrick, *Stalin's Peasants*, p. 193.
105.   Sheila Fitzpatrick, *Stalin's Peasants*, p. 175.
106.   Sheila Fitzpatrick, *Stalin's Peasants*, p. 174-175.
107.   Sheila Fitzpatrick, *Stalin's Peasants*, p. 128-129; Robert C. Tucker, *Stalin In Power*, p. 195.
108.   Sheila Fitzpatrick, *Stalin's Peasants*, p. 143.
109.   Roy Medvedev, *Let History Judge*, p. 249.
110.   Sheila Fitzpatrick, *Stalin's Peasants*, p. 137.
111.   Robert Conquest, *The Harvest of Sorrow*, p. 342.
112.   Alec Nove, *An Economic History of the USSR*, p. 243.
113.   R.W. Davies, ed., *The Economic Transformation of the Soviet Union*, p. 121.
114.   Robert Conquest, *The Harvest of Sorrow*, p. 183; Sheila Fitzpatrick, *Stalin's Peasants*, p. 67.
115.   Sheila Fitzpatrick, *Stalin's Peasants*, p. 66.
116.   Robert C. Tucker, *Stalin In Power*, p. 202.
117.   Robert Conquest, *The Harvest of Sorrow*, p. 181.
118.   Moshe Lewin, *The Making of the Soviet System*, p. 180.
119.   Robert Conquest, *The Harvest of Sorrow*, p. 181.
120.   Sheila Fitzpatrick, *Stalin's Peasants*, p. 192.
121.   Robert Conquest, *The Harvest of Sorrow*, p. 180.
122.   Roy Medvedev, *Let History Judge*, p. 222.
123.   Alec Nove, *An Economic History of the USSR*, p. 186.

124.   Robert C. Tucker, *Stalin In Power*, p. 200.
125.   Robert C. Tucker, *Stalin In Power*, p. 203.
126.   Alec Nove, *An Economic History of the USSR*, p. 187.
127.   Robert C. Tucker, *Stalin In Power*, p. 203.

Chapter 15
Russian Industry and the Revolution

1.   R. W. Davies, *The Economic Transformation of the Soviet Union*, pp. 1-2.
2.   Sheila Fitzpatrick, *Stalin's Peasants*, p. 19.
3.   Alec Nove, *An Economic History of the USSR*, p. 6.
4.   R. W. Davies, *The Economic Transformation of the USSR*, p. 9.
5.   Alec Nove, *An Economic History of the USSR*, p. 47.
6.   Richard Pipes, *The Russian Revolution*, p. 692.
7.   Richard Pipes, *The Russian Revolution*, p. 692.
8.   Richard Pipes, *The Russian Revolution*, p. 694.
9.   Alec Nove, *An Economic History of the USSR*, p. 83.
10.   Alec Nove, *An Economic History of the USSR*, p. 92.
11.   Alec Nove, *An Economic History of the USSR*, p. 99.
12.   Alec Nove, *An Economic History of the USSR*, pp. 238-239.
13.   Richard Pipes, *The Russian Revolution*, p. 678.
14.   Richard Pipes, *The Russian Revolution*, pp. 678-679.
15.   Alec Nove, *An Economic History of the USSR*, p. 62.
16.   Alec Nove, *An Economic History of the USSR*, p. 63.
17.   The exact figure is disputed. The VSNKh official figure was 4,420, although 4,547 is cited as well. Alec Nove, *An Economic History of the USSR*, p. 63; Richard Pipes, *The Russian Revolution*, p. 692.
18.   Richard Pipes, *Russia Under the Bolshevik Regime* (New York: Alfred A. Knopf, 1993), p. 373.
19.   Richard Pipes, *The Russian Revolution*, pp. 686-687.
20.   Richard Pipes, *The Russian Revolution*, p. 693.
21.   The number was 42 according to Pipes. Richard Pipes, *The Russian Revolution*, p. 693. White gives a figure of 52. James D. White, *The Russian Revolution 1917-1921*, p. 223.
22.   Alec Nove, *An Economic History of the USSR*, p. 92.
23.   Richard Pipes, *The Russian Revolution*, p. 694.
24.   Alec Nove, *An Economic History of the USSR*, p. 92.
25.   Alec Nove, *An Economic History of the USSR*, p. 76.
26.   Richard Pipes, *Russia Under the Bolshevik Regime*, p. 379.
27.   Alec Nove, *An Economic History of the USSR*, p. 60.
28.   R. W. Davies, *The Economic Transformation of the Soviet Union*, p. 6.
29.   Richard Pipes, *Russia Under the Bolshevik Regime*, p. 687.

Chapter 16
The New Economic Policy and the Five-Year Plans

1.   Richard Pipes, *Russia Under the Bolshevik Regime*, pp. 400-401.
2.   Richard Pipes, *Russia Under the Bolshevik Regime*, p. 388.
3.   Richard Pipes, *Russia Under the Bolshevik Regime*, p. 391.
4.   Richard Pipes, *Russia Under the Bolshevik Regime*, p. 400.
5.   Alec Nove, *An Economic History of the USSR*, p. 110.
6.   R. W. Davies, *The Economic Transformation of the Soviet Union*, p. 84.
7.   Alec Nove, *An Economic History of the USSR*, p. 112.
8.   R. W. Davies, *The Economic Transformation of the Soviet Union*, p. 84.

9. Richard Pipes, *Russia Under the Bolshevik Regime*, p. 397.
10. Alec Nove, *An Economic History of the USSR*, pp. 89, 228.
11. Richard Pipes, *The Russian Revolution*, pp. 206-207.
12. Alec Nove, *An Economic History of the USSR*, p. 85.
13. Alec Nove, *An Economic History of the USSR*, p. 84; R. W. Davies, *The Economic Transformation of the Soviet Union*, p. 165.
14. R. W. Davies, *The Economic Transformation of the Soviet Union*, p. 136.
15. Richard Pipes, *Russia Under the Bolshevik Regime*, p. 371.
16. R. W. Davies, *The Economic Transformation of the Soviet Union*, p. 135.
17. Alec Nove, *An Economic History of the USSR*, p. 135.
18. Alec Nove, *An Economic History of the USSR*, pp. 135, 144.
19. Alec Nove, *An Economic History of the USSR*, pp. 139-140.
20. Alec Nove, *An Economic History of the USSR*, p. 137.
21. Alec Nove, *An Economic History of the USSR*, pp. 133-134.
22. Alec Nove, *An Economic History of the USSR*, p. 194.
23. Robert C. Tucker, *Stalin In Power*, pp. 95-96.
24. Robert C. Tucker, *Stalin In Power*, p. 100.
25. Alec Nove, *An Economic History of the USSR*, p. 213.
26. Alec Nove, *An Economic History of the USSR*, p. 144.
27. Alec Nove, *An Economic History of the USSR*, p. 214.
28. Alec Nove, *An Economic History of the USSR*, p. 212.
29. Alec Nove, *An Economic History of the USSR*, p. 203.
30. Robert C. Tucker, *Stalin In Power*, p. 261.
31. Robert C. Tucker, *Stalin In Power*, p. 97.
32. R. W. Davies, *The Economic Transformation of the Soviet Union*, pp. 143, 147-148.
33. R. W. Davies, *The Economic Transformation of the Soviet Union*, pp. 148-150.
34. Robert C. Tucker, *Stalin In Power*, p. 191.
35. Robert C. Tucker, *Stalin In Power*, p. 195.
36. Alec Nove, *An Economic History of the USSR*, pp. 228, 231.
37. Roberta T. Manning, "The Soviet economic crisis of 1936-1940 and the Great Purges," *Stalinist Terror*, p. 116.
38. Roberta T. Manning, *Stalinist Terror*, p. 127.
39. Alec Nove, *An Economic History of the USSR*, p. 250.
40. Roberta T. Manning, *Stalinist Terror*, p. 140.
41. Alec Nove, *An Economic History of the USSR*, p. 251.
42. Alec Nove, *An Economic History of the USSR*, p. 259.
43. Alec Nove, *An Economic History of the USSR*, p. 263.
44. Alec Nove, *An Economic History of the USSR*, p. 259.

Chapter 17
The Role of Scarcity in Political and Economic Controls

1. Moshe Lewin, *The Making of the Soviet System*, p. 180.
2. Sheila Fitzpatrick, *Stalin's Peasants*, p. 66.
3. Sheila Fitzpatrick, *Stalin's Peasants*, pp. 144-145.
4. U.S. figures from *Historical Statistics of the United States, Colonial Times to 1970, Bicentennial Edition, Part 1* (Washington, D.C.: U.S. Bureau of the Census, 1975), p. 8.
   Figures for the Soviet Union are from the *1932 Commerce Year Book, Vol. II*, (Washington, D.C.: U.S. Bureau of the Census, 1933), p. 261.
   Figures for Germany are from the *1930 Commerce Year Book, Vol. II*, (Washington, D.C.: U.S. Bureau of the Census, 1931), p. 240.

5. Output figures for the U.S. are from *Historical Statistics of the United States, Colonial Times to 1970, Bicentennial Edition, Part 1* (Washington, D.C.: U.S. Bureau of the Census, 1975), pp. 511 (wheat, corn, oats, barley), 513 (rye), and 516 (sugar beets). Output figures for Russian and Germany are from U.S. Department of Commerce Yearbooks for the years 1928 through 1932.

Russian wheat, rye, corn, oats, barley, and sugar beet figure sources:

Year	Yearbook	Page
1926	1928	546
1927	1928	546
1928	1932	262
1929	1932	262
1930	1932	262

German wheat, rye, corn, oats, barley, and sugar beet figure sources:

Year	Yearbook	Page
1926	1929	291
1927	1929	291
1928	1930	291
1929	1930	107
1930	1932	107

6. Figures for U.S. iron ore production are from *Historical Statistics of the United States*, p. 599.

Russian ore figures from U.S. Department of Commerce Yearbooks:

Year	Yearbook	Page
1926	1928	546
1927	1928	546
1928	1932	262
1929	1932	262
1930	1932	262

German ore figures from U.S. Department of Commerce Yearbooks:

Year	Yearbook	Page
1926	1932	265
1927	1932	265
1928	1932	265
1929	1932	265
1930	1932	265

7.　　U.S. figures for pig iron are from *Historical Statistics of the United States*, p. 599.

Russian figures from U.S. Department of Commerce Yearbooks:

Year	Yearbook	Page
1926	1932	265
1927	1932	265
1928	1932	265
1929	1932	265
1930	1932	265

German figures from U.S. Department of Commerce Yearbooks:

Year	Yearbook	Page
1926	1929	292
1927	1929	292
1928	1929	292
1929	1932	110
1930	1932	110

8.　　U.S. figures for steel production are from U.S. Department of Commerce Yearbooks:

Year	Yearbook	Page
1921-25	1932	696
1927	1932	696
1928	1932	696
1929	1932	696
1930	1932	696

Russian figures from U.S. Department of Commerce Yearbooks:

Year	Yearbook	Page
1926	1932	265
1927	1932	696
1928	1932	696
1929	1932	696
1930	1932	696

German figures from U.S. Department of Commerce Yearbooks:

Year	Yearbook	Page
1926	1929	292
1927	1932	696
1928	1932	696
1929	1932	696
1930	1932	696

9. U.S. figures for coal production are from *Historical Statistics of the United States*.
    Anthracite and bituminous production has been combined from pages 592 (anthracite) and 589 (bituminous).

    Russian figures from U.S. Department of Commerce Yearbooks:

Year	Yearbook	Page
1926	1932	265
1927	1932	265
1928	1932	265
1929	1932	265
1930	1932	265

    German figures from U.S. Department of Commerce Yearbooks:

Year	Yearbook	Page
1926	1929	292
1927	1929	292
1928	1929	110
1929	1932	243
1930	1932	110

10. U.S. figures for copper production are from *Historical Statistics of the United States*, p. 602.

    Russian figures from U.S. Department of Commerce Yearbooks:

Year	Yearbook	Page
1926	1932	265
1927	1932	265
1928	1932	265
1929	1932	265
1930	1932	265

    German figures from U.S. Department of Commerce Yearbooks:

Year	Yearbook	Page
1926	1930	243
1927	1930	243
1928	1930	243
1929	1932	110
1930	1932	110

11. U.S. figures for lead production are from *Historical Statistics of the United States*, p. 603.

German figures are from U.S. Department of Commerce Yearbooks:

Year	Yearbook	Page
1926	1932	698
1927	1932	698
1928	1932	698
1929	1932	698
1930	1932	698

12. U.S. figures for oil production are from *Historical Statistics of the United States*, p. 593.

Russian figures from U.S. Department of Commerce Yearbooks:

Year	Yearbook	Page
1926	1932	265
1927	1932	265
1928	1932	265
1929	1932	265
1930	1932	265

13. The figure for Germany's geographical area is from the *1932 Commerce Year Book, Vol. II*, p. 105.
The figure for railroad lines is from p. 701.
The figure for Russia's geographical area is from the *1932 Commerce Year Book, Vol. II*, p. 261.
The figure for railroad lines is from p. 702.
14. Alec Nove, *An Economic History of the USSR*, p. 3.
15. R. W. Davies, *The Economic Transformation of the Soviet Union*, p. 2.
16. Alec Nove, *An Economic History of the USSR*, pp. 4, 7, from P. Bairuch, *Annales* (Paris), November-December 1965.
17. Alec Nove, *An Economic History of the USSR*, p. 9.
18. Richard Pipes, *Russia Under the Bolshevik Regime*, p. 379.
19. Alec Nove, *An Economic History of the USSR*, p. 48.
20. R. W. Davies, *The Economic Transformation of the Soviet Union*, pp. 166-167; Roberta T. Manning, *Stalinist Terror*, pp. 127-128.
21. Robert Conquest, *The Harvest of Sorrow*, p. 181.
22. Richard Pipes, *The Russian Revolution*, p. 838.
23. Richard Pipes, *The Russian Revolution*, p. 836.
24. Roberta Manning, *Stalinist Terror*, pp. 123, 125.
25. Robert C. Tucker, *Stalin In Power*, pp. 249-250.

Chapter 18
Background to Fascism and an Overview of Nazi Germany

1. Stanley G. Payne, *A History of Fascism, 1914-1945*. (Madison: The University of Wisconsin, 1995), p. 217.
2. Stanley G. Payne, *A History of Fascism*, p. 171.
3. William Carr, *A History of Germany: 1815-1990*, Fourth Ed., (New York: Edward Arnold, 1991), p. 56.

4. Stanley G. Payne, *A History of Fascism*, p. 89.
5. Stanley G. Payne, *A History of Fascism*, p. 104.
6. Alec Nove, *An Economic History of the USSR*, p. 112.
7. Moshe Lewin, *The Making of the Soviet System*, p. 219.
8. Daniel Guerin, *Fascism and Big Business*, (New York: Pathfinder Press; 1973), p. 215.
9. Stanley G. Payne, *A History of Fascism*, pp. 115-116.
10. William Carr, *A History of Germany*, p. 35.
11. William Carr, *A History of Germany*, p. 65.
12. William Carr, *A History of Germany*, p. 107.
13. William Carr, *A History of Germany*, p. 240.
14. William Carr, *A History of Germany*, p. 254.
15. William Carr, *A History of Germany*, p. 263.
16. Stanley G. Payne, *A History of Fascism*, p. 171.
17. William Carr, *A History of Germany*, p. 269.
18. William Carr, *A History of Germany*, p. 271.
19. William Carr, *A History of Germany*, pp. 270-271.
20. William Carr, *A History of Germany*, p. 278.
21. William Carr, *A History of Germany*, p. 273.
22. Klaus P. Fisher, *Nazi Germany: A New History*, (New York, The Continuum Publishing Company, 1995), p. 72.
23. Klaus P. Fisher, *Nazi Germany: A New History*, pp. 127, 131, 143.
24. Jackson J. Spielvogel, *Hitler and Nazi Germany: A History*, 3rd ed. (Upper Saddle River, N.J.: Prentice-Hall, Inc., 1988), p. 34.
25. Stanley G. Payne, *A History of Fascism*, p. 154.
26. Klaus P. Fisher, *Nazi Germany: A New History*, p. 164.
27. Jackson J. Spielvogel, *Hitler and Nazi Germany: A History*, p. 46.
28. Klaus P. Fisher, *Nazi Germany: A New History*, p. 204.
29. Klaus P. Fisher, *Nazi Germany: A New History*, pp. 203-204.
30. Jackson J. Spielvogel, *Hitler and Nazi Germany: A History*, p. 53.
31. Klaus P. Fisher, *Nazi Germany: A New History*, pp. 215-216.
32. Lewis L. Lorwin, *National Planning In Selected Countries*, (Washington, D.C.: National Resources Planning Board, 1941), Table I, p. 39.
33. Jackson J. Spielvogel, *Hitler and Nazi Germany: A History*, p. 54.
34. Jackson J. Spielvogel, *Hitler and Nazi Germany: A History*, p. 53.
35. Klaus P. Fisher, *Nazi Germany: A New History*, p. 224.
36. Klaus P. Fisher, *Nazi Germany: A New History*, p. 227.
37. Lewis L. Lorwin, *National Planning In Selected Countries*, Table I, p. 39.
38. Klaus P. Fisher, *Nazi Germany: A New History*, p. 237.
39. Lewis L. Lorwin, *National Planning In Selected Countries*, Table I, p. 39.
40. Klaus P. Fisher, *Nazi Germany: A New History*, p. 246.
41. Klaus P. Fisher, *Nazi Germany: A New History*, p. 247.
42. Klaus P. Fisher, *Nazi Germany: A New History*, p. 249.
43. Lewis L. Lorwin, *National Planning In Selected Countries*, Table VI, p. 13.

Chapter 19
The Nazi Dictatorship (1933 - 1939)

1. Klaus P. Fischer, *Nazi Germany*, p. 243.
2. Klaus P. Fischer, *Nazi Germany*, p. 255.
3. Klaus P. Fischer, *Nazi Germany*, pp. 270-271.
4. Jackson J. Spielvogel, *Hitler and Nazi Germany*, pp. 102-104.

5.   Klaus P. Fischer, *Nazi Germany*, p. 274.

6.   Klaus P. Fischer, *Nazi Germany*, p. 290.

7.   Jackson J. Spielvogel, *Hitler and Nazi Germany*, p. 86.

8.   J. Noakes and G. Pridham, eds., *Nazism 1919-1945: Volume 2, State, Economy and Society 1933-1939*, (Exeter, England: University of Exeter Press, 1995), p. 216.

9.   Lewis L. Lorwin, *National Planning In Selected Countries*, Table VI, p. 13; Table I, p. 39.

10.   Lewis L. Lorwin, *National Planning In Selected Countries*, Table VI, p. 13.

11.   Noakes and Pridham, *Nazism 1919-1945*, p. 277.

12.   Jackson J. Spielvogel, *Hitler and Nazi Germany*, p. 272-273. Fischer estimates that there were 1,000 businesses destroyed and that the number of those sent to concentration camps was around 26,000. Klaus P. Fischer, *Nazi Germany*, p. 392.

13.   Klaus P. Fischer, *Nazi Germany*, p. 499.

14.   Klaus P. Fischer, *Nazi Germany*, p. 511.

15.   Richard Grunberger, *The 12-Year Reich: A Social History of Nazi Germany 1933-1945*, (New York: Da Capo Press, 1995), p. 186.

Chapter 20
German Economic Resources and the German Economy

1.   U.S. iron ore production figures from *Historical Statistics of the United States*, p. 599.
Russian ore figures from the U.S. Department of Commerce Yearbooks:

Year	Yearbook	Page
1926	1928	546
1927	1928	546
1928	1932	262
1929	1932	262
1930	1932	262

German ore figures from U.S. Department of Commerce Yearbook for 1932, p. 265.

2.   U.S. figures for pig iron are from *Historical Statistics of the United States*, p. 599.
Russian ore figures from U.S. Department of Commerce Yearbook for 1932, p. 265.
German ore figures are from the U.S. Department of Commerce Yearbooks:

Year	Yearbook	Page
1926	1928	546
1927	1928	546
1928	1932	262
1929	1932	262
1930	1932	262

3.   U.S. figures for steel production are from pages 377 and 696 of the 1932 yearbook.
German figures are from the U.S. Department of Commerce Yearbooks:

Year	Yearbook	Page
1926	1929	292
1927	1932	696
1928	1932	696
1929	1932	696
1930	1932	696

Russian figures are from the U.S. Department of Commerce Yearbooks:

Year	Yearbook	Page
1926	1932	265
1927	1932	696
1928	1932	696
1929	1932	696
1930	1932	696

4. U.S. figures for coal production are from *Historical Statistics of the United States*. Anthracite and bituminous production has been combined from pages 592 (anthracite) and 589 (bituminous). German figures are from the U.S. Department of Commerce Yearbooks:

Year	Yearbook	Page
1926	1932	265
1927	1932	265
1928	1932	265
1929	1932	265
1930	1932	265

Russian figures are from the U.S. Department of Commerce Yearbooks:

Year	Yearbook	Page
1926	1929	292
1927	1929	292
1928	1929	110
1929	1932	243
1930	1932	110

5. U.S. figures for copper production are from *Historical Statistics of the United States*, p. 602. German figures are from the U.S. Department of Commerce Yearbooks:

Year	Yearbook	Page
1926	1930	243
1927	1930	243
1928	1930	243
1929	1932	110
1930	1932	110

Russian figures are from the U.S. Department of Commerce Yearbooks:

Year	Yearbook	Page
1926	1932	265
1927	1932	265
1928	1932	265
1929	1932	265
1930	1932	265

6. U.S. figures for lead production are from *Historical Statistics of the United States*, p. 603. German figures are from the U.S. Department of Commerce Yearbooks:

Year	Yearbook	Page
1926	1932	698
1927	1932	698
1928	1932	698
1929	1932	698
1930	1932	698

7. J. Noakes, *Nazism 1919-1945*, p. 291.
8. Richard Grunberger, *The 12-Year Reich*, p. 204.
9. William Carr, *A History of Germany*, p. 289.
10. Klaus P. Fischer, *Nazi Germany*, p. 132.
11. Richard Grunberger, *The 12-Year Reich*, p. 170.
12. Richard Grunberger, *The 12-Year Reich*, p. 173.
13. Richard Grunberger, *The 12-Year Reich*, p. 4.
14. Richard Grunberger, *The 12-Year Reich*, p. 4.
15. Richard Grunberger, *The 12-Year Reich*, p. 4, from Robert A. Brady, *The Spirit and Structure of German Fascism*, (New York; 1937), p. 13.
16. Richard Grunberger, *The 12-Year Reich*, p. 5.
17. William Carr, *A History of Germany*, p. 129.
18. J. Noakes, *Nazism: 1919-1945*, pp. 322-323.
19. J. Noakes, *Nazism: 1919-1945*, pp. 318-321.
20. Richard Grunberger, *The 12-Year Reich*, p. 5.
21. William Carr, *A History of Germany*, p. 327.
22. J. Noakes, *Nazism: 1919-1945*, p. 357.
23. J. Noakes, *Nazism: 1919-1945*, p. 358.
24. William Carr, *A History of Germany*, pp. 327-328.
25. J. Noakes, *Nazism: 1919-1945*, p. 267.
26. J. Noakes, *Nazism: 1919-1945*, p. 275.
27. J. Noakes, *Nazism: 1919-1945*, pp. 268-269; 317-318.
28. J. Noakes, *Nazism: 1919-1945*, pp. 272-273, 276; Spielvogel, *Hitler and Nazi Germany*, p. 93.
29. Klaus P. Fischer, *Nazi Germany*, p. 377.
30. Richard Grunberger, *The 12-Year Reich*, p. 178.
31. Jackson J. Spielvogel, *Hitler and Nazi Germany*, p. 95.
32. J. Noakes, *Nazism: 1919-1945*, p. 291.
33. J. Noakes, *Nazism: 1919-1945*, p. 292.
34. Richard Grunberger, *The 12-Year Reich*, p. 179, from *Frankfurter Zeitung*, 24 October 1937; J. Noakes, *Nazism: 1919-1945*, p. 315.
35. Richard Grunberger, *The 12-Year Reich*, p. 170.
36. Daniel Guerin, *Fascism and Big Business*, (New York: Pathfinder, 1994), p. 215.
37. Richard Grunberger, *The 12-Year Reich*, p. 176.
38. J. Noakes, *Nazism: 1919-1945*, p. 315.
39. Richard Grunberger, *The 12-Year Reich*, p. 177.
40. J. Noakes, *Nazism: 1919-1945*, p. 313.
41. Alec Nove, *An Economic History of the USSR*, p. 134.
42. T.S. Ashton, *The Industrial Revolution: 1760-1830*, (London, Oxford University Press; 1968), p. 29.
43. William Carr, *A History of Germany*, p. 67.

44. William Carr, *A History of Germany*, p. 66.
45. William Carr, *A History of Germany*, p. 65.
46. William Carr, *A History of Germany*, p. 129.
47. William Carr, *A History of Germany*, p. 130.
48. William Carr, *A History of Germany*, p. 129.
49. William Carr, *A History of Germany*, p. 137.
50. William Carr, *A History of Germany*, p. 167.
51. William Carr, *A History of Germany*, p. 167.
52. William Carr, *A History of Germany*, p. 167.
53. William Carr, *A History of Germany*, p. 168.
54. William Carr, *A History of Germany*, pp. 168-169.
55. William Carr, *A History of Germany*, pp. 271, 288.
56. William Carr, *A History of Germany*, p. 270.
57. William Carr, *A History of Germany*, p. 288.

Chapter 21
The United States and the Great Depression

1. *Historical Statistics of the United States, Colonial Times to 1970, Bicentennial Edition*, (Washington, D.C., U.S. Bureau of the Census, 1975), Table I: Series D 85-86, Unemployment: 1890 to 1970, Historical Statistics, Part 1, p. 135.
2. Nell Irvin Painter, *Standing at Armageddon: The United States, 1877-1919*, (New York: W.W. Norton & Company, 1987), p. 116.
3. Edward Robb Ellis, *A Nation In Torment: The Great American Depression 1929-1939*, (New York: Kodansha International, 1995), p. 219.
4. Edward Robb Ellis, *A Nation In Torment*, pp. 220-221.
5. Edward Robb Ellis, *A Nation In Torment*, p. 221.
6. Charles P. Kindleberger, *The World In Depression: 1929-1939*, (Los Angeles: University of California Press, 1986), pp. 1-6.
7. Charles P. Kindleberger, *The World In Depression*, p. 104.
8. *Historical Statistics of the United States*, Series D 85-86, Part 1, p. 135.
9. *Historical Statistics of the United States*, Series D 85-86, Part 1, p. 135.
10. *Who Built America? Working People and the Nation's Economy, Politics, Culture, and Society*, Vol. 2, Joshua Freeman et al. (New York: Pantheon Books, 1992) p. 271.
11. *Historical Statistics of the United States*, Series D 85-86, Part 1, p. 135.
12. *Who Built America?*, Vol. 2, Joshua Freeman, pp. 274-277.
13. *Who Built America?*, Vol. 2, Joshua Freeman, p. 275.
14. Charles P. Kindleberger, *The World In Depression*, p. 45.
15. *Who Built America?*, Vol. 2, Joshua Freeman, p.322; Klaus P. Fischer, *Nazi Germany*, p. 215.
16. Allan Nevins and Henry Steele Commager, *A Pocket History of the United States*, (New York: Pocket Books, 1992), p. 405.
17. Charles P. Kindleberger, *The World In Depression*, pp. 43, 50.
18. Charles P. Kindleberger, *The World In Depression*, p. 53.
19. Charles P. Kindleberger, *The World In Depression*, pp. 54, 59.
20. Charles P. Kindleberger, *The World In Depression*, p. 59.
21. Charles P. Kindleberger, *The World In Depression*, p. 95.
22. Charles P. Kindleberger, *The World In Depression*, p. 105.
23. Charles P. Kindleberger, *The World In Depression*, pp. 102, 106.
24. Charles P. Kindleberger, *The World In Depression*, p. 105.

25. *Who Built America?*, Vol. 2, Joshua Freeman, p. 321.

26. *Who Built America?*, Vol. 2, Joshua Freeman, p. 319.

27. *Who Built America?*, Vol. 2, Joshua Freeman, pp. 105, 106.

28. Charles P. Kindleberger, *The World In Depression*, pp. 112-113.

29. Charles P. Kindleberger, *The World In Depression*, p. 231.

30. Michael Barone, *Our Country: The Shaping of America from Roosevelt to Reagan*, (New York: The Free Press, 1990), p. 44.

31. *Who Built America*, Vol. 2; pp. 319-322.

32. Robert E. Hall and John B. Taylor, *Macroeconomics: Theory, Performance, and Policy*, (New York: W.W. Norton & Company, 1991), p. 30.

33. Charles P. Kindleberger, *The World In Depression*, pp. 78-82.

34. Allan Nevins and Henry Steele Commager, *A Pocket History of the United States*, p. 423.

35. *Who Built America*, Vol. 2; pp. 349-350; *A Pocket History of the United States*, p. 424.

36. Charles P. Kindleberger, *The World In Depression*, p. 84.

37. Carl Abbott, *Urban America in the Modern Age: 1920 to the Present*, (Arlington Heights, IL: Harlan Davidson, Inc., 1987), p. 2.

Chapter 22
American Democracy and Patterns in Economic Development

1. Allan Nevins, *A Pocket History of the United States*, p. 99.

2. Allan Nevins, *A Pocket History of the United States*, p. 287.

3. *Who Built America*, Vol. 2, p. 265.

4. *Who Built America*, Vol. 2, p. 499.

5. Donald Rutherford, *Routledge Dictionary of Economics*, (New York: Routledge, 1995), p. 223.

6. Tom Kemp, *Historical Patterns of Industrialization*, Second Ed., (New York: Longman Publishing, 1993), p. 69.

7. Nell Irvin Painter, *Standing at Armageddon: The United States, 1877-1919*, (New York: W.W. Norton & Company, 1987), p. 116.

8. Allan Nevins, *A Pocket History of the United States*, p. 264.

9. Allan Nevins, *A Pocket History of the United States*, pp. 263-266.

10. Jeffrey Madrick, *The End of Affluence: The Causes and Consequences of America's Economic Dilemma*, (New York: Random House, 1995), pp. 57-58.

11. Allan Nevins, *A Pocket History of the United States*, p. 287.

12. Daniel Yergin, *The Prize: The Epic Quest for Oil, Money, and Power*, (New York: Touchstone Books, 1992), p. 500.

13. U.S. Department of Commerce, *1932 Commerce Yearbook*, Vol. 2, (Washington, D.C.: Commerce Department, 1933), pp. 692-693.

14. Allan Nevins, *A Pocket History of the United States*, p. 262.

15. Carl Abbott, *Urban America in the Modern Age: 1920 to the Present*, (Arlington Heights, IL: Harlan Davidson, Inc., 1987), p. 2.

16. Jeffrey Madrick, *The End of Affluence*, p. 30.

17. Allan Nevins, *A Pocket History of the United States*, p. 270.

18. Thomas L. Purvis, *A Dictionary of American History*, (Cambridge, MA: Blackwell Publishers, Inc., 1995), p. 382.

19. Thomas L. Purvis, *A Dictionary of American History*, p. 316.

20. "Unemployment: 1890 to 1970," *Historical Statistics of the United States, Colonial Times to 1970, Bicentennial Edition*, (Washington, D.C.: Bureau of the Census, 1975), Part 1, p. 8.

21. Jeffrey Madrick, *The End of Affluence*, p. 55.

22. Charles P. Kindleberger, *The World In Depression*, p. 281.

23. "Unemployment: 1890 to 1970," *Historical Statistics of the United States, Colonial Times to 1970, Bicentennial Edition*, (Washington, D.C.: Bureau of the Census, 1975), Part 1, p. 8.
24. Allan Nevins, *A Pocket History of the United States*, p. 440.
25. Roy Rosenzweig, Cons. Ed., *Who Built America*, Vol. 2, pp. 473, 491.
26. Roy Rosenzweig, Cons. Ed., *Who Built America*, Vol. 2, p. 506.
27. Jeffrey Madrick, *The End of Affluence*, pp. 34-35.
28. Roy Rosenzweig, Cons. Ed., *Who Built America*, Vol. 2, p. 504.
29. Roy Rosenzweig, Cons. Ed., *Who Built America*, Vol. 2, p. 504.
30. Roy Rosenzweig, Cons. Ed., *Who Built America*, Vol. 2, pp. 504-505.
31. Michael Barone, *Our Country: The Shaping of America from Roosevelt to Reagan*, (New York: The Free Press, 1990), p. 599.
32. Michael Barone, *Our Country*, pp. 600-601.
33. Michael Barone, *Our Country*, p. 579.
34. Michael Barone, *Our Country*, p. 581.
35. Roy Rosenzweig, Cons. Ed., *Who Built America*, Vol. 2, pp. 635-636.
36. Allan Nevins, *A Pocket History of the United States*, p. 626.
37. Roy Rosenzweig, Cons. Ed., *Who Built America*, Vol. 2, p. 638.
38. T. S. Ashton, *The Industrial Revolution: 1760-1830*, (New York: Oxford University Press, 1968), p. 60.
39. T. S. Ashton, *The Industrial Revolution*, p. 61.
40. T. S. Ashton, *The Industrial Revolution*, p. 61.
41. Jeffrey Madrick, *The End of Affluence*, pp. 43-44.
42. Jeffrey Madrick, *The End of Affluence*, p. 45.
43. "Transportation and Communication: Railways," *1932 Commerce Yearbook*, (Washington, D.C.: U.S. Department of Commerce, 1933), Vol. 2, pp. 701-702.
44. Jeffrey Madrick, *The End of Affluence*, p. 45.
45. *1932 Commerce Yearbook, Vol 2*, (Washington, D.C.: U.S. Department of Commerce, 1933), p. 696.
46. Tom Kemp, *Historical Patterns of Industrialization*, pp. 69-70.
47. Daniel Yergin, *The Prize: The Epic Quest for Oil, Money & Power*, (New York: Touchstone, 1992), p. 27.
48. Figures for pig iron from the *1932 Commerce Yearbook, Vol 2*, (Washington, D.C.: U.S. Department of Commerce, 1933), p. 695; Figures for crude oil production from the *1932 Commerce Yearbook, Vol 2*, (Washington, D.C.: U.S. Department of Commerce, 1933), pp. 693-694; Motor vehicle statistics from *Historical Statistics of the United States, Colonial Times to 1970*, Part 2, p. 716.
49. *1932 Commerce Yearbook, Vol 2*, (Washington, D.C.: U.S. Department of Commerce, 1933), pp. 701-702.
50. *Historical Statistics of the United States, Colonial Times to 1970*, Part 2, pp. 957-958.
51. *Historical Statistics of the United States, Colonial Times to 1970*, Part 1, pp. 587-588.
52. Series D 233-682, "Detailed Occupation of the Economically Active Population: 1900 to 1970," *Historical Statistics of the United States, Colonial Times to 1970*, Part 1, pp. 140-145.
53. Series G 416-469, "Personal Consumption Expenditures by Type of Product: 1929 to 1970," *Historical Statistics of the United States, Colonial Times to 1970*, Part 1, pp. 316-319.
54. Charles P. Kindleberger, *The World In Depression*, p. 84.
55. *1932 Commerce Yearbook, Vol 2*, (Washington, D.C.: U.S. Department of Commerce, 1933), p. 667.
56. Series K 532-537, "Irish Potatoes and Sweet Potatoes - Acreage, Production and Price: 1849 to 1970," *Historical Statistics of the United States, Colonial Times to 1970*, Part 1, pp. 514-515.
57. Series K 583-594, "Meat Slaughtering, Production and Price: 1899 to 1970," *Historical Statistics of the United States, Colonial Times to 1970*, Part 1, pp. 520-521.
58. Allan Nevins, *A Pocket History of the United States*, pp. 314-315.
59. Allan Nevins, *A Pocket History of the United States*, pp. 316-318.

60. Allan Nevins, *A Pocket History of the United States*, pp. 317-318.
61. Allan Nevins, *A Pocket History of the United States*, p. 318.
62. "Series K 392-406, Value of Agricultural Raw Materials in Constant (1967) Dollars: 1900 to 1969," *Historical Statistics of the United States*, Part 1, p. 497.
63. Allan Nevins, *A Pocket History of the United States*, pp. 99-100.
64. Charles Sellers, *The Market Revolution: Jacksonian America, 1815-1846*, (New York: Oxford University Press, 1991), p. 45.
65. Charles Sellers, *The Market Revolution*, pp. 45-46.
66. Charles Sellers, *The Market Revolution*, pp. 45-46.
67. Charles Sellers, *The Market Revolution*, p. 71.
68. Charles Sellers, *The Market Revolution*, pp. 132-133.
69. Charles Sellers, *The Market Revolution*, p. 133.
70. Charles Sellers, *The Market Revolution*, p. 134.
71. Charles Sellers, *The Market Revolution*, pp. 136; 143-144.
72. Charles Sellers, *The Market Revolution*, p. 137.
73. Thomas L. Purvis, *A Dictionary of American History*, pp. 306-307.
74. R.C. Simmons, *The American Colonies: From Settlement to Independence*, (New York: W.W. Norton & Company, 1976), pp. 188-194.
75. Charles Sellers, *The Market Revolution*, p. 156.
76. Charles Sellers, *The Market Revolution*, pp. 343-344.
77. Charles Sellers, *The Market Revolution*, p. 347.
78. Charles Sellers, *The Market Revolution*, p. 354; Thomas L. Purvis, *Dictionary of American History*, p. 307.
79. Charles Sellers, *The Market Revolution*, p. 355.
80. Thomas L. Purvis, *Dictionary of American History*, p. 307.

Chapter 23
The Global Market: More Profits, Less Employment, Never-Ending Competition

1. Jeffrey Madrick, *The End of Affluence: The Causes and Consequences of America's Economic Dilemma*, (New York, Random House, 1995), p. 5.
2. Louis Uchitelle and N.R. Kleinfield, *New York Times Special Report: The Downsizing of America*, (New York: Times Books, 1996), p. 16.
3. Michael Barone, *Our Country*, p. 518; Bennett Harrison and Barry Bluestone, *The Great U-Turn: Corporate Restructuring and the Polarizing of America*, (BasicBooks, 1990), p. x., Calculated from the Council of Economic Advisers, *Economic Report of the President, 1989* (Washington, D.C.: U.S. Government Printing Office, January 1989), p. 389.
4. Michael Barone, *Our Country*, p. 533.
5. Brian J.L. Berry, Edgar C. Conkling and D. Michael Ray, *The Global Economy in Transition*, 2nd. Ed., (Upper Saddle River, NJ: Prentice Hall, 1997), p. 468.
6. Charles W.L. Hill, *International Business: Competing in the Global Marketplace*, (Times Mirror Higher Education Group, 1997), p. 8.
7. William Greider, *One World, Ready or Not: The Manic Logic of Global Capitalism*, (New York: Simon & Schuster, 1997) pp. 57, 103.
8. William Greider, *One World, Ready or Not*, p. 115.
9. William Greider, *One World, Ready or Not*, p. 72.
10. William Greider, *One World, Ready or Not*, pp. 112-114.
11. Bennett Harrison, *The Great U-Turn*, p. 11.
12. Louis Uchitelle, *The Downsizing of America*, pp. 17, 21.
13. Louis Uchitelle, *The Downsizing of America*, p. 6.
14. Louis Uchitelle, *The Downsizing of America*, pp. 5-6, 18, 20.

15. Kirkpatrick Sale, *Rebels Against the Future: The Luddites and Their War on the Industrial Revolution Lessons for the Computer Age*, (New York, Addison-Wesley Publishing Company, 1996), p. 23.

16. John P. Hoerr, *And the Wolf Finally Came: The Decline of the American Steel Industry*, (Pittsburgh: University of Pittsburgh Press, 1988), p. 521.

17. John P. Hoerr, *And the Wolf Finally Came*, p. 87.

18. John P. Hoerr, *And the Wolf Finally Came*, pp. 84-85; 163-164.

19. John P. Hoerr, *And the Wolf Finally Came*, pp. 86-87.

20. Brian J.L. Berry, Edgar C. Conkling, and D. Michael Ray, *The Global Economy In Transition*, 2nd ed., (Upper Saddle River, NJ: Prentice Hall, 1997), p. 222.

21. John P. Hoerr, *And the Wolf Finally Came*, p. 85.

22. Brian J.L. Berry, *The Global Economy In Transition*, p. 228.

23. Brian J.L. Berry, *The Global Economy In Transition*, p. 230.

24. Allan Nevins, *A Pocket History*, p. 264.

25. Brian J.L. Berry, *The Global Economy In Transition*, p. 230.

26. John P. Hoerr, *And the Wolf Finally Came*, pp. 570, 606.

27. John P. Hoerr, *And the Wolf Finally Came*, pp. 97, 99, 100.

28. William Greider, *One World, Ready or Not*, p. 29.

29. John P. Hoerr, *And the Wolf Finally Came*, pp. 93-94, 99, 107.

30. John P. Hoerr, *And the Wolf Finally Came*, p. 100.

31. Bennett Harrison, *The Great U-Turn*, p. 23.

32. Charles W.L. Hill, *International Business*, p. 467.

33. Brian J.L. Berry, *The Global Economy in Transition*, p. 281.

34. Norman Gaither, *Productions and Operations Management*, 7th Ed., (Belmont, CA: Duxbury Press, 1996), pp. 650-679.

35. Norman Gaither, *Productions and Operations Management*, p. 615.

36. John P. Hoerr, *And the Wolf Finally Came*, pp. 323, 471.

37. John P. Hoerr, *And the Wolf Finally Came*, pp. 238, 242.

38. John P. Hoerr, *And the Wolf Finally Came*, p. 94.

39. John P. Hoerr, *And the Wolf Finally Came*, p. 416.

40. *1932 Commerce Yearbook*, U.S. Department of Commerce, Vol 2., (Washington, D.C.: U.S. Govt. Printing Office, 1933), p. 696.

41. John P. Hoerr, *And the Wolf Finally Came*, pp. 99, 100.

42. John P. Hoerr, *And the Wolf Finally Came*, pp. 97-100.

43. John P. Hoerr, *And the Wolf Finally Came*, p. 215.

44. John P. Hoerr, *And the Wolf Finally Came*, pp. 416-418.

45. John P. Hoerr, *And the Wolf Finally Came*, p. 607.

46. Brian J.L. Berry, *The Global Economy in Transition*, p. 282.

47. Michael Barone, *Our Country*, p. 599.

48. Charles W.L. Hill, *International Business*, p. 467.

49. Brian J.L. Berry, *The Global Economy in Transition*, p. 242.

50. Brian J.L. Berry, *The Global Economy in Transition*, p. 281.

51. Brian J.L. Berry, *The Global Economy in Transition*, p. 282.

52. Norman Gaither, *Productions and Operations Management*, p. 180.

53. Norman Gaither, *Productions and Operations Management*, p. 173.

54. Charles W.L. Hill, *International Business*, p. 11.

55. Norman Gaither, *Productions and Operations Management*, p. 208, citing Gavin Wright, "Where America's Industrial Monopoly Went," *Wall Street Journal*, December 20, 1990, A14.

Chapter 24
The New World Economic Order

1. Brian J.L. Berry, *The Global Economy in Transition*, p. 2.
2. Charles P. Kindleberger, *The World in Depression, 1929-1939*, p. 84.
3. Charles Freeman, *Egypt, Greece and Rome: Civilizations of the Ancient Mediterranean*, (New York: Oxford University Press, 1996), p. 22.
4. Martyn Lyons, *Napoleon Bonaparte and the Legacy of the French Revolution*, p. 228.

INDEX

Abbaye prison, 120, 125
Acropolis, 62, 66
Actium, battle of, 94, 102
administration des Finances, 138
Aegospotami, 69
Ager Gallicus, 99
Agesilaus, 83
Agricultural Adjustment Act (1933), 426
Agricultural Adjustment Administration, 427
Agricultural crisis, (Russia) (1927-1929), 222-224
agricultural debt:
  Athens, 64-65, 235
  Germany, 361, 395 (peasant debt), 408
  Rome, 98, 104
  Russia, 235, 236, 241, 340, 341, 477
  U.S., 426, farm debt, 428, 477;
    Colonial period, 432, 450;
    Jacksonian era, 452; after Civil War, 438, 449
agricultural production (U.S.), 447,
  during Depression, 448
  economic weaknesses of, 477
agriculture (U.S.),
  market development and, 450-455
  mechanization of, 448-450
  New Deal programs, 450
  output vs financial survival, 447
Agrippa, 94
Alcibiades, 81
Alcmaeonids, 66, 76
Alexander II, Czar, 184
Alexander III, Czar, 184
Alexandra, Empress, 171
Alsace-Lorraine, 412
American Relief Administration (ARA), 212
Androcles, 77
Antiochos III, king of Syria, 92
Antiphon of Rhamnus, 76, 77
Antonov, Alexander, Admiral, 212
Antonov, General Vladimir, 194
Antony, Marcus Antonius, 94, 487
Appian Way, 99
Appius Claudius, 99
Aqua Anio Vetus, 101
Aqua Marcia, 101

Aqua Appia, 99, 101
Arab oil embargo (1973), 457
arbitrage (wage competition), 459, 463
Arcadia, 81, 84
archonship, 63-66, 68-69, 73
Arginusae, 69
Argives, 81
Argolis, 81
Argos, 81-83
Aristides, The Just, 71
Aristotle, 62
Artaxerxes, 83
Article 4, 187
Article 107 (Russian penal code), 247
assemblies (French), 118
assemblies (Roman), 95-97
Assembly (Athenian), 61, 65-70
Assembly of Notables (France), 118, 119, 149
Assembly (Spartan), 85, 86
assignat, 145, 147, 148, 154
Athens, see generally Chapter 4
  Argos and, 81, 82, 83
  building campaign of 435 B.C., 69
  Empire, 72, 75
  Four Hundred, 69, 75, 77, 78
  Sparta and, 80-83, 84, 86, 87
  Thirty, 70, 75, 77,78
atomic bomb, 440, 475
Attica, 64, 67, 72, 73, 77, 81, 82
Augereau, 132
Aurora, 164
Austria, 124, 126, 145
Austro-Hungarian army, 195
autarchy (Germany), 395, 396, 400, 406
automobile industry:
  global competition in, 440-442
  globalization and, 442-443, 458-459, 460
  overcapacity in, 460-461
  U.S., 441-442

Babeuf, Francois-Noël, 132, 156
Babylon, 83
bagmen, 242
bank specie reserves, 452-455

Bank of the United States, first, 451
    second, 451, 452, 453, 454
Bank of France, 134
bankruptcy of the French government, 150
Bardyiae, 108
Barentin, 118
Barras, 132
barrièrs, governmental customs posts, 120
Bastille, 117-121, 142, 153
Benjamin, Metropolitan of Petrograd, 214
Berdiansk, 244
Beria, Lavrenty, 229
Bibulus, 109-110
Bismarck, Otto von, 361-365
Black Death, 33, 35
Black Repartition, 184-185, 239, 240
Bloody Sunday, 173, 302
Boeotians, 67
Bolsheviks, 160-170, 171-173, 179-185, 187, 188
189-208, 210-212, 230, 233, 239-247, 272, 284,
285, 295-297, 301-307, 313-314, 317-318, 320-
321 333, 338, 339, 341, 342, 343, 344, 347
Bolshevik Central Committee, 162, 181, 183
bomb plot, 135
Bourdeaux, 127
bread rationing (Russia), 1918, 242
bread prices (France), 144, 145
bread shortages, in Paris, 130, 145-146, 148, 149,
152, 153, 154, 155
Brest-Litovsk Treaty, 189, 194, 195, 303
Breteuil, Baron de, 120
Brienne, 139, 140, 141, 142
Britain, 126
Britain, commercial treaty and, 143
bronze, early use, 17
Brunswick, Duke of, 124
Bukharin, Nikolai, 218, 221-222, 223, 228, 254-
255, 257, 258, 259
Bulygin Constitution, 173
Bureau of General Police, 129
Bury, J. B., 73
business cycle, 41, 46

Caelius, 112, 113
Caesar Augustus, 13, 90, 92, 94, 102, 104, 113, 114
Caesar, Julius:
    assassination of, 38, 91
    Cicero and, 96, 109
    Clodius and, 112
    Pompey and, 94, 109
    Senate and, 95

    street violence and, 13, 109-113
    Triumvirate and, 93
    unemployment problem and, 104
Calonne, 139
Campania, 100
canal transport, 444
Caprivi, General Leo von, 409-410
Capua, 108, 113
Carnegie, Andrew, 464, 478
    competitive environment and, 51, 52, 53, 54,
464, 478, 482, 486
    strike - treatment of workers, 49, 478
Carrier, 130
cartelization, see trusts.
cartels:
    Germany, 358-359, 401; (1850-1920s), 411, 413
    cartelization under Nazis, 394, 403, 406
    Italy, 359
Carthage, 92, 100
Carystus, 68
Catholic Church, 123, 134
Catiline conspiracy, 93, 96, 104, 108, 109, 110, 113
Cato the Younger, 104, 109, 111, 112
Cato the Elder, 92
censor, 96
central committee (France), 125
Central Committee (Russia), 181, 183, 263, 264, 265,
266, 268
Central Executive Committee (Bolshevik), 168,192,
225, 228
Chalcidace, 83
Chalcidian League, 83
Chalcidians, 67, 71
Champ de Mars massacre, 153
Chaumette, 146
Cheka, 169, 190, 191, 200-203, 204, 205, 212, 217, 243,
244, 245, 302
Chernov, Victor, 189
China, 440
Chios, 69
Chisholm, George, commercial geographer, 21,   48
Chrysler Corporation, 441, 470
church, Bolshevik attacks on, 212-214, 215
CIA, 27, 39
Cicero, 95
    Catiline conspiracy and, 93, 96, 109
    Clodius and, 110-112
Cimbri, 103
Cimon, 68
Cinadon, conspiracy of, 86-88
Cinna, 93, 103, 104, 108

Cisalpine Gaul, 93, 94, 110
Cispius, Marcus, 111
Civil Code of Law (France), 134
Civil Constitution of the Clergy, 123
Civil War (American), 434
Civil War, (Russian), see Chapter 11; see Russia
Cleisthenes, 66, 67, 72, 74, 76
Cleombrotus, Spartan king, 79, 85
Cleomenes, Spartan king, 66
Cleopatra, 94, 102
Cleophon, 71
clipper ships, 446
Cloaca Maxima, 91
Clodius, 104, 110, 113
  Cicero and, 110-111
  Milo and, 111-112
Cnidus, 83
Coast (Shore) party, 65
coffee, shortages of (France), 145
cohortes urbanae (Roman security force), 13, 38,
  113, 114
coins, first introduced in Lydia, 59
collections crisis, 256-257
collective, 231, 232, 233, 236, 240, 243, 246, 250,
  256, 259, 260, 261, 262, 263, 264, 265, 267, 270,
  271, 272, 273, 274, 276, 277, 278, 281, 282, 283,
  284, 285, 286, 287, 288, 289, 291
Collectivization:
  generally, see Chapter 14, 230, 231, 232, 233,
    258-259
  administration, 272-275, 278-279, 281, 285-286,
    286-289
  deaths from, 232
  dekulakization, 232-233, 241, 261-262, 270,
    271, 274
  Dizzy with Success, 271
  famine (1932-1934), 277-279, 281-281
  five-stalks law, 276-277, 326
  June-Dec. 1929, 260-261
  kulak policy, 261-265
  livestock losses, 261-262, 290
  reasons for, 262-263
  25,000-ers, 270
  statistics on, 232-233, 271, 275, 280, 283, 326
  Terror campaign (1930), 228, 265-271
  Terror campaign (1932-1933), 276-277, 280-282
collegia, 110, 113, 114
colonization (Roman), 103, 104, 106, 107
comitia curiata, 97
comitia centuriata, 97

comitia, 97
comitia tributa, 97
Commissariat of Food, 243
Commission of Twelve (France), 127
Committee of Public Safety (France), 127, 128, 129,
  130, 146, 150, 154
Committee of Public Safety (Russia), 166
Committees of the Poor, 243
commune, 233, 234, 235, 236, 237, 238, 239, 240,
  241, 272, 273
commune (France), 125, 126, 127, 147, 154
communism, definition of, 22, 23
Communism, 172
Companies of the Sun, 130
Companies of Jesus, 130
competition:
  efficiency of resource use and, 483-485
  in France, 136, 137, 156
  in the global marketplace, 42-44, 49, 458-461,
    468, 469, 472, 474, 477, 478, 480, 483, 484
  price competition, 45
concentration camps:
  Germany, 379, 381, 384
  Russia, 30, 191, 192, 202, 203, 350
concilium plebis, 97, 99
Confederacy of Delos (See Delos, Confederacy of)
Confederation Congress, 451
Congress of Soviets, 163, 167, 168
  All-Russian, First, 187
  Second, 187, 189, 239
  Third, 189
  Fourth, 189
  Fifth, 190
Congress (U.S.), 426, 439, 440, 442, 447, 451, 452,
  454
Congress of the Confederation, 431
Conon, 62, 83
Conquest, Robert, 232, 267
Constituent Assembly (France), 122, 123
Constituent Assembly (Russia), 167-170, 172, 181-
185, 189, 193, 195
Constitution of 1793, 135, 149, 155, 156
Constitution (France), 122, 124, 131, 133
consul (Roman), 95, 96
consulship (Roman), 95
Contact Commission, 187
Continental Congress, 431, 433
controls (France), 144, 145, 146, 147, 148, 151, 152,
  153, 154

Convention (France), 126, 127, 128, 130,131,132, 135, 136, 145, 146, 148, 149, 150, 151, 152, 153, 154, 155
Corinth, 69, 82, 83
Cornelii, 93, 108
Coronea, 83
corporation, early use (U.S.), 451
Cosa, 112
Cossacks, 165, 193, 194, 196, 205, 240
cost (resource) theory of unemployment, 41-42
costs, production, 43
council of elders, 251
Council of Areopagus, 65, 68, 73
Council of Five Hundred, 67, 68
Council of Four Hundred, 67
Council of Five Hundred (404 B.C.), 70
Council of People's Commissars (Sovnarkom), 168, 189, 202, 215
Council of Elders (Gerusia) (Sparta), 85
Council of State (France), 133
Council of Five Hundred (France), 131, 133
Council of Elders (France), 131
Councils (France), 131, 132, 133
counter-terror (France), 130-131, 154, 155
Crassus, 93, 94, 109, 111, 112, 113, 487
Creusis, 79
Crimea, 198
Crimean Peninsula, 192, 198
Crimean War, 234
Critias, 77
Croessus, king of Lydia (560-546 B.C.), 59
Crusade, First, 475
Crystal Night (Germany), 384
Cunaxa, battle of, 83
cursus honorum, 96
customs posts, attacks on (France), 120
Cyme, 69
Cyrus, 83
Cyzicus, 69
Czar, 173, 174, 175, 176, 177, 178, 180, 182, 183, 184, 188, 190, 193, 230, 234, 236, 237, 239, 246, 302, 340, 342
Czar's abdication, 171, 173, 179
Czech Legion, 195, 197

Damasias, 65
Danton, 117, 125, 129, 148, 151
Darius, 67
Day of Tiles, 141
debt:
  Athens, 64-65, 235
  Rome, 98, 99, 104, 109

France, governmental, 134, 138-142, 150
Germany, 361;
  agricultural, 408; business, 388, 423;
  deficit financing, 366, 388, 397;
  governmental, 398-401;
  industrial, 370, 388; war debt, 365
Russia: foreign investment, 223, 295, 306, 324
  governmental, 189, 295, 299, 306, 316, 323-324, 341
  peasant debt (1905), 340, 261, 270, (1917), 241
  Stolypin and, 235, 241;
U.S., 479
  agriculture, 424
  business and, 424
  call money loans (1920s), 420-422
  Colonial period, 432, 450
  consumer debt, 441, (1996), 479
  installment debt, 419
  Jacksonian era, 453-455, 479
  overreliance on credit (1920s), 417-418, 420, 439
  Panic of 1819 and, 452-453
Decalea, 77
Declaration of the Rights of Man and the Citizen, 122
Deere, John, 448
dekulakization, 232-233, 241, 261-262, 270, 271, 274
Delos, Confederacy (League) of, 63-64, 68, 72
Denikin, General, 196, 197, 205, 206
depression of 1785-1786, 432, 450
Descombes, 146, 147
Desmoulins, Camille, 120
dictatorship, definition of, 22-23
dictator, 92, 93, 94, 96, 99
dictatorship of the proletariat, 171
Directory, First (France), 132, 135, 149, 155;
  Second, 132-133, 135
Dizzy with Success, 268, 269
Dolabella, 113
Domitius, Lucius, 111-112
Don, 193, 194, 195
drought, in Russia (1920-21), 212
Drusus, Marcus Livius, 93, 103
Duma, 171, 174-175, 176, 177, 178, 180, 186;
  First, 175, 177; Second, 175; Third, 175;
  Fourth, 175-176
Durnovo, Peter, Minister of the Interior, 186
Dutch Republic, 126
Dzerzhinskii, 201, 203

ecology, as market concept, 479-483
Egypt, 32, 37, 55, 72, 94, 100, 102, 104, 477, 483, 484, 485, 486
  Napoleon and, 133
Ekaterinburg, 190
Ekaterinodar, 194
Ekaterinoslav, 200, 206
Eleusis, 70
Eleven, 70
Emancipation loan, 236
Emancipation Edict of 1861, 234, 235, 236, 237, 238
émigrés, 123, 124, 131, 134
employment demand, components of labor market, 46-48
Epaminondas, 79
epeunaktai, 87
Ephialtes, 68, 76
Ephorate, 85, 86
ephors, 85, 86, 88
Epirus, 92
Epitadeus, 88
equites, (knights) (Roman), 98
Equitius, 106
Erie Canal, 444
Estates General, 118
Estonia, 167
Etruria, 109
Etruscans, 108
Euboea, 71
Eurymedon, 68
executions, during Stalinist era, 159, 161
Executive Committee (Russia), 192, 209, 225
failure of delivery, concept relating to scarcity, 34-35
failure of participation, concept relating to unemployment, 34-35
famine:
  Germany, 360
  Russia (1891-92), 232, 345; (1921), 248, 253, 311, 313; (1932-1933), 277, 279-280, 300, 326-327
Farben, I.G., 406
fascism:
  definition of, 23, 24, 352-355
  labor unrest and, 355-357;
  Nazism, see generally Chapter 18;
  private property and, 405-406
  violence and, 354-355
FBI, 39
February 26 Incident (Japan), 355
Feraud, 135, 149

Ferdinand, Archduke, assassination of, 238
fertile crescent, 55
feudalism in France, 122
Fifteenth Party Congress, 256
First World War, 231, 237, 238, 245
  shortages in Russia, 175-180
Fitzpatrick, Sheila, 241, 270, 277, 278, 279
Five Hundred (France), 131, 133
Five Hundred (Athens), 70
Five Thousand (Athens), 69
five-year plans, 294, 299-300, 312, 320-325, 342
Five-Year Plan:
  First, 299, 300, 312, 318, 321-323, 325-326
  Second, 299-300, 326-328
  Third, 300, 328, 331
Five-year's Truce, 69
Flaminius, Gaius, 99-100
Flesselles, 153
Fleury, Joly de, 138
flour riots of 1837 (U.S.), 40, 454, 455
flour, shortages of (Paris), 142, 144, 146, 147, 154
Flour War, 117, 136, 137, 138
food consumption (U.S.), 450
food riots (France), 136, 137, 143, 144, 145, 149, 152, 153, 155
food shortages:
  France, 135, 136, 137, 142, 143, 145, 146, 147, 150, 151, 152, 153, 154, 155, 156
  Russia, 176, 177, 209, 223, 232, 238, 239, 242, 252, 296, 297, 305, 310, 311, 312, 313-314, 324, 344, 345, 346
Food Commission, 146
food supply detachments, 242, 243, 245
forced requisitioning:
  France, 148,
  Russia, 222, 245, 248, 250
Ford, Henry, 420, 439
Ford Motor Co., 441
Fordney-McCumber tariff, 418-419
forty-nine year plan, 235, 236, 241
Forum, 91, 104, 108, 110, 111, 112
Fouché, Joseph 134
Foulon, Joseph François, 121, 153
Four Hundred, Council of (Athens) (508 B.C.), 67
Four Hundred, Council of (Athens) (411 B.C.), 69, 75, 77, 78
Fourteenth Party Congress, 220, 252, 253, 255
Franco, General Francisco, 353
free market, in grain (France), 137
French Revolution, see Chapters 7 & 8.
Frunze, Mikhail, 197

fuel shortages (Russia), 176, 177, 209, 223, 232, 238, 239, 242, 252, 296, 297, 305, 310, 311, 312, 313-314, 324, 344, 345, 346
Fulvius Flaccus, 106
Fundamental Laws (Russia), 175

gardes françaises, French Guard, 121
Garfield, James A., 434
Gaul, 92, 94, 99, 100
Gauls, 91, 94
General Motors, 441
General Maximum Law (France), 128, 146, 147, 151, 154
Germany:
  see generally Chapters 18, 19, and 20; see Adolf Hitler
  agriculture, 394-395, 408
  Bismarck and, 361-365
  business and industry under the Nazis, 392-394, 406
  comparison with Russia, see Chapter 17, 335-337
  Empire, 362
  Enabling Act, 375-377
  Federal Diet, 360
  Franco-Prussian War, 362, 412
  Frankfurt Parliament, 360-361
  German Confederation, 360-362
  Hitler's government, 374-375, 381-382
  industrialization, 356, 407-408
  Nazi defense spending, 395-398
  Nazi economic planning, 382-384
  Nazi Jewish policy, 384-385
  Nazi Party, 367-373
  Nazi police state, 377-381
  Nazism and, 352-355
  New Plan, 398-399
  population, 335, 358
  railroads, 337
  resources, see Chapter 17, 333-351, 335-337, 352, 386-389, 407-408
  Revolution of 1848-1849, 360
  rural, 356
  Russia and, 189, 384-385, 386-387, 391, 394, 397, 404
  Second Four-Year Plan, 400-401, 404
  unemployment, 354, 357, 358, 370, 372, 373
  unification (1814-1871), 359-362
  Weimar Republic, 362-372
  World War I and, 362-363, 411-413
Gerusia (Council of Elders), 85

Gestapo, 13, 38, 379, 380, 381
Girondin party, 128, 145, 151, 153, 154
Glaucia, Gaius Servilius, 106, 107, 113
Glavlit, 214, 215
globalization, 442-443, 458-459, 460, 475, 489
  competition and, 459-462
  labor costs and, 463
  labor markets and, 477
  layoffs and, 461-462
  steel industry and, 463-470
  unemployment and, 478
goods famine, 258, 319
Göring, Hermann, 375, 379, 380, 383
Gosplan, State Planning Commission, 228, 298, 299, 321
GPU, State Political Administration, 217, 221
Gracchi, 90-91, 95, 104, 105, 113, 114
Gracchus, Gaius, 90, 103, 105, 106
Gracchus, Tiberius, 90, 92, 102, 103, 105, 106, 113
grain collections (Russia), 222, 223, 243, 248, 250, 251, 256, 257, 258, 259, 280, 282, 313, 315
grain controls (France), 143, 144, 146, 148, 152, 153
grain crisis of 1928, 256-257
grain distributions (Rome), 91, 103, 104, 106, 107, 108, 109, 110, 111
grain prices (Russia), 222, 228, 257, 319, 320, 324
Gratidianus, Marius, 108, 109
Great Crash, 414, 416-423, 422, 423, 424
Great Depression:
  see generally Chapter 21, 414, 424, 425, 430, 439
  agriculture and, 425-428
  automobile production, 416-417, 419
  call money loans, 420-423
  credit and, 417-418, 419, 420, 421, 422, 423, 424, 426, 428
  deflation, 424;
  factory automation and, 415-416
  Federal Reserve and, 420, 422
  Florida land boom (1925), 419-420
  Hatry empire, 421-422
  recession of 1920-1922, 414, 418
  unemployment, 414, 418, 422, 423, 424
Great Fear (France), 121
Great Purges, 159, 283, 327, 328, 331
Greider, William, 459
gross domestic product (GDP), 40, 426
gross national product (GNP), 40, 426
growth theory of unemployment, 40-41
Guchkov, Alexandr, Minister of War, 181
Guillotin, Dr. Joseph-Ignace, 116

guillotine, 116, 117, 124, 125, 126, 128, 129, 130, 131

hailstorm of 1788 (France), 141, 142
Hamilton, Alexander, 433
Hannibal, 90, 92, 100
Harappa (Indian city), 5
harvest of 1913 (Russia), 231, 238, 248
Haymarket riot (1886), 39, 434
Hébertistes, 147, 151
hektemoroi (sixth-parters), 49, 52, 64, 65, 73, 98, n 235
helots, 81, 85, 86, 87, 88, 89
Henriot, 119, 152
Hill party (Athens), 65, 67, 73
Himmler, Heinrich, 375, 379, 380, 383
Hindenburg, Paul, 364, 371, 372, 373, 374, 375, 377, 380
Hipparchus, 66, 76
Hippias, 66, 76, 78
Histiaea, 71
Hitler, Adolf:
  generally, 3, 13, 14, 351, 363
  administrator, 381
  agriculture and, 394, 395
  beerhall putsch and, 367, 368, 369
  cabinet, 375
  chancellor, 359
  comparison with Stalin, 29, 30, 31, 358
  Enabling Act and, 375, 376-377, 379
  Göring and, 379
  governmental organization and, 381
  Hindenburg and, 373, 374, 375, 380
  industrial policy and, 393, 402
  Jewish policy, 384-385
  labor and, 352, 357
  Nazi Party (1930-1933) 371, 372, 373
  Nazi Party (1919-1923) 364-366, 368, 369
  Nazi Party (1924-1929) 369, 370, 371
  Nazism and, 353, 354
  opposition parties and, 380
  political skills, 31, 357, 368
  political power, 352, 354, 357
  public works projects and, 13
  rearmament, 383, 400
  SA and, 380, 381
  small business and, 392
  unemployment and, 372, 382, 388, 396
  victims of, 25, 352
  World War I and, 363-364, 412
Hittites, iron use, 16

hoarding (France), 146, 151, 154
Homestead strike (1892), 39, 49, 50, 434, 464, 465, 478
homoioi (Peers), 84
Hoover, Herbert, 212
hoplite, 79, 80, 86, 88
hunger of 1936-37, 232
hunter-gatherer societies, economies of, 55-57
Hyperbolus, 77
hypomeiones (Inferiors), 84
Hypsaeus, 112
Hysiai, 81

Iaroslavl, 190, 191, 201
imperium, 95, 96, 97
Indies Company, 129
Indulgents, 129
Indus civilization, 55
Industrial Revolution, 407, 436
industrialization (Russia): see Chapters 15 & 16; 223, 227, 228; (1905), 237; 252, 253-256, 257, 258, 261, 263, 267, (Czarist policy), 295; 299, 312, 318, 321, 322, 323, 324, 326, 328
Inferiors (hypomeiones), 84, 86, 87, 88
inflation:
  Athens, 75
  France, 137, 142, 145, 146, 154
  Germany, 366, 367, 369, 383, 388, 389, 390, 396, 409, 413
  Rome, 103
  Russia, 176, 238, 243, 296, 307, 311, 314, 324, 344
  shortages and, 40
  U.S., 424, 440, 441, 442, 452, 454
inputs, in production process, 42
insurrectionary committee (France), 127
insurrectionary commune (France), 125-126
Ionian Greeks, 68, 83
iron, Age of Iron, 16; early use, 16
Isagoras, 66, 74
Ispolkom, Provisional Executive Committee, 179, 180, 181, 182, 183, 186, 187
Ithome, Mount, 81, 84
Iudenich, General Nikolai, 197
Jackson, Andrew, 453-454
Jacobin Party, 130, 132, 134, 135, 145
Jacobin coup, 155
Jerusalem, 475
Jews:
  Russia, 201, 206
  Germany, 30, 353, 368, 371, 380, 381, 384, 385
  Hitler's policies, 384-385

job, economic concept of, 51
Jugartha, 92
Jugerthine war, 103
Juno Regina, 101
Jupiter Stator, 101

Kadet Party (Konstitutional Democrats) KD, 184
Kaledin, Cossack leader, 193
Kalinin, Mikhail "Papa," 210
Kamenev, Lev B., 159, 215, 216, 217, 218, 219, 220, 221, 222, 228, 229, 321, 327
Kaplan, Fannie, 200, 202
Kennedy, John F., 434
Kerensky, Alexander, 163-165, 179, 180, 181, 182, 183
KGB, 23, 27, 38, 39
Khabalov, S.S., General, 179
Kiev, 200
Kirov, Sergei, 158, 159, 160, 228
kleroi, 86, 87, 88
kleros, 87, 88
knights (Athens), 65
knights (Rome), 93, 94, 98
Kolchak, Aleksandr, 197
Komsomol Central Committee, 220
Komuch government, 195
Kornilov, General Lavr, 163, 181, 182, 183, 184, 194
Kremlin, 165, 166, 167, 190, 191
Kronstadt, 164, 165, 166, 167, 190, 191, 208, 209-211, 212, 246
Krypteia (Spartan secret police), 38, 80, 86, 88; execution of helots (424 B.C.), 1, 25
Kuban steppes, 194, 198
kulak, defined, 224; 225, 226, 227, 228, 232, 233, 241, 242, 247, 250, 254
   campaign against, 261, 271, 274, 275, 284, 318
Kynosoura, 80

La Revellière, 132
labor market, 46-48
Lacedaemonians, 80
Laconia, 80, 81, 84
Laelius, Gaius, 101
Lafayette, Marquis de, 122
land ownership, in Russia, 233-234
Land Decree, 240, 241
landlords, in Russia, 233, 235, 246, 250
Latin League, 91
Launay, Bernard de, 118, 121, 153
Laurium silver mines, 61, 63, 64, 68, 72, 74, 77

Law of 22 Prairial, 129, 130
Law of April 10, 149, 155
Law of Suspects, 128, 151
League of Delos (see Delos, Confederacy of), 63, 68, 72
lean production, 471
Lebedus, 69
Left SR, 190, 201, 202
Left Opposition, 219, 254
Legislative Assembly (France), 123-124, 125, 126
Leipsydrion, 66
Lenin, V.I.:
   generally, 162, 164, 168, 169, 170, 222
   (1921-1924), 212, 213, 214, 215, 216, 217
   agricultural policy, 239, 240, 241, 248, 252, 297, 305, 313, 338, 344, 348
   assassination attempts, 191, 200,
   Bolshevik takeover, 189
   Civil War and, 200, 201, 211
   death of, 215-218
   industrial policy, 297, 298, 300, 303, 304, 305, 307, 308, 314, 316, 317, 319, 322, 324, 328, 347
   labor policy, 308, 309
   NEP and, 246, 247, 248, 253, 297, 298, 311, 312-314
   organizer, 171, 172, 181, 185
   Stalin and, 215-219
   Terror and, 202, 203
   Trotsky and, 213, 214, 216, 217, 218, 219
   War Communism and, 242, 243, 244, 245, 246, 297, 308, 310, 311, 338
Leningrad, 158, 159, 220, 228, 280
Leningrad Center, 158, 159
Leonidas, Spartan king, defense of Thermopylae (480 B.C.), 1, 61
Leopold, Emperor, 124
Lepanto, battle of (1571), 475
Lepidus, Marcus Aemilius, triumvir, 94
Lepidus, Marcus Aemilius, 93, 108, 113
Leuctra, battle of, 79-80, 84, 85, 88
Lex Licinia, 103
Licinius, 99
Limnai, 80
Lincoln, Abraham, 434, 435
Lindet, Robert, 154
lit de justice, 140, 141
livestock population, (Russia), 233, 268
livre, 145
livret (passbook), 134
location choices, 464-466

Long Walls, 62
Long Strike, 50
Louis XVI, 116, 118, 121, 122, 123, 124, 125, 135, 137, 140, 142, 144, 150;
  execution of, 126, 145, 150
Luca, 111
Lucerne, lion of, 116
Lucullus, 109
Luddites, 462-463
Ludlow massacre (1914), 39, 434
Lycurgan reforms, 86, 89
Lycurgus, 86
Lyons, 127, 128, 131, 143, 144, 146, 152, 153
Lysander, Spartan admiral, 69, 70, 77, 82, 83

Macedonia, 62, 66
Macedonian wars, 92
Machecoul, 127
Madrick, Jeffrey, 457, 461
magistracy (Rome), 94-96
magistrates (Rome), 95-97
Mai-Maevskii, General, 196
Makhno, Nestor, 206
Mantinea, 82, 83
Marat, 145
Marathon, battle of (490 B.C.), 61, 67-68;
Marathon, Pisistratus' army and, (540-39 B.C.), 66, 67-68
Marcian Aqueduct (Aqua Marcia), 101
Marie-Antoinette, 128, 129
Marius, Gaius, 103, 107, 108
market
  competition and efficiency, 483-485
  ecological concept of, 479-483
  efficiency of resource use, 483-486
  labor and technology, 477-479
  labor dependence on, 479
  weaknesses of, see Chapter 24, 476-477
market saturation, 408, 459-463
Marseilles, 127, 131
Marsian (Social) War, 93
Martial Law against Tumults, 123
Marx, Karl, 171
Marxist theory, 252, 253
mass production, 470-471
maximum (France), 145, 146, 147, 148, 151, 154
Maya, 5-6
McCarthy, Joseph, 435
McCarthy period, 39, 435
McCormick, Cyrus, 449
McKinley, William, 434

meat prices (France), 148, 154
mechanization, in Russian agriculture, 246, 250, 262, 288
Medontids, Athenian noble family, 64
Medvedev, Roy, 232, 262
Megacles, 66
Megalopolis, 84
Megara, 65, 487
Meiggs, Russell, 73
Mein Kampf, 369
Melos, 71
Memmius, 106, 107
Mensheviks, 169, 179, 185, 190, 212
Menzhinskii, V. R., 168, 169
Mesabi range, 465, 467, 468
Messene, 81, 84
Messenia, 80, 81, 84, 85, 86, 87, 88, 89
Messenian revolt (650 B.C.), see Sparta, 28
Messoa, 89
Methymna, 69
microprocessor, 472
Miletus, city of, 67, 69
Military-Revolutionary Committee, see Milrevkom.
Mills, Ogden, Treasury Secretary, 420
Milo, Titus Annius, 111-112
Milrevkom, (Military-Revolutionary Committee), 162, 163, 183
mir, 233, 236, 241, 251, 252, 270, 272, 273
Mirabeau, 118-119
Mithridates VI, 93, 107, 108, 109
Mohenjo-daro, Indian city, 5, 37
Molly Maguires, 50
Monarchical Club, 144
monopoly (U.S.), 438, see trusts
  concept of, 6, 8-12, 17
Montagnard (Mountain party), 131, 145, 149
Moscow, 158, 159, 161, 162, 165, 166, 167, 168, 176, 185, 186, 190, 191, 195, 196, 197, 198, 201, 202, 203, 205, 206, 211, 212, 213, 214, 218, 219, 225, 227, 228, 229, 238-239, 242, 243, 244, 245, 251, 281, 283, 308, 318, 344,   346
Moscow Revolutionary Committee (MRC), 165
Moscow show trials, 159
Moscow Soviet, 175, 186
Munychia, 77
Muscadins, 149, 155
Mycale, 68
Mycenae, 80
Mytilene, 69, 71

Nantes, 128, 130

Napoleon Bonaparte, 117, 132, 155, 487
  bomb plot and, 134, 135, 155-156
  Consul, 133, 134
  Emperor, 117
National Assembly (France), 116, 118, 119, 121,
National Assembly (France), 122, 123, 144
National Guard (France), 116, 123, 125, 127, 131-132, 147, 149, 153, 155
nationalization of industry:
  Germany, 358, 359
  Russia, 242, 296, 297, 301, 203-304, 306, 307, 310
Naxos, 68, 83
Nazi Party, see generally chapters 18 & 19, 379-380, 381, 384;
  Jews and, 382, 384-385
  labor unrest and, 355-357
  private property and, 405-406
  SA (Storm Detachment), 352, 357, 374, 375, 377,
  SS (Schuzstaffeln), 352, 353, 375, 379, 380, 381, 384
  violence and, 354-355;
Necker, Jacques, Minister of Finance, 119, 120, 121, 138, 139, 142, 143, 144, 148
New Opposition, 220
New Economic Policy (NEP) (Russia),
  see Chapter 16, 245, 246-247, 297
  agriculture and, 247-256
  industry and, 297, 298, 300, 304, 307, 311, 312-320, 321
nexus (Rome), 98
Nicholas II, Czar, 171, 173, 174, 175, 176, 177, 178, 179, 190
Nicholas I, Czar, 180
Nikolaev, Leonid, 158
Nîmes, 131
NKVD, (People's Commissariat of Internal Affairs), 158, 159, 228, 229
Nonius, 106

Octavian (Caesar Augustus), 13, 90, 91, 92, 94
Octavius, Gnaeus, 104, 106, 108
October Manifesto, 174, 175
October Revolution, see Chapter 9, 160, 162, 165, 172
Okhrana, 180
Opimius, 106
optimates, 95
Orchomenus, 81
Order No. 1, 187
Orël, 196
Organization of Petroleum Exporting Countries

(OPEC), 20, 442
Orleans, Duke of, 119, 120, 140
ostracism, 68, 71
outputs, 42
overcapacity, 408, 472
  auto industry and, 460-461
  steel industry and, 468, 469
overproduction, 459-463, 463-470, 472, 474
  in steel, 469

Palais Royal, 120
Pallene, 76
Palmer, A. Mitchell, Attorney General, 435
Panic of 1819, 414, 451-453, 455
Panic of 1837, 414, 454-455
Panic of 1873, 414, 455
Panic of 1893, 53, 414, 455, 436-437, 438, 455
Panic of 1907, 414
Papen, Franz von, 372, 373, 374, 375, 376
Paris sections, 147, 149, 150, 152, 154, 155
Parisian Guard, 149, 155
parlements, 139, 140, 141
Parthenon, 62, 69, 71, 486
Parthians, 94, 487
Party Conference, Sixteenth, 232
Party Congress, Tenth, 244, 246
Party Congress, Twelfth, 248
Party Congress, Fourteenth, 252, 253, 255
Party Congress, Fifteenth, 256
Party Congress, Sixteenth, 259
passports, internal (Russia), 234, 235, 236, 279
patricians, 95-100
Pavlovskii Regiment, 178, 179
Peace of Nicias, 81
Peasants' Land Bank, 235, 237, 241
Peers, 84, 85, 87
Peloponnese, 80, 81, 83, 87, 89
Peloponnesian War, 62, 69, 73, 74, 76, 81, 82
Pericles:
  building program, 69, 70, 71, 72, 74
  leadership, 74, 76
  League funds and, 70, 75
perioeci, 84, 85, 87
Perseus, 92
Persia:
  Athens and, 61, 62, 63, 66, 67, 69, 71, 72, 76
  Sparta and, 62, 82, 83
Peter and Paul fortress, 164
Petra, Jordanian city, 6, 17, 483, 485
Petrograd Soviet, 179, 187
Petrograd (St. Petersburg), 162, 163, 164, 165,

Petrograd (Con'd) 166, 167, 168, 170, 171, 176, 177, 178, 179, 180, 182, 183, 187, 190, 191, 193, 196, 209, 210, 214, 215, 239, 242, 243, 301, 302, 305, 310, 311
Petrograd Defense Committee, 210
Petrovskii, Grigorii, 202
phalanx, 79, 86
Phanias of Lesbos, 64
Pharnabazus, 83
Philip V, 92, 100
Philippine Insurrection, 439
Phoenicia, 68, 72, 83
Phrynichus, 77
Pichegru, General, 149
Pipes, Richard, 234, 239, 241, 242, 243
Pisistratus, 65, 66, 67, 73, 76, 78
Pitane, 80
Plain party, 65, 66
Plataea, battle of, 63, 68
Plato, 62
plebeians (plebs) (Rome), 91, 92, 96, 97, 98, 99, 101, 102, 105
Plutarch, 65, 73, 74, 76, 78, 88
Pocaea, 69
Poetelius, 99
pogroms, 205
Poland, 175, 189, 198, 359, 364, 397
Polemarkhos, 87
Police Ministry (France), 134
Police Legion, 155
Politburo, 215, 216, 219, 220, 221, 222, 224, 228, 263, 264, 268, 297, 312, 321
Polydoros, Spartan king, 87
Pompey (Gnaeus Pompeius Magnus), 93, 94, 108, 109, 111, 112, 113
  Clodius and, 111, 112
  Triumvirate and, 109, 112
pontifices, 99
Pope, 123
populares (Rome), 95
population, Russia, 233, 237, 260, 294, 335
potestas, 96
Potidaea, 71
Preobrazhensky, Evgeni, 254
pressure cooker societies, 27
price competition, 45-46
price controls (France), 144, 145, 146, 148, 151, 152, 153, 154
principate, 94, 114
product demand, components of product market, 46-48

product market, 48
production, six factors involved in, 43
productivity:
  agricultural:
    Athens, 72
    Germany, 386, 396, 408
    Rome, 91, 101
productivity
    Russia, 230-231, 235, 236, 245, 247, 249, 251, 256, n 261, 262, 268, 269, 274, 284, 285, 287-291, 292, 293, 327
    Sparta, 87,
    U.S., 449, 450, 453, 455, 477
  costs of, 481
  effect of competition on, 52, 53, 55, 460, 468
  industrial:
    Germany, 408
    Russia, 249, 292, 308, 329; Stakhanov movement and, 329-330
    U.S., 419, 463
  markets and employment, 389-392
  measuring, 230-231
  output and, 485
  prices and, 468
  profit motive and, 230-231, 285, 287-291, 293, 488
  specialization and, 58
  technology, labor and employment, 462-463, 486
protectionism (Germany), 409-411
Provisional Committee, 162, 164, 166-167, 168, 169, 170, 171, 175
Provisional Government, 179, 180, 181, 182, 183, 184, 185, 187, 188, 192, 193, 204, 209, 239, 241
Provisional Revolutionary Committee, 210
Prussia, France and, 124, 125, 126, 145
public works programs:
  Athens, 70-71, 72, 74, 75
  Germany, 382, 388, 396, 397, 401
  Rome, 98, 99, 101, 103, 104
Pullman strike (1894), 50
Punic War, Third, 92
Punic War, First, 92, 99, 101
Punic War, Second, 92, 100
Pylos, 81
Pyrrhus, king of Epirus, 92

railroad strike of 1877, 39, 49, 50
railroads (U.S.), 444-445
Rathenau, Walter, 366
Reagan, Ronald, 442

Recession of 1982, 442, 469
Red Army, 194, 196, 197, 198, 199, 204, 205, 206, 208, 212, 241, 243, 244, 245, 246, 271, 305, 310
Red Guard, 164, 165, 181, 204
Red Terror, 191, 203
redistribution of land (Russia), 234, 239, 240
Reed, John, 162
Reichsrat, 362-364
Reichstag, 362, 364, 374, 375, 376, 377, 378, 382
Reichstag fire, 375, 377, 379
Reign of Terror (France), 25, 116, 126-130, 131, 132, 135, 145, 146, 147, 149, 150-151, 152, 154, 155
representative assembly (France), 125
republic, French, 126
Republic of Virtue, 129
resource mechanism, see Chapter 3, 1, 25-28, 31-36
resource (cost) theory of unemployment, 41-43
resources:
  definition of, 15-19
  measuring, 19-22
Reubell, 132
Réveillon riots (1789), 36, 39, 40, 119, 120, 136, 143, 144, 152
Revolution of 1848-1849 (Germany), 360
Revolution of 1905, 173-174, 186, 237
Revolutionary Army (France), 154
Revolutionary Committee (Russia), 165
revolutionary committees (France), 121
Revolutionary Tribunal (France), 127, 129
Revolutionary Tribunals (Russia), 203, 242
Richelieu, Cardinal, 118
right deviationists, 222, 228
Robespierre, 117, 129, 130, 146, 147, 148, 150, 151, 152, 154
Rockefeller, John D., 53, 479, 480
Röhm, Ernst, 380
Rome, see Chapter 6 generally
  debt in, 98, 99, 104, 107
  inflation in, 102, 103, 111
  repression, 113
  shortages in, 98, 102, 103, 104, 107, 109, 110, 111, 487
  unemployment in, 12, 13, 90, 102, 103, 104, 114
  violence in, 90, 99, 101, 105-108, 109, 110, 111, 112, 113
Roosevelt, Franklin D., 439
Rostov, 193, 194, 196, 198
roundabout method of production, 56

Rufus Caelius, 112
rural uprisings (1918), 243
Russia, see generally Chapters 9-17, see Joseph Stalin; see Lenin
  agriculture
    after Civil War, 245-246
    under Czar, 231-232;
    Collectivization
Russia
  agriculture:
    Collectivization:
      (June 1929-Dec.), 260-261; see Chapter 14, 232-233, 260-293;
      Collectivization campaign, 261-284
      Communist policies, 222-229;
      grain crisis of 1928, 256-258
      see New Economic Policy, 248-252, 312-320
      pre-1917, 233-239
    Bolshevik rule, see Chapter 12
      agriculture and, 239-241
      church and, 212-214
      famine (1921), 212;
      takeover, 162-170;
    Civil War, see Chapter 11,
      military campaigns, 192-199, 208
      Red Terror, 191, 202-203, 243-250
      repression, 200-203
    Collectivization, see Chapter 14
    Czar, 184, end of monarchy, 173-175
    famine, 232
    First World War and, 175-180
    Germany and, 189, 384-385, 386-387, 391, 394, 397, 404
    industry:
      (1860-1913), 294-295
      five-year plans, 299-300, 320-332
      nationalization, 296-297
      trust system, 298, 307-308
      War Communism, 300-311
    Kronstadt, 208-211
    population, 204, 233, 237, 260, 294, 335
    pre-Revolution, political parties, 184-188
    Provisional Government, 162, 164, 166, 167, 168, 169, 170, 180-184, 185
    resources, see Chapter 17, 333-351
    Revolution of 1905, 173-175
    victims of Communism, 161
  Russian Soviet Socialist Republic, 189
  Russian grain output, (1913), 231
  Ruzskii, N. V., General, 178
  Rykov, 222, 228, 257, 258

SA (Sturmabteiling), 352, 357, 374, 375, 377, 378, 379-380, 381, 384
Sacred Band, 79
Sade, Marquis de, 118
Saguntum, 92
Saint-Just, 128
Saint-Lazare, monastery of, 121, 152
Salamis, battle of, 61, 63, 68
Salvidienus, Rufus, 113
Samnite War, Third, 92, 99
Samnite War, Second (Great), 91
Samnites, 91
Samos, 70, 77, 82
Sarajevo, 238
Sardinia, 100
Sardis, 67
Saturninus, 103, 106, 107, 113
Sauvigny, Bertier de, 121, 153
Savinkov, Boris, 190, 201
scarcity, "absolute" (scarcity of goods), 40
scarcity, "relative" (inflationary), 40
Schacht, Hjalmar, Dr., 400, 401
Schleicher, Kurt von, General, 372, 373, 374
Scipio Africanus, 90, 92
Scipio Aemilianus, 92, 105
scissors crisis, 248-249
Scott, Howard, (Technocracy movement), 415-416, 462, 463
Scyros, 71
secessio (secession), 98
Second Congress of Soviets, 163, 167, 185, 187, 189
Second Directory, 132, 133, 135
secret police, function of, 37-38
Segista, 69
Seisactheia, 65, 235
Seleucid Empire, 92
Selinus, 69
Senate (Roman), 90, 91, 93, 94-96, 97, 98, 99, 100, 103, 105, 106, 107, 108, 109, 110, 111, 112, 113, 114
Senate (France), 133, 134
senatus consultum ultimum, 96, 106-113
September massacres, 125, 127
Sertorius, 93, 108
Sevastopol, 192
Seventeenth Party Congress, 228
Sextus, 99
Shakhty, 160
Shays' Rebellion, 432-433, 435, 450
Sherman Antitrust Act, 339, 438

Shore (Coast) party, 65, 66
show trials (1936), 249
Shuia, 213
Siberia, 182, 195, 196, 197, 222, 224, 234, 235, 244, 256, 259, 265
Sicily, 92, 100, 102, 103
silicon chip, 471
Sixteenth Party Conference, 223
sixth-parters (hektemoroi), 49, 52, 64, 65, 73, 98
slave uprising (West Indies), 145, 153
Slave Revolt, Second, 92
Slave Revolt, First, 92
Smolnyi, 163, 164
Social (Marsian) War, 93, 103, 107
Social-Democratic Workers' Party, 185
Socialist Revolutionary Party (SR), 165, 166, 169, 172, 184, 185, 190, 191, 195, 214
Socrates, 62, 63, 70, 75
Solon, 63, 235
  archonship and, 63
  background, 64
  economic conditions and, 64, 65, 66, 67, 70, 72, 73, 76, 78
  reforms, 65, 66, 67
soviet, 180, 184, 186, 187-188, 190, 192, 195, 210, 239, 251, 272-273, 286, 303
  Congress of Soviets, 187, 189, 190, 239
  Ispolkom and, 187
  Moscow Soviet, 175, 186
  origins of, 185-186
  Petrograd Soviet, 179, 187, 209
  St. Petersburg Soviet, 186, 187,
Soviet Union, see Russia.
Sovnarkom, 168, 169, 189, 202, 215
Spain, 92, 93, 108, 109, 353, 355, 475, 481
Spanish-American War, 438-439
Sparta, see generally Chapter 5
  Argos and, 81, 82, 83
  Athens and, 1, 61, 62, 63, 74, 76, 77, 80, 81, 82, 83, 84
  conspiracy of Cinadon, 86, 87, 88
  earthquake and, 28, 81, 87, 88
  governmental structure, 85, 86
  Messenia and, 28, 80-81, 84, 86, 87, 88, 89
  Persia and, 1, 61, 62
  social classes, 84-85
  Spartano-Messenian wars, 80, 81, 86, 87, 88, 89
  Tegea and, 81
Spartacus, 93, 109, 113
Spartano-Messenian War, First, 80, 87
Spartano-Messenian War, Second, 81, 86, 87, 88, 89

Spartano-Tegeatan wars, 81
Spartiatai, 84
specialization:
  in early economies, 57, 58
  in Rome, 100
Specie Circular (1837), 454
Sphacteria, 80
SR (Socialist Revolutionary Party), (origins of),
    184; 165, 166, 169, 172, 184, 185, 190, 191, 195,
    201, 202, 214
SR Combat Organization, 185, 191
SS, 352, 353, 375, 379, 380, 384
St. Petersburg, 162, 173, 176, 186
St. Petersburg Soviet, 186, 187
Stalin, Joseph:
  agricultural policy, 22-228, 232-233, 241, 247,
    334, 344, 348
  Bukharin and, 221
  Collectivization, see Chapt. 14,
  industrial policy, see Chapter 15, 294, 299-300,
    320-332, 345, 347
  Kamenev & Zinoviev, 215, 220, 221
  Lenin and, 215, 216, 217
  Purge trials, 158-159, 228-229
  Trotsky and, 218-221
  victims of, 25, 161-162
starvation plot (France), 147
State Bank (Russia), 168, 200
State Council, 190
steel industry (U.S.), 463-470
Stenyclarus Plain, 80-81
Stolypin, Pëtr Ivanovich, 234, 235, 236, 237, 238,
    241
Stolypin's reforms, 238, 240
Stresemann, Gustav, 365, 367, 369
strip farming, 237, 240, 241
Stürmer, Boris, 177
Subsistence Commission, 146, 154, 156
substitution, monopoly and, 9, 10, 11, 17
Suetonius, 104
sugar, shortages (France), 145, 153
Sulla, 93, 94, 95, 104, 105, 107, 108, 109, 113
Sulpicius Rufus, 93, 107, 108
Sumer, 32, 37, 54, 483, 484
supply and demand, laws of, 42, 43, 50, 53, 56
Susa (Persia), 83
Swiss guard, 116, 117, 125, 153
Syracuse, 69, 76, 82, 92
syssitia (Spartan military mess), 84, 87

Tabularium, 104

Tambov revolt, 212, 245
Tarantines, 92
Taras, 92
Tarquinius Superbus (Tarquin the Proud), 91,
    94, 95
Taurida Palace, 180, 181
tax in kind, 243, 244
tax policy (Germany), 402-403
tax policy (Russia), 222, 226, 246, 247, 248, 251,
    253-254
Taygetos, 80
teamsters (zeugitae), 65, 68
Technocracy movement, 415-416, 462
technological resources (U.S.), 447
Tegea, 81, 82, 84
Temple (France), 125
Tenth Party Congress, 211, 246
Teos, 69
Terpander, 87
Terror campaigns (Stalin) (1930), 228, 265-271;
    (1932-1933), 280
Terror (Red Terror) (Russia) (1918-1920), 191, 202,
    203, 243, 350
Terror (Reign of Terror) (France), 25, 116, 126-130,
    131, 145-148, 149, 150-152, 154, 155
Thasos, 63, 68
Thebes:
  Athens and, 63, 82
  Sparta and, 79-80, 82, 83, 84, 89
Themistocles, investment of Laurium silver in fleet,
    61, 72, 74
Theramenes, 77
Thermopylae, battle of (480 B.C.), 1, 61
thetes, 65, 73
Third Estate, 118, 143
Thirteenth Party Congress, 219, 220
Thirty (404-403 B.C.), 70, 75, 77, 78
Thrace, 71, 83
Thurii, 92
Thyrea, 81
Tiber river, 90, 91
Tikhon, Patriarch, 212-213
tin, 17, 18
Tiryns, 81
Tissaphernes, 83
Titus Annius Milo (see Milo)
Tomsky, Mikhail, 222, 257, 258
total quality management (TQM), 45, 467
Toulon, 127, 141
Trans-Siberian railroad, 195
Transcontinental Railroad, 436, 445-446

transportation resources (U.S.), 443-447
tribes of Athens, 67, 72
tribes of Rome, 97, 107
tribunate, 97, 110
Tribunate (France), 133
tribunes (tribuni plebis), 97, 98, 99, 102, 104,
    106, 110, 111
trittyes, Athenian districts, 67, 76
Triumvirate, First, 93, 94, 109, 111, 112
Triumvirate, Second, 94, 105
triumvirs, 93, 94
triumvirs (France), 132
troika, (Stalin, Kamenev & Zinoveiv), 215, 216,
    218
Trotsky, Leon:
  (1921-1938), 210, 213, 214, 215, 216, 217
  in Civil War, 195, 196, 197
  Lenin and, 218-220
  Stalin and, 217, 218-221
Truman, Harry S., 440
trusts:
  Germany, see cartels
  Russia:
    Communist policies (1918-1922), 298, 307- 308,
        328, 341, 358
    Czarist policy, 294-295, 339
    generally, 339-340
    glavki, 307, 308
    NEP and, 314
    syndicates, 339
    VSNKh, 296, 297, 298, 299, 304, 307, 399
  U.S., 438; Standard Oil, 438
Tsaritsyn, 194, 196
Tucker, Robert, 257, 262
Tuileries, 116, 120, 124, 125, 126, 145, 153
Tukhachevskii, General Mikhail, 210, 211, 212
Turgot, Anne-Robert, 137, 138, 152
Turkish Wall, 198, 199
Twelfth Party Congress, 218
Twelve Tables, 99
twenty five-thousanders, 225, 270
Two Thirds Law, 131

Uglanov, N.A., 222
Ukraine, 194, 197, 206, 208, 226, 228, 234, 245, 263,
    267, 276, 279, 280, 282
unemployment, 1, 7, 12, 31, 34, 35, 39
  Athens, 71, 74, 78, 478
  economic growth and, 40-41, 46
  France, 36, 119, 142, 143, 152, 157, 478
  Germany, 13, 14, 29, 40, 352, 354, 355, 357, 366,
    368, 370, 371, 372, 373, 382, 385, 387, 388, 390,
    392
  globalization and, 461-462, 478
  market and, 389
  resources and, 41, 54-55
  Rome, 12, 13, 14, 39, 90, 102, 103, 104, 114, 478
  Russia, 190, 308, 310, 311, 314, 315, 324, 346
  U.S., 40, 413, 414, 415, 418, 422, 423, 424
  violence and, 39-40
Union of Soviet Socialist Republics, 189
United States,
generally, see chapters 21 & 22, 1, 2, 45, 477
  as democracy, 2, 23, 27, 39-40
  auto industry and, 470-471
  economic growth, 457, 463
  globalization and 457-458, 467, 474, 477-479
  Great Depression, see chapter 21,
  Great Crash, 416-423
  labor unrest, 39, 49, 50, 440
  resources and, 18, 457, 465-466, 473, 481
  steel industry, 463-470
  unemployment and, 40, 414, 429, 438, 439,
      440, 441, 442, 453, 454, 455, 457, 458, 459,
      461, 476, 478
uranium, as resource, 15-16
Urban, Pope, 475
urbanization, (U.S.), 428-429
Uritskii, M. S., 169, 191
U.S. Steel Corporation, 464, 470

Valmy, 125, 126
Veii, 91, 99
Vendée uprising, 126-127
Venusia, 92
Versailles, 122, 136, 144, 153
Versailles Treaty, 397, 411-412, 418
village, distinguished from commune, 233-234
violence:
  Athens, 65-66, 67, 70, 75, 76, 77
    governmental response, 66, 70, 78
  France, 30, 36, 49, 116, 117, 119-121, 123, 124,
      125, 127, 131-132, 134, 135, 136, 137, 141, 143-
      144, 145-146, 149, 150-151, 152-154, 155
    response, 30, 116-117, 122, 127-128, 130,
  Germany, 29, 39-40, 43, 354, 360-361, 363, 364-
      365, 366, 367
    response, 14, 25, 29, 352, 361, 363
  problem of measuring, 27
  relationship to resources, 1
  relationship to unemployment, 1, 39
  resource mechanism and, 1, 25

response of governments to, 25-28, 31, 37-39
Rome, 13, 25, 39, 49, 90, 102, 105-112
  response, 13, 106, 113-114
Russia, 29, 158, 160, 173-174, 177-178, 185, 190,
    191, 208-210, 212, 227-228
  response, 25, 29-30, 175, 190, 191-192. 200-203,
    209-212, 228-229
societal response, 1
Sparta, 80-81, 84, 87, 88
  response, 1, 25, 28, 80, 88
U.S., 39, 40, 50, 432-433, 434
  response, 50, 433, 435
violence mechanism, 27
Vladivostok, 195
Volunteer Army, 192-199, 204, 205, 206, 208
Volynskii Guard Regiment, 186
wage controls, (France), 147, 148
War Communism, 241-245, 247, 256, 258, 288,
    294, 297, 300, 301-311, 313, 315, 319
War of Independence, American, 137-138, 431

Wheatcroft, S.G., 232
White Army, Northwestern, 197
White armies, 192-207
White Terror (France), 130-131
Wilson, Woodrow, 418
Winter Palace, 163, 164, 165, 173, 194
Witte, Sergei, 174
workers' brigades, 257
Wrangel, Petr, General, 196, 198, 199, 204, 208

Zama, battle of, 92
Zaporozhets, Ivan, 158
zemstvo system, 180, 184
Zemstvo Liberals, 184
zeugitae (teamsters), 68-69
Zinoviev, G. Y., 159, 202, 210, 215, 216, 217, 218,
    219
  Stalin and, 159, 215-222, 228, 229, 321, 322, 327,
    328
Znamenskii Square demonstration, 178, 187

Order Form

Poverty, Wealth Dictatorship, Democracy:
Resource Scarcity and the Origins of Dictatorship
By Jack Barkstrom
ISBN: 0-9610224-0-X
Price: $21.95

Postal orders only:

Please send this form together with a check or money order to:

Pericles Press
Attn: Book Orders
8200 South Quebec Street
Suite A-3, #159
Englewood, CO 80112
U.S.A.

No. copies: _____

Sales tax: Please add 7.6% for orders shipped to Colorado addresses.

Shipping:
US: $5.00 for the first book plus $2.00 for each additional copy.
International: $20.00 for 1st book; $5.00 for each additional copy (Estimate).

Make checks payable to: **Pericles Press**

Shipping Information:

Name: _____

Address: _____
_____
City: _____ **State:** _____ **ZIP:** _____
Country: _____
Telephone: _____

e-mail address: _____

Thank you for your order.

www.periclespress.com